# HOTELS AND COUNTRY INNS
of Character and Charm
# IN FRANCE

Hunter Publishing, Inc.
www.hunterpublishing.com

HUNTER PUBLISHING, INC.
130 Campus Drive, Edison NJ 08818
(732) 225 1900, (800) 255 0343; fax (732) 417 0482


*IN CANADA*
Ulysses Travel Publications
4176 Saint-Denis
Montreal, Quebec H2W 2M5 Canada
(514) 843 9882, ext. 2232; fax 514 843 9448


ISBN 1-55650-899-9
Fourth Edition

For complete information about the hundreds of other travel guides offered
by Hunter Publishing, visit our website at **www.hunterpublishing.com**


**Hotels and Country Inns
of Character and Charm in France**
Translator: Brent Keever, Anne Noris
Front cover photograph: Manoir de Butin (Normandie)
photo by François Tissier
Back cover: Au Claire de la Plume (Rhône Alpes)
photo by Marcus Robinson

**Special Sales**
Hunter Travel Guides can be purchased in quantity at special discounts. For
more information, contact us at the address above.

Printed in Italy by Litho Service
10 9 8 7 6 5 4 3 2 1

**HUNTER** RIVAGES

# HOTELS AND COUNTRY INNS
of Character and Charm
# IN FRANCE

*Conceived by*
Jean and Tatiana de Beaumont
Véronique De Andreis
Anne Deren
and Jean-Emmanuel Richomme

*Project editor*
Jean de Beaumont

*Guide advisor*
Michelle Gastaut

Hunter Publishing, Inc.
www.hunterpublishing.com

The 581 hotels presented in this new edition represent the fruit of a lot of rigorous fieldwork. As a result:

• 53 new establishments have been chosen.
• 41 hotels have been taken out.
• And all the practical information and descriptions have been updated.

In keeping with our defininition of what constitutes "charm," the chosen inns run the scale from the simplest comfort to the greatest luxury. Thus, there is a great variety in levels of "charm," but the level of quality is always there.

We have arranged the hotels according to region, and then alphabetized them according to department and municipality. The page number corresponds to the number of the inn that is marked on the road maps, in the table of contents, in the index, and in the listing of the 210 hotels that have rooms at under 400 Francs a night.

All you have to do is find the place that suits you best. Read the text carefully: it describes the hotel's general ambiance and does not hesitate to mention any flaws.

Please keep in mind that:

• The stars included in the practical information correspond to the system of classification of the French Ministry of Tourism, and not to any ranking system devised by the authors of this guide.
• You cannot demand the same level of quality from a room at 200 Francs as you would from one which costs 800 Francs or more.
• The prices listed are, of course, subject to change by the hotel during the course of the year.

Due to lack of space, we could not systematically inform you of the prices of all single rooms, charge for extra guests, or full board (2 meals). Do not hesitate to ask the hotel itself. Also, we recommend that you ask about the half board (1 meal) rate, which sometimes changes according to number of guests and length of stay. (Half board could also be obligatory for a stay of a certain duration or in summer.)

For places to stay in Paris, see the Hunter Rivages Guide to *Hotels of Character and Charm in Paris.*

**Last but not least, hotel managers often cancel a reservation if the client has not arrived before 6 or 7 PM. If you will be late, it is important to warn the hotel.**

If you are won over by an inn or hotel that is not in our guide, and which you think deserves to be chosen, please let us know so that we might include it.

Similarly, if you are disappointed by one of our hotels, do not hesitate to let us know about it.

Mail can be sent to:

Jean de Beaumont
Editions Rivages
106, bd. Saint-Germain
75006 Paris
FRANCE
Phone (from the US) : 0-11-33-1-44-41-39-90
Fax (from the US): 0-11-33-1-44-41-39-69

You can also contact us on the Guides Rivages' website at:
http://www. guidesdecharme.com

Or get in touch via our US website at
http://www.hunterpublishing.com

Thank you very much.

# C O N T E N T S

Hotels listing by region

Map of France

Road maps

Hotels:

# HOTELS LISTING BY REGION

## ALSACE - LORRAINE

### BAS-RHIN

### HAUT-RHIN

## GIRONDE

## LANDES

# A U V E R G N E - L I M O U S I N

## ALLIER

# B U R G U N D Y

# B R I T T A N Y

## CÔTES-D'ARMOR

## FINISTÈRE

## ILE-ET-VILAINE

## MORBIHAN

# C E N T R E   -   L O I R E   V A L L E Y

## CHER

## LOIRET

# C H A M P A G N E - P I C A R D I E

## AISNE

## AUBE

## MARNE

## MEUSE

## OISE

## SOMME

# C O R S I C A

# F R A N C H E - C O M T É

## JURA

# I L E - D E - F R A N C E

## SEINE-ET-MARNE

## YVELINES

## ESSONNE

# L A N G U E D O C - R O U S S I L L O N

## AUDE

## GARD

## HÉRAULT

## LOZÈRE

## PYRÉNÉES-ORIENTALES

# NORD - PAS - DE - CALAIS

## NORD

# N O R M A N D Y

## CALVADOS

## EURE

# P A Y S   D E   L A   L O I R E

## LOIRE-ATLANTIQUE

## MAINE-ET-LOIRE

## SARTHE

## VENDÉE

# P O I T O U - C H A R E N T E S

## CHARENTE

## CHARENTE-MARITIME

## DEUX-SÈVRES

## VIENNE

## BOUCHES-DU-RHÔNE

# R H Ô N E - A L P E S

## AIN

* The prices given in parentheses are those for a double room, sometimes with half board. For more details, please refer to the specific page.

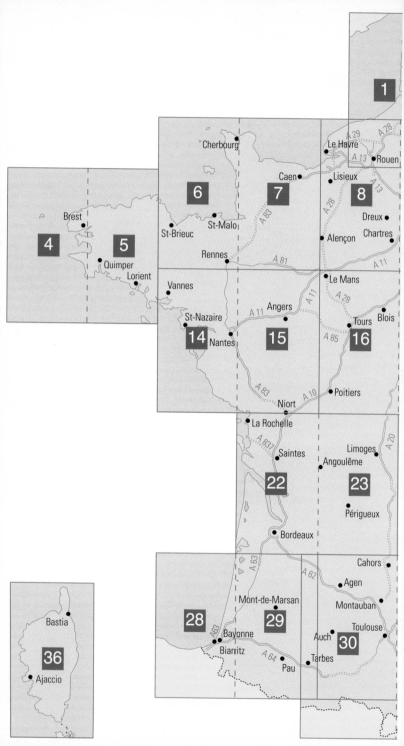

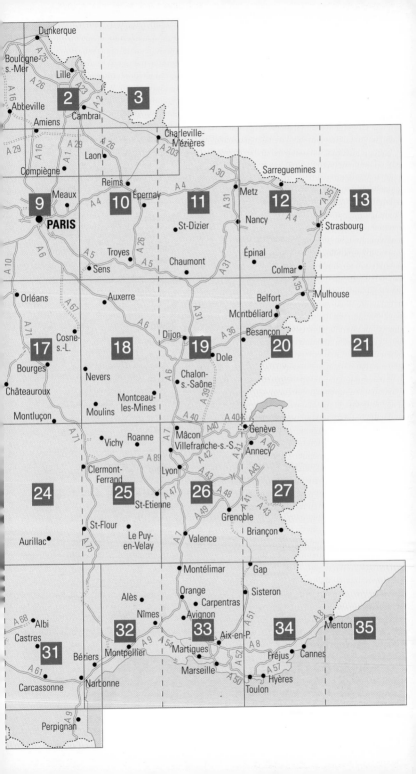

# KEY TO THE MAPS

Scale : 1:1,000,000

maps 30 and 31 : scale 1:1,200,000

## MOTORWAYS

A9 - L'Océane

Under construction
projected

## ROADS
Highway
Dual carriageway
Four lanes road
Major road
Secondary road

## TRAFFIC
National
Regional
Local

## JUNCTIONS
Complete
Limited

## DISTANCES IN KILOMETRES
On motorway     10
On other road   10

## BOUNDARIES
National boundary
Region area
Department area

## URBAIN AREA

**Town**

**Big city**

**Important city**

Medium city

Little city

VILLAGE

## AIRPORTS

## FORESTS

## PARKS
Limit
Center

*Cartography*

*Created by*

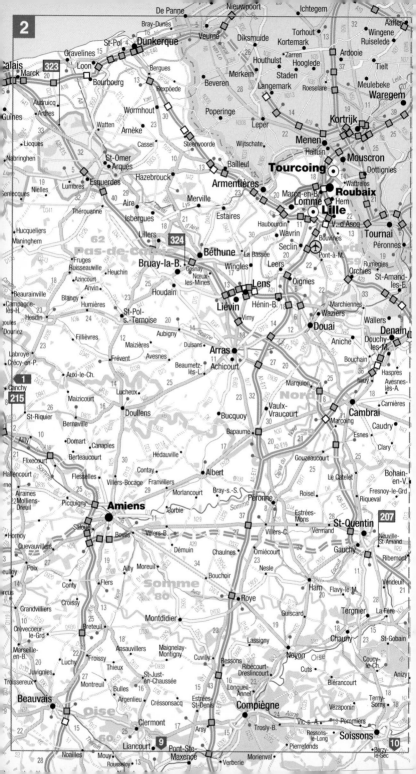

**4**

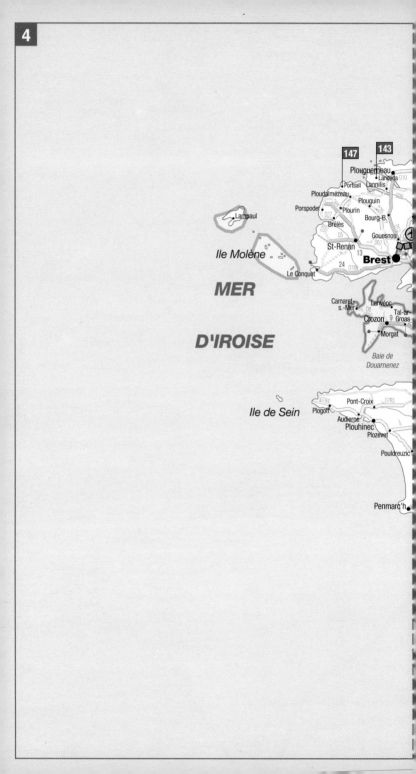

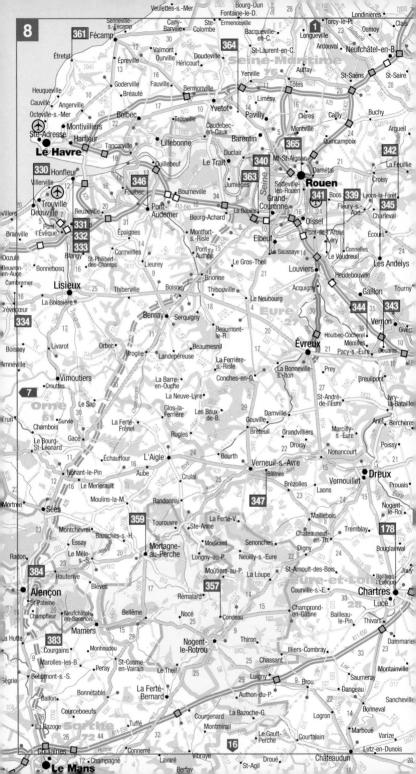

Foucarmont · Liomer · Hornoy · Saleux · Boves · Villers-B. · Villers-C. · Verr

**1** · Quevauvillers · Démuin · Chaulnes · Omiécourt · 23 · Nesle

26 · Mortemer · Aumale · Thieulloy · Poix · 19 · Ailly · Moreuil · Bouchoir · Roye · Guiscard · 19

Abancourt · Sarcus · Grandvilliers · Conty · Flers · Croissy · Montdidier · 23 · Lassigny · Cuts

Formerie · Feuquières · Crèvecoeur-le-Grd · Luchy · Froissy · Thieux · Maignelay-Montigny · Cuvilly · Ressons · Ribécourt-Dreslincourt · Longueil-Annel

Forges-les-Eaux · Songeons · Marseille-en-B. · Juvignies · St-Just-en-Chaussée · Estrées-St-Denis · Compiègne

Gournay-en-Bray · Troissereux · Bulles · Argenlieu · Cressonsacq · Arsy · Trosly-B.

Neuf-Marché · **Beauvais** · Montreuil · Clermont · Liancourt · Pont-Ste-Maxence · Verberie · Crépy-en-V. · Villers-Cotterêts

Morgny · Sérifontaine · St-Denis-le-Ferment · Noailles · Mouy · Rousseloy · Nogent-s.-O. · Creil · Senlis · Fontaine-Chaalis · Baron · Vaumoise

Étrépagny · Gisors · Chaumont-en-V. · Méru · Montataire · Chantilly · Ermenonville · Nanteuil · Acy · La Ferté Milo

Dangu · St-Clair · Écos · Lierville · Amblainville · Chambly · Beaumont-s.-Oise · Luzarches · Fosses · Le Plessis-B. · Étrépilly

Bonnières · Aincourt · Vétheuil · Vigny · Pontoise · Cergy · Auvers-s.-Oise · Domont · Goussainville · Dammartin-en-G. · Meaux

Mantes · Limay · Meulan · Triel · Poissy · St-Germain-en-Laye · Montmorency · St-Denis · Mitry-Mory · Esbly · Lagny · Crécy-la-Chap. · Coulommie

Longnes · Épône · Maule · Nanterre · **Paris** · Bobigny · Créteil · Ozoir-la-F. · Neufmoutiers-en-Brie · Mortcerf

Septeuil · Thoiry · Beynes · Les Clayes · **Versailles** · Ivry · Gretz · Brie-Comte-R. · Rozay · Vaudoy

Houdan · Montfort-l'A. · Trappes · Voisins-le-Br. · **Palaiseau** · Guignes · Mormant · Nangis

Condé-s.-V. · St-Léger-en-Yv. · Dampierre · Chevreuse · Orsay · Montlhéry · **Évry** · Corbeil · Melun · Le Châtelet-en-Br. · Donnemarie Dontil

Rambouillet · Cernay · Limours · Arpajon · Dammarie-les-Lys · Perthes-en-Gâtinais · Barbizon · Fontainebleau · Montereau

Épernon · Maintenon · Orphin · St-Arnoult-en-Y. · St-Chéron · Étréchy · La Ferté-Alais · Bouville · Milly-la-Forêt · Moret-s.-Loing · Flagy · Voulx

Gallardon · Ablis · Dourdan · Authon-la-Pl. · Étampes · Mespuits · Ury · Montigny-s.-Loing · Villecerf · Lorrez-le-Bocage-Pr.

Houville-la-Br. · Voise · Sainville · Saclas · Méréville · La-Chapelle-la-R. · Nemours · Égreville · Chéroy

Fresnay-l'Évêque · Pussay · Angerville · Sermaises · Mainvilliers · Malesherbes · Souppes-s.-Loing · St-Valérien

Voves · Andonville · Charmont-en-B. · Puiseaux · Château-Landon · Dordives · Domat

Cormainville · Janville · Toury · Outarville · Pithiviers · Beaumont-du-G. · Préfontaines · Ferrières · Griselles

Orgères-en-Beauce · Artenay · Neuville-aux-Bois · Ascoux · Boynes · Beaune-la-R. · Corbeilles · Courtenay

Patay · Sougy · Chevilly · Courcy · Chambon-la-F.

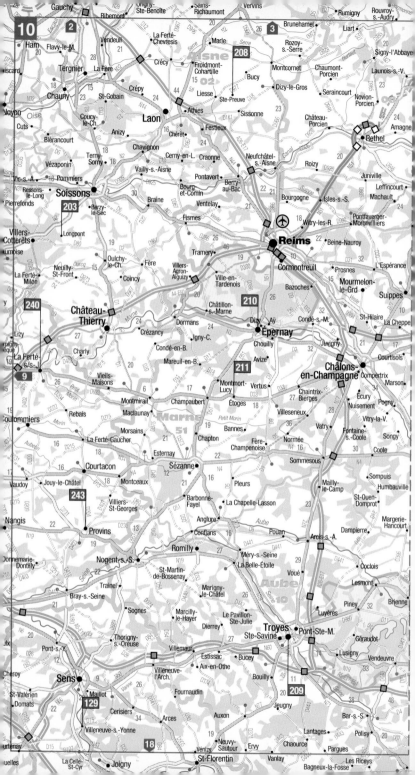

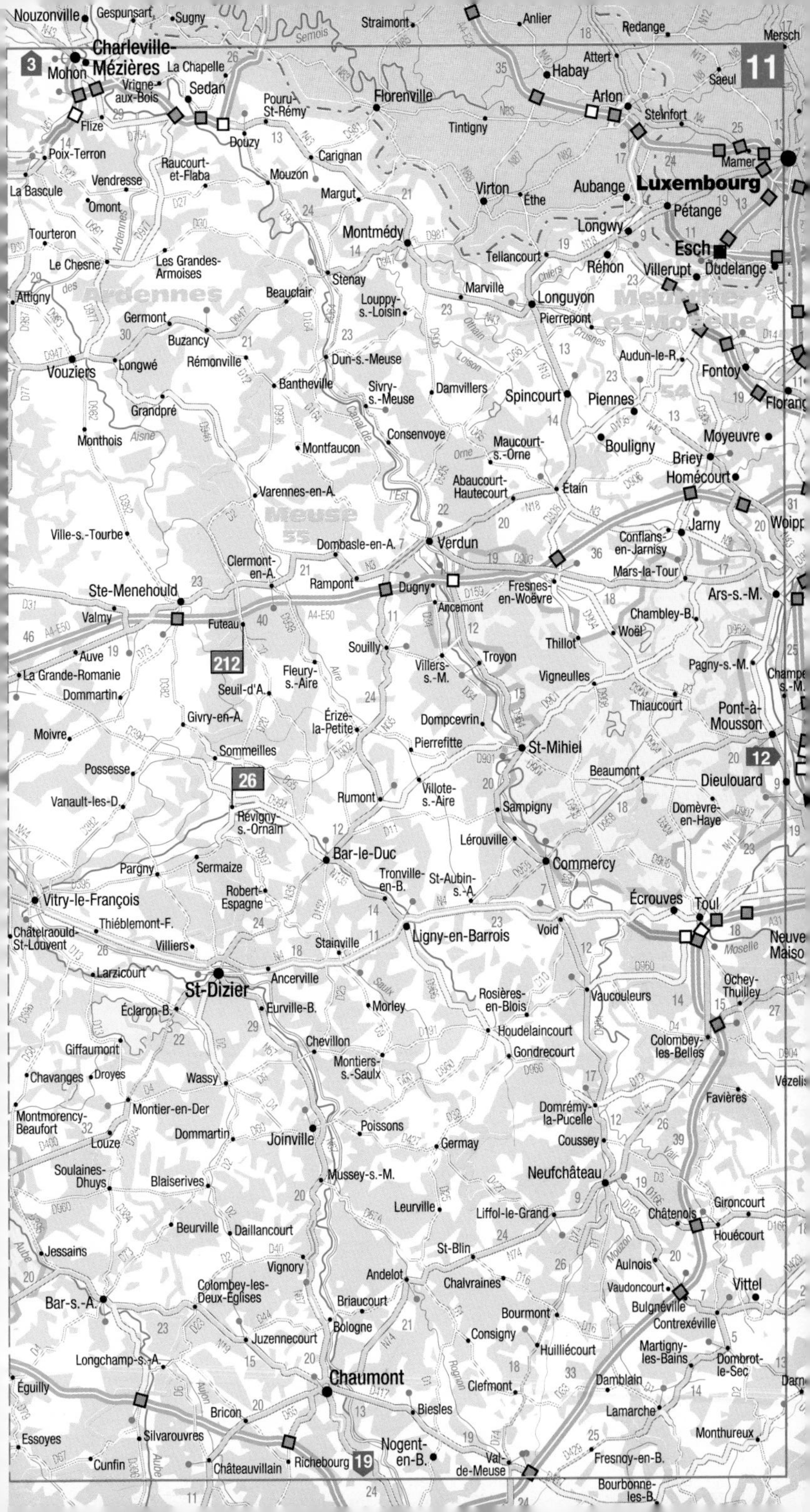
11
3
12
19
26
212
Nouzonville
Gespunsart
Sugny
Semois
Straimont
Anlier
Redange
Mersch
Charleville-Mézières
Mohon
La Chapelle
Vrigne-aux-Bois
Sedan
Habay
Attert
Saeul
Florenville
Arlon
Flize
Pouru-St-Rémy
Tintigny
Steinfort
Douzy
Carignan
Mamer
Poix-Terron
Raucourt-et-Flaba
Vendresse
Mouzon
Virton
Éthe
Aubange
Luxembourg
La Bascule
Omont
Margut
Pétange
Longwy
Tourteron
Montmédy
Esch
Tellancourt
Réhon
Villerupt
Dudelange
Le Chesne
Les Grandes-Armoises
Stenay
Ardennes
Attigny
Beauclair
Louppy-s.-Loisin
Marville
Longuyon
Meurthe-et-Moselle
Germont
Pierrepont
Buzancy
Audun-le-R.
Vouziers
Longwé
Rémonville
Dun-s.-Meuse
Fontoy
Bantheville
Sivry-s.-Meuse
Damvillers
Spincourt
Piennes
Florange
Grandpré
Monthois
Aisne
Consenvoye
Maucourt-s.-Orne
Bouligny
Moyeuvre
Montfaucon
Briey
Abaucourt-Hautecourt
Étain
Homécourt
Varennes-en-A.
Meuse
55
Jarny
Woippy
Ville-s.-Tourbe
Verdun
Conflans-en-Jarnisy
Dombasle-en-A.
Clermont-en-A.
Mars-la-Tour
Rampont
Dugny
Fresnes-en-Woëvre
Ars-s.-M.
Ste-Menehould
Ancemont
Valmy
Futeau
Chambley-B.
Woël
Thillot
Auve
Souilly
Troyon
La Grande-Romanie
Fleury-s.-Aire
Villers-s.-M.
Vigneulles
Pagny-s.-M.
Dommartin
Seuil-d'A.
Thiaucourt
Pont-à-Mousson
Givry-en-A.
Érize-la-Petite
Dompcevrin
Moivre
Sommeilles
Pierrefitte
St-Mihiel
Possesse
Beaumont
Dieulouard
Vanault-les-D.
Rumont
Villote-s.-Aire
Sampigny
Revigny-s.-Ornain
Domèvre-en-Haye
Lérouville
Bar-le-Duc
Pargny
Sermaize
Commercy
Tronville-en-B.
St-Aubin-s.-A.
Vitry-le-François
Robert-Espagne
Écrouves
Toul
Thiéblemont-F.
Châtelraould-St-Louvent
Villiers
Stainville
Ligny-en-Barrois
Void
Neuves-Maisons
Moselle
Larzicourt
Ancerville
St-Dizier
Rosières-en-Blois
Vaucouleurs
Ochey-Thuilley
Éclaron-B.
Eurville-B.
Morley
Houdelaincourt
Giffaumont
Chevillon
Gondrecourt
Colombey-les-Belles
Chavanges
Droyes
Montiers-s.-Saulx
Wassy
Vézelise
Montier-en-Der
Favières
Montmorency-Beaufort
Domrémy-la-Pucelle
Louze
Dommartin
Joinville
Poissons
Germay
Coussey
Soulaines-Dhuys
Blaiserives
Mussey-s.-M.
Neufchâteau
Leurville
Liffol-le-Grand
Châtenois
Gironcourt
Beurville
Daillancourt
Houécourt
Jessains
Vignory
St-Blin
Aulnois
Andelot
Chalvraines
Vittel
Vaudoncourt
Bar-s.-A.
Colombey-les-Deux-Églises
Briaucourt
Bulgnéville
Bourmont
Contrexéville
Bologne
Consigny
Juzennecourt
Huilliécourt
Martigny-les-Bains
Dombrot-le-Sec
Longchamp-s.-A.
Chaumont
Clefmont
Damblain
Éguilly
Bricon
Biesles
Lamarche
Essoyes
Silvarouvres
Monthureux
Nogent-en-B.
Fresnoy-en-B.
Cunfin
Châteauvillain
Richebourg
Val-de-Meuse
Bourbonne-les-B.
Aube

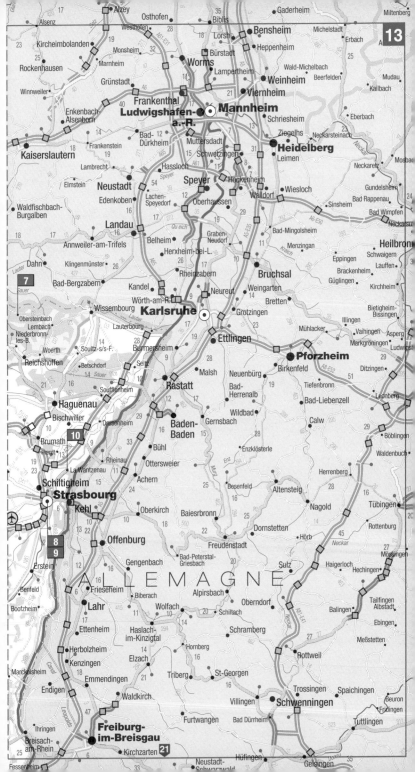

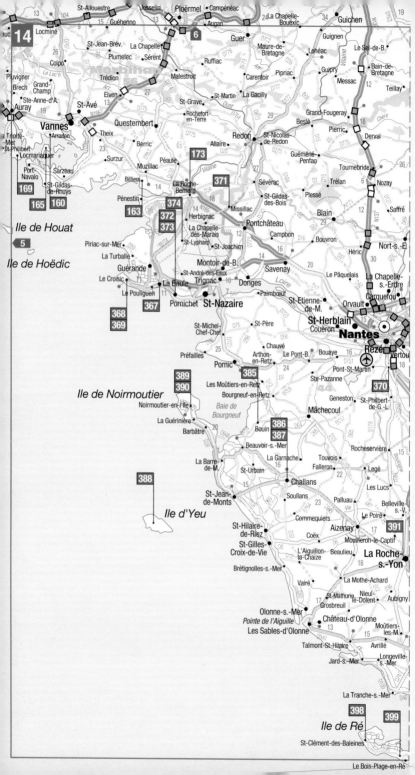

7

Janzé
St-Poix
Entrammes
Coulans-
St-Denis-
d'Orques
Loué
Brûlon
N15

Retiers
La Couyère
Thourie
La Guerche-de-B.
Cossé-le-Vivien
Quelaines
Meslay-
du-Maine
Ruillé-
Froid-Fonds
Grez-en-
Bouère
Bouëssay
Auvers-
le-H.
Asnières-
s.-Vègre

Chelun
St-Aignan-
s.-Roë
Craon
Château-Gontier
Bazouges
Sablé-s.-S.
Solesmes
Malicorne-
s.-Sarthe
381

Martigné-
Ferchaud
Rougé
Chemazé
Bierné
St-Denis-
d'Anjou
377
Miré
Précigné
Clermont-
Créans

Châteaubriant
Pouancé
Vergonnes
Renazé
Daon
La Jaille-
Yvon
Châteauneuf-
s.-Sarthe
Daumeray
La Flèche

La Croix-L.
Combrée
Segré
Champigné
Tiercé
Durtal
Clefs
380

Issé
Moisdon-
la-R.
St-Julien-
de-V.
Challain-la-
Potherie
Le Lion-
d'Angers
Grez-Neuville
Briollay
Seiches
Chevire-
le-Rouge
Baugé

La Mailleraye-
de-Bretagne
Riaillé
Candé
Vern-d'A.
Montreuil-Juigné
Avrillé
375
Jarzé
Bauné
Beaufort-
en-V.
Moulherne

Joué-s.-
Erdre
St-Mars-
la-Jaille
Le Louroux-
Béconnais
Bécon-les-Granits
St-Barthélemy-d'Anjou
Trélazé

Teillé
Belligné
Villemoisan
Angers
Les Ponts-de-Cé
St-Mathurin-
s.-Loire
Longué-Jumelles
Neuillé

Ligné
Varades
Ingrandes
St-Georges
Brissac-
Quincé
376
Les Rosiers
Gennes
378
379
Saumur

Ancenis
Champtoceaux
Montjean
La Pommeraye
St-Florent-
le-V.
Beaulieu
N.-D.-
d'Allençon
Thouarcé
Chènehutte-
Trèves-Cunault
St-Martin-
de-la-Place
Allonnes

Le Loroux-
B.
St-Laurent-
des-A.
Montrevault
St-Laurent-
de-la-P.
Martigné-
Briand
Milly
Doué-
la-F.
Montreuil-
Bellay
Roiffé

Vallet
Beaupréau
Gesté
Chemillé
Jallais
Les Trois-
Moutiers

Monnières
Clisson
St-Macaire-
en-M.
392
Montfaucon
Trémentines
Vihiers
Le Puy-
Notre-Dame
Ternay

Aigrefeuille-
s.-Maine
Cugand
Tortou
La Romagne
Cholet
Nuaillé
Vezins
Cléré-
s.-Layon
St-Pierre-à-Champ

Montaigu
Tiffauges
Mortagne-s.-S.
La Verrie
St-Laurent-
s.-Sèvre
Maulévrier
Les Aubiers
Moûtiers-s/s-
Argenton
Argenton-Ch.
Thouars
Pas-de-Jeu
16

St-Denis-
la-C.
La Gaubretière
Bazoges
Mauléon
La Butte
St-Varent
St-Jouin-
de-Marnes
Moncontour

Les Herbiers
St-Fulgent
Les Épesses
St-Michel-
Mt-Mercure
Flocellière
Cerizay
Bressuire
Boussais
Airvault
La Grimaudière

Les Essarts
L'Oie
Mouchamps
Pouzauges
La-Forêt-s.-S.
Chiché
Chanteloup
Amailloux
Clessé
St-Loup-
Lamairé
Thénezay

Ste-
Cécile
St-Vincent-
Sterlanges
Chavagnes-
les-R.
St-Pierre-
du-Chemin
Moncoutant
Neuvy-Bouin
Parthenay
La Ferrière-
en-P.

La Ferrière
Les Loges
Chantonnay
Mouilleron-
en-P.
La Châtaigneraie
Loge-
Fougereuse
L'Absie
Secondigny

Bournezeau
La Chaize-
le-Vicomte
Thouarsais-
Bouildroux
St-Maurice-
des-Noués
Fenioux
Vasles

Mareuil-s.-Lay-
Dissais
Ste-Hermine
Mervent
Mazières-
en-Gâtine
Vausseroux
Benassay
405

Le Champ-St-Père
Pouillé
Mouzeuil
L'Hermenault
L'Orbrie
Coulonges-
s.-l'Autize
Champdeniers-
St-Denis
Ménigoute
Sanxay

Luçon
Les Quatre-
Chemins
Morelles
393
Fontenay-
le-Comte
St-Hilaire-
des-Loges
Villiers-
en-Plaine
St-Maixent-
l'École
Cherveux
Pamproux
Jazeneuil

St-Denis-du-P.
Chaillé-les-Marais
Velluire
Doix
La Mothe-
St-Héray

Triaize
St-Michel-
en-l'Herm
Maillezais
Benet
Maillezais
Coulon
La Crèche
Chey

L'Aiguillon-
s.-Mer
Marans
L'Île-d'Elle
Gué-de-Velluire
Niort
Aiffres
Beaussais
Lezay

St-Martin-
de-Ré
Villedoux
St-Xandre
Lagord
Courçon
St-Hilaire-
La-Palud
404
22
Mauzé-s.-
le-M.
Usseau
Beauvoir-s.-Niort
Melle

La Rochelle
Prahecq
Coulon

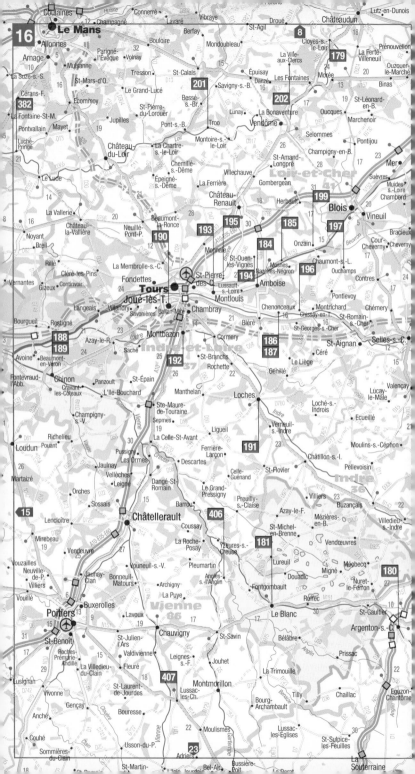

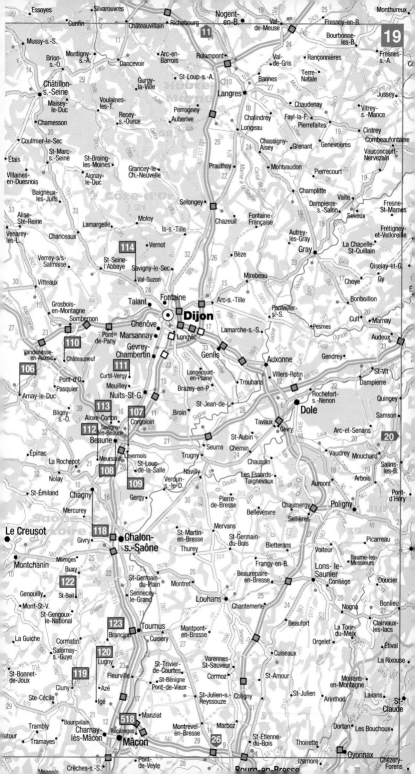

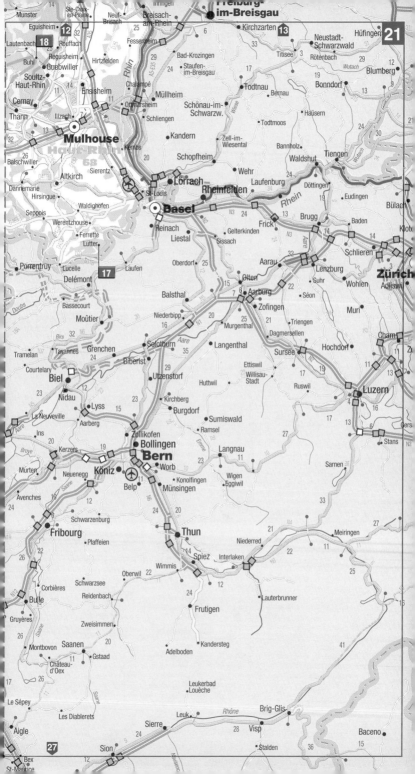

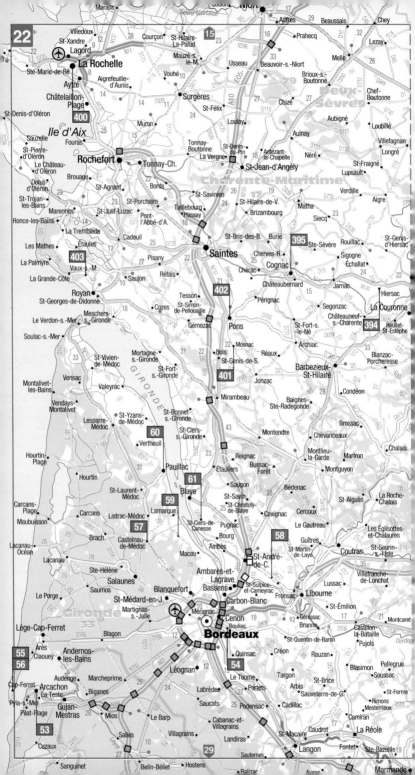

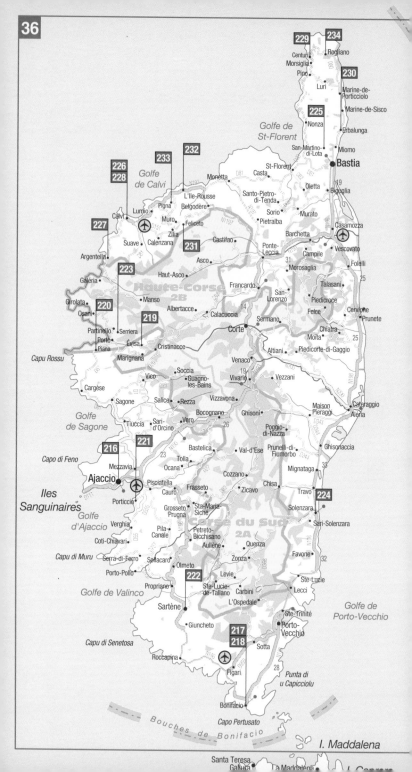

# ZinckHôtel

67140 Andlau (Bas-Rhin)
13, rue de la Marne
Tel. (0)3.88.08.27.30 - Fax (0)3.88.08.42.50 - M. and Mme Zinck

**Category** ★★★ **Rooms** 14 with telephone, bath or shower, WC and 4 with TV – 1 for disabled persons. **Price** Single and double 310-600F / 47,26-91,47€. **Meals** Breakfast 40F / 6,10€, served 8:00-10:00. No restaurant. **Credit cards** Visa, Eurocard and MasterCard. **Pets** Dogs not allowed. **Facilities** Parking. **Nearby** Alsatian wine route, from Marlenheim to Thann, church in Andlau and church of Sainte-Marguerite in Epfig. **Open** All year.

Situated in an 18th-century mill that was then changed into a sock shop, this hotel, nestled in the village, expresses the taste and fancy of its owners, who have outfitted 14 evocatively-named rooms. The "Colonial," "Jazzy," and "Baroque" rooms are witty and colorful. The "Japanese" suite is more sober, and the "Alsatian" is very warm and inviting. Every room, bathrooms included, offers only the greatest comforts and modern-day accommodations. When possible, breakfast is served on the patio, or in the huge, former production room, furnished in a modern design that perfectly accentuates the light wood and steel of the building. Lovers of the pre-industrial age can ask Monsieur Zinck about the function of the imposing wheel -- frozen in time -- in front of the back wall, or get some explanations about the many related objects from that period on display. Not far away, a smashing little walled-in orchard serves everyone as a restful, summer salon. High-quality accommodations at a reasonable price. For your meals, we recommend a few good neighbouring restaurant *Winstub*: *Le Relais de la Poste* and the *Caveau Val d'Eleon* in Andlau; or, 2 kilometers away in Mittelbergheim, the *Hotel Gilg*.

***How to get there*** (*Map 12*): *39km south of Strasbourg via A 352, dir. Selestat, exit Mittelbergheim.*

1

## Hôtel Arnold

67140 Itterswiller (Bas-Rhin)
98, route du Vin
Tel. (0)3.88.85.50.58 - Fax (0)3.88.85.55.54 - Mme Arnold
Web: www.oda.fr/aa/arnold

**Category** ★★★ **Rooms** 28 and 1 apartment (2-6 pers.) with telephone, bath or shower, WC, TV and minibar. **Price** Double 430-630F / 65,55-96,04€; apart. 930-1600F / 141,78-243,92€. **Meals** Breakfast 50F / 7,63€, served 7:30-10:30; half board 410-520F / 62,50-79,27€ (per pers.). **Restaurant** Closed Sunday evening and Monday. Service 11:30AM-2:30PM, 7:30PM-9:00PM; mealtime specials 130-365F / 19,82-55,64€. Seasonal menu. Specialties: Noisette de chevreuil; civet de sanglier; choucroute, baeckeoffe; foie gras. **Credit cards** Amex, Visa, Eurocard and MasterCard. **Pets** Dogs not allowed. **Facilities** Parking. **Nearby** Alsatian wine route from Marlenheim to Thann, church in Andlau, church of Sainte-Marguerite d'Epfig. **Open** All year.

The *Hôtel Arnold* lies in the heart of the Alsatian vineyards at the foot of the Vosges Mountains. It is composed of three buildings in the most traditional Alsatian style. Windows and balconies overflow with flowers. The bedrooms, which are decorated in an accommodating way, are very comfortable, bright and quite large. The great attraction of most rooms is their large balcony and view over the vineyards. The entrance, hallways, breakfast room and lounge (upstairs) are warm and prettily decorated. On the *Réserve* side, the bedrooms are more attractive but the view is not as good. Intent on maintaining Alsatian traditions, the Arnold family will invite you to try the regional specialties in the restaurant. You can also buy them in the hotel's shop, which offers wines, foie gras and other products from the family estate.

***How to get there*** *(Map 12): 41km south of Strasbourg via A35; take the Mittelbergheim exit, and then head toward "Ville" until you get to Itterswiller.*

## Hôtel Neuhauser

Les Quelles
67130 Schirmeck (Bas-Rhin)
Tel. (0)3.88.97.06.81 - Fax (0)3.88.97.14.29
M. Neuhauser

**Category** ★★ **Rooms** 11 and 5 chalets with telephone, bath or shower, WC and TV. **Price** Single and double 300-600F / 45,73-91,47€; chalet 700F-900F / 106,71-137,20€ (2-4 pers.). **Meals** Breakfast 50F / 7,63€, served 8:00-10:00; half board 360-550F / 54,88 à 83,85€ (per pers., 3 days min.). **Restaurant** With air-conditioning. Service 12:00PM-2:00PM, 7:00PM-9:00PM; mealtime specials 110-300F / 16,77-45,73€, also à la carte. Specialties: Foie gras maison; filet de lapereau farçi; noisette de chevreuil forestière. **Credit cards** Visa, Eurocard and MasterCard. **Facilities** Heated swimming pool (except in winter) and parking. **Nearby** Belvédère de la Chatte Pendue. **Open** All year.

The *Neuhauser* and the few small houses in this tiny hamlet are ringed on all sides by fields and forest, an isolated location ensuring total peace and quiet. The rooms are well-kept; the oldest are traditionally furbished with rustic furniture and exposed beams. The *premier étage* rooms are a bit outmoded but charming nevertheless; those of the *second étage* are too spartan, and we don't recommend them (except Number 16). Our favorite rooms - large, cheerful, and with beautiful terraces - have been recently set up in another building. There are also five little chalets with a lounge, kitchenette and terrace, perfect for families. The cuisine, served in a large dining room with a panoramic view of a little valley, is varied and copious. The wine list, too, deserves your attention, as do the liqueurs and *eaux de vie*. This is an attractive hotel with a heated, covered swimming pool where you can enjoy this splendid site even during off-season.

***How to get there*** *( Map 12 ): 56km south of Strasbourg via A35 and A352, then N420 or D392. In Schirmeck, take the road for Les Quelles via Labroque-Albret.*

# Hôtel Gilg

7140 Mittelbergheim (Bas-Rhin)
1, route du Vin
Tel. (0)3.88.08.91.37 - Fax (0)3.88.08.45.17
M. Gilg

**Category** ★★ **Rooms** 15 with telephone, bath, WC and TV. **Price** Double 250-400F / 38,11-60,98€. **Meals** Breakfast 40F / 6,10€, served 7:30-10:00. **Restaurant** Service 12:00PM-2:00PM, 7:00PM-9:00PM; mealtime specials 105-375F / 16,01-57,17€, also à la carte. Specialties: Filet de sandre et langoustines poêlées avec ravioles ouvertes. **Credit cards** All major. **Pets** Dogs allowed. **Facilities** Parking. **Nearby** Barr, church in Andlau, church of Sainte-Marguerite in Epfig, Mont Sainte-Odile. **Closed** Jan 11 – Feb 3, Jun 21 – Jul 7 and Tuesday evening and Wednesday.

This imposing *Winstub* is one of the oldest in Alsace at the intersection of two tiny streets in a typical wine-producing village. A superb spiral staircase, constructed in 1614 by the Strasbourg cathedral stone masons , leads you to the rooms. On each landing, there are a few old and impressive wardrobes which have served generations of travelers. The *premier étage* rooms are often spacious and very well renovated in a pleasing yet restrained style. The small and quainte *deuxième étage* rooms have the charm of the inns of yesteryear with their slightly old-fashioned sheets and window treatments. All is calm and well-kept-up. Meals are taken in the large dining room with its spread-out tables, elegantly set and surrounded by sculpted, Alsatian chairs. Amidst this beautiful traditional decor, you will sample wonderfully flavourful and well-prepared food. This hotel's warm reception and other qualities make it a welcoming destination in the heart of wine country, close to the beautiful villages of Alsace.

*How to get there* *(Map 12): 37 km north of Colmar via A35. Take exit 13 and then the traffic circle to Zellwiller.*

4

## Relais des Marches de l'Est

67280 Oberhaslach (Bas-Rhin)
24, rue de Molsheim
Tel. (0)3.88.50.99.60 - Fax (0)3.88.48.74.88
Mme Weber

**Category** ★★ **Rooms** 9 with telephone, bath or shower, WC and TV. **Price** Single and double 190-250F / 28,97 à 38,11€. **Meals** Breakfast 30F / 4,58€, served 7:00-10:30; half board 250F / 38,11€ (per pers.). **Restaurant** For residents only, by reservation. Service from 7:00PM; mealtime specials 80-160F / 12,21-24,39€. Specialties: Tarte flambée; choucroute; baeckeoffe. **Credit cards** Not accepted. **Pets** Dogs allowed. **Facilities** Parking. **Nearby** Alsace Wine Route, Mont Sainte-Odile, Barr, church in Andlau, church of Sainte-Marguerite in Epfig – Wantzenau golf course. **Open** All year.

Sculptors as well as hoteliers, Bénédicte and Sylvain have succeeded in creating a personal, warm atmosphere here. On the street side, however, the hotel is unremarkable, with its pink Alsatian sandstone, and unobtrusive, as if it were afraid to be discovered too easily. Inside, the rooms on the ground floor have a "refined bistrot" ambiance, with the bread oven as the central element. On weekends, guests can observe as baeckeoffe and flamed tarts come out of the oven (reserve two days in advance). Upstairs, the bedrooms have old stone walls and the antique beds have been modernized for comfort; an old wardrobe, pretty fabrics and impeccable bathrooms complete the furnishings. The result is simple and charming, even if the tiled floors call out for the warmth of a few rugs. In the morning, you have a choice of two kinds of breakfast, which is served in the garden in good weather. This is a very pleasant hotel, and ideal for discovering the Hasel Valley and the Nideck region. Prices are more than reasonable.

***How to get there*** *(Map 12): 24km south of Strasbourg, toward Saint-Dié.*

## Hôtel A la Cour d'Alsace

67210 Obernai (Bas-Rhin)
3, rue de Gail
Tel. (0)3.88.95.07.00 - Fax (0)3.88.95.19.21 - Mme Hager - M. di Mattéo
Web: www.cour-alsace.fr

**Category** ★★★★ **Rooms** 43 and 1 suite with telephone, bath or shower, WC, cabel TV and Minibar – Elevator. **Price** Double 680-830F / 103,67-126,53€, suite 1500F / 228,67€. **Meals** Breakfast (buffet) 60-80F / 9,16-12,21€, served 7:00-10:00; half board 900-1060F / 127,20-161,59€ (per pers., in double). **Restaurant** Service 12:00PM-2:00PM, 7:00PM-9:00PM; mealtime specials 170-335F / 25,92-51,07€, also à la carte. **Credit cards** All major. **Pets** Dogs not allowed. **Facilities** Parking. **Nearby** Alsace Wine Route, church in Andlau, church of Sainte-Marguerite in Epfig, Mont-Saint-Odile; Barr – Wantzenau golf course. **Open** Jan 24 – Dec 22.

This magnificent hotel is composed of several adjoining houses grouped around a very old courtyard and built against the ramparts of Obernai. Whether you are in the *Petite France* or the *Petite Suisse*, the bedrooms are elegant, very comfortable and of varying sizes (which justifies the price differences). The style is light colors with pale or beige tints, panelling and furniture of natural wood and white eiderdowns, all contributing to a refined ambiance. For lunch or dinner you have a choice between the gastronomic restaurant or the charming *Winstub*. You can have a drink in the garden at any time, which has lovely flowers and is niched among the old moats running the length of the hotel. This is an impeccable, genuinely luxurious hotel where you can be assured of excellent cuisine and professional, attentive service.

*How to get there* ( *Map 12* ): *24km south of Strasbourg.*

## Hôtel Anthon

67510 Obersteinbach (Bas-Rhin)
40, rue Principale
Tel. (0)3.88.09.55.01 - Fax (0)3.88.09.50.52
Mme Flaig

**Category** ★★ **Rooms** 9 with telephone, bath and WC (1 with shower, 7 with minibar). **Price** Double 350F / 53,36€. **Meals** Breakfast 60F / 9,16€, served 8:00-10:00. **Restaurant** Service 12:00PM-2:00PM, 18:30-9:00PM; mealtime specials 135-380F / 20,58-57,93€, also à la carte. Specialties: Foie gras frais de canard, game in season. **Credit cards** Visa, Eurocard and MasterCard. **Pets** Dogs allowed. **Facilities** Parking. **Nearby** Lake at Hanau, Châteaux of Lutzelhardt and Falkenstein – 18-hole golf course in Bitche. **Closed** Jan, Tuesday and Wednesday.

Hôtel Anthon is nestled in Obersteinbach, a picturesque litle village in the heart of the northern Vosges national park. It offers nice rooms, though of differing degrees. The first-floor rooms are very well-renovated, well-lit, simple and cheerful. Some of them have amusing beds tucked into alcoves, traditionally Alsatian, that run the length of the same wall. The second-floor rooms are waiting their turn and will soon boast the same look. A small "suite" is even on the board. All the rooms are quiet and look out on the garden where it is not rare to catch a deer frolicking at the base of the fruit trees before running back to the wooded slopes of the Vosges forest. The roomy dining room is designed like a rotunda lit up by great picture window that gives you the impression that you are eating in the middle of a garden in full bloom. (Some tables are set up outside, as well.) The food served lives up to its gastronomic reputation, and we recommend it without a moment's hesitation. Peaceful and hospitable, this hotel is perfect for restful vacations.

***How to get there*** *(Map 13): 66km north of Strasbourg via A4 and D44 to Haguenau, then D27 to Lembach, and D3 to Obersteinbach.*

## Hôtel du Dragon

67000 Strasbourg (Bas-Rhin)
2, rue de l'Ecarlate - 12, rue du Dragon
Tel. (0)3.88.35.79.80 - Fax (0)3.88.25.78.95 - M. Zimmer
Web: www.dragon.fr - E-mail: hotel@dragon.fr

**Category** ★★★ **Rooms** 32 with telephone, bath, WC and TV – Wheelchair access. **Price** Single and double 430-655F / 65,55-99,85€, 510-940F / 77,75-143,30€. **Meals** Breakfast 62F / 9,46€, served 6:45-10:00. No restaurant. **Credit cards** All major. **Pets** Dogs not allowed. **Nearby** La Wantzenau, Alsace Wine Route, foire aux vins – 18-hole golf courses in Illkirch-Graffenstaden and Plobsheim. **Open** All year.

Even though we tend to think that charm comes from vibrant and varied colors, the *Hôtel du Dragon*, which has opted for an unabashedly modern design, is not in the least lacking in charm. Behind the walls of this 18th-century house, the monochrome grey decorations and "modern-look" furniture create a rather chilly atmosphere, but the friendly, welcoming staff and the beautiful contemporary paintings quickly compensate for that. The very comfortable bedrooms face onto one of the quiet streets of the historic quarter. There is no restaurant, but delicious breakfasts are served on pretty china from the *Café Coste*. (If you admire the paintings, some are for sale.) As far as restaurants go, trust Monsieur Zimmer's sound advice, but be sure to visit *Chez Yvonne*, one of the most popular wine bars in the city; the *Pont Corbeau*, as well as the *Strissel* for outstanding sauerkraut. The atmosphere of the *Dragon* and Monsieur Zimmer's courteous management make the hotel a favorite with the European Community officials who come to Strasbourg frequently.

**How to get there** *(Map 13): In the center of Strasbourg via the Quai Saint-Nicolas and the Quai Ch. Frey.*

# Hôtel Gutenberg

67000 Strasbourg (Bas-Rhin)
31, rue des Serruriers
Tel. (0)3.88.32.17.15 - Fax (0)3.88.75.76.67
M. Pierre Lette

**Category** ★★ **Rooms** 42 (28 with air-conditioning) with telephone, bath, WC and cable TV – Elevator.
**Price** Double 330-540F / 50,31-82,32€, 3 pers. 460F / 70,13€. **Meals** Breakfast 43F / 6,56€,
served 7:00-10:00. No restaurant. **Credit card** Visa. **Pets** Dogs not allowed. **Facilities** Parking.
**Nearby** *Petite France*, Christmas market; La Wantzenau; Alsace Wine Route, local festivities – 18-hole
golf courses in Illkirch-Graffenstaden and Plobsheim. **Closed** 2 Jan – 9 Jan.

The *Hôtel Gutenberg* is in a beautiful building erected in 1745, very close to
the cathedral, whose steeple you can see from the entry. Monsieur Lette
loves his hotel and has quite naturally left many family heirlooms in the lobby,
hallways, and rooms. If you take the stairs, you can see the military engravings
from the First and Second Empire before getting to the rooms. These rooms
have just been completely renovated and soundproofed; some have air-
conditioning, and all are of differing sizes according to the floor. The sixth floor
rooms are duplexes, situated under the exposed beams of the roof, and have a
charming view over the neighborhood's old rooftops and the maze of ancient
streets. The lower-floor rooms are more typical in size, but some are very big
indeed, such as the "Baldaquin" which has two windows and a French window
that opens onto the central balcony with its spray of geraniums. All the
decorations are appealing, with wallpaper that matches the running frieze, thick
carpeting, and antique engravings. A tasteful success that also graces the
pleasant bathrooms. Good breakfast with real orange juice and kind hospitality.

***How to get there*** *(Map 13): In the center of town, near the cathedral. You must
go through the place du Corbeau , in the direction of the Gutenberg parking lot.*

## Relais de la Poste

67610 La wantzenau (Bas-Rhin)
21, rue du Général-de-Gaulle
Tel. (0)3.88.59.24.80 - Fax (0)3.88.59.24.89 - M. Daull

**Rooms** 17 (8 with air-conditioning) and 2 apartments with telephone, bath or shower, WC and TV – Elevator; 1 for disabled persons. **Price** Single and double 400-650F / 60,98-99,09€, apart. 850F / 129,58€. **Meals** Breakfast 50F / 7,63€, served 7:00-10:00; half board 750F / 114,34€ (per pers.). **Restaurant** Closed Saturday lunchtime, Sunday evening and Monday. Service 12:00PM-2:00PM, 7:00PM-10:00PM; mealtime specials 175F / 26,68€ (lunchtime except Saturday and Sunday), 235-445F / 35,83-67,84€, also à la carte. Specialties: Foie gras frais à la gelée de muscat; loup grillé aux herbes de Provence; caille désossée farcie aux morilles; soufflé glacé au kirch. **Credit cards** All major. **Pets** Dogs allowed. **Facilities** Parking. **Nearby** Strasbourg, Alsace Wine Route, local festivities – 18-hole La Wantzenau golf course. **Open** Jan 22 – Aug 30 and Sep 12 – Jan 2.

North of Strasbourg in a village of charming half-timbered houses, this former postal-relay station and country bistrot, built in 1789, has today added an inn to its gastronomic restaurant: Since 1986, under the direction of the owner and impassioned chef Jérôme Daull, the *Relais de la Poste* has been one of the outstanding gourmet tables of the region. The twenty small bedrooms, which Monsieur Daull is progressively arranging, are decorated in rustic Alsatian style; some have a small alcove that hides away the television, while others enjoy a small living room and a balcony. All the bathrooms are equipped with a hairdryer and an enlarging mirror, but they could do with a more modern facelift. There is a restful bar with honey-colored panelling and Spanish-style fabrics, and for intimate dinners, you can ask for a private dining room decorated with Alsatian frescos.

*How to get there (Map 13): 15km northeast of Strasbourg via A4 exit Reichett, then N 363 towards Lauterbourg, exit Wantzenau.*

## Le Colombier

68000 Colmar (Haut-Rhin)
7, rue Turenne
Tel. (0)3.89.23.96.00 - Fax (0)3.89.23.97.27
Mme Lejeune

**Category** ★★★ **Rooms** 24 with air-conditioning, telephone, bath (some with whirlpool) or shower, WC, safe, minibar and cable TV – Elevator; 2 for disabled persons. **Price** Double 560-910F / 85,37-138,73€; suite 1190-1400F / 181,41-213,43€. **Meals** Breakfast 65F / 9,90€, served 7:30-11:30. No restaurant. **Credit cards** All major. **Pets** Dogs allowed. **Nearby** Issenheim altarpiece at the Unterlinden Museum in Colmar, Alsace Wine Route, Neuf-Brisach, Munster, Trois-Epis – 18-hole golf course in Ammerschwihr. **Closed** Christmas holidays.

Located in the old quarter of *La Petite Venise* criss-crossed by several canals, the beautiful *Le Colombier* is installed in a large Renaissance building with its original winding stone staircase, surprisingly graceful and light. Shapes, materials and colors have been tastefully combined in decorating the bedrooms, which are equipped with modern amenities. Italian furniture lends the rooms a note of elegane and refinement. Located on four floors, the charming rooms range from small to very large; some are beneath the eaves and overlook the street or the inner courtyard with its old half-timbering and a cool fountain. In winter, a large fire crackles in the lounge fireplace. The breakfasts are excellent. Good restaurants include: *Caveau Saint-Jean, Winstub Brenner, Les trois poissons* and *La Chaudron*. For more gastronomic fare: *Le Fer Rouge* and *Garbo*.

***How to get there*** *(Map 12): In the center of Old Colmar.*

## La Maison des Têtes

68000 Colmar (Haut-Rhin) - 19, rue des Têtes
Tel. (0)3.89.24.43.43 - Fax (0)3.89.24.58.34
M. and Mme Rohfritsch
E-mail: les-tetes@rmcnet.fr

**Category** ★★★★ **Rooms** 18 with telephone, bath (some with jacuzzi) or shower, WC, satellite TV, safe and minibar – Elevator; 1 for disabled persons. **Price** Double 565-980F / 86,13-149,40€; 3 pers. 1050-1500F / 160,07 à 228,67€. **Meals** Breakfast 67F / 10,22€, served 7:15-10:00/11:00; half board 690-900F / 105,19-137,20€ (per pers., 3 days min.). **Restaurant** Closed Sunday evening and Monday. Service 12:00PM-2:00PM, 7:00PM-9:30PM; mealtime specials 160-340F / 24,39-51,83€, also à la carte. **Credit cards** All major. **Pets** Dogs allowed (+60F / 9,15€). **Facilities** Parking. **Nearby** Alsace Wine Route; Neuf-Brisach – 18-hole golf course in Ammerschwihr. **Closed** Winter holidays.

In the heart of Colmar between the Dominican Church and the Unterlinden Museum, the *Maison des Têtes* is the former Wine Exchange, a beautiful Rhine Renaissance building with a façade of 105 masks of grotesque figures. Last year, this restaurant, famed for its regional cuisine and its magnificent, late 19th-century wood panelling added a hotel which, though entirely new, is well-integrated into the old part of the building. The lobby stands on the vestiges of the Colmar wall, built between 1216 and 1220. The eighteen bedrooms surround a small paved courtyard with a young climbing vine. They contain a small corridor leading to the toilet, the storage space, and finally to the bedroom with white cob-style walls and mat-varnished pine furniture. The bathrooms feature a pink sandstone floor, and a bathtub and independent shower in the largest rooms. Those on the *premier étage* are the smallest. Note also the duplexes with a small lounge below and the bedroom upstairs. Gourmets will love a few meals--and then a room--at the *Maison des Têtes*.

***How to get there*** *(Map 12): In town center.*

## Hostellerie Le Maréchal

68000 Colmar (Haut-Rhin)
4-6, place des Six-Montagnes-Noires
Tel. (0)3.89.41.60.32 - Fax (0)3.89.24.59.40
M. and Mme Bomo

**Category** ★★★★ **Rooms** 30 with air-conditioning, telephone, bath or shower, WC and satellite TV.
**Price** Double 550-1200F / 83,85-182,94€, suite 1500F / 228,67€. **Meals** Breakfast 85F / 12,96€,
served 7:30-10:00. **Restaurant** Service 12:00PM-2:00PM, 7:00PM-10:00PM; mealtime specials 195-
380F / 29,73-57,93€, also à la carte. Specialties: Croustillant de pigeonneau au foie gras de canard;
julienne de légumes; Barholdi en feuilleté à l'escalope de foie de canard frais. **Credit cards** All major.
**Pets** Dogs allowed (+40F / 6,09€). **Facilities** Parking (+40F / 6,09€). **Nearby** Issenheim altarpiece
at the Unterlinden Museum in Colmar, Alsace Wine Route, Neuf-Brisach, Trois-Epis – 18-hole golf
course in Ammerschwihr. **Open** All year.

*Petite Venise*, Colmar's most charming area, is precisely where you will find *Le
Marechal*, composed of four venerable, half-timbered houses which border
the canals. Inside, the beams and stones go well with the Louis XIII furniture in
the lounge and dining room. The rooms are elegant, comfortable and well-
equipped, and though some are rather small and overfurnished, this fits in
perfectly with the cozy atmosphere of the hotel. Some rooms boast exposed
half-timber walls, while others look out on the canal. In our opinion, the price
is a little high for the size of the rooms, but justifiable once you consider the
luxurious bathrooms and the excellent upkeep of this establishment, which is
right in the middle of a highly touristic area. In summer, a little patio at the
water's edge becomes part of the long dining room that runs along the Lauch.
The candlelight dinners, the specialities, and the warm and attentive hospitality
still make *Le Maréchal* a good stopping-off-place in the city.

***How to get there*** *(Map 12): In the center of old Colmar.*

# Le Caveau d'Eguisheim

68420 Eguisheim (Haut-Rhin)
3, place du Château-Saint-Léon-IX
Tel. (0)3.89.23.72.00 - Fax (0)3.89.23.68.80
Emmanuel Nasti

**Category** ★★★ **Rooms** 12 with telephone, bath, WC, TV and minibar – 1 for disabled persons. **Price** Double 495-780F / 75,46-118,91€; 3 pers. 1050-1280F / 160,07-195,13€. **Meals** Breakfast 55F / 8,38€, served 7:30-10/11:00; half board 465F / 70,89€ (per pers.). **Restaurant** Closed Tuesday lunchtime and Nov 11 – Jul 1, Wednesday. Service 12:00PM-2:00PM, 7:00PM-9:45PM; mealtime specials 165-375F / 25,15-57,17€, also à la carte. **Credit cards** All major. **Pets** Dogs allowed (+50F / 7,62€). **Nearby** Issenheim altarpiece at the Unterlinden Museum in Colmar, Alsace Wine Route – 18-hole golf course in Ammerschwihr. **Open** Feb 14 – Jan 1.

You will find *Le Caveau d'Eguisheim* on the town square of one of the most charming medieval villages on the old wine merchant trails. In our opinion, this is one of the best restaurants in Alsace. Olivier Nasti, the young manager, excels in both the bold and the traditional; in the dining room, his brother Emmanuel offers passionate advice about the wines. Emmanuel, an architect, also drew up the hotel's blueprints (across the street, in a 17th-century house). Rather than recreate a former interior in a structure in which nothing was salvageable, the two brothers opted for a modern look. Beautiful green, coral and turquoise recycled wallpaper, comfortable beds, particle-board furnishings, beautiful bathrooms decorated with Italian tiles, contemporary art works by friends. This is a real success! Add to this a nightly fruit plate and often a little dessert, as well as an excellent breakfast every morning (served in the square in the summer, next to a fountain and the stunning little castle of the counts of Eguisheim) and you will know why this address is really worth the trip.

***How to get there*** *( Map 12): 5 km from Colmar, via the west bypass, and then the Eguisheim exit.*

## Les Hirondelles

68970 Illhaeusern (Haut-Rhin)
33, rue du 25-Janvier
Tel. (0)3.89.71.83.76 - Fax (0)3.89.71.86.40
Mme Muller

**Category** ★★ **Rooms** 19 with air-conditioning, telephone, shower, WC and TV. **Price** Double 260-300F / 39,64-45,73€. **Meals** Breakfast 38F / 5,80€, served 8:00-10:00; half board 270-295F / 41,16-44,97€ (per pers.). **Restaurant** (only for residents). Closed Nov 1 – Easter. Service from 7:30PM. Specialties: Traditional country cooking, Alsatian specialties. **Credit cards** Visa, Eurocard and MasterCard. **Pets** Small dogs allowed. **Facilities** Tennis communal ( 20F / 3,04€ /hour), parking. **Nearby** Colmar, Alsace Wine Route from Marlenheim to Thann, Haut-Koenigsbourg – 18-hole golf course in Ammerschwihr. **Closed** Feb.

*L*es Hirondelles is a huge, former farm lying near the famous *Auberge de l'Ill* restaurant and the lovely Ill River. The bedrooms are located in a large outbuilding which has been entirely refurbished. Reasonable and comfortable, the are well-kept-up but suffer from a lack of good lighting, which makes them seem a bit somber, especially in those rooms that are decorated in drab colors. Decorated for comfort and practicality, they are furnished with new but typically Alsatian wardrobes of polychromed wood. You may choose between rooms giving onto flowery balconies and the courtyard, or a more rural view over small vegetable gardens. There is a welcoming lounge on the ground floor where breakfast is served, along with good dinners based on regional cooking. A reasonably priced stop not far from the vineyards.

*How to get there* *(Map 12): 12km north of Colmar via RN83 towards Strasbourg.*

## Auberge Les Alisiers

68650 Lapoutroie (Haut-Rhin)
5, rue Faude
Tel. (0)3.89.47.52.82 - Fax (0)3.89.47.22.38
M. and Mme Degouy

**Category** ★★ **Rooms** 16 with telephone, bath (shower jet) or shower and WC. **Price** Single and double 190-450F / 28,97-68,60€. **Meals** Breakfast (buffet) 45F / 6,87€, served 7:30-10:00; half board 320-400F / 48,78-60,98€. **Restaurant** Closed Monday evening except for guests on half board, and Tuesday. Service 12:00PM-1:45PM, 7:00PM-8:45PM; mealtime specials 89-230F / 13,72-35,05, also à la carte. Specialties: Cervelas rôti sur salade de choucroute; kouglof façon pain perdu. **Credit cards** Visa, Eurocard and MasterCard. **Pets** Dogs allowed. **Facilities** Parking. **Nearby** Colmar, Alsace Wine Route from Marlenheim to Thann – 18-hole golf course in Ammerschwihr. **Closed** Jan.

The *Auberge Les Alisiers* lies 700 meters up in the mountains; the view from it over the Hautes Vosges and the Béhine Valley is stunning, and the hotel itself is very pleasant. The small bedrooms are intimate, comfortable and well-kept; one has a small private terrace. A warmly decorated lounge is at your disposal where, in winter, you can cozy up to a crackling fire before heading to dinner. The dining room is delightful, with several pieces of antique furniture and an impressive panoramic view. You will enjoy excellent, very reasonably priced cuisine. From your table in the evening, you might see several deer grazing at the edge of the woods, a bird of prey circling over the valley and the chef's assistant fishing a beautiful trout out of the fishtank. This is a very friendly hotel whose relaxed and informal atmosphere is largely created by the hospitable owners.

***How to get there*** *( Map 12): 19km northwest of Colmar via N415; at Lapoutroie go left in front of the church and follow the signs for 3km.*

## Auberge et Hostellerie Paysanne

68480 Lutter (Haut-Rhin)
Tel. (0)3.89.40.71.67 - Fax (0)3.89.07.33.38
Christiane Litzler

**Category** ★★ **Rooms** 16 with telephone, bath or shower, WC, TV. **Price** Single 230-440F / 35,06-67,08€. **Meals** Breakfast 38F / 5,80€, served 7:00-9:30; half board 280-430F / 42,69-65,5€. **Restaurant** Service 11:30-2:00PM, 18:30-9:00PM; mealtime specials 48-95F/ 7,32-14,48€ (lunch); 125-230F / 19,06-35,06€ (evening), also à la carte. **Credit card** Visa. **Pets** Dogs allowed. **Facilities** Parking. **Nearby** Medieval city of Ferrette, Bale, Museums of Mulhouse, Hiking trail. **Closed** 2 weeks in end Jan – beg Feb.

Lutter is at the base of the first Jura foothills, with a tree-lined brook that flows from a mountain sping. This is two inns in one, managed with love, humor, and energy by Carmen Guerinot and his daughter Christiane. The main house is a sturdy structure with a slightly lackluster façade, fortunately brightened up by a cascade of geraniums. This is where you find the restaurant, with its good traditional cuisine, and, on the *premier étage*, a few very modest rooms. We recommend Numbers 6 and 7 and discourage Numbers 4 and 5. The most beautiful rooms are 200 meters away in an old farmhouse from Sundgau (17th cent.), saved from demolition and moved here, beam by beam, to the field and orchard that border the village. These rooms are beautiful, comfortable, and cozy with their wooden highlights, traditional furnishings, and low ceilings (except for Numbers 17 and 19, whose superb spaciousness includes the slope of the roof). You'll love the peace and quiet here, across from a very well-cared-for garden. Howerer, breakfast is served at the inn. But isn't a little walk the best way to work up a good appetite?

***How to get there*** *( Map 20): Take Mulhouse-Bale highway to the Hesingue - Saint Louis exit to Folgensbourg, Bettlach, Oltingue, and then, Lutter.*

# Hostellerie Saint-Barnabé

Murbach 68530 Buhl (Haut-Rhin)
Tel. (0)3.89.62.14.14 - Fax (0)3.89.62.14.15
M. and Mme Orban
E-mail: hostellerie.st.barnabe@wanadoo.fr

**Category** ★★★ **Rooms** 27 with telephone, bath or shower, WC, TV and minibar. **Price** Single and double 382-595F / 58,32-90,71€, suite 895-1100F / 136,44-167,69€. **Meals** Breakfast (buffet) 65-75F / 9,91-11,43€ (in room), served 7:30-10:30. **Restaurant** With air-conditioning. Closed Sunday evening Nov – Mar and Monday and Wednesday lunchtime. Service 12:00PM-1:30PM, 7:00PM-9:00PM; mealtime specials 158-398F / 24,12-60,76€, also à la carte. Specialties: Triologie de foie gras; variante de l'ocean; pigeon rotie au miel. **Credit cards** All major. **Pets** Dogs allowed (+35F / 5,34€). **Nearby** Lauch Valley, Murbach Abbey, Unterlinden Museum in Colmar, Automobile and Rail Museums in Mulhouse, Alsace Wine Route – 9-hole Rouffach golf course. **Closed** Jan 16 – Feb 25, Sunday evening from Nov – May.

You can find this hotel in a beautiful, wooded vista, just a stone's throw from the abbey of Murbach. The *Hostellerie* has several dining rooms, lounges, and smoking rooms with beautiful views of its forest setting. The atmosphere is tranquil and the decoration is classic. The bedrooms are attractive and very comfortable, with elegant bathrooms. (Rooms 11, 16 and 20 can be noisy during mealtimes). Nature lovers will enjoy the smaller but truly smashing *Pavillon Vert* rooms on the ground floor, and families will relish them because they have communicating doors. Note also the irresistible *Chalet* room with a cheerful fireplace. The fabrics throughout have been beautifully chosen. The regional cuisine is excellent - you are served on the terrace in summer - and there is a delightful choice of Alsatian wines. The owners are young and friendly.

***How to get there*** *( Map 20): 3km from Guebwiller. Go straight through the center of town to Buhl; then turn left for Murbach.*

## Hôtel Le Clos Saint-Vincent

68150 Ribeauvillé (Haut-Rhin)
Route de Bergheim
Tel. (0)3.89.73.67.65 - Fax (0)3.89.73.32.20
Familie Chapotin

**Category** ★★★★ **Rooms** 12 and 3 apartments, with telephone, bath, WC, TV, safe and minibar. **Price** Single and double 800-1000F / 121,96-152,45€, apart. 1100-1225F / 167,69 à 186,75€. **Meals** Breakfast incl., served 8:15-10:30; half board 1300-1600F / 198,18-243,92€. **Restaurant** Closed Tuesday and Wednesday. Service 12:00PM-2:00PM, 7:00PM-8:30; mealtime specials 260F / 39,64€, also à la carte. Specialties: Rognons au pinot noir; cailles farcies à la marjolaine. **Credit cards** Visa, Eurocard and MasterCard. **Pets** Dogs allowed (+30F / 4,58 €). **Facilities** Covered swimming pool, parking. **Nearby** Hunawihr, swan reproduction center, ruins of the Château of St-Ulrich, Riquewihr, Alsace Wine Route from Marlenheim to Thann, Le Haut-Koenigsbourg; local festivities: Wine Festival in Jul-Aug, Minstrel Festival in Sep, Baroque Music Festival in autumn – 18-hole golf course in Ammerschwihr. **Open** Mar 15 – Nov 15.

In the heart of the Riesling wine country, the *Clos Saint Vincent* looks out on the Alsace plateau, the Black Forest, and to the east, the Alps. This hotel is composed of three stories. On the first story there is a lobby and a pleasant restaurant with a panoramic view. The bedrooms, with *Directoire*-style or rustic furniture, are bright, very comfortable and totally quiet. The tasteful fabrics lend much to the decoration. There is a very beautiful covered swimming pool.

***How to get there*** *(Map 12): 19km north of Colmar via N83 and D106 towards Ribeauvillé, then D1b towards Bergheim (follow the signs).*

## Hostellerie des Seigneurs de Ribeaupierre

68150 Ribeauvillé (Haut-Rhin)
11, rue du Château
Tel. (0)3.89.73.70.31 - Fax (0)3.89.73.71.21 - Mme Barth

**Category** ★★★ **Rooms** 10 with telephone, bath or shower and WC. **Price** Double 630-730F / 96,04-111,29€; suite 780-930F / 118,91-141,78€. **Meals** Breakfast incl., served 8:00-11:00. No restaurant. **Credit cards** Amex, Visa. **Pets** Dogs not allowed. **Nearby** Hunawihr, swan reproduction center, ruins of the Château of Saint-Ulrich, Riquewihr, Alsace Wine Route from Marlenheim to Thann, Le Haut-Koenigsbourg; local festivities: Wine Festival in Jul-Aug, Minstrel Festival in Sep, Baroque Music Festival in autumn — 18-hole golf course in Ammerschwihr. **Open** Mar 6 — end Dec.

The *Hostellerie des Seigneurs de Ribeaupierre* is a remarkable small hotel in one of the most beautiful villages of Alsace. There are several delicious rooms in this 18th-century auberge, which is located outside the town center. All are charming and comfortable, with beautiful old regional furniture, soft beds, light-colored woodwork and half-timbering, and ravishing fabrics. The bathrooms are superb and there is a lovely corner sitting area in many rooms. On the ground floor, there is a small lounge where a fireplace is often blazing; several steps down, you come to the breakfast room. Breakfasts are delicious and copious and you may also ask for brunch, with cold cuts, eggs and, as this is Alsace, a slice of *foie gras*. This is a magnificent hotel, where you are greeted warmly by the owners, two very dynamic sisters. For restaurants, we suggest the gastronomic *La Winstub Zum Pfifferhüs*, reserved for non-smokers; and the simpler *La Flammerie* (delicious *jambonneau*) and *L'Auberge Zahnacker*. And three kilometers out of town, the *Winstub du Sommelier*.

***How to get there*** *(Map12): 19km north of Colmar via N83 and D106 towards Ribeauvillé. Once there, head toward Haute-Ville and the parish church of Saint-Grégoire.*

## Hôtel A L'Oriel

68340 Riquewihr (Haut-Rhin)
3, rue des Écuries-Seigneuriales
Tel. (0)3.89.49.03.13 - Fax (0)3.89.47.92.87 - Mme Wendel
E-mail: oriel@club.internet.fr

**Category** ★★ **Rooms** 19 with bath. or shower, WC and TV. (17 with minibar) **Price** Double 395-530F / 60,22-80,80€, 3 pers. 680F / 103,67€. **Meals** Breakfast 54F / 8,24€, served 8:00AM-12:00PM. No restaurant. **Credit cards** All major. **Pets** Dogs allowed (+60F / 9,15€). **Nearby** Riquewihr, Hunawihr, Alsace Wine Route from Marlenheim to Thann; Le Haut-Kœnigsbourg – 18-hole golf course in Ammerschwihr. **Open** All year.

The ramparts of Riquewihr are powerless against the mobs of tourists that lay siege to this most classic of medieval villages along the wine trails of Alsace. So avoid visiting this spot during the day and choose the "Trojan horse" strategy -- let yourself get trapped behind the old walls at day's end and spend the night there. You will then have the chance to canvas the village's tiny streets in total peace and quiet, after the last buses have pulled up stakes and before the next morning's arrivals pull in. The Oriel , an old 18th-century house with traditional furnishing, is a bit off of the beaten path of the main street. Surrounding a little, interior court with exposed half-timbers where you can have a drink in summer, the rooms are simple, small and pleasant with their light wallpaper, plain or with tiny figures, and appointed with either antique furniture or modern pieces in the Louis-Philippe style. Number 2 is our favorite, 19 is a suite with a mezzanine, and 18 and 20 are great for families. All in all, the hotel is pleasing, homey, and not in the least pretentious. A fun bar is in the basement brightened up by orange walls and beautiful, colored tableclothes. Open and friendly reception.

***How to get there*** *( Map 12 ) 19 km north of Colmar on N 83; take the Riquewihr exit.*

# Hôtel Au Moulin

68127 Sainte-Croix-en-Plaine (Haut-Rhin)
Tel. (0)3.89.49.31.20 - Fax (0)3.89.49.23.11
M. and Mme Wœlffle

**Category** ★★ **Rooms** 16 and 1 suite with telephone, bath, WC and TV – Elevator; wheelchair access.
**Price** Single and double 240-420F / 36,59-64,03€, suite 500F / 76,22€. **Meals** Breakfast 50F /
7,62€, served 7:30-10:00. No restaurant. **Credit cards** Visa, Eurocard and MasterCard. **Pets** Dogs
allowed (+30F / 4,57€). **Facilities** Parking. **Nearby** Colmar, Eguisheim, Munster, Alsace Wine Route
from Marlenheim to Thann – 18-hole golf course in Ammerschwihr. **Open** End Mar – Nov 2.

This former grain mill is on the banks of the old Thur, also known as the
"Canal of the 12 Mills" (two of which are still in operation). It was built
in the 16th-century, heavily renovated, and then turned into a hotel in 1982. It's
a great, old white building with window boxes filled with bright geraniums. The
Woelffle family lives in the middle houses. Everything is centered around a
pretty, closed-in courtyard with flowering bushes and a beautiful stone well,
near which breakfast is served in summer. The rooms look out either on the
Vosges forest or on the fields (for three rooms in another building look out on
the courtyard). They are decorated modestly - some a bit behind-the-times,
others a bit more cheerful, but most rooms are roomy and all are well-tended.
Our favorite is Number 401, in white and blue with an expansive view. This is
a simple and agreeable place with reasonable prices, where you will receive a
friendly welcome. For dinner, head back to Eguisheim and treat yourself to the
excellent *Caveau d'Eguisheim*. A bit further away, in Colmar, *La Maison des
Têtes*, serves hefty portions of regional cuisine, and *Au Fer Rouge*, has a high
reputation and prices to match.

***How to get there*** *(Map 12): 6 km south of Colmar via N 422, then take D 1
toward Sainte-Croix-en-Plaine. Head south on A 35 and take Exit 27 toward
Herrlisheim.*

## Auberge La Meunière

68590 Thannenkirch (Haut-Rhin)
30, rue Sainte-Anne
Tel. (0)3.89.73.10.47 - Fax (0)3.89.73.12.31
M. Dumoulin

**Category** ★★ **Rooms** 20 with telephone, bath or shower, WC and TV – Elevator. **Price** Double 290-390F / 44,21-59,46€. **Meals** Breakfast (buffet) 40F / 6,10€, served 8:00-9:30; half board 255-350F / 38,87-53,36€. **Restaurant** Service 12:15PM-2:00PM, 7:15PM-9:00PM; mealtime specials 95-235F / 13,72-35,83€, also à la carte. Specialties: Médaillon de lotte sur lit de choux; foie gras poêlé au miel; noisettes de marcassin; poires pochées au vin rouge d'Alsace. **Credit cards** Amex, Visa, Eurocard and MasterCard. **Pets** Dogs allowed (+20F / 3,05€). **Facilities** Health center and sauna (150F / 22,87€ for 2 pers.), mountain bikes, billiard and parking. **Nearby** Haut-Koenigsbourg, Ribeauvillé, Riquewihr, Kaysersberg – 18-hole golf course in Ammerschwihr. **Open** Mid Mar – 19 Dec.

It is impossible not to notice the typically Alsatian façade of this lovely auberge in the little village of Thannenkirch in the foothills of the Vosges. You will find the same charm in the dining room, with its almond-green table linens and low ceilings and the wooden partitions that create several little intimate corners. The bedrooms, some furnished with antiques and some in more modern style, all have the same cozy and comfortable feel. Instead of numbers, the bedroom doors have enameled plaques inscribed with women's names. We particularly liked the *Sophie* and *Joséphine* rooms with their glassed-in balconies looking over the countryside towards the fortress of Haut-Koenigsbourg in the distance. The view is superb from the large terrace, where meals are also served.

***How to get there*** *(Map 12): 25km north of Colmar via N83 to Guémar, N106 and D42.*

# Hôtel Crystal

54000 Nancy (Meurthe-et-Moselle)
5, rue Chanzy
Tel. (0)3.83.17.54.00 - Fax (0)3.83.17.54.30
M. Gérard Gatinois

**Category** ★★★ **Rooms** 56 (20 with air-conditioning) with telephone, bath or shower, WC and TV – 1 for disabled persons. **Price** Single and double 330-460F / 50,31-70,13€. **Meals** Breakfast 45F / 6,86€, served 6:30-10:00. No restaurant. **Credit cards** Visa, Amex, Diners. **Pets** Dogs allowed (30F / 4,58€). **Facilities** Parking. **Nearby** Stanislas Place, museums, tropical aquarium and botanical garden in Nancy; Château in Haroué **Open** Jan 3 – Dec 31.

Not far from the famous Stanislas Place, a masterpiece of architecture and 18th-century ironwork, you will find the perfect little hotel for your stop-overs in Nancy. Its turn-of-the-century façade, at first banal, has been intelligently redone. The furnishings and interior decorations are strictly contemporary and play with the contrasts between straight lines and curves, and mixes brightly colored yellow and green walls with the furniture and dark wood flooring. Near the bar and the skylights which recall winter gardens, the armchairs, upholstered in blue, green and yellow tartan Kenzo upholstering bring together the hotle's three main colors. A few rooms decorated in yellow and orange, all the others are decked out in the same color scheme. Even the smallest rooms are comfortable, with their thick carpeting, ravishing bathrooms, and stylish furnishings, -designed by the local architect Jean-Philippe Nuel. Double-paned windows keep out the noise from the street, ensuring your peaceful night's rest. Make sure to only take the renovated rooms. (The others will be brought up-to-date very soon.) A warm welcome awaits. Many restaurants nearby, including the famouus 1900 bistro *Excelsior* and the out-standing *Cap-Marine*.

***How to get there*** *(Map 12): Via A 31, take the Nancy-Center exit and head toward Centre-Gare.*

# Château d'Adoménil

Rehainviller 54300 Lunéville (Meurthe-et-Moselle)
Tel. (0)3.83.74.04.81 - Fax (0)3.83.74.21.78
M. Million

**Category** ★★★ **Rooms** 8 and 4 duplexes (with air-conditioning) with telephone, bath, WC, TV and minibar. **Price** Single and double 550-900F / 83,85-137,20€, suite and duplex 1100-1200F / 167,69-182,94€. **Meals** Breakfast 80F / 12,20€, served 8:00-10:30; half board from 790F / 120,43€ (per pers., 3 days min.). **Restaurant** Closed Sunday evening, Monday and Tuesday lunchtime Nov 1– Apr 15, and Sunday evening, Monday lunchtime and Tuesday lunchtime Apr 16 – Oct 31. Service 12:15PM-1:30PM, 7:30PM-9:30PM; mealtime specials 250-465F / 38,11-70,89€, also à la carte. Specialties: Croustillant de langoustines au vinaigre balsamique; assiette lorraine. **Credit cards** All major. **Pets** Dogs allowed. **Facilities** Swimming pool and parking. **Nearby** Château in Lunéville, Crystal Museum in Baccarat, Stanislas Place, School of Nancy Museum and Emile Gallé Museum in Nancy, Saint-Etienne Cathedral in Toul. **Closed** Jan 2 – Feb 10.

In just a few years, Monsieur Million has managed to make the *Adoménil* one of the region's most beautiful establishments. His culinary skills and the gastronomical wonders he whips up here contribute to this reputation, but, for all that, we mustn't forget the quality of the rooms either. You can choose between the delightful, classically-decorated rooms in the castle, with their beautiful, regional furniture; and the rooms more recently set up in the former stables. Extremely luxurious, these stable rooms brilliantly blend antique and neoclassical furnishing, beautiful fabrics, and subtle lighting effects. The bathrooms are just as much of a treat. Outside, there is the expanse of a seven-acre park. The little railway nearby only infrequently breaks the calm of this place. Excellent breakfasts, generously stacked with Viennese pastries. Only the greatest hospitality here.

***How to get there*** *( Map 12 ): 30km southeast of Nancy via N4 to Lunéville; 3km south of Lunéville via D914.*

## La Maison Forte - Restaurant Les Agapes

55800 Revigny-sur-Ornain (Meuse)
6, place Henriot-du-Coudray
Tel. (0)3.29.70.56.00 - Fax (0)3.29.70.59.30
M. and Mme Joblot

**Category** ★★ **Rooms** 6 and 1 suite, with telephone, bath or shower, WC – Room for disabled persons. **Price** Double 350-700F / 53,36-106,71€. **Meals** Breakfast 55F / 8,38€, served 7:30-10:00 **Restaurant** Service 12:00PM-1:30PM, 7:30PM-9:15PM, mealtime specials 165F (lunchtime week days) 235, 320F / 25,15, 35,83, 48,78€, also à la carte. Specialties: Pot-au-feu de foie gras au vinaigre balsamique. **Credit cards** All major. **Pets** Dogs allowed. **Facilities** Parking **Nearby** Bar-le-Duc, Argonne forest, Trois-Fontaines Abbey, Saulx valley, kayaking, Benedictine Abbey and sacred art museum at Saint-Mihiel – 18-hole golf course at Combles. **Closed** Aug 1 – 15.

Born and bred in Alsace, Danièle and Jean-Marc Joblot fell in love with this medieval mansion and have spared no expense to make their dream come true. First off, there is the restaurant, in a beautiful room with a stone fireplace (often in service), high exposed-beam ceilings, terra-cotta tiles, and wrought-iron armchairs. The food is savoury, perfectly-balanced, and magnificiently enhanced by subtle sauces. Jean March has forgotten nothing from his days with A. Dutournier of the *Carré des Feuillants*. The seven rooms, have just been set up in wings. Comfortable and pleasingly decorated with rustic furniture, beautiful materials, and colorful fabrics, these rooms boast a "refined country" look. In summer, the huge patio that looks over the courtyard is dressed out in teak furniture and parasols. The meals are served there, breakfast included, and it's a real pleasure to have your coffee while admiring the view from the entryway where, in the background, the village is starting to come to life.

***How to get there*** *(Map 11): Via A 4, take the Chalons-St-Etienne-au-Temple exit, an then head toward Bar-le-Duc.*

## Auberge du Kiboki

57560 Turquestein (Moselle)
Route du Donon (D 993)
Tel. (0)3.87.08.60.65 - Fax (0)3.87.08.65.26
M. Schmitt

**Category** ★★ **Rooms** 14 with telephone, bath or shower, WC and TV. **Price** Double 450-500F / 68,60-76,22€; suite 700F / 106,71€. **Meals** Breakfast (buffet) 55F / 8,38€, served 8:00-10:00; half board 430F / 65,55€ (per pers. in double room, 3 days min.). **Restaurant** Service 12:00PM-2:00PM, 7:00PM-9:00PM; à la carte 120-220F / 18,29-33,54€. Specialties: Regional cooking; foie gras maison; frog. **Credit cards** Visa, Eurocard and MasterCard. **Pets** Dogs not allowed. **Facilities** Covered swimming pool, whirlpool, sauna, tennis and parking. **Nearby** Dabo Rock, crystal factories, potteries in Niderviller. **Closed** Mid Feb – Mar 20 and Monday, Tuesday, Wednesday from Nov 15 – Jan 15.

In the middle of the forest in the Turquestein-Blancrupt Valley, criss-crossed by many marked footpaths, lies the traditional *Auberge du Kiboki*. A very cozy atmosphere is created by the warm decor in this hotel. The dining rooms are very appealing: one is bright with checked tablecloths, matching curtains and lampshades; the other is decorated in soft colors and has a handsome, large china cabinet filled with local pottery. There you will sample savoury, local traditional cooking. The comfortably furnished bedrooms reflect the same style, with warm beige and brown tones, canopied beds, and antique wardrobes. This genuine forest inn is an ideal place for a restful stay. The cuisine is excellent, and the owners are very hospitable, all making the Kiboki one of the outstanding hotels in this guide.

***How to get there*** *( Map 12 ): 73km west of Strasbourg via A35 and D392 towards Saint-Dié; at Schirmeck D392 towards Donon and D993 towards Turquestein-Blancrupt.*

# Hostellerie des Bas-Rupts et Chalet Fleuri

Les Bas-Rupts
88400 Gérardmer (Vosges)
Tel. (0)3.29.63.09.25 - Fax (0)3.29.63.00.40 - M. and Mlle Sylvie Philippe
E-mail: basrupts@wanadoo.fr

**Category** ★★★ **Rooms** 32 with telephone, bath or shower, WC and TV. **Price** Single and double 450-900F / 68,60-137,20€, suite 1200F / 182,94€. **Meals** Breakfast 90F / 13,74€, served 7:00-10:00; half board 580-750F / 88,42-114,34€. **Restaurant** Service 12:00PM-2:00PM, 7:00PM-9:30PM; mealtime specials 180-450F / 27,44-68,60€, also à la carte. Specialties: Tripes au riesling; aiguillettes de canard; andouille fumée sur choucroute. **Credit cards** Amex, Visa, Eurocard and MasterCard. **Pets** Dogs allowed (+50-100F / 17,62-25,24€). **Facilities** Swimming pool, tennis, garage, parking. **Nearby** Les Cuves Waterfall, Longemer Lake, Retournemer Lake, Epinal — 18-hole golf course in Epinal. **Open** All year.

The *Hostellerie des Bas-Rupts*, with its flower-bedecked chalet and famous restaurant, is located just outside Gérardmer, once a favorite Alsace-Lorraine resort where the well-heeled enjoyed spending time (and money in the casino). The nostalgic town was almost completely destroyed at the end of World War II. The *Hostellerie des Bas-Rupts* is a veritable celebration of flowers, which are found painted on beams, doors, bedsteads; and in fresh and dried bouquets throughout, adding lots of comfort and atmosphere to the comfortable bedrooms in the annex. In the hotel itself, the rooms have just been redone with a completely charming "Austria in the Vosges" look. The service is both professional and extremely courteous.

*How to get there (Map 12): 56km west of Colmar via D417 and D486 towards La Bresse.*

## Le Manoir au Lac

88402 Gérardmer (Vosges)
59, chemin de la droite du lac
Tel. (0)3.29.27.10.20 - Fax (0)3.29.27.10.27
Mme Marie-Luce Valentin

**Category** ★★★★ **Rooms** 6 and 1 suite, with telephone, bath, WC, safe, minibar and satellite TV.
**Price** Double 700-1300F / 106,71-198,18€, suite (2 pers.) 1500F / 228,67 (pers. supp. 200F /
30,49€). **Meals** Breakfast 80F / 12,21€. No restaurant. **Credit cards** Visa, Amex, Diner's Club. **Pets**
Dogs not allowed. **Facilities** Parking. **Nearby** Gérardmer Lake, skiing in winter; cathedral of Saint-
Dié – 18-hole golf course in Epinal. **Open** All year.

A century ago, Guy de Maupassant loved staying here, and one can easily
imagine him passing his time on the hotel's patio, gazing at the lake that
lazily extends some 20-odd meters below. Since that time, this little hotel has
been redone from head to toe, making it respectably luxurious while keeping
the best kind of warm and "homey" feeling. The rooms, decorated in an up-to-
date yet classic manner (with stylish furnishings, parquetry, thick comforters),
are found on two floors. Extremely comfortably and perfectly kept-up, these
rooms are all very well soundproofed, which is a necessity, given the hidden,
though sometimes noisy road that is nearby. Some are quite large, while those
under the rooftop, which are pretty even if a bit dark, are a bit smaller and
cheaper. On the ground floor, a very nice salon with a well-stocked library
extends into a veranda which opens out to the patio. Depending on the time of
day, you can have a drink or take your breakfast over a good book. Why not a
little Maupassant?

***How to get there*** *(Map 12): Leaving Gérardmer, on the road leading to
Remiremont.*

## Chalets des Ayés

88160 Le Thillot (Vosges)
Chemin des Ayés
Tel. (0)3.29.25.00.09 - Fax (0)3.29.25.36.48
M. Marsot

**Category** ★★★ **Rooms** 2 and 17 chalets (4-10 pers.), with bath or shower, WC and TV – Guest phone; wheelchair access. **Price** Double 340-420F / 51,83-64,03€, chalets 1200-4800F / 182,94-731,8€ (4-10 pers.). **Meals** Breakfast 55F / 8,38€, served 8:00-10:00. No restaurant. **Credit card** Visa. **Pets** Dogs allowed only in the chalets. **Facilities** Swimming pool, tennis (38F / 7,79€) and parking. **Nearby** Cross-country and downhill skiing, riding, mountain bikes, walks. **Open** All year.

The *Chalets des Ayes* is not actually a hotel. It does however provide a practical and pleasant solution to the problem of lodging in the wild and seductively beautiful Vosges region, where it is sometimes hard to find a hotel with rural charm. Two comfortable bedrooms are at your disposal (we prefer the one overlooking the valley), along with very well equipped, pleasantly appointed small chalets, which won the First Prize in the Vosges *département* for houses with beautiful flower gardens. Strictly speaking, they are rented by the week but, like the bedrooms, may be reserved for several nights. You can enjoy a magnificent view from the garden and the swimming pool. And if you wish to go out for dinner, you can choose between the *Vicenza*, a pleasant farm/pizzeria, or the more gastronomically sophisticated *Restaurant des Sapins*.

***How to get there*** *(Map 20): 51km west of Mulhouse via N66 towards Remiremont and towards Mulhouse to Le Thillot. Go past the Intermarche for 200 meters, then take a left. Follow the signs.*

## Auberge de la Cholotte

Les Rouges-Eaux 88600 Bruyères (Vosges)
Tel. (0)3.29.50.56.93 - Fax (0)3.29.50.24.12
Mme Cholé

**Rooms** 5 with bath or shower and WC. **Price** Double 450F / 68,60€. **Meals** Breakfast incl.; half board and full board 400-500F / 60,98-76,22€ (per pers., 3 days min., special rates for children). **Restaurant** Service 12:00PM-2:00PM, 7:00PM-9:00PM; mealtime specials 150F / 22,87€, also à la carte. Specialties: Jambon cuit au foin; rapées de pomme de terre; tarte aux myrtilles. **Credit cards** Visa, Eurocard and MasterCard. **Pets** Dogs allowed. **Facilities** Parking. **Nearby** Skiing in winter, Cathedral and Cloisters of Saint-Dié, Epinal, Gérardmer Lake – 18-hole golf course in Epinal. **Closed** Jan, Sunday evening and Monday in low season.

Nestled in a small valley, the *Auberge de la Cholotte* is an irresistibly charming 18th-century farmhouse. In the bedrooms, which have been carefully restored, fabric and wall colors are tastefully coordinated in shades of yellow, blue and soft green, with an occasional brighter color. There are permanent art exhibits on view and a collection of regional objects, along with 19th-century furniture and handsome old Alsatian pieces in polychromed wood. All combine to create a cheerful, refined atmosphere in the comfortable lounges and the two small dining rooms. Concerts are often given in a third, larger dining room with 18th-century panelling and a Steinway piano. The simple bedrooms are charming, and one has a whirlpool bath. All have a pretty view of the flower garden and the pines which cover this magnificent countryside. Only one thing mars this pretty picture: the real lack of personnel, which is explained by the small capacity of the inn, but might cause you some problems when you arrive.

***How to get there*** *( Map 12 ): 15km west of Saint-Dié via D420, towards Bruyères.*

## Hôtel de la Fontaine Stanislas

Fontaine-Stanislas - 88370 Plombières-les-Bains (Vosges)
Tel. (0)3.29.66.01.53 - Fax (0)3.29.30.04.31
M. and Mme Bilger

**Category** ★★ **Rooms** 16 with telephone (14 with bath or shower, 12 with WC and 9 with TV).
**Price** Double 200-325F / 30,49-49,55€. **Meals** Breakfast 39F / 6,10€, served 7:30-9:30; half board
and full board 265-325F / 40,40-49,55€, 320-415F / 48,78-63,27€ (per pers., 3 days min.).
**Restaurant** Service 12:00PM-1:30PM, 7:00PM-9:00PM; mealtime specials 94-205F / 14,33-31,25€, also
à la carte. Specialties: Caille en crapaudine au crillon des Vosges. **Credit cards** All major. **Pets** Dogs
allowed (+25F / 3,81€). **Facilities** Parking. **Nearby** Epinal, Valleys of the Augronne and the Semouse,
Guéhand Waterfall, la Feuillée Nouvelle — 18-hole golf course in Epinal. **Open** Apr 1 – Oct 14.

Four generations of the same family have run this hotel, lost in the wild,
which charmed us with its 50s style. First, pay attention to the truly good
and healthy food (with well-aged wines at a reasonable price) served in a dining
room full of character with its light wood furnishings, huge picture windows,
high wainscotted ceilings and beautiful table linens. As far as the rooms go, the
impression is a bit different. Look away from the furniture (with its fake-wood
lamination so popular 30 years ago) a few drab curtains and bed covers, and
feast your eyes on the gorgeous, sylvan view. The utilities have been recently
improved, the hallways have been cheered up, and the upkeep is impeccable.
For the moment, we strongly recommend Rooms 2, 3, 4, and 7. Number 18 is
for families. In the annex, Rooms 11 and 20 look like they could have wound
up as Jacques Tati sets. Friendly service on the patio with the valley rolling
below. Unforgettably kind hospitality.

***How to get there*** *(Map 20): 30 km south of Epinal via D 434. At Xertigny, take
D3, D63, and D20. At Granges-de-Plombières, take the forest road on the right.*

## Auberge du Val Joli

88230 Le Valtin (Vosges)
Tel. (0)3.29.60.91.37 - Fax (0)3.29.60.81.73
M. Laruelle

**Category** ★★ **Rooms** 17 with telephone, 13 with bath or shower, WC and TV, 9 with minibar. **Price** Single and double 150-420F / 22,87-64,03€. **Meals** Breakfast 42F / 6,47€, served 8:00-10:00; half board 241-660F / 36,60-100,62€. **Restaurant** Service 12:30PM-2:00PM, 7:30PM-9:00PM; mealtime specials 60-270F / 9,16-41,16€, also à la carte. Specialties: Truite fumée maison; pâté lorrain; tarte aux myrtilles. **Credit card** Visa. **Pets** Dogs allowed (+20F / 3,05€). **Facilities** Tennis, parking and garage (30F / 4,58€). **Nearby** Cathedral of Saint-Dié, Gérardmer Lake – 18-hole golf course in Epinal. **Closed** Sunday evening and Monday except during holidays.

The little village of Valtin has only 99 inhabitants, and the mayor is also the owner of this auberge which stands at the bottom of one of the prettiest valleys of the Vosges. You only have to open the door to feel its character: low ceilings, beams, flagstones, and a fireplace create a completely authentic atmosphere. The dining room is very attractive with its many small windows and particularly its carved wood ceiling which is the work of an Alsatian carpenter. The comfort of the bedrooms and their bathroom facilities vary. They would be improved with more decoration. The four new rooms are cheerful and comfortable with their little, flower-bedecked balcony that looks out on the mountains; but the more out-of-date rooms in the old building still have all their charm, just like the old dining room. Even if the road passes just in front, there is no noise. A kind welcome at an unpretentious place in a beautifully conserved village.

***How to get there*** *(Map 12): 40km west of Colmar via D417 (by the Schlucht pass) to Le Collet, then right on D23 to Le Valtin.*

# Les Griffons

Le Bourg
24310 Bourdeilles (Dordogne)
Tel. (0)5.53.45.45.35 - Fax (0)5.53.45.45.20
M. and Mme Lebrun

**Category** ★★★ **Rooms** 10 with telephone and bath. **Price** Single and double 420-490F / 64,03-74,70€. **Meals** Breakfast 45F / 6,87€, served 8:15-10:00; half board 375-420F / 57,17-64,03€ (per pers., 3 days min.). **Restaurant** Closed Sunday evening and Monday lunchtime, Tuesday lunchtime in high season. Service 12:30PM-2:00PM, 7:30PM-9:00PM; mealtime specials 125-199F / 19,06-30,33€; also à la carte. Specialties: Escalope de foie gras aux pruneaux; magret mariné aux navets confits; lotte à la piperade; croustillant aux cèpes. **Credit card** Visa. **Divers Pets** Dogs allowed (+40F / 6,10€). **Facilities** Parking. **Nearby** Bell tower of the abbey church in Brantôme; Peiro-Levado dolmen; Bourdeilles; Châteaux of Puymarteau; Saint-Jean-de-Côle; Chancelade Abbey; Saltgourde estate; Marsac – 18-hole golf course in Périgueux. **Open** Easter – Nov 1.

The Dronne flows peacefully by this superb village lorded over by one of the region's most beautiful castles. Below it, at the foot of a 13th-century bridge, the hotel benefits from a truly attractive location. Large, smooth white stones and antique wood highlights beautify the interior. The rustically decorated dining room opens out to a patio, where you can eat your summer meals surrounded by greenery. The very recently renovated rooms are soberly decorated. You can find plain walls in pastel tones, amusing and colorful wall lamps, stylish furnishings, and, in some, exposed beams and a beautiful stone fireplace. A welcoming place that is attentively looked after.

***How to get there*** *(Map 23): 22 km north of Périgueux, 9 km from Brantôme on the CD 78 - Bourdeilles. Via A 10, take the Angoulême exit; Via A 20, take the Limoges exit.*

## Le Chatenet

Le Chatenet
24310 Brantôme (Dordogne)
Tel. (0)5.53.05.81.08 - Fax (0)5.53.05.85.52
M. and Mme Laxton
E-Mail: chatenet@wanadoo.fr

**Category** ★★★ **Rooms** 10 with telephone, bath, WC (4 with TV) – 1 for disabled persons (–20%). **Price** Double 500-590F / 76,22-89,94€, suites 810F / 123,48€. **Meals** Breakfast 60F / 9,16€, served 8:30-10:00. No restaurant. **Credit cards** Visa, Access, Eurocard and MasterCard. **Pets** Dogs allowed. **Facilities** Heated swimming pool, tennis, billiard, parking at hotel. **Nearby** Bell tower of the abbey church in Brantôme, "Peiro-Levado" dolmen; Châteaux of Hierce; Puymarteau and Saint-Jean-de-Côle; Chancelade Abbey; Saltgourde estate; Marsac – 18-hole golf course in Périgueux. **Open** Apr – Nov.

Nestled in the pretty countryside near Brantome, the *Chatenet*, whose owner, Philippe Laxton, describes as "a family home open to friends and friends of friends," is a wonderful place to stay. In buildings representative of beautiful 16th-century architecture, you will find superb bedrooms with upholstered walls, very tasteful furnishings and modern bathrooms. The lounge and dining room are inviting but in summer, guests often prefer the loggia, mainly because of the excellent breakfasts served there. There is no restaurant but there are many good ones nearby, including *Le Moulin de l'Abbaye*, *Les Frères Charbonnel* (highly rated in Michelin and Gault-Millau), and *Le Saint Marc*. This is a beautiful and very welcoming hotel.

***How to get there*** *(Map 23): 27km north of Périgueux, 1.5km from Brantôme via CD78 towards Bourdeilles.*

# Domaine de la Roseraie

24310 Brantôme (Dordogne)
Tel. (0)5.53.05.84.74 - Fax (0)5.53.05.77.94
M. Roux
E-mail: domaine.la.roseraie@wanadoo.fr

**Category** ★★★ **Rooms** 8 and 2 suite (4 with air-conditioning) with telephone, bath, WC and TV – Wheelchair access. **Price** Double 540-730F / 82,32-111,29€, suite 920-950F / 140,25-144,83€. **Meals** Breakfast 65F / 9,90€, served 7:30-10:30; half board 540-760F / 82,32-115,86€. **Restaurant** Service 12:00PM-15:00, 7:00PM-9:00PM; mealtime specials 165-295F / 25,15-44,97€, also à la carte. Specialties: Foie gras mi-cuit "maison"; saumon mariné à l'huile de noisettes; pavé de foie gras pané aux truffes; tournedos de canard aux poires rôties au sauternes. **Credit carts** All major. **Pets** Dogs allowed. **Nearby** Bell tower of the abbey church in Brantôme, Villars caves ; Bourdeilles; Château of Saint-Jean-de-Côle; Chancelade Abbey; Saltgourde estate; Marsac – 18-hole golf course in Périgueux. **Open** Mid Mar – Jan.

Nestled in the countryside outside Brantôme, *La Roseraie* is composed of two buildings set at an angle and a Perigourdine tower which protects a charming little courtyard full of lawn furniture. When it's sunny, you can take your breakfast and drink cool beverages next to the roses and geraniums. Inside, the *Roseraie* is very inviting. There are two lounges (one is brightened with a lovely log fire in winter) which are furnished with pleasant, comfortable, period furniture and decorated with Impressionist-style paintings. The bedrooms and baths are equally attractive and impeccably clean. Families should note the splendid duplex suite. All rooms are on the ground floor and have independent entrances. Last but not least, it is beautifully quiet here.

***How to get there*** *( Map 23): 27km north of Périgueux via D939; in the center of the town, 1km towards Angoulême.*

## Le Relais du Touron

24200 Carsac-Aillac (Dordogne)
Tel. (0)5.53.28.16.70 - Fax (0)5.53.28.52.51
Mme Carlier - M. Amriah

**Category ★★ Rooms** 12 with telephone, bath or shower, WC and TV. **Price** Double 295-375F / 44,97-57,17€, 3 pers. 430-485F / 65,55-73,94€. **Meals** Breakfast 38F / 5,80€, served 8:00-10:00; half board 310-346F / 47,26-52,61€. **Restaurant** Closed lunchtime (except Jul – Aug) and Thursday; mealtime specials 95-140F / 14,48-21,34€, also à la carte. Specialties: Foie gras d'oie poélé aux pommes câramélisées; feuilleté d'escargots aux cèpes; filet d'agneau au beurre de foie gras; sandre à l'orange. **Credit cards** Visa, Eurocard and MasterCard. **Pets** Dogs allowed. **Facilities** Swimming pool, parking. **Nearby** Walk along the valley of the Enéa from Carsac to Sainte-Nathalène, old town and house of La Boétie in Sarlat – 9-hole golf course in Vitrac. **Open** Apr 1 – Nov 14.

Protected from the road by a curtain of trees, the *Relais du Touron* looks like a simple, homey little country inn. The comfortable, functional, and well-looked-after rooms are divided up between two buildings, but they all look out on a lushly green vista. In the rustic, slightly quaint lounge, you can read and relax during rainy or really hot days. A veranda has just been set up outside next to the swimming pool. This is the perfect place to have breakfast, lunch, and dinner. The *Relais du Touron* serves the traditional cuisine of the area, which we have unfortunately not had the opportunity to sample. Just a few minutes from the tourist hot-spot of Sarlat, the *Relais du Touron* is a handy address at a reasonable price.

***How to get there*** *(Map 23): 75 km southwest of Périgueux, just until Sarlat. Then take D 704 toward Gourdon (600 m before the village of Carsac).*

# Manoir d'Hautegente

24120 Coly (Dordogne)
Tel. (0)5.53.51.68.03 - Fax (0)5.53.50.38.52
Mme Hamelin and Patrick Hamelin

**Category** ★★★ **Rooms** 10 and 4 duplexes (with air-conditioning), with telephone, bath, WC, TV and minibar. **Price** Double and duplex 530-1100F / 80,80-167,69€. **Meals** Breakfast 70F / 10,67€, served 8:30-10:00; half board 550-850F / 83,85-129,58€ (per pers., by reservation in Jul – Aug). **Restaurant** Service from 8:00PM; mealtime specials 250-380F / 38,11-57,93€, also à la carte. Specialties: Brasière de ris de veau aux écrevisses; poêlée de cèpes sur son foie gras et sauce aux truffes. **Credit cards** Visa, Eurocard and MasterCard. **Pets** Dogs allowed. **Facilities** Heated swimming pool, fishing, parking. **Nearby** Lascaux caves, Abbey of Saint-Amand-de-Coly; Sarlat. **Open** Mar – Nov.

A one-time textile mill and forge of the warrior monks of Saint Amand-du-Coly and the property of the Hamelin family for almost three centuries, this noble Perigord manor has, over several years, become a refined stopping place in a beautiful valley where graceful old walnut and oak trees line the roads. Ducks roam freely along the banks of the winding, babbling brook in front of the manor, soon to become delicious *foie gras* and *confit*, for sale at the reception desk. The wonderful rooms, like the series of lounges, have all been tastefully decorated with family furniture in a perfect blend of style and comfort. The fabric wall drapes and curtains are splendid, especially in the *Liserons* room, which is very large and has a private balcony overlooking the river. You will receive a warm and attentive welcome at this very charming hotel.

***How to get there*** *(Map 23): 30km southwest of Brive via the N 89 toward Périgueux. At Lardin-Saint-Lazare, take the D 704 then the D 62 toward Sarlat-Souillac.*

## Hôtel Cro-Magnon

24620 Les Eyzies-de-Tayac (Dordogne)
Tel. (0)5.53.06.97.06 - Fax (0)5.53.06.95.45
M. and Mme Leyssales

**Category** ★★★ **Rooms** 18 and 4 apartments, with telephone, bath or shower and WC (TV on request). **Price** Double 350-550F / 53,36-83,85€; suites 600-800F / 91,47-121,96€. **Meals** Breakfast 50F / 7,63€, served 8:00-10:00; half board 350-505F / 53,36-76,99€ (per pers., 3 days min.). **Restaurant** Closed Wednesday lunchtime except national holidays. Service 12:00PM-2:00PM, 7:00PM-9:15PM; mealtime specials 140-280F / 21,34-42,69€, also à la carte. Specialties: Escalope de foie de canard au vinaigre de cidre; salade d'escargots et fèves à l'oie séchée; croustillant d'anguilles aux châtaignes; truffes en croustade. **Credit cards** All major. **Pets** Dogs allowed (+30F / 4,57€). **Facilities** Swimming pool, parking. **Nearby** Les Eyzies: Cave and National Museum of Prehistory in Les Eyzies; Bara-Bahau cave and Proumeyssac chasm; Limeuil; Lascaux Cave in Montignac; *bastides* of Belvès tour in Montferrand-du-Périgord (130 km) — 18-hole La-Croix-de-Mortemart golf course in Le Bugue. **Open** May 9 – Oct 9.

This old coach house inn has been in the family for generations. The two reception rooms, whose colors harmonize with the open stonework and old furniture, are charming. There is a small museum in one. You can choose between a pretty dining room in local style or another, more modern, one which opens onto a shady terrace. Excellent regional cuisine is complemented by a well-chosen wine list. The bedrooms are comfortable and elegantly decorated. The main road, very busy during the summer, runs past the hotel, so we recommend the quieter annex rooms, which all look out on the two-acre park and its charming swimming pool.

***How to get there*** *(Map 23): 45km southeast of Périgueux via N89 and D710, then D47.*

# Hôtel Les Glycines

24620 Les Eyzies-de-Tayac (Dordogne)
Tel. (0)5.53.06.97.07 - Fax (0)5.53.06.92.19
Maud and Pascal Lombard

**Category** ★★★ **Rooms** 23 with telephone, bath and WC. **Price** Double 360-410F / 54,88-62,50€. **Meals** Breakfast 50F / 7,63€, served 8:00-10:00; half board 395-450F / 60,22-68,60€ (per pers., 3 days min.). **Restaurant** Closed Saturday lunchtime except national holidays. Service 12:00PM-2:00PM, 7:30PM-9:30PM; mealtime specials 135-280F / 20,58-42,69€, also à la carte. Specialties: Filet de bœuf aux morilles. **Credit cards** All major. **Pets** Dogs allowed. **Facilities** Swimming pool, parking. **Nearby** Les Eyzies: Cave and National Museum of Prehistory in Les Eyzies; Le Bugue, Bara-Bahau cave and Proumeyssac chasm; Limeuil – 18-hole La-Croix-de-Mortemart golf course in Le Bugue. **Open** Apr – mid Oct.

Along the road, near the entry to the famous hamlet of Eyzies, this large house is a great stop-over during off-peak-season months (avoid July and August), when the traffic is still light. The exterior tastefully blends stone, wood, and burgeoning greenery which sprouts up from every corner (with an outstanding bower of wisteria and some beautiful trimmed linden trees which shade the patio). The lounge and bar have a restful atmosphere and are furnished and decorated with great care. The lovely dining room opens onto the garden, but meals may also be taken on a new veranda that opens onto the yard with the pool just below. All the bedrooms are very comfortable, but many are time-worn (notably, Room 30), where as others have just been renovated in a more up-to-date style. Let's make it clear that *Les Glycines* has just changed owners and refurbishing projects are on the board for next year. That's good news.

***How to get there*** *(Map 23): 45km southeast of Périgueux via N89 and D710, then D47.*

# Le Moulin de la Beune

24620 Les Eyzies-de-Tayac (Dordogne)
Tel. (0)5.53.06.94.33 - Fax (0)5.53.06.98.06
M. and Mme Soulié

**Category** ★★ **Rooms** 20 with telephone, bath or shower and WC. **Price** Double 288-358F / 43,96-54,65€. **Meals** Breakfast 40F / 6,10€, served 8:00-10:30; half board 340-440F / 51,83-67,08€ (per pers., 2 days min.). **Restaurant** Closed Tuesday lunchtime and Wednesday. Service 12:00PM-2:30PM, 7:00PM-9:30PM; mealtime specials 108-350F / 16,48-53,36€, also à la carte. Specialties: Pigeonneau cuit en cocotte; foie gras frais. **Credit cards** All major. **Pets** Dogs allowed. **Facilities** Parking. **Nearby** Les Eyzies: Cave and National Museum of Prehistory in Les Eyzies; Le Bugue, Bara-Bahau cave and Proumeyssac chasm; Limeuil; Cave Lascaux in Montignac — 18-hole La-Croix-de-Mortemart golf course in Le Bugue. **Open** May — end Oct.

Just below the road, in one of the most visited places in France, this former mill is astonishingly quiet and calm. The little patios in the garden, with the lullaby babble of the Beune that winds about the mill, are restful and inviting. Set up in the foyer, the lounge encircles a large fireplace. Nearby, a room graced with little tables and chestnut armchairs serves as a breakfast or pre-dinner drink nook, according to the hour. The rooms, and the bathrooms as well, are neatly and nicely decorated. The white-painted walls have a restful look. The restaurant, *Au Vieux Moulin*, occupies another adjacent mill which has been just as thoughtfully restored. This is where the house's special bread is made. The truffle-based Périgourdine specialties are served in a large dining room accented by stone and exposed beams, or in the garden, walking distance from the prehistoric cliffs. A friendly, homey, and professional welcome.

***How to get there*** *(Map 23): 45km southeast of Périgueux via N89 and D710, then D47; in the middle of the village.*

# Le Château

24150 Lalinde-en-Périgord (Dordogne)
Tel. (0)5.53.61.01.82 - Fax (0)5.53.24.74.60
M. Gensou

**Category** ★★★ **Rooms** 7 with telephone, bath, WC and TV. **Price** Double 300-900F / 45,73-137,20€.
**Meals** Breakfast 68F / 10,37€, served 8:00-10:00; half board 340-660F / 51,83-100,62€ (per pers.,
obligatory in summer). **Restaurant** Closed Monday except evening in Jul – Aug; mealtime specials
125-300F / 19,06-45,73€; also à la carte. Specialties: Escargots farcis au foie gras et beurre de noix.
**Credit cards** All major. **Pets** Dogs allowed. **Facilities** Swimming pool. **Nearby** Vézère valley and
Dordogne valley. **Closed** Dec 20 – mid Feb; 3rd week in Sep and Sunday evening from Nov – end Mar.

Lording over the Dordogne, this hotel is situated in an impressive and calm place, not far from the town square of this graceful little town. From the other bank of the river, the 15th-century structure, remodelled and enlarged in the 19th-century, almost looks like a backdrop for an opera. The inside is cozy with its small, charmingly out-of-date lounge and well-lit dining room which opens out to the riverside patio where a little swimming pool has been installed, and where meals are served. Comfortable and decorated in reserved colors, most of the rooms look directly, or indirectly, out on the Dordogne. One of them is small indeed, but its price is in keeping with an attic-like room. Monsieur Gensou, a self-proclaimed regionalist whose wine list only carries the names of local vintages and Bordelais, works at the stoves each day to carefully cook up the house specialities based on the fine, local products he knows so well. A really great place.

***How to get there*** *(Map 23): 20 kms east of Bergerac in the Dordogne valley heading toward Sarlat via D 29.*

# Domaine de la Barde

24260 Le Bugue (Dordogne)
Route de Périgueux
Tél. 05.53.07.16.54 - Fax (0)5.53.54.76.19
M. Darnaud

**Category** ★★★ **Rooms** 18 with telephone, bath or shower, WC and TV – 2 for disabled persons. **Price** Double 440-1090F / 67,08-166,17€. **Meals** Breakfast (buffet) 68F / 10,36€, served 8:00-10:30. **Restaurant**. Menus 140-190F / 21,34-28,97€. **Credit cards** Visa, Eurocard and MasterCard. **Pets** Dogs allowed on request (+50F / 7,63€). **Facilities** Swimming pool, tennis, sauna (60F / 9,16€), parking. **Nearby** Le Bugue: cave of Bara-Bahau and chasm of Proumeyssac; Limeuil; Museum of Prehistory in Eyzies; Cadouin Abbey; *bastides* of Belvès tour in Montferrand-du-Périgord (130 km) – 18-hole Croix-de-Mortemart golf course. **Open** Apr – end Oct.

This 14th-century estate, renovated in the 19th-century and rehabilitated by its present owners, blends comfort and luxury. The *Domaine*'s bedrooms, are named after plants (*Bleuet, Les Physalis*); the history estate's (*Le Colombier, Maître Pierre*, and *La Belle Meunière*,) located in the mill; or after the hill that can be seen from the window (*Bara-Bahau*). The rooms are located in three different buildings: in the manor house, containing the smallest room to the most luxurious; in the old nut-oil mill, featuring more rustic but delightful rooms with modern accommodations (some have an independent entrance overlooking the garden); and the most recent bedroom, *La Forge*, which is located in a small, mansard-style house. Then there is the beautiful park relaxing and the replanted formal garden that looks as it must have centuries ago. For dinner, a restaurant with a patio has just been installed in a huge building, a bit away. We hope that it will live up to the great beauty of this area.

***How to get there*** *(Map 23): 47km southeast of Périgueux via N89 to Niversac, D710 to Bugue.*

# Hôtel du Manoir de Bellerive

24480 Le Buisson-de-Cadouin (Dordogne)
Route de Siorac
Tel. (0)5.53.22.16.16 - Fax (0)5.53.22.09.05 - M. Clevenot

**Category** ★★★ **Rooms** 24 with air-conditioning with telephone, bath or shower, WC, TV and minibar. **Price** Single and double 480-1150F / 73,18-175,32€. **Meals** Breakfast 60-85F / 9,16-12,21€, served 8:00-11:00. **Restaurant** Service 12:00PM-2:00PM and 7:30PM-10:00PM mealtime specials 150-420F / 22,87-64,03€, also à la carte. **Credit card** Visa. **Pets** Dogs allowed. **Facilities** Swimming pool, tennis, sauna and hamman (120F / 18,29€), parking. **Nearby** Le Bugue, Limeuil – 18-hole golf course in la-Croix-de-Mortemart. **Closed** Jan 1 – mid Feb.

Along the Dordogne, this hotel has a beautiful lawn in the style of an English landscape garden. On the ground floor, an enormous, columned hall opens out to the lounge, the bar, and the dining room. A double-winding staircase leads you to your room. The biggest rooms are on the first story. Other large and modern rooms, extremely comfortable and outfitted with luxurious bathrooms, are in the orangery. All the decor is very sophisticated. Patinated paintings, *trompe-l'oeil* marble treatments, superb fabric bear witness to an incredible effort in which the old and the new light-heartedly dance together (Although there is ordinary furniture in some rooms.). All are quiet, except for a few rooms which suffer a bit from the nearby road. Once the weather turns good, breakfast is served on the patio that looks out on the Dordogne which winds at the foot of the grounds. This beautiful place is known for its kitchen, in the masterful hand of Bruno Marien. Music (sometimes a bit too much) accompanies your meals in the dining room. Professional hospitality awaits.

***How to get there*** *( Map 23 ): 47km southeast of Périgueux via N89 to Niversac, D710 to Le Bugue, and D31.*

# La Métairie

24150 Mauzac (Dordogne)
Tel. (0)5.53.22.50.47 - Fax (0)5.53.22.52.93
M. Heinz Johner

**Category** ★★★ **Rooms** 10 with telephone, bath, WC and TV (7 with minibar). **Price** Double 450-750F / 68,60-114,34€, suite 950-110F / 144,83-169,22€. **Meals** Breakfast 60F / 9,14€, served 8:00-11:00; half board 450-550F / 68,60-83,85€ (per pers., 2 days min.). **Restaurant** Service 12:30PM-1:45PM, 7:30PM-9:00PM; mealtime specials 150-300F / 22,87-45,73€, also à la carte. **Credit cards** Visa, Eurocard and MasterCard. **Pets** Dogs allowed. **Facilities** Swimming pool, bicycle, parking. **Nearby** Vézère prehistoric valley, Châteaux of the Dordogne valley; Bergerac vineyards; Les Eyzies – 18-hole la-Croix-de-Mortemart golf course in Le Bugue. **Open** Apr – end Oct .

A few kilometers from the famous horseshoe-shaped *Cingle de Trémolat*, in a beautiful valley where great loops of the Dordogne River wind through a mosaic of cultivated fields, lies *La Métairie*. Set up in a pretty country house, this tastefully furnished hotel enjoys a nice view and a very well-cared-for garden with a swimming pool, around which you can leisurely have your lunch in summer. The rooms are split up between the different wings of the house. All are comfortable, simple, and pleasant. Some of them have recently been renovated in a restrained, country look, while others are awaiting their new decor. Little patios, separated by flourishing hedges, are in front of the rooms which are at garden level. Next to the dining room, the lounge is often warmed up by a crackling fire. You will be pleasantly welcomed, and the flavorful and appetizing food in the restaurant will not fail to delight you.

***How to get there*** *(Map 23): 68km south of Périgueux via N89 and D70 to Le Bugue, then D703 and branch for Mauzac.*

# Hôtel de La Ferme Lamy

24220 Meyrals (Dordogne)
Tel. (0)5.53.29.62.46 - Fax (0)5.53.59.61.41
M. Bougon

**Category** ★★★ **Rooms** 12 (2 with air-conditioning) with telephone, bath or shower, WC and TV (10 with minibar) – 1 for disabled persons. **Price** Double 360-850F / 54,88-129,58€. **Meals** Breakfast 50F / 7,63€. No restaurant. **Credit cards** All major. **Pets** Dogs allowed (35F / 5,34€). **Facilities** Swimming pool – Parking. **Nearby** Sarlat, Valley of Vézère (Prehistory route), Dordogne Valley (castles), Bergerac vineyard, Les Eyzies, Museum of Tobacco in Bergerac, Limeuil, Le Bugue – 18-hole Croix-de-Mortemart golf course in Bugue. **Open** All year.

As its name indicates, this hotel is an old farmhouse, close to the the magnificent sites of the Dordogne and the Vézère Valleys and reflecting their remote, ethereal atmosphere. Standing on a shady, green hilltop where you will enjoy a beautiful panorama of the region, the *Ferme Lamy* offers peace and quiet, and total relaxation. Located in various buildings, the twelve recently opened bedrooms have comfortable amenities while retaining their original charm. There is a wide choice of rooms, depending on whether they are located in the outbuildings or in the main house: we prefer the latter. The breakfast of jam, buns, and homemade bread can be taken on the beautiful, shaded patio. There is no restaurant in the hotel, but you can strike a half-board deal with one of the neighboring restaurants, which makes *La Ferme Lamy* a very attractive place to stay indeed. For a dinner close to the hotel, we recommend the *Ferme Auberge la Rhonie*, three minutes away on foot, or *La Metairie*, which is 4 kms away. But Monsieur Bougon will suggest many other good places to you.

***How to get there*** *( Map 23 ): 12km west of Sarlat to Périgueux via D6 then D47, in Bénivès, take the road to the left via C3 towards Meyrals.*

# La Roseraie

24290 Montignac-Lascaux (Dordogne)
11, place d'Armes
Tel. (0)5.53.50.53.92 - Fax (0)5.53.51.02.23
M. Guimbaud

**Category** ★★★ **Rooms** 14 with telephone, bath or shower, WC and TV. **Price** Double 350-490F / 53,36-74,70€. **Meals** Breakfast 50F / 7,63€; half board 350-440F / 53,36-67,08€ (per pers., obligatory in summer). **Restaurant** Closed 1 Nov – Easter. Service 12:00PM-2:00PM, 7:00PM-9:30PM; mealtime specials 100-250F / 15,24-38,11€; also à la carte. Specialties: Foie gras frais chaud aux fraises; confit; tournedos sauce Périgueux. **Credit cards** All major. **Pets** Dogs allowed. **Facilities** Swimming pool. **Nearby** Lascaux, abbey of Saint-Amand-de-Coly, Sarlat, manor of Eyrignac, Hautefort – 18-hole golf course in Brive-la-Gaillarde. **Open** Apr – Nov.

On the quai of the Vézère, which cuts through this village next to the Lascaux caves, *La Roserie*'s façade, looked at from the square, looks like that of a big, beautiful, 18th-century home. But from the river, the hotel presents a shaded patio that extends out into a wonderful garden, bursting with roses, in which you find the swimming pool. This is the summertime dining area; the rest of the time, meals are served in two small dining rooms separated by a lounge. The rooms, set up on the upper stories, are all pleasant and different. Ask first for those that look out on the garden or on the Vézère, and the more youthful and cheerful ones, which have been redecorated in pretty fabrics and hand-painted furnishings. Reserve, also, the two big rooms with parquetry and riverside view for your stays. The owner, who cans his own Périgord victuals, will offer you home-grown, local culinary specialities. A peaceful, and mouthwatering, place to stay.

***How to get there*** *( Map 23): 37km southwest of Brive-la-Gaillarde via N89 to Périgueux then to Condat; follow towards Lascaux.*

## La Plume d'Oie

Au Bourg 24250 La Roque-Gageac (Dordogne)
Tel. (0)5.53.29.57.05/53.28.94.93 - Fax (0)5.53.31.04.81
Mark and Hiddy Walker

**Rooms** 4 with telephone, bath, WC, TV and minibar. **Price** Single and double 375-450F / 57,17-68,60€. **Meals** Breakfast 65F / 9,90€ (+10F / 1,52€ in room), served 8:00-9:30. **Restaurant** Service 12:15PM-1:15PM, 7:30PM-9:30PM; mealtime specials 195-395F / 29,73-60,22€, also à la carte. **Credit cards** Visa, Eurocard and MasterCard. **Pets** Dogs allowed (+25 or 40F / 3,81 or 6,10€). **Nearby** Old Town and La Boétie's house in Sarlat, Châteaux of Puymartin and Commarques, Carsac, Lascaux – 9-hole golf course in Vitrac. **Closed** Nov 15 – Dec 20, Jan 25 – Mar and Monday.

L*a Plume d'Oie* is a restaurant with an excellent reputation to which four charming bedrooms have just been added. Light and bright, comfortably modern, they are decorated with pretty chestnut furniture and cream-colored fabrics with occasional splashes of color; the bathrooms are impeccable. Three rooms open onto the river, which is just across the narrow street. Built on the flank of a gigantic cliff right on the Dordogne, La Roque-Gageac is a superb site. There's another side to the coin, however: you hear the traffic a little, which can be a problem in the high season - July and August. If you want complete silence, it's best to reserve the bedroom looking out on the cliff. Succulent breakfasts are served. A jovial, lively, and kind welcome from the owners.

***How to get there*** *( Map 23 ): 8km south of Sarlat-la-Canéda.*

# Hôtel L'Abbaye

24220 Saint-Cyprien-en-Périgord (Dordogne)
Rue de l'Abbaye-des-Augustins
Tel. (0)5.53.29.20.48 - Fax (0)5.53.29.15.85
M. and Mme Schaller

**Category** ★★★ **Rooms** 24 with telephone, bath or shower and WC (TV on request). **Price** Double 400-700F / 60,98-106,71€, suite 750F / 114,34€. **Meals** Breakfast 60F / 9,16€, served 8:00-10:00; half board 390-600F / 59,46-91,47€ (per pers.). **Restaurant** Service 7:30PM-9:30PM; mealtime specials 155-360F / 23,63-54,88€, also à la carte. Specialties: Foie gras poêlé aux fruits; œufs brouillés aux truffes; feuilleté d'asperges. **Credit cards** Amex, Visa. **Pets** Dogs allowed. **Facilities** Swimming pool, parking. **Nearby** Cave of Proumeyssac, Sarlat, Le Bugue, Château of Campagne, Les Eyzies – 9-hole golf course in Rochebois. **Open** Apr 16 – Oct 14.

All the beauty of deepest Périgord can be found in the landscape of Saint-Cyprien. Against a horizon of hills and forest, the little medieval city is perched on the hillside that rolls down to the Dordogne. This large, 18th-century house, with its distinguished, naturally preserved stones, was named after the old abbey of the Augustines. The lounge, installed in a 16th-century kitchen, has kept its sink, its huge fireplace, and bread oven. The rest of the house is much more classical. The rooms, all different, are very comfortable, but we like those on the upper stories of the main house. In one of the annexes, two large rooms look out on a very nice, little interior courtyard (Avoid the rooms that look out on the road.). Everywhere you look, the decoration rebounds with the spirit of a big country house, where the living is good. Pleasant garden in terrace with a swimming pool. Very, fine, light food, cooked by Yvette Schaller. Thoughtful and warm welcome.

***How to get there*** *(Map 23): 54km southeast of Périgueux via N89 and D710 to Le Bugue, then D703 and D35 to St-Cyprien.*

# Hostellerie Saint-Jacques

24470 Saint-Saud-Lacoussière (Dordogne)
Tel. (0)5.53.56.97.21 - Fax (0)5.53.56.91.33
M. and Mme Babayou

**Category** ★★★ **Rooms** 18 and 3 apartments, with telephone, bath or shower and WC, TV and minibar. **Price** Double 350-450F / 53,36-68,60€, apart. 700F / 106,71€. **Meals** Breakfast 50F / 7,63 €, brunch by the swimming pool; half board 320-400F / 48,78-60,98€ (per pers., 2 days min.); in apart. (family with 2 children) 1290-1500F / 196,66-228,67€. **Restaurant** Closed Sunday evening and Monday, and Nov 15 – Mar. Service 12:30PM-1:30PM, 7:00PM-9:00PM, 10:00PM in Jul and Aug; mealtime specials 120-290F / 18,29-44,21€, also à la carte. Specialties: Cannelloni de cèpes à la mie de pain; lasagnes de foie gras poêlé, émulsion de truffe. **Credit cards** Amex, Visa. **Pets** Dogs allowed. **Facilities** Heated swimming pool, tennis, parking. **Nearby** Brantôme Abbey, Saint-Jean-de-Côle – 18-hole Saltgourde golf course. **Closed** Nov 15 – Mar and Sunday evening and Monday.

The *Hostellerie Saint-Jacques* has the generous proportions of an 18th-century Périgourdine house. The bedrooms all have different fabrics and furniture and are comfortable, cheerful, bright and decorated with a great amount of taste and imagination. Some have a small corner lounge where the bookshelves (worthy of Arsène Lupin), open up to give access to the luxurious bathroom. Downstairs, the dining room has a Provençal air with its elegant yellow and blue decor, but the cuisine is nevertheless authentically Périgourdine. Made with local farm products, it is excellent and light. In the summer, a few tables are set out under the maples. Make a note of the special reductions for "Weekend Getaways" or "Nature Break" (5 days, from 2990 Francs for 2 people with half-board).

***How to get there*** *( Map 23 ): 58km north of Périgueux via N21 to La Coquille, then D79.*

## Le Chaufourg en Périgord

24400 Sourzac (Dordogne)
Tel. (0)5.53.81.01.56 - Fax (0)5.53.82.94.87
M. Dambier

**Rooms** 8 and 2 suites (5 with air conditioning) with telephone, bath, WC and TV (4 with minibar).
**Price** Double 870-1300F / 132,63-198,18€, suite from 1550F / 236,30€. **Meals** Breakfast 85F /
12,96€, served 8:00-11:00. **Restaurant** For residents only, by reservation; also à la carte **Credit
cards** Amex, Visa, Diners. **Pets** Dogs allowed on request. **Facilities** Swimming pool, parking. **Nearby**
Saint-Emilion, Brantôme, Bergerac, Périgueux, Echourgnac and forest of la Double, Chancelade Abbey
– 18-hole golf course in Périgueux. **Open** All year (im winter by reservation).

This very beautiful and elegant 17th-century family mansion is not really a
hotel: *Le Chaufourg en Périgord* is M. Dambier's childhood home, which
he has restored "to create the elegant decor I dreamed of for entertaining." You
will, not surprisingly, find everything here you could wish for when you travel:
a great sense of comfort, tasteful furnishings (featured in many French
interior-decoration magazines), warm hospitality, and those extra details that
make all the difference. There is a billiard table at your disposal, and a wealth
of information on making the most of your visit to this enchanting part of the
Périgord. The garden overlooking the Isle River is wonderful and will afford
you many marvelous moments, whether lazing about the pool, reading or
dreaming in the shade of the grounds, or taking a boat ride down the river.
Served on reservation, dinners highlight the specialties of the Périgord's
renowned cuisine.

***How to get there*** *(Map 23): 30km southwest of Périgueux via N89, towards
Mussidan.*

## Le Vieux Logis

24510 Trémolat (Dordogne)
Tel. (0)5.53.22.80.06 - Fax (0)5.53.22.84.89
M. Giraudel
E-mail: le.vieux.logis@wanadoo.fr

**Category** ★★★★ **Rooms** 24 with telephone, bath, WC, TV, and minibar. **Price** Single and double 840-1420F / 128,06-216,48€; apart. 1750F / 266,79€ **Meals** Breakfast 95F / 14,48€, served 8:00-11:00. **Restaurant** Service 12:00PM-2:00PM, 7:30PM-9:30PM, also à la carte; mealtime specials 195-400F / 29,73-60,98€. **Credit cards** All major. **Pets** Dogs allowed. **Facilities** Swimming pool, parking. **Nearby** Tobacco Museum in Bergerac, Lanquais, bastide town of Sainte-Foy-la-Grande – 9-hole Rochebois golf course in Vitrac. **Open** All year.

For four centuries, the same family has lived on this superb estate, which was made into a hotel by M. Giraudel's mother. The different buildings are all charming: In addition to the main building, there is the tobacco barn, the lodge, and the gardener's house. No two bedrooms are alike but they have one point in common:, they are extremely comfortable, quiet and elegantly decorated down to the last detail; the antique furniture and the souleiado Provençal fabrics go together beautifully. The two dining rooms are magnificent. One is small, with pale wood panelling; the other is immense, overlooked by a balustraded lounge (the former hayloft). Gourmets will love it, and so will those who appreciate interior design. A smoking bar has just been added this year, so tobacco lovers can now serenely puff away to their heart's content.

***How to get there*** *(Map 23): 54km south of Périgueux via N89 to Niversac. D710 to Le Bugue and D81.*

## Villa Térésa-Hôtel Semiramis

33120 Arcachon (Gironde)
4, allée de Rebsomen
Tel. (0)5.56.83.25.87 - Fax (0)5.57.52.22.41 - Mme Baurès

**Category** ★★★ **Rooms** 20 with telephone, bath, WC and TV on request. **Price** Double 520-750F / 79,27-114,34€. **Meals** Breakfast 68F / 10,38€; half board 570F / 86,90€. **Restaurant** By reservation. Service 8:00PM-9:00PM; menu 180F / 27,44€. **Credit cards** Visa, Eurocard and MasterCard. **Pets** Small dogs allowed (+40F / 6,09€) except in the restaurant. **Facilities** Swimming pool, parking. **Nearby** Bassin d'Arcachon: Pyla Dunes; Cap Ferret; lakes of Hourtins-Carcans, Lacanau; Bordeaux; Bordelais. **Open** All year.

In 1860, the Pereire banking family built a vast "urban park" on the dune belt of Arcachon. It was a fabulous ensemble of neo-Gothic, Moorish, Colonial, Swiss and other villas which were frequented by the aristocracy, the *haute bourgeoisie* and the high flyers of the medical world. Saved from ruin and classed as a historic monument, Térésa has been brilliantly restored. In the lobby, wood panelling runs around decorative compositions in earthenware tiles, continuing up the stairway and to gallery upstairs. The comfortable bedrooms, in the *Villa* and in a small house near the swimming pool, are not well-soundproofed. Those in the *Villa* are soberly decorated in pastel shades. The turret room, surrounded by windows in arcades, enjoys an immense terrrace. The pavilion bedrooms have prettier fabrics and beautiful carpets; the pleasant lounge is decorated with squat armchairs. The dining room is bright and elegant, and each evening on reservation a set menu is served, based on fresh market produce. Elegantly enhanced by pretty dishes and embroidered tablecloths, the breakfasts are outstanding and original. For a fish dinner in town, try *Chez Yvette*.

***How to get there*** *( Map 22 ): 60 km southwest of Bordeaux. In the "winter city".*

## Hauterive Hôtel Saint-James

33270 Bouliac (Gironde)
3, place Camille-Hostein
Tel. (0)5.57.97.06.00 - Fax (0)5.56.20.92.58
M. Amat

**Category** ★★★★ **Rooms** 18 with air-conditioning, telephone, bath, WC, TV and minibar. **Price** Single and double 800-1050F / 121,96-160,07€, suite 1300-1650F / 198,18-251,54€. **Meals** Breakfast 100-120F / 15,24-18,29€, served from 7:00. **Restaurant** Service 12:00PM-2:00PM, 8:00PM-10:00PM; mealtime specials 400F / 60,98€, also à la carte. Specialties: Fondant d'aubergines au cumin. **Credit cards** All major. **Pets** Dogs not allowed. **Facilities** Swimming pool, tennis, parking. **Nearby** Museum of Contemporary Art, Museum of Fine Art, Le Bordelais — 18-hole Cameyrac golf course, 18-hole Bordelais golf course. **Closed** Jan.

No run-of-the-mill modern architecture here. Conceived by the architect Jean Nouvel, Jean-Marie Amat's restaurant is, year after year, for fine French gastronomy. The hotel is three smallish buildings decked out as old tobacco drying sheds, joined by a passageway. Their large windows look down on the vineyards, the Garonne, Bordeaux, and the organization of the beds always keeps this view in sight. The decor is white and cream, brightly colored carpets with gray flashes. This high-tech comfort (which you have to get the hang of) combines bunches of flowers, sculptures and books for the intimacy of a private house: what could have been cold, is warm instead. An excellent bistrot looks out on the elegant interior courtyard next to the restaurant. Fine food at a modest price. A stunning place with many ardent admirers.

***How to get there*** *( Map 22): 5km east of Bordeaux. Keep on the bypass until Exit 23 to Bouliac, take a right at the first light, a left at the next light, go past the police station. At the top of the hill, take a right toward the church. The hotel is across from the post office, in the village square.*

## La Maison du Bassin - Le Bayonne

Lège 33970 Cap-Ferret (Gironde)
5, rue des Pionniers
Tel. (0)5.56.60.60.63 - Fax (0)5.56.03.71.47

**Rooms** 7 with telephone, shower and WC. **Price** 550-750F / 83,85-114,34€. **Meals** Breakfast 50F / 7,63€, served until 11:30. **Restaurant** *Le Bistrot du Bassin*. Closed Tuesday except Jul and Aug. Service 8:00PM-23:00; mealtime specials 170-210F / 25,92-32,01€. **Credit cards** Amex, Visa, Eurocard and MasterCard. **Pets** Small dogs allowed. **Nearby** Bordeaux, Bordelais (renowned worldwide for its wines) – 18-hole Lacanau golf course. **Closed** Beg Jan – beg Mar.

After Saint Tropez and the Island of Ré, now it's Cap Ferret, the summer vacation spot popular with Bordeaux families that has become the fashionable new resort of France. The *Maison du Bassin* looks like something out of an interior decoration magazine: the building itself with its beautiful wood façade in the tradition of this oyster-farming area, the bedrooms with objects and old furniture evoking a theme: *Louisiane, Cabane de Pêcheur, Maison du Bassin*. Our favorite is Room 3, *Cabine de Bateau*, which overlooks the water. Each room is supplied with elegant dressing gowns and toiletry articles. The charm of this small hotel also lies in its restaurant looking out over the water, which features local specialties and a magnificent dessert trolley. Its colonial bar, *Le Tchanqué*, is delightful, too, and the young staff is efficient and friendly. Relaxed and warm welcome from a dynamic staff. Don't miss out on these other addresses: on Cap Ferret, *Fredelian*, for its famous ice cream and cannelet pastry; *Chez Hortense*, for a special mussel recipe; *Le Sail Fish*, with excellent cuisine and a popular night-owl atmosphere; the *Hôtel de la Plage* in L'Herbe; and in *La Vigne*, the Wharrfzazate. Don't miss a drink at the *Pinasse Café* or *L'Escale*.

***How to get there*** *(Map 22): 65km southwest of Bordeaux.*

## Hôtel des Pins

33950 Cap-Ferret (Gironde)
23, rue des Fauvettes
Tel. (0)5.56.60.60.11 - Fax (0)5.56.60.67.41
M. Rohr

**Category** ★★ **Rooms** 14 with telephone, bath or shower, WC. **Price** Double 329-445F / 50,15-67,83€. **Meals** Breakfast 38F / 5,80€; half board 285-310F / 43,45-47,26€ (per pers.). **Restaurant** Service 7:00PM-23:00, mealtime specials 110F / 16,77€; also à la carte. Specialties: Pavé de morue fraîche à l'aïoli; thon grillé à la bordelaise; brochette de magret à l'orange; agneau de Pauillac; assiette aux trois saumons; escargots; piquillos. **Credit cards** Visa, Eurocard and MasterCard. **Pets** Dogs allowed by reservation. **Facilities** Parking. **Nearby** Pyla Dunes, fishing; Bordeaux, Bordelais – 18-hole golf course in Lacanau. **Open** Apr – Nov 11.

The *Hotel des Pins* is a charming small turn-of-the-century hotel built in the Arcachon style and renovated in its original spirit. Set in the midst of a garden full of hortensia and rose bushes in a quiet neighborhood in the heart of Cap-Ferret, the hotel is midway between the beaches of the Arcachon Basin, 50 yards away, and those of the Atlantic, 700 yards distant. It has the atmosphere of a traditional family home, with panelled walls in the old-style bedrooms. Dinners, offering several excellent specialties, are served in summer on the terrace high above the shady garden. On your return from the beach, be sure to stop off at *Fredelian*, Cap Ferret's famous spot for homemade pastries and ice cream.

***How to get there*** *( Map 22): 65km southwest of Bordeaux via D106 to Lège, Cap Ferret.*

## Château du Foulon

33480 Castelnau-de-Médoc (Gironde)
Tel. (0)5.56.58.20.18 - Fax (0)5.56.58.23.43
M. and Mme de Baritault du Carpia

**Rooms** 5 with bath and WC. **Price** Double 450-600F / 68,60-91,47€. **Meals** Breakfast incl. No restaurant. **Credit cards** Not accepted. **Pets** Dogs not allowed. **Facilities** Parking. **Nearby** Médoc peninsula on the left bank of the Garonne, then the Gironde (day trip, 150km), Mouton-Rothschild Museum in Pauillac; Ocean beach (30 km) — 18-hole Bordelais golf course, 18-hole Bordeaux-le-Lac golf course. **Open** All year.

The *Château du Foulon* stands at the end of a long avenue of trees which leads into a wood and then an immense park where you will discover magnificent peacocks and snow-white swans. This castle is the height of elegance. M. and Mme de Baritault, who will greet you with great hospitality, have tastefully decorated each bedroom with beautiful antique furniture. There are also two charming apartments, ideal for a long stay. Breakfasts are served at a large table in the magnificent dining room, a model of elegance and refinement. For dinner or for discovering the region, your hosts will give you a wealth of good advice.

***How to get there*** *( Map 22): 28km northwest of Bordeaux via D1 to Le Verdon, then go north to Foulon.*

## Hostellerie du Vieux Raquine

Lugon
33240 Saint-André-de-Cubzac (Gironde)
Tel. (0)5.57.84.42.77 - Fax (0)5.57.84.83.77
Mme de Raquine

**Category** ★★★ **Rooms** 10 with telephone, bath or shower and WC (5 with TV). **Price** Single and double 480-720F / 73,18-109,76€. **Meals** Breakfast 60F / 9,16€, served 8:00-10:00. No restaurant. **Credit cards** Visa, Eurocard and MasterCard. **Pets** Dogs not allowed. **Facilities** Parking. **Nearby** Church of Saint-André-de-Cubzac, Château of Bouilh, Bourg, Saint-Emilion – 18-hole Bordeaux golf course. **Closed** Jan 10 – Feb 10.

Fresh air, peace, and quiet are guaranteed at this hotel, whose ground floor covers the whole top of a hill. Completely renovated, it is furnished in an old-fashioned style. The bedrooms are impeccably kept and all are at ground level. There are two reception rooms including the one used as the dining room; it has windows all along one side opening onto a large terrace with an outstanding view of the vineyards of Fronsac, bordered by the Dordogne in the distance. From there, you can easily criss-cross most of the great vineyards of Bordelais, or even take in the Medoc region and sample the *bac de Blaye*. A homey and venerable place to stay, kept spotless by Mme Raquine, who makes the hotel feel like a family house. For fine dining, try the local restaurants near the hotel -- *Au Sarment* in Saint-Gervais or, a bit further away, *Au Bord d'Eau* in Fronsac.

*How to get there* (*Map 22*): *23km northeast of Bordeaux; A10 St-André-de-Cubzac exit, D670.*

## Le Pavillon de Margaux

33460 Margaux (Gironde)
Tel. (0)5.57.88.77.54 - Fax (0)5.57.88.77.73
Mme Laurent and Mme Gonzalez

**Rooms** 14 with telephone, bath, WC, TV and minibar – 1 for disabled persons. **Price** Single and double 480-660F / 73,18-100,62€. **Meals** Breakfast (buffet) 60F / 9,16€, served 7:30-10:00; half board 330F / 50,31€ (per pers.). **Restaurant** Closed Wednesday lunchtime in low season. Service 12:00PM–2:00PM, 7:30PM-10:00PM; mealtime specials 95-270F / 14,48-41,16€, also à la carte. Specialties: Poêlée de langoustines au jambon de canard fumé et dés de foie gras chaud; crépinette de daurade rôtie aux champignons. **Credit cards** Amex, Visa, Eurocard and MasterCard. **Pets** Dogs allowed. **Facilities** Parking. **Nearby** Médoc; Bordelais; Bordeaux – 36-hole Médoc golf course. **Closed** Jan.

The name Château Margaux alone is enough to bring to mind the entire noble family of the great Médoc wines. And there is nothing like staying at the *Pavillon de Margaux* when you tour the cellars of the château (open every day except Saturday, Sunday, and holidays). Built two years ago on the site of the former village school, the hotel exemplifies the 19th-century architecture of the village of Margaux. Classically decorated and restful, the bedrooms offer comfortable accommodations. Chef Frank Launay's specialties, genuine and without frills, are served in a beautiful dining room, but with the first good weather, you can enjoy meals on the shady terrace overlooking the famous vineyards. The dynamic young staff is attentive to your every need.

***How to get there*** *(Map 22): 30km northwest of Bordeaux, A 10 to Mérignac, exit number 7 towards Pauillac.*

## Château Cordeillan-Bages

33250 Pauillac (Gironde)
Tel. (0)5.56.59.24.24 - Fax (0)5.56.59.01.89
M. Alain Rabier

**Category** ★★★★ **Rooms** 25 with telephone, bath, WC, TV and minibar – Wheelchair access; elevator. **Price** Single and double 760-350F / 115,86-205,81€. **Meals** Breakfast 80-100F / 12,21-15,24€ (buffet), served 7:30-10:30; half board 730-1145F / 111,29-174,55€ (per pers. in double room). **Restaurant** Closed Saturday lunchtimes and Monday. Service 12:15PM-2:00PM, 7:30PM-9:30PM, mealtime specials 195-390F / 29,73-59,46€, also à la carte. Specialties: Foie chaud poêlé; pêche confite cordon de porto réduit. **Credit cards** All major. **Pets** Dogs allowed. **Facilities** Parking. **Nearby** Médoc; Bordelais; Bordeaux – 36-hole Médoc golf course. **Closed** Dec and Jan.

On the left bank of the Garonne, this 17th-century charterhouse stands on the small Médoc peninsula which is strung out with hundreds of world-famous wine châteaux and vineyards: Château Margaux, Château Lafite, Mouton Rothschild, to mention only the three *premiers grands crus classés* of the tiny village of Pauillac. Renovated in 1989, *Château Cordeillan-Bages* has retained its original Médoc character, while offering modern amenities. The twenty-five bedrooms, located in the recently built wings around a quiet, inner garden, are elegantly decorated in cheerful colors. The salons are lovely and the large dining room, whose terrace overlooks the vineyards, reminds us that this is where the Bordeaux School of Oenology gives courses in wine tasting to amateurs and professionals alike. An expert *sommelier* will advise you on wines to accompany your meal, and the best ones to buy.

*How to get there (Map 22): 45km northwest of Bordeaux, A 10 dir. Mérignac, exit number 7 to Le Verdon; on leaving Ezines, take D1, Route des Châteaux.*

## La Closerie des Vignes

Village des Arnauds
33710 Saint-Ciers-de-Canesse (Gironde)
Tel. (0)5.57.64.81.90 - Fax (0)5.57.64.94.44
Mme Robert

**Category** ★★ **Rooms** 9 with telephone, bath, WC and TV. **Price** Double 440F / 67,08€. **Meals** Breakfast 45F / 6,87€, served 8:00-10:00; half board 400F / 60,98€ (per pers., 3 days min.). **Restaurant** Closed Sunday evening and Tuesday in low season. Service 12:00PM-1:30PM, 7:30PM-9:00PM; mealtime specials 140 and 180F / 21,34 and 27,44€, also à la carte. Specialties: Gambas flambées au whisky; saumon à l'orange; magret confit; canard au miel et aux épices; foie gras; clafoutis. **Credit cards** Visa, Eurocard and MasterCard. **Pets** Dogs allowed. **Facilities** Swimming pool, parking. **Nearby** Citadel in Blaye, Bourg, cave of Pair-non-Pair near Prignac, Château de Bouilh, Church of Saint-André-de-Cubzac. **Open** May 1 – Oct 31.

The *Closerie des Vignes* is not an old building but this small *auberge* is truly delightful and the ambiance so welcoming and friendly that it cries out to be included in this guide. Lying amid vineyards, it is very comfortable and admirably well-cared-for. Its decor includes modern furniture, soft pastel colors, pretty floral fabrics, and comfortable sofas and chairs. The dining room, whose color scheme is not to our liking but where one can eat very well, opens onto the vineyards and there is a pleasant swimming pool for summer visitors. Ask for a room away from the kitchen, which is somewhat noisy.

***How to get there*** *( Map 22 ): 8km southeast of Blaye via D669 to Villeneuve, then D250. Don't confuse this town with Saint-Ciers-sur-Gironde.*

# Le Couvent des Herbes

40320 Eugénie-les-Bains (Landes)
Tel. (0)5.58.05.06.07 - Fax (0)5.58.51.10.10
M. and Mme Guérard

**Category** ★★★★ **Rooms** 8 with telephone, bath, WC, TV and minibar. **Price** Double 1500-1800F / 228,67-274,41€; suite 1800-2200F / 274,41-335,39€. **Meals** Breakfast 150F / 22,87€, served 7:30-10:30; "Theme weeks" (price on request). **Restaurant** *Les Prés d'Eugénie* Closed Monday and Thursday evening. Service 12:00PM-2:30PM, 7:00PM-10:30PM; mealtime specials 600-800F / 91,47-121,96€, also à la carte. **Credit cards** All major. **Pets** Dogs allowed (+200F / 30,48€). **Facilities** Swimming pool, tennis, sauna, health center, parking. **Nearby** Aire-sur-Adour, Mont-de-Marsan – 18-hole golf course in Mont-de-Marsan. **Closed** Jan 5 – Feb 25.

This village in the heart of Gascony which was made famous in the 19th-century by Empress Eugénie, who came here to take the waters. *Le Couvent aux Herbes* is a former 18th-century convent and girls' boarding school lying on the edge of a lovely park lush with magnolias, palms, and banana trees. It has been exquisitely restored by Christine Guérard of *Les Prés d'Eugénie* in the village, which is famous for the cuisine of her husband, Michel, as well as for her own gracious hospitality and decorative talents. Mme Guérard has decorated the *Couvent aux Herbes* with soft, refined, harmonious touches throughout the eight exquisite bedrooms/salons. They are so beautiful we wanted to try them all: *Le Temps des Cerises* for its delicious scent of old roses; *Belle Nonnette* for its magnificent oak beams; or, *Jardin Secret,* which opens onto the luscious herb garden for which the hotel is named. If a week's slimming and exercising is part of your vacation plan, this is the place to come to.

***How to get there*** *(Map 29): 25km south of Mont-de-Marsan via D124 towards Pau. Pau Airport 45km away, Bordeaux 150km.*

## Les Logis de la Ferme aux Grives

40320 Eugénie-les-Bains (Landes)
Tel. (0)5.58.05.05.06 - Fax (0)5.58.51.10.10
M. and Mme Guérard

**Category** ★★★ **Logis-suites** 4 with telephone, bath, WC, TV and minibar. **Price** Double 1700-2200F / 259,16-335,39€. **Meals** Breakfast in lounge 120F / 18,29€, served 8:30-10:00; "Theme weeks" (price on request). **Restaurant** Closed Monday evening and Tuesday except Jul 10 – Aug 28 and national holidays. Service 12:00PM-2:00PM, 8:00PM-10:30PM; mealtime specials 195F / 29,73€. Specialties: Côte de saumon à l'atre. **Credit card** Visa. **Pets** Dogs allowed (+200F / 30,48€). **Facilities** Swimming pool, tennis, health center, parking. **Nearby** Cathedral; Samadet pottery museum – 9-hole golf courses 1.5 km away. **Closed** Jan 6 – Feb 4.

Does the little village of Eugénie deserve yet another listing in our guide? Any place that accents quality and charm really deserves our attention, which is the case with *Les Logis*. This old farmhouse, restored in the finest regional tradition, has walls of polished stone gathered from the Adour River, big stone fireplaces and terra-cotta floors. There are two dining rooms: the *Café du Village*, where you can sample the excellent wines of the region and enjoy the chef's special; and the large *auberge* dining room where a beautiful menu highlights homestyle recipes. Plump, farm-raised Landes chickens roast on the spit and hams hang to cure. Fresh vegetables and breads are displayed on a butcher block. The bedrooms are in a stately house, where Christine Guérard has resurrected a new and poetic ambiance, in a lady's salon style. The rooms look like those of an aristocratic, country manor. The house's old and patinated materials, antique furniture, pictures and art objects, and bathrooms as beautiful as salons make this address irresistible. Warm hospitality. Full of extras.

***How to get there*** *( Map 29): 25km south of Mont-de-Marsan via D 124, dir. Pau. Pau Airport 45km away, Bordeaux 150km.*

# La Maison Rose

40320 Eugénie-les-Bains (Landes)
Tel. (0)5.58.05.05.05 - Fax (0)5.58.51.10.10
M. and Mme Guérard - MM. Hardy and Leclercq

**Category** ★★ **Rooms** 27and 5 suites, with telephone, bath, WC and TV. **Price** Single and double 500-650F / 76,22-99,09€, suite with kitchen 750-950F / 114,34-144,83€. **Meals** Breakfast 90F / 13,72€, (buffet), served 8:00-9:30; full board 720-1000F / 109,76-152,45€ (per pers., 3 days min.). **Restaurant** Service 1:00PM and 8:00PM; menu 195F / 29,73€, diet cooking. **Credit cards** All major. **Pets** Dogs allowed (+100F / 15,24€). **Facilities** Swimming pool, tennis, health center, parking. **Nearby** Aire-sur-Adour cathedral and organs – 9-hole golf courses in 1,5 km. **Closed** Jan 3 – Feb 6 and Dec 9 – 18.

Michel and Christine Guérard have always been successful at combining their respective arts. There is Michel's gastronomic art, of course, which has made his *Prés d'Eugénie* into one of the greatest restaurants in France. And Christine's art of gracious hospitality has made the couple's three houses in Eugénie into models of charm. While *Les Prés* has a colonial touch and *Le Couvent des Herbes* has become one of their prettiest hotels, *La Maison Rose* is decorated in a more country manner. We especially like this one for its "Feather Weight, Feather Price" menu, with its four to five daily thermal treatments and the possibility of following a slimming regime, for a reasonable full-room-and-board price. Throughout your stay, you can enjoy the long-time famous cooking of the master chef, or a rustic festive meal at *La Ferme aux Grives*, the couple's third auberge. You can also take a thermal bath at the superb *Ferme Thermale*.

***How to get there*** *( Map 29): 25km south of Mont-de-Marsan via D124 towards Pau. Pau Airport 45km away, Bordeaux 150km.*

## Pain, Adour et Fantaisie

40270 Grenade-sur-Adour (Landes)
14-16, place des Tilleuls
Tel. (0)5.58.45.18.80 - Fax (0)5.58.45.16.57
M. Garret

**Category ★★★ Rooms** 11 with air-conditioning, telephone, bath (9 with whirlpool), WC, TV, safe and minibar – Wheelchair access. **Price** Double 380-800F / 57,93-121,96€, apart. 1300F / 198,18€. **Meals** Breakfast 75F / 11,45€; "Weekend of charm" 2750F / 419,23€ (per 2 pers.); "Fantaisy Gala" (per 2 pers.) 1430F / 218,00€ (except Jul – Aug). **Restaurant** Closed Sunday evening and Monday except national holidays. Service 12:00PM-2:00PM, 8:00PM-10:00PM; menu 165-360F / 25,15-54,88€, also à la carte. **Credit cards** All major. **Pets** Dogs allowed (+50F / 7,63€). **Facilities** Parking, garage (+50F / 7,63€). **Nearby** Landes de Gascogne Regional Park, Bastides tour; tours of chais du Bas Armagnac and Madiran organized by hotel – 9- and 18-hole golf courses in Mont-de-Marsan. **Open** All year.

On the village side, this superb, half-timbered 17th-century *auberge* looks out onto the arcades of the large public square. On the river side, a cool, shady terrace (a summer dining spot), the large traditional balconies and certain bedrooms look out directly onto the river Adour. Here is a place of peace and pleasure. The bedrooms, with evocative names from nature, are vast and bright. Decorated with great talent, they all have charm and character; and the bathrooms are well-equipped. Original old wood panelling graces the dining room. You will enjoy the culinary specialties of Philippe Garret, who brings off the *tour de force* of offering excellent cuisine at astonishingly reasonable prices. This is yet another very good auberge, and is reason enough to make the trip to the Landes.

***How to get there*** *(Map 29): 15km south of Mont-de-Marsan via N 124. Pau Airport 45km away, Bordeaux 150km.*

# La Vieille Auberge

40300 Port-de-Lanne (Landes)
Place de l'Eglise
Tel. (0)5.58.89.16.29 - Fax (0)5.58.89.12.89
M. and Mme Lataillade

**Category** ★★★ **Rooms** 10 with telephone, bath or shower and WC (3 with TV). **Price** Single and double 230-450F / 35,06-68,60€, suite 500-600F / 76,22-91,47€. **Meals** Breakfast 50F / 7,63€, served 8:30-10:30; half board 320-450F / 48,78-68,60€ (per pers.). **Restaurant** Service 12:00PM-1:30PM, 7:30PM-9:00PM; mealtime specials 120-250F / 18,29-38,11€, also à la carte. Specialties: Magret; saumon à l'oseille; matelote d'anguilles; confits de canard et de porc avec frites à l'ail. **Credit cards** Not accepted. **Facilities** Swimming pool, fishing, parking. **Nearby** Biarritz, Peyrehorade, abbey of Arthous, Sorde Abbey; Romanesque church in Cagnotte; Bonnat and Basque museums in Bayonne – 18-hole Hossegor golf course. **Open** Jun 15 – Sep 15.

**B**oth M. Lataillade and his father were born in this old coaching inn whose rustic beams, walls, and floors bear the mark of time. The inviting reception rooms are disturbed only by the slow rhythm of an antique pendulum clock or occasional music from an old piano. The bedrooms, located in the former stables and barns, are charming and comfortable, and there is a lovely garden with a swimming pool. M. Lataillade has built up an interesting museum, which is in the old hay barn. It contains objects retracing the history of the port of Lanne and its seafarers, who were known as *Gabariers*. *La Vieille Auberge* is a friendly Gascon inn, where you will enjoy Mme Lataillade's homemade preserves at breakfast.

***How to get there*** *( Map 29): 30km northwest of Bayonne via N117; on the church square.*

## Auberge des Pins

40630 Sabres (Landes)
Route de la Piscine
Tel. (0)5.58.08.30.00 - Fax (0)5.58.07.56.74
M. and Mme Lesclauze

**Category** ★ ★ **Rooms** 25 with telephone, bath (8 with wirlpool) or shower and WC (21 with TV). **Price** Single and double 300-450F / 45,73-68,60€, suite 500-600F / 76,22-91,47€. **Meals** Breakfast 50F / 7,63€, served 7:30-10:00; half board 320-450F / 48,78-68,60€ (per pers., 3 days min.). **Restaurant** Service 12:00PM-2:00PM, 7:30PM-9:00PM; mealtime specials 100-400F / 15,24-60,98€, also à la carte. Specialties: Soupe de pêches; foie gras poêlé, pointes d'asperges; filets de rouget; langoustines aux cèpes. **Credit cards** Visa, Eurocard, MasterCard and Amex. **Pets** Dogs not allowed. **Facilities** Parking. **Nearby** Church in Sabres, local history museum in Marquèze, Les Landes de Gascogne Regional park. **Closed** Sunday evening and Monday in low season.

Set in a village lost in the middle of the vast forest of the Landes region, this inn continues to follow the best tradition, passed down from generation to generation, of high-quality hotel service, and flawless hospitality. The bedrooms in the main building have every comfort and an old-fashioned charm, but the bedrooms in the newer building blend very well with the old ones and are our favorites. They are large, light, airy, and elegantly modern, with lovely fabrics, superb bathrooms, and a small terrace. The dining room, with its antique furniture, copperware, ceramics, and fireplace laden with a collection of rare old Armagnacs, is a place to linger in over the beautiful cooking of Michel Lesclauze, who uses the best local produce to make truly memorable meals. A real success. We heartily recommend this address.

*How to get there (Map 29): 40km east of Mimizan via D44.*

# Le Square

47220 Astaffort (Lot-et-Garonne)
5, place de la Craste
Tel. (0)5.53.47.20.40 - Fax (0)5.53.47.10.38
M. Latrille

**Category** ★★★ **Rooms** 14 with air-conditioning, telephone, bath, WC, TV and minibar – 2 for disabled persons. **Price** Single and double 310-630F / 47,26-96,04€. **Meals** Breakfast 50F / 7,63€, served 8:00-10:00. **Restaurant** Closed Sunday evening and Monday. Service 12:00PM-2:00PM, 7:30PM-10:00PM; menu 130-190F / 19,82-28,97€, also à la carte. **Credit cards** All major. **Pets** Small dogs allowed. **Nearby** Agen, bastides of Villeneuve-sur-Lot and of Beauville, Prades, Auvillar, Nérac, Farmer's Market Monday in Astaffort. **Open** All year.

This year has seen many changes at *Le Square*: A new manager, six more rooms, and very attentive decoration, at a price in keeping with the heightened comfort. Regulars might not feel at home at first, but this place really deserves a second look. Here is a brand-new, growing, village hotel that contains precious touches of refinement and comfort. The rooms are delightful, tastefully matching up warm colors and brand-name prints that reflect the decoration trends of today The bathrooms, in the same color schemes, are superb. There are two dining rooms where you can sample the cuisine of Michel Latrille. One dining room opens onto a small terrace where you can have your meals in summer; in the other, which is cool and informal, you are served on warmly colored enameled-lava tables. Add to this a cast-iron pergola intertwined with ivy and honeysuckle in summer. A charming place right next to Agen.

*How to get there* ( *Map 30* ): *16km south of Agen via RN 21. Via A62, take Agen exit No 7.*

## Château de Lassalle

47310 Moirax-Laplume (Lot-et-Garonne) - Brimont
Tel. (0)5.53.95.10.58 - Fax (0)5.53.95.13.01
M. and Mme Laurens

**Category** ★★★ **Rooms** 14 with telephone, bath, WC and TV. **Price** Double 490-1090F / 74,70-166,17€. **Meals** Breakfast 70F / 10,67€; half board 550-730F / 83,85-111,29€ (per pers., 3 days min.). **Restaurant** Closed Thursday in low season. Service 12:00PM-3:00PM, 8:00PM-10:00PM, mealtime specials 155-220F / 23,63-33,54€. Specialties: Croustillant d'agneau au romarin à la Blanche d'Armagnac. **Credit cards** Visa, Eurocard, MasterCard, Amex. **Pets** Dogs allowed in kennel. **Facilities** Swimming pool, Ball-Trap, parking. **Nearby** Agen; Bastides of Condom, Fourcès, Lectoure; Prades; Auvillar; Nérac. **Closed** Some days in Jan and Feb.

Seven kilometers from Agen, at the end of a lane of great oaks, this beautiful, 17th-century manor house is surrounded by a huge park, rolling with valleys. Before opening the hotel, Jacqueline was a fashion designer, and Jean-Pierre was in advertising. But now, they express their talents in the *Château de Lassalle*. It's hard to describe everything in detail, but we loved the matching of beautiful antique furniture and contemporary paintings, one-of-a-kind objects found in antique yards, the choice of fabrics, and the high-quality, delicately accented materials. Enormous or more cozy, each comfortable room has its own style. Even the smallest ones will please you. Meals are served on the veranda. Let Jean-Pierre, a true lover of fine food and wine, give you some suggestions. Jacqueline works her miracles in the kitchen; here as well, her artistic sensibility and rigorous execution helps her add a creative touch to the classic specialities of the region. A high-quality, endearing address, the perfect place to stay while you get to know the area.

***How to get there*** *(Map 30): In Agen, towards. traffic circle on highway, then towards Auch for 3km. Turn right to Moirax; on leaving Moirax, go 5km.*

## Les Terrasses du Petit Nérac

47600 Nérac (Lot-et-Garonne)
7, rue Sédérie
Tel. (0)5.53.97.02.91 - Fax (0)5.53.65.65.98
Mme Kuiper

**Rooms** 6 with telephone, bath, WC and TV. **Price** Single and double 240-350F / 36,59-53,36€. **Meals** Breakfast 40F / 6,10€. **Restaurant** Service 12:00PM-3:00PM, 7:00PM-10:00PM, mealtime specials 100-150F / 15,24-22,87€, also à la carte. Specialties: Fish and foie gras maison. **Credit cards** Amex, Visa, Eurocard and MasterCard. **Pets** Dogs allowed. **Nearby** Agen; Bastides of Villeneuve-sur-Lot and of Beauville; Prades; Auvillar; Nérac. **Open** Feb – end Nov.

A stone's throw from the château where Henri IV stayed as a youth, this restaurant with several rooms is installed in a small house in the old part of Nérac on the banks of the Baïse, a lovely river offering popular sightseeing cruises. Two dining rooms spill over to the river's edge in good weather. There, you'll have a front-row seat for watching the boats, the old houses on the opposite bank, and the summer sky, while you eat meals of generous portion at a reasonable price. The establishment only has four rooms, two on the riverside and two on the road with less stunning views, but which are particularly appreciated by those who are "early to bed", because they are quieter. They are decorated in a simple, colorful, and pleasant way. A friendly and attentive welcome awaits.

***How to get there*** *(Map 30): 28km west of Agen via D 656, towards Nérac; on the edge of the Baïse River.*

## Les Loges de l'Aubergade

47270 Puymirol (Lot-et-Garonne)
52, rue Royale
Tel. (0)5.53.95.31.46 - Fax (0)5.53.95.33.80 - M. Trama
E-mail: trama@aubergade.com - Web: www.aubergade.com

**Category** ★★★★ **Rooms** 10 with air-conditioning, telephone, bath, WC, TV, safe and minibar – Wheelchair access. **Price** Double 880-1410F / 134,16-214,95€. **Meals** Breakfast 90F / 13,72€, served 8:00-10:00; half board 2100F / 320,14€ (2 pers., 3 days min.). **Restaurant** Closed Sunday evening and Monday. Service 12:00PM-2:00PM, 7:30PM-9:30PM; mealtime specials 200F / 30,49€ (lunch except weekend and national holidays), 280-680F / 42,69-103,67€, also à la carte. Specialties: Corona trama et sa feuille de tabac au poivre. **Credit cards** All major. **Pets** Dogs allowed (+100F / 15,24€). **Facilities** Swimming pool, jacuzzi, mountain bikes, parking (70F / 10,67€). **Nearby** Agen, Villeneuve-sur-Lot, Beauville; Prades, Auvillar (pottery museum), Nérac – 9-hole Saint-Ferréol golf courses. **Closed** Winter holidays.

We no longer need to introduce you to Miche Trama, whose French cuisine is truly "star-spangled," but we often forget that, at *L'Aubergade*, room can also come with board. And in this area as well, quality awaits. Installed in the living quarters, ten spacious and sunny rooms await your approval in an old house of the counts of Toulouse (13th-century). Furbished with lots of character by Madame Trama, these rooms blend the warm tones of terra-cotta with highlights of lively color (often in royal blue). Like their bathrooms, every room is an invitation to relax and enjoy. Their placement around a patio with a jacuzzi only makes them all the more attractive. Next to the fortified village of Puymirol, this is a high-class address with a very professional reception.

***How to get there*** *(Map 30): 20km east of Agen. Via A62 exit Valence-d'Agen, towards Golfech le Magistère, turn right, follow signs.*

## Château de Scandaillac

Saint-Europe-de-Born 47210 Villeréal (Lot-et-Garonne)
Tel. (0)5.53.36.65.40 - Fax (0)5.53.36.65.40
M. and Mme Woehe

**Rooms** 6 no smoking rooms with bath, telephone. **Price** Double 490-590F / 74,70-89,94€. **Meals** Breakfast 59F / 8,99€, served 9:00-10:30. **Restaurant** Closed Thusday. Service at 8:00PM; menu 131F / 19,88€. **Credit cards** Visa, Eurocard and MasterCard. **Pets** Dogs allowed by reservation. **Facilities** Swimming pool, bicycle, parking. **Nearby** Montflanquin; Château of Biron; Monpazier; Bastide-Cadouin; Bonaguil; Bergerac. **Open** Mar – end Oct.

The little, operetta drawbridge that leads to the inner courtyard of the Scandillac perfectly symbolizes the ambiance of this vigorously renovated castle, which has left one wing in its authentically Renaissance style with a 12th-century chapel and lots of other antique touches, including transom windows, exposed beams, and original flooring. The antique furniture, often in the stye of Louis XIII, has something bright and theatrical about it. The rooms, with their elegant fabrics, are perfectly comfortable and impeccably maintained with a suberb view. You, like us, will be just as charmed by the true kindness and availability of Maren and Klaus Woehe who go to the greatest lengths to make your stay a pleasant one. They offer precious advice to help you discover the region, or book a restaurant table or tour, and they put out a remarkable breakfast and dinner buffet (only one menu with free drink). A pleasant place to stay, a particular favorite with foreign travelers.

***How to get there*** *(Map 23): 50km north of Agen toward Villeneuve-sur-Lot. At Cancon, head toward Montflanquin, then D153 until Saint-Vivier where the hotel is indicated 30km south of Bergerac.*

# Hôtel Ithurria

64250 Aïnhoa (Pyrénées-Atlantiques)
Tel. (0)5.59.29.92.11 - Fax (0)5.59.29.81.28
Famille Isabal

**Category** ★★★ **Rooms** 27 with telephone, bath, WC and TV. **Price** Single and double 400-600F / 60,98-91,47€. **Meals** Breakfast 50F / 7,63€, served 8:00-10:30; half board 520-600F / 79,27-91,47€ (per pers., 3 days min.). **Restaurant** Service 12:00PM-2:00PM, 7:00PM-9:00PM; mealtime specials 170-260F / 25,92-39,64€, also à la carte. **Credit cards** All major. **Pets** Dogs allowed. **Facilities** Parking. **Nearby** Biarritz; Anglet and forest of Chiberta; Forest of Iraty; Arcangues; Bidart, Saint-Jean-de-Luz — 18-hole Biarritz golf course, 18-hole Chiberta golf course in Anglet. **Closed** Nov — Mar and Wednesday except in Jul and Aug.

Nestling among the gentle rolling hills of the Basque Country and in the heart of Aïnhoa, rated "One of the Most Beautiful Villages of France", the *Hôtel Ithurria* is a big inn which opens onto the Place de l'Eglise, where Basque *pelote* is played. It is a traditional family hotel where guests can enjoy a quiet vacation, pleasant hospitality, and gourmet cuisine. You will find a large choice of comfortable bedrooms, all attractive while differing in size and decoration. In the spacious dining room, where delicious, creative Basque cuisine is served with a smile, local color is created by traditional floor tiles, the fireplace, and the sculptured wood door lattices. Add a delightful small bar and an immense swimming pool at the back of the garden and you'll understand why the *Ithurria* is a favorite spot with those who love the good life.

*How to get there (Map 28): 25km south of Saint-Jean-de-Luz via D918.*

## Hôtel Laminak

64210 Arbonne (Pyrénées-Atlantiques)
Route de Saint-Pée
Tel. (0)5.59.41.95.40 - Fax (0)5.59.41.87.65
M. and Mme Proux

**Category** ★★★ **Rooms** 12 with telephone, bath or shower, WC, TV and minibar – Wheelchair access. **Price** Double 350-590F / 53,36-89,94€. **Meals** Breakfast 55F / 8,38€, served 8:00-11:00. No restaurant. Snacks available in evening on request. **Credit cards** Amex, Visa, Eurocard and MasterCard. **Pets** Dogs allowed (+50 F / 7,63€). **Facilities** Parking. **Nearby** Biarritz, Anglet and the forest of Chiberta, Arcangues, Bidart, Saint-Jean-de-Luz – 18-hole golf courses in Arcangues and Bussussary. **Open** Mar 15 – Nov 15.

Perched on a hilltop on the edge of Biarritz between the Atlantic and the Pyrenees, this 18th-century Basque farmhouse has just been entirely converted into a charming small hotel. The *Laminak* is surrounded by rolling countryside which is calm, peaceful, and bursting with leisure activities, such as hiking or fly-fishing. The beaches of Biarritz are also nearby. The bedrooms have been carefully decorated, combining the latest amenities with original touches which lend an individual character to each. Some are larger and have corner sitting areas, but all are in exquisite taste. You can enjoy a copious, elegant breakfast in the colonial-style winter garden, which also serves light snacks. There are many good restaurants nearby, including *L'Epicerie d'Ahetze* and *Les Frères Ibarboure* in Bidart; in Biarritz, *Campagne et Gourmandise* is famous for its cuisine, its charm, and its view, and *La Tantine de Burgos* for its Basque and Spanish ambiance.

***How to get there*** *(Map 28): 4km south of Biarritz. Via A63 and then take Exit 4 toward Biarritz-La Negresse, then D 255 towards Arbonne.*

## Chez Chilo

64130 Barcus (Pyrénées-Atlantiques)
Tel. (0)5.59.28.90.79 - Fax (0)5.59.28.93.10
M. and Mme Chilo

**Category** ★★ **Rooms** 11 and 1 apartment with telephone, bath or shower, WC and TV. **Price** Double 300-650F / 45,73-99,09€. **Meals** Breakfast 45F / 6,87€; half board 450-800F / 68,60-121,96€ (2 pers., 3 days min.). **Restaurant** Closed Sunday and Monday in low season. Service 12:00PM-2:00PM, 7:30PM-10:00PM; mealtime specials 120-300F / 18,29-45,73€, also à la carte. Specialties: Carré d'agneau de lait "Axuria" aux raviolis de fromage de brebis, pèche blanche farcie à la glace pistache au sabayon de Jurançon mœlleux. **Credit cards** All major. **Pets** Dogs allowed. **Facilities** Swimming pool, parking. **Nearby** Châteaux of Moumour and Aven, Saint-Blaise-Hospital, Pau — Golf course in Artiguelouve. **Closed** Jan 5 – Feb 3, Sunday evening and Monday in low season.

You have to have an adventurous spirit to turn off onto this tiny winding road in the heart of the green Béarn mountains. Yet it's only a few kilometers from the villages of Aramits and Lanne, immortalized in Alexandre Dumas's *The Three Musketeers*. You won't regret your detour. Awaiting you in this beautiful countryside is a restaurant offering sumptuous cuisine and a hotel worthy of the most discriminating tastes. This family *auberge* has recently been enlarged and redecorated with taste and originality by young Mme Chilo, whose husband is the chef. The bedrooms, all now renovated, combine charm with simplicity. And the welcome is extremely courteous.

***How to get there*** *(Map 29): 16km of Oloron-Sainte-Marie. In Oloron, head toward "centre ville", then the D24 in front of the "polyclinique Oçomendy" on rue des Basques. Leaving the village, head toward Mauléon-Licharre.*

## Château du Clair de Lune

64200 Biarritz (Pyrénées-Atlantiques)
48, avenue Alan-Seeger
Tel. (0)5.59.41.53.20 - Fax (0)5.59.41.53.29
Mme Beyrière

**Category** ★★★ **Rooms** 18 with telephone, bath, WC, TV and minibar. **Price** Château rooms or in the hunting lodge: 450-750F / 68,60-114,34€ (2 pers.), 650 and 700F (3 pers.), 780-850F / 118,91-129,58€ (4 pers.). **Meals** Breakfast 60F / 9,15 €, served 8:00-11:00. No restaurant. **Credit cards** All major. **Pets** Dogs allowed (+45F / 6,87€). **Facilities** Parking. **Nearby** Rock of the Virgin, Anglet and the Forest of Chiberta, Arcangues, Bidard – 18-hole Biarritz golf course, 18-hole Chiberta golf course in Anglet. **Open** All year.

This turn-of-the-century house stands in a very quiet park above Biarritz. It is the sort of house which conjures up nostalgic memories of childhood. The bathrooms and bathtubs have the huge proportions of another era, and the floor tiles and basins are antique. The large lounge on the ground floor opens onto and merges with the garden: cheerful, airy, and bright, it is furnished with yellow sofas and a grand piano. The dining room is where guests breakfast together around a large table. This lovely family house on the Basque coast, though a hotel, feels as if it were your own. At the edge of the property, you will find a restaurant on an 18th-century farm. We also recommend *Campagne et Gourmandises*, for its cuisine and lovely view.

***How to get there*** *(Map 28): 4km south of the town center via the Pont de la Négresse and D255 (Arbonne route).*

# Hôtel Villa L'Arche

64210 Bidart (Pyrénées-Atlantiques)
Chemin Camboénéa
Tel. (0)5.59.51.65.95 - Fax (0)5.59.51.65.99 - Mme Salaignac

**Category** ★★★ **Rooms** 8 with telephone, bath or shower, WC, TV and minibar. **Price** Double 490-830F / 74,70 à 126,53€. **Meals** Breakfast 60F / 9,16€, served to 12:00PM. No restaurant; Room service. **Credit cards** Visa, Eurocard and MasterCard. **Pets** Dogs allowed (+50F/ 7,63€). **Facilities** Covered parking.(50F / 7,63€) **Nearby** Biarritz, Anglet and the Forest of Chiberta, Arcangues, Bidart, Saint-Jean-de Luz – 18-hole Arcangues golf course. **Open** Feb 15 – Nov 15.

This small hotel alone is worth making a long detour for. For how is it possible to find a more enchanting location than this flower-covered cliff with a stairway leading directly to the beach? When Bernadette Salaignac transformed her house into a hotel, she might have been content with simply the location, but she also put an enormous amount of talent into decorating the comfortable bedrooms. A bay window opens onto each terrace where you can have breakfast (delicious) and, from six terraces, there is a view of the ocean. Those who prefer breakfast in the salon enjoy the same view with classical music in the background. Here too, the decoration is very tasteful, with blue and white checkered sofas, chairs painted in pearl grey, old paintings, collector's objects, all slyly observed through the window by a pig and a saddle horse. This very homey atmosphere is echoed at the reception and you will certainly leave the *Villa* with a promise to return. There is no restaurant in the hotel, but there are good addresses nearby, including *La Tantina della Playa, Les Frères Ibarboure, La Ferme de l'Ostalapia* and *La Cucaracha*.

***How to get there*** *(Map 28): RN 10 between Biarritz (7 km) and Saint-Jean-de-Luz. In Bidart center, rue de l'Ouhabia to Embruny.*

# Lehen Tokia

64500 Ciboure (Pyrénées-Atlantiques)
Chemin Achotarreta
Tel. (0)5.59.47.18.16 - Fax (0)5.59.47.38.04
M. Personnaz

**Rooms** 6 with telephone, bath or shower, WC and TV. **Price** Single and double 500-950F / 76,22-144,83€; suite 1200-1400F / 182,94-213,43€. **Meals** Breakfast 50F / 7,63€, served 8:30-10:00. No restaurant. **Credit cards** Visa, Eurocard and MasterCard. **Pets** Dogs allowed. (+30 F / 4,58€). **Facilities** Swimming pool, sauna, parking. **Nearby** Saint-Jean-Baptiste Church in Saint-Jean-de-Luz, coastal road, Ciboure, Bayonne, Biarritz – 18-hole Nivelle and Chantaco golf courses. **Closed** Mid Nov – mid Dec.

Built in 1925, this splendid Basque villa has recently been classed as a Historic Monument, notably because of its remarkable stained glass. The original owner used to come here on vacation with his family. Today, *Lehen Tokia* is open to guests. The interior has been refurbished, but the original decoration is intact. There is a subtle combination of magnificent objects and Art Deco furniture with antique regional furniture and family paintings (which explains why young children, are not admitted). The rooms are of superb size. You enter the vestibule, then go up several steps to the lounge, which in turn is surrounded by an elegant curving stairway leading to the bedrooms. Ravishingly beautiful and very comfortable, most have a marvelous view out over the Atlantic. The bedroom in the garden near the swimming pool has only a few pieces of Art Deco furniture but is not lacking in charm. The suite and the lounge boast a bow-window from which you can see the entire harbor of Saint-Jean-de-Luz. You'll fall in love with this unique place.

***How to get there*** *( Map 28): 2km from Saint-Jean-de-Luz. On A 63, exit Saint-Jean-de-Luz south.*

# Hôtel Arcé

64430 Saint-Etienne-de-Baïgorry (Pyrénées-Atlantiques)
Tel. (0)5.59.37.40.14 - Fax (0)5.59.37.40.27
M. Arcé

**Category** ★★★ **Rooms** 22 with telephone, bath or shower, WC and TV. **Price** Single and double 390-750F / 59,46-114,34€; suite 1130F / 172,27€. **Meals** Breakfast 50F / 7,63€, served 7:45-10:30; half board 440-800F / 67,08-121,96€ (per pers., 3 days min.). **Restaurant** Closed Monday lunchtime in low season except national holidays. Service 12:30PM-1:45PM, 7:30PM-8:30PM; mealtime specials 110-215F / 16,77-32,78€, also à la carte. Specialties: Truite en petits filets marinés au citron et son tartare; morue fraîche sauce piperade et pommes vinaigrette; ris d'agneau et cèpes dorés en persillade. **Credit cards** Visa, Eurocard and MasterCard. **Pets** Dogs allowed. (+100F / 15,24€). **Facilities** Heated swimming pool, tennis, parking. **Nearby** Petite Nive Valley, Saint-Jean-Pied-de-Port, dolmens, Cromlechs – 18-hole Souraïde golf course. **Open** Mid Mar – mid Nov.

This old inn, typical of the region and luxuriously restored, has been managed by the same family for the last five generations. The large picture windows are in keeping with the beautiful proportions of the dining room, and outside, long terraces are laid out at the water's edge. The bedrooms are extremely comfortable, newly decorated and overlook the river and the Pyrenees. A variety of reading matter is even supplied. Bouquets of flowers are placed all over the hotel. The little annex is a pleasing addition, with its balconies overhanging the river: you can fish without even leaving your bedroom! You will enjoy classic regional cooking and a very friendly welcome.

***How to get there*** *(Map 28): 50km southeast of Bayonne via D932 and D918 to Saint-Martin-d'Arossa, then D948 to St-Etienne-de-Baïgorry.*

# Hôtel Arraya

64310 Sare (Pyrénées-Atlantiques)
Place du village
Tel. (0)5.59.54.20.46 - Fax (0)5.59.54.27.04 - M. Fagoaga
E-mail: hotel@arraya.com - Web: www.arraya.com

**Category** ★★★ **Rooms** 20 with telephone, bath or shower, WC and satellite TV. **Price** Single and double 395-595F / 60,22-90,71€, suite 755-855F / 115,10-130,34€. **Meals** Breakfast 50F / 7,63€, served 8:00-10:30; half board 790-995F / 120,43-151,69€. **Restaurant** Service 12:00PM-2:00PM, 7:30PM-10:00PM; mealtime specials 135-190F / 20,58-28,97€, also à la carte. Specialties: Méli-mélo de gambas et ris d'agneau aux girolles; chipirons entiers poêlés et marmelade de crabe; gratin de fraises et de framboises au sabayon d'orange. **Credit cards** Amex, Visa, Eurocard and MasterCard. **Pets** Dogs not allowed. **Facilities** Parking. **Nearby** Villa Arnaga in Cambo, Espelette, Ascain, Saint-Jean-de-Luz, Bonnat and Basque museums in Bayonne – 18-hole La Nivelle and Chantaco golf courses. **Open** Mid Apr – mid Nov.

Do not be put off by the Arraya's somber façade, which is typical of the region. This superb Basque hotel, set on the corner of two streets in the center of the village, is made up of three old houses; the garden, invisible from the street, effectively screens out the noise. On the ground floor, the lovely lounges and the comfortable dining room are charming with rustic furniture and bright bowls of flowers. The bedrooms are all different bute equally attractive: the prettiest is on the garden side. There is a boutique selling regional delicacies which you can eat on the spot or take away. The restaurant menu is long and varied, but regional dishes remain the specialties of the house.

***How to get there*** *(Map 28): 28km south of Bayonne via A63, Saint-Jean-de-Luz exit, D918 to Ascain and D4 to Sare.*

## La Devinière

64500 Saint-Jean-de-Luz (Pyrénées-Atlantiques)
5, rue Loquin
Tel. (0)5.59.26.05.51 - Fax (0)5.59.51.26.38
M. Carrère

**Category** ★★★ **Rooms** 8 with telephone, bath and WC. **Price** 500-750F / 76,22-114,34€. **Meals** Breakfast 50F / 7,63€, served all morning. No restaurant. **Credit cards** Visa, Eurocard and MasterCard. **Pets** Dogs allowed on request (+50F / 7,63€). **Nearby** Saint-Jean-Baptiste Church in Saint-Jean-de-Luz, Basque coast road, Ciboure, Bayonne, Biarritz – 18-hole Nivelle and Chantaco golf courses. **Open** All year.

There is no obvious reason why M. and Mme Carrère should have taken on and renovated this residential family hotel - he is a lawyer and she an antiques dealer - other than the pleasure of opening a charming, refined, and tasteful establishment in the heart of Saint-Jean-de-Luz. Good taste and discernment are apparent everywhere. The eight bedrooms are ravishingly pretty and are furnished with beautiful antiques, as are the music room and library, which are open for the use of the guests. The reception might seem a bit out of the ordinary -- when you get your keys, you will also be given a little speech about "house rules" which you should take as more funny than fussy. The pedestrian street and the garden ensure quiet nights even in the heart of the town. The welcome is warm. Breakfast is served in the tea room, which offers homemade pastries, teas and old-fashioned hot chocolate. For fine dining, try *Chez Pablo* (*piperades* and *chipirons*), *Kaïku* for shellfish; and the *Casa Amaya* for its delectables "from the other coast" (that of Bidassoa). In the immediate environs, don't miss the *magret de canard* at the *Ferme Penzia* (open only in summer); *Chez Mattin's ttorro*; or the grilled fish at *Chez Pantxoa* in Ciboure.

***How to get there*** *(Map 28): 15km southwest of Biarritz.*

## Hôtel La Patoula

64480 Ustaritz (Pyrénées-Atlantiques)
Tel. (0)5.59.93.00.56 - Fax (0)5.59.93.16.54
M. and Mme Guilhem

**Category** ★★★ **Rooms** 9 with telephone, bath or shower and WC. **Price** Double 390-510F / 59,46–77,75€. **Meals** Breakfast 60F / 9,16€; half board 350-430F / 53,36-65,55€. **Restaurant** Service 12:00PM-2:00PM, 8:00PM-10:00PM; mealtime specials 100F / 15,24€ (child) 150 and 200F / 22,87 and 30,49€ also à la carte. Specialties: Alose grillée; saumon sauvage; gibier, agneau de lait des Pyrénées; tarte fine aux pommes chaudes caramélisées. **Credit cards** Visa, Eurocard and MasterCard. **Pets** Dogs allowed (+35F / 5,33€). **Facilities** Parking. **Nearby** Villa Arnaga in Cambo, Biarritz, Bonnat and Basque museums in Bayonne – 18-hole Biarritz golf course, 18-hole Chantaco golf course in Saint-Jean-de-Luz. **Closed** Jan 6 – Feb 15 and Monday in low season.

This hotel is set back from the road in a park bordered by the tranquil waters of the River Nive. This romantic view can be enjoyed either from the dining room, from the pergola where breakfast tables are laid in summer, or from the chaise longues in the garden. In the winter, when there are fewer tourists, the dining room with its open fire provides an intimate setting, and people come for the home-style cooking from all over the area. The rooms are spacious and comfortable, but their decoration needs a serious overhaul. Luckily, the excellent breakfasts, the overall quiet, and Madame Guilhem's friendliness still make *La Patoula* a place worth checking out.

***How to get there*** *(Map 28): 11km south of Bayonne via A63, Bayonne-sud exit number 5, towards Cambo-les-Bains, then D982; in the center of Ustaritz, opposite the church.*

## Grand Hôtel Montespan Talleyrand

03160 Bourbon-L'Archambault (Allier)
2-4, place des Thermes
Tel. (0)4.70.67.00.24 - Fax (0)4.70.67.12.00
M. Livertout

**Category** ★★ **Rooms** 53 and 2 apartments with telephone, bath or shower, WC and TV – Elevator. **Price** Single and double 295-420F / 44,97-64,03€, apart. 550-800F / 83,85-121,96€. **Meals** Breakfast 50F / 7,63€, served 7:30-10:00; half board 300-370F / 45,73-56,41€ (per pers., 3 days min.). **Restaurant** Service 12:30PM-1:30PM, 7:30PM-9:00PM; mealtime specials 120-220F / 18,29-33,54€, also à la carte. Specialties: Pièce de bœuf de Charolais façon ducs de Bourbon. **Credit cards** Amex, Visa. **Pets** Dogs allowed. **Facilities** Swimming pool, fitness room, garage. **Nearby** Bourbon; Souvigny Priory, Châteaux of the Besbre Valley and of Lapalisse in Dompierre (half day's journey), triptych of the Maître de Moulins at Notre Dame Cathedral in Moulins – 9-hole Avenelles golf course in Moulins. **Open** Apr – end Oct.

This hotel derives its name from the illustrious guests who came here for the famous thermal baths. It is made up of four adjoining town houses with well-appointed bedrooms. The *Sévigné* and *Talleyrand* rooms are vast, decorated with antique furniture and some have a balcony. The *Capucine* room, with a view over the gardens, is decorated with rattan furniture and elegant floral fabrics. The *Montespan* bedroom is reserved for guests taking the waters. On the ground floor, comfortable reception rooms and a large dining room (good family cooking) look out onto the greenery where in summer you can have breakfast. Another attractive feature of the *Grand Hôtel* is its immense terrace-garden built against the wall and surrounded by a medieval tower. It has a swimming pool, several flower-covered rock gardens, and tables and chaises longues. This is a very pleasant hotel with extremely reasonable prices.

***How to get there*** *(Map 18): 20km west of Moulins.*

83

## Château de Boussac

Target
03140 Chantelle (Allier)
Tel. (0)4.70.40.63.20 - Fax (0)4.70.40.60.03 - M. and Mme de Longueil
E-mail: longueil@club-internet.fr

**Rooms** 5 with bath and WC. **Price** Single and double 600-900F / 91,47-137,2€, suite 950-1100F / 144,83-167,69€. **Meals** Breakfast 55F / 8,38€, served 8:00-10:00; half board 1300F / 198,18€ (per pers., 5 days min.). **Restaurant** Set meal in the evening only and by reservation; menu 260-320F / 39,64-48,78€, incl. wine and alcohol. **Credit cards** Amex, Visa, Eurocard and MasterCard. **Pets** Dogs allowed (free). **Facilities** Parking. **Nearby** Church of Sainte-Croix and museum of the Vine in Saint-Pourçain-sur-Sioule, triptych of the Maître de Moulins at Notre Dame cathedral in Moulins – 18-hole golf course in Montluçon. **Open** Apr – Nov 15.

The many faces of this beautiful château blend medieval austerity with the grace of the 18th-century. In this one-of-a-kind hotel, lost in the Bourdon countryside, the owners receive you like friends and spontaneously include you in their aristocratic country life. Each very comfortable bedroom is superbly furnished with antiques (often Louis XV or Louis XVI), family mementos, and beautiful fabrics. The lounges have been charmingly restored. Finally, the large dining room table sets the scene for festive dinner parties which are very popular with sportsmen in the hunting season. The elegant silverware, the conversation, and the cuisine all contribute towards making each evening a lovely and memorable event.

*How to get there (Map 25): 40km south of Moulins via A71, number 11 Montmarault D46 exit, then D42 to Boussac (between Chantelle and Montmarault).*

## Le Grenier à Sel

03100 Montluçon (Allier)
10, rue Sainte-Anne
Tel. (0)4.70.05.53.79 - Fax (0)4.70.05.87.91
M. Morlon

**Rooms** 5 with telephone, bath or shower, WC and TV. **Price** Double 500-600F / 76,22-91,47€. **Meals** Breakfast 55F / 8,38€, served from 7:30; half board on request (3 days min.). **Restaurant** Closed like the hotel. Service 12:30PM-2:00PM, 7:30PM-10:00PM; mealtime specials 120-390F / 18,29-59,46€, also à la carte. Specialties: Chausson de morilles; canette fermière à la Duchambais. **Credit cards** All major. **Pets** Dogs allowed (+25F / 3,81€). **Facilities** Parking. **Nearby** Oak forest of Tronçais, Evaux-les Bains, Château of Boussac, Château of Culan. **Closed** Sunday evening and Monday, in summer and national holidays.

Like a small haven of greenery and tranquillity in the heart of old Montluçon, this large hotel with its pointed roofs dates from the 16th century, which perhaps explains the majesty of the great trees shading the delicious small garden which the dining room overlooks. In fact, the ï is known especially for its restaurant, which was taken over several years ago by Jacky Morlon (and his wife) on his return to his native region after stints with several leading French chefs. Madame and Monsieur Morlon have had the hotel decorated very tastefully: antique furniture, decorative objects, and paintings create an atmosphere of charming comfort and discreet luxury. The two bedrooms on the *premier étage* upstairs are spacious and bright, with ultra-modern bathrooms. The rooms on the last floor have mansard roofs but are equally well-equipped. A pleasant stay awaits you in this beautiful hotel.

***How to get there*** *( Map 17): 332km south of Paris via A 10 until Orléans and A 71, to Bourges. In the old town, beside the theater.*

## Hôtel de Paris

03000 Moulins (Allier)
21, rue de Paris
Tel. (0)4.70.44.00.58 - Fax (0)4.70.34.05.39 - M. Chaupitre

**Category** ★★★ **Rooms** 23 and 4 suites, with telephone, bath, WC, minibar and TV – Elevator **Price** Single and double 350-650F / 53,36-99,09€, suites 800F / 121,96€. **Meals** Breakfast 55F / 8,38€, served 7:00-11:00, half board on request (3 jours min.) **Restaurant** Service 12:15PM-1:45PM, 7:15PM-9:15PM; mealtime specials 150F / 22,87€ (weekdays), 180-450F / 27,44-68,60€, also à la carte. **Credit cards** All major. **Pets** Dogs allowed. **Facilities** Swimming pool, parking. **Nearby** Anne de Beaujeu musuem – 9-hole golf course. **Closed** Mid Jul – 31 and Jan 2 – 25.

Along the legendary N 7, the town of Moulins, with its many historically-conserved medieval relics around the cathedral, marks the border between the Auvergne region and Burgundy. Nearby, you will find the slightly austere façade of the *Hôtel de Paris*. The establishment experienced its days of glory before sinking, into a state of sweet desuetude. Today, Pascal Chaupitre (the former right-hand man of Bernard Loiseau), breathes new life into the hotel. First, the restaurant and its vast, classically decorated dining room, where you can sample food that is well-balanced and almost impossibly savory. You won't be able to stop talking about it. Next, the rooms, furbished in two quiet distinct styles. You have the "standards", modest but witty rooms with modern furnishing and orangish fabrics; and the "superiors", which are huge and have kept their retro furniture while livening it up with pretty, new upholstery. You will find this charming country touch in the elegant lounge and bar as well. Last, but not least, outside you have a patio with swimming pool and a large garden which raises the quality of life at this beautiful stop even more.

**How to get there** *(Map 18): Via A 71, take Montmarault exit, then N 7. At Moulins, head towards "gare". Hotel in town center.*

86

# Le Tronçais

03360 Saint-Bonnet-Tronçais (Allier)
Avenue Nicolas-Rambourg
Tel. (0)4.70.06.11.95 - Fax (0)4.70.06.16.15
M. and Mme Bajard

**Category** ★★ **Rooms** 12 with telephone, bath or shower and TV. **Price** Double 280-370F / 42,69-56,41€. **Meals** Breakfast 38F / 5,80€, served 8:00-10:30; half board 260-340F / 39,64-51,83€ (per pers., 3 days min.). **Restaurant** Service 12:00PM-1:30PM, 7:30PM-9:00PM; mealtime specials 100-190F / 15,24-28,97€, also à la carte. Specialties: Terrine d'anguille aux mûres; sandre au gratin;côte de veau aux cèpes; game. **Credit cards** Visa, Eurocard and Masterᵣᵣ ᵣd. **Pets** Dogs allowed only in bedrooms. **Facilities** Tennis, parking. **Nearby** Oak forest of Tronçais, Château d'Ainay-le-Vieil, Château Meillant – 18-hole Nassigny golf course. **Closed** Nov 15 – Mar 15, Sunday evening and Monday in low season.

Once the private house of a forge owner, the *Tronçais* is located in a park that borders a pond at the edge of one of the largest and most famous national forests in France. Inside, the hotel is pleasant, very quiet, and quite refined. The bedrooms are tastefully appointed, comfortable, and many are huge. There are rooms also in a small annex; we find them small, but they have just been redone.The graveled garden in front of the two buildings serves as the terrace and bar in the summer. The meals are excellent, light, and appetizing (the portions are on the small side) and are served in a charming dining room. The hotel grounds stretch all the way to the banks of the lake, in which you can fish. But it is the nature walks in the forest, in which one can meet up with does, deer, wild boar, or even great, many-centuries-old oaks as high as cathedrals, that stand out as the principle high-points of this address.

***How to get there*** *(Map 17): 45km north of Montluçon. On A71 Forêt-de-Tronçais exit, then N144 and D978A to Tronçais.*

## Château d'Ygrande

03160 Ygrande (Allier)
Le Mont
Tel. (0)4.70.66.33.11 - Fax (0)4.70.66.33.63 - M. Tissier

**Category** ★★★ **Rooms** 16 with telephone, bath, WC and TV. **Price** Single and double 500-700F / 76,22-106,71€. **Meals** Breakfast 55F / 8,38 €, served 7:00-10:30; half board 560F / 85,37€ (3 days min.) **Restaurant** Service 12:00PM and 7:30PM; mealtime specials 140-200F / 21,34-30,49€, also à la carte. **Credit cards** Visa, Amex. **Pets** Dogs allowed. **Facilities** Billiard, sauna, jacuzzi, mountain bike, parking. **Nearby** Oak forest of Tronçais; Château d'Ainay-le-Vieil, Château Meillant; riding – 18-hole Nassigny golf course. **Closed** Jan 10 – Feb 20.

You leave the thick forest of Tronçais, follow the road, lined by huge paddocks, for a few more kilometers, then to the château's courtyard. The whinnying of a horse greets you. There is the crunch of gravel, and then, surprise! On the other side of the foyer, French doors open out upon a sublime vista as far as the eye can see. Nothing but meadows, woods, and lakes. And to really enjoy this, there are a few tables outside where you can have a drink before going to the restaurant where you will enjoy a flavorful and artfully concocted cuisine with an excellent choice of fine wines. The general look is rather refined -- stylish furnishings (18th and early 19th-century), gold-highlighted wainscotting frames panels of silk, prints, and art objects. On the first floor, the large rooms boast selected, sometimes antique, furniture. These comfortable, well-lit rooms are our favorites. We recommend the second-floor rooms just as strongly (not those with skylights), with their beams, beautiful colored fabrics, and nice bathrooms. Recently opened to the general public, this is a remarkable and very hospitable place.

***How to get there*** *(Map 17): 45km north of Montluçon. Via A 71 Saint-Amand-Montrond exit, then N 144 and D 978 to Ygrande. Follow signs.*

## Auberge de Concasty

15600 Boisset (Cantal)
Tel. (0)4.71.62.21.16 - Fax (0)4.71.62.22.22
Mme Causse

**Category** ★★★ **Rooms** 14 and 1 suite with telephone, bath, WC and TV. **Price** Double 330-520F / 50,31-79,27€; suite 620-760F / 94,52-115,86€. **Meals** Breakfast 52-82F / 7,92-12,50€, served 9:00-11:30; half board 340-460F / 51,83-70,13€ (per pers., 2 days min.). **Restaurant** By reservation. Closed Wednesday except for residents. Service 12:30PM-1:30PM, 8:00PM-9:00PM; mealtime specials 160-200F / 24,39-30,49€. **Credit cards** All major. **Pets** Dogs allowed (+40F/ 6,10€). **Facilities** Heated swimming pool, whirlpool, Turkish bath, billiard, parking. **Nearby** Audillac, valleys of the Lot and the Truyère, Champollion Museum in Figeac, 18-hole golf in Haute Auvergne. **Open** Feb – Nov 14 and Dec – mid Jan.

The *Auberge de Concasty* is an old family mansion surrounded by its farm and fields. It has been completely restored and equipped with a swimming pool and whirlpool. Around the inn you will find many marked hiking paths and a beautiful golf course, which has just opened. The inn nonetheless looks like a traditional family vacation house. Comfort everywhere you look, just as much in the rooms as in the ground-floor lobby and in the prettily decorated salons. At Concasty, Mme Causse will delight you with fine seasonal cuisine featuring local specialties, (*cèpe* mushrooms, *foie gras*). You can also enjoy a good Auvergnat breakfast. A great place to stop or stay-over while in Cantal, with marked hiking trails all around the hotel as well as a superb, recently opened golf course only 15 kms away.

***How to get there*** *(Map 24): 25km southwest of Aurillac. In Aurillac via Cahors/Montauban by N122 for 20km; then in Manhes, turn left on D64 and follow signs.*

# Hôtel Beauséjour

15340 Calvinet (Cantal)
Tel. (0)4.71.49.91.68 - Fax (0)4.71.49.98.63
M. Puech

**Category** ★★ **Rooms** 12 with telephone, bath or shower, WC and satellite TV. **Price** Single and double 250-300F / 38,11-45,73€. **Meals** Breakfast 40-60F / 6,10-9,16€, served 9:00-11:30; half board 250-300F / 38,11-45,73€ (per pers.). **Restaurant** Closed Sunday evening and Monday in low season, Monday lunchtime in high season (except national holidays). Service 12:30PM-2:00PM, 8:00PM-9:30PM by reservation, mealtime specials 95F, 140F-300F / 14,48, 21,34-45,73€. **Credit cards** Visa, Eurocard and MasterCard. **Pets** Dogs allowed. **Facilities** Parking. **Nearby** Audillac, valleys of the Lot and the Truyère, Champollion Museum in Figeac, Conques. **Closed** Mid Jan – Mar, Sunday evening and Monday in low season.

The Pueches are natives of this region and despite his growing reputation as a gourmet chef, Louis-Bernard preferred renovating this hotel, which was built by his parents, rather than setting up in a more prestigious place or a more accessible region far from his roots. The building is nothing special but the modern interior is pleasant. It is discreet and perfectly well-kept, as are the bedrooms, which offer excellent value for the price when you consider their size and comfort. The outstanding features of the *Beauséjour* begin with the restaurant and the big, bright dining room overlooking greenery and a few village houses. Gourmets come from far and wide to savor the chef's fine, imaginative cuisine in a friendly atmosphere. There are superb culinary discoveries in the offing, and the prices are reasonable.

***How to get there*** *(Map 24): 34km south of Aurillac via Rodez. Take the D 920 until Lafeuillade; then Calvinet-Conques via D 610.*

## Auberge du Vieux Chêne

15270 Champs-sur-Tarentaine (Cantal)
34, route des Lacs
Tel. (0)4.71.78.71.64 - Fax (0)4.71.78.70.88
Mme Moins

**Category** ★★ **Rooms** 15 with telephone, bath or shower, WC and TV. **Price** Double 350-480F / 53,36-73,18€. **Meals** Breakfast 50F / 7,63€, served 8:00-10:00; half board 300-400F / 45,73-60,98€, (per pers., 3 days min.). **Restaurant** Service 12:00PM-1:30PM, 7:00PM-8:30PM; mealtime specials 140-230F / 21,34-35,06€, also à la carte. Specialties: Foie gras d'oie maison, confit de canard aux lentilees vertes du Puy, escalope de saumon-l'oseille. **Credit cards** Diners, Visa. **Pets** Dogs allowed. **Facilities** Parking. **Nearby** Bort-les-Orgues, Bort dam and Château de Val, gorges of the Dordogne from Bort to the Aigle dam (3 hours) — 9-hole Mont-Dore golf course. **Closed** Nov 16 — Mar 14, Sunday evening and Monday except Jul and Aug.

On the edge of the village and far from the road, this old stone and timber farmhouse has been charmingly restored and enlarged. The bedrooms have been beautifully renovated with cheerful, refined colors, coordinated fabrics and wallpapers, and many charming decorative details. One *single*, huge room takes up most of the ground floor, principally dedicated to the dining room, with its rustic and cheerful decor, elegant table linens, line of white curtains, and immense fireplace. To your right, you will find the bar, and in front, the huge shaded patio where breakfast and dinner is served on nice days. (No lunch is served during the week.) The food is truly good, and you will enjoy it against a backdrop of hills and in front of the meadows where a few horses graze. A beautiful place where you will always be heartily welcomed.

***How to get there*** *(Map 24): 93km north of Aurillac via D922 to Bort-les-Orgues, then take D 797, and then D 679.*

## Auberge du Pont de Lanau

Lanau
15260 Chaudes-Aigues (Cantal)
Tel. (0)4.71.23.57.76 - Fax (0)4.71.23.53.84
M. Cornut

**Category** ★★ **Rooms** 8 with telephone, bath, WC and TV. **Price** Single and double 270-360F / 41,16-54,88€. **Meals** Breakfast 37F / 5,64€; half board 280-360F / 42,69-54,88€,(per pers., 3 days min.). **Restaurant** Service 12:30PM-2:00PM, 7:30PM-9:30PM; mealtime specials 95-300F / 14,48-45,73€, also à la carte. **Credit cards** Visa, Eurocard and MasterCard. **Pets** Dogs allowed. **Facilities** Parking. **Nearby** Saint-Flour, gorges of the Truyère. **Closed** Jan and Feb, Monday evening and Tuesday.

Courtesy is the tradition in this old farmhouse-*auberge* built in 1855. In the past, clients were served meals on the left (today the restaurant) and horses were stabled on the right (today the lounge, breakfast room, and bar). The beautifully decorated, rustic restaurant has stone walls and is dominated by an immense fireplace. Guests once slept in bed recesses close to the fireplace to keep warm, and you can still see traces of the original wooden partitions. Today the inn is primarily a restaurant serving very good, refined regional cooking. M. Cornut often prepares specialties which are little known today, or delicious new versions of traditional regional dishes. The eight bedrooms are pleasant, some decorated in floral motifs while others are drenched in salmon pink. They have fabric-covered walls and are well-insulated with double windows. The *auberge* is located beside a country road, so, if you demand silence, you should take a room in the back of the hotel. A lovely place to stay.

*How to get there (Map 25): 20km south of Saint-Flour via D921.*

## Hostellerie de la Maronne

Le Theil
15140 Saint-Martin-Valmeroux (Cantal)
Tel. (0)4.71.69.20.33 - Fax (0)4.71.69.28.22 - Mme Decock
E-mail: hotelmaronne@cfi.fr

**Category ★★★ Rooms** 21 with telephone, bath, WC, minibar and TV. **Price** Single and double 500-680F / 76,22-103,67€, suite 760F / 115,86€. **Meals** Breakfast 60F / 9,16€, served 8:30-10:00; half board 480-550F / 73,18-83,85€. **Restaurant** Service 7:30PM-9:00PM; mealtime specials 150-250F / 22,87-38,11€, also à la carte. Specialties: Escalope de sandre aux mousserons; foie gras chaud au caramel de porto. **Credit card** Visa. **Pets** Dogs allowed (except in restaurant). **Facilities** Swimming pool, tennis, parking. **Nearby** Medieval city of Salers, basilica of Notre-Dame-des-Miracles in Mauriac, Puy Mary. **Open** Apr 3 – Nov 5.

M and Mme Decock have marvelously transformed this 19th-century Auvergnat house into a hotel. Everything has been provided for guests' entertainment and rest: for example, guests watching television sets are provided with headsets so as not to disturb others. The living room, reading room, and bar have been elegantly decorated with comfortable armchairs and some antique furniture. The elegantly modern, comfortable bedrooms are decorated in pale shades, our preferences leaning toward those with a view, which is splendid, particularly from the rooms with large terraces and balconies. (There is also an apartment, which families will enjoy). The cuisine is increasingly renowned and the dining room is beautiful, with a lovely view over the countryside. Walking in the area is a pleasure, and there are tennis courts and a swimming pool. Last but not least, the hospitality and service are charming.

***How to get there*** *(Map 24): 33km north of Aurillac via D922 to Saint-Martin Valmeroux, then D37 towards Fontanges.*

## Auberge de la Tomette

15220 Vitrac (Cantal)
Tel. (0)4.71.64.70.94 - Fax (0)4.71.64.77.11
M. and Mme Chausi

**Category** ★★ **Rooms** 15 with telephone, bath or shower, WC and TV. **Price** Double 290-350F / 44,21-53,36€, suite 430-560F / 65,55-85,37€. **Meals** Breakfast 43F / 6,55€; half board 252-412F / 38,51-62,50€ (per pers., 3 days min.). **Restaurant** Service 12:00PM-2:00PM, 7:00PM-8:30PM; mealtime specials 70-200F / 10,67-30,49€, also à la carte. Specialties: Foie gras maison; carré d'agneau à la crème d'ail; magret au vinaigre de cidre; crépinette de pied de cochon aux craterelles; ris de veau crémaillère; tartes maison. **Credit cards** Amex, Visa. **Pets** Dogs allowed in bedrooms only. **Facilities** Swimming pool, sauna, parking. **Nearby** Conques, Salers, Rocamadour, Cantal Mounts, Château of Anjony, Vic-sur-Cère. **Open** Easter – Dec 31.

Vitrac, surrounded by chestnut plantations, is a beauty spot in the south of the Cantal, and the *Auberge de la Tomette* is right in the heart of the village. The restaurant is located here and in the evening, you can have dinner in the delicious garden behind the inn. The bedrooms are a few steps away in a vast flowery park with a very beautiful view of the countryside. The bedrooms are comfortable, impeccably kept and decorated in a sober, modern style, brightened with pretty fabrics. Note the duplex, which is ideal for families. The atmosphere in the rustic dining room, with its exposed beams and wood panelling, is very friendly, and the cuisine is excellent. Mme Chausi will greet you charmingly and advise you on what to do and where to go in the region. This is a picturesque place to stay, where you become part of the village life.

**How to get there** (*Map 24*): 25km south of Aurillac via N122 towards Figeac; at Saint-Mamet-La Salvetat take D66.

## Auberge Les Charmilles

19120 Beaulieu-sur-Dordogne (Corrèze)
20, boulevard Saint-Rodolphe-de-Turenne
Tel. (0)5.55.91.29.29 - Fax (0)5.55.91.29.30
Mme Perrette

**Category** ★★ **Rooms** 7 and 1 suite with telephone, bath or shower, WC, satellite TV (1 with minibar); 1 for disabled persons. **Price** Single and double 320-440F / 48,78-67,08€. **Meals** Breakfast 40F / 6,10€; half board 280-350F / 42,69-53,36€ (per pers.). **Restaurant** Closed Tuesday evening and Wednesday, except Jul and Aug. Service 12:00PM-2:30PM, 7:00PM-9:00PM; mealtime specials 95-225F / 14,48-34,30€, also à la carte. **Credit cards** All major. **Pets** Dogs allowed. **Nearby** Church in Collonges; village, Turenne; Argentat – 18-hole Coiroux golf course in Aubazine. **Open** All year.

A tributary of the Dordogne encircles the little town of Beaulieu and laps at the patios of the houses near its edge. That's where you'll find the *Charmilles*, an adorable little turn-of-the-century hotel that has recently been done up good as new. With all the imaginable comforts, simply and harmoniusly decorated with a beautiful assortment of colored fabrics, the rooms are a real success. Each has a completely new and impeccable bathroom. Meals are served in a huge dining room, lit up by wide picture windows. The white table linen plays off of the honey-colored parquetry and the ambiance is both refined and calm. Here you'll be served food that is delicate, bringing together both tradition and creativity, with a menu based on fresh produce. In summer, a few tables are set up outside on the patio that gives onto the riverside. Very hospitable and in love with her little hotel, Catherine Perrette has worked in many large establishments before bringing her talents here. Her professionalism extends to even the smallest detail, and we are certain that she will make the *Charmilles* a reputable place to stay in the region.

***How to get there*** *( Map 24 ): 39km south of Tulle on D940.*

# Le Turenne

19120 Beaulieu-sur-Dordogne (Corrèze)
1, boulevard Saint-Rodolphe-de-Turenne
Tel. (0)5.55.91.10.16 - Fax (0)5.55.91.22.42
M. Cavé - Mme Gasquet

**Category** ★★ **Rooms** 15 with telephone, bath or shower, TV and WC. **Price** Double 280-300F / 42,69-45,73€. **Meals** Breakfast 42F / 6,40€; half board 270-290F / 41,16-44,21€ (per pers.). **Restaurant** Closed Sunday evening and Monday in low season. Service 12:15PM-1:30PM, 7:30PM-9:00PM; mealtime specials 75F / 11,43€ (lunch weekdays) 95-370F / 14,48-56,41€ (wine tasting incl.), also à la carte. Specialties: Croustillant de foie gras et cèpes sauce banuyls; filet de perche en matelotte; crépinette de pied de porc à la moutarde violette. **Credit cards** All major. **Pets** Dogs allowed. **Nearby** Collonges, Turenne, Argentat – 18-hole Coiroux golf course in Aubazines. **Closed** Dec – end Feb, Sunday evening in low season.

There are so many superb houses in Beaulieu because in the 13th century a powerful abbey was built here. This hotel occupies a part of its venerable walls, 100 meters from the banks of the Dordogne River. Inside, various vestiges are reminders of the antiquity of the building: many monumental fireplaces, a superb spiral staircase, parts of age-old doors. All confer special charm to the place. Pascal Cavé, the chef, respects the Quercy culinary traditions while lending them a lighter and more delicate touch. His cuisine is marvelous. In winter, there is always a fire crackling in the immense fireplace of the restaurant, while in summer the large ogival French doors open onto a leafy terrace with a few tables. The bedrooms are being renovated in pastel colors with classic furniture. Some look out on the medieval city, others onto the square; all are very quiet. Overall, the hotel is simple, family-style, and the prices are very reasonable.

*How to get there* ( Map 24 ): *39km south of Tulle via D940.*

## Relais de Saint-Jacques-de-Compostelle

19500 Collonges-la-Rouge (Corrèze)
Tel. (0)5.55.25.41.02 - Fax (0)5.55.84.08.51
M. Guillaume

**Category** ★★ **Rooms** 24; 12 with telephone, bath or shower and WC, 4 with TV, 14 in the annex with washroom. **Price** Double 170-310F / 25,92-47,26€. **Meals** Breakfast 40F / 6,10€. **Restaurant** Service 12:30PM-1:30PM, 7:30PM-9:00PM; mealtime specials 100-250F / 15,24-38,11€, also à la carte. Specialties: Feuilleté de Saint-Jacques; filet de bœuf fourré au foie gras; terrine de cèpes au coulis de jambon de pays; crème brulée aux noix; fondant au chocolat. **Credit cards** All major. **Pets** Dogs allowed. **Facilities** Parking. **Nearby** Collonges; Turenne; church in Beaulieu-sur-Dordogne; Argentat – 18-hole Coiroux golf course in Aubazines. **Open** Mid Mar – mid Nov.

Its fascinating medieval houses in red sandstone make Collonges-la-Rouge a very beautiful and much visited place. Located in the heart of the village, the hotel has just been very tastefully restored; the general effect is light and flowery. On the ground floor are two dining rooms, a small reception room furnished with amusing "toad" armchairs, and an intimate bar. The small bedrooms are all very attractive. Excellent cooking is served with a smile. In summer, tables are laid on three lovely shaded terraces. M. and Mme Guillaume's welcome, even in this tourist-ridden town, is reason enough for a visit. Open and home-style hospitality.

***How to get there*** *(Map 24): 45km south of Tulle via D940 and D38 towards Meyssac. The hotel is in the village.*

## La Maison des Chanoines

19500 Turenne (Corrèze)
Route de l'Eglise
Tel. (0)5.55.85.93.43
M. and Mme Cheyroux

**Rooms** 5 and 1 suite with bath and WC. **Price** Double 340-470F / 51,83-71,65€; suite 500-570F / 76,22-86,90€. **Meals** Breakfast 40F / 6,10€, served 7:30-10:00; half board 340-430F / 51,83-65,55€. **Restaurant** Service 12:00PM-2:00PM, 7:30PM-9:00PM; mealtime specials 155 and 195F / 23,63 and 29,73€, also à la carte. Specialties: Escalope de foie gras frais mariné de canard; filet de sandre à l'étuvée de cèpes; moules de bouchot au jus de noix vertes; médaillon de veau du limousin aux girolles. **Credit card** Visa. **Pets** Dogs allowed. **Nearby** Abbey of Aubazines, Uzerches, Argentat, Collonges-la-Rouge, Pompadour stud farm, Beaulieu-sur-Dordogne – 18-hole Coiroux golf course in Aubazines. **Closed** Halloween – Palm Sunday, Tuesday, Wednesday, and Thursday evening in low season.

This 15th century home, with its corbelled façade, flamboyantly gothic door and beautiful spiral staircase illustrates the architecture of Turenne, one of the most beautiful villages in France. *La Maison des Chanoines* is a small restaurant to which six bedrooms have been added; three are in the little house next door. Totally renovated, the rooms are elegant and tastefully decorated with antiques. For their dinner guests' pleasure, M. and Mme Cheyrou have chosen quality over quantity. There is a reasonable number of dishes on the menu, a maximum 16 diners in the beautiful vaulted dining room, and no more than 25 when meals are served beneath the honeysuckle trellis. Fresh products, gastronomic quality and friendly service are guaranteed. We will long remember the *foie gras* simply marinated with truffle and girolle vinegar.

***How to get there*** *( Maps 24): 14km south of Brive-la-Gaillarde. Highway A 20, exit number 52 to Noailles; Turenne 10 mn away.*

## Hôtel du Cèdre

23210 Bénévent-L'Abbaye (Creuse)
Rue de l'Oiseau
Tel. (0)5.55.81.59.99 - Fax (0)5.55.81.59.98
M. and Mme Choukroun

**Category** ★★ **Rooms** 16 with telephone, bath or shower, WC, satellite TV – 1 for disabled persons.
**Price** Double 250-550F / 38,11-83,85€. **Meals** Breakfast 40F / 6,10€, served 8:00-9:30. **Restaurant**
Only for residents. Service 12:00PM-2:00PM and 7:30PM-9:00PM; mealtime specials 68-130F / 10,36-
19,82€; also à la carte. Spécialités: Magret au miel; râble de lapin; pavé de sandre sauce vierge.
**Credit card** Visa. **Pets** Dogs not allowed. **Facilities** Parking. **Nearby** Abbey Bénavent; Guéret Museum.
**Closed** Feb.

In Bénévent-L'Abbaye in the Creuse region, this manor house has refound its
look of yesteryear. Tastefully restored, with blue shutters and exposed stone,
the hotel is flanked by a 150-year-old cedar tree. The rooms, look out on this
tree and either the dark, waters of the swimming pool or a road that never
knows night-time traffic. Light and happy colors, modern furnishing that
brings together wrought-iron beds, wicker, and futon sofas. The bathrooms are,
on the average, large and completely modern. The lounge, with its fireplace lit
during the cold season, is furbished with pleasant checkered couches. The
young chef, Jerome Bellot, who has still to make his mark, whips up dishes in
which the local speciality, chestnuts, make an appearance with wild-honeyed
duck breast or rabbit with walnuts. Dried plants are everywhere -- wheat and
bulrushes gathered up from the wild, or hortensias and roses picked from the
garden -- and are expertly arranged by the lady of the house. A beautiful place
to stay that we recommend without a moment's hesitation.

***How to get there*** *(Map 24): Via A20, take exit 23 (La Souterraine). Then*
*N145, take Grand-Bourg exit, then via D914 until Bénévent.*

# Domaine des Mouillères

Les Mouillères
23250 Saint-Georges-la-Pouge (Creuse)
Tel. (0)5.55.66.60.64 - Fax (0)5.55.66.68.80
Mme Thill-Blanquart

**Category** ★★ **Rooms** 7 with telephone (3 with bath, 4 with WC). **Price** Double 220-380F / 33,54-57,93€. **Meals** Breakfast 45F / 6,87€, served 8:00-9:30. **Restaurant** Only for residents. Service 8:00PM-8:30PM; mealtime specials 90-150F / 13,72-22,87€, also à la carte. Specialties: Cuisse de canard à l'ancienne; civet de lièvre aux cèpes; confit de canard. **Credit card** Visa. **Pets** Dogs not allowed. **Facilities** Parking. **Nearby** Hôtel de Moneyroux and Guéret Museum, Abbey church of Moutier-d'Ahun – 18-hole la Jonchère golf course in Montgrenier-Gouzon. **Open** End Mar – Nov 30.

This old farmhouse is set in an absolutely magnificent countryside of valleys, pastures, small rivers, birch groves, conifer-covered hills and large trees. The hotel's little lounge, dining room, and rooms are very pleasing, with their mix of furniture and decorative objects. Though at times a bit out-of-date, the overall effect is charming. Ask first for the rooms with bathrooms. The others, outfitted with a simple toilet, are well-maintained but of a modest level of comfort. They are all pretty and pleasant, many with satin bedcovers and small, round, skirted tables. Dinners are served in a rustic dining room and feature good first courses, salads and excellent meats (ask for the meat dishes with little sauce.) The owners rent bikes for exploring the superb surrounding countryside. Drinks and meals can be served on the lovely garden terrace. The staff is very courteous. A charming place that appreciates the simple life.

***How to get there*** *( Map 24): 34km south of Guéret via D942 towards Limoges to Pontarion; then towards La Chapelle-Saint-Martial, D3.*

## Hôtel de l'Echo et de l'Abbaye

43160 La Chaise-Dieu (Haute-Loire)
Place de L'Echo
Tel. (0)4.71.00.00.45 - Fax (0)4.71.00.00.22
M. Degreze

**Category** ★★ **Rooms** 10 with telephone, bath or shower, 9 with TV. **Price** Double 300-380F / 45,73-57,93€. **Meals** Breakfast 52F / 7,92€, served 7:30-9:30; half board 320-350F / 48,78-53,36€ (per pers., 3 days min.). **Restaurant** Service 12:00PM-2:00PM, 7:30PM-9:00PM; mealtime specials 95-250F / 14,48-38,11€, also à la carte. Specialties: Flan aux cèpes sauce forestière; mignon de porc à la crème de myrtilles; tournedos de saumon aux lentilles vertes du Puy. **Credit cards** All major. **Pets** Dogs not allowed. **Nearby** Basilica of Notre-Dame du Puy, church of Saint-Laurent and Aiguille au Puy, Mont Mezenc, Mont Gerbier-de-Jonc, village of Arlempdes. **Open** Palm Sunday – Nov 16.

Located in the heart of the enclave of the splendid La Chaise-Dieu abbey, this hotel owes its name to the "Room of Echoes" nearby, which is known for its strange acoustical phenomenon. It is a very old hotel, remarkably well-looked-after by its young owner and a very discrete staff, who are both very hospitable and professional. The small bedrooms are modest yet fetching, and some look out on the abbey's cloister. There is always a contemporary painting exhibit on view in the restaurant dining room, which is decorated in Haute Epoque style. The food is good and healthy, and your full plate is served with pleasure. Lastly, hotel guests, and only hotel guests, can take their meals on the hotel patio, under the shade of umbrellas and right across from the abbey's entrance. A beautiful place to stay at reasonable prices.

***How to get there*** *(Map 25): 35km north of Le Puy-en-Velay.*

## Le Pré Bossu

43150 Moudeyres (Haute-Loire)
Tel. (0)4.71.05.10.70 - Fax (0)4.71.05.10.21
M. Grootaert and Mme Moreels

**Category** ★★★ **Rooms** 10 with telephone, bath or shower and WC. **Price** Double 390-495F / 59,46-75,46 . **Meals** Breakfast 65F / 9,90€, served 8:00-10:00; half board 470-525F / 71,65-80,04€ (per pers.). **Restaurant** (no smoking). Closed lunchtime except Saturday and Sunday, national holidays and Jul – Aug. Service 12:00PM-1:30PM, 7:30PM-9:00PM; mealtime specials 175-360F / 26,68-54,88€, (child 80F / 12,20€), also à la carte. Specialties: menu légumes; pot-au-feu de pigeonneaux; gibier en a utomne. **Credit cards** All major. **Pets** Dogs allowed in bedrooms (+45F / 6,87€). **Facilities** Parking. **Nearby** Basilica of Notre-Dame-du-Puy in Puy-en-Velay, Gerbier-des-Joncs, Mézenc forest – 9-hole Chambon-sur-Lignon golf course in Romières. **Open** Mar 31 – Nov 2.

Located in the lovely village of Moudeyres, this old thatched cottage built in local stone is named for the meadow which surrounds it. The atmosphere is cozy and welcoming. To one side there is a reception room with a large fireplace, TV, and library. In the beautiful stone dining room with its smartly set tables, you will be served outstanding regional gourmet specialties, which are made with fresh produce from the kitchen garden. The bedrooms are very comfortable and attractively furnished, and the garden and terrace overlook the countryside. If you wish to go out for the day, picnic baskets can be prepared, and the welcome is very friendly.

***How to get there*** *( Map 25 ): 25km southwest of Puy. Once at Puy, head toward Valence via D 15, then drive for about 15 kms until Pandreaux. Then take D 36 until Moudeyres via Laussonne.*

## Castel-Hôtel 1904

Rue du Castel
63390 Saint-Gervais-d'Auvergne (Puy-de-Dôme)
Tel. (0)4.73.85.70.42 - Fax (0)4.73.85.84.39
M. Mouty

**Category** ★★ **Rooms** 17 with telephone, bath or shower, WC, TV. **Price** Single and double 330-360F / 50,31-54,88€. **Meals** Breakfast 49F / 7,47€, served 7:30-10:00; half board 290F / 44,21€ (per pers., 3 days min.). **Restaurant** Service from 12:30PM and 7:30PM; mealtime specials 79-269F / 12,04-41,10€, also à la carte. Specialties: Tournedos roulé au hachis de pieds de porc, Sandre, Crêpe Céline. **Credit cards** Visa, Eurocard and MasterCard. **Pets** Dogs not allowed. **Facilities** Parking. **Nearby** Gorges of the Sioule, church in Ménat, Fades viaduct, Mandet Museum and museum of the Auvergne in Riom — 9- and 18-hole Volcans golf course in Orcines. **Open** Easter — Nov 11.

Refurbished as a hotel in 1904, this grand, old house has been run by the same family ever since. All the charm of an old French hotel is to be found in its warm and welcoming rooms, bar and above all its large dining room, whose parquet floors gleam. The fireplaces, the antique furniture as well as the walls and curtains' earthy tan highlights all contribute to the old-fashioned but very charming character of the hotel. The hallways and rooms have all been recently renovated. They are of an often respectable size, decorated in a spryly rustic way, and are comfortable, well-maintained, and at a price that seems very reasonable to us. You have the choice between the hotel's restaurant (closed on Monday), which offers creative cuisine and the *Comptoir à Moustache*, an authentic country bistro. The *Castel-Hôtel 1904* is welcoming and friendly - the kind of place you get attached to.

***How to get there*** *(Map 24): 55km northwest of Clermont-Ferrand via N9 to Châtelguyon, then D227 to Saint-Gervais-d'Auvergne via Manzat.*

# Castel-Marie

87000 Limoges (Haute-Vienne)
43, rue de Nexon
Tel. (0)5.55.31.11.34 - Fax (0)5.55.31.30.17
M. and Mme Longin

**Category** ★★★ **Chambres** 6 with telephone, bath, WC, TV and videorecorder. **Price** Double 750F / 114,34€; suite (4 pers.) 1100F / 167,69€. **Meals** Breakfast 65F / 9,90 €; half board 650F / 99,09€ (per pers.). **Restaurant** Service 12:00PM-1:30PM, 7:30PM-9:00PM; mealtime specials 155F / 23,63€ (lunch weekdays), 199-299F / 30,49-45,73€, also à la carte. **Credit card** Visa. **Pets** Dogs allowed (+60F / 9,16€). **Facilities** Parking. **Nearby** Cathedral and Limoges ceramics museum; factory direct stores – 18-hole golf in Limoges. **Open** All year.

As soon as you find out that a mansion is called "Castel So-and-So", you expect a little castle from the turn-of-the-century, and this hotel is no exception. Set in the middle of a huge, leafy park near the Limoges city limits, this little manor flaunts a subtle charm. The hotel and restuarant, already known by the locals, is also a family house, with all the good points and little flaws. The lounge and dining room are very comfortable, with decor in an updated nineteenth-century style. The rooms are nice, spacious and recently renovated with antique furniture, pier glass, many 18th-century engravings, and big, beautiful bathrooms. On the down side, the upkeep of the park is a bit "so-so", the traffic noise rumbles through shrubbery (but is luckily kept out by the double-paned windows), and the sense for details is more "artistic" than perfectionist. On the plus side, the high-quality food (excellent cuts of limousine beef here) is served expertly under a wonderful glass ceiling. You can also ask for a video cassette at the reception desk to record television programs while you eat so you can watch them later in your room. A truly thoughtful touch.

***How to get there** ( Map 23 ): Near the center of Limoges.*

## Au Moulin de la Gorce

87800 La Roche l'Abeille (Haute-Vienne)
Tel. (0)5.55.00.70.66 - Fax (0)5.55.00.76.57
Bertranet-Bremont Family

**Category** ★★★ **Rooms** 9 and 1 apartment, with telephone, bath, WC and TV. **Price** Double 750-950F / 114,34-144,83€; suite 1300F / 198,18€. **Meals** Breakfast 75F / 11,43€, served from 8:00; half board 1450-1550F / 221,05-236,30€ (2 pers., 3 days min.). **Restaurant** Service 12:00PM-1:30PM, 7:30PM-9:00PM; mealtime specials 275-390F / 41,92-59,46€, also à la carte. Specialties: Harmonie gourmande de homard et foie gras; œufs brouillés aux truffes; foie poêlé aux pommes. **Credit cards** All major. **Pets** Dogs allowed. **Facilities** Parking. **Nearby** Saint Etienne and Limoges, Abbey of Solignac, Church of Saint-Léonard-de-Noblat – 18-hole Porcelaine golf course in Limoges. **Closed** 10 days in Nov and winter holidays.

Travellers looking for charm and comfort will not be disappointed here. Belonging to the same family for twenty years, this 1560 mill and surrounding buildings have become a very pleasant hotel and restaurant. Right in the middle of the countryside, this establishment benefits from an exceptional and totally calm location. The stylish, pleasant, and completely renovated rooms are split up between several buildings. All the rooms are comfortable and well-looked-after. Some are large (there is even a small studio apartment available), while others are a bit smaller, with prices to match. A feeling of cozy comfort reigns over all. When the weather is beautiful, breakfast and lunch is served at the edge of the lake that later bursts into a waterfall, only to wind away through the garden below. Relax in the nice lounge after dinner. Fine dining with an interesting menu and very well-prepared breakfasts. A luxurious and very professional place that knows how to welcome you like one of the family.

***How to get there*** *(Map 23): 30km south of Limoges on D 704, then via D 17.*

## Chez Camille

21230 Arnay-le-Duc (Côte-d'Or)
1, place Edouard-Herriot
Tel. (0)3.80.90.01.38 - Fax (0)3.80.90.04.64
M. and Mme Poinsot

**Category** ★★★ **Rooms** 14 with telephone, bath, WC and TV. **Price** Doubles 395F / 60,22€. **Meals** 50F / 7,62€, served 7:00AM-12:00PM; half board 400F / 60,98€ (per pers.). **Restaurant** Service 12:00PM-14:30PM, 7:30PM-10:00PM; mealtime specials 80-450F / 12,20-68,60€, also à la carte. Specialties: Rissoles d'escargots aux pâtes fraîches et champignons; charolais. **Credit cards** All major. **Pets** Dogs allowed. **Facilities** Garage. **Nearby** Basilica of Saint-Andoche in Saulieu; Château of Commarin; Châteauneuf — 18-hole golf course in Chailly. **Open** All year

*Chez Camille* is a real Burgundy institution and its location in the heart of Arnay-le-Duc does nothing to distract from its charm. The word here is warmth, without one of those long, anonymous hallways but a venerable, old stairwell which mounts up to the rustic, quaint rooms, which are prettily accommodated with antique furniture. You'll feel great here, and you, like us, won't dwell too much on those little signs of aging that are starting to crop up here and there. Dinner time is when the enchantress "Camille" puts her magic to work. Choose your meal while seated in one of the many alcoves of banquet room while your table is set up under the glass ceiling of the stunning dining room, a former closed-in interior courtyard. Stylized service from an attentive and thoughtful staff and remarkable, fresh Provence produce gathered direct from the hotel's own farm. All this for a home-grown, light, and inventive cuisine that is well-prepared (however, during our last stay, a few dishes were a bit overdone). A beautiful place to stay with an outstanding sense of hospitality, and where children under the age of eleven are heartily welcome.

*How to get there* *(Map 19): 28km northeast of Autun via N81.*

## Château de Challanges

Challanges 21200 Beaune (Côte-d'Or)
Rue des Templiers
Tel. (0)3.80.26.32.62 - Fax (0)3.80.26.32.52 - M. Schwarz

**Category** ★★★ **Rooms** 9 and 5 suites, with telephone bath or shower, WC and TV. **Price** Double 530F / 80,80€, suites 800F / 121,96€. **Meals** Breakfast (buffet) 60F / 9,15€, served 8:00-10:00. No restaurant. **Credit cards** All major. **Pets** Dogs allowed in suite. **Facilities** Wine toasting, parking. **Nearby** Hôtel-Dieu, Basilica of Notre-Dame in Beaune; Côte de Nuits; Château of Clos-Vougeot; Nolay; Rochepot – Golf 18-hole Beaune-Levernois golf course. **Open** Mar – Dec (check in before 7:00 PM).

When you get to *Challanges*, don't worry too much about the nearby highway, because the noise of passing cars only faintly reaches the old walls of this castle, protected by a seven-acre park. The interior is decorated in a classic and careful manner with straw-yellow walls, lots of blues, and quite restrained modern furnishings. Elegance is the rule in the common areas, notably in the well-lit dining room where each morning a breakfast buffet is set up. Same level of success in the bedrooms and suites; however, some of the rooms are a bit cramped, so we recommend that you ask first for the chambers that look out on the park entrance. Tiled in white with a matching border frieze, the bathrooms are all very pleasant and add a little something extra to this excellent destination, perfect for your visits to Beaune and the surrounding area. The lack of a restaurant in the hotel is greatly made up for by the high-quality establishments in nearby Beaune. *Le Jardin des Remparts* is a wonderful and tasty place located next to the famous hospices. There is also the excellent *Gourmandin* with its bistrot look and the warm and welcoming *Benaton*. The choice is yours.

***How to get there*** *(Map 19): On A6, take the Beaune exit towards Dole; turn right in 2km to Challanges.*

# Hôtel Le Home

21200 Beaune (Côte-d'Or)
138, route de Dijon
Tel. (0)3.80.22.16.43 - Fax (0)3.80.24.90.74
Mme Jacquet

**Category** ★★ **Rooms** 23 with telephone bath or shower and WC (8 with TV). **Price** Single and double 325-450F / 49,55-68,60€. **Meals** Breakfast 38F / 5,79€. No restaurant. **Credit cards** Visa, Eurocard and MasterCard. **Pets** Dogs allowed. **Facilities** Garage. **Nearby** Hôtel-Dieu, Basilica of Notre-Dame; Côte de Beaune between Serrigny and Chagny; Château of Clos-Vougeot; Nolay; Rochepot – 18-hole Beaune-Levernois golf course. **Open** All year.

As is the case with many built-up areas, the entrance to Beaune is eaten up by huge billboards, but don't let this inconvenience stop you from taking the road to this hotel, which is a bit off the road and is effectively soundproofed. Here you will find a broad range of rooms of greater or lesser size that are, overall, well-decorated. All are well-kept-up and the renovation works, which were necessary, have begun. However, there is still work to be done, notably in a few bathrooms and with the soundproofing of the walls between the rooms. Ask first for those that have just been renovated and avoid, in our opinion, the ground-floor rooms which suffer from the nearby parking lot. Hats off to the beautifully decorated breakfast (Yum!) nook and to the inviting lounge. You can really feel the love that Madame Jacquet and her daughter have for their house. No restaurant in the hotel, but is this really a problem when you have the excellent *Jardin des Remparts* nearby where Roland Chanliaud follows (in his own way) the lessons of Marc Meneau?

***How to get there*** *(Map 19): Via A 6, take A 31 exit 24 "Savigny-les-Beaunes".
At Beaune, toward Dijon; past Saint-Nicolas church.*

# Hôtel Le Parc

Levernois 21200 Beaune (Côte-d'Or)
Rue du Golf
Tel. (0)3.80.22.22.51/03.80.24.63.00 - Fax (0)3.80.24.21.19
Mme Oudot

**Category** ★★ **Rooms** 25 with telephone, TV (19 with shower, 6 with bath, 24 with WC.). **Price** Doubles 200-520F / 30,49-79,27€. **Meals** Breakfast 37F / 5,64€, served 7:30-9:30. No restaurant. **Credit card** Visa. **Divers** Dogs not allowed. **Facilities** Parking. **Nearby** Hôtel-Dieu, Basilica of Notre-Dame à Beaune; Côte de Beaune between Serrigny and Chagny; Château of Clos-Vougeot; Nolay; Rochepot – 18-hole Beaune-Levernois golf course. **Open** Jan 16 – Dec.

The *Hôtel Le Parc* is an old, ivy-covered Burgundian house on the doorstep of the charming international wine capital of Beaune. It has a flowery courtyard where breakfast is served, and a garden with huge, ancient trees. *Hôtel Le Parc* has the feel of a much smaller hotel despite the number of bedrooms. The atmosphere of every bedroom is different, created in one by the wallpaper, in another by a chest of drawers, and in yet another by a quilt. M. and Mme Oudot refurbish the rooms regularly. Those which have just been redecorated have pretty floral-bordered English wallpapers coordinated with the curtains and bedspreads. Some of them are very large and luxurious, and all are in good taste. Although not far from the town, you will feel as if you are in the country, and, most importantly, you will feel most welcome. For restaurants, try the famous *Hostellerie de Levernois*, or in Beaune the elegant *Jardin des Remparts*, the charming *Le Bénaton*, or *Le Gourmandin*.

***How to get there*** (*Map 19*): *4km southeast of Beaune via D970, towards Verdun, Lons-le-Saulnier.*

## Hostellerie du Château

21320 Châteauneuf-en-Auxois (Côte-d'Or)
Rue du Centre
Tel. (0)3.80.49.22.00 - Fax (0)3.80.49.21.27
M. and Mme Hartmann

**Category** ★★ **Rooms** 17 with telephone bath or shower, WC – 1 for disabled persons. **Price** Single and double 270-430F / 41,16-65,55€. **Meals** Breakfast 50F / 7,62€, served 8:00-9:45, half board from 310F / 47,26€ (per pers., 2 days min.). **Restaurant** Closed Monday and Tuesday except in Jul and Aug. Service 12:00PM-1:30PM, 7:00PM-9:00PM; mealtime specials 140-220F / 21,34-33,54€, also à la carte. Specialties: Filet de charolais au foie gras poêlé; escargots de Bourgogne en persillade. **Credit cards** All major. **Pets** Dogs allowed. **Nearby** Château of Commarin; Basilica of Saint-Andoche in Saulieu; Hôtel-Dieu in Beaune – 18-hole château de Chailly golf course. **Closed** Dec and Jan.

Perched on the hilltop of this fortified village, the Hostellerie is adjacent to a very beautiful château, built in the 12th century and restructured in the 15th, which has been photographed and filmed many times. The hostelry has all the character and charm of old inns. The bedrooms are progressively being restored to their original simplicity under the direction of a hard-working young Alsatian couple, André Hartmann and his wife. The rooms are located in two buildings: in the inn itself, offering a pleasant small suite in blue; and in a late-17th-century building a few steps away, where some rooms have a loft and others a roof window to provide light in addition to that of the small windows of the epoch. During the cocktail hour, guests can enjoy drinks on the terrace with a beautiful view of the château turrets. Or watch the daily news in the television lounge. Good homegrown, traditional cooking.

***How to get there*** *(Map 19): 30km northwest of Beaune via A 6 Pouilly-en-Auxois exit, then head toward Bligny/Ouche and Châteauneuf. After you pass the cemetary, take the left on the other side of the canal.*

# Le Manassès

21220 Curtil-Vergy (Côte-d'Or)
Tel. (0)3.80.61.43.81 - Fax (0)3.80.61.42.79
M. Chaley

**Rooms** 12 and 5 in annex, with air-conditioning, with tel., bath, TV and minibar. **Price** Single and double 430F / 65,55€; 580F / 88,42€ in annex. **Meals** Breakfast 50F / 7,62€, served 7:45-10:00. No restaurant. **Credit cards** All major. **Divers** Dogs not allowed. **Facilities** Parking. **Nearby** Abbey of Saint-Vivant and of Cîteaux; château of Clos-Vougeot; Côte de Nuits – 18-hole Dijon-Bourgogne golf course. **Open** Mar – End Nov.

Nestled in a hamlet near the most well-known vineyards of Burgundy, this little hotel, set up a few years ago in a traditional style, has pleasant rooms. Small and sassy in the main house, large and elegant in the annex, these rooms are impeccably well-maintained, the marbled bathrooms included. All are very quiet and many rooms look out on a wild, green valley. A vintner in his own right, Monsieur Chaley is a perfect example of the kind of jolly personality often associated with that profession, and his hospitality, as well as that of his family, is reason in itself to stop at the Manasses. A faint smell clues you into the location of the nearby wine cellar where new vintages are left to age. This wine theme is echoed as well in the beautiful barn that houses an interesting museum dedicated to the arts of the vine. We must also tell you about the exceptional breakfasts here, with Morvan cured ham, Burgundy ham with parsley, slices of salami, and special surprise for wine-lovers, served in a large common room dressed out with beautiful antique furniture and accented by a crackling fireplace in winter. For restaurants, we recommend *L'Auberge du Coteau* at Villars-Fontaine, *Les Gourmets* at Marsannay-la-Côte, *La Sommellerie* at Gevrey Chambertin, and *Chez Robert Losset* at Flagey-Echezaux.

***How to get there*** *(Map 19): 24km northwest of Beaune. A31, Nuits-Saint-Georges exit, D25 and D35.*

## Hôtel Les Magnolias

21190 Meursault (Côte-d'Or)
8, rue Pierre-Joigneaux
Tel. (0)3.80.21.23.23 - Fax (0)3.80.21.29.10

**Rooms** 11 and 1 suite, with telephone, bath. or shower, WC. **Price** Double 450-680F / 68,60-103,67€, suite 850F/ 129,58€. **Meals** Breakfast 48F / 7,31 €, served 8:00-10:00. No restaurant. **Credit cards** All major. **Divers** Dogs not allowed. **Facilities** Parking. **Nearby** Château of Commarin; Basilica of Saint-Andoche in Saulieu; Hôtel-Dieu and Basilica of Notre-Dame in Beaune – 18-hole Château de Chailly golf course. **Open** Mid Mar – Dec.

In this Burgundian village famed for its great Meursault, an amusing Englishman has converted an old winegrowing family's house into a charming place to stay. Surrounded by a lush garden of old roses, sweet william, honeysuckle, and magnolias, the outbuilding offers four bedrooms, including a huge suite with a small private terrace on the ground floor. Often beautiful and big, the other eight rooms are located in the house, each decorated with a special touch, antique furniture, and floral wallpaper, and all redolent of fragrant pots-pourris. Most of the baths are of average size, with a small tub, but they are relaxing and attractively fitted out in grey tones and white marble. You can enjoy breakfast outside in the sun (hoping that the vineyard tractors are not too busily at work.) Good restaurants nearby include *Le Chevreuil* and *Le Centre* in Mersault, and don't forget the splendid restaurants of Beaune, only six kilometers away.

***How to get there*** *(Map 19): 7 km south of Beaune via N 74. Then take the A 6 until the Beaune exit.*

## Le Hameau de Barboron

21420 Savigny-les-Beaune (Côte-d'Or)
Tel. (0)3.80.21.58.35 - Fax (0)3.80.26.10.59
Mme Nominé

**Rooms** 12 with telephone bath or shower, WC, TV and minibar. **Price** Double 550-900F / 83,85-137,20€, suite 1000-1200F / 152,45-182,94€. **Meals** Breakfast (buffet) 65F / 9,90 €, served to 12:00PM. **Restaurant** By reservation. **Credit cards** Visa, Eurocard and MasterCard. **Pets** Dogs allowed. **Facilities** Garage. **Nearby** Hôtel-Dieu, Basilica of Notre-Dame in Beaune; Côte de Beaune between Serrigny and Chagny; Côte de Nuits; Château of Clos-Vougeot; Nolay; Rochepot – 18-hole golf course in Beaune. **Open** All year.

Originally a monastery, the *Barbaron* is set in a remote valley, isolated from the world in keeping with Cistercian tradition. Here too, following the French Revolution in 1789, farming families settled on this immense estate devoted to hunting, cattle grazing, and agriculture. Meticulously restored, the 16th-century buildings, built around a small courtyard, look austere and serious. But once you're inside, the atmosphere is one of warmth, refinement, and conviviality. You might prefer the large suites like *Les Cousins* or *Le Guet du Loup* with their gleaming blue and white bathrooms. Or the more intimate rooms like *Lucien*, which overlooks the orchard and is equipped with a large shower rather than a bathtub. With a sweeping view of the countryside and classical music in the background, the breakfast room has a very charming decor with a fireplace and a floor of wood and ceramic tiles. You will enjoy absolute peace and quiet on this estate inhabited by birds, hares, and even the Barbaron's wild boars.

***How to get there*** *(Map 19): Via the A 6, then take the A 31 exit 4 to Savigny-les-Beaunes.*

## Hostellerie du Val-Suzon

21121 Val-Suzon (Côte-d'Or) - R.N. 71
Tel. (0)3.80.35.60.15 - Fax (0)3.80.35.61.36
M. and Mme Perreau

**Category** ★★★ **Rooms** 17 with telephone bath, WC, satellite TV, safe and minibar. **Price** Double 450-600F / 68,60-91,47€; suite 700-980F / 106,71-149,40€. **Meals** Breakfast 60F / 9,14 €, served 7:30-9:30; half board 485-585F / 73,94-89,38€ (per pers., 3 days min.). **Restaurant** Closed Sunday evening and Monday Oct – mid May. Service 12:00PM-2:00PM, 7:30PM-9:30PM; menu 130-445F / 19,82-67,84€, also à la carte. Specialties: Œufs coque homard et foie gras; millefeuille d'escargots. **Credit cards** All major. **Pets** Dogs allowed (+100F / 15,24€). **Facilities** Parking. **Nearby** Dijon; chartreuse of Champhol; la Côte de Nuits – 18-hole golf course in Beaune. **Open** All year (except mid Nov – mid Dec, Sunday evening and Monday in Oct – mid May).

In a sleepy hamlet at the base of an imposing hill, there is a little inn with a sloping garden that ends under the great trees of the patio. This place is enchanting, and were it not for the N 71 nearby, we would recommend it whole-heartedly. The rooms are located in three buildings. We unhesitatingly recommend those in the *Colombier* which have been recently finished, are elegant, comfortable, and well-soundproofed. Rooms 6 and 7 in the main house are pleasant, spacious, and also worth a look (though they start to get expensive once you ask for extra bedding). Despite their slightly out-of-date decor, the rooms in the large "chalet" located at the top of the garden are also good. The other rooms are small and more ordinary, so we don't recommend them to you. A very nice restaurant on the ground floor, where a few table are prettily set next to a fireplace and flowing, flowery curtains, adds to the warm decoration scheme which rounds out the delicious experience of eating the savory and creative cuisine of Yves Perreau.

*How to get there (Map 19): 15km northwest of Dijon via N71 towards Troyes.*

# Hôtel Saint-Louis et de la Poste

71400 Autun (Saône-et-Loire)
6, rue de l'Arbalète
Tel. (0)3.85.52.01.01 - Fax (0)3.85.86.32.54 - M. Bart Barels
E-mail: louisposte@aol.com

**Category** ★★★★ **Rooms** 31 and 7 suites, with telephone bath or shower and TV. **Price** Double 450-690F / 68,60-105,19€; suite 1250F / 190,56€. **Meals** Breakfast 50F / 7,62€, served 7:00-10:30. **Restaurant** Closed Saturday lunchtime. Service 12:00PM-2:00PM, 7:00PM-9:30PM; mealtime specials 90-165F / 13,72-25,15€ (lunchtime), 165-320F / 25,15-48,78€, also à la carte. Specialties: Pressé de magret et foie gras; filets de rouget poêlés et escalope de foie gras; risotto aux noix; filet de bœuf du Morvan mi-fumé; souflé chaud à la vanille Bourbon. **Credit cards** Amex, Visa. **Pets** Dogs allowed. **Nearby** In Autun: Saint-Lazare Cathedral, museum Rolin; Château of Sully; Couches; Couchard rocks and Brisecou waterfall. **Open** All year.

With its two thousand years of history, the town of Autun has a lot going for it. Founded by the Celtic tribe of Bibracte, it became the "sister city" of Rome before erecting the Saint-Lazare cathedral in the 12th century -- a church which still amazes visitors. The hotel dates from 1655 and has housed many prestigious guests, including Napoléon, whose former room is still available. Nevertheless, this place evokes beautiful memories of the 30s, with a superb cupola in glass brick which lights the main hall, windows done up with stained glass, and a winding staircase. From the most luxurious suites to the simplest bedrooms, all the rooms (except for one) possess a decor in muted tan, brightened up by accessories and little pieces of furniture. They are located around a large interior court covered with ivy where you can take your meals in summer. A great place to stop and stay over, or to wander about a region rich in history, culture, and viticulture. A friendly and smiling reception.

***How to get there*** *(Map 18): 53km northwest of Chalon-sur-Saône on D978.*

## Manoir de Sornat

71140 Bourbon-Lancy (Saône-et-Loire)
Allée de Sornat
Tel. (0)3.85.89.17.39 - Fax (0)3.85.89.29.47
M. Raymond

**Category** ★★★ **Rooms** 13 with telephone bath or shower, WC, TV and minibar **Price** Single and double 350-700F / 53,36-106,71€. **Meals** Breakfast 65F / 9,91€, served 7:30-11:00; half board 450-700F / 68,60-106,71€ (per pers., 3 days min.). **Restaurant** Closed Monday lunchtime. Service 12:00PM-14 h, 7:30PM-9:30PM; mealtime specials 160-430F / 24,39-65,55€, also à la carte. Specialties: Pigeon laqué; filet de bœuf charolais. **Credit cards** All major. **Pets** Dogs allowed except in restaurant (+30F / 4,57€). **Facilities** Parking, helideck. **Nearby** Château of Saint-Aubin-sur-Loire; church of Ternant; abbatia of Paray-le-Monial. **Closed** 4 weeks between mid Jan and mid Feb; Sunday evening in low season.

This house was built in the 19th century by of an affluent Lyonnais who was fond of horse racing at Deauville. He chose a pure Anglo-Norman style of architecture which, though common in Deauville, is unusual here. Adjoining the *Manoir* are the remains of a racecourse where up to World War II the Bourbon Lancy stakes race was run. Many bedrooms are spacious; all are comfortably appointed and tastefully decorated in a restrained modern style. On the park side, some rooms have a terrace where you can enjoy a copious breakfast overlooking large trees with scampering squirrels. The gastronomic reputation of the *Manoir de Sornat* needs no introduction (Michelin gives it a star), and many gourmets make a special trip here for Gérard Raymond's cuisine. You will be served in a large dining room which is to be renovated this year, or on the patio in summer. A beautiful and very pleasing place where you will always find a professional and competent reception.

***How to get there*** *(Map 18): 30km northeast of Moulins via N79 towards Chevagnes, Autun.*

## Château de la Fredière

La Fredière 71110 Céron (Saône-et-Loire)
Tel. (0)3.85.25.19.67 - Fax (0)3.85.25.35.01
Mme Charlier

**Rooms** 10 and 1 suite, with telephone bath or shower, WC, TV. **Price** Double 480-620F / 73,18-94,52€, suite 750F / 114,34€. **Meals** Breakfast 55F / 8,38€; half board and full board 610-1070F / 92,99-163,12€ (2 pers.). **Restaurant** Closed Nov 16 – Mar 15 and Wednesday. Service 12:00PM-2:00PM, 7:30PM-9:00PM; menu and also à la carte. Specialties: Terrine de queues de bœuf; charolais; charlotte aux fraises. **Credit cards** Visa, Eurocard, MasterCard. **Pets** Dogs allowed by reservation (+50F / 7,62€). **Facilities** Swimming pool – 18-hole golf course, parking. **Nearby** Château of Lapalisse; romanesque church in Brionnais. **Closed** Jan.

This small château looks out over a large park, which is itself surrounded by an 18-hole golf course. Madame Charlier and her family welcome their guests as if they were members of the family. Most of the bedrooms and the suite are spacious and bright, and all are quiet and comfortably appointed. The rooms on the first floor have kept their original furniture and perfectly represent the charm of the good old days; recently renovated, the rooms on the *deuxième étage* have received a new lease on life and are decorated in vibrantly colored fabrics. The large salon and fireplace offer a relaxing place to read. Breakfast is served in the bright dining room with a blond parquet floor, or on the terrace in good weather. We had a lovely impression of relaxation and tranquillity in this beautiful hotel and its country setting. Just a few steps away from the château, you will find the pretty dining room, which overlooks a lake and the garden. The *Château de la Frédière* is a beautiful place to stay for a weekend in the country.

*How to get there* *(Map 25): 40km north of Roanne to Marcigny, towards Le Donjon, Lapalisse and follow signs for the golf course.*

## Hostellerie du Château de Bellecroix

71150 Chagny (Saône-et-Loire)
Tel. (0)3.85.87.13.86 - Fax (0)3.85.91.28.62
Family Gautier-Crinquant

**Category** ★★★ **Rooms** 20 with telephone bath or shower, WC, TV and minibar. **Price** Double 580-1000F / 88,42-152,45€. **Meals** Breakfast 70F / 10,67€, served 7:30-10:00; half board 600-950F / 91,47-144,83€ (per pers., 3 days min.). **Restaurant** Service 12:00PM-1:30PM, 7:30PM-9:00PM; mealtime specials 265-350F / 40,40-53,36€, also à la carte. Specialties: Filet de charolais et foie gras chaud; escargots en cocotte lutée. **Credit cards** All major. **Pets** Dogs allowed (+50F / 7,62€). **Facilities** Swimming pool, parking. **Nearby** Hôtel-Dieu, Notre-Dame parish church in Beaune; Côte de Beaune between Serrigny and Chagny; château of Clos-Vougeot; Nolay; Rochepot – 18-hole golf course Beaune-Levernois. **Closed** Dec 19 – Feb 14 and Wednesday except Jun – Sep.

A bit away from the city and the N 6, this hotel is in a little 15th-century castle and the old headquarters of the 12th-century Knights of Malta (Wonderful transom windows and ancient murals). At the entrance, a large, beautifully decorated, panelled reception hall and dining room, decorated with lovely flowered draperies, stylish, comfortable chairs, elegantly laid tables, and reproductions of Old Master paintings. Next to it, in a turret, there is a small, intimate lounge. The comfortable bedrooms occupy two buildings, with some overlooking the five-acre park with a swimming pool. The rooms in the first building are tastefully furnished, often in 18th-century style (we do not recommend 3 and 4). The rooms in the command headquarters evoke a lost era; they are very large and some open out to the garden. Higher price but great. The Bellecroix is a pleasant hotel which constantly strives to improve and succeeds.

***How to get there*** *( Map 19): 15 kms south of Beaune on the N 74, then take the N 6 and the north exit at Chalon-sur-Saône.*

# Hôtel de Bourgogne

71250 Cluny (Saône-et-Loire)
1, rue Porte-des-Prés
Tel. (0)3.85.59.00.58 - Fax (0)3.85.59.03.73
M. and Mme Colin

**Category** ★★★ **Rooms** 15 with telephone bath or shower, WC and TV. **Price** Double 470-1000F / 71,65-152,45€. **Meals** Breakfast 60F / 9,15€, served 7:30-10:00, "Soirée étape gourmande" 1030-1560F / 157,02-237,82€ (2 pers.). **Restaurant** Service 12:00PM-2:00PM, 7:30PM-9:00PM; mealtime specials 130-350F / 19,82-53,36€, also à la carte. Specialties: Croustine de chèvre chaud du Clunisois aux épices douces; sandre rôti sur sa peau. **Credit cards** All major. **Pets** Dogs allowed (+60F / 9,15€). **Facilities** Garage (50F / 7,62€). **Nearby** Abbey and museum in Cluny; caves of Azé; arboretum of Pézanin; Châteaux of Chaumont, Brézé and Cormatin; chapel in Berzé – 18-hole Château de la Salle golf course in Lugny. **Closed** Feb – end Nov.

This hotel was built on part of the site of the ancient Cluny Abbey. However, the number of rooms and the arrangement of the rooms around a small inner garden ensure peace and quiet. There is a pleasantly proportioned living room, where several styles are nicely combined; a large dining room, and gourmet cooking. The comfortable bedrooms are quaintly charming, and there is an inviting bar where breakfasts are served. Everything, including the welcome, contributes to the pleasure of your stay. The 19th-century poet Alphonse de Lamartine enjoyed the hotel, as did the many famous people who have signed the Guest Book for the past thirty years. Let's make iwt clear that the hotel has just been bought up and many improvements are on the board. We hope that they will keep the charm of this beautiful home.

***How to get there*** *(Map 19):24km northwest of Mâcon via N79 and D980. Or take the Mâcon south exit, then head toward Cluny on the expressway.*

## Château d'Igé

71960 Igé (Saône-et-Loire)
Tel. (0)3.85.33.33.99 - Fax (0)3.85.33.41.41
Mme Germond
E-mail: ige@relaischateaux.fr

**Category** ★★★★ **Rooms** 7 and 6 suites, with telephone, bath or shower, WC and satellite TV. **Price** Single and double 495-780F / 75,46-118,91€, suite 975-1195F / 148,64-182,18€. **Meals** Breakfast 75F / 11,43€, served 7:30-11:00; half board +610F / 92,99€ (2 pers.). **Restaurant** Service 12:00PM-2:00PM, 7:30PM-9:00PM; mealtime specials 160F / 16,77€ (lunchtime weekdays), 200-380F / 30,49-48,78€, also à la carte. **Credit cards** All major. **Pets** Dogs allowed (+55F / 8,38€). **Facilities** Parking (+55F / 8,38€). **Nearby** Abbey and museum in Cluny – 18-hole golf course in Lugny. **Open** Mar 1 – Nov 30.

The lush countryside of Mâcon, with its rolling valleys and vineyards perched on exposed slopes makes a beautiful locale for the little village of Igé. With its balconies and flowery courtyards, Igé seems to be sparring with its sublime environs, and its castle-hotel is not the least powerful of arguments in this battle over beauty. With its sturdy 16th-century towers, its bit of moat, and its deliciously romantic garden, this hotel is both homey and subtly luxurious. Highlighted by fabrics and antique furnishing throughout, the rooms are very comfortable, well-kept-up, and outfitted with more or less modern bathrooms, but often suffer from a limited though lush view. (The tower room, set off in a corner of the garden, is superb, with its vaulted ceiling and meticulously sculpted groin.) There is an excellent restaurant occupying several little Louis XIII lounges. Or you may eat on the patio next to a great winter garden with rattan furnishings. Truly friendly hospitality from a family which has run this hotel for two generations.

*How to get there* (*Map 19*)*: Via A 6, take Mâcon exit south. Montceau-les-Mines Cluny road. Exit La Roche-Vineuse, after the town, take a right toward Verzé then Igé.*

# Hôtel La Reconce - Restaurant de la Poste

71600 Le-Bourg-Poisson (Saône-et-Loire)
Tel. (0)3.85.81.10.72 - Fax (0)3.85.81.64.34
M. and Mme Dauvergne

**Category ★★★ Rooms** 6 and 1 suite, with telephone, bath or shower, TV and minibar. **Price** Double 350-430F / 53,36-65,55€, suite 630-680F / 96,04-103,67€. **Meals** Breakfast 55F / 8,38€, served 7:30-10:00. **Restaurant** Closed Monday evening and Tuesday, except Jul and Aug. Service 12:00PM-1:30PM, 7:00PM-9:30PM; mealtime specials 85-500F / 12,96-76,22€, menu for child 60F / 9,15€, also à la carte. Specialties: Bœuf de charolais; nougat glacé. **Credit cards** Amex, Visa. **Pets** Dogs allowed (+50F / 7,62€). **Facilities** Parking. **Nearby** Paray-le-Monial: Church Notre-Dame, museum Hiéron; Brionnais. **Open** All year (except first 3 weeks in Feb and 2 weeks in Oct).

The peaceful village of Poisson is located in the meadows of the Charolais region, mottled by the white cattle that provide the famous meat that one finds on only the best tables. This is the case as well for the *Restaurant de la Poste*. Now, the restaurant has expanded into a large, adjoining house where Madame Dauvergne has prepared seven comfortable rooms, whose colorful fabrics and blond parquetry create an inviting, sweet ambiance. The bathrooms are modern, and two of them are flooded with light during the day. In summer, breakfast is in a covered courtyard that gives out to a delightful little garden. In the other house, a former village cafe, the large dining room looks out on a shaded garden, making mealtime feel like an outdoor party. You will enjoy the delicious, charolais beef, but also a great variety of fish (a reference to the town), as well as the inventive desserts of Jean-Noël Dauvergne. Attentive hospitality with a smile. A beautiful place to rest and relax.

***How to get there*** *(Map 18): 70km west of Mâcon heading toward Moulins on N 79 until Paray-le-Monial; left at first light to Poisson.*

# Hôtel du Cheval Blanc

71390 Saint-Boil (Saône-et-Loire)
Tel. (0)3.85.44.03.16 - Fax (0)3.85.44.07.25
M. and Mme Cantin

**Category** ★★★ **Rooms** 10 and 1 maisonnette, with telephone bath or shower, WC, TV. **Price** Double 370-460F / 56,41-70,13€, extra bed 90F / 13,72€; half board 450F / 68,60€. **Meals** Breakfast 58F / 8,82€, served 8:00-9:30. **Restaurant** Closed Wednesday. Service 12:00PM-1:30PM, 7:00PM-9:00PM; mealtime specials 140-230F / 21,34-35,06€, also à la carte. Specialties: Pot-au-feu de volaille; terrine maison. **Credit card** Visa. **Pets** Dogs not allowed. **Facilities** Bicycle, swimming pool, parking, garage. **Nearby** château of Cormatin, romanesque church, Cluny. **Closed** Feb 15 – Mar 15.

In the southwest of wine-growing Burgundy, at the border of the meadows of Charolais, the countryside around Saint-Boil could easily be found a post card from "Deepest France." At the entrance to the village, the Cheval Blanc was just until recently known only as a restaurant, and you will immediately want to get a seat there once you see the dining room painted in shades of white, yellow and green, accented by pretty objects and bordered by a little garden court where you can eat in the summer. (Monsieur Cantin was a chef at the famous Parisian restaurant, *La Closerie des Lilas*.) Today, after having bought up a little manor house located just across the street, the inn outfitted it with ten luminous, playful, comfortable, and perfectly well-kept rooms. You will also not be disappointed by the excellent breakfasts served outside or in a room decorated in pastels, just like the rooms. A simple and hospitable place, perfect for even a long stay.

***How to get there*** *(Map 19): Via A 6, take Châlon south or Mâcon south exit, then D 981.*

## La Montagne de Brancion

Brancion 71700 Tournus (Saône-et-Loire)
Tel. (0)3.85.51.12.40 - Fax (0)3.85.51.18.64
M. and Mme Million

**Category** ★★★ **Rooms** 18 and 1 suite, with telephone, bath or shower, WC, TV, safe and minibar.
**Price** Double 680-800F / 103,67-121,96€, suite 1100F / 167,69€. **Meals** Breakfast 75F / 11,43€,
served 8:00-9:30/10:00 in room; half board 595-870F / 90,71-132,63€ (per pers.). **Restaurant**
Service 12:00PM-1:30PM, 7:30PM-9:00PM; mealtime specials 180F / 27,44€ (lunchtime except
Saturday and Sunday), 270-370F / 41,16-56,41€, also à la carte. Specialties: local traditional
cooking. **Credit cards** All major. **Pets** Dogs allowed (+50F / 7,62€). **Facilities** Heated swimming pool,
parking. **Nearby** Saint-Philibert Church in Tournus; church in Chapaize; Blanot; Cluny; Taizé; Château
of Cormatin – 8-hole and 18-hole in Château-la-Salle. **Open** 13 Mar – 16 Nov.

Located in a quiet, well-conserved area, this recently built hotel is perched
on a hilltop and enjoys a sweeping view over the vineyards and the pretty
village of Martilly-lès-Brancion. The interior is modern. Open to the rising sun
and looking out over the landscape, the bedrooms are pleasant, simple, and
tranquil. They are being steadily redecorated, and we would pick those most
recently redone, with their happy warm colors, as well as to those which open
out to the pretty little balcony. While the dining room is somewhat too modern,
the service there is professional and pleasant and the cuisine is delectable.
(Meals served on the patio in summer.) A pleasant place to stay, from which
you can head out on your tourist excursions, and where you will be warmly
welcomed with a smile.

***How to get there*** *(Map 19): 13km west of Tournus; A 6 exit Tournus; via D14*
*dir. Briancion. After Martailly-lès-Brancion, follow signs and turn on the left.*

## Domaine du Roncemay

89110 Aillant-sur-Tholon (Yonne)
Tel. (0)3.86.73.50.50 - Fax (0)3.86.73.69.46
M. Christian Adam

**Category ★★★★ Rooms** 15 and 1 suite (4 pers.), with telephone, bath or shower, WC, satellite TV and minibar. **Price** Double 590-750F / 89,94-114,34€, suite 850-1050F / 129,58-160,07€. **Meals** Breakfast 50F / 7,62€, served 7:00-10:00; half board 625-765F / 95,28-116,62€ (per pers.). **Restaurant** Service 12:00PM-2:00PM, 7:00PM-10:00PM; mealtime specials 145-320F / 22,11-48,78€, also à la carte. Specialties: Feuillantine de grenouilles désossées; filet de sandre au chou frisé parfumé au cumin et morilles. Brasserie: Service 12:00PM-18:00; menu 95F / 14,48€. **Credit cards** All major. **Pets** Dogs allowed (+40F / 6,10€). **Facilities** Swimming pool, 18-hole golf course, parking. **Nearby** Abbey of Saint-Fargeau, wine cellars of Joigny, cathedral in Auxerre. **Open** Mid Feb – mid Jan.

Located in the heart of an immense oak forest, next to a beautiful golf course, the *Domaine du Roncemay* will certainly make sports lovers happy, but everyone can find something wonderful here. Set up in old, carefully renovated buildings, the hotel has a sweeping view of the golf course. The lounges and dining room bathe in beautiful sunlight, as well as do most of the rooms which look out on the green (our favorites). The rooms are of a beautiful size, outfitted with furniture and engravings hunted down in antique auctions, are all very warm, and, with their superb bathrooms, offer only the highest comfort. For meals, you can choose between the bistrot with its great, natural vista and the castle's nearby dining room which fits into the league of gourmet restaurants (only open evenings). For breakfast, you will sample old-fashioned jams, homemade from the fruit from the orchard. A place that brings together sport and the tranquility of a beautiful country hotel.

***How to get there*** *(Map 19): Via A 6 Joigny exit, toward Aillant/Tholon, then "Les Ormes" follow signs.*

## La Fontaine aux Muses

89116 La Celle-Saint-Cyr (Yonne)
Tel. (0)3.86.73.40.22 - Fax (0)3.86.73.48.66
Family Pointeau-Langevin

**Category** ★★ **Rooms** 17 with telephone, bath or shower and WC (4 with TV), minibar. **Price** Double 350-410F / 53,36-62,50€, suite 525-630F / 80,04-96,04€. **Meals** Breakfast 38F / 5,86€, served 8:00-10:00; half board 375-535F / 57,17-81,56€ (per pers., 3 days min.). **Restaurant** Closed Monday lunchtime – Tuesday evening. Service 12:30-13:45, 8:00PM-21:15; menu 185F / 28,20€, also à la carte. Specialties: Ragoût de homard au foie gras. **Credit cards** Visa, Eurocard, MasterCard. **Pets** Dogs allowed by reservation. **Facilities** Swimming pool, golf (50F / 7,62€), tennis (35F / 5,34€), parking. **Nearby** Joigny; forest of Othe; Saint-Cydroine; Saint-Florentin. **Open** All year (closed Monday 11:00 – Tuesday 17:00 except by reservation).

A bit outside of a little village, this inviting inn was founded by a couple of artists and is now in the lively hands of their son, Vincent, and his wife. On top of tending the vines and the inn, Vincent livens up the weekend dinners with his musician friendsand turns evenings into veritable jazz concerts. In the lounge bar, you will sit in inviting armchairs around a charming fire. The rooms, decorated in a modest and restrained way, look out on the countryside. To keep the authentic look of the house and its sloping roof, as well as to have more space, the hallway of the top floor kept its sloped ceiling, which might require a bit of acrobatics from tall people. Not far from there, on the golf course, the annex rooms were built in the local style, offering more comfort but less character. Ask for precise information when you reserve your room. A relaxed and friendly atmosphere.

***How to get there*** *(Map 18): 36km northwest of Auxerre via N6 to Joigny, D943 for 7km, then D194. By A6, Joigny (North), Villeneuve-sur-Yonne south exit.*

## Château de Vienne

Prunoy
89120 Charny (Yonne)
Tel. (0)3.86.63.66.91 - Fax (0)3.86.63.77.79
Mme Roumilhac

**Rooms** 13 and 6 suites, with telephone bath, WC, minibar and TV – 3 rooms for disabled persons. **Price** Double 750F / 114,34€; suite 850-1200F / 129,58-182,94€. **Meals** Breakfast incl., served 8:30-10:30. **Restaurant** Service 12:30PM-8:00PM; mealtime specials 170-220F / 25,92-33,54€, also à la carte. **Credit cards** Amex, Visa, Eurocard, MasterCard. **Pets** Dogs allowed. **Facilities** Swimming pool, tennis, parking. **Nearby** Saint-Fargeau; zoological gardens in Boutissaint; Château of Ratilly; Cathedral of Saint-Etienne in Auxerre – 18-hole Roncemay golf course in Aillant-Thoron. **Closed** Jan – end Mar.

Surrounded by 250 acres of parks, the *Château de Prunoy* was built in the purest 17th-century architectural style. The beautiful reception rooms on the ground floor, with stunning 18th-century sculptured woodwork, reflect the rare nature of this setting, which has been entirely designed and decorated by Madame Roumilhac. (During dinner, she goes from table to table to make sure that guests are enjoying their meal.) In one wing, the cheerful country dining room, gives onto a terrace with the great trees in the park. The cuisine is copious, but it is the bedrooms which make the *Vienne* stand out, with the quality and originality of their decor, their spaciousness, and their modern amenities. The view is magnificent, from the bedrooms overlooking the main courtyard as well as from those on the park, whose perspective is lost in the forest. This beautiful château still seems to have much of the atmosphere of a private residence.

***How to get there*** *( Map 18): 40 km northwest of Auxerre (90 mins.) from Paris. Take the A 6 until Exit Joigny/Charny no. 8, then via D 943 toward Montargis, and then take D 16 heading toward Charny until you reach Prunoy.*

# Le Castel

89660 Mailly-le-Château (Yonne)
Place de l'Eglise
Tel. (0)3.86.81.43.06 - Fax (0)3.86.81.49.26
M. ann Mme Bréèrette

**Category** ★★ **Rooms** 12 with telephone, 8 with bath, 3 with shower, 8 with WC. **Price** Double 230-340F / 35,06-51,83€; apart 400F / 60,98€. **Meals** Breakfast 37F / 5,64€, served 8:00-9:30; 1 meal per day. **Restaurant** Closed Wednesday. Service 12:15PM-1:30PM, 7:15PM-8:30PM; mealtime specials 75-170F / 11,43-25,92€, also à la carte. Specialties: Escargots aux noisettes; gratin de framboises. **Credit card** Visa. **Pets** Dogs allowed (+25F / 3,81€). **Nearby** Basilica Sainte-Madeleine in Vézelay; Saussois boulders; Saint-Etienne-d'Auxerre Cathedral; caves of Arcy – 18-hole Roncemay golf course in Chassy. **Open** Mar 16 – Nov 14.

A pretty garden with a lime-shaded terrace awaits you in front of this late 19th-century house. The arrangement of the ground floor means that the lounge lies between the two dining rooms, the whole forming a single area. Around the fireplace are Empire tables and armchairs, and although the furniture in the dining rooms is in a different style, the ensemble is tasteful and effective. Several bedrooms have been renovated and until the others follow suit, we recommend Rooms 6, 9 and especially Number 10, which is very handsome with its blue Jouy fabric and corner lounge. Despite several new carpets, the others are still too lackluster for our taste. Located in a historically preserved site in front of the church of this tiny, typical village, *Le Castel* is a quiet hotel with a very good restaurant, and a bar on the terrace. The owners are friendly and informal.

***How to get there*** *(Map 18): 30km south of Auxerre via A6 exit Auxerre-sud, then N6 dir. Avallon until D 100 on the right via Bazarnes, Mailly-la-ville and Mailly-le-Château.*

## Auberge du Château

89580 Val-de-Mercy (Yonne)
3, rue du Pont
Tel. (0)3.86.41.60.00 - Fax (0)3.86.41.73.28
L. and J. Delfontaine

**Rooms** 4 and 1 suite, with telephone, bath or shower, WC and TV. **Price** Double 380-450F / 57,93-68,60€, suite 600F / 91,47€. **Meals** Breakfast 55 and 70F / 8,38 and 10,67€. **Credit card** Visa. **Pets** Dogs allowed. **Nearby** Saint-Etienne Cathedral and abbey of Saint-Germain in Auxerre; Valley of la Cure; Valley of Ouanne. **Restaurant** Closed Sunday evening and Monday. Service 12:00PM-2:00PM, 7:30PM-10:00PM; mealtime specials 115-255F / 17,53-38,87€, also à la carte. Specialties: Gâteau de crabes et de gambas et sa quenelle de caviar coulis de concombre; noisettes d'agneau parfumées au jus d'agneau et miel d'acacias; larme de chocolat mousse ivoirine et griottine. **Open** Mar 1 – 14 Jan.

Nestled in a quiet Burgundy village, this fetching inn is composed of many small, exposed-stone buildings joined together by a blossoming courtyard and extending out into a pleasant garden. The bedrooms are upstairs and are very tastefully decorated with parquet floors (in all but one), white walls which show off the oldpink of the drapes and bedcovers, and some antique furniture. In good weather, the room with an immense terrace is especially in demand. The restaurant is located in two small lounges and the dining tables are set with rare elegance; only the lighting is somewhat cold. Jacques Delfontaine mans the kitchen stoves, and the result is quite delicious, for simple dishes as well as more sophisticated cuisine. Breakfasts are served either in a lovely corner bar, the garden, or beneath the beautiful roof beams of a room which serves as an art gallery and tea room. This is a charming inn offering reasonable prices and friendly service.

***How to get there*** *( Map 18 ): 18km south of Auxerre via A6, Auxerre Sud exit; then N6 towards Avallon, D85 towards Coulanges-la-Vineuse, D165 to Val-de-Mercy.*

# Auberge La Lucarne aux Chouettes

89500 Villeneuve-sur-Yonne (Yonne)
14, quai Bretoche
Tel. (0)3.86.87.18.26 - Fax (0)3.86.87.22.63
Mme Leslie Caron

**Rooms** 4 with telephone, bath, WC. **Price** Double 490F / 74,70€, suite 760F / 115,86€; loft and duplex 870F / 132,63€. **Meals** Breakfast 60F / 9,15€, served 8:30-10:30. **Restaurant** Closed Sunday evening and Monday, except Jul. Service 12:00PM-2:30PM, 7:00PM-10:00PM; business lunch specials 98F / 15,24€ (lunchtime); mealtime specials 200F / 30,49€. Specialties: Feuilleté d'escargots sur lit de salade verte; mi-cuit au chocolat sur sa crème pistache et coulis de cassis. **Credit cards** Amex, Visa. **Pets** Dogs allowed. **Facilities** Parking. **Nearby** Cathedral; Joigny; Auxerre, Museum of l'Avalonnais. **Open** All year.

The houses of Villeneuve-sur-Yonne are huddled around the beautiful Renaissance church of Notre Dame, and you will find this inn on the town's border. Originally four village houses, the *Lucarne aux Chouettes* has recently been converted into a very charming auberge by Leslie Caron herself. On the ground floor, there is a bar-veranda and a superb dining room whose beams and half-timbering create the essential part of the decor. The cuisine is delicious, inventive, light and refined. (Marc Daniel used to be the chef at Paris's famous restaurant *Lasserre*). The service is attentive and in summer meals are served on the lovely terrace overlooking the quay. The bedrooms are upstairs and all have a beautiful view over the river. Priority has been given to spaciousness, modern amenities, and charm in the bedrooms, where there are antique-style beds, pretty fabrics, family furniture, and paintings. The welcome is very hospitable and friendly.

***How to get there*** *(Map 10): 15km south of Sens. Via A6 exit Courtenay/ Sens, then D15 towards Piffonds and Villeneuve-sur-Yonne.*

## Manoir de Crec'h-Goulifern

Beg-Leguer - Servel
22300 Lannion (Côtes-d'Armor)
Tel. (0)2.96.47.26.17 - Fax (0)2.96.47.28.00
Mme Droniou

**Rooms** 8 with telephone, bath or shower, WC. **Price** Double 380-480F / 57,93-73,18€. **Meals** Breakfast incl., served 8:00-10:00. No restaurant. **Credit cards** Not accepted. **Pets** Dogs not allowed. **Facilities** Tennis, parking. **Alentour** Chapel of Kerfons; Châteaux of Tonquédec, of Kergrist, of Rosambo; chapel of the Sept-Nains – Saint-Samson 18-hole golf course in Pleumeur-Bodou. **Open** All year.

The manor of *Crec'h-Goulifen*, originally an 18th-century farmhouse, lovingly renovated and linked to the presence of Madame Droniou, whose simple, very friendly, clear, and reserved ways (read, wry) still please us immensely. The main room on the ground floor is arranged with regional country furniture, and on the terrace you will be served a copious breakfast to the rhythm of the tick-tock of the clock. The bedrooms, some of which are rather small and dark, are rustic in style and have thick carpets. All are comfortably appointed, scrupulously well-looked-after, but there decor deserves a little freshening up. One large room, located on the upper floor of a neighboring little house, has already been refurbished, and it's our favorite for the time being. There is a smashing garden as well, whose blossoms often win prizes at the regional fair. Peace and quiet guaranteed. For meals, you might try the gastronomic restaurant *Ville Blanche*, ten kilometers away in the town of Ville Blanche; or head toward Trebeurden to taste the excellent food at *Ti Al Lannec*.

***How to get there*** *(Map 5): 6km northwest of Lannion via D21, then towards Servel.*

## Château Hôtel de Brélidy

Brélidy 22140 Bégard (Côtes-d'Armor)
Tel. (0)2.96.95.69.38 - Fax (0)2.96.95.18.03
M. and Mme Yoncourt-Pémezec

**Category** ★★★ **Rooms** 14 with telephone, bath, WC and TV. **Price** Double 390-820F / 59,46-125,01€, suite 1145-1270F / 174,55-193,61€. **Meals** Breakfast 55F / 8,38€, served 8:00-10:00; half board 435-640F / 66,32-97,57€. **Restaurant** Service 7:30PM-9:00PM; mealtime specials 150 and 190F / 22,87 and 28,97€. Specialties: Râble de lapin à la moutarde à l'ancienne et au romarin du jardin. **Credit cards** All major. **Pets** Dogs allowed (+50F / 7,62€). **Facilities** Fishing, mountain bikes, jacuzi, parking. **Nearby** Saint-Tugdual Cathedral in Tréguier, Basilica of Notre-Dame-de-Bon-Secours in Guingamp, Château of Tonquedec, Kergrist, Rosambo – 18-hole Ajoncs d'or golf course in Saint-Quai-Portrieux. **Open** Easter – Nov.

Hidden away in a Breton grove, the Brelidy boasts flowery and carefully cared-for surroundings. Behind its old walls, you will find a traditional and pleasant ambiance. Of course, the lounge's "Country Louis XIII" look is a bit out-of-fashion, but charming all the same, and we understand the owners who decided to focus their attention on the patio that opens out from the dining room. Partially covered, it often affords you the opportunity to taste the culinary specialties of the chef while looking out on the spectacular landscape of hills, woods, hedges, and well-worn paths. No matter what their size, the rooms are all very well-maintained, pleasant, and refined. Some have canopy beds, while others open out to a flowery patio. A hospitable and homey place for nature lovers and those who love peace and quiet.

***How to get there*** *(Map 5): north of Guingamp; on N12 after Guingamp, Lannion-Bégard exit, 300m after the first trafic circle, take D712 towards Tréguier, then 11km on left to Brélidy.*

## Hôtel d'Avaugour

22100 Dinan (Côtes-d'Armor)
1, place du Champ-Clos
Tel. (0)2.96.39.07.49 - Fax (0)2.96.85.43.04
M. Nicolas Caron

**Category** ★★★ **Rooms** 21 and 3 suites, with telephone, bath, WC and TV. **Price** Double 460-850F / 70,13-129,58€, suite 800-1700F / 121,96-259,16€. **Meals** Breakfast (buffet) 52F / 7,92€, served 7:00-10:00. No restaurant. **Credit cards** All major. **Pets** Dogs allowed. **Nearby** Léhon, Pleslin, Pleslin, Pléven, Château of la Hunaudaie, Saint Malo – 18-hole Dinard golf course in Saint-Briac-sur-Mer. **Closed** Mid Nov – mid Dec.

Away from the center of old Dinan, this hotel, located on a slightly noisy square, has a charming garden in back, bursting with flowers, which looks out on the ramparts. When it's nice, you can relax far from the madding crowd or have your breakfast. Try to reserve a room that looks out on this splendid view, bathed in the light of the setting sun. We recommend this hotel to you even more strongly than the year before because all of the garden rooms and suites have been redone. The decoration sports an entirely new look -- cheerful, elegant, and modern-day. The bathrooms have been refurbished with towel heaters, hair dryers, and even a telephone, all this against a backdrop of Italian tiles. The others, that look out on the square, have kept their more classic scheme, but still remain comfortable and well-protected by double-pane windows, for a high level of peace and quiet. The restaurant is under renovation and will not be open this year, but many good restaurants are in Dinan. Try *La Mère Pourcel*, *Les Grands Fosses*, *Fleur de Sel* (right across from the hotel, with good food at the right price), without forgetting *Les Terrasses*, on the old port.

***How to get there*** *( Map 6): 29km south of Saint-Malo (center of Dinan).*

# Le K'loys

22500 Paimpol (Côtes-d'Armor)
21, quai Morand
Tel. (0)2.96.20.40.01 - Fax (0)2.96.20.72.68
Guy Conan

**Category** ★★★ **Rooms** 11 with telephone, bath, satellite TV – Elevator; 1 for disabled persons. **Price** Double 495-595F / 75,46-90,71€; 4 pers 795F / 121,20€. **Meals** Breakfast 50F / 7,62€, served 7:30-10:30. **Restaurant** *L'Islandais* Service 12:15PM-2:00PM, 7:15PM-10:00PM; mealtime specials 98-148F / 14,94-22,56€; also à la carte. Specialties: Seafood, fish, crêpes and galettes. **Credit cards** Diners, Visa. **Pets** Small dogs allowed. **Facilities** Parking. **Nearby** Abbey of Beauport; Guilben Point; Arcouest Point; Lanieff, Kermaria-an-Iskuit Chapel, Lanloup. **Open** All year.

On the dock of Paimpol, this manor house from the end of the last century has just benefitted from a complete interior renovation. As soon as it gets nice, the façade and stoop blossoms with hortensias and geraniums. Top priority has been given to comfort and decor. If the bar, the lounge with its caisson ceiling, and the common areas are a bit too bright, the eleven rooms spread out over three stories are spacious, well-lit, and very pleasant. Decorated in beautiful, colored fabrics, these rooms are cheerful and quite cozy with their stylish or antique furniture. Whether they look out on the port or on the back of the hotel, the chambers are truly comfortable. The well-looked-after bathrooms are tiled or panelled in teak. Breakfast is served in your room or on a veranda that looks out on the back of the house. Before dining at the neighboring restaurant, *L'Islandais*, a very popular place run by the hotel management, you can have a drink at the bar or at one of the little tables set up in front of the hotel. The owner, a really colorful character, well-known in Paimpol, will welcome you warmly. A very relaxed ambiance.

***How to get there*** *(Map 5): 33km east of Lannion via D 786 until Paimpol.*

# Le Manoir du Sphinx

22700 Perros-Guirec (Côtes-d'Armor)
67, chemin de la Messe
Tel. (0)2.96.23.25.42 - Fax (0)2.96.91.26.13
M. and Mme Le Verge

**Category** ★★★ **Rooms** 20 with telephone, bath, WC, Safe and satellite TV – Wheelchair access; elevator. **Price** Double 560-650F / 85,37-99,09€. **Meals** Breakfast 52F / 7,92€, served 7:30-9:30; half board 1100-1270F / 167,69-193,61€ (pour 2 pers.). **Restaurant** Closed Monday lunchtime, except national holidays. Service 12:30PM-2:00PM, 7:30PM-9:30PM; mealtime specials 130-300F / 19,82-45,73, also à la carte. **Credit cards** Amex, Visa. **Pets** Dogs not allowed. **Facilities** Direct access to the sea, parking. **Nearby** Footpath to Ploumanac'h, pink granite coast (Chapel of Notre-Dame-de-la-Clarté), Sainte-Anne-de-Trégastel, boat excursions to the Sept Iles (Ile aux Moines) – 18-hole Saint-Samson golf course in Pleumeur-Bodou. **Closed** Jan 5 – Mar 22.

This turn-of-the-century house is located on a little cliff road above a pink granite coast. To take best advantage of this exceptional locale, every bit of the hotel faces the Bay of Trestrignel. The lounge bar (very nicely renovated last year) and elegant, adjoining dining room look directly down on the ocean; the carefully tended gardens extend down to the rocks, and the rooms equally enjoy this sumptuous view (except for a tiny few that only have a peripheral view of the sea). They are decorated in a restrainedly modern way, usually furbished with English-style, mahogonny furniture. The bathrooms are very well done, and some rooms even have a little corner lounge located in front of bay or bow windows which look directly down on the sea. Everything is perfectly well-kept-up. Savoury food, and exceptionel seafood. The heartiest of welcomes awaits.

***How to get there*** *(Map 5): 11km of Lannion, along the coast.*

## Manoir de Vaumadeuc

22130 Pleven (Côtes-d'Armor)
Tel. (0)2.96.84.46.17 - Fax (0)2.96.84.40.16
M. O'Neill

**Category** ★★★★ **Rooms** 14 with telephone, bath or shower and WC. **Price** Single and double 490-1100F / 74,70-167,69€; suites 850-1250F / 129,58-190,56€. **Meals** Breakfast 50F / 7,62€, served 8:00-10:00; half board 450-745F / 68,60-113,57€ (par pers. 3 j. min.). **Restaurant** By reservation. (guests first); mealtime specials 195F / 29,73€. **Credit cards** All major. **Pets** Dogs allowed (+50F / 7,62€). **Facilities** Parking. **Nearby** Château of la Hunaudaye; Dinan; Saint-Malo; 18-hole Pleslin golf course. **Open** Easter – Jan 5.

An historically registered monument, this 15th-century, granite manor located in the heart of the forest of Hunaudaye has kept all its integrity. You enter into a majestic reception lounge, where you will admire the ceiling and original fireplace. A magnificent staircase leads you to the first-floor rooms. You can only appreciate the flawlessly tasteful furnishings and decorative objects. All the rooms are inviting. Choose those on the first floor. Those under the mansard are just as pleasant and comfortable, but they have kept their quaint, original charm. The very well-tended bathrooms have the charm of bathrooms of yesteryear. The two little bunk houses fitted out as rooms in a simple style are ravishing. Monsieur O'Neill, whose family has owned this manor for many generations, will welcome you with attention and courtesy. He will also give you advice on nearby dining possibilities when the hotel restaurant is closed. An excellent place to stay between surf and turf.

***How to get there*** *(Map 6): 37km east of Saint-Brieuc via N12 to Lamballe; in the village, D28 to Pléven via La Poterie and the Hunaudaye Forest.*

# Le Manoir de Rigourdaine

22490 Plouër-sur-Rance (Côtes-d'Armor)
Route de Langrolay
Tel. (0)2.96.86.89.96 - Fax (0)2.96.86.92.46
M. Van Valenberg

**Category** ★★ **Rooms** 19 with telephone, bath or shower, WC, TV – Wheelchair access. **Price** Double 300-450F / 45,73-68,60€; studio or duplex 390-450F / 59,46-68,60€ (2 pers., +70F / 10,67€, extra bed). **Meals** Breakfast 40F / 6,10€, served 8:00-10:30. No restaurant. **Credit cards** Amex, Visa. **Pets** Dogs on the ground floor (+30F / 4,57€). **Facilities** Parking. **Nearby** Saint-Malo; Pays de Rance and d'Arguenon – 18-hole Saint-Cast golf course, 18-hole Ormes golf course. **Open** Apr 2 – Nov 14.

The location of this old, extensively renovated farmhouse combines the charms of the country with a sweeping view over the blue waters of the Rance Valley 200 meters below. The bedrooms, all of which enjoy this panorama, are new, with English-style wallpaper and a pleasant decor. An old wardrobe here, a chest-of-drawers there and numerous paintings lend a personal touch. Those on the ground floor have a private terrace and are perfect for summer. For families, we recommend the suites, which are especially well-suited for groups. Breakfast is served in a large, rustic-style dining room or on the leafy terrace. The general ambiance is very pleasant, just like the hospitality of the young and attentive Patrick Van Valenberg. There is no restaurant here, but you are not lacking in dining options. Just nearby, in Plouer, *La Vieille Auberge* serves up good local food, and at Saint-Suliac, you will find *La Grève* next to a charming little port. A bit further, but well worth going out of your way for is the excellent *Clos des Chanoines*, located at the Saint-Malo exit on the road to Cancale.

***How to get there*** *( Map 6): 15km northeast of Dinan. On N176 between Dol and Dinan, take the Plouër exit towards Langrolay. Signposted.*

# Ti Al-Lannec

22560 Trébeurden (Côtes-d'Armor)
14, allée de Mezo-Gwen
Tel. (0)2.96.15.01.01 - Fax (0)2.96.23.62.14 - M. and Mme Jouanny
E-mail: ti.al.lannec@wanadoo.fr - Web: www.pro.wanadoo.fr/ti.al.lannec

**Category** ★★★ **Rooms** 29 with telephone, bath, WC and satellite TV – Elevator; wheelchair access. **Price** Double 680-1175F / 103,67-179,13€. **Meals** Breakfast 70-90F / 10,67-13,72€, served 7:15-10:30; half board 615-835F / 93,76-127,29€. **Restaurant** Service 12:30PM-2:00PM, 7:30PM-9:30PM; mealtime specials 115-395F / 17,53-60,22€; also à la carte. Specialties: Suprême de saint-pierre doré, jus aux truffes et pommes boulangères. **Credit cards** All major. **Pets** Dogs allowed (+50F / 7,62€). **Facilities** Fitness-beauty center, parking. **Nearby** Le Castel; Bihit point; the Breton slopes from Trébeurden to Perros-Guirec – Saint-Samson golf course in Pleumeur-Bodou. **Open** Mid Mar – mid Nov.

Year after year, the *Ti Al-Lannec* proves to be an exceptional place, as much because of the quality of its interior decorating as for its wonderful view of the Channel (which is easily accessible by a small path) and terraced gardens. The very comfortable bedrooms are beautifully furnished and decorated, some with English fabrics and wallpaper; most have a sitting area, a charming veranda or terrace. The same care in decoration is evident in the lounges, generously furnished with antiques and decorated with paintings and wall hangings that have been expertly chosen to achieve a very stately, "*maison*" look. Just next door, the elegant dining room opens out into a long veranda overlooking the bay. The service here is perfect and the cuisine excellent. Outside, the gardens descend by terraces. Also, check out the gym facilities, perfect to get you back in shape. A top-of-the-line address, rather expensive, but well-worth the visit.

***How to get there*** *(Map 5): 9km northwest of Lannion via D65.*

## Kastell Dinec'h

22200 Tréguier (Côtes-d'Armor)
Tel. (0)2.96.92.49.39 - Fax (0)2.96.92.34.03
M. and Mme Pauwels

**Category** ★★★ **Rooms** 15 with telephone, bath and WC (9 with TV). **Price** Double 450-540F / 68,60-82,32€. **Meals** Breakfast 65F / 9,91€, served 8:00-10:00; half board 455-530F / 67,84-80,80€. **Restaurant** Service 7:30PM-9:30PM; mealtime specials 130-310F / 19,82-47,26€; also à la carte. Specialties: Bar en croûte de sel; cassolette de moules aux mousserons; crêpes de seigle au homard; crème de Saint-Jacques. **Credit card** Visa. **Pets** Dogs allowed (+50F / 7,62€). **Facilities** Heated swimming pool (May 15 – Sep 15) and parking. **Nearby** Cathedral of Saint-Tugdual and the house of Ernest Renan-Tréguier; Pleubian; Chapel of Saint-Gonéry-Plougrescant; Château de la Roche-Jagu – 9-hole Saint-Samson golf course in Pleumeur-Bodou. **Closed** Oct 12 – 26 and 1 Jan – Mar 20; Tuesday evening and Wednesday in low season.

Hidden away in luxurious green flora, 2km from Tréguier stands this 17th-century manor-farm. The main building - housing a beautiful dining room, a small comfortable lounge, and some of the bedrooms - has two annexes containing the other bedrooms. Together they look onto a lovely garden where drinks and breakfast are served in summer. Highlighted by elegant fabrics, the bedrooms are small but tastefully decorated, some with carefully selected antique furniture. The overall effect is warm and very refined. A really great place which owes a lot to the hospitality of Madame Pauwels as well as to the culinary talent of her husband who holds court in the kitchen to the great pleasure of his food-loving guests.

***How to get there*** *( Map 5 ): 16km east of Lannion via D786, 2km before Tréguier; follow the signs.*

## Le Minaret

29950 Bénodet (Finistère)
Corniche de l'Estuaire
Tel. (0)2.98.57.03.13 - Fax (0)2.98.66.23.72
Mme Kervran

**Category** ★★ **Rooms** 20 with telephone, bath or shower, WC and TV – Elevator. **Price** Double 280-550F / 42,69-83,85€. **Meals** Breakfast 45F / 6,86€, served 8:00-10:00; half board (obligatory in high season) 280-485F / 42,69-73,94€. **Restaurant** Closed Tuesday in Apr – May. Service 12:30PM-2:00PM, 7:30PM-9:00PM; mealtime specials 90-235F / 13,72-35,83€; also à la carte. Specialties: Gigot de lotte au poivre vert; homard grillé-la crème d'estragon. **Credit card** Visa. **Pets** Dogs allowed except in restaurant (+30F / 4,57€). **Facilities** Parking. **Nearby** Quimper; boat trip on the Odet from Quimper to Bénodet; Breton museum and villages; Notre-Dame de Quilinen Chapel. **Closed** 15 Oct – 2 Apr.

An oasis in the midst of traditional Brittany: That is what *Le Minaret* looks like! It is a large white house designed in the 1920s by the architect Laprade; from the top of its real minaret, there's a breathtaking view out over the estuary of the River Odet, where sailboats pass regularly on their way in and out of the port. Even more than the exterior, the interior of the house reminds you of its Oriental character. The bright rooms, three of which have a small terrace, have a view of the sea or the charming small inlet bordering the town of Sainte-Marine. The great curiosity of the house is the Pacha bedroom, decorated in pure Moroccan style with wide windows opening onto the estuary. The mixture of the styles is attractive and lends unusual charm to the hotel. A pretty garden surrounds the house, and the terrace on the seafront also affords a superb view.

***How to get there*** *(Map 5): 16km south of Quimper.*

# La Ferme de Porz-Kloz

Tredudon-Le-Moine
29690 Berrien (Finistère)
Tél. 02.98.99.61.65 - Fax (0)2.98.99.67.36
M. and Mme Berthou

**Rooms** 7 with telephone, bath or shower, WC, 6 with TV and 3 with minibar – 2 for disabled persons.
**Price** Double 260-400F / 39,64-60,98€, 3 pers. 400-460F / 60,98-70,13€. **Meals** Breakfast 40F /
6,10€, served 9:00-11:00; half board 270-340F / 41,16-51,83€ (per pers.). **Restaurant** Only for
residents. Service 7:00PM-8:00PM; menu 110F / 16,77€. Specialties: Fricassée au cidre; épaule
d'agneau aux poireaux; chevreau rôti. **Credit card** Visa. **Pets** Dogs not allowed. **Facilities** Parking.
**Nearby** Plougonven, Saint-Thegonnec, Guimiliau, Lampaul-Guimiliau – 18-hole Saint-Samson golf
course in Plemeur-Bodou. **Open** Apr – Nov.

With sparse, broom-flecked vegetation, and lakes mirroring the changing
skies of Brittany, the Arrée Mounts seem to embody the very soul of the
region's ancient Celtic legends. You will find the welcoming *Ferme de Porz-Kloz*
in this strikingly beautiful site. Its group of buildings once belonged to the Relq
Abbey, the oldest parts dating from the 13th century. Still a working farm, it
supplies the hotel with meat and vegetables for the delectable evening meal,
served in a pleasantly rustic room. Located in three houses, the bedrooms have
a charming country air with their lovely fabrics, a few pieces of antique
furniture, and cozy beds. Room 6, "*La Jabadao*" is a great success, Numbers 8
and 9 are perfect for families, Room 4, the "*Gavotte*" is very cheerful, and
finally, there is the "*Aw Dro*", which is a huge lounge room on the ground floor,
perfect for families. The baths are pleasant despite a few elements that look
rather amateurishly fitted. Picnic lunches can be prepared for hikers.

***How to get there*** *(Map 5): 20km south of Morlaix. In Morlaix, take D769
towards Huelgoat, then Abbaye de Releq, Tredudon; follow signs.*

# Castel Régis

29890 Brignognan-Plage (Finistère)
Tel. (0)2.98.83.40.22 - Fax (0)2.98.83.44.71
Mme Dominique Norgeot

**Category** ★★ **Rooms** 22 with telephone, bath and TV – 1 for disabled persons **Price** Double 300-590F / 45,73-89,94€. **Meals** Breakfast 40F / 6,10€, served 8:00-9:45; half board and full board (obligatory in Jul – Aug) 340-520F / 51,83-79,27€; 470-520F / 71,65-79,27€ (per pers., drink incl., 1 day min.). **Restaurant** Closed Monday lunchtime. Service 12:15PM-1:30PM, 7:30PM-9:00PM; mealtime specials 115-280F / 17,53-42,69€; also à la carte. Specialties: Saint-Jacques; lobster; seafood. **Credit card** Visa. **Pets** Dogs allowed. **Facilities** Swimming pool, tennis, sauna, parking. **Nearby** Pontusual Point; Goulven Church; la Côte des Abers. **Open** Apr 1 – Sep 30.

*C*astel Régis can be found on a little peninsula of sand and rocks. It's actually several houses linked together by a garden. You will find the restaurant in the main house, where, in front of the fishing boats that rock against the backdrop of the setting sun, you can eat a cuisine bursting with flavor. The rooms can be found in the six other houses. Most have just been handily renovated. The furnishing is restrained and comfortable, and the decoration, with its grey and pale blue color scheme, corresponds perfectly with what one finds on the seaside. Some rooms have a superb view of the ocean, while others open out upon the greenery, and still others are perfect for families. A pleasant, hospitable place to stay, wonderfully well-located.

***How to get there*** *(Map 5): 37km nord of Brest via D 788 until Lesneven, then via D 770.*

# Hôtel Ty Mad

29100 Douarnenez (Finistère)
Plage Saint-Jean
Tel. (0)2.98.74.00.53 - Fax (0)2.98.74.15.16
Mme Martin

**Category** ★★ **Rooms** 23 with telephone, bath or shower and WC (TV on request). **Price** Single and double 250-340F / 38,11-51,83€. **Meals** Breakfast 40F / 6,10€, served 8:00-11:00. **Restaurant** service 7:30PM-9:30PM; mealtime specials and also à la carte. **Credit cards** All major. **Pets** Dogs allowed (+28F / 4,26€). **Facilities** Parking. **Nearby** Douarnenez (Port Museum), coast paths of Plomarc'h and Roches Blanches; Beuzec Point; Cap Sizun; Quimper, Locronan, Church of Confort, Pont-Croix and Sainte-Anne-la-Palud – 18-hole l'Odet golf course in Bénodet. **Open** Easter – Oct.

A one-time refuge for many celebrities in search of peace and quiet, this house has counted the likes of Christopher Wood and Max Jacob among its guests, the latter who lived her for more than two years. However, the *Ty Mad* is just a little, modest hotel, but you will certainly understand its attraction when you see the superb view that it has of the Douarnenez Bay. The interior is not lacking in charm either: There is a pretty little lounge with green linden wood flooring, comfortably accommodated in a youthful, cheerful style; and an elegant, panoramic dining room with white table linen and colorful, freshly-cut flowers. As far as the rooms go, let's be honest, they are, for the most part, really small with miniscule showers. But their lighting, simple and youthful decor, and good upkeep make them fetching. Try first to reserve the rooms that look out on the ocean. You can take your dinner here, but the kitchen is in the process of "finding itself" right now, and the frequent changes in staff make it difficult for us to tell you anything clearer on the subject.

***How to get there*** *( Map 5 ): 18km northwest of Quimper via D765; at the Tréboul Yacht Harbor, the hotel is signposted.*

## La Baie des Anges

29870 Landéda (Finistère)
350, route des Anges
Tel. (0)2.98.04.90.04 - Fax (0)2.98.04.92.27 - M. Jacques Briant
E-mail: bdanges@abers-tourisme.com

**Category** ★★★ **Rooms** 18 and 2 suites, with telephone, bath and WC, TV, Safe – 1 for disabled persons. **Price** Double 320-580F / 48,78-88,42€, suite 720F / 109,76€. **Meals** Breakfast 55F / 8,38€, served 7:00AM-1:00PM. No restaurant. **Credit cards** Amex, Visa. **Pets** Dogs allowed +50F / 7,62€. **Facilities** Parking. **Nearby** Boat tours of Abers, parish glebes, sailing, kayaking, riding. **Closed** Jan.

Not far from Aber Wrach, in front of the "Bay of Angels," this little hotel has just been entirely redone by a young couple who will go to any length to make your stay a pleasant one. Decorated in a modern-day spa theme, with light wood, wicker, and white and blue fabrics, the reception lounge and dining room perfectly express the general tone of the place. The ambiance of the rooms is just a bit more "up-tight", but pleasant all the same. Each is furnished in modern furniture, made with natural woods, and beautiful blue and tan patterns highlight the blue carpeting. Pretty pewter light fixtures and nautical engravings add a little extra touch. Very well-lit, many of the rooms look directly out on the sea without suffering the least from noise coming from the local main road, thanks to the double-pane windows. Of course, we highly recommend these rooms over those that look out on the rather humdrum back of the hotel. As you take your leave, the good breakfasts will reinforce your general impression of the place, and you will want to come back soon to breathe the fresh, sea air and listen to the lullaby of the rolling surf.

***How to get there*** *(Map 4): At Brest, take D 13 toward Gouesnou, Lannilis, Landéda and Aber Wrach.*

# Grand Hôtel des Bains

29241 Locquirec (Finistère)
15 bis, rue de l'Eglise
Tel. (0)2.98.67.41.02 - Fax (0)2.98.67.44.60 - M. Van Lier

**Category** ★★★ **Rooms** 36 with telephone, bath, WC, TV — Wheelchair access and 2 rooms for disabled persons; elevator. **Price** Single and double 550-950F / 83,85-144,83€. **Meals** Breakfast (buffet) served 8:00-11:00; half board 830-1230F / 126,53-187,51€ (per pers., 3 days min.). **Restaurant** Service 7:30PM-9:30PM (and Sunday lunchtime); mealtime specials 150-295F / 22,87-44,97€; also à la carte. **Credit cards** All major. **Pets** Dogs allowed (+50F / 7,62€). **Facilities** Heated and covered swimming pool, jacuzzi, sauna, massage, parking. **Nearby** Church and tower of La Pointe de Locquirec; Pink granite coast; Rugged coastine — 18-hole golf course in Lannion. **Open** All year.

Built on one of the most beautiful spots of the Breton Coast, this imposing turn-of-the-century hotel has just had a face lift. Its park on the waterside, which served as a setting for the film *L'Hôtel de la Plage*, is as elegant as in its heyday except that today, it boasts a big plus: a beautiful covered swimming pool. Exposed to the morning sun, almost all the bedrooms overlook the sea (some have a large terrace) and afford guests the spectacle of the clear waters crashing against the rocks, or of the beach, immense at low tide. The rooms are of variable sizes, their extremely comfortable arrangement reminiscent of the 1900s beach-house style. The beautiful decor includes walls painted in delicate shades of grey or grey-beige; lovely pale-blue, dusky rose or lime-green fabrics, white painted furniture… The excellent cuisine is served in a huge, elegant dining room which opens wide onto the garden. After long years of neglect, the superb rebirth of the *Grand Hôtel des Bains* has been a great success. Make sure to reserve a room way ahead of time.

***How to get there*** *(Map 5): 79km east of Brest via E50 to Morlaix, then D796 to Plestin-des-Grèves and Locquirec.*

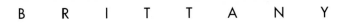

## Manoir de Moëllien

29550 Plonévez-Porzay (Finistère)
Tel. (0)2.98.92.50.40 - Fax (0)2.98.92.55.21
M. and Mme Garet

**Category** ★★ **Rooms** 18 with telephone, bath, WC and TV **Price** Double 360-740F / 54,88-112,81€.
**Meals** Breakfast (buffet) 50F / 7,62€, served 8:00-10:00; half board 370-570F / 56,41-86,90€
(per pers.). **Restaurant** Service 12:30PM-2:00PM, 7:30PM-9:00PM; mealtime specials 126-300F / 19,06-
45,73€; also à la carte. Specialties: Fish and shellfish. **Credit cards** All major. **Pets** Dogs allowed
(+30F / 4,57€). **Facilities** Parking. **Nearby** Saint-Corentin Cathedral and Art Museum in Quimper;
Locronan; Sainte-Anne-la-Palud – 18-hole l'Odet golf course in Bénodet. **Open** Mar 25 – Nov 16.

Invisible from the little road leading to it, this château is hidden by a pine
forest. The dining room is on the ground floor of the main building, built of
stone in the 17th century. It is very Haute Epoque in style with its granite walls,
anitque Breton furnishings, and fresh-cut floors set on lightly-colored table
linen. Next door is a small, intimate bar. In the relaxing first-floor lounge a
stone fireplace takes pride of place. Opposite the noble façade of the manor is
a building housing bedrooms at ground-floor level. They are comfortable,
classic, quiet, and well-kept, and many have a private patio with a beautiful
view of the countryside. The most recent rooms are our favorites, with their
more youthful decoration. Some are duplexes and all have very nice bathrooms.
This is an excellent address, just a few minutes from the beautiful Finistère
coastline, with cooking that has received an excellent reputation

***How to get there*** *( Map 5 ): 20km northwest of Quimper via D63 to Locronan at
the first traffic circle, take Plonévez-Porzay exit; first road on the left.*

# Moulin de Rosmadec

29930 Pont-Aven (Finistère)
Venelle de Rosmadec
Tel. (0)2.98.06.00.22 - Fax (0)2.98.06.18.00
Famille Sébilleau

**Category** ★★ **Rooms** 4 with telephone, bath, WC and TV **Price** Doublex 480F / 73,18€. **Meals** Breakfast 47F / 7,16€. **Restaurant** Service 12:30PM-2:00PM, 7:30PM-9:30PM; mealtime specials 168-400F / 25,61-60,98€ with lobster; also à la carte. Specialties: Fish; Rosmadec grilled lobster. **Credit card** Visa. **Pets** Dogs allowed (+30F / 4,57€). **Nearby** Gauguin-Pont-Aven musuem; Cathedral of Saint-Corentin and Museum of Beaux-Arts à Quimper; Church of Tremalo; Nizon; Kérangosquer; Concarneau "la ville close"; boat rides from Odet and Aven — 18-hole Odet golf course in Bénodet. **Closed** 2 weeks in Nov, Feb; Wednesday; Sunday evening in low season.

You will find the *Moulin de Rosmadec* at the end of a small lane in the charming village of Pont Aven, immortalized by Paul Gauguin. Nestling between two branches of a pretty river, this 15th-century mill is an ideal place to stay in order to explore this marvelous Breton village with fifteen mills in all. The *Moulin*'s four small bedrooms, which are located in the building adjacent to the hotel, are all comfortable, and from them you will hear the peaceful sound of water tumbling through the wheel, which is still in operation. The hotel's restaurant, which is run by the owners' son, has been here for more than sixty years, its reputation deservedly extending beyond Brittany. The beautiful dining room has great character, spilling over into a ravishing veranda which is perfect for breakfast in the sun (unless you prefer the patio with its old moss-covered well.) This is an exceptionally friendly and lovely hotel where you just might be tempted to stay on a while.

***How to get there*** *(Map 5): 37km southeast of Quimper via D783, towards Concarneau.*

## La Demeure Océane

29830 Portsall (Finistère)
Tel. (0)2.98.48.77.42 - Fax (0)2.98.80.52.64
M. and Mme Richard

**Rooms** 6 and 2 duplexes, with shower and WC. **Price** Double 290-370F / 44,21-56,41€; duplex 500F / 76,22€. **Meals** Breakfast 35F / 5,34€, served 8:30-10:00. No restaurant but evening meal for residents only on request. **Credit card** Visa. **Pets** Dogs allowed (+35F / 5,34€). **Facilities** Parking. **Nearby** Coast of Abers Conquet-Brignognan (120 km). **Open** Mar – Oct (except national holidays).

This large, somewhat ordinary village house is surrounded by a garden and is very well-located a hundred meters from an irresistible little port. You will find family-style hospitality, half-way between that of a bed-and-breakfast and a hotel. Recently renovated, the bedrooms are simple, cheerful, impeccably maintained and very bright. On the *premier étage* upstairs, they are classic and decorated with period furniture. On the *second étage*, there is a younger ambiance and some duplex rooms which are ideal for families. You should also know that their is a little apartment with a kitchenette that opens out directly onto the garden -- great for long stays, but we do not recommend it as highly as the rooms. A dinner menu is posted in the lobby every day (by reservation only). The cuisine, served family-style on a communal table, is traditional and of course regularly features fish and shellfish. A great wine lover, M. Richard has built up a very interesting cellar of estate-bottled wines and *grands crus*. This is an occasion to make interesting discoveries. The decoration, however, is a bit ho-hum, and would benefit from a little renovation. Apart from that, the "Ocean Residence" is pleasant, the prices are reasonable and you shouldn't miss a walk to the highly scenic port.

***How to get there*** *(Map 4): 30km north of Brest towards Saint-Renan. In Ploudaimézeau, take the road to Portsall. Signposted.*

# Le Brittany

29681 Roscoff (Finistère)
Boulevard Sainte-Barbe
Tel. (0)2.98.69.70.78 - Fax (0)2.98.61.13.29 - Mme Chapalain

**Category** ★★★ **Rooms** 25 with telephone, bath or shower, WC and TV – 1 for disabled persons; elevator. **Price** Double 590-890F / 89,94-135,68€; apart. 780-1100F / 118,91-167,69€. **Meals** Breakfast 65F / 9,91€, served 7:15-10:30; half board 450-680F / 68,60-103,67€. **Restaurant** *Le Yatchman.* Closed lunchtime Monday, Tuesday and Saturday. Service 12:15PM-2:00PM, 7:15PM-9:15PM; mealtime specials 130-320F / 19,82-48,78€, also à la carte. Specialties: Seafood, fish and shellfish. **Credit cards** Amex, Visa. **Pets** Dogs allowed, except in restaurant. **Facilities** Heated and swimming pool, sauna, parking. **Nearby** Saint-Pol-de-Léon; Léon Châteaux tour trail (Château de Kerouzéré, manoir de Tronjoly, Château de Kerjean) **Open** Mar – Nov.

In the delightful small town of Roscoff, the *Brittany* is the last rampart against the winds that beat in from the Atlantic. The bedrooms are decorated with beautiful old furniture and white fabric wall coverings; they are calm and pleasant, with well-equipped bathrooms. You might want to have breakfast in your room because the breakfast room near the swimming pool can be noisy. The dining room, which is located in a 17th-century manor house, is the most charming and pleasant part of the hotel: Facing due west, it looks out over the sea and its large bay windows bathe the room with light. The hospitality is very British, and the cuisine is typical of the region, with lots of fresh fish; and there is a very good wine list. The bar has the discreet atmosphere of a great hotel. The last stop on the way to Ireland and England, this *auberge* combines the pleasures of a comfortable stopover with the tranquillity of an old Breton house.

***How to get there*** *(Map 5): 25km north of Morlaix.*

## Hôtel de la Plage

29550 Sainte-Anne-la-Palud (Finistère)
Boulevard Sainte-Barbe
Tel. (0)2.98.92.50.12 - Fax (0)2.98.92.56.54
M. and Mme Le Coz

**Category** ★★★★ **Rooms** 30 with telephone, bath or shower, WC, TV, minibar – Elevator.
**Price** Double 840-1400F / 128,06-213,43€, suite 1100-1600F / 167,69-243,92€. **Meals** Breakfast
80F / 12,20€, served 8:00-10:00; half board +350F / 53,36€ (per pers., 2 days min.). **Restaurant**
Service 12:30PM-1:30PM, 7:30PM-9:00PM; mealtime specials 230-420F / 35,06-64,03€, also à la carte.
Specialties: Fish and shellfish. **Credit cards** All major. **Pets** Dogs allowed, except in restaurant.
**Facilities** Swimming pool, tennis, sauna, parking. **Nearby** Cathedral of Saint-Corentin and B
eaux-Arts Museum in Quimper; Locronan; Church of Ploéven – 18-hole Odet golf course in Bénodet.
**Closed** Nov – end Mar.

The small road that leads to this hotel goes right up to the sandy beach
facing a superb bay. The hotel thus well-deserves its name, "The Beach".
Luxurious without being stuffy, it takes maximum advantage of its exceptional
location. The comfortable bedrooms are classically decorated overall, with
beautiful period furniture, paintings, and carpets. Others have been recently
appointed in an especially elegant seaside style; All overlook either the garden
or the ocean. Those with the ocean-view are bit more expensive, but highly
recommend them. (Avoid the rooms in the annex.) You can enjoy a marvelous
panorama from the salon-bar and the restaurant. Spacious bay windows give
you the impression that the hotel is right on the beach: you definitely feel as if
you're on vacation. The Michelin-rated restaurant didn't live up to its
reputation during our last visit. But this was probably just a one-time fluke.

***How to get there*** *( Map 5): 17km northwest of Quimper.*

## Les Grandes Roches

29910 Trégunc (Finistère)
Route des Grandes-Roches
Tel. (0)2.98.97.62.97 - Fax (0)2.98.50.29.19
M. and Mme Henrich

**Category** ★★★ **Rooms** 22 with telephone, bath or shower, WC. **Price** Double 275-420F / 41,92-64,03€; apart. 600F / 91,47€. **Meals** Breakfast 45F / 6,86€, served 8:00-9:30; half board 320-480F / 48,78-73,18€, except Monday (per pers., 3 days min.). **Restaurant** Closed mid Nov – end Mar and Monday. Service 12:30PM-1:30PM (only Sunday and national holidays), 7:15PM-9:30PM; mealtime specials 98-260F / 14,94-39,64€; also à la carte. Specialties: Shellfish, grilled lobster, country lamb. **Credit card** Visa. **Pets** Dogs not allowed. **Facilities** Parking. **Nearby** Pont-Aven; Quimper; Nizon; Concarneau; Nevez; Golf in Cornouaille and Ploemeur – 18-hole Odet golf course in Bénodet and Queven. **Closed** Dec and Jan.

Impressive monoliths greet the guests at the entrance to this inn's garden and echo the historically-registered menhir which juts up from another corner of the property. This recently renovated former farm is composed of many buildings, some built from stone. This very comfortable inn has a bar with a terrace, two dining rooms, and a lounge with a television. The thatched cottages, an unusual and interesting feature, have been very well-restored and turned into apartments with traditional furnishings. The lounges are decorated in an attentive way, with oriental rugs, paintings, and beautiful, regional furniture. Medium-sized and perfectly tended, the rooms are equally well-cared-for, and each has a look all its own. Located near the beaches, this is an inviting address, particularly for our German friends, given the fact that Monsieur Henrich is of German origin, but has adopted Brittany as his home.

***How to get there*** *(Map 5): 28km southeast of Quimper via D783 to Trégunc via Concarneau; (the auberge is just outside the village).*

## Hôtel Richeux

35260 Cancale (Ille-et-Vilaine)
Tel. (0)2.99.89.25.25 - Fax (0)2.99.89.88.47
M. and Mme Roellinger

**Rooms** 13 with telephone, bath, WC, TV and minibar – Elevator; room for disabled persons. **Price** Double 750-1550F / 114,34-236,30€. **Meals** Breakfast 85F / 12,96€, served 8:00-10:00. **Restaurant** Closed Monday and Tuesday lunchtime. Service 12:30PM-2:00PM, 7:30PM-9:30PM; mealtime specials from 110F / 16,77€, also à la carte. **Credit cards** All major. **Pets** Dogs allowed (+50F / 7,62€). **Facilities** Parking. Riding (100 m). **Nearby** Saint-Malo; Côte d'Emeraude; Mont-Saint-Michel – 18-hole golf course in Dinard. **Open** All year.

Wonderful! That's the word that comes to mind once you see this luxurious inn, lovingly run by Jeanne and Olivier Roellinger. Each irresistible room, overlooking the sea or the countryside, has a different ambiance, beautiful antique furniture, a bouquet of flowers, and even a decanter of sherry. The bathrooms are bright and pleasant. You will love the dinner, catch of the day, and homegrown fruits and vegetables. Masterfully prepared and served in the two dining rooms that open out to the garden and the ocean, these meals prove that the Roellingers know how to create awe-inspiring menus, at modest prices. Next door, the lounge, decorated in a modern-day, charming style, is a great place to have your cocktail or coffee; and the magic of the place works here as well. Let's point out that the Roellingers also own the charming little hotel, *Les Rimains*, which will delight those who love the intimate and luxurious. Six smashing rooms, decorated in the English mode (costing between 850 and 950 Francs). There is no lounge nor dining room, but there is a marvelous garden with a little staircase that leads down to the sea and the port of Cancale. Yet another wonderful success to discover.

***How to get there*** *(Map 6): 5 km from Cancale. Head toward Rennes and then toward Mont-Saint-Michel.*

# Hôtel Reine Hortense

35800 Dinard (Ille-et-Vilaine)
19, rue de la Malouine
Tel. (0)2.99.46.54.31 - Fax (0)2.99.88.15.88 - Marc Benoist
E-mail: reine.hortense@wanadoo.fr

**Category** ★★★ **Rooms** 8 and 1 suite, with telephone, bath or shower, WC, TV. **Price** Double 980-1200F / 149,40-182,94€, suite 1800-2200F / 274,41-335,39€. **Meals** Breakfast 70F / 10,67€, served 7:30-10:30. No restaurant. **Credit cards** Amex, Visa. **Pets** Dogs allowed (+60F / 9,15€). **Facilities** Parking. **Nearby** Décollé and Garde-Guérin points; Cézembre and Chausey islands – 18-hole golf course in Dinard. **Closed** Nov 15 – Mar 25 (except Christmas holidays).

All the pomp and circumstance of the Belle Epoque lives again in this mansion built by Prince Vlasov in praise of the woman he loved, Hortense de Beauharnais, the queen of the Netherlands. The lounge, decorated in the style of Napoleon III, and above all the queen's room still contain many souvenirs of the celebrated woman (including her silver bathtub, which is still in use). Antique furniture, precious decorative objects, paintings and *trompe-l'oeil* decorations are everywhere, bringing with them their rich and romantic touch. The lounge's veranda opens out to a terrace that extends down to the sea. Excellent breakfasts served here, and after that last drop of coffee, everyone can walk down to the beach, accessible directly from the hotel. Nine out of the ten rooms look out on this vibrant and irresistible vista. Totally but tactfully renovated, each rivals the other in comfort and seductive charm. Three of the rooms have a private patio-veranda, and the one-of-kind "suite" is composed of two huge rooms which open out to a lounge bathed in sunlight streaming from its six windows! The owner's hospitality adds a youthful and friendly touch to this place, among one of the most cozy and beautiful on the western coast.

*How to get there* (*Map 6*): *In Dinard, next to the Ecluse beach.*

## Hôtel Printania

35801 Dinard (Ille-et-Vilaine)
5, avenue George-V
Tel. (0)2.99.46.13.07 - Fax (0)2.99.46.26.32 - Mme Caro

**Category** ★★ **Rooms** 56 (11 with telephone), bath or shower, WC, TV. **Price** Double 320-450F / 48,78-68,60€. **Meals** Breakfast 40F / 6,10€, served 7:00-10:30; half board 290-360F / 44,21-54,88€ (per pers.). **Restaurant** Service 12:00PM-2:00PM, 7:00PM-9:30PM; mealtime specials 95-135F / 14,48-20,58€; also à la carte. Specialties: Fish, shellfish. **Credit cards** Amex, Visa. **Pets** Dogs allowed. **Nearby** Garde-Guérin point; Château of Saint-Malo; Cézembre and Chausey islands – 18-hole Dinard golf course. **Open** Mar 15 – Nov 20.

Below the peak of Moulinet, the *Hôtel Printania* overlooks a small port and the embarcadero to Saint Malo. A simple, family atmosphere prevails here. We were immediately charmed by the rooms with Breton buffets, the region's typical enclosed beds, their fronts woodworked and copper-studded; old landscape paintings, Louis Philippe armchairs, chandeliers, and objects. A lovely Breton ensemble. The comfortable bedrooms--some delightfully old-fashioned, other more youthful--are all pleasant, especially those overlooking the sea. Others are somewhat small and the view of the street is less attractive. Room 102, with its traditional enclosed bed, is very pleasant, but the recently redone 214 is more classic and deserves mention. The annex rooms were less to our liking. Their furniture is much more modest, even if they all have an ocean view. Breakfasts are served on a veranda that is a little hot in summer. Dinners (order from the menu, avoid the half board) are served in the dining room, Breton, which extends out into a veranda that is very nice in the evenings. Attentive hospitality, but, all the same, we must tell you that the hotel welcomes tourist buses from time to time.

***How to get there*** *(Map 6): 11km southeast of Saint-Malo.*

## Château de la Motte Beaumanoir

35720 Pleugueneuc (Ille-et-Vilaine)
Tel. (0)2.99.69.46.01 - Fax (0)2.99.69.42.49
M. Bernard

**Category** ★★★ **Rooms** 6 and 2 suites, with telephone, bath and WC (TV by request). **Price** Double 800F / 121,96€, suite 900F / 137,20€; apart. (3-4 pers.) 950-1100F / 144,83-167,69€. **Meals** Breakfast 50F / 7,62€, served 8:00-11:00. No restaurant. **Credit card** Visa. **Pets** Dogs allowed. **Facilities** Heated swimming pool, tennis, boating, fishing. **Facilities** Parking. **Nearby** Dinan; Léhon; Cancale; Combourg; Dinard; Saint-Malo; Mont-Saint-Michel – 18-hole golf course and Tronchet golf course. **Open** All year.

Erected in 1410, and then enlarged in the 18th century, the *Château de la Motte Beaumanoir* is one of the very beautiful mansions of Britanny. Bordered by ornamental ponds, surrounded by a park and a wooded estate, this château is majestic, and gets much more inviting and intimate once you enter true peace and calm here. You will enjoy the particularly pleasant rooms, which are spacious, bright, and decorated with taste and the highest level of comfort in mind. The lounge and dining room, where one takes breakfast, are decorated in the same style but are much warmer. You can splash around, in the swimming pool, whose waters seem to flow down into the pond located in front of the castle. Even if the hotel doesn't have its own restaurant, it would be a pity to let that stop you from staying here, because it is such a refined, restful, and charming place. That said, don't forget to see the sights nearby (Saint-Malo, Dinard, Mont-Saint-Michel). Warm hospitality from the *Château*'s young owners.

***How to get there*** *(Map 6): 12km southeast of Dinan via N137; then north of Pleugeuneuc turn right at first crossroads from Dinan, towards Plesder.*

## Manoir de la Rance

Château de Jouvente
35730 Pleurtuit (Ille-et-Vilaine)
Tel. (0)2.99.88.53.76 - Fax (0)2.99.88.63.03
Mme Jasselin

**Category** ★★★ **Rooms** 10 with telephone, bath, WC and TV. **Price** Double 450-800F / 68,60-121,96€; suite 800-1200F / 121,96-182,94€ (– 20 % in Oct to Apr). **Meals** Breakfast 50F / 7,62€, served 7:00-11:00. No restaurant. **Credit card** Visa. **Pets** Dogs allowed +40F / 6,10€. **Facilities** Parking. **Nearby** Rance docks; Dinard; Château and Ville Close in Saint-Malo; Chausey and Cézembre islands; Emeraude coast from Dinard to Val André – 18-hole Saint-Briac-sur-Mer in Dinard, 27-hole golf course in Saint-Malo. **Closed** Jan and Feb.

Facing the Rance and surrounded by trees and flowers, this 19th-century manor occupies in large and lovely grounds. The big lounge is pleasantly furnished in a mixture of styles. The bar and the small living room, where tea is served, have a very homey atmosphere. Refreshments are served outside in the charming gardens and terraces, which have reclining chairs. Located on three floors, all the bedrooms are very comfortable and quiet, and all (but for two) have a stunning view of the Rance and the cliffs. The same goes for the verandah, where the delicious breakfasts are served. Mme Jasselin, the owner, is very friendly. In Dinard, you have the choice between many restaurants, such as *La Salle a Manger* for gourmet dining or *Le Prieuré*. Saint-Malo also offers many possibilities, including, notably, the excellent *Clos des Chanoines* (in La Mettrie-aux-Chanoines).

***How to get there*** *(Map 6): 15km southeast of Saint-Malo via D168, then left after the Rance Dam on D114 to La Jouvente (via La Richardais). The manor is to the left on the way out of the village.*

# L'Ascott Hôtel

35400 Saint-Malo (Ille-et-Vilaine)
Saint-Servan - 35, rue du Chapitre
Tel. (0)2.99.81.89.93 - Fax (0)2.99.81.77.40
M. and Mme Hardouin

**Category** ★★★ **Rooms** 10 with telephone, bath, WC and TV. **Price** Double 400-600F / 60,98-91,47€. **Meals** Breakfast 50F / 7,62€. No restaurant. **Credit cards** Visa, Eurocard and MasterCard. **Pets** Dogs allowed. **Facilities** Parking. **Nearby** Rampart, Château and Ville Close in Saint-Malo; Chausey and Cézembre islands; Jersey and England; Saint-Samson-Dol-de-Bretagne Cathedral. **Open** All year.

Hidden behind this 19th-century mansion is a budding garden that invites you to relax. Away from the center of Saint-Malo, this little hotel possesses an indisputable charm. The hospitality and atmosphere are very refined. No detail has been overlooked. The bedrooms, which are often small though verily prettily decorated, are each named after a racetrack. A restrained feeling reigns throughout. Beautifully colored wall hangings go well with the pretty, coordinated fabrics chosen for the bedcovers and curtains. Some rooms have a small balcony where you can have breakfast. On the ground floor, there is the lounge, as appealing as the rest of the house, and which opens onto the small, lush garden where drinks are served. Near the hotel, you will find *Le Saint Placide*, one of the best restaurants in this part of Saint-Malo; note also the *Métairie de Beauregard*, *La Corderie* and *La Duchesse Anne* in the town. But are favorite still remains *Le Clos des Chanoines*, which is located on the road to Cancale, in La Mettrie-aux-Chanoines.

***How to get there*** *(Map 6): Via N137, take the towards Saint-Servan, then Boulevard Douville and the second street to the left (signposted).*

## Hôtel Brocéliande

35400 Saint-Malo (Ille-et-Vilaine)
43, chaussée du Sillon
Tel. (0)2.99.20.62.62 - Fax (0)2.99.40.42.47
M. and Mme Chombart

**Category** ★★★ **Rooms** 6 and 3 suites, with telephone, bath, WC, TV and minibar. **Price** Double 300-560F / 45,73-85,37€; 4 pers. 500-750F / 76,22-114,34€. **Meals** Breakfast 50F / 7,62€, served until 10:30. **No restaurant** board possible (except during national holidays). **Credit cards** All major. **Pets** Dogs not allowed. **Facilities** Parking and garage. **Nearby** Rampart, Château and Ville Close in Saint-Malo; Chausey and Cézembre islands; Jersey and England; Saint-Samson-Dol-de-Bretagne Cathedral. **Closed** End Nov – Dec 23.

This little Saint-Malo hotel is on the *Chaussée du Sillon*, along the beach. Designed as a private home, it offers attractive bedrooms decorated with Laura Ashley wallpaper and fabrics, and pleasant baths. Small (except for the family suites) but bright and cheerful, most are spacious with a view directly over the ocean; two rooms are on the courtyard. Upstairs on the *premier étage*, the rooms have balconies (the central room a huge terrace) offering a magnificent view of the ocean. The upper rooms are a bit cramped, and we don't recommend them for your stays. The overall effect is very pleasant, but that which makes a beach-side hotel so appealing could also be seen as a bother by those who like desert islands. Very hospitable, Anne-Marie and André-Guy serve good, varied breakfasts, and it's not unusual for guests to be so taken with the friendly atmosphere that they have breakfast at the kitchen table. There is a lovely living/dining room with a huge bow window against which the waves sometimes crash during an equinox. For restaurants, we recommend: *Les Embruns*, *Le Chasse Marée* and *Le Borgne Fesse*.

***How to get there*** *(Map 6): On the Chaussée du Sillon*

# La Korrigane

35400 Saint-Malo (Ille-et-Vilaine)
Saint-Servan - 39, rue Le Pomellec
Tel. (0)2.99.81.65.85 - Fax (0)2.99.82.23.89
Mme Dolbeau

**Category** ★★★ **Rooms** 10 with telephone, bath or shower, WC and TV **Price** Single and double 450-950F / 68,60-144,83€. **Meals** Breakfast 65F / 9,91€, served 8:00-10:00. No restaurant. **Credit cards** All major. **Pets** Dogs allowed (+50F / 7,62€). **Facilities** Parking. **Nearby** Rampart, Château and Ville Close in Saint-Malo; Chausey and Cézembre islands; Jersey and England; Saint-Samson-Dol-de-Bretagne Cathedral. **Open** All year.

This very charming little hotel is nestled away in a totally white, late-19th-century house. The atmosphere is so comfortable that you feel quite at home, and the welcome is warm, discreet and courteous. Everything is restful, exquisitely tasteful and unpretentious. Each bedroom has its own color scheme, with perfectly harmonized colors and fabrics, and lovely furniture and paintings. Each room is accented by furnishings and paintings, and you'll feel great here, even if, prices considered, some of the rooms could do with a little freshening up. (It seems that this is in the works.) Behind the house is a small garden where you can have breakfast or enjoy the sunshine. The large, book-lined living room is an invitation to relax as are the tearoom and bar. *La Korrigane* is better than a hotel: it is your own special pied-à-terre in Saint-Malo. *Le Saint Placide*, *Le Chalut*, *La Corderie* and *La Duchesse Anne* are among some of the good restaurants in this part of Saint-Malo, but we beg of you to try the excellent *Clos des Chanoines*, located just a few minutes away, on the coastal road leading to Cancale.

***How to get there*** *( Map 6): In the center of town, on N137 take the Saint-Servan road.*

## Le Valmarin

35400 Saint-Malo (Ille-et-Vilaine)
7, rue Jean-XXIII
Tel. (0)2.99.81.94.76 - Fax (0)2.99.81.30.03
M. and Mme Pollitzer

**Rooms** 12 with telephone, bath TV and minibar. **Price** Double 550-750F / 83,85-114,34€. **Meals** Breakfast 60F / 9,15€, served 8:00-11:00. No restaurant. **Credit cards** Amex, Visa. **Pets** Dogs allowed (+50F / 7,62€). **Facilities** Private parking until 11:30 PM. **Nearby** Rampart, Château and Ville Close in Saint-Malo; Chausey and Cézembre islands; Jersey and England; Saint-Samson-Dol-de-Bretagne Cathedral. **Open** Winter hollidays – Nov 15 (except Christmas and New Year's Day).

Behind the granite façade of this typical, 18th-century, Saint-Malo manor house, you will find a park full of trees, where you can have your breakfast during nice weather. Well-located, near the Solidor tower and the little port of Saint-Servan (where you can take your dinner with the setting sun), this hotel is really nice place to stay. You will be charmed by the dimensions of the rooms, which have kept their original wainscotting. The entry hall, with its 4-meter-high ceiling, the marble floor, and the majestic wooden staircase set the tone. All the rooms are furnished with antique furniture and tastefully decorated; as is the case with the breakfast room with its blue panelling and the lounge bar that overlooks the park. The most beautiful rooms are on the first floor. With their very high ceilings, they are bright, comfortable, pretty, and well-tended. Some are in need of new wallpaper and new carpeting. The *deuxieme étage* rooms are under the sloping roof, but their size and decor make them very pleasant. (The family room is a true success.) Our favorites look out on the park. The ground-floor rooms, with their basement bathrooms, were less to our liking. Hospitality with a smile.

***How to get there*** *( Map 6): In the town center, in N 137 head, toward Saint-Servan.*

## Le Logis Parc Er Gréo

Le Gréo 56610 Arradon (Morbihan)
9, rue Mané-Guen
Tel. (0)2.97.44.73.03 - Fax (0)2.97.44.80.48
M. and Mme Bermond

**Category** ★★★ **Rooms** 12 with telephone, bath or shower, WC and TV – Wheelchair access. **Price** Double 300-550F / 45,73-83,85€. **Meals** Breakfast 55F / 8,38€, served 8:00-11:00. No restaurant. **Credit cards** All major. **Pets** Dogs allowed (+40F / 6,10€). **Facilities** Swimming pool. **Nearby** Morbihan, Gavrinis and Moines isalnds – 18-hole Carnac golf course in Baden. **Closed** Feb 9 – Mar 9.

Even though the *Logis Parc er Gréo* has been built recently, this small hotel is indeed one of "character and charm," beginning with the welcome you receive. The decoration combines shapes and colors beautifully, with antique furniture here and there, a boat model, or a painting done by an artist friend. Finally, there is the beautiful island setting itself. From the terrace as well as the bedrooms, you have a lovely view of the swimming pool, the fields and trees and, just behind them, one of the small inlets that so charmingly dot the Morbihan Gulf. The bedrooms, which look due south, are a model of taste and comfort. On the ground floor, the living room is also a dining room where excellent breakfasts and dinners are served. When it's sunny, meals are served on the pretty flowery terrace. There is a small winter garden with luxuriant bougainvillia where you can enjoy a view of the countryside whether it rains or shines. Children will particularly appreciate the swimming pool, which has been recently covered by a transparent awning, permitting a longer season of use. All very good and well, even if the glass structure detracts from the natural beauty of the garden a bit.

***How to get there*** *( Map 14): 10km southwest of Vannes via D101 to Le Moustoir, on left, then 6th turn on right.*

## Hôtel Village La Désirade

56360 Belle-Ile-en-Mer (Morbihan)
Tel. (0)2.97.31.70.70 - Fax (0)2.97.31.89.63
Mme Mulon

**Category** ★★★ **Rooms** 24 with telephone, bath, WC and satellite TV. **Price** Double 390-700F / 59,46-106,71€. **Meals** Breakfast (buffet) 70F / 10,67€, served 8:00-11:00; half board 450-600F / 68,60-91,47€ (per pers.). **Restaurant** Easter – Oct 1. **Credit cards** All major. **Pets** Dogs allowed (+40F / 6,10€). **Facilities** Heated swimming pool, parking. **Nearby** Vauban citadel; Donnant bridge; Port-Coton Needles – 18-hole Sauzon in Belle-Ile-en-Mer. **Closed** Nov 11 – Dec 24 and Jan 7 – Feb 15.

In a typical Belle-Ile hamlet, where Monet painted his *Les Aiguilles de Port-Coton*, the little white houses that make up this hotel are themselves brought together like a hamlet around the swimming pool. Built by Madame Mulon in the spirit of Belle-Ile residences, each of these houses counts four rooms, allowing families or groups of friends to stay there in privacy. The decoration is sober, but in good taste. The vibrantly colored chintz makes them feel comfortable all year long. To let everyone live at his or her pace, an appealing breakfast buffet is set up all morning long in a big, ground-floor room, graced with a fireplace tiled in faience. You'll find it all here, even homemade jams. A pleasing sense of relaxation reigns in this "anti-hotel", which respects the independence of each of its guests. In the evening, you will find yourself in the little restaurant, decorated in the same manner, or on the patio to eat dishes made from market-fresh produce or a seafood platter (must order in advance). A quiet place, right next to the seaside.

***How to get there*** *( Map 5): By car, take the Quiberon-Le Palais ferry; by air from Lorient by Finist-Air (20 min. flight); 7km southwest of Le Palais via D190 through Bangor, (the hotel is 2km from Bangor).*

## Petit Hôtel Les Pougnots

Rue du Chemin-Neuf - Le Sauzon
56360 Belle-Ile-en-Mer (Morbihan)
Tel. (0)2.97.31.61.03 - Mme Guillouët

**Rooms** 5 with telephone, shower and WC. **Price** Single and double 470-570F / 71,65-86,90€.
**Meals** Breakfast incl., served 8:30-12:00PM. No restaurant. **Credit cards** Not accepted. **Pets** Dogs not
allowed. **Nearby** Vauban fortifications, cave of l'Apothicairerie, Port Donnan, Port-Coton Needles –
18-hole Sauzon golf course in Belle-Ile-en-Mer. **Open** All year.

The little port of Sauzon, on Belle-Ile, is composed of little white or
colorfully painted houses. It is magical place, bursting with charm, all the
more so because it is protected from the onslaught of tourists that come from
Le Palais or most of the ferries. Located at the end of a little street that leads
right to the port, in a one-story, turn-of-the-century, house bordered by little
gardens and patios, *Les Pougnots* has a beautiful view of the port or of the
island's ocean inlet. With only five rooms, this mini-hotel is just like a comfy,
private home. Breakfasts are served family-style in the dining room/lounge, or
even on the outside patio. Those who like their peace and quiet can have their
breakfasts in their room. The rooms themselves are pleasant and comfortable,
nicelydecorated, modest and well-tended, just like a seaside home shared with
friends. Some open out directly onto the patio or the garden. A charming place,
livened up by the wonderful and interesting Madame Guillouet, who will give
you advice about what to see on Belle-Ile.

***How to get there*** *( Map 5): By car, take the Quiberon-Le Palais ferry; by air from
Lorient by Finist-Air (20 min. flight); 5km from Le Palais, at the port of Le
Sauzon.*

# Domaine de Rochevilaine

56190 Billiers-Muzillac (Morbihan)
Pointe de Pen Lan
Tel. (0)2.97.41.61.61 - Fax (0)2.97.41.44.85
M. Jaquet

**Category** ★★★★ **Rooms** 37 and 3 suites, with telephone, bath, WC and satellite TV – Wheelchair access. **Price** Double 590-1550F / 89,94-236,30€, suite 1700-2500F / 259,16-381,12€. **Meals** Breakfast 70F / 10,67€, served 7:15-10:30; half board 545-1050F / 83,08-160,07€ (per pers., 3 days min.). **Restaurant** Service 12:15PM-1:30PM, 7:15PM-9:30PM; mealtime specials 260-490F / 39,64-74,70€ (with lobster), also à la carte. Specialties: live lobster; fish and fishing. **Credit cards** All major. **Pets** Dogs allowed (+75F / 11,43€). **Facilities** Heated swimming pool, sea spa center and fitnes center and parking. **Nearby** Rochefort-en-Terre; Gulf of Morbihan – 18-hole Kerver golf course. **Open** All year.

The majestic site of the Pointe de Pen Lan, the former ocean lookout post, resembles a little village made up of 15th- and 17th-century buildings. From here, you can take advantage of the view over the Atlantic, whose rolling, sometimes turbulent waves crash against the rocks at the base of this hotel. An establishment in very high standing, the *Rochevilaine* offers spacious bedrooms that are classically elegant. All the rooms are charming; the most attractive are the ones with antique decoration; the suites sometimes have their own private patios. We highly recommend the rooms with an ocean view, and this all the more so because the other rooms are a bit small. For breakfast or dinner, the panoramic restaurant, well-know in Britanny, offers high-quality cuisine that is served professionally. (Try the lobster menu.) A good place for a holiday weekend get-away.

***How to get there*** *(Map 14): 20km southeast of Vannes via the express route (towards Nantes) to Muzillac; then to Billiers and Pointe de Pen Lan.*

## Les Chaumières de Kerniaven

56700 Hennebont (Morbihan)
Route de Port-Louis-en-Kervignac
Tel. (0)2.97.76.76.76 - Fax (0)2.97.76.82.35 - M. de La Sablière
Web: www.chateau-de-locguenole.fr

**Rooms** 11 with telephone, bath, WC, TV and minibar **Price** Single and double 460-690F / 70,13-105,19€. **Meals** Breakfast 76F / 11,58€, served 7:45-10:30. **Restaurant** *Château de Locguénolé*. **Credit cards** All major. **Pets** Dogs allowed (+50F / 7,62€). **Facilities** Heated swimming pool, sauna, hammam and tennis 4 km, parking. **Nearby** Hennebont; citadel and museum of Cie des Indes-Port-Louis – 18-hole Val Queven and Ploemeur golf course. **Open** Mar – Nov.

These two charming thatched-roof cottages are part of the *Château of Locguénolé*. They are located 3km away in the heart of the countryside but all enjoy the advantages of the hotel: a superb swimming pool, sauna, tennis courts, and innumerable private paths along the seafront. You can alternate your stay between the luxurious atmosphere of the château and the calm countryside of your cottage. In the main *chaumière,* the bedrooms are vast and decorated in a style which is both rustic and elegant, with several pieces of smartly waxed antique furniture and exposed-stone walls. On the *premier étage,* the bedrooms have a mezzanine which families will enjoy, while on the ground floor, beautiful log fires crackle in imposing fireplaces (except for one, which we like somewhat less). In the other *chaumière,* the bedrooms are somewhat smaller, decorated in the same spirit and are a little less expensive. You can ask for your breakfast there, unless you prefer having it outdoors. Lunches and dinners are served in the château dining room, which has elegant yellow or blue tablecloths and an 18th-century Aubusson tapestry on one wall. You will enjoy famous cuisine and the especially friendly hospitality refutes the notion that luxury is always stuffy.

***How to get there*** *( Map 5): 5km of Hennebont, via Port-Louis.*

# Le San Francisco

56780 Ile-aux-Moines (Morbihan)
Tel. (0)2.97.26.31.52 - Fax (0)2.97.26.35.59
M. Alexandre Vérien

**Rooms** 8 with telephone, bath or shower, WC and TV. **Price** Single and double 370-605F / 56,41-92,23€. **Meals** Breakfast 47F / 7,17€, served 8:00-11:00; half board 315-430F / 48,02-65,55€ (per pers.). **Restaurant** Service 12:00PM-2:00PM, 7:00PM-8:30PM; mealtime specials 110-240F / 16,77-36,59€, also à la carte. Specialties: Sole et lotte en brick sauce crustacés; noix de Saint-Jacques poêlées sur fondue d'endives. **Cartes de crédit** All major. **Pets** Dogs allowed (+40F / 6,10€). **Nearby** 18-hole Morbihan golf course in La Bretesche. **Open** Mar 26 – Nov.

The Franciscan sisters who used to come here to rest chose the most beautiful location on the island: facing the port, with the dramatic, jagged coast of the Gulf of Morbihan in the distance. The *San Francisco* is also next to the dock, a bit busy during the day, but rediscovers its peace and quiet in the evening. The number of rooms is reasonable, with a pleasant ambiance that is never uptight. All the rooms, are rather confortable and well-decorated in a rather classic way, just like the hotel itself. The nicest rooms look out over the coast. If you hurry, you can reserve the bedroom that has a superb view and a little balcony overlooking the dock. There is a pleasant reception area and a lovely dining room; but with the first rays of sunshine, the high points are the shady terraces to sit back and watch the boats cutting through the waters of the gulf. The *San Francisco* is a pleasant place with kind and courteous hospitality. Discover this little island, where you can easily paddle back to the coast.

*How to get there (Map 14): Via highway E60 (RN 165), exit Vannes-Ouest; then follow signs for Ile aux Moines to boat landing. 5 min. crossing; in winter, 7:00 to 8:00PM; in summer, 7:00 to 10:00PM.*

## Hôtel de la Jetée

56590 Ile-de-Groix (Morbihan)
1, quai Port-Tudy
Tel. (0)2.97.86.80.82 - Fax (0)2.97.86.56.11
Mme Tonnerre

**Category** ★★ **Rooms** 8 with telephone, bath or shower and WC. **Price** Double 290-380F / 44,21-57,93€. **Meals** Breakfast 40F / 6,10€, served 8:00-10:30. No restaurant (in season, light meals and oyster tasting). **Credit cards** Amex, Visa. **Pets** Dogs allowed. **Nearby** Museum in Groix, pointe de l'Enfer, Port Saint-Nicolas, Pen-Men. **Closed** Jan 5 – Feb 15.

A small hotel with one side on the port and the other beaten by the ocean spray, the *Hôtel de la Jetée* stands just at the beginning of the jetty, at the far side of the basin. The ground floor is divided between an attractive café with several pretty tables on the terrace (a meeting place for fishermen and sailors) and an Irish pub where you can enjoy oysters brought in by Monsieur and Madame Tonnerre's son, who has recently set up here as an oyster farmer. The bedrooms are small but really quite charming. They are decorated with handsome wallpaper trimmed with elegant friezes; smartly waxed antique furniture and English-style coordinated fabrics, just like the cheerful, well-kept baths with modern amenities. You'll enjoy a picture-postcard view over the port or the sea, and a small terrace installed on a rock in the back which is reserved for hotel guests; looking out over the immense blue horizon and small creeks of fine sand not far away, one has the delicious feeling of utter peace and solitude. Let it be known that during seasonally hot weather, the low-tide leaves behind lots of salt deposits in the port. If you are looking for air that is a little more refreshing, choose those rooms that look away from the harbor.

*How to get there (Map 5): Boat from Lorient (45 min.); tel. 02 97 21 03 97.*

## Hôtel de la Marine

56590 Ile-de-Groix (Morbihan)
7, rue du Général-de-Gaulle
Tel. (0)2.97.86.80.05 - Fax (0)2.97.86.56.37
Mme Hubert

**Category** ★★ **Rooms** 22 with telephone, bath or shower and WC **Price** Double 218-470F / 32,78-71,65€. **Meals** Breakfast 45F / 6,86€, served 8:00-10:00; half board and full board 249-372F / 38,01-56,79€, 334-466F / 50,99-71,14€ (per pers., 2 days min, reduction in low season). **Restaurant** Service 12:00PM-1:30PM, 7:30PM-9:30PM; mealtime specials 80-140F / 12,20-21,34€, also à la carte. Specialties: Feuilleté de Saint-Jacques; barbecue de poissons; marquise au chocolat. **Credit card** Visa. **Pets** Dogs allowed (+22F / 3,35€). **Facilities** Parking. **Nearby** Museum in Groix, pointe de l'Enfer, Saint-Nicolas Port, Pen-Men. **Closed** Jan.

The *Hôtel de la Marine* is located somewhat high up in the village, several hundred feet from the port. Lovingly decorated by Madame Hubert, a former stylist, it attracts a faithful, congenial clientele each summer. The hotel has just undergone beautiful renovation work, with a charming, boat-gangway decor in the communal rooms. The small lounge is delightfully furnished with antiques, and in the dining room, where you will enjoy good meals for very reasonable prices, the tables are set with attractive, colorful linens; on the fireplace and the shelves is a collection of pottery; in a corner, a shell-encrusted clock is the only reminder of the passage of time. The bedrooms are simple, painted white and brightened with colored curtains and bedspreads. Ask for those facing the sea (especially No 1), but all are very pleasant and comfortable. Outside on the garden terrace, you can enjoy a drink in the shade of the oldest tree on the island.

***How to get there*** *(Map 5): Boat from Lorient (45 min.), tel. 97.21.03.97.*

# Le Petit Hôtel des Hortensias

56470 La Trinité-sur-Mer (Morbihan)
Place de la Mairie
Tel. (0)2.97.30.10.30 - Fax (0)2.97.30.14.54
P. le Gloahec - N. Gautier

**Rooms** 5 with telephone, bath, WC and satellite TV – 1 for disabled persons. **Price** Double 500-850F / 76,22-129,58€. **Meals** Breakfast 58F / 8,85€, served 8:00-11:00. **Restaurant** *L'Arrosoir*, reservation recommended (telephone. 02.97.30.13.58). **Credit card** Visa. **Pets** Dogs allowed (+40F / 6,10€.). **Facilities** Parking. **Nearby** Gulfe of Morbihan, Baie of Quiberon (Belle-Ile, Houat, Hoedic) – 18-hole Saint-Laurent and Baden golf course. **Closed** Jan 8 – Jan 23 and Dec 1 – Dec 18.

We were quite familiar with the *L'Arrosoir Restaurant* in La Trinité-sur-Mer, , which two friendly young people have now converted into the charming *Petit Hôtel des Hortensias*. Both the restaurant and the hotel occupy an outstanding location on the port. Set somewhat back from the hustle and bustle of the quay, the hotel overlooks the entrance to the port. Regatta sailboats, old rigging, oyster-farm pontoons, fishing boats and ocean-racing trimarans provide a permanent spectacle, with yachts sailing in and out of the port in front of the hotel and the restaurant. The yachting crowd of La Trinité, the sailor's Mecca, love to meet there. In fact, it's not unusual to see crack skippers like Laurent Bourgnon, Loïc Peyron and Florence Arthaud at the *Hortensias*. Five chambers await those who have the foresight to reserve in advance. Small, bright, and comfortable, the rooms are decorated in a well-done marine style, which heartily plays blues off of whites. A very pretty and comfortable place to stay.

*How to get there* ( *Map 5*): *30km southwest of Vannes.*

## Hôtel des Trois Fontaines

56740 Locmariaquer (Morbihan)
Tel. (0)2.97.57.42.70 - Fax (0)2.97.57.30.59
M. Jean-Pierre Orain
E-mail: hot3f@aol.com

**Rooms** 18 with telephone, bath or shower, WC and cable TV, 17 with minibar and safe – For disabled persons. **Price** Double 320-600F / 48,78-91,47€. **Meals** Breakfast 55F / 8,38€, served 8:00-11.00. No restaurant. **Credit card** Visa. **Facilities** Parking. **Nearby** Gulf of Morbihan; megalithe site; sailing school, tennis – 18-hole golf course (reduction for residents). **Open** Mar 25 – Nov 14 and Dec 21 – Jan 4.

Locqmariaquer rests on a peninsula at the far reaches of the Morbihan Gulf. This place is superb, on top of its huge beaches, rugged inlets, and coves to weigh anchor, it also has many megalithic relics. When you get to the hotel, don't worry about the proximity of the road (which only serves the village) and forgive these slightly-too-new walls, because the hospitality and interior ambiance will chase those cares away. You will most certainly like the cheerful and restrainedly modern decoration of the little lounge, arranged in a half circle around the fireplace. The same goes for the rooms, with their terra cotta or parquetry flooring, their simple mahagonny furnishings, and their counterpane bedcovers that match the curtains that stand out against the white walls. The most beautiful room has a bow window, perfect for watching the tide come in. Also, just in general, ask for the first-floor rooms which have some beautiful vantage points from which to see the little natural harbor. As soon as the weather gets nice, the patio's teak tables are set up for breakfast, and it's a real pleasure to sip your coffee while taking in the sea air, with the cry of gulls in the distance.

***How to get there*** *(Map 5): Via N 165 (Nantes-Brest), at Auray take Locmariaquer and La Trinité-sur-Mer exit, then D 28 and D 781.*

## Château du Launay

Locuon 56160 Ploerdut (Morbihan)
Tel. (0)2.97.39.46.32 - Fax (0)2.97.39.46.31
Famille Redolfi-Strizzot

**Rooms** 10 with telephone, bath. **Price** Double 600-700F / 91,47-106,71€. **Meals** Breakfast (buffet) 35F / 5,34€, served 8:30-10:30; half board 500F / 76,22€ (per pers.). **Restaurant** Service 8:00PM; mealtime specials 135F / 20,58€. Specialties: Italian and Asian food. **Credit card** Visa. **Pets** Dogs allowed. **Facilities** Swimming pool, parking. **Nearby** Sainte-Noyale; Blavet valley. **Closed** Jan and Feb.

Set right in the middle of the countryside, in a huge park surrounded by forests and meadows, bordered by a lake, this ravishing little 18th-century castle will delight lovers of peace and quiet. Its owners, a young Nepalese and Danish couple, will welcome you here with simplicity and kindness, a bit like the hospitality you would expect from a private home. The comparison doesn't stop there, because in the evenings you will all gather around the guest table to share a meal that is both simple and refined. Lovers might choose to dine alone in the separate little dining room. Livened up by its fireplace, the large, panelled library is inviting, comfortable, and includes many art books. Other lounges, decorated with a light, exotic touch, gives everyone the opportunity to be alone. The entrance hall, with its very scaled-down look, only accents the collection of Far-East sculptures and art objects of the owner's father. The bedrooms are spacious, soberly though elegantly decorated in a thoughtfully minimalist style. They boast creme painting and varnishes, complimented with more colorful partitions, exotic or wrought furniture, huge and comfortable beds, and luxurious bathrooms. A beautiful place, where you can choose to be apart or with others. Telephone ahead before your arrival.

*How to get there (Map 6): 30km from Pontivy.*

# Hostellerie Les Ajoncs d'Or

Kerbachique
56340 Plouharnel (Morbihan)
Tel. (0)2.97.52.32.02 - Fax (0)2.97.52.40.36
Mme Le Maguer

**Category** ★★ **Rooms** 17 with telephone, bath or shower, WC, satellite TV. **Price** Double 350-460F / 53,36-70,13€, suite (4 pers.) 680F / 103,67€. **Meals** Breakfast 41F / 6,25€, served 8:00-10:00; half board 330-390F / 50,31-59,46€ (per pers.). **Restaurant** Service 7:00PM-9:30PM; mealtime specials 110-160F / 16,77-24,39€. Specialties: Seafood and traditional food. **Credit card** Visa. **Pets** Small dogs allowed (+20F / 3,05€). **Facilities** Parking. **Nearby** Carnac (2935 menhirs); Erdeven menhirs; Church of Plouhinec; Belle-Ile – Saint-Laurent golf course in Ploërmel. **Open** Mar 15 – Nov 2.

Hostellerie Les Ajoncs d'Or is a pink granite Breton farmhouse made up of three adjoining buildings and situated outside the village. On the ground floor, a large restaurant with a lovely fireplace happily combines beams, exposed stonework, flowered curtains and pictures. It opens out into another room where breakfast is served (during nice weather, breakfast served outside). Recently renovated, the bedrooms are often brightened with lovely fabrics and beautiful carpets (some could almost be called suites, with their small corner lounge.) All different, the rooms are comfortable and bright. A special mention goes to those rooms and suites above the restaurant and on the ground floor in the adjacent building. You will enjoy good, family-style cooking and a most cheerful welcome from Madame Le Maguer and her daughter, whose family has owned this establishment for two centuries. Their kindness and special personalities just adds more charm to this already charming address.

***How to get there*** *( Map 5): 52km of Lorient via N165 to Auray, then D768 and D781 (between Carnac and Plouharnel).*

# Hôtel de Kerlon

56680 Plouhinec (Morbihan)
Tel. (0)2.97.36.77.03 - Fax (0)2.97.85.81.14
M. and Mme Coëffic
E-mail: kerlon@minitel.net - Web: www.auberge-de-kerlon.com

**Category** ★★ **Rooms** 16 with telephone, 15 with bath or shower, WC and TV. **Price** Double 240-320F / 36,59-48,78€. **Meals** Breakfast 40F / 6,10€, served 8:00-10:00; half board 285-310F / 43,45-47,26€ (per pers.). **Restaurant** Service 7:30PM-9:00PM; mealtime specials 82-160F / 12,51-24,39€, also à la carte. Specialties: Fish, shellfish. **Credit card** Visa. **Pets** Dogs not allowed. **Facilities** Parking. **Nearby** Quiberon; Gulf of Morbihan; Groix Island; Port-Louis – 18-hole Queven golf course and Plœmeur Océan golf course in Saint-Jude. **Open** Mar 15 – Nov 15.

Standing in the heart of the countryside five kilometers from the sea, this inviting little hotel cannot be separated from its owners. The constantly smiling Madame Coeffic takes care of your every need while her husband keeps busy in the kitchen. The rooms are very scantily furnished, though very well-kept-up. Some have new bed throws and curtains that make them slightly more cheerful. The little bathrooms are spotless, and the bedding is excellent. The comfortable lounge-bar and especially the bright dining room are more attractive, the dining tables set with beautiful white linens and bouquets of fresh flowers. The cuisine is good and nutritious, based on fresh local products, with Breton fish and shellfish taking the gastronomic place of honor. You can enjoy a drink while you relax on the terrace facing the garden. Breakfasts are also excellent, changing each day of the week.

***How to get there*** *(Map 5): 30km southeast of Lorient. Leave N165 at Hennebont, "Carnac-Quiberon-Port-Louis" exit, then follow signs Carnac-Quiberon. D194, then D9.*

## Domaine de Bodeuc

56130 La Roche-Bernard (Morbihan)
Tel. (0)2.99.90.89.63 - Fax (0)2.99.90.90.32
M. and Mme Grandpierre

**Category** ★★★ **Rooms** 8 with telephone, bath or shower, WC and TV – Elevator; 1 for disabled persons. **Price** Double 540-590F / 82,32-89,94€. **Meals** Breakfast 50F / 7,62€, served 8:00-12:30PM. **Restaurant** Only for residents, reserve the day before. Closed Jun 15 – Sep 15; mealtime specials 170F / 25,92€. **Credit cards** Amex, Visa. **Pets** Dogs allowed. **Facilities** Heated swimming pool, parking. **Nearby** La Baule; La Brière trails and Guérande marshes; Gulf of Morbihan – 18-hole La Bretesche, Kerver, Saint-Laurent golf course. **Open** All year, by reservation in Nov – Mar.

Nestling in the Breton countryside only twenty minutes from the beaches, this charming hotel stands in a handsome 37-acre park. From the entrance, one feels that this is more like a house than a traditional hotel. Monsieur Grandpierre welcomes you on the doorstep as if you were an old friend of the family, his wife joining him in the friendly greeting. She has arranged the eight bedrooms of the hotel with great taste, adding a lovely touch to the comfortable amenities, the harmonious color schemes, the quality of the fabrics and the choice of antique furniture (a thoughtful finishing touch is the basket of fruit awaiting you in your room.) The bathrooms are equally attractive, bright and well-kept. On the ground floor, a comfortable lounge, classic and cheerful, is the venue for the apéritif or coffee hour. On reservation, Monsieur Grandpierre prepares dinners consisting of simple but savory dishes; he is also responsible for the homemade preserves served with the good breakfast.

***How to get there*** *( Map 14): 40km south of Vannes. A 4 way N 165, exit near La Roche-Bernard (exit Number 16), dir. Redon. Saint-Dolas, by D 34, during 5km then follow the signs.*

## Auberge du Moulin de Chaméron

18210 Bannegon (Cher)
Tel. (0)2.48.61.83.80 - Fax (0)2.48.61.84.92
M. Rommel
E-mail: moulindechameron@wanadoo.fr

**Category** ★★★ **Rooms** 13 with telephone, bath or shower, WC and TV. **Price** Double 350-515F / 53,36-78,51€, suite 680-765F / 103,67-116,62€. **Meals** Breakfast 51 and 85F / 7,62 and 12,96€, served 7:30-10:00. **Restaurant** Service 12:15PM-2:00PM, 7:30PM-9:00PM; mealtime specials 130-195F / 19,82-29,73€, (children 58F / 8,85€), also à la carte. **Specialties:** Seasonal cooking. **Credit cards** Amex, Visa. **Pets** Dogs allowed (30F / 4,57€). **Facilities** Swimming pool, parking. **Nearby** Basilica and Château of Châteauneuf-sur-Cher, Church of Saint-Amand-Montrond, Abbey of Noirlac, Châteaux of Meillant and Ainay-le-Vieil, Bourges – 18-hole Val-de-Cher golf course in Montluçon. **Closed** Nov 16 – end Feb and Tuesday in low season.

Deep in the countryside, this hotel is made up of two buildings joined by a pretty garden. In the heart of the whole, there is the former, 18th-century mill with its machinery left intact, as well as a museum which brings together all the tools of the millers who once worked here. This is where you will find the restaurant, run by Madame and Monsieur Merilleau (who does the cooking), and where you will eat excellent food served in a ravishing and intimate little chamber with a fireplace. In summer, tables are also set up outside, next to a pond. What a pleasure to take your meals in such a pretty setting. The other building houses the rooms. Furnished without any surprises, these rooms are more or less large and some have their own patio, where you can have breakfast. Recently redone, all of the rooms now have comfortable bathrooms. A hospitable place that bathes in charm during nice weather.

***How to get there*** *(Map 17): 42km southeast of Bourges via N76 towards Moulins, then D953 and D41.*

# La Solognote

18410 Brinon-sur-Sauldre (Cher)
Tel. (0)2.48.58.50.29 - Fax (0)2.48.58.56.00
M. and Mme Girard

**Category ★★ Rooms** 13 with telephone, bath or shower, WC and TV. **Price** 350-480F / 53,36-73,18€; apart. (3-4 pers.) 600F / 91,47€. **Meals** Breakfast 60F / 9,15€; half board 900-1050F / 137,20-160,07€ (per 2 pers., 3 days min.). **Restaurant** Closed Tuesday lunchtime, Wednesday lunchtime except in Jul and Aug. Service 12:30PM-2:00PM, 7:30PM-8:30PM; mealtime specials 170-350F / 25,92-53,36€, also à la carte. **Credit card** Visa. **Pets** Dogs not allowed. **Facilities** Parking. **Nearby** Orléans Cathedral, La Source flower gardens in Olivet, Châteaux on the Jacques-Coeur road, Aubigny-sur-Nère, the Berry from La Chapelle d'Angillon to Saint-Martin-d'Auxigny, Sancerre – 18-hole Sully golf course in Viglains. **Closed** Mid Feb – mid Mar, May 12 – 25, Sep 13 – 21, Tuesday and Wednesday in winter.

This pink brick inn, located in a small village in Sologne just fifteen minutes from the National Route 20, is famous for its excellent cuisine, it also has particularly well-done rooms, decorated in a refined, country style. Each room is decorated in a different style, with one or two antique pieces, beautiful fabrics, and polished wooden floors. They are comfortable and very quiet, their bathrooms are well-equipped, and many look out on a small flower garden. There are apartments available for families. The beautiful, ground-floor restaurant, with its old furniture and exposed-beam ceiling is a friendly and warm setting in which to dine. (Don't forget this address during fall and winter, when you can enjoy an interesting selection of wild game.) Last but not least, a special mention should be made of Monsieur and Madame Girard's courteous management and commitment to quality.

*How to get there (Map 17): 60km southeast of Orléans via N20 to Lamotte-Beuvron, then D923 towards Aubigny-sur-Nère.*

# Le Piet à Terre

18370 Châteaumeillant (Cher)
21, rue du Château
Tel. (0)2.48.61.41.74 - Fax (0)2.48.61.41.88
M. Finet and Mme Piet

**Category** ★★ **Rooms** 7 with telephone, bath or shower, WC and TV. **Price** Double 260-350F / 39,64-53,36€. **Meals** Breakfast 40F / 6,10€, served 8:00-9:30; half board 460-580F / 70,13-88,42€ (per pers., 2-3 days min.). **Restaurant** Closed Sunday evening and Monday in low season. Service 12:00PM-13:30PM, 7:30PM-9:00PM; mealtime specials 98F (weekdays) -340F / 14,96-51,83€, also à la carte. Specialties: Foie gras de canard et jus de truffes; pigeon de ferme au foin; moelleux de chocolat mi-ame. **Credit card** Visa. **Pets** Dogs not allowed. **Nearby** Nohant-Vic (Festival of Nohant in June), La Châtre (Museum of George Sand), Abbey of Fontgombault – Dryades golf course in Pouligny-Notre-Dame. **Closed** Feb, Sunday evening and Monday.

How we'd love to find more small village hotels like this one! Located in a quiet spot on a square, the *Piet-à-Terre* looks as prim as it is hospitable. With the talent of a skillful seamstress and great taste, Sylvie Piet has "dressed" each bedroom, skillfully concealing the small size of some. The comfortable beds of certain rooms have beautiful embroidered sheets, the bathrooms are impeccable, and all the rooms (except for two with small roof windows) enjoy a lovely view over the village. Served in two beautiful small dining rooms, the cuisine is the other strong point of the *Piet-à-Terre*. The specialties as well as the set-price meals, made with only the freshest products, are simply prepared so as to enhance the native tastes of ingredients, and yet the chef's original touches make for delicious gastronomic discoveries. The hotel has a promising future in this little-known but highly attractive region.

***How to get there*** ( *Map 17*): *50km southeast of Châteauroux.*

## Château de la Beuvrière

18100 Saint-Hilaire-de-Court (Cher)
Tel. (0)2.48.75.14.63 - Fax (0)2.48.75.47.62
M. and Mme de Brach

**Category** ★★ **Rooms** 15 with telephone, bath or shower and WC (4 with minibar). **Price** Double 350-500F / 53,36-76,22€; suite 700F / 106,71€. **Meals** Breakfast 50F / 7,62€, served 7:30-9:30. **Restaurant** Closed Sunday evening and Monday. Service 12:00PM-2:00PM, 7:30PM-9:00PM; mealtime specials 150-198F / 22,87-30,22€, gastronomic menu 250F / 38,11€, also à la carte. Specialties: Saumon fumé et foie gras frais maison; sandre braisé au beurre de truffes; ris de veau braisés à l'orange. **Credit cards** All major. **Pets** Dogs allowed. **Facilities** Swimming pool, tennis, parking. **Nearby** Saint-Etienne Cathedral, Hôtel Jacques-Coeur in Bourges, Aubigny-sur-Nère – 18-hole La Picardière golf course. **Closed** Dec 15 – Mar 15, Sunday evening.

The château has kept its 2,562-acre estate intact since the Middle Ages. Inherited by the present owners, it is a very charming hotel today. The family furniture is authentic and dates from the 15th to the 19th century – the overall effect is one of excellent quality arranged with perfect taste. Lovely and very well-kept, the bedrooms overlook the grounds. Those on the *premier étage* are almost sumptuous, and if their bathrooms are a bit on the small side this allows room for the wood-panelled bed alcoves. The *deuxième étage* bedrooms have original beams and some have a mezzanine. You will dine sitting on Empire armchairs at a beautifully laid table. The food is as excellent as the decor, and the welcome is informal and cordial.

***How to get there*** *( Map 17): 39km northwest of Bourges via A71, Vierzon-centre exit, then N20 towards Châteauroux exit Nr 7.*

## Le Grand Monarque

28005 Chartres (Eure-et-Loir)
22, place des Epars
Tel. (0)2.37.21.00.72 - Fax (0)2.37.36.34.18
M. Jallerat

**Category** ★★★ **Rooms** 49 and 5 apartments (2 with air-conditioning) with telephone, bath, WC, satellite TV and minibar – Elevator. **Price** Double 600-720F / 91,47-109,76€, apart. 995-1330F / 151,69-202,76€. **Meals** Breakfast (buffet) 60F / 9,15€, served 7:00-10:30. **Restaurant** Service 12:00PM-14:15PM, 7:30PM-10:00PM; mealtime specials 163-295F / 24,88-44,97€ – Light meals served at the bar *Le Madrigal*. **Credit cards** All major. **Pets** Dogs allowed. **Facilities** Parking and garage (50F / 7,62€). **Nearby** In Chartres: Notre-Dame Cathedral, Church of Saint-Pierre, Maison Picassiette, Illiers, Combray (Proust Museum) – 18-hole Maintenon golf course. **Open** All year.

This is the ideal spot for visiting famous Chartres Cathedral and the historic center of the town: Efficiently and professionally staffed, the *Grand Monarque* is a large hotel in a handsome building just at the beginning of Chartres' picturesque, small pedestrian streets. The sizeable lobby is discreetly quiet and decorated in classic good taste. The imposing dining room, where you will enjoy one of the best cuisines of the region, is lent distinction by well-spaced tables, comfortable armchairs, and a beautiful group of 18th- and 19th-century paintings. The large suites, very pleasant for families, as well as the rooms have comfortable amenities; the tasteful decoration--all the rooms are different--includes lovely fabrics, distinctive furniture, and interesting engravings. The rooms are bright and quiet, including the soundproofed rooms overlooking the square. The others are on an interior courtyard.

***How to get there*** *(Map 8): 90km from Paris via A 10 or A11, exit Chartres-Centre.*

## Hostellerie Saint-Jacques

28220 Cloyes-sur-le-Loir (Eure-et-Loir)
35, rue Nationale
Tel. (0)2.37.98.40.08 - Fax (0)2.37.98.32.63
M. and Mme Thureau

**Category** ★★★ **Rooms** 22 with telephone, bath or shower, WC and TV. **Price** Double 360-680F / 54,88-103,67€. **Meals** Breakfast 55F / 8,38€, served 8:00-10:30; half board and full board 490 and 630F / 74,70 and 96,04€ (per pers., in double room). **Restaurant** Service 12:00PM-2:00PM, 7:30PM-9:00PM; mealtime specials 130-175F / 19,82-26,68€. Specialties: Escalope de saumon au vin rouge. **Credit card** Visa. **Pets** Dogs allowed. **Facilities** Boats, table tennis, mountain bikes, parking. **Nearby** Chapel of Yrou at Châteaudun, Vendôme, valley of the Loir (Montoire-sur-le-Loir, Lavardin, Troo, Manoir of Poissonnière) – 9-hole la Bosse golf course in Oucques. **Open** Mid Mar – Nov.

On the village square, the *Hostellerie Saint-Jacques* is a former 16th-century post office. You can go on a boat ride from the shady park that borders the Loir river. Twenty-some comfortable and agreeable rooms are in this peaceful setting. Soberly decorated in cotton prints with stylish furnishings, these rooms are very well soundproofed and non look out on the road. Choose a room in the main building, easy to acces thanks to an elevator. The three, ground-floor rooms in the annex are much more impersonal and their doors are right in front of parking lot. Depending on the season and number of reservations, you can choose between the very beautiful, large dining room, which is refined and a bit majestic and opens out to the terrace where tables are set up during nice weather; and the very charming and more intimate *Petit Bistrot*. The menu there remains unchanged, and the fine food makes the *Hostellerie* a reputed, gourmet address. Very kind hospitality with a smile.

***How to get there*** *(Map 16): 53km north of Blois via D957 to Vendôme, then N10 (going north) to Cloyes-sur-le-Loir.*

## Manoir de Boisvillers

36200 Argenton-sur-Creuse (Indre)
11, rue du Moulin-de-Bord
Tel. (0)2.54.24.13.88 - Fax (0)2.54.24.27.83
M. and Mme Nowakowski
E-Mail: manoir.de.boisvilliers@wanadoo.fr

**Category** ★★ **Rooms** 14 with telephone, bath or shower, 13 with WC and TV. **Price** Double 240-395F / 36,59-60,22€. **Meals** Breakfast 45F / 6,86€, served 7:30-10:00. No restaurant. **Credit cards** Amex, Visa. **Pets** Dogs allowed (+30F / 4,57€). **Facilities** Swimming pool, parking. **Nearby** Pont-Vieux and Saint-Benoît Chapel in Argenton, Château de Nohant-Vic, Georges Sand Museum in La Châtre, Abbey Church of Fontgombault – 18-hole Dryades and Pouligny-Notre-Dame golf courses. **Closed** Dec.

This welcoming hotel in the center of town enjoys an excellent location with its large garden and the immediate proximity of the Creuse River. Taken over by Isabelle and Christophe Nowakowski, it has been rejuvenated with pleasant bedrooms, which are simply decorated in cheerful colors and shared between the hotel and an outbuilding. All the rooms are different, with some overlooking the river; others the garden or the courtyard. Room 5 is very beautiful with its wood panelling and vast proportions. On the ground floor, there is a small modern lounge and breakfast room. There is no restaurant in the hotel, but in July and August, weather permitting, you can serve yourself from the cold buffet, set up in the garden in your honor. If not, we recommend *Le Moulin des Eaux Vives* in Tendu. Youthful and pleasant hospitality.

***How to get there*** *(Map 16): 30km southwest of Châteauroux, Argenton-sur-Creuse exit.*

## Domaine de l'Etape

36300 Le Blanc (Indre)
Route de Bélâbre
Tel. (0)2.54.37.18.02 - Fax (0)2.54.37.75.59
Mme Seiller

**Rooms** 35 with telephone, bath or shower and WC (20 with TV). **Price** Double 240-560F / 36,59-85,37€. **Meals** Breakfast 52F / 7,93€, served 7:00-11:00. **Restaurant** Service 12:30PM-13:30PM, 7:30PM-9:30PM; mealtime specials 130-300F / 19,82-45,73€, also à la carte. Specialties: Salade de homard à l'émulsion d'huile d'olive et de corail; escalope de sandre au vinaigre de cidre. **Credit card** Visa. **Pets** Dogs allowed. **Facilities** Riding, fishing, hunting, boating, parking. **Nearby** Museum of local history in Le Blanc, Châteaux of Azay-le-Ferron, Benedictine Abbey of Fontgombault. **Open** All year.

We loved the truly kind welcome we received at the *Domaine de l'Etape*, a 19th-century mansion standing on a 500-acre estate. The hotel is charming throughout, from the salon with its Louis-Philippe furnishings (a lovely spot for reading or watching television) to the panelled dining room which is often brightened by an open fire. The bedrooms in the main building are the most delightful (notably Numbers 1, 6, and 15), even if some carpets and wallpaper are beginning to look a little frayed. However, Rooms 3, 4, and 14 have just been renovated. In the modern house, the rooms are less personalized though elegant and comfortable, and those on the ground level open directly onto the garden. Finally, there are other bedrooms in a small farmhouse: much too simple for our taste but certainly cool in summer. Add to these fine qualities the gourmet cooking of Daniel Cotar, served on the terrace in summer; an immense lake for fishing and horses which you can ride through the beautiful countryside. A very attractive place.

***How to get there*** *( Map 16): 59km west of Châteauroux via N20 and N151 to Le Blanc, then D10 towards Bélâbre.*

## Château de Bouesse-en-Berry

36200 Bouesse (Indre)
Tel. (0)2.54.25.12.20 - Fax (0)2.54.25.12.30
M. and Mme Courtot-Atterton

**Rooms** 11 with telephone, bath or shower and WC. **Price** Single and double 350-480F / 53,36-73,18€, apart. (2 rooms) 720F / 109,76€. **Meals** Breakfast 60F / 9,15€, served 8:00-10:00; half board 435-495F / 66,32-75,46€ (per pers., 3 days min.). **Restaurant** Service 12:00PM-2:00PM, 7:30PM-9:30PM; mealtime specials 95F / 14,48€ (lunch weekdays), 140-220F / 21,34-33,54€, also à la carte. Specialties: Croquant d'agneau fumé et foie gras; nage de Saint Jacques au coulis de langoustines; pigeon fermier à la sauge. **Credit cards** Amex, Visa. **Pets** Dogs not allowed. **Facilities** Parking. **Nearby** Pont-Vieux and Saint-Benoît Chapel in Argenton, Château of Nohant-Vic, Georges Sand Museum in La Châtre, Abbey Church of Fontgombault – 18-hole Dryades and Pouligny-Notre-Dame golf courses. **Closed** Mid Nov – mid Mar, Monday in low season.

Monsieur and Mme Courtot-Atterton love history and have focused their enthusiasm on the restoration of this superb 13th- and 15th-century château. The bedrooms' names refer to the château's history: *Jeanne d'Arc, Raoul VI de Gaucourt,* etc. The bedrooms are all very large, and often have stone fireplaces bearing coats of arms. Some rooms have been redecorated recently in the style of the Middle Ages, using furniture specially made for the château. Others are in the romantic style of the English 19th century. The hotel is totally comfortable and peaceful. The view cannot have changed for centuries. We particularly admired the dining room, which has pale blue and grey panelling and a 17th-century painting on the ceiling. In summer an excellent breakfast is served outside on the terrace.

***How to get there*** *(Map 17): 33km south of Châteauroux, on D927 between Argenton-sur-Creuse and La Châtre.*

## Château de la Vallée Bleue

Saint-Chartier - 36400 La Châtre (Indre)
Tel. (0)2.54.31.01.91 - Fax (0)2.54.31.04.48
M. Gasquet

**Category** ★★★ **Rooms** 15 with telephone, bath or shower, WC, TV and minibar. **Price** Single and double 390-690F / 59,46-105,19€. **Meals** Breakfast 55F / 8,38€; half board 450-590F / 68,60-89,94€ (per pers., 3 days min.). **Restaurant** Service 12:00PM-13:30PM, 7:30PM-9:00PM; mealtime specials 100F / 15,24€ lunch (except national holidays) 150-295F / 22,87-44,97€, also à la carte. Specialties: Quasi de veau rôti à l'huile de noix et pleurotes; croustillant aux poires épicées; crème vanillée. **Credit card** Visa. **Pets** Dogs allowed (+60F / 9,15€). **Facilities** Swimming pool, health center, mountain bike, putting range, parking. **Nearby** Georges Sand Museum in La Châtre, Château des Maître-Sonneurs in Saint-Chartier, Château of Nohant-Vic – 18-hole Dryades golf course. **Closed** Mid Nov – beg Mar; Mar – end Apr and Oct closed Sunday evening and Monday.

The shadows of George Sand and Chopin lord over this little castle, constructed by the artists' physician in a four-acre park. Paintings and little touches recalling the lives of the famous couple are everywhere, such as the glass placques indentifying the room numbers with the reproduced signatures of the artful lovers. The hotel is characterized by an agreeable level of comfort and stylish furnishings which harmonize with the English-style wallpaper and fabrics. Many rooms, the lounge and elegant dining rooms included, enjoy a splendid view of the countryside with the old roofs of the village far away. Gasquet looks after everything: his restaurant offers excellent, delicately-spiced, seasonal fare, as well as an astounding wine and liqueur list. A charming place, perfect for your longer stays.

***How to get there*** *( Map 17): 27km southeast of Châteauroux via D943 to Saint-Chartier. The hotel is outside the village on the Verneuil road.*

## Le Manoir Les Minimes

37400 Amboise (Indre-et-Loire)
34, quai Charles-Guinot
Tel. (0)2.47.30.40.40 - Fax. 02.47.30.40.77 - M. Eric Deforge
E-mail: manoir-les-minimes@wanadoo.fr

**Category** ★★★★ **Rooms** 11 and 2 suites, with telephone, bath, WC, satellite TV – 1 for disabled persons. **Price** Double 590-820F / 89,94-125,01€. **Meals** Breakfast 58F / 8,85€; half board by reservation. No restaurant; snacks avalaible by reservation in room or on terrace. **Credit cards** Visa, Amex. **Pets** Dogs allowed (+45F / 6,86€). **Facilities** Parking. **Nearby** Château d'Amboise and Manoir du Clos-Lucé, mini-castle park, hot-air ballooning – 18-hole Arbelle golf course (5 km). **Open** All year.

This hotel, a former family estate restored in the traditional manner, has kept the feeling of the large manors of the 18th century. Full of sunlight, the lounges and dining room have have kept some antique pictures and furniture. Elegantly accommodated with a great knack for comfort, the rooms are quite often spacious, accented by beautiful fabrics and well-selected furnishings. On top of this, there is a magnificent view of the Amboise château and the Loire river. Those that look out on the river bank are huge, bathed in light, and isolated from the noise of the road (little traffic) by double-paned windows. In a little house, you can find two ground-floor rooms, simpler but a little dark. A pleasant garden could serve as an evening setting for a light meal (short menu) for those who don't feel like going out. If not, there is a half board agreement with a local restaurant. Lastly, the warm hospitality makes this a perfect place to discover the many cultural and gourmet wonders of the Amboise and surrounding areas.

***How to get there*** *(Map 16): Via A10, take Amboise exit, then D 31. Soon after the bridge over the Loire, take a right toward the town center, and then 2 km along the quai.*

## Le Fleuray

37530 Cangey-Amboise (Indre-et-Loire)
Route Dame-Marie-les-Bois
Tel. (0)2.47.56.09.25 - Fax (0)2.47.56.93.97 - M. and Mme Newington
E-mail: lefleuray.hotel@wanadoo.fr

**Category** ★★ **Rooms** 11 with telephone, bath or shower and WC – 2 with wheelchair access; 1 for disabled persons. **Price** Single and double 375-550F / 57,17-83,85€. **Meals** Breakfast 68F / 10,38€, served 8:00-10:00; half board 410-595F / 62,50-90,71€ (per pers.). **Restaurant** Service 7:30PM-9:30PM; mealtime specials 155-265F / 23,63-40,40€, also à la carte. **Credit card** Visa. **Pets** Dogs allowed (40F / 6,10€). **Facilities** Parking and garage. **Nearby** Château d'Amboise and Manoir du Clos-Lucé, Pagoda of Chanteloup, forest of Amboise. **Closed** Dec 19 – Jan and Feb 12 – 28; November school holidays.

This hotel is, ideally situated on the lush plain overlooking the Loire and the Vouvray vineyards. Each bedroom is decorated in a fresh, English style, with pink-striped wallpaper, floral fabrics, and white tulle bed canopies. Two rooms in the outbuildings have a private terrace on the garden; the others are in the main building. With all the enthusiasm of the self-taught cook, Hazel turns out very copious meals, which are, however, sometimes a bit disappointing. Fortunately, the smiling service of Peter, the pretty dining room with its wood-burning stove, and the pleasant shady terrace makes up for this mixed impression. A charming place which, let's say it again, is really very welcoming.

***How to get there*** *(Map 16): Via A 10, take Exit no. 18 to Amboise/Château-Renault, and then via D 31 to Autrèche (2km); turn left and follow signs for "Dame-Marie-aux-Bois"; in the village turn right onto D74 towards Cangey.*

## Hôtel du Bon Laboureur et du Château

37150 Chenonceaux (Indre-et-Loire)
6, rue du Docteur-Bretonneau
Tel. (0)2.47.23.90.02 - Fax (0)2.47.23.82.01
M. Jeudi

**Category** ★★★ **Rooms** 28 with telephone, bath or shower, WC and satellite TV – 2 for disabled persons. **Price** Double 320-600F / 48,78-91,47€, suite 900-1000F / 137,20-152,45€. **Meals** Breakfast 45F / 6,86€, served 7:30-10:30; half board 400-650F / 60,98-99,09€ (per pers.). **Restaurant** Service 12:00PM-2:00PM, 7:30PM-9:30PM; mealtime specials 160-300F / 24,39-45,73€, also à la carte. Specialties: Blancs de sandre cuits croustillants aux épices; millefeuille de nougatine au chocolat. **Credit cards** All major. **Pets** Dogs allowed. **Facilities** Swimming pool, parking. **Nearby** Château of Chenonceaux, Loire Valley (Châteaux of the Loire), Montlouis-sur-Loire via the Cher Valley – 18-hole Touraine golf course in Ballan-Miré. **Open** Dec 16 – Jan 3 and Feb 16 – Nov 15.

Like a field regularly tended by a good laborer, this hotel, which has been in the same family for four generations, just keeps getting better and better, as evidenced by its latest addition -- a Loire wine bar, which should make many very happy. Located 200 meters from the Château de Chenonceaux, it consists of several buildings on either side of the street, gardens and a swimming pool. The bedrooms are all different, comfortable, prettily decorated and those which have just been renovated are, of course, the most attractive. Some are especially well-designed for families. You will also enjoy three pleasant, restful lounges. The first is English-style and has a bar; the two others are more modern. There is a bright, large dining room where guests enjoy the owner's excellent regional cuisine. Note too that in summer several tables are set out on the terrace in the shade of a large tree. The staff is efficient and very friendly.

***How to get there*** *(Map 16): 35km southeast of Tours; on A10 Tours exit, then via D410, or N76 to Bléré, then D40 to Chenonceaux.*

# La Roseraie

37150 Chenonceaux (Indre-et-Loire)
7, rue de Docteur-Bretonneau
Tel. (0)2.47.23.90.09 - Fax (0)2.47.23.91.59 - M. and Mme Fiorito
E-mail: lfiorito@aol.com

**Category** ★★★ **Rooms** 17 with telephone, 16 with bath or shower and WC, 15 with satellite TV. **Price** Double 280-550F / 42,69-83,85€, family suite 400-650F / 60,98-99,09€. **Meals** Breakfast 38F / 5,80€, served 8:00-10:30; half board +150F / 22,87€ (per pers.). **Restaurant** Service 12:00PM-2:30PM, 7:00PM-9:00PM (10:00PM in high season); mealtime specials 98-170F / 14,96-25,92€, also à la carte. Regional cooking. **Credit cards** All major. **Pets** Dogs allowed. **Facilities** Swimming pool, parking. **Nearby** Loire Valley (Châteaux of the Loire), Château of Chenonceaux, Montlouis-sur-Loire via the Cher Valley – 18-hole Touraine golf course in Ballan-Miré. **Open** Feb 16 – Nov 14.

Recently bought up by a family set on restoring this hotel's former luxury, *La Roseraie* already shows some true improvements. After a thorough cleaning, repainting job, and replacement of bedding and fabrics, the bedrooms are really starting to look wonderful. It's true that the hotel overall is simple, but the decoration is tasteful, the baths well-kept, and most of the bedrooms are quiet (those on the street side get some traffic noise in the morning.) In spring, the *Roserie* opens several bedrooms on a wing overlooking the garden and the terrace, which are connected by a broad exterior passageway on the *premier étage*. In good weather, several dining tables are set out there; otherwise, meals are served in the large, rustic dining room or in the *Rôtisserie*, which is often used for breakfast. The cuisine is copious and the prices reasonable.

***How to get there*** *( Map 16): Via A 10, take Tours exit, then via D140, or N76, to Bléré, and D40 to Chenonceaux. The hotel is in front of the Poste.*

## Agnès Sorel

37500 Chinon (Indre-et-Loire)
4, quai Pasteur
Tel. (0)2.47.93.04.37 - Fax (0)2.47.93.06.37

**Rooms** 6 with telephone, 3 with bath and WC, TV. **Price** 180-250F / 27,44-38,11€ (with basin), 300-450F / 45,73-68,60€ (with bath). **Meals** Breakfast 38F / 5,80€. Snacks avalaible by reservation. Mealtime specials from 70F / 10,67€. **Credit cards** All major. **Pets** Dogs allowed. **Facilities** Bicycle rentals. **Nearby** Loire Valley (Châteaux of the Loire: Chinon, Ussé, Azay-le-rideau), Richelieu, Rabelais country (La Devinière), Coudray-Montpensier Château, Lerné, Château of the Roche-Clermanet – 18-hole Touraine golf course in Ballan-Miré. **Open** All year.

The discreet small hotel *Agnès Sorel*, recently taken over by an enthusiastic, hospitable young couple, offers several bedrooms of varying attraction and amenities. Prices vary depending on whether the room has a bathroom or a simple washroom. We recommend the *Bleu* and the *Rose* Rooms (overlooking the River Vienne and insulated from street noise by double glazing), as well as the *Verte* Room, which has a small terrace. On the ground floor, there is a dining area with charming old-fashioned furniture found in local *brocante* shops; excellent breakfasts are served there, as are afternoon tea and light meals in the evening, on reservation. Because of the small number of rooms, the staff can take special care of the guests: you'll be met at the station if you come by train, the chef will make you a picnic lunch, you can rent a bike...In short, the *Agnès Sorel*, named after the beautiful mistress of Charles VII, is a true hotel of character and charm. For restaurants, you can enjoy the gastronomic *Plaisir Gourmand* or the more folkloric *Hostellerie Gargantua*; good, too, are *Les Années 30* and *L'Océanic*.

***How to get there*** *(Map 16): 48km southwest of Tours via D751.*

## Hôtel Diderot

37500 Chinon (Indre-et-Loire)
4, rue Buffon
Tel. (0)2.47.93.18.87 - Fax (0)2.47.93.37.10
Mme Kazamias

**Category** ★★ **Rooms** 28 (4 in annex) with telephone, bath or shower and WC (TV on request). **Price** Double 250-400F / 38,11-60,98€. **Meals** Breakfast 40F / 6,10€, served 7:30-10:00. No restaurant. **Credit cards** All major. **Pets** Dogs not allowed. **Facilities** Parking. **Nearby** Loire Châteaux: Chinon, Ussé, Azay-le-Rideau, Richelieu, Rabelais country (La Devinière), Château of Coudray-Montpensier, Lerné, Château of la Roche-Clermanet – 18-hole Touraine golf course in Ballan-Miré. **Open** All year.

Located in the center of Chinon, just behind Joan of Arc Square, this hotel is nevertheless truly peaceful and quiet. In the garden courtyard, where breakfast is served in summer, Monsieur Kazmias (born in Cyprus) tends the Mediterranean plants. Next to the entrance, there is the breakfast room with its still-functioning fireplace and exposed beams that remind us of the 15th-century roots of this house, enlarged and modified in the 18th. Here you will eat the excellent "house" jams that sweet-tooths can buy as souvenirs. (All proceeds go to aid Chad.) The rooms are either upstairs or on the ground floor or in various buildings around the courtyard. No two are alike, treated in fabrics or dressed up in wallpaper. Their bathrooms are restrained and well-kept. We highly recommend Rooms 1, 3, and 5. The more ordinary rooms are located in the annex. Great hospitality. No restaurant in the hotel, but you can go to *L'Hostellerie Gargantua*, the *Plaisir Gourmand*, or even *L'Océanic* for dinner.

***How to get there*** *(Map 16): 48km southwest of Tours via D751. Go along the Vienne to the Place Jeanne-d'Arc; on the corner of the Rue Diderot and Rue Buffon.*

## Château de Beaulieu

37300 Joué-lès-Tours (Indre-et-Loire)
67, rue de Beaulieu (D 207)
Tel. (0)2.47.53.20.26 - Fax (0)2.47.53.84.20
M. and Mme Lozay

**Category** ★★★ **Rooms** 19 with air-conditioning, telephone, bath, WC, TV and minibar. **Price** Double 390-780F / 59,46-118,91€. **Meals** Breakfast 58F / 8,85€, until 10:30; half board 800-1200F / 121,96-182,94€ (2 pers., 2 days min.). **Restaurant** Closed Dec 24 evening. Service 12:00PM-14:15PM, 7:00PM-9:30PM; mealtime specials 195-480F / 29,73-73,18€, also à la carte. Specialties: Nems d'écrevisses et son coulis; ananas confit aux épices et sa glace au lait d'amandes. **Credit cards** Amex, Visa. **Divers** Dogs allowed. **Facilities** Tennis and parking. **Nearby** Tours: Palais de l'ancien archevêché, Museum of Fine Art, Cathedral of Saint-Gatien, Château-la-Vallière, Grange de Meslay, Vouvray wine cellars, Loire Valley (Châteaux of the Loire) – 18-hole Touraine golf course in Ballan-Miré. **Open** All year.

Though Tours is nearby, the *Château de Beaulieu* enjoys a country setting, flowery terraced gardens and a panoramic view. Although this 15th-century château, redesigned in the 19th-century, no longer has a great deal of antique furniture, it has been decorated to respect the building's history: the period furniture gains in comfort what it loses in authenticity. The colors are luminous, fine detail everywhere, and the staff is at your beck and call. Prices vary according to room size and the view; all have modern amenities. Some rooms are located in an independent building; our favorites there are Numbers 21 and 22 on the garden level and the spacious *premier étage,* rooms. The cuisine is truly *gastronomique,* cooked with precision for no-nonsense taste.

***How to get there*** *(Map 16): 5km southwest of Tours via A 10. Exit 24 bypass 585, Savonnieres-Villandry exit, then 2 left coming from Bordeaux or Paris.*

## Hôtel George Sand

37600 Loches (Indre-et-Loire)
39, rue Quintefol
Tel. (0)2.47.59.39.74 - Fax (0)2.47.91.55.75
M. and Mme Fortin

**Rooms** 20 with telephone, bath or shower, WC and TV. **Price** Double 260-650F / 39,64-99,09€. **Meals** Breakfast 38F / 5,80€, served 7:00-9:30; half board 490-680F / 74,70-103,67€, (per pers., 3 days min.). **Restaurant** Service 12:00PM-2:00PM, 7:30PM-9:00PM; mealtime specials 95-290F / 14,48-44,21€, also à la carte. Specialties: Pavé de carpe au vin du Lochois; croustillant de pommes au vieux marc de Touraine et framboises. **Credit cards** Visa, Eurocard and MasterCard. **Pets** Dogs allowed (+25F / 3,81€). **Nearby** Château and keep of Loches, Abbey Church of Beaulieu-les-Loches, Montrésor, Indre valley, Cormery, Montbazon, Monts, Saché – 18-hole Touraine golf course in Ballan-Miré. **Open** All year.

At the foot of the impressive Château de Loches, this former 15th-century house once marked the boundary of the medieval town. Entering from the street you will be pleasantly surprised to find that the dining room and its large terrace are on the edge of the river Indre with its large waterfall. With access via an antique spiral staircase, many of the bedrooms still have their original beams and some a beautiful stone fireplace. The most pleasant rooms look out on the river and the public garden. All have just been entirely renovated, sporting double-paned windows and impeccable bathrooms. Although the wallpaper and carpeting is still a bit pretty-pretty and the rustic furniture not very gay (though antique furniture is steadily making an appearance), the price is right and some rooms are great for families. The delicate, traditional cuisine is excellent, culminating with delicious desserts. Warm hospitality.

***How to get there*** *( Map 16): 42km southeast of Tours via N143.*

191

## Domaine de la Tortinière

37250 Montbazon-en-Touraine (Indre-et-Loire)
Les Gués de Veigné
Tel. (0)2.47.34.35.00 - Fax (0)2.47.65.95.70
Mme Olivereau-Capron - M. Olivereau

**Category** ★★★ **Rooms** 21 (3 with air-conditioning) with telephone, bath, WC and TV – For disabled persons. **Price** Double 520-950F / 79,27-144,83€, suite 1050-1400F / 160,07-213,43€. **Meals** Breakfast 80F / 12,20€, served 8:00-11:00; half board 620-1045F / 94,52-159,31€ (per pers.). **Restaurant** Service 12:15PM-1:45PM, 7:30PM-9:15PM; mealtime specials 230-420F / 35,06-64,03€, also à la carte. Specialties: Pigeon de Touraine rôti en salmis et ravioles de cuisses confites au Sainte-Maure; palet d'or au chocolat, glace fleur de thé earl-grey. **Credit card** Visa. **Pets** Dogs not allowed. **Facilities** Heated swimming pool, tennis, boat, mountain bikes on request, parking. **Nearby** Keep of Fouques Nerra in Montbazon, Indre Valley, Cormery, Monts, Saché, Tours Cathedral, Château d'Azay-le-Rideau – 18-hole Touraine golf course in Ballan-Miré. **Open** Mar – Dec 20.

A Renaissance-style château built in 1861, the *Tortinière* is set in a 37-acre park dominating the Indre valley, although it is only 10km from Tours. The two restaurants, the salon and most of the bedrooms are in the château. The bedrooms are all different, superbly decorated, and very comfortable; the ones in old pavillions outside are as beautiful and recommendable as those in the château. There is a beautiful restaurant with a terrace where meals are served in good weather. In autumn, the park is carpeted with cyclamen, and in good weather you can still enjoy the heated swimming pool.

***How to get there*** *(Map 16): 10 km south of Tours on the A 10, take Exit 23 and then the N 10 toward Montbazon. Once at Les-Gués-de-Veigné, turn right at the second traffic light on the road to Ballan-Miré.*

## Château de la Bourdaisière

37270 Montlouis-sur-Loire (Indre-et-Loire)
25, rue de la Bourdaisière
Tel. (0)2.47.45.16.31 - Fax (0)2.47.45.09.11 - M. de Broglie
E-mail: labourd@club-internet.fr

**Rooms** 17, 2 suites and 1 duplex with bath or shower and WC (TV on request) – Elevator. **Price** Single and double 650-1200F / 99,09-182,94€, suite 900-1300F / 137,20-198,18€. **Meals** Breakfast 60F / 9,15€. No restaurant. **Credit card** Visa. **Pets** Dogs allowed. **Facilities** Heated swimming pool, tennis, riding, parking. **Nearby** Tours, Vouvray wine cellars, Loire Valley (Châteaux of the Loire) – 18-hole Touraine golf course in Ballan-Miré. **Closed** 15 days in Feb.

First inhabited by Marie Gaudin, the mistress of Francois the First, then by Gabrielle d'Estrée, the beloved of Henry IV, *La Bourdaisière* is dedicated to a few noble women, and names of the rooms bear witness to this. The rooms are divided up between the outlying houses and the main castle. No two are alike, and all are well-decorated with antique reproductions and graced with quite attractive bathrooms. Breakfast is served in an amusing little room decorated with portraits of the Princess of Broglie's poodles that opens out to a stone balcony where a few tables are set. Beautiful lounge dominated by an impressive fireplace. Great hospitality. Don't leave without strolling through the park and the huge vegetable garden, with its 350 varieties of tomatos, almost as many herbs, its flowers and rose bushes. This is a rare and enchanting place, and if you happen upon Pierre, the gardener, don't hesitate to talk to him. He loves his work. For dinner, aside from the restaurants near the hotel, you can also enjoy fine dining at such places as the large *Jean Bardet*, or *L'Aubiniere*, which is excellent and right next to Saint-Ouen-les-Vignes.

***How to get there*** *( Map 16 ): 11km east of Tours via D152.*

## L'Aubinière

37530 Saint-Ouen-les-Vignes (Indre-et-Loire)
Tél. 02.47.30.15.29 - Fax. 02.47.30.02.44
Odile and Jacques Arrayet

**Rooms** 5 with telephone, bath or shower, WC and TV. **Price** Single and double 460-680F / 70,13-103,67€. **Meals** Breakfast 65F / 9,91€; half board 600-700 F / 91,47-106,71€. **Restaurant** Service 12:15PM-1.30PM, 7:30PM-9:30PM; mealtime specials 195-400F / 29,73-60,98€, also à la carte. **Credit cards** Amex, Visa. **Pets** Small dogs allowed. **Facilities** Parking. **Nearby** Loire Valley (Châteaux of the Loire) Vouvray and Montlouis wine cellars — 18-hole Touraine golf course in Ballan-Miré. **Closed** except 2 weeks in Oct and Feb.

A stone arch along the village's main road gives you entrance to this country inn, mostly renowned for its excellent restaurant. For some years now, the former roadside building has been fashioned into a string of houses, built in the Tour style, that border the park. That's where you will now find the large dining room, which extends into an elegant terrace where meals are served during good weather. In the kitchen, Jacques Arrayet concocts subtle, fragrant and perfectly-cooked seasonal dishes. The decor is fresh, colorful, nicely modern, and the service is proof of professionalism. Same amount of care in the five rooms, which are spacious, very comfortable, furnished in a very pleasant and modern style, with equally well-appointed bathrooms. Add to this calm and cheer a large garden, bursting with flowers, that gently rolls down to the little river where lovers of fishing can try their luck. A charming, discrete little place, *L'Aubiniere* is perfect for excursions to the Loire castles or for touring the nearby vineyards.

***How to get there*** *(Map 16): 30km east of Tours. Via A10, take Amboise-Château-Renault exit, then D 431 toward Saint-Ouen-les-Vignes.*

## Hostellerie Les Perce-Neige

37210 Vernou-sur-Brenne (Indre-et-Loire)
Tel. (0)2.47.52.10.04 - Fax (0)2.47.52.19.08
Mme Chemin
Web: www.perceneige.com - E-mail: brigitte@perceneige.com

**Rooms** 15 with telephone, bath or shower (14 with WC) and TV. **Price** Double 200-300F / 30,49-45,73€. **Meals** Breakfast 33F / 5,03€, served 8:00-10:00; half board 400-520F / 60,98-79,27€ (2 pers.). **Restaurant** Service 12:00PM-2:00PM, 7:30PM-10:00PM; mealtime specials 98-190F / 14,96-28,97€ (children 55F / 8,38€), also à la carte. Specialties: Traditional cuisine. **Credit cards** Amex, Visa, Eurocard and MasterCard. **Pets** Dogs allowed. **Facilities** Parking. **Nearby** Tours, grange de Meslay, Vouvray wine cellars, Loire Valley (Châteaux of the Loire) — 18-hole Touraine golf course in Ballan-Miré. **Closed** Mid Nov — mid Dec and beg Jan — mid Mar.

The *Perce-Neige* ("Snow Drops") is a small, charming, simple hotel located in a lovely winegrowing village on the banks of the Loire just a few minutes from Tours. Decorated in cheerful color schemes, the ground floor contains an inviting bar and two lovely dining rooms where regional specialties are served, always made with fresh local products. Simple but very reasonably priced, the main building's rooms sometimes look a bit out-of-fashion, with their retro furniture painted to match the room's predominant colors. We liked least of all the tiny, dark annex rooms. In spring, the garden is perfumed by a sumptuous wisteria, almost a century old. In summer, you can have dinner in the park, which is shaded with beautiful trees: a veritable invitation to a romantic stroll before or after dinner. Last but not least, the kind welcome adds a little extra something to this little hotel, really practical for your visits to the Loire châteaux.

*How to get there (Map 16): 11km east of Tours, towards Amboise-Blois; in Vouvray, head towards Vernou.*

## Château de Chissay

41400 Chissay-en-Touraine (Loir-et-Cher)
Montrichard
Tel. (0)2.54.32.32.01 - Fax (0)2.54.32.43.80
M. Savry

**Category** ★★★★ **Rooms** 31 with telephone, bath and WC. **Price** Single and double 490-820F / 74,70-125,01€; suite or apartment 920-1500F / 140,25-228,67€. **Meals** Breakfast 65F / 9,90€, served 7:30-10:30; half board 490-680F / 74,70-105,19€ (per pers.). **Restaurant** Service 12:00PM-2:00PM, 7:30PM-9:30PM; mealtime specials 185-295F / 28,20-44,97€, also à la carte. **Credit cards** All major. **Pets Dogs** allowed (+45F / 6,87€). **Facilities** Swimming pool, parking. **Nearby** Tours, Grange de Meslay, Vouvray wine cellars, Loire Valley (Châteaux of the Loire) – 18-hole Touraine golf course in Ballan-Miré. **Open** Mar 15 – Nov 15.

This old fortified château is full of historic memories: Charles VII, Louis XI and the Duke of Choiseul all stayed here. More recently, General de Gaulle spent several days here in June 1940 before going to England. Arranged around a majestic interior courtyard, the reception rooms are decorated with pale oak period furniture, or in Louis XIII style; they are beautifully in keeping with the château. The bedrooms are luxurious, very comfortable, and some are immense. They are classically decorated, mixing styles to an often lovely effect. From the towering vantage point of the château, there is a sweeping view of the park and the swimming pool, and in the distance, the Tours plain traversed by the Cher River, just visible through the trees. The staff at the *Château de Croissy* is pleasant and professional.

***How to get there*** *( Map 16): 35km east of Tours via D40 to Chenonceaux, then D76; 4km before Montrichard.*

196

## Relais des Landes

Ouchamps
41120 Les Montils (Loir-et-Cher)
Tel. (0)2.54.44.40.40 - Fax (0)2.54.44.03.89
M. Badenier and Mme Rousselet

**Category** ★★★ **Rooms** 28 with telephone, bath, WC, TV and minibar. **Price** Single and double 515-785F / 78,51-119,67€. **Meals** Breakfast 65F / 9,91€, served 7:30-10:00. **Restaurant** Service 12:30PM-13:30PM, 7:00PM-9:30PM; mealtime specials 180-295F / 27,44-44,97€, also à la carte. Specialties: Foie gras de canard des Landes maison; folie de homard au pistou; filet de bœuf à la lie de vin; blanc manger aux amandes douces et coulis de fruits rouges. **Credit cards** All major. **Pets** Dogs allowed (+50F / 7,62€). **Facilities** Swimming pool, bicycle rental, parking. **Nearby** Châteaux of Chaumont, Blois, Amboise, Chambord, Beauregard and Chenonceaux – 18-hole la Carte golf course in Onzain, 18-hole Château de Cheverny golf course. **Closed** Dec, Jan and Feb.

Lying in the middle of the countryside in a 24-acre park, the *Relais de Landes* is a 17th-century house which has been restored and is well-kept. The lounge/reception area also houses the bar and offers corners for conversation or reading. The furniture is comfortable in these rooms and in the dining room, where a fire is lit in winter. Next to it, there is a winter garden leading to the lawn where dining tables are also set. In summer, you can have meals in the flower garden beside its small streams. The bedrooms are very comfortable, prettily decorated, and they have beautiful bathrooms. The staff is friendly and helpful.

***How to get there*** (*Map 16*): *15km east of Blois towards Montrichard; follow the signs from Les Montils.*

## Hôtel Les Charmilles

41600 Nouan-le-Fuzelier (Loir-et-Cher)
19, rue de la Grande-Sologne
Tel. (0)2.54.88.73.55 - Fax (0)2.54.88.74.55
M. Coquet

**Category** ★★ **Rooms** 13 with telephone, bath or shower, WC and TV. **Price** Single and double 240-320F / 36,59-48,78€, suite (4 pers.) 480F / 73,18€. **Meals** Breakfast 35F / 5,34€, served 7:30-9:00. No restaurant. **Credit card** Visa. **Pets** Dogs allowed in the ground-floor bedrooms (+30F / 4,57€). **Facilities** Parking. **Nearby** Church of Saint-Viâtre, Château du Moulin, lake road from Saint-Viâtre to Romorantin via Selle Saint-Denis, La Source flower garden in Olivet, Châteaux of Chambord, Cheverny 40km. **Closed** Feb.

Built at the turn of the century, this solid manor house is now a simple, little hotel in the heart of Sologne. So don't demand to much from it, and let yourself be won over by the bucolic environs as well as by the warm welcome you will find. The decor is traditional, but more than half of the rooms have just been freshened up and are very inviting, with comfortable and clean bathrooms. The surrounding area is delightful: The large park has a little, landscaped pond, a stream colonized by ducks that you can cross on log bridges, refreshing corners under stately trees, inviting lawn furniture, and a lawn where you can stretch out. No restaurant here, but, if you don't feel like a picnic, you can find nearby *Le Raboliot* and *Le Dahu* in Nouan; the *Lion d'Or* at Pierrefitte, and *La Perdrix Rouge* in Souvigny. All highly recommended.

***How to get there*** *(Map 17): 44km south of Orléans via N20 towards Vierzon; on the way out of the village D122, via A 71, Lamotte-Beuvron (north) or Sablis (south) exit.*

## Hôtel Château des Tertres

41150 Onzain (Loir-et-Cher)
Route de Monteaux
Tel. (0)2.54.20.83.88 - Fax (0)2.54.20.89.21
M. Valois

**Category** ★★★ **Rooms** 14 with telephone, bath or shower and WC. **Price** Double 400-600F / 60,98-91,47€. **Meals** Breakfast 45F / 6,86€, served 8:00-10:00. No restaurant. **Credit cards** Amex, Visa, Eurocard and MasterCard. **Pets** Dogs not allowed. **Facilities** Bicycles, parking. **Nearby** Châteaux of Chaumont, Blois, Amboise, Chambord, Beauregard and Chenonceaux – 9-hole la Carte golf course in Onzain, 18-hole Château de Cheverny golf course. **Open** Apr – Nov.

This 19th-century château is a beautiful building and charmingly decorated. On the ground floor overlooking the garden and the countryside, the reception area adjoins a lounge with 19th-century furniture. To one side is a very attractive room where a delicious breakfast is served. The overall effect is that of a family house. The bedrooms are very comfortable and pretty. They are regularly redecorated with beautiful fabrics and the latest conveniences. Add to this the very pleasant bathrooms, many accented in chrome and exotic varnished wood. Perfectly calm in a highly touristic area, this is a rare place where you will find the best hospitality and high quality at a good price. The hotel does not serve meals but there are some good restaurants in the village, notably *Le Pont d'Ouchet* and *Le Domaine des Hauts de Loire*, which is more elegant and more expensive.

***How to get there*** *(Map 16): 198km of Paris via A 10, Blois exit; 17km west of Blois via N 152 towards Tours, then towards Monteaux.*

## Domaine de Valaudran

41300 Salbris (Loir-et-Cher)
Tel. (0)2.54.97.20.00 - Fax (0)2.54.97.12.22
Famille Debois-Frogé
E-mail: info@valaudran.com - Web: www.valaudran.com

**Category** ★★★ **Rooms** 31 with telephone, bath, WC, TV and minibar – 2 for disabled persons. **Price** Single and double 390-650F / 59,46-99,09€, apart. 900-990F / 137,20-150,92€. **Meals** Breakfast 70 and 80F / 10,67 and 12,20€; half board 890-1400F / 135,68-213,43€ (per pers., 3 days min.). **Restaurant** Closed Sunday evening and Monday Dec – Mar. Service 12:00PM-13:30PM, 7:30PM-10:00PM; mealtime specials 120-300F / 18,29-45,73€, also à la carte. Specialties: Pigeonneau au chou; moelleux chocolat praliné. **Credit cards** All major. **Pets** Dogs allowed (+60F / 9,15€). **Facilities** Heated swimming pool, mountain bike and parking. **Nearby** "Grand Meaulnes" Museum, Le Grenier Villâtre in Nançay, Bourges, Aubigny-sur-Nère, Sancerre, Chambord, Cheverny – 9-hole Meaulnes golf course. **Open** All year.

At the edge of Salbris, this hotel of brick and stone is typical of the hunting lodges which are part of the charm of the Sologne countryside. Less traditional, the living rooms are elegant and comfortable. In the reception salon, handsome wicker furniture sets the elegant, cheerful, and contemporary decorative style. One side of the house extends into a long veranda where the restaurant tables are set. The fare is mouthwatering. As far as the rooms go, ask for those in the central building. They are medium-sized, brightened up by beautiful colored fabrics, comfortable, and have beautiful bathrooms. Only one hitch: you can't escape the noise of the highway when you are outside. As for pastimes, the Debois know the area perfectly and will recommend all kinds of sports and cultural activities.

***How to get there*** *( Map 17): 56km south of Orléans via A 71, exit Salbris; signs at traffic circle.*

## Château de la Voûte

41800 Montoire-sur-le-Loir (Loir-et-Cher)
Troo
Tel. (0)2.54.72.52.52 - Fax (0)2.54.72.52.52
Véronique and Richard Provenzano

**Rooms** 5 with bath or shower and WC. **Price** Double 430-600F / 65,55-91,47€. **Meals** Breakfast incl., served 8:00-10:00. No restaurant. **Credit cards** Not accepted. **Pets** Dogs not allowed. **Facilities** Parking. **Nearby** Benedictine Abbey of la Trinité and Church of Rhodon in Vendôme, valley of the Loir, Chapel of Saint-Gilles in Montoire, Gué-du-Loir, Lavardin, Saint-Jacques-des-Guérets, Manoir de la Possonière — 9-hole La Bosse golf course in Oucques. **Open** All year.

Leaning against a chalky cliff looking over the Loir, this former manor is in a charming village with underground dwellings. It offers five smashing guest rooms furnished and decorated like days-gone-by. Each has its own look; the smallest, decorated in Jouy canvas is truly charming. The *"Pompadour"* is very roomy, accommodated in the 18th-century style. *"Louis XIII"* has a canopy bed. The *"Empire"* has a small adjoining room, perfect for a child. The overall view is worthy of a 17th-century painting, with the meanderings of the Loir embracing a little medieval church against a backdrop of fields and hills. Breakfast is served in your room or on the patio, and if you cannot have dinner here, there are plenty of restaurants nearby. We recommend first and foremost the stunning *Le Petit Relais*, nicely located next to the church. Good food at a good price, made even better by the welcoming and sparkiling personality of Maryse Sinon. The more classic *Le Cheval Rouge* in Montoire is also a good address.

***How to get there*** *( Map 16): 48km north of Tours via D29 to La Chartre-sur-le-Loir, then right on D305 and D917 to Troo.*

201

## Manoir de la Forêt

Fort-Girard
41160 La Ville-aux-Clercs (Loir-et-Cher)
Tel. (0)2.54.80.62.83 - Fax (0)2.54.80.66.03
Mme Autebon - M. and Mme Redon

**Category** ★★ **Rooms** 19 with telephone, bath or shower, WC and cable TV. **Price** Single and double 300-400F / 45,73-60,98€, suite 510-680F / 77,75-103,67€. **Meals** Breakfast 50F / 7,62€, served 7:15-10:30; half board 450F / 68,60€. **Restaurant** Service 12:15PM-2:00PM, 7:30PM-9:00PM; mealtime specials 160-300F / 24,39-45,73€, also à la carte. Specialties: Foie gras frais au muscat; grenadin de lotte et langoustines au sabayon de champagne; poêlée de ris de veau; sandre au vin de Chinon. **Credit cards** Amex, Visa. **Pets** Dogs allowed. **Facilities** Fishing, parking. **Nearby** Benedictine Abbey of la Trinité and Church of Rhodon in Vendôme, Loire Valley (Châteaux of the Loire), Loire Valley, chapel of Saint-Gilles in Montoire, Gué-du-Loir, Saint-Jacques-des-Guérets, Manoir de la Possonnière – 9-hole la Bosse golf course in Oucques. **Open** All year (closed Sunday evening Oct – Mar).

The former hunting lodge of the Château de la Gaudinière, which dates from the 18th-century, the *Manoir de la Forêt* stands in five acres of wooded grounds with a lake. The lounge/reception sets the scene with its restful atmosphere, fresh flowers, and pleasant furniture. Two living rooms with deep armchairs and sofas are the ideal place for a drink, morning coffee, or afternoon tea. A beautiful, spacious dining room with many windows overlooks the garden (where meals are served in good weather). The cuisine is good, somewhat irregular in quality, but still recommendable. The bedrooms, combining modern amenities with cheerful decoration, all enjoy a view over the park. The staff is hospitable and attentive.

***How to get there*** *(Map 16): 72km northeast of Tours via N10 to 6km past Vendôme, then left via D141 to La Ville-aux-Clercs.*

## Hôtel de l'Abbaye

45190 Beaugency (Loiret)
2, quai de l'Abbaye
Tel. (0)2.38.44.67.35 - Fax (0)2.38.44.87.92
M. Aupetit

**Category** ★★★ **Rooms** 18 with telephone, bath, WC and TV. **Price** Single 520-570F / 79,27-86,90€, suite 560-700F / 85,37-106,71€. **Meals** Breakfast 46F / 6,86€, served 7:00AM-7:00PM. **Restaurant** Service 12:00PM-2:00PM, 7:00PM-9:30PM; menu 190F / 28,97€, also à la carte. Specialties: Traditional cooking. **Credit cards** All major. **Pet** Dogs allowed (+50F / 7,62€ ). **Facilities** Parking. **Nearby** Medieval and Renaissance quarters of Beaugency, Château de Meung-sur-Loire, Basilica and Chapel of Saint-Jacques in Cléry-Saint-André – 18-hole Saint-Laurent-Nouan golf course. **Open** All year.

A discreet nameplate announces that this 17th-century former Augustine convent built on the banks of the Loire opposite the old bridge in Beaugency is a hotel. You will be charmingly welcomed in an immense but comfortable hall. Adjacent to it is a very inviting bar, which is next to the dining room. A tall fireplace, very tasteful rustic furnishings, and windows overlooking the Loire all make it very pleasant, particularly as the cuisine is extremely good (the prices are somewhat high but the very reasonable wine list compensates for this when the bill comes). In the summer, several tables are set out on the extraordinary terrace, whose splendid austerity would not be out of place in an Italian palace. The bedrooms on the *premier étage* upstairs have a mezzanine, thus making good use of the high ceilings. They are comfortable, very elegant and the beautiful Louis XIII period furniture contributes to the authenticity of this truly exceptional hotel.

*How to get there (Map 17): 25km southwest of Orléans via A10, Meung-sur-Loire exit, then N152.*

## Hôtel de la Sologne

45190 Beaugency (Loiret)
Place Saint-Firmin
Tel. (0)2.38.44.50.27 - Fax (0)2.38.44.90.19
Mme Vinauger

**Category ★★ Rooms** 16 with telephone, bath or shower, WC and TV. **Price** Single and double 240-330F / 36,59-50,31€. **Meals** Breakfast 39F / 5,95€, served 7:00-9:30. No restaurant. **Credit cards** Visa, Eurocard and MasterCard. **Pets** Dogs not allowed. **Nearby** Medieval and Renaissance quarters of Beaugency, Château of Chambord, Basilica and Chapel of Saint-Jacques in Cléry-Saint-André – 18-hole les Bordes golf course in Saint-Laurent-Nouan. **Open** Jan 6 – 19 Dec.

This charming hotel in the heart of old Beaugency is very courteously managed by Mme Rogue. The bedrooms are plain but comfortable, and she has equipped them with television sets with headphones (so as not to disturb the neighbors), wall lamps with pretty shades, hairdryers, and, in as many as possible, electric trouser presses. Good breakfast are served in an inviting dining room with exposed beams and a wood stove, often alight. (You can also use it as a lounge, because there are plenty of magazines and newspapers here.). The living room is rustic and welcoming, with a fireplace, old beams, and a huge selection of magazines. There is a pleasant veranda, which is also a lounge and winter garden. For restaurants, we recommend *Le Petit Bateau, Le Relais du Château* and *Le Vieux Fourneau* in Beaugency.

***How to get there*** *(Map 17): 29km southwest of Orléans via A 10, Meung-sur-Loire exit, then N152.*

## Domaine de Chicamour

45530 Sury-aux-Bois (Loiret)
Tel. (0)2.38.55.85.42 - Fax (0)2.38.55.80.43
Mme Merckx

**Category** ★★ **Rooms** 12 with telephone, bath or shower, and WC. **Price** Single and double 400-500F / 60,98-76,22€. **Meals** Breakfast incl., served 8:00-10:00; half board 430F / 65,55€. per pers. **Restaurant** Service 12:00PM-2:00PM, 7:30PM-9:00PM; mealtime specials 100-235F / 15,24-35,83€, also à la carte. Specialties: Foie gras; aumônière de chèvre chaud et son sorbet de tomates. **Credit cards** All major. **Pets** Dogs allowed (+25F / 3,81€). **Facilities** Tennis, riding, bicycles, lawn bowling and parking. **Nearby** Orléans, arboretum and museum in Châteauneuf-sur-Loire, La Source flower gardens in Olivet – 18-hole Orléans golf course. **Open** Mar 16 – Nov 14.

Set in a 20-acre park in the heart of the Orléans National Forest, the small château of Chicamour has been turned into a hotel with the accent on simplicity and elegance. The result is remarkable. The lovely lounge has deep sofas surrounding the fireplace and beautifully chosen curtains and fabrics. The superb collection of paintings and decorative objects helps to make this a special place you will not want to leave. The bedrooms also are beautiful, with pale wood furniture and Laura Ashley fabrics matching the wallpapers and lampshades. They are all comfortable, overlook the park, and have beautiful bathrooms. In the elegant dining room, you will enjoy refined cuisine based on regional produce. The cellar includes a great variety of Loire wines, which are available for purchase.

*How to get there* (Map 17): 39km west of Montargis on N60, between Bellegarde and Châteauneuf-sur-Loire.

## Hôtel de l'Abbaye

02600 Longpont (Aisne)
8, rue des Tourelles
Tel. (0)3.23.96.02.44 - Fax (0)3.23.96.02.44
M. Verdun

**Category** ★★ **Rooms** 11 with telephone, bath or shower, WC (5 with TV). **Price** Double 280-335F / 42,69-51,07€. **Meals** Breakfast "campagnard" 40F / 6,10€, served any time; half board and full board 390-470F / 59,46-71,65€ (per pers., 3 days min.). **Restaurant** Service 12:00PM-2:00PM, 7:30PM-9:00PM; mealtime specials 98-220F / 14,94-33,54€, also à la carte. Specialties: grilled meat; canard aux cerises; game and mushrooms in season. **Credit cards** All major. **Pets** Dogs allowed. **Facilities** Bicycle rental. **Nearby** Abbey and Château of Longpont; Château, Hôtel de Ville and Alexandre Dumas museum in Villers-Cotterêts, Château of Vierzy, forest of Retz – 9-hole Valois golf course in Barbery. **Open** All year.

In the heart of the Retz forest, Longpont and its remarkable hotel are worth going out of your way for. Right on the square, this little, friendly inn, with its truly nice owner, also serves as the village cafe. It is also a meeting place for hikers and hunters. Around the large, hardwood tables on the ground floor, a sense of relaxed liveliness reigns. Home-style, seasonal cooking is served, as well as good grilled meat. When weather permits, meals are served in the garden. The very simple rooms are quiet, well-kept, and in progress, as far as their decoration goes. Some look out on the forest, while others peer on the abbey. A quite small television room and reading lounge are at your disposal. You will find a lot of brochures about the region here, but if you want to know more, just ask Monsieur Verdun. An inviting little place, genuine and simple, not far from Paris.

***How to get there*** *(Map 10): 20km south of Soissons via N2 towards Villers-Cotterêts, then D2.*

## Hostellerie Le Château

Neuville-Saint-Amand
02100 Saint-Quentin (Aisne)
Tel. (0)3.23.68.41.82 - Fax (0)3.23.68.46.02
M. Meiresonne

**Category** ★★★ **Rooms** 13 with telephone, bath, WC and TV (6 with minibar) – 2 for disabled persons. **Price** Single and double 330-390F / 50,31-59,46€. **Meals** Breakfast 45F / 6,86€, served from 7:30. **Restaurant** Service 12:00PM-1:30PM, 7:00PM-9:00PM; mealtime specials 125-350F / 19,06-53,36€, also à la carte. Specialties: Cassolette d'escargots crème d'ail et poivrons; mélange de ris et rognons au genièvre de Houlles; assiette gourmande. **Credit cards** All major. **Pets** Dogs not allowed. **Facilities** Parking. **Nearby** Antoine-Lécuyer Museum (pastels by Quentin de la Tour), college and Hôtel de Ville of Saint-Quentin – 9-hole le Mesnil golf course. **Closed** Saturday lunch and Sunday evening, 3 weeks in Aug.

In northern France, the château is known as the most importance house in the village. This château lies in the heart of a beautiful wooded park. The ground floor rooms are occupied by its famous restaurant, while other pleasantly furnished rooms extend into a modern wing with bay windows and a view of the park. Viewed from the outside, however, the architectural effect is disappointing. The comfortable, pleasantly furnished bedrooms are very attractive, with pastel wall fabrics. The bathrooms are lovely. The rooms in the modern building are more run-of-the-mill, but huge, and a great value for the price. At the *Hostellerie*, you will enjoy a restful stay and welcoming hospitality.

***How to get there*** *( Map 2): 1km south of Saint-Quentin via A 26, exit number 11, to Lain via RN44. In Neuville-Saint-Amand village, on the right after the church.*

## Château de Barive

Sainte-Preuve
02350 Liesse (Aisne)
Tel. (0)3.23.22.15.15 - Fax (0)3.23.22.08.39
M. Bergman

**Category** ★★★★ **Rooms** 14 with telephone, bath or shower, WC and TV. **Price** Double 480-880F / 73,18-134,16€. **Meals** Breakfast 75F / 11,43€, served from 7:30; half board from 500F / 76,22€ (per pers.). **Restaurant** Service 12:00PM-2:00PM, 7:00PM-9:30PM; mealtime specials 185-350F / 28,20-53,36€, also à la carte. Specialties: Ravioles de crustacés servis dans leur nage; filet de saint-pierre aux truffes et aux poireaux. **Credit cards** All major. **Pets** Dogs not allowed. **Facilities** Heated swimming pool, sauna, tennis. **Nearby** Laon Cathedral, Abbey of Prémontrés, forest of Saint-Gobain, ruins of abbeys of Le Tortoir and Saint-Nicolas-aux-Bois. **Closed** Mid Dec – end Jan and Tuesday.

Surrounded by countryside in the middle of a 500-acre estate, this 17th-century château, first a hunting lodge, then a boarding house, has now been fully restored and opened as an impeccable hotel. The bedrooms are large and extremely comfortable, with thick eiderdowns and luxuriously fitted bathrooms. There is no period furniture, but some fine copies recreate something of the historic atmosphere of the château. The big breakfast room opens onto the surrounding greenery and is arranged rather like a winter garden. The lounge and dining room are still a little formal, but both rooms are comfortable, and the gourmet cuisine served in the latter certainly contributes much to the atmosphere. Hotel facilities include a large heated indoor swimming-pool, a sauna and a tennis court, so a stay here provides the perfect opportunity to get back into shape. The hospitality is friendly and attentive, and the service gracious.

***How to get there*** *(Maps 3 and 10): 18km east of Laon via D977.*

## Le Champ des Oiseaux

10000 Troyes (Aube)
20, rue Linard-Gonthier
Tel. (0)3.25.80.58.50 - Fax (0)3.25.80.98.34
Mme Boisseau

**Category** ★★★ **Rooms** 12 with telephone, bath or shower, WC and TV – 1 for disabled persons. **Price** Single and double 480-950F / 73,18-144,83€. **Meals** Breakfast 70F / 10,67€, served from 7:30. No restaurant. **Credit cards** All major. **Pets** Dogs not allowed. **Facilities** Parking (50F / 7,62€). **Nearby** In Troyes: Saint-Urbain Basilica, Saint-Pierre Cathedral and Saint-Paul Cathedral, Museum of Contemporary Art; Lake and forest of Orient; factory direct clothing stores – 18-hole Troyes-La Cordelière golf course. **Open** All year.

The only thing "new" about this new hotel is its ultra-modern amenities: The half-timbered houses that make up "The Birds' Song" are among the oldest in Troyes, dating from the 16th and 17th centuries. Renovated at the request of the new owners by the Compagnons du Devoir--an exclusive guild of élite French workers--the houses are especially admirable for their elegant proportions. Around a small medieval inner courtyard, you will find twelve bedrooms with evocative names: The *Marinot*, *Bengali* and the *Bleue Rooms* are marvels, all very comfortably appointed and furnished with taste and elegance. Only *Les Perroquets* has a somewhat less desirable location. Excellent breakfasts are served in a beautiful dining room where an open fire burns in winter; in summer, there is a delicious small garden for the breakfast service. Amiable, attentive, and hospitable, Madame Boisseau has succeeded in her wish to make *Le Chant des Oiseaux* into a hotel like a home. For meals, we suggest the gastronomic *Le Clos Juillet*; *Les Matines* and *L'Auberge de Sainte-Maure*.

***How to get there*** *(Map 10): 158km southeast of Paris via A 5 exit Troyes-Centre, then towards Centre-Ville, Cathédrale.*

## Le Clos Raymi

51200 Epernay (Marne)
3, rue Joseph-de-Venoge
Tel. (0)3.26.51.00.58 - Fax (0)3.26.51.18.98 - Mme Woda
E-mail: closraymi@wanadoo.fr

**Rooms** 7 with telephone, bath or shower, WC and satellite TV. **Price** Double 570-840F / 86,90-128,06€. **Meals** Breakfast 75F / 11,43€, served 8:00-11:00. No restaurant. **Credit cards** Visa, Eurocard and MasterCard. **Pets** Small dogs allowed (+40F / 6,10€). **Facilities** Parking. **Nearby** Wine Museum (Champagne) and Champagne tours (Moët et Chandon, Pol Roger, Mercier, de Castellane) in Epernay; Hautvillers (abbey where Dom Pérignon invented Champagne); Verzy and in the fouêt: "les Faux de Verzy"; Reims – 18-hole golf course in Doumans. **Open** All year.

The Champagne vineyards are one of the main tourist attractions of France, with Rheims and Epernay sharing the production of the festive wine. And so if you'd like to visit the cellars, taste various Champagnes, or buy them directly from the vineyard or the Champagne producer, you should not miss a new hotel called *Le Clos Raymi*. This beautiful house was built by the Chandon family of Champagne fame and has been converted into a beautiful small hotel which has conserved all the elegance and intimate atmosphere of the original house. Madame Woda has decorated it exquisitely, esentially with Art Deco furniture, beautiful Cubist paintings, and engravings by Jouve, a well-known painter of animals in the 1930s. The rooms, always graced with fresh flowers, are very cozy, with their bathrooms full of amenities. The equally well-appointed lounge is the perfect place to enjoy a glass of champagne. Enjoy the garden in summer for a delicious breakfast. High-quality and great hospitality.

*How to get there* ( *Map 10): 26km south of Reims.*

## Château d'Etoges

51270 Etoges par Montmort (Marne)
Tel. (0)3.26.59.30.08 - Fax (0)3.26.59.35.57
Mme Filliette-Neuville

**Rooms** 20 with telephone, bath or shower and WC (TV on request). **Price** Double 600-800F / 91,47-121,96€, suite 1200F / 182,94€. **Meals** Breakfast 70F / 10,67€, served 7:00-11:00; half board 530-830F / 80,80-126,53€, (per pers., 2 days min.). **Restaurant** By reservation. Service 12:00PM-2:00PM, 7:30PM-9:30PM; mealtime specials 180-340F / 27,44-51,83€. Specialties: Foie gras de canard maison; filets de rougets au champagne et jus d'airelles; délice de Reims et sa crème au ratafia. **Credit cards** All major. **Pets** Dogs allowed (+40F / 6,10€). **Facilities** Parking. **Nearby** Champagne Museum in Epernay, Abbey of Hautvillers (where Dom Perignon invented champagne) – 18-hole La Vitarderie golf course in Dormans, 18-hole Val-Secret golf course in Château-Thierry. **Open** All year.

The splendid *Château d'Etoges* dates from the 17th-century. Completely surrounded by water, it is set against a low hill beneath where springs emerge as elegant fountains. The interior of the château is equally enchanting; it has been refurbished with good taste to retain the building's character and provide modern amenities. There is a grand staircase, as well as spacious lounges with decorative panels, delightful percale tablecloths in the dining room, and superb bedrooms. Some are big and sumptuous, others more intimate, but in each there is a delightful blend of antique furniture, pretty materials, and romantic views over the moat. A warm, personal welcome at the *Château d'Etoges* evokes a way of life in a more graceful age. It is an ideal base for exploring the Champagne vineyards.

*How to get there (Map 10): 40km west of Châlons-en-Champagne via D933.*

# A l'Orée du Bois

Futeau 55120 Clermont-en-Argonne ( Meuse)
Tel. (0)3.29.88.28.41 - Fax (0)3.29.88.24.52
M. and Mme Aguesse

**Category** ★★★ **Rooms** 13 and 1 apartment with telephone, bath, WC and TV. **Price** Single and double 325-380F / 49,55-57,93€, apart. 520F / 79,27€. **Meals** Breakfast 52F / 7,92€, served 7:30-11:00; half board 440F / 67,08€ (per pers., 3 days min.). **Restaurant** Only for residents. Closed Tuesday and Sunday evening in low season. Service 12:00PM-1:30PM, 7:00PM-8:30PM; mealtime specials 120F / 18,29€ (in week), 165-365F / 25,15-55,64€, also à la carte. Specialties: Rognons de lapin aux champignons; bourgeon de sapin glacé. **Credit card** Visa. **Pets** Dogs allowed (+40F / 6,10€). **Facilities** Parking. **Nearby** Argonne Forest, Varennes-en-Argonne, Lachalade Abbey. **Closed** Jan, All Saints' Day school holidays, Sunday evening and Tuesday in low season.

With a beautiful forest at the back, the small *Orée du Bois* looks out over a beautiful, peaceful countryside. The interior decoration is pleasant and is lent character by traditional old furniture. Located in a recently built wing, the bedrooms are on the ground floor facing the lawn and all have a very beautiful view. They are large and decorated in a classically rustic style, brightened up by flowery, pastel fabrics. Seven new rooms, very colorful with antique furnishings, have been set up in a neighboring house. These are our favorites. The dining room with large bay windows has the most beautiful view. M. Aguesse turns out such regional specialties as fricassée of crayfish, while his wife, who oversees the dining room, will advise you very competently on wines.

***How to get there*** *(Map 11): 40km west of Verdun via A 4, exit Sainte-Menehould. Then take N3 towards Verdun to Islettes, then D2 on the right, towards Futeau.*

## Le Prieuré

60950 Ermenonville (Oise)
Chevet de l'Eglise
Tel. (0)3.44.54.00.44 - Fax (0)3.44.54.02.21
M. and Mme Treillou

**Category** ★★★ **Rooms** 11 with telephone, bath or shower, WC, TV and minibar. **Price** Double 450-500F / 68,60-76,22€. **Meals** Breakfast 50F / 7,62€. No restaurant. **Credit cards** All major. **Pets** Dogs allowed. **Nearby** Châalis Abbey, Ermenonville forest, Astérix Park, Eurodisney. **Closed** Feb.

Surrounded by a stunning, English-style garden, Le Prieuré is located at the foot of Ermenonville's church. Monsieur and Madame Treillou will pay a lot of attention to you here, and you will feel like you are in a comfortable, private home. Bursting with pictures, knick-knacks, and antique furniture, the ground-floor reception areas are also highlighted by a beautiful, black-and-white tiled floor. In winter, a crackling fireplace creates a friendly atmostphere. More or less large, the rooms are warm and comfortable. Some of the top-floor rooms have sloped ceilings and display beautiful beams. A few pieces of antique furniture gives them an authentic charm, and the fabrics chosen for the bed throws and curtains are in tune with their ambiance. Often small, the bathrooms are functional and well-tended. You can have a pleasant meal at *L'Hermitage*, just 100 m from the hotel. Close to Paris, this charming, little place is the perfect weekend destination.

***How to get there*** *(Map 9): 45km northeast of Paris via A1, exit Survilliers, towards Villepinte, then Ermenonville.*

## Auberge Le Fiacre

Routhiauville 80120 Quend (Somme)
Rue des Pommiers - Route de Fort-Mahon
Tel. (0)3.22.23.47.30 - Fax (0)3.22.27.19.80 - M. Masmonteil

**Category** ★★★ **Rooms** 11 with telephone, bath, WC and TV – Wheelchair access. **Price** Double 390-430F / 59,46-65,55€, apartment 460-860F / 70,13-131,11€. **Meals** Breakfast 50F / 7,62€, served 8:00-10:00; half board 390-450F / 59,46-68,60€ (per pers., 2 days min.). **Restaurant** Service 12:00PM-2:00PM, 7:00PM-9:30PM; mealtime specials 110-220F / 16,77-33,54€, also à la carte. Specialties: Agneau de pré-salé de la baie de Somme. **Credit cards** All major. **Pets** Dogs not allowed. **Facilities** Mountainbike rentals, parking. **Nearby** Beaches of Quend and Fort-Mahon (3km) – 18-hole Belle Dune golf course. **Closed** Mid Jan – mid Feb.

Standing in the midst of the Picardie countryside, this old *auberge* is located in a hamlet which is quiet day and night. The buildings, which have been very well restored, surround a charming dovecote and a beautifully tended garden. Well-known in the region for their excellent restaurant, the owners have opened eleven bedrooms, half of them downstairs on the garden. All are comfortable, quite spacious, and furnished with an attention to detail, if not to decoration. The hotel has expanded, investing in a house next door, where two two-room apartments and a similar duplex have been set up. The delicious homemade pastries and the good breakfast coffee are served in an attractive dining room; the restaurant has a beautiful old-farm decor, with a fireplace and period furniture. M. Masmonteil himself is the excellent chef and his elegant and discreet wife, a great wine connoisseur, will guide you in your choice of wines. In good weather, the owners plan to set up several tables outside as well as chaises-longues on the lawn.

*How to get there* (Map 1): 30 south of Le Touquet; in Quend-ville, take towards Fort-Mahon. Turn at the Routhiauville traffic circle.

## Hôtel Jean-de-Bruges

80135 Saint-Riquier (Somme)
18, place de l'Eglise
Tel. (0)3.22.28.30.30 - Fax (0)3.22.28.00.69 - Mme Stubbe
E-mail: jeandebruges@minitel.net

**Category** ★★★ **Rooms** 8 and 1 suite, with telephone, bath, WC, minibar and TV. – Elevator. **Price** Single and double 450-650F / 68,60-99,09€. **Meals** Breakfast 60F / 9,15€, served 7:15 (8:00 weekend) -10:00. **Restaurant** Service 12:00PM-2:00PM, 7:30PM-9:00PM. Salade; flamiche (40-90F / 6,10-13,72€). **Credit cards** All major. **Pets** Dogs not allowed. **Facilities** Parking (50F / 7,62€). **Nearby** Somme – Golf course in Abbeville, Quend and Nampont. **Closed** Jan.

A few kilometers from Abbeville, the medieval city of Saint-Riquier, not far from the Somme Bay, is home to a flamboyantly gothic abbacy, a belfry, and the brothers' hospital. Right next to the church, a Belgian couple has turned the former hostel of Pierre le Prestre, an abbot, into a charming little house, impeccably and soberly decorated. The eight rooms, which carry the names of the abbots who headed the abbey, are of medium size; some look out on the church square or on the interior courtyard. All follow a white color-scheme, with chalky stone walls, damask curtains and bedcovers, antique furniture with modern, patinated highlights, Loom furnishings, and spotless bathrooms. You enjoy your breakfast in the tea room under the glass ceiling, with much to choose from. Have your pre-dinner or after-dinner drink in the little lounge with its English sofas, clubhouse atmosphere, and regal, late-17th-century sideboard. Even if the hotel doesn't have a restaurant, cold-cut plates and keenly prepared salads are offered at noon and in the evening.

***How to get there*** *(Map 1): Via A 16 Paris-Calais, take exit 22, road for Saint-Riquier for 8km. Fot those coming from Arras, take D925.*

## Hôtel Dolce Vita

20000 Ajaccio (Corse-du-Sud)
Route des Sanguinaires
Tel. (0)4.95.52.42.42 - Fax (0)4.95.52.07.15
M. Federici

**Category** ★★★ **Rooms** 32 with telephone, bath, WC, TV and minibar. **Price** Double and triple 735-1170F / 112,05-178,37€. **Meals** Breakfast 75F / 11,43€, served 7:00-10:00; half board and full board (obligatory in Jul and Aug) 1395-1845F / 212,67-281,27€ (per 2 pers.). **Restaurant** Service 12:30PM-1:45PM, 7:30PM-9:30PM; menu 200F / 30,49€, also à la carte. Specialties: Raviolis au broccio, fricassée de langouste. **Credit cards** All major. **Pets** Dogs allowed (+70F / 10,67€). **Facilities** Swimming pool, water skiing, beach. **Nearby** Gulf of Ajaccio via the Route des Iles Sanguinaires, Les Milelli, Château of Punta, Bastelica. **Open** Easter – Nov 1.

The *Dolce Vita* is a modern hotel whose superb location compensates for the functional style of its architecture. The terraces of the *premier étage* bedrooms all overlook luxuriant vegetation. All the rooms look out on the sea and are located on two levels; the lower gives direct access to a small beach built on the rocks. The hotel is very comfortable and the bathrooms have all the usual facilities. There are flowers everywhere and it is a pleasure to stroll among the bougainvillea, oleanders and palm trees. The dining area is composed of a large interior room, which is used in winter, and a spacious terrace which overlooks the sea. The Dolce Vita's high-quality food is famous, and comes with stylish service, all of which is reflected in the prices. At night, with the swimming pool floodlit, the twinkling lights in the trees and the glimmer of lights across the bay, the scene is reminiscent of Hollywood.

***How to get there*** *( Map 36): 8km west of Ajaccio via the Route des Sanguinaires. Ajaccio-Campo dell'Oro Airport 15km away, tel. (0)4.95.21.03.64.*

## Hôtel du Centre Nautique

20169 Bonifacio (Corse-du-Sud)
Quai Nord
Tel. (0)4.95.73.02.11 - Fax (0)4.95.73.17.47

**Rooms** 10 with air-conditioning, telephone, shower, WC, TV and minibar. **Price** Double 450-1050F / 68,60-160,07€. **Meals** Breakfast 50-60F / 7,62-9,15€. **Restaurant** Service 12:15-3:00PM, 7:00PM-12:00AM. Specialties: Fish. **Credit cards** All major. **Pets** Dogs allowed. **Facilities** Parking. **Nearby** Boat trip to the sea caves, Sdragonato Cave and tour of the cliffs, Santa-Manza Gulf — 18-hole golf course in Sperone. **Open** All year.

This hotel on Bonifacio harbor lies below the upper town and looks out over the moored boats. Despite its name it is a place that gives a cordial welcome to tourists as well as to sailing enthusiasts. The high ceilings have made it possible to convert the rooms into small duplexes. On the lower level there is a small living room and on the mezzanine the bedroom and bathroom. It is more like a studio than a conventional hotel bedroom and perfect for inviting your neighbors in for cocktails. Some units have a view over the garden and over the port (they're somewhat noisier, but how marvelous to lie in bed and watch the comings and goings of the boats and the seagulls careening above them!). You can have breakfast on the terrace overlooking the sailboats and yachts. For restaurants, aside from the hotel's own, note the several addresses given for the *Hôtel Genovèse* on the next page.

***How to get there*** *(Map 36): On the port. Figari Airport 21km away, tel. (0)4.95.71.00.22*

# Hôtel Genovese

20169 Bonifacio (Corse-du-Sud)
Quartier de la Citadelle
Tel. (0)4.95.73.12.34 - Fax (0)4.95.73.09.03

**Category** ★★★ **Rooms** 14 with air-conditioning, telephone, bath, WC, TV and minibar. **Price** Double 700-1500F / 106,71-228,67€, suite 950-1700F / 144,83-259,16€. **Meals** Breakfast 70-80F / 10,67-12,20€, served 7:30-11:00. No restaurant. **Credit cards** All major. **Pets** Dogs allowed. **Facilities** Parking. **Nearby** Boat trip to sea caves, cave of Sdragonato and tour of the cliffs, gulf of Santa-Manza – 18-hole golf course in Sperone. **Open** All year.

Set out along the walls of the Bonifacio ramparts, this hotel is in an old naval building and has a beautiful view of the sea, the town, and the harbor. It is luxuriously and elegantly furnished. The rooms are set around a delightful courtyard and are decorated in pastel shades with flowered curtains. The bathrooms have comfortable amenities. Room 2 also has a balcony which overlooks the port. There is no restaurant but the ground floor has a breakfast area and a lounge where a handsome white settee blends delightfully with the stone walls. An additional asset is that the hotel is fully air conditioned. *La Caravelle* is the popular fish restaurant; *Le Voilier* and *Le Stella d'Oro* (upstairs) are favorites with the anybody who's anybody in the area. Let's also add the extraordinary *Chez Marco*, right on the water's edge on the Tonnara beach, which is known for its excellent and Pantagruelian servings of shellfish, grilled fish, and bouillabaisse.

***How to get there*** *(Map 36): In Bonifacio, turn right immediately on leaving the road to the Citadelle. Figari Airport 21km away, tel. (0)4.95.71.00.22.*

# L'Aïtone

20126 Evisa (Corse-du-Sud)
Tel. (0)4.95.26.20.04 - Fax (0)4.95.26.24.18
M. Ceccaldi

**Category** ★★ **Rooms** 32 with telephone, bath or shower, WC and satellite TV. **Price** Double 200-550F / 30,49-83,85€. **Meals** Breakfast 38F / 5,80€, served 8:00-9:30; half board and full board 250-550F / 38,11- 83,85€ (per pers, 3 days min.). **Restaurant** Service 12:00PM-2:00PM, 7:30PM-10:00PM; mealtime specials 95-160F / 14,48-24,39€, also à la carte. Specialties: Terrine de sanglier; porc aux châtaignes; omelette broccio et menthe; truites. **Credit cards** Amex, Visa. **Pets** Dogs allowed. **Facilities** Swimming pool, garage, parking. **Nearby** Waterfall and pool in the forest of Aïtone, gorges of the Spelunca, forest of Aïtone, calanques of Piana, villages of Ota and Vico, Girolata. **Closed** Dec.

The *Aïtone auberge* is 2550 feet above sea level; in driving to it, you just may meet up with a horde of half-wild pigs roaming on the road (they finish up in delicious Corsican *charcuterie*.). The building, whose modern architecture is completely lacking in charm, nevertheless enjoys a superb location, with its large swimming pool overlooking the beautiful Spelunca Valley. The rooms, large and small, are decorated rather off-handedly; yet the rooms are really comfortable and well-tended; those in the new part have a balcony each, with a beautiful view over the Gulf of Porto. The good, family-style meals are served in the dining room or on the panoramic terrace; you can enjoy a very convivial bar with a warm open fire as soon as the weather cools off. This is a good place to stay in the mountains, where you are nevertheless near the Gulf of Porto.

***How to get there*** *(Map 36): 23km east of Porto via D84. Ajaccio-Campo dell'Oro Airport 70km away.*

# Capo Rosso

20115 Piana (Corse-du-Sud) - Route des Calanques
Tel. (0)4.95.27.82.40 - Fax (0)4.95.27.80.00 - M. Camilli-Ollivier
E-mail: caporosso@wanadoo.fr

**Category** ★★★★ **Rooms** 57 with telephone, bath or shower, WC, minibar and satellite TV – Wheelchair access. **Price** Double 350-450F / 53,36-68,60€. **Meals** Breakfast 50F/ 7,62€, served 7:30-10:00; half board 450-565F / 68,60-86,13€ (per pers., obligatory in sommer). **Restaurant** Service 12:00PM-1:30PM, 7:30PM-10:00PM; mealtime specials 100-380F / 15,24-57,93€, also à la carte. Specialties: Fish, spiny lobster, corsica products. **Credit cards** All major. **Pets** Dogs not allowed. **Facilities** Swimming pool, parking. **Nearby** Calanques of Piana, boat to Girolata (dep. Porto), villages of Ota, Evisa and Vico, Lava peak, route de Ficajola. **Open** Apr 2 – Oct 14.

Built in the 1970s, the "Red Cape" is surrounded by flowers and overlooks one of Corsica's most sumptuous panoramas: the red rocks of Piana tumbling down to the sea and forming a succession of small gulfs, capes and mini-peninsulas. The hotel's modern architecture is obviously not typically Corsican, but the site is used to optimum advantage: The swimming-pool area offers a superb viewpoint from which to admire the Gulf of Porto, and every bedroom has a small terrace. Well-kept and comfortable, they have just been redecorated, bathrooms included. A whole family helps run the establishment, some going fishing to supply the restaurant; others doing the cooking or handling the reception. Extending out onto a terrace, the panoramic dining room is rather fussily decorated in pale pink, pearl grey and mother-of-pearl. Good, very copious meals are served in an atmosphere of warmth and good humor. There are many sights to see in the area, including a beautiful drive to the fine sands of Arone Beach.

***How to get there*** *(Map 36): 71km north of Ajaccio via D 81. Ajaccio Airport, on the inlet road.*

# Le Maquis

20166 Porticcio (Corse-du-Sud)
Tel. (0)4.95.25.05.55 - Fax (0)4.95.25.11.70
Mme Salini

**Category** ★★★★ **Rooms** 27 with air-conditioning, telephone, bath, WC, TV and minibar. **Price** Double 900-2700F / 137,20-411,61€, suite 1200-5400F / 182,94-823,22€. **Meals** Breakfast included served 7:00-10:30. **Restaurant** Service 12:30PM-2:00PM, 8:00PM-10:00PM; also à la carte. **Credit cards** All major. **Pets** Dogs allowed (+100F / 15,24€). **Facilities** Heated swimming pool, tennis, gym, private beach, parking. **Nearby** Gulf of Ajaccio via the Route des Iles Sanguinaires, Les Milelli, Château of la Punta, Bastelica. **Closed** Jan 4 – Feb 5.

Wonderfully located on a little inlet from the Ajaccio gulf, 2 km after Porticcio, *Le Maquis* is doubtless one of the most beautiful places in Corsica. With its pretty, protected, and accommodating fine sand beach, the refined decoration and service, the comfortable common areas, and the rooms (Choose the seaview chambers with terrace.), make this a perfect place for comfortable and restful stays. The terrace, the covered swimming pool and the tennis court complete the picture. At noon, there is a delicious buffet lunch on the terrace and in the evenings an excellent menu, changed every day, is served. What more could we want? Mme Salini has made *Le Maquis* a marvelous oasis on a coast that unfortunately has been rather spoiled. But if you do want to leave the hotel, you can explore the beautiful interior of Corsica. However, we hope that customers will be welcomed more courteously than we were when we asked for the new rates.

***How to get there*** *( Map 36): 18km southeast of Ajaccio via N196, D55 along the coast. Ajaccio-Campo dell'Oro Airport.*

# La Villa Piana

20100 Sartène (Corse-du-Sud)
Route de Propriano
Tel. (0)4.95.77.07.04 - Fax (0)4.95.73.45.65
Mme Abraini

**Category** ★★ **Rooms** 31 with telephone, bath or shower, WC – 2 for disabled persons. **Price** Single and double 250-440F / 38,11-67,08€. **Meals** Breakfast 38F / 5,80€, served 7:30-10:30. **Restaurant** Snack June – Aug. Service 12:00PM-9:00PM. Small menu. **Credit cards** All major. **Pets** Dogs not allowed. **Facilities** Swimming pool, tennis, parking. **Nearby** Museum of Prehistory in Sartène and Levie, Campomoro Scenic outlook, Filitosa, Olmeto, Sollocaro. **Open** Apr 11 – Oct 14.

Several minutes from the beaches of Propriano, the *Villa Piana* faces the very beautiful village of Sartène. It is a recent construction of ochre plaster, surrounded by Mediterranean vegetation covering the hillside. Pretty and comfortable, the bedrooms are pleasant, the baths beautiful. Some rooms have a private terrace brightened with pink oleander. Behind the hotel, a path leads up to a lovely overflow swimming pool surrounded by olive trees and lavender. Just next to it is a small stone bar which serves light meals for guests who prefer to stay by the pool rather than go out for lunch. Otherwise, there are plenty of restaurants, in both Sarthène and Propriano (note *Le Lido*, on the water.) A young, efficient staff adds a plus to the *Villa Piana*, which is recommendable for either a short visit or a longer holiday. Very near the hotel, you can enjoy good Corsican specialties at *L'Auberge Santa Barbara*.

***How to get there*** *(Map 36): Between Ajaccio and Portovecchio (about 70km). Ajaccio Airport or Figari Airport.*

# Hôtel L'Aiglon

20147 Serriera (Corse-du-Sud)
Tel. (0)4.95.26.10.65 - Fax (0)4.95.26.14.77
M. Colonna-Ceccaldi

**Category** ★★ **Rooms** 18 with telephone, bath or shower (8 with WC). **Price** Single and double 210-370F / 32,01-56,41€. **Meals** Breakfast 35F / 5,34€, served 8:00-9:30; half board and full board 200-360F / 30,49-54,88€ (per pers.). **Restaurant** Service 12:30PM-2:00PM, 8:00PM-9:30PM; mealtime specials 90-150F / 13,72-22,87€, also à la carte. Specialties: Omelette au broccio; daube de sanglier; cannellonis à la corse; cabri; fiadone. **Credit cards** Visa, Eurocard, MasterCard. **Pets** Dogs allowed. **Facilities** Parking. **Nearby** Waterfall and pool in the Forest of Aïtone, Gorges of the Spelunca, Forest of Aïtone, calanques of Piana, boat to Girolata, villages of Ota and Vico. **Open** Apr 16 – Oct 14.

The *Hôtel L'Aiglon*, built about thirty years ago out of Porto stone, is a place for those who love nature and quiet. It is set in the heart of the *maquis*. To reach the hotel, you take a winding road across hilly countryside; but it is not as isolated as this might suggest for the sea is only five kilometers away. Because it is patronized by a regular clientele, the bedrooms have not been updated. They are quite simple and the furniture is very 1950s -- a bit dated as a look, but one that will soon become a rarity. The bathrooms are behind rather thin partitions. To one side of the building there are six bedrooms, one bungalow, each enjoying a ground-floor terrace on the garden. The regular clients of *L'Aiglon* add to the peaceful atmosphere of the place, and the moderate rates are interesting if you wish to explore the interior of Corsica or want inexpensive proximity to the sea.

***How to get there*** *(Map 36): 5km north of Porto via D81; follow signs. Calvi - Sainte-Catherine Airport 80km, tel. (0)4.95.65.08.09, or 85 km from Ajaccio - Campo del Oro airport, tel. 08.02.80.28.02.*

## Hôtel La Solenzara

20145 Solenzara (Corse-du-Sud)
Tel. (0)4.95.57.42.18 - Fax (0)4.95.57.46.84
M. Lucchini

**Category** ★★ **Rooms** 25 with telephone, bath or shower, WC (18 with TV) - Rooms with Wheelchair access. **Price** Single and double 270-450F / 41,16-68,60€. **Meals** Breakfast 35F / 5,34€, served 6:45-11:00. No restaurant. **Credit cards** All major. **Pets** Dogs allowed. **Facilities** Swimming pool, parking. **Nearby** Aiguilles de Bavella, museum in Aléria, Gulf of Porto-Vecchio. **Open** All year (by reservation in low season).

You'll find this small family-run hotel at the mouth of the Solenzara River very near fine sandy beaches. Built in the 18th-century in the Genoese style by a wealthy man of the village, the hotel has conserved its original beautifully proportioned façade, its spacious, high ceilings and the 19th-century frescos in Room 11, on the street side. Located at the far side of the village, the *Solenzara* is in a limited-speed zone, which keeps traffic noise to a minimum. An elegant lobby furnished with several antiques gives access to the bedrooms. Often large (some are ideal for families), the rooms are simple, their Provençal-style drapes nicely contrasting with the white stucco walls. Our favorites overlook the sea: As they're no more expensive, it's best to reserve them in advance. Other smaller rooms are located in a neighboring house; less expensive, they nevertheless can be recommended. You can enjoy a flowery terrace around a charming overflow swimming pool near a pleasant bar/tea room, and cheerful, informal service.

***How to get there*** *(Map 36): 38km north of Porto Vecchio. Figari Airport, tel. 04.95.71.00.22.*

## Hôtel de la Corniche

San-Martino-di-Lota
20200 Bastia (Haute-Corse)
Tel. (0)4.95.31.40.98 - Fax (0)4.95.32.37.69
Mme Anziani

**Category** ★★ **Rooms** 19 with telephone, bath or shower and WC (10 with TV). **Price** Double 320-490F / 48,78-74,70€. **Meals** Breakfast 40-45F / 6,10-6,86€, served 7:30-10:00; half board and full board 320-410F / 48,78-62,50€ (per pers.). **Restaurant** Closed Sunday evening and Monday, Oct – end Mar. Service 12:00PM-2:00PM, 7:30PM-9:30PM; mealtime specials, also à la carte. Specialties: Pageot du golfe en étuvée de fenouil confit olives vertes; pastizzu du cap Corse et son coulis d'orange caramélisé. **Credit cards** All major. **Pets** Dogs not allowed. **Facilities** Swimming pool. **Nearby** Romanesque Cathedral of La Canonica and San Parteo Church, villages of Cap Corse from Bastia to Saint-Florent. **Open** Feb 1 – Dec 20.

This hotel at San Martino-di-Lota lies along a winding road ten minutes drive from Bastia. It has been owned by the same family since 1935 and has incomparable views of the sea. The first thing you will notice is the beautiful terrace and its splendid plane trees. Meals are served here in beautiful weather and on clear days you can see as far as the Italian coast. The cooking, from a young and talented chef, is itself worth the trip. You will dine on the best local products prepared with a level of finesse and creativity that is sometimes missing from more reputable establishments. The bedrooms are excellent for their price range; they are tastefully and comfortably decorated with classic wooden furniture and attractive bathrooms, and all look out to the sea. An excellent place, perfectly calm, where you will find the warmest and friendliest hospitality and service.

***How to get there*** *(Map 36): 6km north of Bastia via D80, then D131 at Pietranera. Bastia-Poretta Airport, tel. (0)4.95.54.54.54.*

# Hôtel Balanéa

20260 Calvi (Haute-Corse)
6, rue Clemenceau
Tel. (0)4.95.65.94.94 - Fax (0)4.95.65.29.71
M. Ceccaldi

**Category** ★★★ **Rooms** 37 with air-conditioning, telephone, bath, WC and TV (31 with minibar).
**Price** Double 320-1610F / 48,78-245,44€. **Meals** Breakfast 60F/ 9,16€, served 7:30-10:30. No
restaurant. **Credit cards** All major. **Pets** Dogs allowed (+100F / 15,24€). **Nearby** Citadel of Calvi,
tour of the villages of Balagne (Calenzana, Zilia, Montemaggiore, Sant'Antonino, church of the Trinity
in Aregno, convent of Corbara), Scandola national park – 9-hole Lumio golf course. **Open** All year.

Located on the harbor in Calvi, the *Balanéa* is the most pleasant hotel in the
center of town. The modern, standard rooms are very comfortable,
spacious, with all the amenities. There main attraction comes from their
marvelous views of the fort and citadel (some have a terrace or balcony). All
the rooms are air-conditioned with double-paned windows, making for
pleasant sleeping in the hot summer party season. Those that look out on the
road are smaller and darker, and only have a fan. Likewise, we advise you to
have breakfast in your room, the dining room lacking similar appeal. The
*Balanéa* is the only hotel open in Calvi during the winter, and is one of the
good destinations along the Corsican coastline. We recommend dinner on the
marvelous terrace of *La Signoria* and the hip piano-bar of *Chez Tao*, where
you'll have an unforgettable good time.

***How to get there*** *( Map 36): on the port in Calvi. Calvi-Sainte-Catherine Airport
7km, tel. (0)4.95.65.08.09*

## Marina d'Argentella

20260 Calvi (Haute-Corse)
L'Argentella
Tel. (0)4.95.65.25.08 - Fax (0)4.95.65.25.12
M. Grisoli

**Rooms** 25 with bath and WC. **Price** Double with half board 350-450F / 53,36-68,60€ (per pers.), reduced rate for children. **Meals** Breakfast incl. **Restaurant** Service 12:30PM-14:30, 8:00PM-10:00PM; mealtime specials 130F / 19,82€, also à la carte. **Credit cards** Visa, Eurocard and MasterCard. **Pets** Dogs allowed. **Facilities** Parking. **Nearby** Citadel of Calvi, tour of the villages of Ballagne (Calenzana, Zilia, Montemaggiore, Sant 'Antonino, Church of the Trinity in Aregno, convent of Corbara), Scandola regional park – 9-hole Lumio golf course. **Open** End May – Oct 3.

The Argentella is a very special place, not only because it is so beautifully located on the beach of Crovani Bay, but also because of Pierre and Dorine's friendly hospitality. The bedrooms, which are in small bungalows in a eucalyptus grove, are simple but charming, and all have comfortable bathrooms. You can have lunch *à la carte*, but the dinner menu offers family-style cooking. Swimming, windsurfing, picnics and boat excursions are offered by the hotel. At seven in the evening, you can join in the traditional volleyball game and then enjoy a drink as you admire the wonderful sunset. The Argentella is ideal for a family vacation; note the special slimming week in June.

***How to get there*** *(Map 36): 22km south of Calvi towards Porto by coast road. Calvi-Sainte-Catherine Airport 25km away, tel. (0)4.95.65.08.09.*

## Auberge Relais de la Signoria

20260 Calvi (Haute-Corse)
Route de la forêt de Bonifato
Tel. (0)4.95.65.93.00 - Fax (0)4.95.65.38.77
MM. Ceccaldi

**Category** ★★★ **Rooms** 20 with telephone, bath, WC, TV and minibar. **Price** Single and double 700-1400F / 106,71-213,43€; suite 1200-1600F / 182,94-243,92€. **Meals** Breakfast 100F / 15,24€, served 8:00-11:00. **Restaurant** Service 12:00PM-1:30PM (weekend), 7:30PM-10:30PM (at lunchtime in Jul and Aug grill until 2:00PM in front of the swimming pool); mealtime specials 250F / 38,11€, also à la carte. Specialties: Gâteau de magret fumé; saint-pierre en chausson et tapenade verte; macaronnade de brousse. **Credit cards** Amex, Visa. **Pets** Dogs allowed. **Facilities** Swimming pool, tennis, hammam, parking. **Nearby** Citadel of Calvi, tour of the villages of Balagne (Calenzana, Zilia, Montemaggiore, Sant'Antonino, Church of the Trinity in Aregno, convent of Corbara), Scandola national park – 9-hole Lumio golf course. **Open** End Mar – Oct 15.

This very pleasant hotel, not far from one of the island's most charming ports, is housed in a beautiful old house on a large estate planted with palm trees and eucalyptus. The owners have hospitably furbished the place for the guests while all the while keeping its original splendor. The rooms in the main building are the most pleasant and comfortable ones, but you will not feel deprived if you have one in the annex. Dine by candlelight under the canopy of palm trees on the terrace, and there you may lavish in the coolness of the evening to your heart's content. This beautiful hotel is perfectly quiet even in the middle of August.

***How to get there*** *(Map 36): 5km from Calvi on the airport road. Calvi-Sainte-Catherine Airport 2km, tel. (0)4.95.65.08.09.*

# Le Vieux Moulin

20238 Centuri-Port (Haute-Corse)
Le Port
Tel. (0)4.95.35.60.15 - Fax (0)4.95.35.60.24
M. Alessandrini

**Rooms** 14 with telephone, bath or shower, WC and TV. **Price** Single and double 300-350F / 45,73-53,36€; half board 385F / 58,69€ (per pers., obligatory in summer). **Meals** Breakfast 34F / 5,34€, served 8:30-11:00. **Restaurant** Service 12:00PM-3:00PM, 7:30PM-11:00PM; mealtime specials 145-310F / 22,11-47,26€, also à la carte. Specialties: Fish, shellfish, bouillabaisse. **Credit cards** All major. **Pets** Dogs allowed. **Facilities** Parking. **Nearby** Le Cap Corse from Bastia to Saint-Florent (Canari, Nonza, Saint-Florent…). **Open** Feb 16 – Nov 14.

The minuscule port of Centuri is an absolute must, a model of its kind that unfortunately is rarely found today on the continent. Local fishermen bring in lobsters, anchovy, crabs, and an abundance of marvelous products which are served for very reasonable prices at the *Vieux Moulin* and other village restaurants. Fronting on a huge terrace beneath feathery old tamarisks, this beautiful house is located slightly above the port. Built in the 19th-century by an uncle of the owner who had made a fortune in America, it has retained much of its original character and charm, especially in the lobby and the upstairs salon. The bedrooms in the house are the warmest in winter (Numbers 5 and 6 have a very beautiful view), while the rooms in the modern annex enjoy the use of a shady terrace, which is lovely in summer; all are simply furnished but well-kept and pleasant. The garden is a delightful place for a drink or a meal surrounded by Mediterranean fragrances and the panorama of the fishing boats coming and going.

***How to get there*** *(Map 36): 50km north of Bastia. Bastia-Poretta Airport, tel. (0)4 95 54 54 54.*

# Hôtel Castel Brando

20222 Erbalunga (Haute-Corse)
Tel. (0)4.95.30.10.30 - Fax (0)4.95.33.98.18
M. and Mme Piéri

**Category** ★ ★ ★ **Rooms** 15 and 6 apartments with air-conditioning, telephone, bath, WC and TV, kitchenette and safe – Wheelchair access. **Price** Double 380-630F / 57,93-96,04€, apart. 530-880F / 80,80-134,16€ (per 3-4 pers). **Meals** Breakfast 35F / 5,34€, served 8:00-11:00. No restaurant. **Credit cards** Amex, Visa. **Pets** Dogs allowed. **Facilities** Swimming pool, parking. **Nearby** Bastia, romanesque Cathedral of La Canonica and San Parteo Church, villages of Cap Corse from Bastia to Saint-Florent. **Open** Mar 14 – Nov 14.

Joëlle and Jean-Paul Piéri, who were born in this picturesque fishing village, have restored a beautiful and charming house here, lending it comfort and personality. You can live here at your own pace and the apartments with kitchenette are especially recommendable for long stays. The shady park has a swimming pool, but if you prefer the sea, the pebble beaches in Erbalunga or Piétracorba are nearby. Fairly new to the hotel business, M. and Mme Piéri have quickly become real professionals. They are very enthusiastic and will give you a warm welcome - as well as tips for discovering and enjoying the real Corsica. Erbalunga itself is classed as a preserved site and has inspired numerous painters, and the *Castel Brando*, in our opinion, has become one of the most charming, if not the most charming hotel in Corsica. For dinner, the owners will give you their special addresses. We recommend *La Citadelle* and *Le Romantique* in Bastia; and in Erbalunga, overlooking the sea, *Le Pirate*.

***How to get there*** *(Map 36): 9km north of Bastia. Bastia-Poretta Airport tel. (0)4.95.54.54.54.*

## Grand hôtel Mare e Monti

20225 Feliceto (Haute-Corse)
Tel. (0)4.95.63.02.00-02 - Fax (0)4.95.63.02.01
M. Renucci

**Category** ★★ **Rooms** 18 with telephone, (16 with bath or shower and WC). **Price** Double 310-350F / 47,26-53,36€; apart. (4 pers.) 630F / 96,04€. **Meals** Breakfast 40F / 6,10€, served 8:00-10:00; half board 266-313 F / 40,40-47,78€ (per pers., 3 days min.). **Restaurant** Not managed by the hotel. **Credit cards** All major. **Pets** Dogs allowed. **Facilities** Parking. **Nearby** Citadel of Calvi, tour of the villages of Ballagne (Calenzana, Zilia, Montemaggiore, Sant 'Antonino, Church of the Trinity in Aregno, convent of Corbara). **Open** Apr – Sept 30.

This lovely house, which lies between the sea and the mountains, was built in 1870. Behind the hotel there are steep rocky cliffs, and in the distance one can see the sea behind Ile Rousse. The lobby with its painted ceiling, the delightful Louis-Philippe lounge, the lovely Corsican lounge, and the large stairway have great character and charm. The bedrooms are appointed more simply but their amenities have been renovated. For the moment, ask for those with beautiful high ceilings on the *second étage*; as well as those on the *troisième étage*, which have just been renovated. M. Renucci, whose family has lived here for generations, gives a cordial welcome to all his guests and the traditional, delicious cuisine provided by his chef is an attraction for people who want to know a more authentic Corsica than that found in its seaside resorts.

*How to get there (Map 36): 26km northeast of Calvi via N197 to beyond Alcajola, then right on D13 to Feliceto via Santa Reparata. Calvi-Sainte-Catherine Airport, Tel. (0)4.95.65.08.09.*

# La Bergerie

Monticello 20220 Ile-Rousse (Haute-Corse)
Route de Monticello
Tel. (0)4.95.60.01.28 - Fax (0)4.95.60.06.36
M. Caumer

**Category** ★★ **Rooms** 19 (2 air-conditioning) with telephone, bath or shower and WC. **Price** Single and double 260-420F / 39,64-64,03€. **Meals** Breakfast 35F / 5,34€, served 8:00-10:00; half board 330-420F / 50,31-64,03€ (per pers., 5 days min.). **Restaurant** Service 12:00PM and 7:30PM; also à la carte. Specialties: Brochettes de liche; araignées farcies; omelette aux oursins; sardines farcies **Credit cards** Visa, Eurocard and MasterCard. **Pets** Dogs allowed. **Facilities** Swimming pool, parking. **Nearby** Citadel of Calvi, tour of the villages of Ballagne (Calenzana, Zilia, Montemaggiore, Sant'Antonino, church of the Trinity in Aregno, convent of Corbara). **Open** Mar 15 – 31 Oct (closed Monday in low season).

*La Bergerie* is an old sheep farm converted into a small hotel 800 meters from Ile Rousse and the beach. Located in several buildings, the bedrooms have rough white walls and are plainly decorated. Each however has a small terrace. We recommend the rooms with a view over the sea, particularly as they're no more expensive. On the flip side, be sure to avoid Rooms 1 to 5, which are dark and bleak. In good weather, you can enjoy the lovely quiet swimming pool surrounded by flowers. The owner is an enthusiastic fisherman and delights his guests with dishes he creates using his catch of the day. These might include such refined dishes as sea-urchin omelette and sea-anemone fritters, and several Moroccan specialties. With the first rays of sunshine, meals are served outdoors on the shady terrace; otherwise, the dining room is in the small rustic shepherd's house. The atmosphere is relaxed and friendly.

***How to get there*** *(Map 36): 24km northeast of Calvi via N197 to L'Ile Rousse. Calvi-Sainte-Catherine Airport, tel. (0)4.95.65.08.09.*

## La Casa Musicale

20220 Pigna (Haute-Corse)
Tel. (0)4.95.61.77.31-81 - Fax (0)4.95.61.74.28
M. Jérome Casalonga
E-mail: casa.musicale.pigna@wanadoo.fr

**Rooms** 7 with telephone, bath or shower and WC. **Price** Single and double 195-380F / 29,73-57,93€; 3 pers. 300-400F / 45,73-60,98€. **Meals** Breakfast 30F / 4,57€, served 8:00-11:00. **Restaurant** Service 8:00PM-10:30PM; also à la carte. Regional cooking. **Credit card** Visa. **Pets** Dogs allowed. **Nearby** Citadel of Calvi, tour of the villages of Balagne (Calenzana, Zilia, Montemaggiore, Sant'Antonino, church of the Triniy in Aregno, convent of Corbara). **Closed** End Dec – end Feb; Monday in low season.

Patiently renovated, the ravishing hillside village of Pigna invites you to wind through its cobblestone lanes and discover a few artisans' ateliers, a small panoramic square, and… *La Casa Musicale*, overlooking a magnificent countryside of trees and sea. The hotel was originally a venue for concerts and art courses; success was such that the owners decided to set dining tables out on the terrace and in the old olive- and grape-press for those who wished to stay for lunch or dinner. The traditional cooking was good, the atmosphere delightful, lots of guests would have enjoyed spending the night and, not wanting to disappoint them, Monsieur Casalonga soon opened several bedrooms. They are very simple but the magic of the place, the extraordinary view over the sea and hills, the colorful bedspreads, the wall frescos all make the rooms very pleasant. Two have a terrace (one of which is reached by a ladder.) Last but not least, the concerts still are given, once or twice a week depending on the season.

***How to get there*** *(Map 36): 8km southwest of Ile-Rousse. Calvi-Sainte-Catherine Airport, tel. (0)4.95.65.08.09.*

233

# U Sant' Agnellu

20247 Rogliano (Haute-Corse)
Tel. (0)4.95.35.40.59 - Fax (0)4.95.35.40.59
M. and Mme Albertini

**Rooms** 9 with bath and WC. **Price** Double 280-370F / 42,69-56,41€. **Meals** Breakfast 30F / 4,57€; half board 250-300F / 38,11-45,73€ (per pers.). **Restaurant** Service 12:00PM-2:30PM, 7:30PM-11:00PM; mealtime specials 90F / 13,72€, also à la carte. Specialties: Brandade; boulettes au broccio; cannelonis; tourte Sant'Agnellu; langoustes; cabri; rôti de veau. **Credit cards** All major. **Pets** Dogs allowed. **Nearby** Riding, Chemin des Douaniers, villages of Cap Corse from Bastia to Saint-Florent. **Open** Easter – Oct.

Young M. and Mme Albertini set up a restaurant in this old town hall in 1984 and three years later converted it into a hotel. They deserve encouragement for their delicious cuisine at unbeatable prices, as well as for the charming bedrooms. With white stucco walls and solid wooden furniture, the accommodations are simple but very comfortable and the tiled bathrooms are impeccable. Five bedrooms look out onto the sea and the others onto the mountains. In good weather, meals are served on the panoramic terrace: the spacious indoor dining room with its semicircle of large windows also has beautiful views. Visitors who enjoy old buildings will find much to interest them in this picturesque 12th-century village, which has two churches, a convent and the ruins of a château as well as various Genoese towers.

***How to get there*** *(Map 36): 42km north of Bastia via D80 towards Maci-w naggio (free bus from port of Macinaggio to the hotel). Bastia Airport, tel. (0)4.95.54.54.54.*

## Castan Relais

25000 Besançon (Doubs)
6, square Castan
Tel. (0)3.81.65.02.00 - Fax (0)3.81.83.01.02 - M. Dintroz

**Rooms** 10 with telephone, bath, WC, satellite TV and minibar (5 with air-conditioning) — 1 for disabled persons. **Price** Double 580-980F / 88,42-149,40€. **Meals** Breakfast 60F / 9,15€, served 7:30-10:30. No restaurant. **Credit cards** Amex, Visa. **Pets** Dogs allowed. **Facilities** Parking. **Nearby** Citadel and Fine Art Museum in Besançon, Salines Royales of Arc and Senans, Museum of Courbet in Ornans — 18-hole Chevillotte golf course. **Closed** 1 weekend in Dec and 3 weeks in Aug.

Standing on a promontory far above a bend in the Doubs River, the old citadel of Besançon boasts a number of town houses, including that occupied by the *Relais Castan*, which has been in the same family for four centuries. Well-located in the historic quarter near the Porte Noire (a 2nd-century Roman arcade) and Saint Jean Cathedral, this beautiful 17th- and 18th-century house has been converted into a small luxury hotel. The eight bedrooms are named after a theme: the Guillaume Tell, Victor Hugo, and Pasteur rooms pay homage to the local Franche-Comté culture; the Trianon and the Régence honor Louis XIV, who made the Franche-Comté part of France; and if you want to succumb to the pleasure of a Roman bath, ask for the Olympe or the Pompéi room. Many thoughtful details add to the pleasure of the *Relais*: a basket of fresh fruit in your room, and a delicious breakfast which you can enjoy in the trophy room. With all its positive qualities, the *Relais* does lack a touch of warmth. For restaurants, try *Mungo Park*, an excellent (one Michelin star) restaurant of the city and the region; *Le Vauban*, with a superb view over the citadel; and *Le Chaland*, on a boat.

***How to get there*** *(Map 20): In the center of town, follow signs for Citadelle and Conseil Régional.*

## Hôtel Taillard

25470 Goumois (Doubs)
Tel. (0)3.81.44.20.75 - Fax (0)3.81.44.26.15
M. Taillard
Web: www.hoteltaillard.com

**Category** ★★ **Rooms** 22 with telephone, bath or shower and WC (6 with minibar). **Price** Single 275-520F / 41,92-79,27€, apart. 650-780F / 99,09-118,91€. **Meals** Breakfast 55F / 8,38€, served 8:00-9:30; half board 350-600F / 53,36-91,47€ (per pers., 3 days min.). **Restaurant** Service 12:00PM-1:30PM, 7:00PM-9:30PM; mealtime specials 135-360F / 20,58-54,88€, also à la carte. Specialties: Escalope de foie gras poêlée au miel de pays et griottines de Fougerolles. **Credit cards** Visa, Eurocard and MasterCard. **Pets** Dogs allowed (40F / 6,10€). **Facilities** Parking. **Nearby** Circuit from Maîche (D437) to Gière and Indevillers, Slopes of Goumois via the gorges of the Doubs to the Echelles de la Mort, art and clock making museums in Besançon – 18-hole Prunevelle golf course. **Open** Apr – mid Nov.

Four generations have lived in this keenly hospitable mansion, located in the Jura countryside on a valley. All is peace and quiet here, and you can still hear the tinkling of cowbells. The Doubs river still makes fishermen and hikers happy. Most of the rooms have a balcony that overlooks the mountains, but the similarity stops there, because the newly-renovated rooms are of a markedly superior quality. So we don't just recommend Room 16, but all of the Résidence apartments, which are large, cheerful, and truly well-done. Take notice of the fine cuisine, whose imaginative selections keeps that local, homegrown flavor and whose "light" menu will delight the greatest gastronome. The service is praiseworthy as well, and the panoramic dining room with its view of the loaming Swiss slopes on the horizon is definitively delightful. All of this makes the *Taillard*, which keeps getting better and better, a perfect place for your stays.

***How to get there*** *(Map 20): 53km south of Montbéliard via D437 towards Maîche, at Maison Rouge D437b to Goumois (near the church).*

## Hôtel Le Lac

25160 Malbuisson (Doubs)
"Au Village"
Tel. (0)3.81.69.34.80 - Fax (0)3.81.69.35.44
M. Chauvin

**Category** ★★★ **Rooms** 54 with telephone, bath or shower, WC, TV, 2 with minibar – Elevator. **Price** Single and double 250-380F / 38,11-57,93€, suite 700-900F / 106,71-137,20€. **Meals** Breakfast 50F / 7,62€, served 7:30-9:45; half board and full board 230-520F / 35,06-79,27€ (per pers. 3 days min.). **Restaurant** Service 12:00PM-2:00PM, 7:00PM-9:00PM; mealtime specials 105-255F / 16,01-38,87€, also à la carte. Specialties: Fish, morilles. **Credit cards** Diners, Visa. **Pets** Dogs allowed (+35F / 5,34€). **Facilities** Parking. **Nearby** Château of Joux, Saline Royale of Arc and Senans; Le Saut du Doubs, Museum of Courbet in Ornans, Besançon. **Closed** Mid Nov – mid Dec except weekends.

Lying between a lake and a forest, this imposing turn-of-the-century building has retained its traditional *Vieille France* atmosphere. The cuisine and the reception are very much a family affair, with everyone lending a helping hand. Beginning with Grandfather Chauvin, who makes his rounds to see if everyone is happy in the dining room. Then there are the two chefs who man the stoves, their wives overseeing the service in the elegant, classic dining room. Highlighting the products of the region and fish from the lake, the chef duo turn out excellent meals. In the same building, the *Restaurant du Fromage* offers a 35-Franc chef's special in the beautiful wood-paneled decor of a Swiss chalet, while in the tea room, you can enjoy ice cream from the famous Paris *glacier,* Berthillon. The comfortable, cozy bedrooms do not all enjoy a view of Saint Point Lake which, if you wish, you should request. It's also possible to have a room with a balcony.

***How to get there*** *(Map 20): 75km south of Besançon.*

# Hôtel de France

39220 Les Rousses (Jura)
Tel. (0)3.84.60.01.45 - Fax (0)3.84.60.04.63
Mme Petit

**Category ★★★ Rooms** 31 with telephone, bath or shower and TV. **Price** Double 300-580F / 45,73-88,42€. **Meals** Breakfast 50F / 7,62€; half board and full board 355-595F / 54,12-90,71€ (per pers., 2 days min.). **Restaurant** Service 12:15PM-3:00PM, 7:15PM-9:30PM, mealtime specials 155-455F / 23,63-69,36€. Specialties: Terrine de volaille de Bresse aux truffes et au foie gras; glacé au marc du Jura. **Credit cards** All major. **Pets** Dogs not allowed. **Nearby** Ski: 200m from the ski lift – 18-hole Rochat golf course, riding, hiking, lake. **Closed** End Nov – mid Dec and Jun 4 – 23.

The Petit family has been running this hotel for more than thirty years. It is a large chalet whose balconies overflow with flowers in summer. Once you're inside the front door, you will love the *Hôtel de France*; the large lounge with its wood panelling and beautiful exposed ceiling beams beckons you to take a seat by the large stone fireplace. On the left, the dining room is bright and welcoming. The chef, Jean-Pierre Durcrot, who was Roger Petit's apprentice and trained with famous Paris chefs, puts all his considerable talent in the service of the hotel's clientele. Meals are served on the large shady terrace in summer. All the bedrooms are simply and comfortably decorated and have a view of the forest. You can enjoy total relaxation here after a vigorous day of cross-country or downhill skiing. Mme Petit is very friendly and hospitable.

***How to get there*** *(Map 20): 85km southwest of Pontarlier via D72 to Chaffrois; D471 to Champagnole and N5 via Morez.*

## Hostellerie Les Pléiades

77630 Barbizon (Seine-et-Marne)
21, Grande-Rue
Tel. (0)1.60.66.40.25 - Fax (0)1.60.66.41.68
Sophie Vermersch

**Category** ★★★ **Rooms** 23 with telephone, bath (1 with shower), WC and satellite TV. **Price** Double 320-550F / 48,78-83,85€. **Meals** Breakfast 45F / 6,86€; half board 390-490F / 59,46-74,70€. **Restaurant** Service 12:30-2:30PM, 7:30PM-9:30PM; mealtime specials 195F / 29,73€, menu-dégustation 290F / 44,21€, also à la carte. Specialties: Local produce. **Credit cards** All major. **Pets** Dogs allowed. **Facilities** Parking. **Nearby** Museum of Théodore Rousseau, Museum of Auverge Ganne; Milly-la-forêt; forest and palace of Fontainebleau – 18-hole Fontainebleau golf course. **Open** All year.

Located on the main road of the charming village of Barbizon, the *Hostellerie* lodged many important figures in politics, arts, and literature between the two wars. The traces of Millet, Theodore Rousseau, Ziem, and landscape artists are still here. The classically, soberly decorated dining room opens onto a pleasant, shady patio in summer. Here you will eat inventive fine food and enjoy a warm and cozy lounge/bar corner. The least expensive rooms are those that are awaiting renovation (avoid the bathrooms with clanking toilets). *La Villa* next door, a 2-star hotel, offers more modern rooms that are too impersonal to our taste. Sophie Vermersch, who has just taken over management of the hotel from her father, informs us of upcoming and sweeping renovations. We await the results so we can be more positive about this beautifully located place not more than an hour from Paris.

***How to get there*** *(Map 9): 57km southeast of Paris via A6 to Fontainebleau exit, then N37 and D64 to Barbizon.*

## Château des Bondons

77260 La Ferté-sous-Jouarre (Seine-et-Marne)
47-49, rue des Bondons
Tel. (0)1.60.22.00.98 - Fax (0)1.60.22.97.01
M. Busconi

**Category** ★★★ **Rooms** 14 with telephone, bath, WC, satellite TV and minibar. **Price** Double 500-550F / 76,22-83,85€, suite 800-1000F / 121,96-152,45€, apart. 550-800F / 83,85-121,96€. **Meals** Breakfast 60F / 9,15€. No restaurant. **Credit cards** All major. **Pets** Dogs allowed (+50F / 7,62€). **Facilities** Parking. **Nearby** Jouarre, Eurodisneyland. **Open** All year.

Set in a vast park, this small 19th-century château was sinking into oblivion before the Busconis thoroughly renovated and resuscitated it. The reception rooms on the ground floor look out onto the surrounding gardens. The entrance hall has an elaborate marble mosaic floor and the same geometrical patterns can be seen in the ivory inlay of the panelling. In the dining-room there is delightful panelling inlaid with small landscape pictures. You will find a wealth of 18th-century-style furniture – modern copies, but elegant. The lounge is vast and bright, but the tiled floor could do with a few rugs. A beautiful wooden staircase leads up to the bedrooms which are extremely warm and cozy, with thick carpets and lovely flowered fabrics. The bedrooms are individually decorated and have luxuriously equipped bathrooms. Rooms 4 and 8 are particularly noteworthy (albeit more expensive). You will enjoy an friendly welcome and excellent, hearty breakfasts. *F* is the best restaurant in town. Or choose *L'Auberge du Petit Morin* in Mourette.

**How to get there** *( Map 10): 65km east of Paris via A4, Ferté-sous-Jouarre exit, then N3; in the village Châlons-sur-Marne heading towards Montménard.*

## Au Moulin

77940 Flagy (Seine-et-Marne)
2, rue du Moulin
Tel. (0)1.60.96.67.89 - Fax (0)1.60.96.69.51
M. and Mme Scheidecker

**Category** ★★★ **Rooms** 10 with telephone, bath and WC. **Price** Double 350-520F / 53,36-79,27€.
**Meals** Breakfast 55F / 8,38€, served 7:45-11:00; half board 385-455F / 58,69-69,36€ (per 2 pers.,
4 days min.). **Restaurant** Service 12:15-14:15, 19:15-21:15; mealtime specials 160-250F / 24,39-
38,11€, also à la carte. **Credit cards** All major. **Pets** Dogs allowed. **Facilities** Parking. **Nearby** Palace
and forest of Fontainebleau, Moret-sur-Loing – 18-hole La Forteresse golf course. **Closed** Sep 12 –
24 and Dec 19 – Jan 21, Sunday evenings and Monday (except Easter, Monday evening and Tuesday).

After many transformations, this former, 13th-century flour mill, still in
operation up until the 40s, has refound its look of yesteryear. Beneath the
stucco façade the ancient masonry was uncovered in excellent condition, as
well as the original half-timbering, the cob walls, the ground-floor stonework
and the beautiful vaulted gable. The hotel accommodates guests in ten fully
equipped and carefully decorated bedrooms. The dining room looks out onto
the river, and there is also a terrace and a garden. Dinner is served by
candlelight in the evening and log fires are lit in winter. Just one hour from
Paris, you will find a courteous and hearty welcome here, in a place where calm,
comfort, and the countryside all come together.

***How to get there*** *(Map 9): 88km southeast of Paris via A6, Fontainebleau exit,*
*then N6 for 18km; at the traffic lights turn right onto D403 and immediately on*
*your left D120.*

## Hostellerie Le Gonfalon

77910 Germigny-L'Evêque (Seine-et-Marne)
2, rue de L'Eglise
Tel. (0)1.64.33.16.05 - Fax (0)1.64.33.25.59 - Mme Colubi

**Rooms** 10 with telephone, bath, WC, TV and minibar. **Price** Single and double 280-380F / 42,69-57,93€. **Meals** Breakfast 55F / 8,38€, served 7:30-10:30. **Restaurant** Service 12:00PM-1:30PM, 7:30PM-9:00PM; mealtime specials 198F / 29,93€ from Thursday to Friday and 260-350F / 39,64-53,36€ also à la carte. **Credit cards** All major. **Pets** Dogs allowed. **Facilities** Bicycle rental (80F / 12,19€), parking. **Nearby** Forest of Montceaux. **Closed** Jan, Sunday evening and Monday.

In the heart of Brie country and right on the Marne River, an unremarkable village *auberge* in 1977 was transformed into a beautiful country inn by Mme Line Colubi, already a reputable *Cordon Bleu* chef. Behind the plain façade of the Gonfalon, you discover a cool terrace out of a summer's dream, shaded by enormous century-old linden trees and surrounded by luxuriant vegetation overlooking the banks of the Marne. *Bons vivants* come here especially for Mme Colubi's delicately sauced specialties, which are served either on the delicious terrace or in the elegant Louis XIII dining room with its warm woodwork and beautiful log fires in winter. There are ten comfortable, very quiet bedrooms upstairs; ask for those with a large private terrace-conservatory overlooking the trees and the river (especially Number 2). For a more youthful, brighter decoration, request the mansard rooms on the *deuxième étage*. The delicious breakfasts, with hot homemade brioches and fruit juice, are served either in your room, the dining room, or on the terrace in good weather. The friendly waitresses are discreet and professional. Less than an hour from Paris, this is a beautiful place for your gastronomic weekends.

***How to get there*** *(Map 9): 60km east of Paris via A4 to Meaux, then N3 to Trilport and D97.*

## Hostellerie Aux Vieux Remparts

77160 Provins (Seine-et-Marne)
3, rue Couverte - Ville Haute
Tel. (0)1.64.08.94.00 - Fax (0)1.60.67.77.22
M. Roy

**Category** ★★★ **Rooms** 25 with telephone, bath or shower, WC, TV and minibar. **Price** Double 395-750F / 60,22-114,34€. **Meals** Breakfast 55F / 8,38€, served 7:00-11:00; half board 450-650F / 68,60-99,09€ (per pers.). **Restaurant** Service 12:00PM-2:30PM, 7:30PM-9:30PM; mealtime specials 170-360F / 25,92-54,88€, also à la carte. Specialties: Petite salade de langoustines tièdes gaspacho de tomates; lasagnes de homard breton et ragoût de coquillages; pomme de ris de veau piquée de foie gras braisée au beurre mousseux; confiture de vieux garçon. **Credit cards** All major. **Pets** Dogs allowed (+60F / 9,15€). **Facilities** Parking. **Nearby** Ramparts, tower of César, Church of Saint-Quiriace in Provins, falconery show, knight's tournament, Church of Saint-Loup-de-Naud – 18-hole Fontenaille golf course. **Open** All year.

L ocated in the most beautiful part of medieval Provins, the *Hostellerie Aux Vieux Remparts* has twenty-five bedrooms in an adjoining modern building. Successfully blending in with the splendid high city, this building does not clash too much. In the comfortable, quiet bedrooms, the modern decor includes quilted bedcovers, carpets, and many white-lead pieces of furniture. In the restaurant, you will have the choice between a highly reputed gastronomic menu or the bistrot fare, which is served in a beautiful half-timbered 16th-century house, or on the terrace in summer. The decoration is in strict keeping with the traditional character of the village and tables are also set up in a very charming small courtyard in good weather. The *Hostellerie* is very lovely and extremely professional, and you will be warmly welcomed.

***How to get there*** *(Map 10): 86km southeast of Paris via A4, then D231 to Provins.*

## L'Auberge du Château

78720 Dampierre (Yvelines)
1, Grande-Rue
Tel. (0)1.30.47.56.56 - Fax (0)1.30.47.51.75
Sylvie and Christophe Blot

**Category** ★★ **Rooms** 14 with telephone, bath, WC, TV. **Price** Single and double 350-600F / 53,36-91,47€. **Meals** Breakfast 50F / 7,62€, served 8:00-10:30. **Restaurant** Service 12:00PM-2:30PM, 7:30PM-8:30PM; mealtime specials 190-300F / 28,97-45,73€, also à la carte. Specialties: inventive food; menu changes every 3 weeks. **Credit cards** All major. **Pets** Dogs allowed (+60F / 9,15€). **Nearby** Châteaux of Dampierre, Breteuil, Versailles. **Closed** Some days, at the end of Dec, of Feb, and of Aug.

Next to the Rambouillet forest, almost directly across from the superb, 13th-century Dampierre château, this is the inn you've dreamed of for your stays near Paris. Sylvie and Christophe Blot took up the inn a little more than a year ago, and their restaurant already enjoys a well-deserved gourmet reputation. A prize student of Marc Meneau and of *Troisgros*, Christophe works wonders in the kitchen, and helps Sylvie in the dining room for service whose quality and speed is out of this world. The same goes for the decor, with the pleasant mix of rustic, antique furniture with beautiful, orangish yellow upholstery, against of white walls and large, checker-style windows that overlook the terrace, the road, and the château's stately walls. The rooms are equally well-done, and you will love their fresh, country-style simplicity. Most overlook the main road, but they have double-paned windows, and night traffic is quite light. (Lovers of perfect silence should choose Rooms 7, 8, 10, or 11.) All are pleasant and worth recommending. A particularly warm welcome.

***How to get there*** *(Map 9): 30km from Paris via A 13 toward Dreux, then A12. At Rambouillet take N 10 to Trappes, Mesnil-Saint-Denis and Dampierre.*

## Domaine du Verbois

78640 Neauphle-le-Château (Yvelines)
38, avenue de la République
Tel. (0)1.34.89.11.78 - Fax (0)1.34.89.57.33
M. and Mme Boone

**Category ★★★ Rooms** 20 with telephone, bath, WC, satellite TV, 10 with minibar – 1 for disabled persons. **Price** Single and double 590-690F / 89,94-105,19€, suite 860F / 131,11€. **Meals** Breakfast 68F / 10,36€, served 7:15-1:00PM. **Restaurant** Closed Sunday evening. Service 12:00PM-2:00PM, 7:30PM-9:30PM; mealtime specials 155F / 23,63€, also à la carte. Specialties: Poularde Houdan; barbue au jus de viande; Neauphleen. **Credit cards** All major. **Pets** Dogs allowed (+60F / 9,15€). **Facilities** Parking and garage (60F / 9,15€). **Nearby** Visit of the Grand-Marnier cellars, Versailles, Giverny, Auvers – 18-hole Isabella golf course, 18-hole Saint-Nom golf course. **Closed** Aug 14 – 26 and Dec 21 – 29.

Right next to Versailles, this hotel enjoys an exceptionally sweeping view that stretches out beyond a three-acre estate. The series of salons, whose dimensions have been conserved, maintains the feeling of large 19th-century homes. In good weather, meals are served on the large patio that overlooks the park and the countryside. The rooms, named after Greek goddesses, are all comfortable and very prettily accommodated. The most roomy are on the upper floor, but all are agreeable and bright. You will doze off peacefully while flipping through the owner's collection of art magazines from the 50s and 60s. With the many conferences always held in the private lounges, the hotel always treats its guests attentively. A charming place whose luxurious comfort remains a good value. You will be welcomed by a competent staff, under the direction of Monsieur Boone, who loves this house as if it had been in his family forever.

***How to get there*** *(Map 9): 29km west of Paris, via A13 to Dreux, A12 to Saint-Quentin-en-Yvelines, N12 Neauphles-le Château exit and Verbois (2km).*

## Hôtel de France

91670 Angerville (Essonne)
2, place du Marché
Tel. (0)1.69.95.11.30 - Fax (0)1.64.95.39.59
Mme Tarrene

**Rooms** 17 with telephone, bath or shower, WC and TV – Elevator. **Price** Single and double 440-540F / 67,08-82,32€. **Meals** Breakfast 48F / 7,39€; half board 430F / 65,55€ (per pers.). **Restaurant** Service 12:00PM-2:00PM, 7:30PM-9:30PM; mealtime specials 150F / 22,87€. **Credit cards** Amex, Visa. **Pets** Dogs allowed. **Facilities** Parking. **Nearby** Juine Valley and Château of Méréville, Chalouette Valley and Chalou-Moulineu Valley, Château of Farcheville, Dourdan (Place of Marché-aux-grains). **Open** All year.

There is a big family of *Hôtels de France* with their opulent façades occupying the main square of provincial towns. In Angerville, the comparison stops there as the interior decoration of this hotel is much more tasteful than that generally found in this kind of establishment. The hotel in fact is made up of five small, very old houses, joined together around a leafy courtyard with several tables in summer. Charmingly decorated and insulated from street noise by double-glazing, the bedrooms are all different, with a small 18th-century wardrobe in one, a Louis-Philippe chest-of-drawers in another, a scattering of engravings, and famous-name fabrics, all creating an intimate, tasteful atmosphere. On the ground floor, the savory fare of Madame Tarrene is served in an elegant dining room. Depending on the hour, you can enjoy breakfast and drinks in a charming room with a sofa and armchairs, a stone fireplace, and a warm log fire in winter. A hospitable place that owes a lot to the kindness of its owners.

***How to get there*** *(Map 9): 40km south of Paris via N20 to Etampes, 15km south of Etampes.*

## Auberge de l'Ile du Saussay

91760 Itteville (Essonne)
Route de Ballancourt
Tel. (0)1.64.93.20.12 - Fax (0)1.64.93.39.88 - M. Lebrun
Web: www.auberge-saussay.com

**Category** ★★★ **Rooms** 7, 2 apartments (4 pers.), 13 suites with telephone, bath or shower, WC, TV, minibar and safe. **Price** Single and double 370-470F / 56,41-71,65€, apart. 900F / 137,20€. **Meals** Breakfast 45F / 6,86€, served 7:00-10:30. **Restaurant** Closed Monday. Service 12:00PM-2:30PM, 7:00PM-10:00PM; mealtime specials 125-225F / 19,06-34,30€, also à la carte. **Credit cards** All major. **Pets** Dogs allowed. **Facilities** Parking. **Nearby** Dourdan, Arpajon and Renarde Valley, château of Farcheville. **Closed** Aug and Monday.

Monsieur Lebrun was immediately captivated by the beautiful setting of the *Auberge de l'Ile de Saussay*. Although the Auberge is very contemporary in design, the surrounding lakes and trees make it perfectly charming. Three different categories of accommodations are proposed, but all enjoy modern amenities, tasteful decoration, and large bay windows opening onto a terrace with a view of the lake or, in the back, trees and a small inlet. You have a choice of bedrooms, suites with a small living room and bedroom on the mezzanine, or apartments with two bedrooms and a living room. The overall effect is lovely. The entire inn is lovely, restful, and the dinners are excellent. You will enjoy your meal in front of the lake, shimmering with the relfection of the great trees. A true pleasure for the eye as well as the palate, which makes *L'Ile du Saussay* an excellent place to stay.

***How to get there*** *(Map 9): 40km south of Paris via N20 to Etampes; then, after Arpajon, towards La Fertais-Alais.*

247

# Hôtel de la Cité

11000 Carcassonne (Aude)
Tel. (0)4.68.71.98.71 - Fax (0)4.68.71.50.15
M. Jacques Hamburger

**Category** ★★★ **Rooms** 61 with air-conditioning, telephone, bath or shower, WC, satellite TV, videorecorder – Elevator; 1 for disabled persons. **Price** Double 1450-2050F / 221,05-312,52€, suite 2300-3200F / 350,63-487,84€. **Meals** Breakfast 130F / 19,82€, served 7:00-10:30. **Restaurant** Service 12:00PM-2:30PM, 7:00PM-10:00PM; mealtime specials 120-450F / 18,29-68,60€, also à la carte. **Credit cards** All major. **Pets** Dogs allowed. **Facilities** Swimming pool. **Facilities** Parking (90F / 13,72€). **Nearby** La Cité, Church of Saint-Vincent and Church of Saint-Nazaire in Carcassonne, Château of Pennautier – 18-hole Auriac golf course in Carcassonne. **Closed** Dec – beg Jan.

After considerable refurbishing, the *Dame Carcas* hotel has recently changed into the *Hôtel de la Cité*, part of the Orient-Express group. The newly-created group has become the palace that Caracassonne was missing. The hotel's standing has gone up, but the prices have shot up as well, and the former regulars might not be able to follow suit. The rooms display two different styles. Some of the more classic rooms have kept their cream panelling and their Louis XVI furniture; other newly redone rooms boast a highly-accomplished decor with contemporary revisions of medieval furnishing (stately woods, cast iron, elegant fabrics). Take notice of the view of the plain beyond the ramparts, the boxwood gardens, and the restrained atmosphere of the hallways and reception rooms. You may choose between the reputed restaurant and chic bistrot for dinner. Either way, gourmet dining is in your future.

*How to get there* ( *Map 31*): The hotel is inside the walls.

## Château de Cavanac

11570 Cavanac (Aude)
Tel. (0)4.68.79.61.04 - Fax (0)4.68.79.79.67
M. and Mme Gobin

**Category** ★★★ **Rooms** 15 with telephone, bath or shower, WC, safe and TV – Elevator, 1 for disabled persons. **Price** Single and double 350-525F / 53,36-80,04€. **Meals** Breakfast (buffet) 45F / 6,86€ . **Restaurant** Service 8:00PM-10:00PM; mealtime specials 198F / 29,93€ (wine incl.), also à la carte. Specialties: Foie gras maison; baron d'agneau au four-bois; fromages de pays-l'huile et au miel. **Credit card** Visa. **Pets** Dogs not allowed. **Facilities** Swimming pool, tennis, sauna, fitness center, parking. **Nearby** La Cité, Church of Saint-Vincent and Church of Saint-Nazaire in Carcassonne, Château of Pennautier – 9-hole Auriac golf course in Carcassonne. **Closed** Mid Jan – mid Feb.

A winegrowing family's château for generations, this splendid 17th-century edifice has now been converted into a magnificent hotel by its young owner. The bedrooms are huge, with a scattering of antique furniture and beautiful fabrics to conserve their original charm; most rooms overlook the vineyard or the surrounding countryside. They are equipped with gleaming, modern bathrooms. Installed in the former stables, the immense dining room, with its fireplace, antique copper objects and a superb butcher's block, creates a lovely, inviting atmosphere in which to enjoy elaborate regional specialties and wines from the property. Intimate and charming, the breakfast room with its pedestal tables still looks like an old kitchen (no room service). On your way to the tennis court or the swimming pool, don't miss a visit to the wine cellars. A beautiful place to stay, just five minutes from the historic city of Carcasonne.

*How to get there (Map 31): 7km south of Carcassonne. From Toulouse Carcassonne-ouest exit; depuis Narbonne, Carcassonne-est exit, towards hospital "hôpital", Saint-Hilaire and Cavanac road.*

## Clos des Souquets

11200 Fabrezan (Aude)
Tel. (0)4.68.43.52.61 - Fax (0)4.68.43.56.76
M. Julien

**Rooms** 4 and 1 studio with bath, WC and TV on request. **Price** Double 280-395F / 42,69-60,22€, studio 480F / 73,18€. **Meals** Breakfast 45F / 6,86€; half board 330-395F / 50,31-60,22€ (per pers.). **Restaurant** Closed Sunday evening. Service 12:15-14:15, 7:30PM-9:30PM; mealtime specials 100-185F / 15,24-28,20€, also à la carte. Specialties: Fish and regional cooking. **Credit card** Visa. **Pets** Dogs allowed. **Facilities** Swimming pool, bicycle and parking. **Nearby** Saint-Just Cathedral in Narbonne, mountain of la Clape, African reserve of Sigean, abbey of Fontfroide, Lagrasse, Corbières Wine Route, Carcassonne – 9-hole Auriac golf course in Carcassonne. **Open** Apr 1 – Nov 1.

Nestling in the heart of the tranquil village of Fabrezan, this is a small *auberge* unlike any other. It is composed of a group of buildings centered around the restaurant area, which opens out onto a patio and a swimming pool. You will find two bedrooms on the ground floor, giving onto a courtyard with olive trees; a large, all-white studio, reminiscent of a Greek house, which is located upstairs in a converted barn; two other rooms open out onto their own small, shaded terraces. These two terraces then give out onto a second swimming pool, reserved for the guests of those rooms alone. Monsieur Julien's inventive cuisine makes abundant use of fish and shellfish, a delicious plus adding to the feeling of relaxation created by his and Madame Julien's warm hospitality. This is a place you won't want to leave.

*How to get there ( Map 31): 25km of Carcassonnne and Narbonne. On A 61 take exit Lezignan-Corbières, dir. Fabrezan. In Fabrezan, dir. Lagrasse.*

## Hostellerie du Grand Duc

11140 Gincla (Aude)
2, route de Boucheville
Tel. (0)4.68.20.55.02 - Fax (0)4.68.20.61.22
M. and Mme Bruchet

**Category** ★★ **Rooms** 12 with telephone, bath or shower, WC, hairdryer, TV and safe. **Price** Single and double 270-360F / 41,16-54,88€. **Meals** Breakfast 42F / 6,40€, served 8:00-11:00; half board 330-350F / 50,31-53,36€ (per pers., 3 days min.). **Restaurant** Closed Wednesday lunchtime except Jul and Aug. Service 12:15-2:00PM, 7:30PM-9:00PM; also à la carte. Specialties: Baignades de sépiole au Fitou; cailles au muscat; faux-filet au foie gras et aux griottes; duo de lotte et saumon sur fondue de poireaux; gratin de fruits. **Credit cards** Visa, Eurocard and MasterCard. **Pets** Dogs allowed. **Facilities** Parking. **Nearby** Forest of Fanges, Saint-Paul-de-Fenouillet, Belvianes, Saint-Paul-de-Fenouillet, gorges of Galamus. **Open** Apr – Nov 11.

This immense, old manor house is in the little village of Gincla, in this Cathar country that has seen so many changes. Well-restored by its young and friendly owners, the *Hostellerie* now claims charm at still reasonable prices. You will find warm hospitality and ten very clean rooms which go from very traditional (with leafy-patterned wallpaper) to more modern looks. Three new rooms are in the newly-opened annex, and renovations works will soon be in the offing. The restaurant displays a rustic decor, with bleached walls, exposed stone, and joisted ceilings to enjoy local and inventive dining. The little lounge and bar are pleasant and inviting. In summer, breakfasts and candlelight dinners can be taken in the garden, next to a stone reflecting pool.

***How to get there*** *(Map 31): 63km northwest of Perpignan via D117 to Lapradelle, then D22 to Gincla.*

## La Buissonnière

Hameau de Foussargues - 30700 Aigaliers (Gard)
Tel. (0)4.66.03.01.71 - Fax (0)4.66.03.19.21
M. Robberts and Mme Küchler
E-mail: la.buissonnière@wanadoo.fr

**Rooms** 6 and 2 apartments (2-3 pers.) with kitchen, telephone, bath or shower, WC, minibar and TV on request. **Price** Double 500-674F / 76,22-102,10€, apart. 525-900F / 80,04-137,20€. **Meals** Breakfast incl., served 8:30-10:00. **Credit cards** Visa, Eurocard and MasterCard. **Pets** Dogs not allowed. **Facilities** Swimming pool and parking. **Nearby** Le Duché, Church of Saint-Etienne and Saint-Théodorit in Uzès; pont du Gard; Nîmes; Avignon – 9-hole golf course in Uzès, 18-hole glof course (20km). **Open** All year (by reservation in winter).

A few kilometers from Uzès, this old, rugged stone house has been restored with a deep respect for authenticity always in mind, without ever forgetting comfort and fine decoration. The overall effect is a great success. The bedrooms are spacious, some with a fireplace and others with a mezzanine. The apartments have a small kitchen. Mediterranean decoration lends a personal touch to each room, but all have a small terrace where breakfast is served, unless you prefer to dine with others in the cool of the courtyard. Lavender, pink oleander, and olive trees all create a lovely decor in the garden and an inviting place to relax.

***How to get there*** *(Map 32): 7km from Uzès, towards Arles; in 6km towards Aigaliers, go 800m, turn right at the intersection, then left immediately, and follow signs.*

## Hôtel Les Arcades

30220 Aigues-Mortes (Gard)
23, bd Gambetta
Tel. (0)4.66.53.81.13 - Fax (0)4.66.53.75.46
E-mail: info@les-arcades.fr - Web: www.les-arcades.fr

**Rooms** 9 with air-conditioning, telephone, bath, WC and TV. **Price** Double 500-650F / 76,22-99,09€.
**Meals** Breakfast incl. **Restaurant** Closed Monday and Tuesday lunchtime in low season. Menus 135-250F / 20,58-38,11€, also à la carte. Specialties: Gardiane de taureau à l'ancienne; huîtres chaudes; filet de taureau grillé; croustillant aux fruits. **Credit cards** All major. **Pets** Small dogs allowed. **Nearby** The Camargue, Arles, Saintes-Maries-de-la-Mer (gypsies' pilgrimage May 24 – 25), Tarascon, Nîmes, Montpellier. **Closed** Mar 1 – 15 and Nov 15 – 30.

We loved this 16th-century house set in a quiet street in the old town. Inside, everything is neat and charming. A lovely aged and patinated paint effect, in colors ranging from lime green to brown, enhances the corridors and the bedrooms, where curtains, bedspreads and antique furniture are in perfect harmony. The bedrooms are vast, with high, elaborate ceilings and tall mullioned windows, and fully equipped bathrooms provide all the modern comforts. Breakfast and dinner – which are excellent – are served in a pleasant dining room with an ancient terra-cotta tiled floor. It opens on one side into a little garden, and on the other into an arcade where a few tables are set up. A warm, family atmosphere prevails.

***How to get there*** (*Map 32*): *48km west of Arles towards Saintes-Maries-de-la-Mer, then D58.*

# Hôtel Les Templiers

30220 Aigues-Mortes (Gard)
23, rue de la République
Tel. (0)4.66.53.66.56 - Fax (0)4.66.53.69.61
M. and Mme Alary

**Category** ★★★ **Rooms** 11 with air-conditioning, telephone, bath or shower, WC and satellite TV –
Wheelchair access. **Price** Double 450-800F / 68,60-121,96€, suite 600-960F / 91,47-146,35€.
**Meals** Breakfast 55F / 8,38€, served from 8:30. **Restaurant** Service 8:30PM-10:00PM, à la carte.
**Credit cards** All major. **Pets** Dogs allowed (50F / 7,62€). **Facilities** Garage. **Nearby** La Camargue,
Arles, Les Sainte-Marie-de-la-Mer (gypsies' pilgrimage May 24 – 25), Tarascon, Nîmes, Montpellier.
**Closed** End Oct – beg Mar (except New Year's Day).

The owners have made an elegant hotel in the center of Aigues-Mortes out
of what was once a dilapidated 17th-century merchants' house. Natives of
Nîmes, they are in love with the region, the city, the hotel, and their work -
which is a very recent discovery for them - and they are anxious to share their
enthusiasm in every way with their guests. After their tasteful restoration of the
house, the couple searched the region for Provençal as well as 50s furniture
(like the leather club chairs in the bar), which lends each bedroom a personal
touch, as do the family portraits on the walls. Some rooms look out onto the
street but are nevertheless very quiet except on holidays: Aigues-Mortes is a
pedestrian town. We liked other rooms for their view onto the interior
courtyard and a cool fountain. A former garage now houses the new
restaurant, with its chic bistrot look, where you can taste simple, good food like
leg of lamb, beef ribs, or filet of mullet in olive oil.

***How to get there*** *(Map 32): 48km west of Arles, towards Saintes-Maries-de-la-
Mer, then D58.*

## Demeures du Ranquet

Tornac 30140 Anduze (Gard)
Tel. (0)4.66.77.51.63 - Fax (0)4.66.77.55.62
M. and Mme Majourel
E-mail: ranquet@mnet.fr

**Rooms** 10 (some with air-conditioning), telephone, bath, WC, TV and minibar – Wheelchair access.
**Price** Single and double 600-900F / 97,57-137,20€. **Meals** Breakfast 80F / 12,20€, served from
7:30; half board 620-720F / 91,47-109,76€ (per pers., 3 days min.). **Restaurant** Service 12:00PM-
1:30PM, 7:30PM-9:30PM; mealtime specials 200-380F / 30,49-57,93€, also à la carte. Specialties:
Daurade rose en croûte de sel et fenouil braisé-l'huile d'olive; épaule d'agneau au four gratin de
pommes de terre-l'ancienne; beignets d'aubergines sucrées avec glace au miel. **Credit cards** Diners,
Visa. **Pets** Dogs allowed. **Facilities** Swimming pool, golf practice green, cooking lessons, parking.
**Nearby** Prafance, Bamboo Grove, Générargues, Luziers, Mas-Soubeyran (Desert Museum), Trabuc
Cave, Saint-Jean-du-Gard. **Open** Mar 11 – Nov 10.

W elcoming celebrity guests hasn't gone to the heads of this charming
couple. The glitterati who have appreciated their genuine hospitality keep
coming with a faithfulness that still surprises the owners. And yet, if you are
swept away by the little houses spread out under the trees, as well as by their
delicious names (Pistachio, Vanilla, and Licorice) and harmonious decor, you
will let yourself be charmed by the informal and original ambiance. The menu
is full of variety, swarming with ideas. Wine lovers will also be pleased. Overall,
there is a skilled mix of qualities tthat comes from both the love these people
have for their difficult profession and their deep, open interest in such things as
painting and gardening. One last thing: No matter what, do not miss the
breakfasts!

***How to get there*** *( Map 32 ): 47km northwest of Nîmes, towards Alès; 6km south
of Anduze on D982, on the road to Sainte-Hippolyte-du-Fort.*

## Hostellerie Le Castellas

30210 Collias (Gard)
Grand' Rue
Tel. (0)4.66.22.88.88 - Fax (0)4.66.22.84.28
M. and Mme Aparis

**Category** ★★★ **Rooms** 15 and 2 suites with air-conditioning, telephone, bath or shower, WC, TV and minibar. **Price** Double 650-800F / 99,09-121,96€, suite 1000F / 152,45€. **Meals** Breakfast 80F / 12,2€, served 7:30-11:00; half board 650-850F / 99,09-129,58€. **Restaurant** Service 12:00PM-2:00PM, 7:00PM-9:15PM; mealtime specials 178-360F / 26,84-54,88€, also à la carte. Specialties: Foie gras poêlé et gâteau de pommes de terre à la truffe; suprême de pigeon rôti-la provençale, champignons et jus de ses abats. **Credit cards** All major. **Pets** Dogs allowed (+50F / 7,62€). **Facilities** Swimming pool, parking. **Nearby** Pont du Gard, Uzès, Nîmes – 9-hole golf course in Uzès. **Closed** Jan 7 – Mar 9.

In a little street in the center of Collias, two venerable 17th-century dwellings house the *Hostellerie Le Castellas*. Making admirable use of the arrangement of the houses, Madame Aparis has succeeded in transforming the enclosed courtyard into an oasis of greenery and flowers, hiding a small swimming pool farther down, with space for four or five chaise-longues. A favorite haunt of artists and sculptors, the second house offers bedrooms with outstanding interior decoration, some with fabulous bathrooms (One even enjoys the use of a terrace-solarium on the roof with a bathtub in the center!). More classic, the bedrooms in the main house are also lovely and have all the amenities. Excellent dinners, refined and inventive, are served on the terrace in summer, in the shade of large parasols or an arbor. Friendly and very attentive reception. A great place to stay.

***How to get there*** *( Map 33 ): 26km northeast of Nîmes via A9, Remoulins exit; at Remoulins D981 then D112 to Collias.*

## La Vieille Fontaine

30630 Cornillon (Gard)
Tel. (0)4.66.82.20.56 - Fax (0)4.66.82.33.64
M. Audibert

**Category** ★★★ **Rooms** 8 (4 with air-conditioning) with bath, WC, TV and minibar. **Price** Double 550-850F / 83,85-129,58€. **Meals** Breakfast 55F / 8,38€, served 8:00-10:00; half board 550-700F / 83,85-106,71€ (per pers., 3 night min.). **Restaurant** Service 12:00PM-1:30PM, 7:30PM-9:30PM; mealtime specials from 195F, also à la carte. Specialties: Moules farçies-la Diable, soupe au pistou in season; gratiné de langoustines; civet de porcelet. **Credit cards** Amex, Visa. **Pets** Dogs allowed (+50F / 7,62€). **Facilities** Swimming pool. **Nearby** Avignon; Orange; Uzès; pont du Gard; musée d'Art moderne de Bagnols-sur-Cèze; village of Roque-sur-Cèze; abbey church in Goudargues; gorges of Cèze and Ardèche; well of Orgnac; Anduze bamboo grove. **Closed** Jan and Feb.

Restaurant owners for more than twenty years, M. and Mme Audibert have discovered a new calling as hotel keepers. Within the walls of the former medieval castle of Cornillon, they have integrated a very modern structure with eight bedrooms decorated by Mme Audibert. There are two bedrooms per floor. Upstairs, the original small medieval apertures have been kept, providing lovely cool air in the summer. Your climb up to the last floor is rewarded with the view from pleasant balconies, which look out over the château walls and the valley. To reach the swimming pool, you must climb up a terraced garden which is not advisable for people who have difficulty walking. Those who do stroll through the beautiful, carefully arranged garden, however, do not regret it!

***How to get there*** *(Map 33): 45km northwest of Avignon via A9, exit Tavel to Bagnols-sur-Cèze; then D980 towards Barjac. On A7, take Bollène exit.*

## Hôtel Imperator Concorde

30900 Nîmes (Gard)
Quai de la Fontaine
Tel. (0)4.66.21.90.30 - Fax (0)4.66.67.70.25
M. Creac'h

**Category** ★★★★ **Rooms** 63 with air-conditioning, telephone, bath or shower, WC, TV, minibar – Elevator. **Price** Single and double 680-850F / 103,67-129,58€, suite 1900F / 289,65€. **Meals** Breakfast 80F / 12,20€, served 7:00-11:00. **Restaurant** Service 12:30PM-1:45PM, 7:30PM-9:45PM; mealtime specials and also à la carte. **Credit cards** All major. **Pets** Dogs allowed. **Nearby** Arènes, Maison Carrée, art museum and Carré d'Art in Nîmes, Pont du Gard, Château of Villevieille in Sommiéres, Chapel of Saint-Julien-de-Salinelles – 18-hole Haut-de-Nîmes golf course. **Open** All year.

Well-located in the town center very near the beautiful Jardin de la Fontaine gardens, the *Hôtel Imperator Concorde* is an institution in Nîmes: It is here that the most famous toreros and bullfight aficionados stay during the *féria*. The hotel, which has undergone renovation, has lost some of its sparkle, but the bedrooms, especially those on the *troisième étage*, are more spacious and more comfortable. They are very carefully decorated, with a fine mix of 19th-century furniture and beautiful reproductions. The fabrics and color schemes go well with the style of each room. Take a room on the garden side, even if the air-conditioning insulates the other rooms from the noise of the quay. The pleasantly decorated bar and restaurant overlook the walled garden behind the hotel. Meals are served either on the modern veranda or the large shady terrace. The cuisine is inventive and subtly seasoned, and the set menu at lunch offers a large number of specialities. The staff is very courteous.

***How to get there*** *(Map 32): In the town center, between the Jardin de la Fontaine and the Maison Carrée.*

## Royal Hôtel

30000 Nîmes (Gard)
3, boulevard Alphonse-Daudet
Tel. (0)4.66.58.28.27 - Fax (0)4.66.58.28.28
Mmes Riera and Maurel

**Category** ★★★ **Rooms** 23 with telephone, bath or shower, WC and TV. **Price** Single and double 250-480F / 38,11-73,18€. **Meals** Breakfast 40F / 6,10€, served 7:00AM-12:00PM. **Restaurant** *La Bodeguita*. Service 12:00PM-3:00PM, 7:30PM-11:30PM; mealtime specials and à la carte. Specialties: Spanish cooking. **Credit cards** Amex, Visa, Eurocard and MasterCard. **Pets** Dogs allowed (+40F / 6,09€). **Nearby** Maison Carrée, art museum in Nîmes, Pont du Gard, Château of Villevieille in Sommiéres, Chapel of Saint-Julien-de-Salinelles – 18-hole Haut-de-Nîmes golf course. **Open** All year.

The pretty Assas square, renovated by Martial Raysse, is right next to the Maison Carree and the quai de la Fontaine. This is where you will find this little hotel often visited by artists and creators, who appreciate its relaxed decor and ambiance. The rooms are always outfitted in an elegant style, scaled-down and very chic. Their 1950s furniture in wood or wrought, plays against the white walls and fabrics, while the great blades of a ceiling fan lightly move the air. The back rooms are more monastic, but quieter, especially in summer, when the hotel's restaurant, *La Godeguita*, sets up a few tables on the square. You will eat Spanish specialities, and the tapas bar stays open late. Jazz and Flamenco concerts happen on Thursday nights in a young and friendly ambiance. But national holidays bring a bit of craziness to the hotel and the whole town itself. A very charming place at reasonable prices.

*How to get there (Map 32): In the town center.*

## Auberge du Pont Romain

30250 Sommières (Gard)
2, rue Emile-Jamais
Tel. (0)4.66.80.00.58 - Fax (0)4.66.80.31.52 - Famille Michel

**Category** ★★★ **Rooms** 19 with telephone, bath or shower and WC — Elevator. **Price** Single and double 300-480F / 45,73-73,18€. **Meals** Breakfast 60F / 9,15€, served 7:45-10:00; half board 365-450F / 55,64-68,60€. **Restaurant** Service 12:00PM-1:30PM, 8:00PM-9:30PM; mealtime specials 125F / 19,06€ (weekdays) 180-250F / 27,44-38,11€ (children 98F / 15,01€), also à la carte. Specialties: Petit gris des garrigues au roquefort. **Credit cards** All major. **Pets** Dogs allowed. **Facilities** Swimming pool, parking. **Nearby** Château de Villevieille, Chapel of Saint-Julien-de-Salinelles, Church of Notre-Dame-des-Pommiers in Beaucaire, Pont du Gard, Nîmes — 18-hole Nîmes-campagne golf course. **Closed** Jan 15 — Mar 15.

The street-side façade of the *Auberge du Pont Romain* really needs a facelift to brighten up a building that was a carpet factory in the 19th-century, then a laundry, then, until 1968, a distillery. But as soon as you walk through the porch you enter a different world. The garden is a saving grace, full of trees and flowers that cheer up the old factory. It is a pleasant setting for a terrace and a swimming pool, and leads down to the Vidourle River. Is it the vastness of the bedrooms that might prompt memories of dormitories? Those that overlook the garden are decorated in a rustic and outdated manner. Those who like the modern look might prefer the *Provençales* but should most often be pleased with a view of the village. The ground-floor lounges and restaurant have kept a lot of their character. You will eat hefty portions of traditional cuisine, crowned with excellent pastries (notably, chocolate treats). A most warm welcome. The only hotel in France graced with a factory chimney.

***How to get there*** *( Map 32 ): 28 km southwest of Nimes on the D 40. Or on the A 9 off of the Lunel exit.*

## Hostellerie du Seigneur

30126 Tavel (Gard)
Place du Seigneur
Tel. (0)4.66.50.04.26
Mme Bodo

**Rooms** 7 with basin. **Price** Double 185F / 28,20€. **Meals** Breakfast 35F / 5,34€, served 8:00-9:30; half board 240F / 36,59€. **Restaurant** Closed evening Oct – Mar. Service 12:15-2:00PM, 7:15PM-8:30PM; mealtime specials 98-145F / 15,08-22,11€. Specialties: Cuisse de canard au vin de pays; langue de porcelet au poivre vert; charlotte maison. **Credit cards** Visa, Eurocard and MasterCard. **Pets** Dogs allowed. **Nearby** Avignon; Villeneuve-lez-Avignon; Lubéron. **Open** Mid Jan – mid Nov (closed Thursday).

This is an excellent, friendly hostelry, located off the main roads in the small village of Tavel, which has given its name to one of the heady, beautifully colored rosés of the Côtes du Rhône vineyards. The *Hostellerie du Seigneur* was installed more than thirty years ago in the former town hall of the village across from a little square at the bottom of the road, which lends it a special charm. Dating from the 18th-century, the hostelry has cool, tastefully appointed rooms and the beautiful stone of the stairway bears witness to the generations who have passed through here. M. Bodo is mainly known for his good regional cooking, but you are also invited to stay in one of the seven, antique-furnished rooms. One important point however -- the bathrooms and toilets are in the hall and not in the rooms, lending an ambinance of houses from days gone by. A simple, hospitable place to stay, with some beautiful and genuine touches.

**How to get there** *(Map 32): 12km north of Avignon. On A9, Roquemaure exit, towards Tavel.*

## Hôtel Marie-d'Agoult

30700 Uzès (Gard)
Château d'Arpaillargues
Tel. (0)4.66.22.14.48 - Fax (0)4.66.22.56.10 - M. and Mme Savry
Web: www.lcm.fr/savry

**Category** ★★★ **Rooms** 28 (23 with air-conditioning) with telephone, bath, WC, TV and minibar. **Price** Single and double 400-850F / 60,98-129,58€, suite 900-1150F / 137,20-175,32€. **Meals** Breakfast 65F / 9,91€, served 7:30-10:30; half board 460-810F / 70,13-123,48€ (per pers.). **Restaurant** Service 12:30-2:00PM, 7:30PM-9:30PM; mealtime specials 145-230F / 22,11-35,06€, also à la carte. Specialties: Filets de rougets au basilic. **Credit cards** All major. **Pets** Dogs allowed (+60F / 9,15€). **Facilities** Swimming pool, tennis, parking. **Nearby** Le Duché, churches of Saint-Etienne and Saint-Théodorit in Uzès, Pont du Gard, Nîmes, Avignon – 9-hole golf course in Uzès, 18-hole golf course 20km away. **Open** Apr 1 – Nov 1.

A bit away from Uzès, this hotel is in the beautiful 18th-century Château d'Arpaillargues, once the home of Marie de Flavigny, Franz Liszt's companion. The bedrooms are comfortably furnished and tastefully decorated. Eleven ground-floor bedrooms have a terrace that opens out to the garden, the other rooms are on the upper floors of the magnanerie. A small duplex in the annex enjoys a covered loggia. Elegance and professional service are also among the star qualities of this hotel. The extremely high standards of everything here make up for the somewhat formal atmosphere that prevails. A pleasant bar area, lunch by the swimming-pool, and breakfast and dinner in the garden in summer make a stay here a delightful prospect. Add to all this a light and refined fare, and you will understand why the *Marie-d'Agoult* might make a most pleasant place to stay.

***How to get there*** *(Map 33): 40km west of Avignon via N100 to Remoulins (on A9, Remoulins exit), then D981 to Uzès and D982 (westward) to Arpaillargues (4km).*

## Le Mas d'Oléandre

Saint-Médiers - 30700 Uzès (Gard)
Tel. (0)4.66.22.63.43 - Fax (0)4.66.22.63.43
Famille Vandekerckhove-Desmet
E-Mail: oleandre@provence-sud.com

**Rooms** 3, 2 apartments and 1 studio, with bath or shower and WC. **Price** Double 350F / 53,36€, apart. 500F / 76,22€ (per 2 pers.) 810 F / 123,48 € (per 4-5 pers.). **Meals** Breakfast 45F / 6,87 €, served 9:00-10:00. No restaurant. **Credit cards** Not accepted. **Pets** Dogs not allowed. **Facilities** Swimming pool, parking. **Nearby** Le Duché, churches of Saint-Etienne and Saint-Théodorit in Uzès, Pont du Gard, Nîmes, Avignon – 9-hole golf course in Uzès. **Open** Mar 16 – Oct 31.

A secluded location and a stunning view are the main features of this hotel tucked away at the end of a peaceful little village. All around it, cypresses, vineyards, and hills combine to create a beautifully harmonious landscape and that may be what kept the owners from returning to their native Germany once they had set eyes on it. This doesn't feel like a hotel at all. The farmhouse has been carefully restored to make your stay as pleasant as possible. The bedrooms are comfortable and welcoming, two practical small apartments and a studio enable you to accommodate relatives and children. All three lodgings come with a little kitchen. All invite a long stay. The hotel is an ideal base for exploring the beautiful Uzès area, and the swimming pool proves an irresistible invitation to laze in the sun. In the evening your hosts will gladly indicate the best local restaurants, including *L'Auberge de Cruvier*, or *Le Fou du Roi* in Pougnadoresse, and for dinner *L'Auberge Saint-Maximin* in Saint-Maximin.

***How to get there*** *(Map 33): 40km west of Avignon via N100 and D981 to Montaren, then D337 to Saint-Médiers; (the Mas is on the edge of the hamlet).*

## La Bégude Saint-Pierre

30210 Vers - Pont du Gard (Gard)
Tel. (0)4.66.63.63.63 - Fax (0)4.66.22.73.73
M. Griffoul
E-mail: bruno.griffoul@enprovence.com

**Rooms** 29 with air-conditioning, telephone, bath, WC, TV, hairdryer, safe and minibar – Wheelchair access. **Price** Double 350-680F / 53,36-103,67€, suite 800-1300F / 121,96-198,18€. **Meals** Breakfast 75F / 11,43€, served 7:00-10:30; half board +245F / 37,35€ (per pers., 3 days min.). **Restaurant** Service 12:00PM-2:00PM, 7:30PM-9:30PM (10:00PM in summer); mealtime specials 170-300F / 25,92-45,73€, also à la carte. Specialties: Symphonie gardoise-l'emulsion de tapenade et huile d'olive; saumon fumé par nos soins. **Credit cards** All major. **Pets** Dogs allowed (+40F / 6,10€). **Facilities** Swimming pool, parking. **Nearby** Pont du Gard, Uzès, Nîmes, Avignon. **Open** Sunday evening and Monday end Oct – end Mar.

L*A Bégude* used to be a postal relay station with a twin farmhouse next door. The owner of an auberge in a village near Uzès, M. Griffoul has extensively restored this pretty Provençal *bégude*, creating a comfortable, luxurious hotel with a swimming pool, bedrooms with large terraces, a bar, a restaurant and a grill for the summer. We especially liked Room 31 for its unusual spaciousness, and Number 15 for its charming mezzanine. The rooms' simple, Provençal decor includes Souleïado fabrics and regional furniture. The lounges and dining rooms are decorated with similar traditional charm, conferring homogeneity to the style of this recently inaugurated hotel, and that's almost a shame. Of course, particular care is given to the food, for Monsieur Griffoul is still in charge of the kitchen. In summer, you should know that there is a barbecue grill next to the pool..

*How to get there (Map 33): 25km northeast of Nîmes via A9, exit Remoulins, then D981 towards Uzès.*

## Château de Madières

Madières
34190 Ganges (Hérault)
Tel. (0)4.67.73.84.03 - Fax (0)4.67.73.55.71 - M. and Mme Brucy
E-mail: madieres@wanadoo.fr

**Category** ★★★★ **Rooms** 12 with telephone, bath or shower, WC, TV and minibar. **Price** Double 650-1300F / 99,09-198,18€, suite 1350-1500F / 205,81-228,67€. **Meals** Breakfast 85-120F / 12,96-18,29€, served 8:30-10:30; half board 670-1000F / 102,14-152,45€ (per pers., 3 days min.). **Restaurant** Service 12:30-2:00PM, 7:30PM-9:00PM; mealtime specials 195-395F / 29,73-60,22€, also à la carte. Specialties: Minute de Saint-Jacques; filet de bœuf; soufflé de rougets. **Credit cards** All major. **Pets** Dogs allowed (extra charge). **Facilities** Heated swimming pool, fitness room, parking. **Nearby** Gorges of the River Vis, Navacelles Circus, Church of Saint-Guilhem-le-Désert. **Open** Apr 8 – Nov 2.

Set on the southern slopes of the Cévennes among the gorges of the River Vis, this 14th-century fortified house juts out like a balcony on the side of the mountain, only 40 minutes away from the Cirque de Navacelles. The splendid *Château de Madières* has been carefully restored. The bedrooms are luxuriously equipped and look out onto a patio. They are extremely comfortable, pleasant, and finely decorated. The elegant lounge still has a Renaissance fireplace and leads out onto a terrace overlooking the river and the village. There are two dining-rooms (one with panoramic views) in which to enjoy Mme Brucy's excellent cooking. In summer, meals can be served by the swimming-pool which has just been completed on a terrace below the hotel.

***How to get there*** *(Map 32): 60km northwest of Montpellier via D986 towards Le Vigan to Ganges, then D25 towards the Cirque de Navacelles, Lodève (18km from Ganges).*

## Bastide Les Aliberts

Les Aliberts 34210 Minerve (Hérault)
Tel. (0)4.68.91.81.72 - Fax (0)4.68.91.22.95
M. and Mme Bourgogne
E-mail: aliberts@wanadoo.fr - Web: www.aliberts.web-france.net

**Rooms** 5 cottages (4-8 pers.) with kitchen, lounge, bath, WC. **Price** Cottage (1 week) 3000-6200F / 457,35-946,56€ (8-9 pers.), 3500-8000F / 533,57-1219,59€ (4-5 pers.), 4500-11000F / 687,02-1679,38€ (6 pers.) - if possible: 450F / 68,60€ (2 pers. /day), 800F / 121,96€ (3-4 pers. /day). **Meals** Breakfast incl. **Evening meals** By reservation. Mealtime special 120F / 18,29€. **Credit cards** Not accepted. **Pets** Dogs not allowed. **Facilities** Swimming pool (Apr – Oct), parking. **Nearby** Minerve, Châteaux Cathares in Lastours, Carcassonne, abbey of Lagrasse, abbey of Fontfroide, African reserve of Sigean, Minervois vineyard. **Open** All year.

*L*es Aliberts is composed of a group of farmhouses which have been converted into five small individual houses accommodating four to nine people. Very comfortable, well-equipped, and prettily decorated, they're a perfect vacation home for a week or more. (During off-season, it is possible to stay here for one night, which is why we made an exception and included this address in our collection, even though it really isn't a hotel.) A large, barrel-vaulted room in the bastide serves as a living room, and what a lovely place in which to curl up in front of the fire in winter, or to take refuge within its cool walls in summer. The charm of *Les Aliberts* owes much to its friendly, hospitable owners and to the village of Minerve itself, which has been described as "a prow of burnt rock washed up in the blue of heaven like an arc from the deluge; a village… which reigns over a desert of scrub and stones, indented with gorges, punctured with grottos, scattered with dolmens and remote farmhouses."

***How to get there*** *( Map 31 ): 45km northwest of Carcassonne via N113 and D610 to Homps, then D910 to Olonzac and D10 to Minerve (heading north).*

## Relais Chantovent

34210 Minerve (Hérault)
Tel. (0)4.68.91.14.18 - Fax (0)4.68.91.81.99
Mme Evenou

**Rooms** 7 with shower (1 with bath) and WC. **Price** Single and double 200-260F / 30,49-39,64€.
**Meals** Breakfast 30F / 4,57€, served 8:00-10:00; half board 320F / 48,78€ (per pers., 3 days min.).
**Restaurant** Service 12:30-2:00PM, 7:30PM-9:00PM; mealtime specials 100-230F / 15,24-35,06€.
Specialties: Croustillant aux deux saumons sur coulis de poivrons doux. **Credit cards** Visa, Eurocard
and MasterCard. **Pets** Dogs allowed. **Nearby** Minerve, Cathares Châteaux of Lastours, Carcassonne,
abbey of Lagrasse, abbey of Fontfroide, African reserve of Sigean, Minervois vineyard. **Closed** Feb –
Mar 15; Monday in Jul, Aug and Sep; Sunday evening and Monday in low season.

Minerve is a village high up between the gorges of the rivers Cesse and
Briand, and the hotel buildings are scattered in its narrow alleys. The
annex is a tastefully restored old village house next to the "post-office library"
and the rooms are as charming as the ones in the main building. Two of them
share a terrace, and the one in the attic has kept its original layout, with the
bathroom more or less in the room; all have charm and character. The rooms
facing the restaurant have been redecorated and renovated, with fabrics and
contemporary lithographs brightening the decor. The restaurant, with a view
over the limestone Briand Valley, serves good regional cuisine (on the terrace
in good weather.) The village and its surroundings are splendid and the
welcome is very friendly.

***How to get there*** *( Map 31): 45km northwest of Carcassonne via N113 and D160*
*to Homps, then D910 to Olonzac and D10 to Minerve (northward).*

## Hôtel Le Guilhem

34000 Montpellier (Hérault)
18, rue Jean-Jacques-Rousseau
Tel. (0)4.67.52.90.90 - Fax (0)4.67.60.67.67
M. Charpentier

**Category** ★★★ **Rooms** 33 (15 with air conditioning), telephone, bath, WC, satellite TV, minibar – Elevator. **Price** Double 360-700F / 54,88-106,71€. **Meals** Breakfast 52F / 7,92€, served 7:00-1:00PM. No restaurant. **Credit cards** Diners, Visa, Amex. **Pets** Dogs allowed. **Facilities** Parking (+40F / 6,10€). **Nearby** Montpellier historical center. **Open** All year.

Well-hidden on a little alley in the heart of the historical district of Montpellier next to the Arc de Triomphe, this little hotel has been set up in a former, 16th-century house. The little reception area, with its high hospitality, opens to the upper floors' sunny yellow hallways. Most of the rooms overlook the peaceful rear of the hotel, with its garden full of birds, across from the medical school and the cathedral whose bells mark the hour but do not toll at night. The rooms are white with a colored border and antique furnishing, not at all cutesy, with a touch of cheerful red fabrics, yellow or blue bedthrows, and table skirts. The bathrooms are also white and modern, and are outfitted with either bathtub or shower. Breakfast is served in your room with a bouquet of flowers and newspaper, or on a patio, awash in the light of the rising sun, seated in striped director's chairs. There is no restaurant, but the *Petit Jardin* next door sets up tables under its awnings. There is also the *Maison de la Lozère* with its 16th-century cellars, or the *Isadora*. Parking fee for the Peyrou-Pilot lot.

***How to get there*** *(Map 32): Via A9, take Montpellier east. Follow signs until "Centre historique", go under the arc de Triomphe. 2nd street on the right after courthouse.*

## Bergeries de Pondérach

34220 Saint-Pons-de-Thomières (Hérault)
Route de Narbonne
Tel. (0)4.67.97.02.57 - Fax (0)4.67.97.29.75
M. Gilles Lentin

**Rooms** 7 with telephone, bath, 1 with minibar – 1 for disabled persons. **Price** Double 350-490F / 53,36-74,70€. **Meals** Breakfast 48F / 7,32€, served 7:30-10:30; half board 700-850F / 106,71-129,58€ (for 2 pers., 3 days min.). **Credit cards** Diners, Visa, Eurocard and MasterCard. **Pets** Dogs allowed (+80F / 12,20€). **Facilities** Parking, garage. **Nearby** Béziers; Espinousse Mounts; Carcassonne. **Restaurant** Service 12:00PM-2:00PM, 8:00PM-9:00PM; mealtime specials 98-230F / 14,96-35,06€, also à la carte. Specialties: Rougets au noilly; confit de canard maison; salade de langoustines aux épices; champignons. **Open** Mar – end Nov.

Nestled in the verdant heart of a Languedoc national park, this former, 18th-century farmhouse overlooks a tiny river. The reception areas and rooms are set up around a pleasant interior courtyard. Each room has a terrace, and every room has been made "as a good as new." To get them back into shape, the owners used stunning, cheerful colors, chose beautiful fabrics, and excellent bedding. The pastel bathrooms are just as carefully arranged. In the summer, the courtyard makes a great place for dinner and, sometimes, classical music concerts are organized by the hotel. (The rooms look out on the other side, toward the country.) Furbished in a more traditional manner, the lounge bar and dining room display a more outdated style, personalized by many paintings from the owner's former days as a gallery director. Mouthwatering seasonal food, made only from the freshest ingredients. Very warm hospitality.

*How to get there* ( *Map 31*): *50km west of Béziers on N 112.*

## Ostalaria Cardabela

34725 Saint-Saturnin-de-Lucian (Hérault)
10, place de la Fontaine
Tel. (0)4.67.88.62.62 - Fax (0)4.67.88.62.82
M. David Puch

**Rooms** 8 with telephone, bath or shower, TV by reservation. **Price** Single and double 350-480F / 53,36-73,18€. **Meals** Breakfast 60F / 9,15€, served from 7:00-10:30. **Restaurant** Le Mimosa in Saint-Guiraud (2 km). Service 12:00PM-1:30PM, 8:00PM-9:30PM; mealtime specials 190F / 28,97€ (lunchtime except Saturday and Sunday) 290F / 44,21€ (evening and Sunday). **Credit cards** Visa, Eurocard and MasterCard. **Pets** Dogs not allowed. **Nearby** Lodève; Hérault Valley: Villeneuvette, Brissac, Saint-Guilhem-du-Désert. **Open** Mar – Nov.

While studying the outside of this inn in the heart of an old village, the passing guest could not even guess all the qualities that are hidden behind the cramped façade and heavy entrance door. Inside, you will find ravishing rooms with terra-cotta or painted cement tile flooring, wicker and wrought iron furniture, red and yellow regional fabrics, contemporary wall lamps also in wrought iron, and impeccable white bathrooms. The upper-floor rooms are large, but, outside of the "*Cardabela*," have a limited view. Less of a problem for the rooms above, whose windows reach the top of the neighboring houses. Carefully prepared, breakfast can be taken in your room or at the guest table on the ground floor, and on the terrace in summer. The hotel has no garden, but why not go enjoy the excellent food and unforgettable regional wine list of *Le Mimosa* restaurant, associated with the hotel though 2 km away. A very beautiful and hospitable place.

*How to get there* (*Map 32*): 10km north of Clermont-l'Hérault.

## La Villa d'Eléis

34210 Siran (Hérault)
Avenue du Château
Tel. (0)4.68.91.55.98 - Fax (0)4.68.91.48.34
M. Lafuente - Mme Rodriguez

**Category** ★★★ **Rooms** 12 with telephone, bath or shower, WC, 6 with TV and minibar – Elevator; 1 for disabled persons. **Price** Single and double 350-700F / 53,36-106,71€. **Meals** Breakfast 60F / 9,15€, served 8:00-11:00. **Restaurant** Closed Sunday evening and Monday from Oct – Apr. Service 12:00PM-2:30PM, 7:30PM-10:00PM; also à la carte. Specialties: Morue safranée à la languedocienne, fondue de tomate au basilic et huile d'olive, tarte tiède de lisette. **Credit cards** Visa, Eurocard and MasterCard. **Pets** Dogs allowed (+35F / 5,33€). **Facilities** Tennis and parking. **Nearby** Abbey of Fontfroide, Natural Park of Haut-Languedoc, Minerve, Lastours. **Closed** 2 weeks in Feb.

Set in the heart of the Minervois vineyards, one of the most beautiful regions of Languedoc, Siran is a quiet village of pale stone houses. *La Villa d'Eléis* was originally a farmhouse built by wealthy winegrowers on the ramparts which once surrounded the village. The *Villa* is now a beautiful country inn, transformed by Bernard Lafuente and Marie-Hélène Rodriguez, who are well-known for their hotel restoration. Here, modern accommodations combine harmoniously with the old charm and character of the place. Whether the bedrooms overlook the vines or the village, each has its special personality and predominant color. All have lovely bathrooms and are beautifully restful. The elegant meals of Bernard Lafuente (awarded two trophies in 1998) are served in a large dining room, or in the shady garden. Small concerts or readings are occasionally given in the interior courtyard. An atmosphere of well-being and relaxation reigns at the *Villa*, a welcome respite after a day of visiting the splendid sites of the region.

***How to get there*** *( Map 31): 20km northwest of Lezignan; A1 Lézignan-Corbières exit to Olonzac, Pépieux, Siran.*

# La Lozerette

48400 Cocurès (Lozère)
Tel. (0)4.66.45.06.04 - Fax (0)4.66.45.12.93
Mme Pierrette Agulhon

**Category** ★★ **Rooms** 21 with telephone, with bath or shower, WC, TV. **Price** Double 290-420F / 44,21-64,03€. **Meals** Breakfast 40F / 6,10€, served 8:00-11:00; half board 285-375F / 43,45-57,17€ (per pers., 3 days min.). **Credit cards** All major. **Pets** Dogs allowed (except in restaurant). **Facilities** Parking and garage. **Nearby** Cévennes National Park (information center at Florac); gorges of Tarn de Florac-Millau near Sainte-Enimie; Mont Lozère. **Restaurant** Closed Tuesday (except for residents, 1 mealtime special) and Wednesday afternoon, except Jul-Aug. Service 12:00PM-1:30PM, 7:30PM-9:15PM; mealtime specials: 90-250F / 13,72-38,11€, also à la carte. Specialties: Panade de morue en habit vert-l'ail doux; selle d'agneau des Causses au romarin; pied de veau en crépine au genièvre. **Open** Easter – Nov.

Certainly don't let yourself be put off by the slightly drab façade of this little village inn. You would pass up a charming place of indisuptable quality. The vast majority of the rooms have just had a facelift, and what a success. Beautiful light oak parquetry has replaced most of the carpetting, lighting is assured by elegant pewter wall fixtures, the fabrics are elegant and cheerful, matresses firm, and the bathrooms are just as agreeable. The huge, beautiful, ground-floor dining room invites you to taste succulent cuisine. Trust Pierrette Agulhon for the wines -- she is a reputed wine steward and the hotel's owner. Pleasant, shady terrace and very friendly atmosphere.

***How to get there*** *(Map 32): 38km from Mende. 5.5km northwest of Florac on N 106 and D 998.*

## Domaine de Barres

48300 Langogne (Lozère)
Tel. (0)4.66.69.71.00 - Fax (0)4.66.69.71.29
M. and Mme Bigot

**Category** ★★★ **Rooms** 20 with telephone, bath, WC, TV. and minibar – Elevator; 4 for disabled persons. **Price** Double 390-430F / 59,46-65,55€. **Meals** Breakfast 50F / 7,62€, served 7:30-10:30; half board and full board 750-1050F / 114,34-160,07€ (2 pers., 3 night min.). **Restaurant** Closed Sunday evening and Monday in low season. Service 12:30-1:30PM, 7:30PM-9:30PM; mealtime specials 98-260F / 21,34-48,78€, also à la carte. **Credit cards** All major. **Pets** Dogs allowed (+50F / 7,62€). **Facilities** Covered swimming pool, sauna, parking. **Nearby** Romanesque church in Langogne; Mende; Marvejols; La Margeride – Golf course. **Open** Mid Mar – mid Nov.

This is an unexpected hotel, located north of the Lozère, in the wild Margeride next to Naussac Lake. The 18th-century, country squire's house, surrounded by a golf course, perfectly represents the successful joining of classical architecture and contemporary decor, thanks to the talents of J.M. Wilmotte, who furbished both the interior and the exterior. (Including a superb covered swimming pool lit by a system of collapsible lamps in summer.) A great, unified decorating scheme characterizes the place. Spacious areas on the ground floor with light oak, parquetry, beige walls, sober furnishing, and black-and-white photographs of the Lozère landscape. A tranquil atmosphere that is livened up by flowers on the dining room tables and the green upholstery of the lounge's armchairs. Very comfortable rooms decorated the same way. Promising fare that we haven't had the chance to taste yet. (The chef has worked for the finest French restaurants -- *Troisgros, Greuze, La Tour d'Argent* --and we would put faith in that.) A beautiful, inviting and stunning place to discover.

*How to get there* ( *Map 25*): *47km northeast of Mende; 3km from Langogne.*

## Château de la Caze

La Malène 48210 Sainte-Enimie (Lozère)
Tel. (0)4.66.48.51.01 - Fax (0)4.66.48.55.75
Sandrine and Jean-Paul Lecroq
E-mail: chateau.de.la.Caze @ wanadoo.fr

**Category** ★★★ **Rooms** 12, 1 apartement and 6 suites, with telephone, bath, WC, TV, minibar in suites – 1 for disabled persons. **Price** Double 500-950F / 76,22-144,83€, suite 750-1400F / 114,34-213,43€. **Meals** Breakfast 70F / 10,67€, served 8:00-10:00; half board 465-690F / 70,89-105,19€ (per pers., 2 days. min). **Restaurant** Closed Wednesday and Thursday evening in low season. Service 12:30-2:00PM, 7:30PM-9:30PM; mealtime specials: 130-320F / 19,82-48,78€, also à la carte. Specialties: Selle d'agneau de Lozère; gâteau-la châtaigne et au chocolat amer. **Credit cards** Amex, Visa. **Pets** Dogs not allowed except in restaurant. **Facilities** Swimming pool, parking (30F / 4,57€). **Nearby** Cévennes National park; Mont Lozère. **Closed** Nov 15 – Mar 15, Wednesday in low season.

You can only fall in love with the architecture of this 15th-century château. The Tarn canyons widen up a bit here, almost as to let a little sunlight warm the old walls of La Caze and make the water dance with emerald and turquoise reflections. Before going into the Château, a waterfall greets the visitor and spills its clear water into waters teeming with fish. Then the opening door reveals a wide hallway with a stone floor polished by the centuries. The hall opens out onto the lounge bar and medieval-style dining room, where good, healthy, seasonal food is served. The rooms are on the two top floors, and some enjoy a crenellated balcony that overlooks the Tarn. Antique or retro furniture adds comfort to this timeless charm. On the other side of the garden, another building houses some superb suites that have just been successfully renovated in the southern style. Youthful and pleasant hospitality.

*How to get there (Map 32): 46km south of Mende; 3km northeast of La Malène, on D 907 bis.*

## Hôtel Chantoiseau

48220 Vialas (Lozère)
Tel. (0)4.66.41.00.02 - Fax (0)4.66.41.04.34
M. Patrick Pagès

**Category** ★★★ **Rooms** 8 with bath or shower, WC, TV and minibar. **Price** Single and double 299-450F / 45,67-68,60€. **Meals** Breakfast 50F / 7,62€, served 8:00-10:00; half board 520F / 79,27€ (per pers., 3 days min.). **Restaurant** Service 12:00PM-1:30PM, 7:00PM-8:30PM; mealtime specials 100-500F / 15,24-76,22€, also à la carte. Specialties: Ravioles au pélardon; carré d'agneau; suprême au chocolat. **Credit cards** All major. **Pets** Dogs not allowed. **Facilities** Swimming pool, parking. **Nearby** Ridgeway to Alès via Portes; La Garde de Guérin, Florac. **Closed** Sep – Jun 1, Tuesday evenings and Wednesday.

With one of the outstanding gastronomic restaurants (one Michelin star) of the region, *Chantoiseau* is a converted 17th-century postal relay station lying at an altitude of 1800 feet in a region of steep escarpments that already evoke the Mediterranean: a sunny place to stay on the doorstep of the Cévennes National Park. Overlooking the valleys and mountains, the bedrooms are comfortable but dark and small, the architecture obliging. The dining room retains the austere character of houses in the area: walls built from large slabs of granite, deep embrasures, the warm presence of wood. It commands beautiful views over the valley. The menu features specialties of the Cévennes only, prepared by the owner whose talent has earned wide recognition, and who has chosen the finest wines to accompany them. The wine list is outstanding, ranging from modest but charming *vins de pays* to great wines.

***How to get there*** *(Map 32): Northwest of Alès via D906, towards Genolhac; in Belle-Poèle, D998 to Vialas.*

## La Regordane

La Garde-Guérin 48800 Villefort (Lozère)
Tel. (0)4.66.46.82.88 - Fax (0)4.66.46.90.29
M. Nogier

**Category** ★★ **Rooms** 15 with telephone, bath, WC, 10 with TV. **Price** Single and double 280-350F / 42,69-53,36€. **Meals** Breakfast 37F / 5,64€, served 8:00-10:00; half board 270-320F / 41,16-48,78€ (per pers.). **Restaurant** Service: 12:00PM-2:00PM, 7:30PM-9:00PM; mealtime specials 98-180F / 14,96-27,44€, also à la carte. Specialties: Maôuche aux pruneaux; manouls loréziens; foie gras maison au gros sel; truite du mont Lozère et lentilles vertes du Puy; carré d'agneau et tomates confites-la cannelle. **Credit cards** Visa, Diners Club. **Pets** Dogs allowed (+20F / 3,05€). **Facilities** Parking. **Nearby** Cévennes National park; Mont Lozère (from mas de la Barque to col de Finiel), sources of the Allier and Tarn; gorges of Tarn, Sainte-Enimie. **Open** Easter – end Sep.

Between Mont Lozère and the Chassezac canyons, La Garde-Guerin is a walled village located on a rocky plateau. The inn is in a former 16th-century noble mansion and owes its name to the Regordane Way, a pre-Roman road that joined the Midi to the Massif Central region. Behind the austerity of these walls lies wonderful, renovated rooms, with honey-colored parquetry, and their sober decoration accented by beautiful fabrics and antique accessories. All look out on the old walls of the village, with at times a view of the countryside. You will also enjoy a pleasant lounge, full of character, with its monumental fireplace and 19th-century furnishing. Excellent food is served in the vaulted dining room, or in the interior courtyard in summer. An incredible place, remarkably well-tended by two devoted brothers.

***How to get there*** *( Map 32 ): 55km from Alès on D 906.*

## La Terrasse au Soleil

66400 Céret (Pyrénées-Orientales)
Route de Fontfrède
Tel. (0)4.68.87.01.94 - Fax (0)4.68.87.39.24
B. and P. Leveillé-Nizerolle

**Category** ★★★★ **Rooms** 13 and 7 suites with air-conditioning, telephone, bath, WC, hairdryer, TV, minibar and safe. **Price** Double 740-1435F / 112,81-218,76€, suite 770-1855F / 117,39-282,79€ **Meals** Breakfast incl., served 7:30-10:30; half board 1040-1535F / 158,55-234,01€. **Restaurant** Service 12:30PM-2:00PM, 7:30PM-9:30PM; mealtime specials 160-380F / 24,39-57,93€ (gastronimic menu). Specialties: Etuvée de girolles-la catalane; rosés des Pyrénées poêlés **Credit cards** All major. **Pets** Dogs allowed. **Facilities** Heated swimming pool, tennis, par-3 golf course, parking, helicopter pad. **Nearby** Museum of Modern Art and Church of Saint-Pierre in Céret, Cabestany, Prats-de-Mollo, Perpignan – 27-hole Saint-Cyprien golf course, 18-hole Falgos golf course. **Open** All year.

*La Terrasse au Soleil* is an old farmhouse which has been completely restored. It occupies an enviable position crowning the village among cherry trees. The rooms have an exceptional view of the mountains, and some suites are outfitted with a corner lounge, and sometimes even a terrace. We still prefer the rooms on the *premier étage* rather than those at ground level on the garden. The *La Cerisaie* restaurant will delight you with its excellent cuisine; for lunch, it also proposes a simpler brasserie menu, in addition to the dessert menu: don't miss the superb mille-feuille pastry. In good weather meals can be served in the garden. A heated swimming-pool, tennis court, and the golf course (no extra charge) will add further to your enjoyment of the hotel, a charming and informal place to stay.

***How to get there*** *( Map 31): 31km southwest of Perpignan via A9, Le Boulou exit, then D115 towards Céret; it's 2km from the center of the village via D13f towards Fontfrède.*

277

# Le Mas des Trilles

66400 Céret-Reynès (Pyrénées-Orientales)
Tel. (0)4.68.87.38.37 - Fax (0)4.68.87.42.62
M. and Mme Bukk

**Category** ★★★ **Rooms** 10 with telephone, bath, WC and TV – 1 for disabled persons. **Price** Double and suite 520-1100F / 79,27-167,69€. **Meals** Breakfast 70F / 10,67€, served 8:30-10:30; half board 520-810F / 79,27-123,48€ (per pers.). **Restaurant** Service 8:00PM; mealtime specials 190-235F / 28,97-35,83€. Specialties: Seasonal cooking. **Credit cards** Visa, Eurocard and MasterCard. **Pets** Dogs allowed (extra charge). **Facilities** Heated swimming pool, parking. **Nearby** Museum of Modern Art and Church of Saint-Pierre in Céret, Quilhac and the Château of Peyrepertuse, Perpignan – 27-hole Saint-Cyprien golf course, 7-hole Amélie-les-Bains golf course, 18-hole Falgos golf course. **Open** Easter – Oct 9.

The *Mas des Trilles* is an old house surrounded by a garden with fruit trees. From the swimming pool, when there is a lot of traffic and the wind is blowing in the wrong direction, the rumble of cars on the road above the hotel can sometimes be heard. The bedrooms, however, are quiet at all times. Inside, the house has been fully refurbished and tastefully decorated: there are terra-cotta floors, sponge painted or whitewashed walls, and each fabric has been carefully chosen by Mme Bukk to blend in with, and round off, the decor. The bedrooms have lovely bathrooms; many have a private terrace where breakfast (which always includes fresh fruit) can be served. Dinner (for residents only) is in a charming dining room or on the terrace. Friendly hospitality adds to the pleasant homey atmosphere that prevails. This is a beautiful, comfortable hotel that is enjoying more and more success.

***How to get there*** *(Map 31): 31km southwest of Perpignan via A9, Le Boulou exit, then D115 towards Céret (do not go into Céret); 2km after Céret towards Amélie-les-Bains .*

## Hôtel Casa Païral

66190 Collioure (Pyrénées-Orientales)
Impasse des Palmiers
Tel. (0)4.68.82.05.81 - Fax (0)4.68.82.52.10
Mmes De Bon and Lormand

**Category** ★★★ **Rooms** 28 with air-conditioning, telephone, bath or shower, WC, satellite TV and minibar. **Price** Single and double 360-760F / 54,88-115,86€, junior-suites 810-960F / 123,48-146,35€. **Meals** Breakfast (buffet) 60F / 9,15€. No restaurant. **Credit cards** All major. **Pets** Dogs allowed (+30F / 4,57€). **Facilities** Swimming pool, parking (+40F / 6,10€). **Nearby** The Vermeille coast between Argelès-sur-Mer and Cerbère, Balcon de Madeloc, mountain road between Collioure and Banyuls, Château of Salses, Museum of Modern Art in Céret – 27-hole Saint-Cyprien golf course. **Open** Apr – end Oct.

*Casa Païral* is hidden in a small dead-end street, right in the center of Coullioure, just a few minutes from the beach, restaurants, and cafés. It is perfectly quiet. This luxurious 19th-century town house was built in a Moorish style with wrought ironwork, marble, and ceramic tilework. On the patio, lush vegetation grows in the shade of a stately palm tree and a hundred-year-old magnolia tree. All the rooms are comfortable, though unfortunately badly soundproofed, which is often the case in old houses. Ask for the ones in the main house, which are nicer. The very pleasant breakfast room and lounges open onto the walled garden and swimming pool. This hotel is very much in demand, so you will need a reservation. For dinner, try the fish at *Tremail*, or *La Marinade*, for its pretty terrace on the town square. Last but not least, don't forget the excellent *Relais des Trois Mats*, the gourmet address in Collioure.

***How to get there*** *(Map 31): 26km southeast of Perpignan via N114.*

## Relais des Trois Mas

66190 Collioure (Pyrénées-Orientales)
Route de Port-Vendres
Tel. (0)4.68.82.05.07 - Fax (0)4.68.82.38.08
M. de Gelder

**Category ★★★★ Rooms** 23 with air conditioning with telephone, bath, WC, satellite TV, minibar, safe. **Price** Double 540-1140F / 82,32-173,79€, suite 1300-2380F / 198,18-362,83€. **Meals** Breakfast 90F / 13,72€, served 8:30-10:30; half board 665-965F / 101,38-147,11€ (per pers.). **Restaurant** Service 12:30PM-2:00PM, 7:30PM-9:00PM; mealtime specials 195-395F / 29,73-60,22€, also à la carte. Specialties: Anchois frais de Collioure marinés; compotée d'oignons; poivrons et vinaigrette de Banyuls. **Credit cards** Visa, Eurocard, MasterCard. **Pets** Dogs allowed (+88F / 13,43€). **Facilities** Swimming pool, jacuzzi, parking. **Nearby** Vermillion Coast between Argelès-sur-Mer and Cerbère; Madeloc plateau; mountain road between Collioure and Banyuls; Salses Château; Céret Museum of Modern Art – 27-hole Saint-Cyprien golf course. **Closed** Nov 13 – Dec 21.

How could you dream of a better place from which to appreciate the town of Collioure? The hotel is located directly in front of the bay and medieval citadel of this town. Its rooms are split up among many structures that mingle with the rocky slope and are joined together by passageways or stairwells bordered terraces, both big and small, that are bursting with luxuriant, meridianal flora. Each room is named after a famous painter who came to Collioure for inspiration. The decoration is pleasant, with sponge-painted pastel walls, many cream-colored furnishings set off by the room's main colors, and comfortable bathrooms with whirlpool baths. Everywhere you look, the vista is superb, even from the swimming pool and jacuzzi. You don't have to go far for dinner. The hotel's panoramic restaurant offers excellent, delicate, inventive, and masterfully prepared cuisine. Very professional and pleasant service.

*How to get there* ( Map 31 ): 26km southeast of Perpignan on N 114.

## Auberge L'Atalaya

Llo - 66800 Saillagouse (Pyrénées-Orientales)
Tel. (0)4.68.04.70.04 - Fax (0)4.68.04.01.29
M. and Mme Toussaint

**Category** ★★★ **Rooms** 12 and 1 suite with telephone, bath or shower, WC, satellite TV, safe and minibar. **Price** Single and double 495-620F / 75,46-94,52€, suite 768F / 117,25€. **Meals** Breakfast 65F / 9,91€, served 7:30-10:30; half board and full board 490-740F / 74,70-112,81€ (per pers., 3 days min.). **Restaurant** Closed Monday and Tuesday lunchtime in low season. Service 12:30PM-2:30PM, 7:30PM-9:30PM; mealtime specials 165-390F / 25,15-59,46€, also à la carte. **Credit cards** Visa, Eurocard and MasterCard. **Pets** Dogs allowed in the bedrooms. **Facilities** Swimming pool, solarium, parking. **Nearby** Ski in Eyne, Odeillo solar furnace, lake of Les Buoillouses north of Mont-Louis, gorges of the river Aude, Château de Quérigut – 18-hole Real Club de Cerdana golf course, 9-hole golf course in Font-Romeu, 18-hole Fontanals golf course (15km). **Closed** Nov 5 – Dec 20.

Llo is the most typical pastoral village of the Cerdagne region on the border between Andorra and Spain, which can be seen from some of the bedrooms. Clustered around its watchtower - called an atalaya in old Castilian - and the ruins of its 11th-century castle, the village stands above the gorges of the River Sègre. Needless to say, its location is one of the memorable features of the Auberge. The mansion is gorgeous, with the traditional schist architecture covered with vines, overlooking the valley. The little rooms are sweet and comfortable. The dining room opens out onto the Spanish mountain chain, and the food is a reminder of the local traditions. In summer, meals are served outside on a terrace among geraniums and hollyhocks, and there is now also a swimming-pool. In winter, there are eight ski resorts nearby. This is a genuine and simple place to stay.

***How to get there*** *( Map 31 ): 90km west of Perpignan via N116 to Saillagouse, then D33.*

# La Maison des Consuls

09500 Mirepoix (Ariège)
Tel. (0)5.61.68.81.81 - Fax (0)5.61.68.81.15
M. Garcia

**Category** ★★★ **Rooms** 7 (1 with air-conditioning) and 1 suite with telephone, bath, WC, TV and minibar. **Price** Double 420-680F / 64,03-103,67€. **Meals** Breakfast 40 and 60F / 6,10 and 9,15€, served 7:15AM-12:00PM. No restaurant. **Credit cards** Visa, Eurocard and MasterCard. **Pets** Dogs allowed (+40F / 6,10€). **Nearby** Cathedral of Mirepoix; Sainte-Foy Tower; Châteaux of Lagarde and of Caudeval, Montségur and Foix; caves of mas d'Azil. **Open** All year.

*L*a Maison des Consuls is a historic residence located on the medieval square for which Mirepoix is famous. The hotel's letterhead reads "Unrestricted View of the 13th century"; this is a figurative way of saying that four of the seven bedrooms recently decorated with antique furniture look out over the "*couverts*" and their magnificently preserved framework. Each room has its own style, from the 18th century to today, and all are very comfortable with beautiful bathrooms. Breakfast is served in a beautiful, rustic, ground-floor dining area. The *Cafe des maquignons* opens out onto a verdant and calm little courtyard. For dinner, we recommend the excellent *Auberge Louis XIII*, just a few minutes away. Before going there, take the time to stroll around this extraordinary little town, have a drink at one of the many cafes set up under the shelters, and watch life at Mirepoix pass by. A wonderful moment, particularly if you do so on market day.

***How to get there*** *( Map 31): 59km southwest of Carcassonne via D119.*

## Hôtel Eychenne

09200 Saint-Girons (Ariège)
8, avenue Paul-Laffont
Tel. (0)5.61.04.04.50 - Fax (0)5.61.96.07.20
M. and Mme Bordeau

**Category** ★★★ **Rooms** 42 with telephone, bath or shower, WC, cable TV and 16 with minibar. **Price** Double 300-575F / 45,73-87,66€. **Meals** Breakfast 49F / 7,47€, served 7:00-11:00; half board and full board 380-585F / 57,93-89,18€ (per pers., 3 days min.). **Restaurant** Closed Sunday evening and Monday from Nov – Mar. Service 12:15PM-1:30PM, 7:45PM-9:30PM; mealtime specials 140-320F / 21,34-48,78€, also à la carte. Specialties: Foie de canard frais aux raisins; pigeonneau au fitou; gigot de lotte safrané; soufflé au grand-marnier. **Credit cards** All major. **Pets** Dogs allowed. **Facilities** Swimming pool, parking (20F / 3,05€). **Nearby** Saint-Lizier, Montjoie, Romanesques churches in the valley of Couserans in Oust and Cominac, Ercé Chapel in Garbet Valley, Castillon, Audressein, Sentein, Ayet, Ourtjou-les Bordes. **Closed** Dec – Jan 31, Sunday evening and Monday from Nov – end Mar except national holidays.

Managed by the Bordeau family for generations, the *Hôtel Eychenne* has preserved its atmosphere of the past while offering the latest in modern amenities. In the two lounges, small bar, and dining room, the furniture, family objects and pictures create a friendly atmosphere. Most of the comfortable bedrooms, which are not very large, are furnished with antiques. Some have a beautiful view out over the Pyrénées. The cuisine – savory specialties of the Southwest – warrants a visit here. In summer, meals are served in the dining room which looks onto a garden, or lighter fare is available by the swimming pool. Breakfasts are generous. The staff is friendly and attentive.

***How to get there*** *( Map 30): In Saint-Girons, head towards Foix and follow the signs.*

## Hôtel du Vieux Pont

12390 Belcastel (Aveyron)
Tel. (0)5.65.64.52.29 - Fax (0)5.65.64.44.32
Nicole and Michèle Fagegaltier

**Category** ★★★ **Rooms** 7 with telephone, bath, TV and minibar – 1 for disabled persons. **Price** Single and double 420-490F/ 64,03-74,70€. **Meals** Breakfast 55F/ 8,38€, served 8:30-10:00; half board 450-500F/ 68,60-76,22€ (per pers.). **Restaurant** Service 12:15PM-1:30PM, 7:45PM-9:00PM; mealtime specials 145-380F/ 22,11-57,93€; also à la carte. Specialties: Seasonal and farm-fresh food. **Credit cards** Visa, Eurocard and MasterCard. **Pets** Dogs allowed (+30F / 4,57€). **Facilities** Parking. **Nearby** Rodez; Sauveterre-de-Rouergue; Ségala plateau, Lévezou lakes; Causse Comtal. **Closed** Jan and Feb, Sunday evening and Monday except Jul – Aug.

With its old bridge that spans the river and its old lauze and stone houses at the foot of a feudal castel, Belcastel is truly one of the most beautiful villages of Aveyron. The restaurant is on the left bank in the childhood home of Nicole and Michèle Fagegaltier who, following their parents and grandparents, delight their guests and perform unforgettable culinary feats. Such success takes nothing away from the simplicity and kindness of these two sisters, who never stop improving the place. Thus, not long ago, seven irresistible rooms have been set up on the other side of the bridge in an old house next to the church. Unquestionably comfortable, they all are simply and beautifully decorated with light oak flooring, quilted white bedding, elegant curtains, and one or two little pieces of antique furniture. Add dazzling white bathrooms and a great river view, and you'll see why stays at the *Hôtel du Vieux Pont* are always too short.

*How to get there* ( *Map 31*): *25km west of Rodez.*

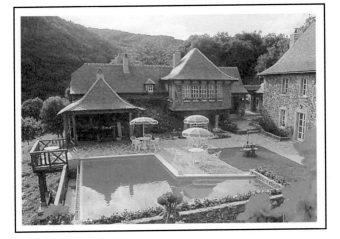

## Hôtel Longcol-en-Aveyron

12270 La Fouillade-Najac (Aveyron)
Route de Monteils
Tel. (0)5.65.29.63.36 - Fax (0)5.65.29.64.28
Famille Luyckx

**Category** ★★★ **Rooms** 18 and 1 studio (with kitchen) with telephone, bath or shower, WC, satellite TV and minibar. **Price** Single and double 650-900F / 99,09-137,20€. **Meals** Breakfast 75F/ 11,43€, served 7:00-11:00. **Restaurant** Closed Monday and Tuesday lunchtime. Service 7:30PM-9:30PM; mealtime specials 210F and 295F / 32,01 and 44,97€. **Credit cards** Amex, Visa. **Pets** Dogs allowed. **Facilities** Heated swimming pool, tennis, fishing, helicopter pad, parking. **Nearby** Château of Najac, Gorges of the Aveyron, Carthusian Monastery, Pénitents Noirs Chapel and Place of Notre-Dame in Villefranche-de-Rouergue. **Open** Mid Feb – mid Nov.

This old Rouergue country house is like a miniature village sitting on a wild mountain pass with the Aveyron flowing below. Recently restored and decorated beautifully, each room is furnished with Oriental objects, antique rugs and furniture, and old studded doors - all elegantly arranged and comfortable. The lounge and billiards rooms are particularly gracious, a corner fireplace and large leather armchairs creating a convivial atmosphere. The bedrooms are all individually decorated, bright, and cheerful. All have views of either the swimming pool or the valley. In summer you can fish in the river that runs through the property and can enjoy lunch by the pool, looking out over the beautiful countryside. The staff is pleasant in keeping with the quality of the place and the cooking of Francis Caradaillac.

***How to get there*** *(Map 31): 19km south of Villefranche-de-Rouergue towards Monteils on D47. After the bridge, towards La Fouillade on D638 for 2,5km.*

## L'Oustal del Barry

12270 Najac (Aveyron)
Place du Bourg
Tel. (0)5.65.29.74.32 - Fax (0)5.65.29.75.32 - Mme Miquel
E-mail: oustald.caramail.com - Web: www.loustaldelbarry.com

**Category** ★★ **Rooms** 20 with telephone, bath or shower, WC and TV – Elevator. **Price** Double 320-420F / 48,78-64,03€. **Meals** Breakfast 50F / 7,62€, served 8:00-10:30; half board and full board 270-455F / 41,16-69,36€ (per pers., 2 days min.). **Restaurant** Service 12:30PM-2:00PM, 7:30PM-9:30PM; mealtime specials 140-260F / 21,34-39,64€, also à la carte. **Credit cards** Amex, Visa. **Pets** Dogs allowed. **Facilities** Parking. **Nearby** Château of Najac, Gorges of the Aveyron, carthusian Monastery, Pénitents Noirs Chapel and Place of Notre-Dame in Villefranche-de-Rouergue. **Closed** Jan – Mar, Monday (except national holidays) from Apr – Jun and Oct.

Five generations of the same family have presided over the *Oustal del Barry*, which has all the charms of a traditional French hotel. On the whole the bedrooms are rustic but with a curious mixture of other styles, principally Art Deco. The dining room has a panoramic view of the flowers and greenery of the 6-acre grounds and the fortress of Najac. A vegetable garden cultivated by Mme Miquel grows several types of herbs used in the excellent cuisine, which also incorporates other local produce and is whipped up by the young Remy Simon, who was a chef at the famous *Jardin des Sens* in Montpellier. The kindness of your hosts will make you regret leaving this simple and charming hotel. Hotel rates include free admission to the swimming pool at Najac, one hour of tennis a day and the use of mountain bikes.

***How to get there*** *(Map 31): 24km south of Villefranche-de-Rouergue via D922, then D239.*

## Hôtel du Midi-Papillon

12230 Saint-Jean-du-Bruel (Aveyron)
Tel. (0)5.65.62.26.04 - Fax (0)5.65.62.12.97
M. and Mme Papillon

**Category** ★★ **Rooms** 18 and 1 suite with telephone, 12 with bath, 5 with shower and 18 with WC.
**Price** Double 134-207F / 20,58-32,01€, suite 338F / 51,83€. **Meals** Breakfast 25F / 3,81€, served
8:00-10:00; half board and full board 197-268F / 29,73-41,16€ (per pers. in double, 3 days min.).
**Restaurant** Service 12:30PM-2:00PM, 7:30PM-9:00PM; mealtime specials 76-211F / 11,43-32,01€,
also à la carte. Specialties: Cassolette d'escargots aux grisets en croûte; gâteau de homard au foie
gras. **Credit cards** All major. **Pets** Dogs allowed. **Facilities** Heated swimming pool, whirlpool. **Nearby**
Millau Belfry, old Montpellier, Gorges of the Tarn. **Open** Palm Sunday – Nov 11.

Saint-Jean-du-Bruel is a great stop along the Dourbie canyons, on the road
to Mont Aigoual, the highest peak of the Cévennes. The hotel is an old
coach inn, run by the same family for four generations. Well-situated on an
outcrop above the river, it offers an outstanding picture-postcard view of the
old village houses and a stone bridge. Here you will find all the good things
about a fine French inn -- comfort and good taste. Breakfasts and meals are
excellent, fashioned in a traditional or more elaborate way with homegrown
vegetables and fowl, and homemade jams, *foie gras*, and cold cuts. Jean-Michel
Papillon is at the stove. He spent a year with Michel Bras at *Laguiole* and hasn't
stoped enchanting food lovers. All the rooms have been renovated,
personalized with a special piece of furniture, a rug, or an antique engraving,
and each has a waterside balcony. Astonishingly good prices and warm
hospitality at this charming address.

***How to get there*** *( Map 32): 99km northwest of Montpellier via N109 and N9 in
the towards of Le Caylar to La Cavalerie, then D999 (as you enter the village).*

## Le Sénéchal

12800 Sauveterre-de-Rouergue (Aveyron)
Tel. (0)5.65.71.29.00 - Fax (0)5.65.71.29.09
M. Truchon

**Category ★★★ Rooms** 11 with air-conditioning, telephone, bath, WC, TV and minibar – Elevator; 1 for disabled persons. **Price** Double 580F / 88,42€, duplex 790F / 120,43€, suite 950F / 144,83€. **Meals** Breakfast 75F / 11,43€; half board 560-600F / 85,37-91,47€ (per pers., 3 days min.). **Restaurant** Closed Monday, Tuesday lunchtime and Wednesday lunchtime except public holidays, Jul and Aug. Service 12:00PM-2:00PM, 7:30PM-9:30PM; mealtime specials 140-480F / 21,34-73,18€, also à la carte. Specialties: Terrine de queues de bœuf en gelée à l'orange; tournedos de pied de porc en écailles de truffes; mousse de verveine fraîche et son sorbet. **Credit cards** All major. **Pets** Dogs allowed. **Facilities** Heated and covered swimming pool. **Nearby** Rodez, Plateau Le Ségala, lakes of Levézou and villages of Saint-Beauzély, Combéroumal, Castelnau-Prégayrols, Montjaux, Chestnut Festival on Nov 1, Saint-Christophe's Feast Day in Jul, Light Festival in Aug. **Closed** Jan and Feb.

A little museum retells the history of Sauveterre-de-Rouergue, a royal, fortified village which has conserved its checkerboard look, its passageways, its fortifications, and its church-dungeon. In the heart of the lovely Aveyron countryside, the big, brand-new *Sénéchal* is a haven of refinement and hospitality. The bedrooms, decorated in pale lemon colors, are very spacious, and look out over gentle hillsides. Spacious, too, are the bathrooms, the lounge, and the dining room. Decor is modern and comfortable, with some antique furniture. The cuisine is delicious, inventive, and subtly spiced: a true feast. Last but not least, the genuine, warm hospitality won us over to the inn's many qualities.

***How to get there*** *( Map 31): 32km southwest of Rodez.*

## Auberge du Poids Public

31540 Saint-Félix-Lauragais (Haute-Garonne)
Tel. (0)5.61.83.00.20 - Fax (0)5.61.83.86.21
M. and Mme Taffarello

**Category** ★★★ **Rooms** 10 with telephone, bath or shower, WC, TV and minibar. **Price** Double 330-550F / 50,31-83,85€. **Meals** Breakfast 50F / 7,62€, served 8:00-10:00; half board 670-880F / 102,14-134,16€ (per 2 pers.). **Restaurant** Closed Sunday evening from Oct – Apr. Service 12:00PM-1:30PM, 7:30PM-9:30PM; mealtime specials 140-340F / 21,34-51,83€, also à la carte. Specialties: Terrine de foie gras cuit au torchon; gigotin d'agneau de lait des Pyrénées; croustillant aux fruits rouges. **Credit cards** All major. **Pets** Dogs allowed. **Facilities** Parking. **Nearby** Cathedral of Saint-Papoul, Toulouse-Lautrec Museum in Albi, Toulouse, Pastel road, Midi Canal road – 9 and 18-hole golf courses in Toulouse. **Closed** Jan.

Located on the outskirts of the village, this old inn makes a pleasant stopping place. The bedrooms are fairly large and simply furnished with some antique pieces. They are renovated from year to year, and have modern bathrooms. The largest even has air-conditioning. Six of them enjoy a beautiful view. Most are quiet; the few that look onto the street are only used if the others are full. There is a private bar-lounge. Depending on the time of year lunches and dinners are served either in the large, bright and prettily decorated dining room or in the shade of wide umbrellas on the lovely terrace. In either case the marvelous view is enhanced by outstanding cuisine, some of the best in the region.

***How to get there*** *(Map 31): 40km southeast of Toulouse; on the bypass of Toulouse via Revel towards Saint-Orens, exit number 18.*

## Hostellerie des Sept Molles

31510 Sauveterre-de-Comminges (Haute-Garonne)
Tel. (0)5.61.88.30.87 - Fax (0)5.61.88.36.42
M. Ferran
E-mail: 7.molles@hostellerie-7-molles.com - Web: www.hostellerie-7-molles.com

**Category** ★★★ **Rooms** 19 with telephone, bath, WC, TV and minibar – Elevator. **Price** Single and double 420-780F / 64,03-118,91€, suite 900-1100F / 137,20-167,69€. **Meals** Breakfast 75F / 11,43€, served 8:00-11:00; half board and full board 580-860F / 88,42-131,11€ (per pers., 3 days min.). **Restaurant** Service 12:00PM-1:30PM, 7:30PM-9:30PM; mealtime specials 195-310F / 29,73-47,26€, also à la carte. Specialties: Foie chaud de canard poêlé à la pêche blanche; cèpes; truite du vivier. **Credit cards** All major. **Pets** Dogs allowed. **Facilities** Swimming pool, tennis, parking. **Nearby** Saint-Bertrand-de-Comminges, Montréjeau, Gallo-Roman villa of Montmaurin – 18-hole Lannemezan golf course, 9-hole golf course in Luchon. **Closed** Mid Feb – mid Mar.

The seven watermills, perched on the banks of the Roussec, gave a particular touch to this pretty corner of Comminges. The mills have disappeared but the millstones remain and lend their name to the hotel. The immediate surroundings are superb: meadows, vines, and groves of trees surround the house. The spacious, luminous bedrooms are furnished in traditional style. Some rooms evoke an English feel with their flowery fabrics, while others flaunt a more assertive style, like those with Empire furniture. The little suites have kept their charm of yesteryear. There is a warm ambiance in the dining room and reception rooms. The cuisine, both traditional and modern, is made largely from homemade products, including sausages from the hotel's own pig farm, trout from the fish tank, *foie gras* and pastries. The staff is welcoming and friendly.

***How to get there*** *(Map 30): 100km southwest of Toulouse. 74km southeast of Tarbes via A64, N117 to Saint-Gaudens, then D8 to Valentine and D9 (follow signs).*

## Hôtel des Beaux-Arts

31000 Toulouse (Haute-Garonne)
1, place du Pont-Neuf
Tel. (0)5.34.45.42.42 - Fax (0)5.34.45.42.43 - M. Courtois de Viçose
E-mail: hba@internetclub.fr

**Category** ★★★ **Rooms** 20 with air-conditioning, telephone, bath or shower, WC, TV and minibar – Elevator. **Price** Single and double 490-980F / 74,70-150,92€, suite 1000F / 152,45€. **Meals** Breakfast 85F / 12,96€, served 7:00-10:00. Snack available. **Credit cards** All major. **Pets** Dogs not allowed. **Facilities** Parking: Esquirol. **Nearby** In Toulouse: Fondation Bemberg, Basilica of Saint-Cernin, Jacobins church, Museum of Saint-Raymond and Museum of Augustins, Le Capitole (Hôtel de Ville), bastide of Grenade, Cathedral of Lombez – 9-18-hole golf course in Toulouse. **Open** All year.

The only part of the past that this refined hotel kept is the 18th-century façade, as well as the bedrooms' unique view out over the Garonne River, the Hôtel Dieu and the Pont Neuf, especially magnificent at sunset. Twenty bedrooms with ultra-modern amenities, discreetly and tastefully decorated, have been designed to make the Beaux-Arts a place of relaxation in the center of the city: Double windows and air-conditioning make for rest and relaxation in all seasons. The most delightful room is like a cozy loft, opening onto the sky and the river. If you don't want to go out for meals, the *Brasserie Flo* in the same building will serve you in your room. The breakfast-buffet is set out in a small vaulted room in the basement--a typical Toulouse cellar. For restaurants, try the gastronomic *Les Jardins de l'Opéra*; *La Frégate*, *La Brasserie des Beaux-Arts*, or *La Bascule*.

***How to get there*** *( Maps 30 and 31): In Toulouse, at the end of the Pont-Neuf.*

## Hôtel des Trois Lys

32100 Condom (Gers)
38, rue Gambetta
Tel. (0)5.62.28.33.33 - Fax (0)5.62.28.41.85 - Mme Manet
E-mail: hoteltroislys@minitel.net

**Category** ★★★ **Rooms** 10 with air-conditioning, telephone, bath or shower, WC and TV. **Price** Single and double 260-580F / 39,64-88,42€. **Meals** Breakfast 45F / 6,86€, served 7:30-10:00. **Restaurant** Closed in Feb, Sunday evening and Monday except Jul and Aug. Service 12:00PM-2:00PM, 7:30PM-10:00PM; mealtime specials 100-170F/ 15,24-25,92€, Chef's special (lunchtime) 50F/ 7,62€, also à la carte. Specialties: Fish; confit de canard; magret. **Credit cards** All major. **Pets** Dogs allowed. **Facilities** Swimming pool, garage. **Nearby** Armagnac Museum in Condom, Châteaux, Collegiate Church of La Romieu, Jazz festival in Marciac (August) – 18-hole Guinlet golf course in Eauze. **Closed** Feb.

A former, 18th-century private mansion, this establishment has really held onto its homey character, thanks to the kindness and attentiveness of Madame Manet. The ten rooms are done in coordinated colors and furnished with antiques or excellent reproductions finished in splendid fabrics. The rooms are big - some very big - and a few retain their wood panelling and Louis XV alcoves; double doors, thick carpeting, and double windows ensure absolute silence. The bathrooms are also beautiful, with gleaming taps, colored tiles, and soft lighting. A monumental stone staircase leads from the bedrooms to the ground floor where breakfast is served. Prettily redecorated this year, the dining room overlooks both the little courtyard (meals often served under the shade of umbrellas) and the back of the hotel in front of the swimming pool. A very pleasant address at smart prices.

*How to get there* *(Map 30): 40km south of Agen.*

## Château de Fourcès

32250 Fourcès (Gers)
Tel. (0)5.62.29.49.53 - Fax (0)5.62.29.50.59
Mme Barsan

**Category** ★★★ **Rooms** 15 with telephone, bath or shower, WC and TV. **Price** Double 465-870F / 70,89-132,63€, suite 925-1245F / 141,02-189,80€. **Meals** Breakfast 60F / 9,15€, served 8:00-10:00; half board 500-630F / 76,22-96,04€ (per pers.). **Restaurant** Closed Feb. Service 12:00PM-2:00PM, 8:00PM-10:00PM; mealtime specials 135F / 20,58€ (week), 175-230F / 26,68-35,06€, also à la carte. Specialties: Foie gras en terrine, magret, games in season, mushrooms, pigeon. **Credit cards** All major. **Pets** Dogs allowed. **Facilities** Swimming pool, parking. **Nearby** Museum of Armagnac in Condom, Châteaux, churches and bastide town in Armagnac; boat trip on the Baïse in Condom – 18-hole Guinlet golf course in Eauze. **Open** All year.

On the route through the old fortified villages called *bastides* that dot the Armagnac region, Fourcès, built in the 11th century, is one of the smallest. Nevertheless, it boasts all the charm of traditional bastide architecture, including the half-timbered houses encircling its square, its arcades, and the castle that today is the beautiful *Château de Fourcès* hotel. The noble, austere edifice is surrounded by fields sloping to the riverside. Inside, a restful atmosphere is created by the elegance and refinement of the decor and the mullioned windows. The bedroom walls are made of the region's traditional blond stone, or decorated in pastel shades; the rooms are furnished with antiques and offer all the amenities, even though some have only a shower room. After our last visit, however, we have a slight reservation about the professionalism and quality of the dinner. We might have just been luckier for lunch, because service was great at *L'Auberge de Fourcès* on the village square. A great chance to see one of the most charming architectural wonders of southern France.

*How to get there ( Map 30): 50km south of Agen. 12km west of Condom.*

# Hôtel de Bastard

32700 Lectoure (Gers)
Rue Lagrange
Tel. (0)5.62.68.82.44 - Fax (0)5.62.68.76.81
M. Arnaud

**Category** ★★ **Rooms** 27 and 2 suite with telephone, bath or shower, WC and TV. **Price** Double 260-380F / 39,64-57,93€; suite 590-690F / 89,94-105,19€. **Meals** Breakfast 48F / 7,32€; half board 270-500F / 41,16-76,22€ (per pers., 3 days min.). **Restaurant** Service 12:15PM-1:30PM, 7:30PM-9:30PM; mealtime specials 88-300F / 13,43-45,73€, also à la carte. Specialties: Foie frais, magret. **Credit cards** All major. **Pets** Dogs allowed (+15F / 2,28€). **Facilities** Swimming pool, parking. **Nearby** Château of Gramont; Châteaux, churches and bastides of Armagnac; Flaran, Larresingle, Fourcès, Tillac, Bassoues, Lavarders; Collegiate Church of La Romieu; jazz festival in Marciac (August) – 9-hole Fleurance golf course. **Open** Feb 7 – Dec 19.

Lectoure is a magnificent small fortified town overlooking the undulating countryside of the Gers. Setting out to explore the narrow streets lined with old houses, you will come across a large carved stone gateway which is the entrance to this 18th-century house. A large paved terrace with a swimming pool overlooks the village rooftops and open countryside. This view can be seen from the reception rooms, which are beautifully decorated, with pretty fabrics, high ceilings, and handsome 18th-century style furniture. The bedrooms are small but comfortable; choose a room on the *premier étage* and make sure that the hotel is not giving a wedding party if it is a weekend! This year, there is a new, pleasant lounge bar, as well as mouthwatering cuisine. A hospitable and charming place to stay.

*How to get there (Map 30): 35km north of Auch via N21.*

## Château de Projan

32400 Projan (Gers)
Tel. (0)5.62.09.46.21 - Fax (0)5.62.09.44.08
M. Bernard Vichet - Mme Christine Poullain

**Rooms** 9 (4 with shower or bath and WC). **Price** Single and double 300-650F / 45,73-99,09€. **Meals** Breakfast 45F / 6,86€, served 8:00AM-12:00PM; half board 280-430F / 42,69-65,55€ (per pers., 3 days min.). **Evening meals** Only by reservation for non-residents. Service from 8:00PM; mealtime special 110F / 16,77€. **Credit cards** Visa, Eurocard and MasterCard. **Pets** Small dogs allowed on request (+40F / 6,10€). **Nearby** Landes and Gascony Regional Parks; bastides; Lourdes (1hr); Château of Mascaraas, Museum of Vic-Bilh, the ocean 1 1/2 hr. away, jazz festival in Marciac (August). **Open** Easter – mid Nov (in winter by reservation).

The beautiful old *Château de Projan* is located in a 7-1/2-acre park on a rocky spur overlooking the two Valleys of the Lees. The present owners, who are veritable patrons of the arts, have gathered an impressive collection of contemporary art, which is exhibited throughout the château; combined with several imposing 17th- and 18th-century pieces of furniture, the overall effect is warm and inviting. The bedrooms, impeccably renovated and tastefully decorated, vary from vast to tiny. Some ultra-modern designer baths were cleverly integrated into the château, where space was available. Finally, for those rooms without bathrooms, don't be scared: Projan has made the collective, antique thermal baths both up-to-date and charming. This place really deserves going out of your way for.

***How to get there*** *(Map 29): A 64, exit Pau. 40km north of Pau via N134 to Sarron, and D646 towards Riscles.*

## Auberge du Bergerayre

32110 Saint-Martin-d'Armagnac (Gers)
Tel. (0)5.62.09.08.72 - Fax (0)5.62.09.09.74
Mme Sarran

**Category ★ Rooms** 10 with telephone, bath or shower, WC, 7 with TV. **Price** Single and double 300-425F / 45,73-64,79€. **Meals** Breakfast 35F / 5,34€; half board and full board 255-310F / 38,87-47,26€ (obligatory in Jul and Aug) and full board 335-400F / 51,07-60,98€ (per pers.). **Restaurant** Closed Tuesday evening and Wednesday. Service 12:00PM-2:30PM, 7:30PM-9:00PM; mealtime specials 80-200F / 12,20-30,49€, also à la carte. Specialties: Foie gras de canard sur le grill; magret fourré de foie sur lit de cèpes et pommes de terre; pastis gascon. **Credit cards** Diner's, Visa, Eurocard and MasterCard. **Pets** Dogs allowed. **Facilities** Parking. **Nearby** Landes and Gascony Regional Parks; bastides; Lourdes (1hr); Château of Mascaraas, Museum of Vic-Bilh, jazz festival in Marciac (Aug) – 18-hole Quintet golf course, 18-hole Bigone golf course. **Open** All year.

The Auberge du Bergeraye is a typical house of the Gers *département:* simple, solid, and planted in the midst of vineyards and fields. At the foot of the *auberge* is a lake, and in the distance the Pyrénées appear, splendid and mysterious. You will find fourteen bedrooms here, some in the old auberge, others around the swimming pool, and the most recent in another building which has just been renovated. Each decorated individually, the rooms are quiet and comfortable. A discreet garden shades a large swimming pool, which the guests love. Pierrette Sarran, who is a cooking teacher from November to April, turns out a generous *cuisine de terroir,* employing products from neighboring farms and conferring on this delicious *auberge* the charm of the past.

***How to get there*** *( Map 29 ): 35km southeast of Mont-de-Marsan towards Aire-sur-l'Adour, then N134; at the traffic circle, head towards Nogaro/Riscle and follow signs.*

## Domaine de Bassibé

32400 Ségos (Gers)
Tel. (0)5.62.09.46.71 - Fax (0)5.62.08.40.15
M. and Mme Lacroix

**Category** ★★★★ **Rooms** 11, 7 suites with telephone, bath, WC and TV. **Price** Double and suite 650-980F / 99,09-149,40€. **Meals** Breakfast 75F / 11,43€; half board 640-805F / 97,57-122,72€ (per pers.). **Restaurant** Closed Tuesday and Wednesday lunchtime except in hight season. Service 12:00PM-2:00PM, 7:30PM-10:00PM; mealtime specials 160-240F / 24,39-36,59€, also à la carte. Specialties: Cou de canard farci aux champignons et foie gras; salade originale de poulet grillé aux condiments à la façon d'Alexandre Dumas. **Credit cards** All major. **Pets** Dogs allowed. **Facilities** Swimming pool, bicycle, parking. **Nearby** Landes and Gascony Regional Parks; bastides; jazz festival in Marciac (Aug) – 18-hole Mont-de-Marsan golf course, 18-hole golf course in Pau, Tursan golf course (8km). **Closed** Jan – end Mar and Tuesday, Wednesday lunchtime in low season.

The *Domaine de Bassibé* was built in the old family mansion of a large farming estate. The ancient trees in the park and the carefully tended garden grace it with the reassuring atmosphere of tradition. Modern conveniences and elegance are also the key words in the bedrooms and bathrooms in the *Maison Vieille* as well as in the more recent *Maison des Champs* facing it. The rooms overlook the fragrant honeysuckle garden or, as far as the eye can see, the gentle hills of the Gers. There is no set time for breakfast, which you can enjoy in the flower garden in summer. Elegant meals accompanied by well-chosen wines are served around the large swimming pool shaded by great oak trees or in the pleasant dining room installed in the old wine press. Attentive hospitality with a smile at this beautiful, genuine, and charming place to stay.

***How to get there*** *(Map 29): 40km southeast of Mont-de-Marsan towards Aire-sur-l'Adour, then N134. Airport and TGV (train) in Pau, 40km away.*

## Claude Marco

Lamagdelaine 46090 Cahors (Lot)
Tel. (0)5.65.35.30.64 - Fax (0)5.65.30.31.40
M. and Mme Marco

**Rooms** 4 with air conditioning, telephone, bath with whirlpool bath, WC, satellite TV and minibar.
**Price** Double 550-580F / 83,85-88,42€; suite 680F / 103,67€. **Meals** Breakfast 60F / 9,15€, served
8:00-11:00. **Restaurant** Closed Sunday evening and Monday except Jun 15 – Sep 15. Service 12:00PM-
2:00PM, 7:30PM-9:30PM, mealtime specials 140F / 21,34€ (lunchtime), 200-295F / 30,49-44,97€;
also à la carte. Specialties: Foie gras au sel; tatin de foie gras; pot-au-feu de canard; filet de bœuf
aux morilles. **Credit cards** All major. **Pets** Dogs allowed. **Facilities** Swimming pool, parking. **Nearby**
Cahors; Cahors wine route from Mercues to Montcabrier; Lot and Célé valleys. **Closed** Jan – Mar 5,
Sunday evening and Monday in low season.

*C*laude Marco is well-known and highly rated in all the French gastronomic
guides. The addition of several bedrooms now gives us the opportunity to
include his address in our guide and to suggest a true gourmet stay in an inn of
character and charm. This beautiful old Quercy building and balcony are
covered in greenery; inside, the lounges and dining room are located in superb
barrel-vaulted rooms of pale-yellow stone, while the bedrooms have been
installed in the garden, around the swimming pool. They are fresh, cheerful,
elegant, and very comfortable, as are the the bathrooms with whirlpool
bathtubs. In the restaurant, you may choose between the *Menu Quercynois* if
you wish to discover the regional specialties; the *Menu Surprise*, which is made
up depending on the best products from the market that day, and the chef's
inspiration; and finally the *Carte des Saisons*, for seasonal specialties. The
delicious cuisine aside, remember that you are in a very beautiful region, which
has many natural and touristic sites of interest.

**How to get there** *(Map 30): 7km from Cahors via D653 towards Figeac.*

## Chez Marcel

46100 Cardaillac (Lot)
Rue du 11-Mai-1944
Tel. (0)5.65.40.11.16 - Fax (0)5.65.40.49.08
M. B. Marcel

**Rooms** 5. **Price** Double 160F / 24,39€. **Meals** Breakfast 30F, / 4,57€, served all morning; half board and full board 210-260F / 32,01-39,64€ (per pers., 3 days min.). **Restaurant** Closed Sunday evening and Monday except in Jul and Aug. Service 12:00PM-1:30PM, 7:00PM-8:30PM; mealtime specials 80-180F / 12,20-27,44€, also à la carte. Specialties: Foie gras; omelette aux cèpes ou truffes; cou de canard farci; truite aux croûtons; agneau des Causses; gâteau aux noix; profiterolles à la menthe et à la crème. **Credit cards** Visa, Eurocard and MasterCard. **Pets** Dogs allowed in restaurant. **Facilities** Parking on the Place du Fort. **Nearby** "Musée Eclaté" in Cardaillac, Valleys of the Lot and the Célé (Figeac-Cahors-Figeac). **Closed** 2 weeks in Oct and Feb, Sunday evening and Monday in low season.

Praised as among one of the "Most Beautiful Villages in France," Cardaillac still has many relics from the Middle Ages and the Holy Wars. Today, the community is working hard to preserve the authenticity of the sites. The grocery store still stands in as tobacco store and newspaper shop, and the village bar-restaurant, *Chez Marcel*, has some rooms for visitors who might like to stay over. On the ground floor, two large restaurant rooms with tables dressed in Vichy red and white welcome local regulars for good meals cooked with local, traditional produce. Upstairs, the little bedrooms sport country-style furniture found by the present owner's father. They all have the quaint charm of country hotels of the past. Each has a sink, and all share one shower room which should be soon redone. Relaxed, homey atmosphere at this charming hotel at less than 200 Francs.

***How to get there*** *( Map 24): 9 km northwest of Figeac on N 140, and then, on the right, D 15.*

## Château de la Treyne

Lacave 46200 Souillac (Lot)
La Treyne
Tel. (0)5.65.27.60.60 - Fax (0)5.65.27.60.70
Mme Gombert

**Category** ★★★★ **Rooms** 14, 2 apartments, with air-conditioning, telephone, bath, WC and TV. **Price** Double 750-1650F / 114,34-251,54€, apart. from 1850F / 282,03€. **Meals** Breakfast 90F / 13,72€, served all the morning; half board 850-1260F / 129,58-192,09€ (per pers., obligatory in summer). **Restaurant** Closed Tuesday and Wednesday lunchtime. Service 12:30PM-2:00PM, 7:30PM-10:00PM, mealtime specials 220F / 33,54€ (lunchtime, wine and coffee incl.) 320-420F / 48,78-64,03€, also à la carte. Specialties: Langoustines au vinaigre de framboises; chartreuse de pintade aux girolles. **Credit cards** All major. **Pets** Dogs allowed. **Facilities** Swimming pool, tennis, canoeing/kayaking, parking. **Nearby** Quercy region of the Dordogne from Souillac to Saint-Céré, Rocamadour, Padirac – 9-hole Rochebois golf course in Vitrac. **Open** Easter – mid Nov.

Overlooking the Dordogne, the *Château de la Treyne* enjoys an exceptional location. A beautiful forest (a great place to stroll) surrounds the château, which itself has a French garden and a tree grove, which hides a large, clear pool and a tennis court. The hotel is a 17th-century structure of human proportions, and where you'll feel at ease, whether in the lounges, in the bar, or in the magnificient dining room where candlelight dinners take place. In summer, dinner moves out to the terrace which looks over the river, and guests linger there late to enjoy the peaceful, refreshing evening. No matter what their view, the rooms (some are large) are all particularly pleasant, comfortable, very prettily furnished, and tastefully decorated. Each has its own genuine charm. A precious place, where subtle luxury and charm mix wonderfully together.

***How to get there*** *(Map 23): 37 km south of Brive-la-Gaillarde on N 20 or A 20 until Souillac, then take D 43 for 5 km until La Treyne.*

## Le Pont de l'Ouysse

46200 Lacave (Lot)
Tel. (0)5.65.37.87.04 - Fax (0)5.65.32.77.41
M. and Mme Chambon

**Category** ★★★ **Rooms** 13 with air-conditioning, telephone, bath, WC, TV and minibar. **Price** Single and double 750-800F / 114,34-121,96€, suite 900F / 137,20€. **Meals** Breakfast 70F / 10,67€, served 8:00-10:00; half board 750-800F / 114,34-121,96€ (per pers.). **Restaurant** Closed Monday lunchtime and Tuesday lunchtime; Monday evening in low season. Service 12:30PM-2:00PM, 7:30PM-9:00PM; also à la carte. Specialties: Ecrevisses; foie gras; pigeon aux cèpes; poulette rôtie aux truffes. **Credit cards** All major. **Pets** Dogs allowed. **Facilities** Swimming pool, parking. **Nearby** Quercy region of the Dordogne from Souillac to Saint-Céré, Rocamadour, Padirac – 9-hole Rochebois golf course in Vitrac. **Open** Mar – Nov 10.

Drowned in verdant nature, at the foot of a rocky peak, this hotel overlooks a few meters of the Ouysse which flows to meet the Dordogne a bit downstream. The completely refurbished interior has warm, tastefully up-to-date decorations. Bordered by a veranda, the ground floor is heated by warm colors -- salmon for the lounge, and ochre for the dining room. All the bedrooms look out on the terrace, shaded by a linden and a chestnut tree, where meals are served during good weather. The comfortable rooms, with their discreet or colorful wallpaper, boast pleasant bathrooms. Choose the upper rooms (a bit calmer for when the murmur of the terrace dinner lasts longer than it should), or those with a little terrace. The excellent restaurant menu is not very long, but often changes according to the imaginative knack of Monsieur Chambon. His wife makes sure that your welcome is a friendly one.

***How to get there*** *(Map 23): 37 km south of Brive-la-Gaillarde on N 20 until Souillac, then take D 43.*

## Domaine de Saint-Géry- La Petite Auberge

46800 Lascabanes (Lot)
Tel. (0)5.65.31.82.51 - Fax (0)5.65.22.92.89
Pascale and Patrick Duler

**Rooms** 4 and 1 apartment with telephone, bath, WC. **Price** Double from 590F / 89,94€, apart. 1050F / 160,07€. **Meals** Breakfast 95F / 14,48€, served 8:30-10:00; half board 480-930F / 73,18-141,78€ (per pers., obligatory in Jul and Aug). **Restaurant** Closed Monday and Tuesday except in Jul and Aug. Service 8:00PM-9:00PM, mealtime specials 195-450F / 29,73-68,60€. Specialties: Filet de porc au basilic; marquise au chocolat. **Credit cards** Visa, Eurocard and MasterCard. **Pets** Dogs allowed (+45F / 6,86€). **Facilities** Swimming pool, parking. **Nearby** Cathedral of Saint-Etienne in Cahors, Cahors wine route (château de Bonaguil), valley of the Lot and the Célé (Saint-Cirq-Lapopie). **Closed** Jan 10 – Mar 15, Monday and Tuesday except Jul – Aug.

This is an *auberge* but it is above all Patrick and Pascale Duler's home where you will share with them the atmosphere of the past. The beautiful farm buildings surrounding the *auberge* are used for the farm. Acres of grain, a wild-boar farm, several black Gascon pigs, ducks, and a vegetable garden provide the basis for hearty meals prepared and served with discreet charm by Pascale. The dinners served at a communal table, in the lounge, or on the adjoining terrace in summer, are moments of great pleasure. For proof, you only need to see the smiles when guests gather around the dessert buffet. (You should know that the "suggestions" for half board are extra.) Very pretty rooms with country furniture have been tastefully arranged, offering you space, quiet and comfort. A charming place to stay, where you might, however, not find someone on hand: with only five rooms, it is difficult to find full-time staff.

***How to get there*** *( Map 30): 18 km southwest of Cahors on N 20, heading toward Toulouse, then a right toward Montcuq for 500 m, then Labastide Marnhac on D 7 for 15 km. Follow the signs.*

## Relais Sainte-Anne

46600 Martel (Lot)
Rue du Pourtanel
Tel. (0)5.65.37.40.56 - Fax (0)5.65.37.42.82
Mme Lachèze

**Category** ★★★ **Rooms** 13 with telephone, bath or shower, WC, TV and 8 with minibar – 1 for disabled persons. **Price** Single and double 200-780F / 30,49-118,91€. **Meals** Breakfast 55F / 8,38€, served 8:00AM-12:00PM. No restaurant. **Credit cards** All major. **Pets** Dogs allowed (+50F / 7,62€). **Facilities** Heated swimming pool, parking. **Nearby** Rocamadour, Padirac, caves of Lacave, Dordogne Valley, Collonges-la-Rouge, abbey of Aubazines - Music festival in summer. **Open** End Mar – Mid Nov.

Don't be surprised to find a chapel here: The *Relais Sainte-Anne* was once a boarding house for nuns. There are 13 lovely bedrooms located in several recently renovated buildings. All have very modern conveniences but each room is individually decorated in sober, elegant fabrics and colors. The largest room has a fireplace and a large terrace. All around the *Relais*, there is a walled-in, old garden with a lovely terrace, small paths, and a beautiful swimming pool surrounded by a lawn. Breakfast can be served in your room, in the breakfast room which has a fireplace or, in good weather, on the terrace. In summer, classical music concerts are performed in the chapel. The *Relais Sainte-Anne* radiates with turn-of-the-century charm.

***How to get there*** *( Map 23): 30km south of Brive.*

## Hostellerie Le Vert

Le Vert - 46700 Mauroux (Lot)
Tel. (0)5.65.36.51.36 - Fax (0)5.65.36.56.84
M. and Mme Philippe

**Category** ★★ **Rooms** 7 with telephone, bath or shower, WC and TV. **Price** Double 290-400F / 44,21-60,98€. **Meals** Breakfast 38F / 5,80€, served 7:30-10:30; half board 325-380F / 49,55-57,93€ (per pers., 3 days min.). **Restaurant** Closed Thursday and Friday lunchtime. Service 12:00PM-1:15PM, 7:30PM-8:30PM; mealtime specials 100-180F / 15,24-27,44€, also à la carte. Specialties: Foie gras frais aux fruits frais;agneau du Quercy; poêlée de cèpes aux petits gris. **Credit cards** Amex, Visa, Eurocard and MasterCard. **Pets** Dogs allowed (+25F / 3,81€). **Facilities** Swimming pool, parking. **Nearby** Cathedral of Saint-Etienne in Cahors, Cahors wine route (château de Bonaguil), Valley of the Lot. **Open** Mid Feb – Nov 11.

The *Hostellerie Le Vert* is located in the great, rolling outdoors. The hotel is an old converted farmhouse. Its windows shed a soft and gentle light on the spacious, comfortable and refined interior. A lovely terrace looks out over the surrounding countryside - a pleasant spot for a summer breakfast. The cuisine is very good. In summer, ask for the bedroom that has been made in Room 6, set up in the former vaulted cellar, which is cool and unusual, even if its bathroom is a little austere. Above it, a large, bright new bedroom has just been added, with a beamed ceiling, stone floor, a beautiful fireplace, and a piano. The bedrooms in the main hotel are not so original but are no less inviting and comfortable, especially Rooms 3 and 4, which are very spacious and prettily furnished. Pleasant and tranquil atmosphere.

***How to get there*** *( Map 30): 37km west of Cahors via D911 to Puy-l'Evêque, then D5 towards Mauroux.*

## Hostellerie La Source Bleue

Touzac - 46700 Puy-l'Evêque (Lot)
Tel. (0)5.65.36.52.01 - Fax (0)5.65.24.65.69
M. and Mme Bouyou
E-mail: sourcebleue@wanadoo.fr

**Category** ★★★ **Rooms** 15 and 1 suite with telephone, bath, WC and TV – Wheelchair access. **Price** Double and suite 335-550F / 51,07-83,85€. **Meals** Breakfast 35F / 5,34€, served all morning; half board from 290F / 44,21€ (per pers. in double, 2 days min.). **Restaurant** Closed Wednesday lunchtime. Service 12:00PM-1:30PM, 7:30PM-9:15PM; mealtime specials 100-220F / 15,24-33,54€, also à la carte. Specialties: Saint-Jacques au safran; feuilleté de foie gras; agneau du Quercy; nougat glacé. **Credit cards** Amex, Visa, Eurocard and MasterCard. **Pets** Dogs allowed (+30F / 4,57€). **Facilities** Swimming pool, sauna (100F / 15,24€), health center, boat, bicycle rentals, parking. **Nearby** Marguerite-Moréno museum, Cahors wine route (château de Bonaguil) – 18-hole La Chapelle golf course in Auzac, 18-hole Castelnaud-de-Gratecambe golf course, Roucous golf course (18km). **Open** Mar 26 – Dec 16.

Hostellerie La Source Bleue, in a converted 14th-century paper mill on the left bank of the Lot, has been tastefully restored by its owners. The bedrooms, some with modern furniture, are comfortable, and the bathrooms are impeccable. (However, avoid Room 3.) Four new bedrooms have been added in the tower and decorated with antique furniture. The restaurant, located at the entrance to the park, is separate from the hotel. The cooking is refined and served in a beautiful dining room, with the soft lilt of well-chosen music in the background. The service is attentive but discreet. The gardens and park of "The Blue Spring" are beautiful with their many species of trees, including an impressive bamboo forest.

***How to get there*** *(Map 30): 39km west of Cahors via D911 towards Fumel/Villeneuve-sur-Lot; at Touzac, cross the Lot.*

## Domaine de la Rhue

La Rhue
46500 Rocamadour (Lot)
Tel. (0)5.65.33.71.50 - Fax (0)5.65.33.72.48
M. and Mme Jooris

**Category** ★★★ **Rooms** 14 (some with air-conditioning) with telephone, bath or shower, WC and 4 with TV. **Price** Single and double 380-580F / 57,93-88,42€, apart. (4 pers.) 680F / 103,67€. **Meals** Breakfast 45-65F / 6,86-9,91€, served 8:00-10:00. No restaurant. **Credit cards** Visa, Diner's. **Pets** Dogs allowed (+30F / 3,96€). **Facilities** Swimming pool, hot-air ballooning, parking. **Nearby** Old town, Francis Poulenc Museum in Rocamadour, Dordogne Valley, Lascaux caves, Padirac chasm – 9-hole Montal golf course in Saint-Céré. **Open** Palm days – Oct 17.

This hotel is located in the splendid stables of a château which is surrounded by beautiful rolling countryside. The vast entrance hall still has its original paving and traces of the stalls. Next to the fireplace, antique furniture, and a few armchairs invite you to kick back and relax. Also, not far away, breakfast is served on pretty tables (you can also take breakfast in your room or in the garden.) The rooms and their very comfortable bathrooms are found on the upper stories and in the surrounding buildings. They are prettily decorated, with beatufiul fabrics, vintage furniture, parquetry, or soft carpeting. Some of the rooms on the ground floor are like small houses with a private terrace (two have small kitchens.). From there, following the bushy path, you can go directly to Rocamadour. If you need some advice about restaurants, don't hesitate to ask the owners about the good eateries in the area.

***How to get there*** *(Map 24): 55km south of Brive-la-Gaillarde via N20 towards Cressensac, then N140; 1km before junction with D673, take the road on the right.*

## Château de Roumégouse

Rignac 46500 Gramat (Lot)
Tel. (0)5.65.33.63.81 - Fax (0)5.65.33.71.18
M. and Mme Laine

**Category** ★★★★ **Rooms** 15 (2 with air-conditioning) with telephone, bath, TV, minibar. **Price** Double 650-1000F / 99,09-152,45€; suite 1200-1400F / 182,94-213,43€. **Meals** Breakfast 65F / 9,91€, served 8:00-10:00; half board (obligatory in summer) 1020-2300F / 155,50-350,63€ (1-2 pers.). **Restaurant** Closed Tuesday (except Jul-Aug). Service 12:30PM-1:45PM, 7:30PM-9:45PM; mealtime specials 105-350F / 16,01-53,36€; also à la carte. Specialties: Foie gras chaud; purée à la truffe; côtes de canard; pastis aux pommes. **Credit cards** Amex, Visa, Eurocard, MasterCard. **Pets** Dogs allowed. **Facilities** Swimming pool, parking. **Nearby** Rocamadour; Dordogne Valley; Lascaux caves; Padirac chasm – 9-hole Montal golf course in Saint-Céré. **Open** Easter – Oct 19.

Built in the 19th century on the ruins of a very old castle, this hotel is a true family home surrounded by a 5-acre park. Now changed into a hotel, the *Roumegouse* is wonderfully furbished, and each room is personalized by beautiful antique furniture, decorative objects and selected paintings. There is the Napoleon III lounge, the little, tower library/bar, the two dining rooms, the veranda, and fifteen irresistible rooms. All are different, bright, furnished with antiques, and very comfortable, with decoration in natural color schemes, beiges, and delicate highlights. (Each winter, Luce makes lampshades that go with each rooms decor.) Fresh-cut flowers follow the changing of the seasons; you'll even find them on your breakfast plate. In summer, the meals, majestically prepared by Jean-Louis, are served on the terrace, resplendent in white geraniums that dominate the countryside. A charming and very tasteful place to stay, where you will come back with friends.

***How to get there*** *( Map 24): 35 km north of Figeac on N 140. 4 km from Gramat.*

## Hôtel Beau Site

46500 Rocamadour (Lot)
Tel. (0)5.65.33.63.08 - Fax (0)5.65.33.65.23
M. Martial Menot
E-mail: beausite.rocamadour@wanadoo.fr

**Category** ★★★ **Rooms** 43 (21 with air-conditioning) with telephone, bath or shower, WC, TV – Elevator. **Price** Double 390-690F / 59,46-105,19€. **Meals** Breakfast 55F / 8,38€, served 7:00-9:30/10:00; half board 300-380F / 45,73-57,93€ (per pers.). **Restaurant** Service 12:00PM-2:00PM, 7:00PM-9:00PM (7:30PM-9:30PM in summer); mealtime specials 115-275F / 17,53-41,92€, also à la carte. Specialties: Foie gras de canard à croque sel. **Credit cards** All major. **Pets** Dogs allowed. **Facilities** Garage. **Nearby** Rocamadour, Padirac, caves of Lascaux – 9-hole Saint-Céré golf course. **Open** Feb 6 – Dec 31.

Rocamadour is world famous not only because pilgrims have been coming here since the Middle Ages, but because of its extraordinary location on a gigantic outcrop overlooking the cliffs' limestone plateaux. The well-named "Beautiful Site" hotel stands in the very heart of the medieval city where, once the throngs have emptied the tiny pedestrian streets aroound 7 P.M., you will be one of the rare people to whom Rocamadour offers its true face. The lobby has a distinctly medieval, Haute Epoque style with, hidden behind the central stairway, two small vaulted lounges which are much appreciated in summer. The bedrooms are pleasant with a beautiful view. Our favorites are in the main house; the others are in front, above the restaurant. They have been renovated in a discreetly modern style, with attractive color schemes. Good regional cuisine is served in the panoramic restaurant, in the dining room or on the terrace.

***How to get there*** *(Map 24): Via A 20 take the Rocamadour-Rodez exit 12 km south of Brive, then the N 140 and the D 673. Once in the village, follow direction "Cité medievale" then take the pedestrian street from the first fortified gate until the hotel's parking lot.*

## Hôtel Les Vieilles Tours

Lafage - 46500 Rocamadour (Lot)
Tel. (0)5.65.33.68.01 - Fax (0)5.65.33.68.59
M. Zozzoli
E-mail: roger.zozzoli@wanadoo.fr

**Category** ★★ **Rooms** 18 with telephone, bath or shower and WC. **Price** Double 300-480F / 45,73-73,18€. **Meals** Breakfast 45-65F / 6,86-9,91€, served 8:00-11:00; half board 360-450F / 54,88-68,60€. **Restaurant** Closed lunchtime except Sunday and national holidays. Service 7:30PM-9:00PM; mealtime specials 125-320F / 19,06-48,78€, children 56F / 8,54€, also à la carte. Specialties: Foie gras au Cahors; escalope de foie gras; dos d'esturgeon; croustillant de magret de canard au miel et à la vanille. **Credit cards** Visa, Amex. **Pets** Dogs allowed (+30F / 4,57€). **Facilities** Swimming pool, parking. **Nearby** Old town, Francis Poulenc Museum in Rocamadour, Padirac chasm, Lascaux caves – 9-hole Saint-Céré golf course. **Open** Palm Sunday – mid Nov.

Three kilometers from Rocamadour, this very well-restored manor (the oldest part of which dates back to the 13th century) enjoys peace, quiet, and an exceptional view of the Alzou and Ouysse valleys. The reception and dining room have their original stone walls and the tables are tastefully laid. There are bedrooms in both the old building and its modern annex, which was built in the local style. Pleasantly furnished, with some 19th-century pieces, the bedrooms are all different. Eight of them have just been rehabilitated and brightened up; the renovation program continues on this year. In the kitchen, Frederique Colot works with regional products and his creativity changes according to the season. Its very worthwhile half board plan, the kindness and availability of the staff, and the two acres that surround this hotel make this an ideal place to rest and relax.

***How to get there*** *(Map 24): 53km south of Brive via N20 to Cressensac, then N140 and D673; 3km from Rocamadour, in the towards Payrac/Gourdon.*

# Auberge du Sombral

46330 Saint-Cirq-Lapopie (Lot)
Tel. (0)5.65.31.26.08 - Fax (0)5.65.30.26.37
M. and Mme Hardeveld

**Category** ★★ **Rooms** 8 with telephone, 5 with bath, 5 with shower. **Price** Single and double 300-400F / 45,73-60,98€. **Meals** Breakfast 48F / 7,32€, served until 9:30. **Restaurant** Service 12:00PM-2:00PM, 7:30PM-9:00PM; mealtime specials 100-280F / 15,24-42,69€, also à la carte. Specialties: Truite au vieux Cahors; feuilleté d'asperges aux morilles; escalope de foie chaud aux pommes; terrine de foie de canard confit. **Credit cards** Visa, Eurocard and MasterCard. **Pets** Dogs allowed. **Nearby** Saint-Etienne Cathedral, Cahors wine route from Cahors to Bonaguil by the Lot Valley, valleys of the Lot and the Célé. **Closed** Nov 11 – end Mar, Tuesday evening and Wednesday.

In the heart of this superb, historically-registered village that overlooks the Lot valley, the *Auberge du Sombral* should be an example to other hotels located in highly touristic areas. Set up in a pretty, simply decorated house, this hotel is run by owners who obviously love their work and are the reason for the comfortable, agreeable feeling that reigns here. A tiny corner lounge, heated by a fireplace, is set up in the reception area. Next door, two dining rooms, pleasantly lit in the evening, offer a tranquil place to taste good produce and tastefully, delicately cooked meals. The service is both attentive and warm and is one of the high points of this address. Whether large or medium-sized, the rooms are comfortable, soberly decorated, and cheered up by paintings from regional artists that also hang in the restaurant. At the end of the day, the visitors flee the village, peace and calm moves in, and you have but to enjoy the tranquility of the evening.

***How to get there*** *(Map 31): 33 km east of Cahors on D 653 heading toward Saint-Gery, then via D 662.*

## La Pergola

65170 Saint-Lary-Soulan (Hautes-Pyrénées)
Tel. (0)5.62.39.40.46 - Fax (0)5.62.40.06.55
M. Mir

**Category** ★★ **Rooms** 22 with bath or shower, WC, TV – Elevator; 1 for disabled persons. **Price** Single and double 280-360F/ 42,69-54,88€. **Meals** Breakfast 40F/ 6,10€, served 7:30-10:00; half board and full board 240-395F/ 36,59-60,22€ (per pers.). **Restaurant** Service 12:00PM-2:30PM, 7:00PM-9:30PM; mealtime specials 100-250F / 15,24-38,11€; also à la carte. Specialties: Terrine de foie gras; truite; magret de canard; agneau; chevreau. **Credit cards** All major. **Pets** Dogs not allowed. **Facilities** Parking. **Nearby** Skiing; thermal bath; Aure Valley: Arreau, Cadéac, Ancizan, Bazuz-Aure, Vieille-Aure; National Park of Spain. **Closed** Nov.

At 827 meters in altitude at the entrance to the Néouvielle nature reserve, Saint-Lary is a low-mountain town equally well-known for its thermal baths. A bit away from the main road and just after a well-manicured garden, the *Pergola* is the perfect hotel to enjoy this pleasant Pyrenese locale. Almost entirely renovated, it has still kept its family feeling, thanks to the friendly hospitality and some older pieces of furniture placed here and there to warm up the contemporary look of the reception area, restaurant, and hallways. The rooms, often quite large, are outfitted in a simple, elegant, and functional way. Very comfortable and perfectly well-tended, they all look out on the garden and the mountains. Some have access to a huge, southern exposure terrace. The food, breakfast included, is excellent, and, in summer, meals are served under the "pergola" that gave the hotel its name. A high-quality place to stay that we do not hesitate to recommend to you.

*How to get there* ( *Map 30*): 30 km from Lannemezan on D 929.

## Château d'Aiguefonde

81200 Aiguefonde (Tarn)
Rue du Château
Tel. (0)5.63.98.13.70 - Fax (0)5.63.98.69.90 - P. de Vilder - H. Goens

**Category** ★★★★ **Rooms** 8 with telephone, bath, satellite TV, CD player – 1 for disabled persons. **Price** Single and double 750-1000F/ 114,34-152,45€; suite 1250F/ 190,56€. **Meals** Breakfast incl.; half board 635-790F/ 96,81-120,43€ (per pers., 4 days min.). **Restaurant** By reservation. Service 1:00PM-2:30PM, 7:00PM-9:15PM; mealtime specials 250F / 38,11€, also à la carte. Specialties: Joues de lotte sauce hollandaise; rognons d'agneau au foie gras; gauffres d'Espérandieu. **Credit cards** All major. **Divers Pets** Dogs allowed (private kennel). **Facilities** Swimming pool, parking and garage (2 cars). **Nearby** Goya Museum in Castres; Sidobre and Lacaune Mounts, Castres to Mazamet – 18-hole la Barouge golf course in Pont-de-l'Arn. **Open** End May – end Sep.

At the foot of the Black Mountain, the *Château d'Aiguefonde* was redone in the 18th century, when the boxwood garden, designed by Le Notre, was added on. The interior sports a sumptuous, monumental stairway with *trompe-l'oeil* decorations, Flemish and Dutch paintings, Persian rugs, and antique furniture which gracefully mixes with unusual, contemporary pieces. The very comfortable rooms enjoy the same outstanding attentiveness and furnishing. To give you a feel for the mood, CD players replace televisions -- a pleasant idea in keeping with the originality and artistry of the place. For dinner, the hotel offers succulent seasonal cuisine served in the coziness of a little dining room decorated with beautiful, Aubusson tapestries. In summer, breakfasts are served in the midst of the boxwood garden, and, to not miss a beat, the swimming pool is designed like an Italian reflecting pool. Here is the perfect place to spread out in the sun and watch the waterfalls that spray their last mist next to your very own chaise longue.

***How to get there*** *(Map 31): 5 km from Mazamet.*

## Hostellerie Saint-Antoine

81000 Albi (Tarn)
17, rue Saint-Antoine
Tel. (0)5.63.54.04.04 - Fax (0)5.63.47.10.47
MM. Rieux and son

**Category** ★★★★ **Rooms** 48 with air-conditioning, telephone, bath, WC, TV and minibar. **Price** Double 450-750F / 68,60-114,34€, suite 850-950F / 129,58-144,83€. **Meals** Breakfast 60F / 9,15€; half board 420-720F / 64,03-109,76€ (per pers.). **Restaurant** Closed Sunday. Service 7:00PM-9:30PM; menu 140F / 21,34€, also à la carte. Specialties: Foie gras; salade d'écrevisses; daube de bœuf à l'albigeoise; tournedos Périgueux; tarte à l'ancienne; glace aux noix. **Credit cards** All major. **Pets** Dogs allowed (+30F / 4,57€). **Facilities** Swimming pool and tennis in "La Réserve", parking. **Nearby** Cathedral of Sainte-Cécile, Toulouse-Lautrec Museum in Albi, Viaur viaduct, Ambialet, Gaillac, Cordes – 18-hole golf course in Albi. **Open** All year.

Founded in the 18th-century and run by the same family for five generations, this inn was restored in 1960, which might explain its underwhelming exterior. The roomy reception areas are much more appealing, especially thanks to the personal touch that comes from the elegant furniture. The bedrooms are extremely comfortable, quiet, well-designed, and many have a view of the flower garden. Some of the larger ones have a lounge area. On the ground floor the dining room opens onto the garden. A breakfast buffet is served on the veranda. You will enjoy good traditional cooking, attentive service, and warm hospitality.

*How to get there* (*Map 31*): *In the town center.*

## Le Castel de Burlats

81100 Burlats (Tarn)
8, place du 8-Mai-1945
Tel. (0)5.63.35.29.20 - Fax (0)5.63.51.14.69
M. Dauphin

**Rooms** 10 with telephone bath or shower, WC and TV – 1 for disabled persons. **Price** Single and double 350-420F / 53,36-64,12€; suite 450-680F / 68,60-103,67€. **Meals** Breakfast 40F / 6,10€; half board 340-420F / 51,83-64,12€ (per pers., 3 days min.). **Restaurant** For residents and only by reservation. Service from 7:30PM; mealtime specials 100-180F / 15,24-27,44€. Specialties: Fois gras maison. **Credit cards** All major. **Pets** Dogs allowed. **Facilities** Parking and garage. **Nearby** Castres (Goya Museum; Goya festival in July); Mount of Sidobre; Albi (Cathedral and Toulouse-Lautrec museum) – 18-hole La Barouge golf course in Albi and 9-hole golf course in Mazamet. **Open** All year.

Located at the start of the Agout valley that runs to the granite mount of Sidobre, the village of Burlats has existed since the 12th century. The hotel is in the château of the local lords and is surrounded by a beautiful, French-style park. With its impressive 13th-century tower and austere, U-shaped, renaissance façade, the hotel leans into the slope and faces the romanesque church. Recently opened after a very successful renovation, the *Castel* offers huge rooms, decorated in light, often blue and yellow, tones, beautifully furnished with Louis-Philippe furniture. Comfortable, well-kept-up, with impeccable bathrooms, they are there to please, and that includes their value for the money. You will also enjoy an immense lounge, pool lounge, and dining room that faces a terrace with century-old camelias. Madame Dauphin is in the kitchen and offers up two savory specials that change every evening. She, with her husband, takes the upkeep of the hotel and the quality of the reception very seriously. A really wonderful place with a great future ahead of it.

*How to get there ( Map 31): 5 km from Castres.*

## Auberge de la Halle

81170 Cordes (Tarn)
Place de la Halle
Tel. (0)5.63.56.18.84 - Fax (0)5.63.56.19.09
Mme Anne-Marie Aizes-Lopez

**Rooms** 5 with telephone, bath, WC, TV. **Price** Doubles 250-450F / 38,11-68,60€; extra bed 50F / 7,62€. **Meals** Breakfast 38F / 5,80€; half board and full board 195-270F / 29,73-41,16€ (per pers.). **Restaurant** Service: 12:00PM-2:00PM, 7:00PM-9:30PM; mealtime specials 85-175F / 12,96-26,68€; also à la carte. Specialties: Cassoulet; daube cordaise; croustade. **Credit cards** All major. **Pets** Dogs allowed. **Nearby** Cordes site; Vindrac-Alayrac; Villefranche-de-Rouergue; (Cathedral and Toulouse-Lautrec Museum). **Open** All year.

With its steep streets, its medieval houses, and its sweeping view, Cordes is one of the most beautiful villages of southwest France. At the very top, in the market square, this is the inn to discover this little town. Of course, the artisinal, and local produce shop that neighbor the hotel feels a bit like a "tourist-trap." All the same, during holiday season, the inn gets caught up in the frenzy, and lovers of peace and quiet might be disappointed. Off season, the *auberge* can be a handy stop-over. We highly recommend the two rooms in the 13th-century, Colen tower (former counsel tower), with their expansive view over all the region, their transom windows framed by two stone benches, their roominess, and their antique furniture. The others are simpler but still useful, once you consider their price. Hearty traditional cuisine (which could afford to be a bit lighter) is served in the rustic dining room, with its dizzying view of the valley below.

*How to get there ( Map 31 ): 80 km northeast of Toulouse and 25 kms north of Albi.*

## Cuq en Terrasses

Cuq-le-Château 81470 Cuq-Toulza (Tarn)
Tel. (0)5.63.82.54.00 - Fax (0)5.63.82.54.11
M. and Mme Whitmore

**Rooms** 7 and 1 apartment (duplex) with telephone, bath or shower, WC and TV. **Price** Rooms and suites 550-750F / 83,85-114,34€, apart. 1000F / 152,45€. **Meals** Breakfast 65F / 9,91€, served 8:30-10:00. **Restaurant** By reservation. Service 12:00PM-2:30PM, 7:30PM-9:30PM; mealtime specials 150F / 22,87€ (lunch), 180F / 27,44€ (dinner). Specialties: Vichyssoise; gazpacho; mousse de saumon fumé; filet mignon de veau à l'estragon et aux baies roses; noisettes d'agneau aux deux poivrons. **Credit cards** Diner's, Visa, Eurocard. **Pets** Dogs allowed. **Facilities** Swimming pool. **Nearby** Albi, Carcassonne, Castres market in Revel – 18-hole Fiac Golf Course. **Closed** Jan 6 – Feb 6.

This ancient house spreads out over an enchanting terraced hillside. From the terraces and the garden swimming pool, you will have a superb view over the patchwork of rich valleys the locals call *Le Pays de Cocagne*, the land of abundance. *Le Cuq en Terrasse* has been magnificently restored and decorated by an English architect and his wife. Tasteful decoration in the bright bedrooms and baths make this a very beautiful hotel, in which traditional decor has been skillfully combined with the most modern amenities. You will enjoy the sheer serenity of the place, from the terrace to the shady nooks around the swimming pool. Breakfasts are generous and elegant, and Zara Whitmore serves delicious regional cuisine. There is an excellent choice of wines, and the owners are friendly and considerate.

***How to get there*** *(Map 31): 35km east of Toulouse, towards Castres. In Cuq, head towards Revel for 2km. On A61, exit number 17.*

## Demeure de Flore

81240 Lacabarède (Tarn)
Tel. (0)5.63.98.32.32 - Fax (0)5.63.98.47.56
M. Francesco di Bari

**Category** ★★★ **Rooms** 10 and 1 suite with telephone, bath, WC and TV – Wheelchair access. **Price** Single and double 390-500F/ 59,46-76,22€, suite 850F/ 129,58€. **Meals** Breakfast 60F/ 9,14€; half board 470-500F / 71,65-76,22€ (per per., 3 days min.). **Restaurant** Closed Sunday evening and Monday from Oct – Mar 31, except national holidays. Service 12:00PM-1:30PM, 7:30PM-9:00PM; mealtime specials 130-175F / 19,82-26,67€, also à la carte. Specialties: Regional cooking. **Credit cards** Visa, Eurocard and MasterCard. **Pets** Small dogs allowed (+70F/ 10,67€). **Facilities** Swimming pool, parking, garage. **Nearby** Goya museum in Castres, Sidobre and the Monts Lacaune de Castres in Mazamet – 18-hole La Barouge golf course in Pont-de-l'Arn. **Open** All year.

This small hotel is hidden from the road by lush vegetation. Indoors, the decor is elegant; antique furniture, paintings and curios combine to create a warm and cozy atmosphere. The comfortable bedrooms are all individually decorated with colorful designer fabrics and antiques bought locally. The bathrooms are modern and luxuriously equipped. Our favorite rooms are those with a small terrace and access to the garden and swimming pool, the perfect place to relax while enjoying the view of the meadows and hills. Finally, you don't have to go out for dinner, because mouthwatering southern cuisine is served to the guests, with a smile, in a delightful dining room. A wonderful address at reasonable prices.

*How to get there (Map 31): 15km east of Mazamet via N112.*

# La Métairie Neuve

81660 Pont-de-L'Arn (Tarn)
Tel. (0)5.63.97.73.50 - Fax (0)5.63.61.94.75
Mmew Tournier

**Category** ★★★ **Rooms** 14 with telephone, bath, WC, TV and minibar. **Price** Double 390-480F / 59,46-73,18€. **Meals** Half board 300-550F / 45,73-83,85€ (per pers., 3 days min.). **Restaurant** Closed Saturday and Sunday Oct 1 – Mar 30. Service 7:30PM-9:00PM; mealtime specials 95 and 120F / 14,48 and 18,29€. Specialties: Regional cooking. **Credit cards** Diner's, Visa, Eurocard and MasterCard. **Pets** Dogs allowed. **Facilities** Swimming pool, parking. **Nearby** Goya Museum in Castres, Sidobre and the Monts Lacaune de Castres in Mazamet – 18-hole La Barouge golf course in Pont-de-l'Arn. **Open** Jan 20 – Dec 13.

This lovely old farmhouse is on the outskirts of a village which is expanding with commercial developments, but the hotel remains in a leafy, quiet area. The bedrooms are all well-equipped and elegantly furnished; the colors are harmonious and the old furniture blends perfectly with the more modern pieces. Some rooms, located in a small wing, have just been redone in a refined, well-done countryside style. The very hospitable Madame Tournier has set up her hotel like a home, with many corner lounges and a lot of pleasant little touches. A huge, open barn expands the dining room and let's one eat dinner while enjoying the swimming pool and large garden. The restaurant is running a bit slow right now, but is still the right choice for those who don't want to go out for dinner.

***How to get there*** *(Map 31): 19km southeast of Castres via N112 towards Mazamet.*

## Domaine de Rasigous

81290 Saint-Affrique-les-Montagnes (Tarn)
Tel. (0)5.63.73.30.50 - Fax (0)5.63.73.30.51
M. and Mme Fons Pessers

**Rooms** 5 and 3 suite with telephone, bath or shower, WC and TV – 1 for disabled persons. **Price** Double 400-500F / 60,98-76,22€; suite 600 and 750F / 91,47 and 114,34€. **Meals** Breakfast 55F / 8,38€, served from 8:00. **Restaurant** By reservation, for residents, from 7:00PM; mealtime specials 140F / 21,34€. Seasonal cuisine. **Credit cards** All major. **Pets** Dogs allowed. **Facilities** Swimming pool, parking and garage. **Nearby** Goya Museum in Castres, Sidobre, mounts of Lacaune and Castres in Mazamet – 18-hole Mazamet golf course. **Open** Jan 2 – Dec 14.

Set in the beautiful green countryside of the southern Tarn, this large 19th-century house has been skillfully renovated by its new owners, who have a fine appreciation for the comfort and charm of the past. With hospitality and efficiency, they have created the warm atmosphere of a vacation house here, offering quiet and relaxation. You will find five bedrooms and three suites in which no detail has been overlooked. Beautiful antique furniture and paintings make them seem like guest rooms in a home, and all have ultra-modern baths. The marriage of past and present is achieved with special flair in the garden full of flowers and in the park with its century-old shade trees. Dinners, reserved for residents, feature generous, light cuisine with an abundance of fresh seasonal vegetables.

*How to get there ( Map 31): 18km west of Mazamet, dir. Toulouse, La Bruiguière. Go 12km, then towards Dourgne. 2km from Sainte-Affrique, on the left.*

## Le Lys Bleu

82140 Saint-Antonin-Noble-Val (Tarn-et-Garonne)
29, place de la Halle
Tel. (0)5.63.30.65.06 - Fax (0)5.63.30.62.27
M. Risi-Charlot

**Category** ★★★ **Rooms** 11 with telephone, bath or shower, WC, TV and minibar. **Price** Single and double 390-540F / 59,46-82,32€. **Meals** Breakfast 60F / 9,15€; half board 380-460F / 57,93-70,13€ (per pers., 3 days min.). **Restaurant** Service 12:30PM-2:30PM, 7:30PM-11:00PM; mealtime specials 100F / 15,24€ (lunchtime), 190-290F / 28,97-44,21€, also à la carte. Specialties: Foie gras aux épices; magret aux mangues; boudin blanc truffé et sorbet à la truffe (in winter); poissons et homards en arrivage direct; duo de mousses exotiques en millefeuille. **Credit cards** Visa, Eurocard and MasterCard. **Pets** Dogs allowed. **Facilities** Parking and garage. **Nearby** In Saint-Antonin-Noble-Val: Prehistory Museum, Varen, Abbey of Beaulieu, villages in Bonette Valley (Caylus, Chapelle-Livron), Montauban (Ingres Museum), Lauzerte, Montpezat-de-Quercy, Caussade. **Open** All year.

The former prosperity of Saint-Antonin-Noble-Val is still reflected in the town's elegant terrace on the edge of the Aveyron River, and in its beautiful houses, one of which is the *Lys Bleu*. Offering the tranquility of the town as it must have been in the past, eleven simple bedrooms are discreetly appointed and have small baths. Downstairs, you can relax in several corner lounges and on a small, cool patio where breakfast is served in summer. The hotel's restaurant, located two houses farther on, is truly delightful, offering delicious cuisine complemented by a large, somewhat baroque dining room where an open fire crackles in winter; in summer, you can enjoy dinner until 11 P.M. in the tropical garden. It all makes for a rare and welcoming atmosphere.

***How to get there*** *(Map 30): 45km northeast of Montauban, towards Gorges de l'Aveyron and Saint-Antonin-Noble-Val.*

## Résidences du Golf des Roucous

82110 Sauveterre (Tarn-et-Garonne)
Tel. (0)5.63.95.83.70 - Fax (0)5.63.95.82.47
M. and Mme Finance

**Rooms** 5 maisonnettes with 2 rooms and bath, WC, TV – Wheelchair access. **Price** Maisonnettes (4 pers.) 450-580F / 68,60-88,42€. **Meals** Breakfast 40F / 6,10€, served 8:00-10:00. **Restaurant** For guests only. Service: 12:00PM-3:00PM, 7:00PM-10:00PM; mealtime specials 100F / 15,24€; also à la carte. Specialties: Foie gras de canard; salade d'oranges. **Credit card** Visa. **Pets** Dogs not allowed. **Facilities** 9-hole golf course, swimming pool, tennis, parking. **Nearby** Moissac, Cahors, Lot Valley, fortified village. **Open** All year.

Deep in the Quercynois countryside, in a lost valley far away from the beaten path, the *Golf des Roucous* is a haven of peace and quiet. If golfers people the green on the weekends, you can laze about by the pool or eat in the huge lounge or garden. Five wooden dollhouses serve the guests. Each can house four people and includes a kitchenette with dining nook, a comfortable, little lounge brightened by patchwork, one bedroom for a couple, and another with two beds. The bathrooms are small but warm and functional. In the lounge where the golfers meet, there is a well-stocked shop and tables to eat the good and simple fare, ordered *à la carte*. Salads with blue cheese or mozarella are very hearty, with chicken curry, *magret de canard*, and even *foie gras*. Warm and discreet welcome for a restful stay in the green.

***How to get there*** *(Map 30): At Cahors head toward Castelnau-Montratier on D 19. Once in Sauveterre, follow the billboards.*

## Auberge du Bon Fermier

59300 Valenciennes (Nord)
64, rue de Famars
Tel. (0)3.27.46.68.25 - Fax (0)3.27.33.75.01
M. Beine

**Category** ★★★★ **Rooms** 16 with telephone, bath, WC, TV and minibar. **Price** Single and double 480-700F / 73,18-106,71€. **Meals** Breakfast 45F / 6,86€, all the morning. **Restaurant** Service 12:00PM-2:30PM, 7:00PM-10:30PM; mealtime specials 128-275F / 19,51-41,92€, also à la carte. Specialties: Langue Lucullus; cochon de lait à la broche. **Credit cards** All major. **Pets** Dogs allowed (+50F / 7,62€). **Facilities** Parking (+50F / 7,62€). **Nearby** Remains of the ancient abbey in Saint-Amand-les-Eaux, fortifications of Le Quesnoy, the Helpe valley; Watteau Museum in Valence – 9-hole golf course in Valenciennes. **Open** All year.

Stop off at the *Auberge du Bon Fermier* for a comfortable evening in what used to be a royal carriage house in the 17th-century, on the road from the Tuileries to Brussels. It has been an inn since 1840, and is now registered as an historic monument, scrupulously restored by its present owners. The red bricks of the outer walls and many inner ones, the exposed beams, and the oak floors all help recreate the atmosphere of that era. The rooms are all spacious and enchanting, and each has a sitting area. The quietest ones are on the park. Modern conveniences have been carefully blended into the decor. The restaurant serves regional specialties but also features fresh lobster and a wide range of spit-roasted meats. The atmosphere is somewhat theatrical, but this is nonetheless a place not to be missed.

***How to get there*** *(Map 3): In the town center, between the "Place du Canada" and the town hall.*

## Château de Cocove

Cocove
62890 Recques-sur-Hem (Pas-de-Calais)
Tel. (0)3.21.82.68.29 - Fax (0)3.21.82.72.59

**Category** ★★★ **Rooms** 22 with telephone, bath or shower, WC and TV. **Price** Single and double 455-735F / 69,36-112,05€. **Meals** Breakfast 50F / 7,62€, served 7:30-10:30; "weekend gastronomic" 2360F / 359,78€ (2 pers., 2 night). **Restaurant** Service 12:30PM-2:30PM, 7:30PM-9:30PM; mealtime specials 145-375F / 22,11-57,17€, also à la carte. **Credit cards** All major. **Pets** Dogs allowed (+45F / 6,86€). **Facilities** Sauna (35F / 5,34€), parking. **Nearby** Basilica of Notre-Dame and Sandelin museum in Valenciennes; blockhouse in Eperlecques; Church of Saint-Eloi and museum in Hazebrouck; the "Bourgeois de Calais", art and lace museum in Calais – 27-hole Saint-Omer golf course in Lumbres. **Open** All year (closed Dec 25).

Only a few minutes from Calais, this 18th-century château is deep in the countryside surrounded by an extensive English-style park. You will enjoy youthful and charming hospitality here. The interior has been beautifully restored in keeping with the age of the building. In the same spirit the dining room has been converted from the old stables, its wide doors replaced by bay windows; pale subdued decor adds to the elegance of the room. The bedrooms are bright and quiet and some are very large; there are occasional antiques. Renovation of the rooms is being completed, and we are already very satisfied with the result as regards the cheerful, elegant decoration as well as the modern amenities. Before leaving, wine lovers can visit the cellars and buy from a large selection of excellent wines at reasonable prices.

***How to get there*** *(Map 2): 17km southeast of Calais: from Calais by A26, number 2 Ardres-Licques exit. Or via N43 towards Saint-Omer.*

## Chartreuse du Val Saint-Esprit

62199 Gosnay (Pas-de-Calais)
1, rue de Fouquières
Tel. (0)3.21.62.80.00 - Fax (0)3.21.62.42.50 - M. and Mme Constant
Web: lachartreuse.com - E-mail: lachartreuse@gofornet.com

**Category** ★★★★ **Rooms** 56 with telephone, bath, WC, TV and minibar. **Price** Double 400-900F / 60,98-137,20€, suite 1800F / 274,41€ (1-2 pers.). **Meals** Breakfast 65F / 9,91€, served 6:30-10:00. **Restaurant** Service 12:00PM-2:30PM, 7:00PM-10:00PM; mealtime specials 185F / 28,20€ (weekdays); 285-365F / 43,45-55,64€, also à la carte. Specialties: Médaillons de homard et ravioles de Royans dans un bouillon à la tomate au basilic; foie gras rôti et caramélisé au miel; filet d'esturgeon grillé; vinaigrette de lentilles et beurre battu. **Credit cards** All major. **Pets** Dogs allowed (+45F / 6,86€). **Facilities** Parking. **Nearby** Golf course at Aa. **Open** All year.

A t first sight this splendid brick and stone edifice, with its great courtyard and large park, may seem rather austere. This first impression is, however, immediately dispelled by a warm and friendly welcome and the refinement of the interior decoration. Most of the rooms are vast, and the *premier étage* bedrooms with impressive high-ceilings are extremely comfortable, with beautiful bathrooms. Lavish amounts of attention have been devoted to features such as bedspreads, curtains an,d wallpapers which all blend to perfection. The *deuxième étage* rooms tend to be less bright, but this makes them more cozy and intimate. The breakfast room is delightful, with a row of arched windows overlooking the gardens. The hotel has added new bedrooms which match the charm of the older ones. A recent *brasserie* service has been added for simple meals.

***How to get there*** *(Map 2): 5km south of Béthune via A26, number 6 exit, heading towards Les Chartreuses.*

# Hôtel Cléry

62360 Hesdin-l'Abbé (Pas-de-Calais)
Tel. (0)3.21.83.19.83 - Fax (0)3.21.87.52.59
Catherine and Didier Legros

**Category** ★★★ **Rooms** 22 with telephone, bath or shower, WC and satellite TV. **Price** Double 345-870F / 52,59-132,63€. **Meals** Breakfast 55-65F / 8,38-9,91€, served 7:00-10:30. **Restaurant** For residents only. Service 7:00PM-9:30PM; mealtime specials 145-250F / 22,11-38,11€, also à la carte. **Credit cards** All major. **Pets** Dogs not allowed. **Facilities** Tennis, mountain bike rentals, parking. **Nearby** Castle-museum and national marine center in Boulogne-sur-Mer; Opal coast, Cap Gris-Nez, Cap Blanc-Nez – 18-hole golf course in Hardelot. **Open** Feb 1 – Dec 10.

Legend has it that Napoléon stayed at this small château. There are three rooms on the ground floor: a large, light room where breakfast is served, a bar and a beautiful room where you can sit in deep leather armchairs by an open fire. An elegant staircase with a Louis XV style, wrought-iron banister leads to the *premier étage*. The bedrooms are comfortable and the decor simple. The rooms on the *deuxième étage* have gently sloping mansard roofs, but whether they look out on the chestnut trees in the park or on the drive, all the bedrooms are quiet. Behind a beautiful paved courtyard filled with flowers, seven bedrooms are located in the former stables, four of which are on the ground floor. Finally, a bit away, there is a pavilion containing two bedrooms. A short distance from the national highway, the hotel is conveniently located on the road to England. In case you don't want to eat in the hotel, *La Matelote* in Boulogne is very good; simpler fare is served at *l'Huitrière* and *Chez Jules*; and at the *Centre National de la Mer*, you can enjoy delicious shellfish at the *Grand Pavois*.

***How to get there*** *(Map 1): 9km southeast of Boulogne via N1. 1 km from Exit No 28, Isques-Samer, on A 16.*

## Auberge de la Grenouillère

La Madelaine-sous-Montreuil
62170 Montreuil-sur-Mer (Pas-de-Calais)
Tel. (0)3.21.06.07.22 - Fax (0)3.21.86.36.36 - M. Roland Gauthier
E-mail: auberge.de.la.grenouillere@wanadoo.fr

**Category** ★★★★ **Rooms** 3 and 1 apartment with telephone, bath, WC – Rooms for disabled persons. **Price** Double 400-500F / 60,98-76,22€, apartment: 600F / 91,47. **Meals** Breakfast 50F / 7,62€, served from 8:30. **Restaurant** Closed Tuesday and Wednesday in low season. Service 12:00PM-1:45PM, 7:00PM-9:30PM; mealtime specials 160F / 24,39€ (except weekend) 400F / 60,98€, also à la carte. Specialties: Frog. **Credit cards** All major. **Pets** Dogs allowed. **Facilities** Parking (+50F / 7,62€). **Nearby** Remains of the ancient abbey in Saint-Amand-les-Eaux; fortifications of Le Quesnoy, the Helpe valley; Watteau Museum in Valence – 9-hole golf course in Valenciennes. **Closed** Jan and Tuesday, Wednesday except Jul and Aug.

Hidden away on the verdant banks of the Canche, at the foot of the ramparts of the Montreuil-sur-Mer fortress redone by Vauban, this delicious inn is made up of many small white houses. Originally a farm, this inn now offers four country rooms with refined comforts and beautiful bathrooms. It is the food that will first attract you here, because Roland Gauthier has quite a rating in the Michelin guide. In the biggest house, several dining rooms are outfitted with frogs in mind. Of course, you find these frogs on the plates and on the tables, but also in the guise of eclectic objects and 1930 frescos on the walls of the largest dinning hall, in which a great fireplace creates a truly warm atmosphere. The cooking is inventive, light, full of flavor, and makes much use of the fish from the nearby sea. Add to this the warm, discrete, and friendly hospitality. You will not be able to pass up the pleasures of the *Auberge de la Grenouillère*.

***How to get there*** *(Map 1): 13 km south of Touquet. 2.5 km from Montreuil on D 917 or D 139.*

## Auberge de la Boule d'or

Le Bourg
14430 Beuvron-en-Auge (Calvados)
Tel. (0)2.31.79.78.78 - Fax (0)2.31.39.61.50

**Rooms** 3 with bath or shower and WC. **Price** Double 250F / 38,11€. **Meals** Breakfast 35F / 5,34€, served 8:30-10:00. **Restaurant** Service 12:30PM-2:00PM, 7:30PM-9:00PM; mealtime specials 99-175F / 15,24-26,68€, also à la carte. Specialties: Andouille de vire chaude; rognons de veau à la graine de moutarde; poulet vallée d'Auge, salade normande au chèvre chaud; tarte aux pommes à l'ancienne. **Credit card** Visa. **Pets** Dogs not allowed in no smoking room. **Nearby** Lisieux, la pays d'Auge at Deauville and Lisieux at Cabourg, cider trails. **Closed** Jan; Wednesday in low season.

Beuvron-en-Auge is a delightful little Norman village with half-timbered houses. It has been carefully conserved and is considered to be one of the most beautiful villages of France. This little inn is the jewel in the crown of the village square. In summer, the geranium-bedecked façade is a feast for the eyes. You but push the door open and you are already inside the traditional dining room, cheered up with pink tableclothes and sparkling glassware. After having taken over from the owners for whom they worked for many years, this young staff had the heart to keep the warm spirit of this place, continue with the specialities that made it famous, while all the while adding a new, youthful spark. Upstairs, the three simple and affordable rooms sport brand-new bedding. For fine dining, cheerful hospitality, and the glories of the Auge area, the *Boule d'Or* is worth the stop.

***How to get there*** *(Map 7): 25 km west of Lisieux on N 13, Exit no. 29 toward Dozule. Follow the signs.*

## Hostellerie du Château de Goville

14330 Le Breuil-en-Bessin (Calvados)
Tel. (0)2.31.22.19.28 - Fax (0)2.31.22.68.74
M. Vallée

**Category** ★★★ **Rooms** 12 with telephone, bath or shower, WC and minibar. **Price** Double 550-650F / 83,85-99,09€, suite 750F / 114,34€. **Meals** Breakfast 65F / 9,91€, served 8:30-11:30; half board from 550F / 83,85€ (per pers., 2 days min.). **Restaurant** *Le Baromètre*. Closed Tuesday in low season except by reservation. Service 12:30PM-2:00PM, 7:30PM-9:30PM; mealtime specials 145-250F / 22,11-38,11€, also à la carte. **Credit cards** All major. **Pets** Dogs allowed (+75F / 11,43€). **Facilities** Parking. **Nearby** Bayeux tapestry and cathedral, Châteaux of Vaulaville and of Fontaine-Henry, D-Day beaches – 27-hole Omaha Beach golf course. **Open** All year.

The *Château de Goville* has all the character and charm of a private home. It has belonged to Monsieur Vallée's family since 1813 and the owner is greatly attached to the setting, the furniture and the objects which have been left by the generations preceding him. The interior decoration is outstandingly elegant: All furniture, objects, and pictures are antiques. The bedrooms are especially charming and decorated with great taste and thought; each has its special personality. Our favorites are those on the *premier étage*, but all are attractive. On the upper floors, you will find collections of dolls which are either antiques or Monsieur Vallée's own creations. The salon, Napoléon III in style, is very inviting and comfortable for afternoon relaxation or cocktails. The dinners, illuminated by real candles in an immense crystal chandelier, are enchanting. The produce and bread are homemade, and all the recipes are made with fresh ingredients. Monsieur Vallée's hospitality puts a lovely finishing touch on the *Château de Goville*, making it one of the most charming hotels in Normandy.

***How to get there*** *( Map 7): 38km northwest of Caen via N13 to Bayeux, then D5 towards Molay-Littry, singposted before Molay.*

## Ferme Hôtel La Rançonnière

14480 Crépon (Calvados)
Entre Arromanches et Creully
Tel. (0)2.31.22.21.73 - Fax (0)2.31.22.98.39
Mmes Vereecke and Sileghem

**Category** ★★ **Rooms** 35 with telephone, bath or shower, hairdryer, WC and satellite TV. **Price** Single and double 295-480F / 44,97-73,18€, in "La Ferme de Mathan" 420-580F / 64,03-88,42€. **Meals** Breakfast 48F / 7,31€, served 7:30-10:00; half board 320-465F / 48,78-70,89€ (per pers.). **Restaurant** Service 12:00PM-2:00PM, 7:00PM-9:30PM; mealtime specials 98-280F / 15,24-42,69€, also à la carte. Specialties: Homard frais flambé; soupière du pêcheur. **Credit cards** All major. **Pets** Dogs allowed. **Facilities** Parking. **Nearby** Bayeux tapestry and cathedral, Châteaux of Creullet and of Creully, Church of Saint-Loup-Hors, abbey of Mondaye – 27-hole Omaha Beach golf course. **Open** All year.

The Bessin region is full of old manor houses and Crépon has more than its share in terms of both numbers and quality. You enter this old farm through a crenellated carriage gate into a vast courtyard around which are the reception, restaurant, and the bedrooms of the hotel. The interior is decidedly rustic with wooden furniture and exposed timbers everywhere. Comfortable bedrooms have small windows and old furniture whose dark tones are at times a little heavy. We particularly like Rooms 2, 3, 5, 6, 7, 9, 18, 24, 28, 29 and for families we like Rooms 8, 23, 25, 31 and 32. Note also the *Ferme de Mathan*, 300 feet away, where several bedrooms have just been opened, the largest being also the most attractive. On the other hand, avoid the annex rooms (located 10 km away), which are best suited for small groups. The excellent restaurant is very popular in the region. The *Rançonnière* seems to get better and better, and you couldn't ask for a warmer welcome.

***How to get there*** *(Map 7): 21km northwest of Caen (exit number 7) via D22 towards Creully/Arromanches. In Creully take a right at the church and go 3km.*

# L'Augeval

14800 Deauville (Calvados)
15, avenue Hocquart-de-Turtot
Tel. (0)2.31.81.13.18 - Fax (0)2.31.81.00.40 - Mme Guilbert

**Category ★★★ Rooms** 32 (8 with air-conditioning) with telephone, bath (26 with whirlpool), WC, satellite TV and minibar – 2 for disabled persons. **Price** Double 420-850F / 64,03-129,58€; suite 880-1400F / 134,16-213,43€. **Meals** Breakfast 60F / 9,15€; buffet 80F / 12,20€; half board +200F / 30,49€ (per pers.). **Restaurant** with air-conditioning. Service 12:00PM-2:30PM, 7:00PM-10:30PM; mealtime specials 160-380F / 24,39-57,93€, also à la carte. Specialties: pomme farcie au foie gras; brochette d'ananas sauce et glace au chocolat lacté. **Credit cards** All major. **Pets** Dogs allowed on request (+40-80F / 6,10-12,20€). **Facilities** Heated swimming pool, small fitness center and garage (5 places) in the hotel (+50F / 7,62€). **Nearby** Deauville; Honfleur; Houlgate; Cabourg – 27 hole New-Golf golf course and 9-18-hole Saint-Gatien golf course in Deauville. **Open** All year.

A ten-minute walk from the center of Deauville, *L'Augeval* is a typical turn-of-the-century villa which has been enlarged and renovated by the present owners. The comfortably appointed bedrooms are arranged with classic contemporary furniture harmoniously set off by a sober, tasteful décor. Five rooms have direct access to the small garden and to the swimming pool located on the side near the road to the racetrack, which is unfortunately very busy in summer. Guests who enjoy a quiet, equestrian setting should ask for the bedrooms at the back with a view of the Hippodrome stables (Numbers 107, 108, 207, 208). The most spacious rooms are those with a lounge and a balcony. Monsieur Moutier turns out elaborate gastronomic cuisine based on regional recipes, served outside in good weather. You will enjoy friendly, efficient service at this traditional hotel.

***How to get there*** *(Map 8): 211km of Paris via A 13, Pont-Levêque exit to Deauville. Beside the racecourse.*

# L'Absinthe

14602 Honfleur (Calvados)
1, rue de la Ville
Tel. (0)2.31.89.39.00 - Fax (0)2.31.89.53.60
M. and Mme Ceffrey

**Category** ★★★ **Rooms** 6 and 1 suite with telephone, bath (whirlpool), WC and satellite TV – 1 for disabled persons. **Price** Double 550F / 83,85€ (just 1)-750F / 114,34€; suite 1350F / 205,81€. **Meals** Breakfast 65F, served 8:00-11:00. **Restaurant** Closed mid Nov – mid Dec. Service 12:15PM-2:30PM, 7:15PM-9:30PM; mealtime specials 169-350F / 25,92-53,36€. **Credit cards** Diner's, Visa, Eurocard and MasterCard. **Pets** Dogs allowed (+40F / 6,10€). **Facilities** Garage in the hotel (+40F / 6,10€). **Nearby** Old dock, Greniers à sel, Church of Sainte-Catherine, museum of Eugène-Boudin in Honfleur; Deauville; Trouville – 27 hole New-Golf golf course and 9-18-hole Saint-Gatien golf course in Deauville. **Closed** Mid Nov – mid Dec.

This small hotel is just off the Place Eugène Boudin, not an area of peace and quiet but all the bedrooms are well-soundproofed. The quietest rooms are in the back or on the side (Numbers 4, 5, and 6). From the reception area and lounge, with its imposing stone fireplace, and the bar, you can admire the elegant decoration, worthy of a magazine cover. Throughout the hotel, handsomely patinated antique materials have been used in the restoration of this former 16th-century rectory. Beautiful and comfortably appointed, the bedrooms are rather small, except for the suite beneath the eaves. The rooms are decorated with Nobilis fabrics in discreet colors, and furniture, objects and rugs found in local antique shops. The breakfast room, illuminated by a veranda, is more simply decorated with rattan furniture. You will be warmly greeted by the owners, who have long welcomed guests to their fish restaurant just in front.

***How to get there*** (*Map 8*): *Via A 13, take the Beuzeville exit, then towards Honfleur. Opposite the harbour (parking near the hotel).*

## Hôtel l'Ecrin

14602 Honfleur (Calvados)
19, rue Eugène-Boudin
Tel. (0)2.31.14.43.45 - Fax (0)2.31.89.24.41
Mme Blais

**Category** ★★★ **Rooms** 26 with telephone, bath or shower, WC, TV and minibar. **Price** Double 420 à 900F / 64,03-137,20€, suite 990F / 150,92€. **Meals** Breakfast 55F / 8,38€, served 8:00-11:00. No restaurant. **Credit cards** All major. **Pets** Dogs not allowed. **Facilities** Sauna (+55F / 8,38€), parking. **Nearby** Old dock, Church of Sainte-Catherine, Eugène Boudin Museum in Honfleur, Deauville, Trouville – 27-hole New-Golf, 18- and 9-hole Saint-Gatien golf courses in Deauville. **Open** All year.

This elegant Napoléon III house and its garden make a restful place to stay in the center of the charming fishing port of Honfleur. The ground-floor rooms have retained their late-19th-century design and much of the style of the time. The reception office with its large fireplace is stunning. The lounge, where the gilt woodwork echoes that of the armchairs, is filled with pictures, drapes, and carpets. Breakfast is served on the veranda overlooking the garden, which is filled with flowers in summer. Ask for a room in the house. On the *premier étage*, families will enjoy the suite with two bedrooms. On the top floor, the rooms have mansard roofs; Numbers 11 and 12 are delightful, while Numbers 7 and 9 are waiting to be renovated. Simple or more comfortable, the rooms in the outbuildings overlook the courtyard and the cars parked just in front, and so, cannot be recommended. The hotel staff is extremely pleasant. For dinner, we recommend *L'Absinthe* and *L'Assiette Gourmande*, the two gourmet restaurants of Honfleur, but there is also *L'Hostellerie Lechat* and *Le Petit Mareyeur*.

***How to get there*** *(Map 8): 97km west of Rouen via A13, Beuzeville exit, then D22 (in the town center).*

## Le Manoir de Butin

14600 Honfleur (Calvados)
Phare du Butin
Tel. (0)2.31.81.63.00 - Fax (0)2.31.89.59.23
M. Hervé Delahaye

**Category** ★★★★ **Rooms** 9 with telephone, bath, WC, TV and minibar. **Price** Double 640-1970F / 97,57-300,32€. **Meals** Breakfast 65F / 9,91€, served 7:30-11:00; half board 565-1230F / 86,13-187,51€ (per pers., restricted to menu). **Restaurant** Closed Monday and Tuesday lunchtime. Service 12:30PM-2:00PM, 7:30PM-9:30PM; mealtime specials 128-265F / 19,82-40,40€, also à la carte. **Credit cards** Amex, Visa, Eurocard and MasterCard. **Pets** Dogs allowed (+80F / 12,20€). **Facilities** Parking. **Nearby** Old dock, Church of Sainte-Catherine, Eugène-Boudin Museum in Honfleur, Deauville, Trouville – 27- hole New-Golf golf course, 18-hole Saint-Gatien golf course and 9-hole golf course in Deauville. **Open** All year.

The owners of Normandy's luxurious *Chaumière* have now opened *Le Manoir de Butin*, a hotel in the same spirit very near the sea. Set in a beautiful park full of trees and flowers, the house is a handsome residence with traditional Norman half-timbering. The interior is somewhat enclosed, creating an atmosphere of intimacy and tranquil comfort, antique furniture, and tastefully chosen fabrics further the feeling of comfort. The passage of time will doubtless confer the hotel with the charm of *La Chaumière*. The beautiful bedrooms open onto the countryside or the sea. Meals are served on the terrace in summer. If the hotel has no more vacancies, *La Chaumiere*, another great hotel in Honfleur, might be able to put you up (tel: 02.31.81.63.20).

***How to get there*** *(Map 8): 97km west of Rouen via A 13, exit 28, then exit Honfleur, towards Deauville via the coast.*

## Au Repos des Chineurs

14340 Notre-Dame-d'Estrées (Calvados)
Chemin de l'Eglise
Tel. (0)2.31.63.72.51 - Fax (0)2.31.63.62.38 - Mme Steffen
E-mail: au-repos-des-chineurs@wanadoo.fr

**Category** ★★ **Rooms** 10 with telephone, bath (2 with whirlpool) or shower and WC. **Price** Double 500-650F / 76,22-99,09€; suite (4 pers.) 1000F / 152,45€. **Meals** Breakfast 60F / 9,15€, served 8:00-11:00. **Restaurant** and tea room. Service 10:00-7:30PM. Specialties: Assiette du chineur, bouquets de saveurs salées or sucrées. **Credit cards** Diners, Visa, Eurocard and MasterCard. **Pets** Dogs allowed. **Meals** Parking. **Nearby** Bernay (museum), Château de Broglie, Le Pays d'Auge de Lisieux in Deauville and Le Pays de Lisieux in Cabourg by Vimoutiers and camembert country. **Open** Mid Dec – beg Mar, except by reservation for weekends.

On the edge of a street but quiet at night, this postal relay station from the 17th and 18th centuries, dominated by a beautiful 16th- and 18th-century church, has been resuscitated thanks to Mme Steffen's hard work and sure taste. Lying in the heart of the Pays d'Auge region, the country inn is an attractive and pleasant place to stay, offering a tea room, lovely bedrooms, and a *brocante*, a shop selling old furniture and objects, in this case from the 18th and 19th centuries. The chests-of-drawers, tables, wardrobes, and objects which furnish the inn are all for sale at the "Antique-Hunter's Rest", but they remain as décor until they find a new owner. The reception area includes a pleasant lounge, and the tea room is totally charming with its exposed beams and big fireplace, its small tables set with pretty dishes for your breakfast and light snacks. Comfortable, simple but very tasteful, the bedrooms named after flowers are cheerful, their floors dyed to match the carpets, the wallpaper friezes, and the fabrics (the beds are queen, not king, size.) Dressing growns await you in the pretty bathrooms.

*How to get there (Map 7): 23km south of Cabourg.*

## Auberge Saint-Christophe

14690 Pont-d'Ouilly (Calvados)
Tel. (0)2.31.69.81.23 - Fax (0)2.31.69.26.58
Gilles and Françoise Lecœur

**Category** ★★ **Rooms** 7 with telephone, bath or shower, WC and TV. **Price** Double 280F / 42,69€.
**Meals** Breakfast 40F / 6,10€, served 8:00-9:30; half board 295F / 44,97€,(per pers., 2 days min.).
**Restaurant** Service 12:00PM-1:30PM, 7:30PM-9:00PM; mealtime specials 98-250F / 15,24-38,11€,
also à la carte. Specialties: Bœuf ficelle à la crème de camembert; salade tiède de queues de
langoustines; crème brûlée. **Credit cards** Amex, Visa, Eurocard and MasterCard. **Pets** Dogs allowed
(+25F / 3,81€). **Facilities** Parking. **Nearby** Castle of Falaise, 'La Suisse Normande', Thury-Harcourt,
Clécy (Châteaux of La Pommeraye and Placy), Oëtre rock, gorges of Saint-Aubert, Château of
Pontécoulant – 18-hole Clécy-Cantelou golf course. **Closed** 1 week in Nov, 1 in Sep, Sunday evening
and Monday.

At the end of a little road, this hotel is in an elegant house in the *Suisse Normande*. Its interior has been carefully designed for the comfort and well-being of the guests. Plants and flowers adorn every corner. There is a small lounge, a breakfast room which becomes a bar in the evening and out-of-the-way covies set up for those who want even more peace and quiet. The light-colored rooms are small, as are their bathrooms. Renovated a while ago, they are still not well-soundproofed against interior noise, though they do look out on the beautiful garden. In good weather, lunch can be taken on the terrace, and you will like the cuisine as much as we did. Very pleasant hospitality from the young owners.

***How to get there*** *( Map 7): 26km south of Caen via D562 towards Flers, or N158 towards Falaise, then D1; 1.5km from Pont-d'Ouilly via D23 towards Thury-Harcourt.*

## La Chenevière

Escures-Commes
14520 Port-en-Bessin (Calvados)
Tel. (0)2.31.51.25.25 - Fax (0)2.31.51.25.20
M. Esprabens

**Category** ★★★★ **Rooms** 20 with telephone, bath, WC, TV and minibar – Elevator; wheelchair access. **Price** Double 890-1290F / 135,68-196,66€. **Meals** Breakfast incl. **Restaurant** Mealtime specials 170-420F / 25,92-64,03€, also à la carte. Specialties: Langoustines rôties aux graines de sésame; blanc et noir de turbot au jus de carottes et de madras; carré d'agneau de pays rôti; feuillantine de pommes au caramel de cidre. **Credit cards** Amex, Visa, Eurocard and MasterCard. **Pets** Dogs allowed (+165F / 25,15€). **Facilities** Parking. **Nearby** Epaves museum in Commes, Port-en-Bessin, Cathedral of Bayeux – 27-hole Omaha Beach golf course. **Closed** Jan 3 – Feb 8.

Very near Port-en-Bessin, Arromanches, and D-Day Beaches, this is an elegant mansion surrounded by a beautifully kept park with venerable trees. The interior resembles a private home which has been furnished to please the eye as well as to provide the comfort you crave after a tiring drive. You will find a succession of very pretty, bright rooms which are generously decorated with light fabrics, collections of paintings (old seals, architectural drawings) and handsome objects that evoke Merry Old England. The bedrooms, with efficient soundproofing, are furnished with the same tasteful style and attention to comfort and decorated in a floral theme. The bathrooms are luxurious. All the windows look out on the lawn and flowers. This magnificent place to stay is also a gourmet destination. Warmest hospitality.

***How to get there*** *(Map 7): 8km north of Bayeux via D6, head toward Port-en-Bessin.*

## Château de Sully

14400 Sully-Bayeux (Calvados)
Route de Port-en-Bessin
Tel. (0)2.31.22.29.48. - Fax (0)2.31.22.64.77.
M. and Mme Brault

**Category** ★★★ **Rooms** 23 with telephone, bath or shower, WC, and satellite TV. – 1 for disabled persons. **Price** Double 520-690F / 79,27-105,19€; suites 850-950F / 129,58-144,83€. **Meals** Breakfast 65-75F / 9,91-11,73€, served 8:00-11:00; half board 1000-1170F / 152,45-178,37€ (2 pers.). **Restaurant** Service 12:00PM-1:45PM, 7:30PM-9:30PM; mealtime specials 150-360F / 22,87-54,88€; also à la carte. **Credit cards** All major. **Pets** Dogs not allowed. **Facilities** Tennis, fitness room, billiard; parking. **Nearby** Deauville; Caen; D-Day Beaches; Houlgate – 27-hole golf course. **Open** Mar 11 – Nov 24.

A bit away from Bayeux, a few kilometers from the sea, the 18th-century *Château de Sully* continues to stand proud between its grounds and its delightful, flowery, walled-in garden. There are fourteen rooms in the château done up in warm tones and antique furniture, offering comfort that is both modern and restrained. Nine other rooms are in a little manor in the park, just a bit away. (Some of these have a little, private patio.) The lounge bar and pool room are warm and relaxing, as is the large, covered, heated swiming pool. The dining room has just been enlarged into a magnificient space with a veranda that opens out into a smoking lounge. All this opens out directly onto the garden. This is a true feast for the eyes, which goes well with the gourmet fare of the young chef, Alexandre Bourdas. A beautiful place to stay between the treasures of Bayeux and famous Normandy beaches.

***How to get there*** *( Map 7): from Bayeux, take D 6 toward Port-en-Bessin. The hotel is 2 km away, on the right.*

## Hôtel Victoria

Tracy-sur-Mer 14117 Arromanches (Calvados)
Tel. (0)2.31.22.35.37 - Fax (0)2.31.22.93.38
M. and Mme Selmi

**Category** ★★ **Rooms** 14 with telephone, bath or shower, WC and TV. **Price** Double 340-580F / 51,83-88,42€. **Meals** Breakfast 42F / 6,41€, served 7:30-10:00. No restaurant. **Credit cards** Visa, Eurocard and MasterCard. **Pets** Small dogs allowed. **Facilities** Parking. **Nearby** Port-en-Bessin, D-Day Beaches, Bayeux, cathedral and tapestry of the Queen Mathilde — 27-hole Bayeux golf course (10km). **Open** Apr — end Sep.

Two kilometers from the sea and from the modest town of Arromanches, today famous as a D-Day landing site on June 6, 1944, the *Victoria* is a small country hotel, pretty and well-kept. The bedrooms are in the two wings and in the central building, where you will find the largest and most pleasant accommodations (except for the *Verte* room, which is best for families.) Furnishings include some antiques, and all rooms have a lovely view over the countryside or the garden full of flowers. Don't neglect the rooms on the *second étage*, which have low ceilings and are often illuminated only by a small roof window, but whose decoration is especially warm and inviting. The rooms in the wings, however, are more ordinary, except for the smallest ones beneath the eaves, which are more intimate and reasonably priced. The traditionally decorated lounge is Regency in style, with gilt wood, bric-a-brac, crystal chandeliers... Breakfasts are served outdoors in good weather.

***How to get there*** *(Map 7): 10km north of Bayeux; 2,5km before Arromanches, follow signs on D516.*

## Le Moulin de Connelles

27430 Connelles (Eure)
40, route d'Amfreville-sur-les-Monts
Tel. (0)2.32.59.53.33 - Fax (0)2.32.59.21.83 - M. and Mme Petiteau
E-mail: moulindeconnelles@cofrase.com

**Category** ★★★★ **Rooms** 7 and 6 suites with telephone, bath, WC, TV and minibar. **Price** Single and double 650-850F / 99,09-129,58€; suite 850-1000F / 129,58-152,45€. **Meals** Breakfast 70F / 10,67€, served 7:30-10:30. **Restaurant** Closed same dates as hotel. Service 12:30PM-2:00PM, 7:30PM-9:00PM; mealtime specials 140-315F / 21,34-48,02€ (child 70F / 10,67€), also à la carte. Specialties: croustillant de langoustines et petits légumes parfumés aux épices. **Credit cards** All major. **Pets** Dogs allowed. **Facilities** Heated swimming pool, tennis, Mountain bikes, boating, parking. **Nearby** Lery Poses recreation center (water skiing, golf, sailing…), Church of Notre-Dame in Louviers; cathedral of Rouen; Monet Museum in Giverny – 18-hole Vaudreuil golf course. **Closed** Jan and Sunday evening and Monday from Oct 1 – May 1.

A beautiful lawn and flower gardens on the banks of the Seine surround the *Moulin de Connelles*, an old mill which was converted into a lovely home and, then, into a luxurious hotel. The *Moulin* is extremely comfortable, with thick carpets, a handsome decor of soft green and gold-yellow tones, coordinated fabrics, and superb bathrooms. Many bedrooms and the restaurant look out on an enchanting river scene, where the Seine winds in and out of its course and finally forms several lush green islands. It's a lovely place for strolling or having a drink before dinner, and the hotel will happily lend you a boat to explore it all up close, including the resident moorhens.

***How to get there*** *(Maps 1 and 8): Via A 14 and A 13 heading toward Rouen, Louviers exit, towards N15, Saint-Pierre-du-Vauvray, Andé, Connelles.*

## Le Manoir des Saules

27370 La Saussaye (Eure)
2, place Saint-Martin
Tel. (0)2.35.87.25.65 - Fax (0)2.35.87.49.39
M. Monnaie-Metot

**Rooms** 7 and 2 apartments with telephone, bath or shower, WC and TV – 1 for disabled persons. **Price** Double 580-780F / 88,42-118,91€, apart. 880-1280F / 134,16-195,13€. **Meals** Breakfast 75F / 11,43€. **Restaurant** Closed Sunday evening and Monday except national holidays. Service 12:00PM-2:00PM, 8:00PM-9:30PM; mealtime specials 185-365F / 28,20-55,64€, also à la carte. Specialties: Foie gras, ragoût de homard frais, fish. **Credit cards** All major. **Pets** Dogs allowed. **Meals** Parking. **Nearby** Château of Champ-de-Bataille, Château and arboretum of Harcourt, Collegial Church of La Saussaye, Abbey of Bec-Hellouin – 18-hole Champ-de-Bataille golf course. **Closed** Winter holidays and beg Oct.

With its half-timbering, turrets, and recessed walls, the *Manoir des Saules* is as Norman as they come. The decoration is highly colorful and cheerful. The bedrooms are delightfully appointed with a mixture of antiques and Louis XV copies, amusing old objects, and heavy drapes which are coordinated with silky bedspreads. All the rooms are beautifully kept, including the bathrooms. A lovely lounge in blue and cream colors is an intimte, cozy place for a drink. Adjacent to it, the dining room with its smartly set tables serves excellent cuisine which is based on fresh, seasonal products. In charming weather, you can of course have meals outside on the terrace amidst the flowers. You will always receive very friendly and attentive service.

***How to get there*** *( Map 8): South of Rouen, 4km from Elbeuf via D840, towards Le Neubourg. On A13, Pont-de-l'Arche exit.*

## Hôtel du Golf

Golf du Vaudreuil
27100 Le Vaudreuil (Eure)
Tel. (0)2.32.59.02.94 - Fax (0)2.32.59.67.39
Mme Launay

**Category** ★★ **Rooms** 20 with telephone, bath or shower, 17 with WC and TV, 10 with minibar. **Price** Double 230-350F / 35,06-53,36€. **Meals** Breakfast 30-45F / 4,57-6,86€, served 7:00-11:00. No restaurant. **Credit cards** Amex, Visa, Eurocard and MasterCard. **Pets** Dogs allowed (+25F / 3,81€). **Facilities** Parking, 18-hole golf course. **Nearby** Rouen, Château Gaillard. **Open** All year.

The Château de Vaudreuil was destroyed during the Revolution and all that remains of it are two buildings beside an avenue that leads nowhere. The castle grounds, whose ends are lost in the horizon, have been changed into a superb golf course, and one of the pavilions became a hotel. It is quiet here, and you can enjoy views over the greens from the breakfast room and the living room. The bedrooms, with big windows, have just been redone (except for three), and a delicate palette of colors was chosen for them. All are furnished in the simplest way, while all the while remaining pleasant. The upper floor rooms are smallish, but the top-floor rooms are clearly much larger. The decor is modern but elegant. There is no restaurant at the hotel but golfers can eat at the golf club.

***How to get there*** *( Map 8): 15km southeast of Rouen via A13, exit 18 or 19; then D77 to the entrance of Vaudreuil.*

## La Licorne

27480 Lyons-la-Forêt (Eure)
27, place Benserade
Tel. (0)2.32.49.62.02 - Fax (0)2.32.49.80.09
M. and Mme Brun

**Category** ★★★ **Rooms** 19 with telephone, bath or shower, WC and satellite TV. **Price** Double and apart. 405-790F / 61,74-120,43€. **Meals** Breakfast 60F / 9,15€, served 8:00-11:00; half board 420-595F / 64,12-90,71€ (per pers.). **Restaurant** Closed same dates as hotel and Sunday evening and Monday in low season, Monday and Tuesday lunchtime in high season. Service 12:30PM-2:00PM, 7:30PM-9:00PM; mealtime specials 205F / 31,25€. Specialties: rognon de veau marchand de vin; tarte Tatin. **Credit cards** All major. **Pets** Dogs not allowed. **Facilities** Parking, mountain bike rental. **Nearby** Lyons forest, Château of Martainville, Abbey of Fontaine-Guerard and Mortemer. **Open** Jan 21 – Dec 19.

On the square of this charming village, a popular spot on the weekends, you can't miss the pink half-timbered façade and blue shutters of *La Licorne*, a former postal relay station that has been welcoming travelers since 1610. The interior decoration combines antique with rustic contemporary styles: The stairway leading to the bedrooms is itself an antique. The bedrooms are comfortable and plainly decorated. Our favorites are those overlooking the interior courtyard and those with bathtubs. You should avoid the smallest rooms (Numbers 2, 3, and 9) and enjoy the apartments with a lounge. Depending on the number of guests, you will have the choice of two dining rooms: one small and charming to the left of the entrance; the other installed in a rustic outbuilding. The cuisine is traditional and the chef's specialties are fine regional recipes. The *Licorne* is a pleasant inn from which to discover the region and take lovely walks in the forest. Best to reserve ahead for the weekend.

***How to get there*** *(Map 8): 21km east of Evreux. A13 Gaillon-les-Andelys exit then D316, to Les Andelys.*

## Château de Brécourt

27120 Pacy-sur-Eure (Eure)
Route de Vernon à Pacy
Tel. (0)2.32.52.40.50 - Fax (0)2.32.52.69.65 - M. Savry and Mme Langlais
E-mail: chato-brecourt@club-internet.fr

**Category** ★★★★ **Rooms** 30 with telephone, bath, shower and WC. **Price** Single and double 490-960F / 74,70-146,35€, suites 1155-1680F / 176,08-256,11€. **Meals** Breakfast 78F / 12,20€, served 7:00AM-12:00PM; half board 530-960F / 80,80-146,35€. **Restaurant** Service 12:00PM-2:00PM, 7:30PM-9:30PM; mealtime specials 190F / 28,97€ (lunchtime except national holidays), 235-360F, 235-360F / 35,83-54,88€; also à la carte. Specialties: Pavé de bar cuit vapeur en couscous et petite ratatouille; aile de canard caramélisée au miel de romarin, ravioles aux pommes. **Credit cards** All major. **Pets** Dogs allowed (+60F / 9,15€). **Facilities** Swimming pool, whirlpool, tennis, parking. **Nearby** A.G. Poulain Museum and Church of Notre-Dame in Vernon, Château of Gaillon, Monet Museum and American Art Museum in Giverny – 9-hole golf course in Gaillon. **Open** All year.

On the threshold of Normandy and only sixty kilometers from Paris, this magnificent Louis XIII château with its symmetrical wings stands on the edge of a 55-acre park. The interior still charms with its original distinctive character highlighted by ravishing 17th-century floor tiles in the corridors and in many bedrooms. The rooms offer comfortable amenities as well as handsome antique furniture in most, painted ceilings, and tall windows overlooking the lush expanse of the immense park. Served in two highly elegant dining rooms, the delicious cuisine, of course, gives a place of honor to Norman specialties. Excellent hospitality that manages to avoid the stuffiness one might expect from an address such as this.

***How to get there*** *(Map 8): 21km east of Evreux via N13, Pacy-sur-Eure exit, then D181 and D533. 70km west of Paris via A13, number 16 Vernon exit.*

# La Ferme de Cocherel

Cocherel 27120 Pacy-sur-Eure (Eure)
Route de la vallée de l'Eure
Tel. (0)2.32.36.68.27 - Fax (0)2.32.26.28.18
M. and Mme Delton

**Rooms** 2 with bath or shower and WC. **Price** Double 600-800F / 91,47-121,96€. **Meals** Breakfast 60F / 9,15€ served 8:15-9:30. **Restaurant** Closed Tuesday and Wednesday. Service 12:00PM-2:00PM, 7:30PM-9:00PM; meal time special 220F / 33,54€, also à la carte. Specialties: craquelin de queue de bœuf aux navets confits. **Credit cards** All major. **Pets** Dogs allowed. **Facilities** Parking. **Nearby** Historical village of Cocherel, Château of Bizy, Monet Museum in Giverny; Château of Anet – 18-hole Vaudreuil golf course. **Closed** 3 weeks in Jan, 2 weeks in Sep, Tuesday and Wednesday.

Cocherel saw one of the most beautiful victories of Du Guesclin. Today, nothing reminds us of those troubled times. The delightful hamlet is reflected calmly in the waters of the Eure. The hotel is only separated from the river by a little local road. The *Ferme* consists of several picturesque Norman houses with old tile roofs. The largest is reserved for the acclaimed gastronomic restaurant, where the tables are set in a room decorated like an elegant winter garden. You will enjoy succulent meals made with fresh products bought in the local market or from nearby farms. The three bedrooms, opening onto a carefully tended flower garden, are on the ground floor in separate houses; they are decorated with several pieces of rustic or lacquered cane furniture, floral fabrics, and a few engravings. The breakfasts are excellent. This is truly a beautiful country inn.

***How to get there*** *( Map 8 ): 7km northwest of Pacy-sur-Eure via D836, towards Louviers. On A13, number 16 exit towards Vernon on D 181 toward Pacy, take a very quick right onto D 57 heading toward Cocherel.*

## La Chaîne d'Or

27700 Petit-Andelys (Eure)
27, rue Grande
Tel. (0)2.32.54.00.31 - Fax (0)2.32.54.05.68
Mme Foucault

**Category** ★★★ **Rooms** 10 with telephone, bath or shower, WC and TV. **Price** Double 420-760F / 64,12-115,86€. **Meals** Breakfast 75F / 11,43€, served 8:00-10:00. **Restaurant** Closed Sunday evening and Monday. Service 12:00PM-2:00PM, 7:30PM-9:30PM; mealtime specials 150-330F / 22,87-50,31€, also à la carte. Specialties: Miroir d'huîtres normandes au raifort; langoustines royales croquant de pommes de terre; plaisir au chocolat chaud et sirop de jasmin. **Credit cards** Amex, Visa, Eurocard and MasterCard. **Pets** Dogs allowed. **Facilities** Parking. **Nearby** Church of Notre-Dame and Château Gaillard in Les Andelys, Giverny – 18-hole Vaudreuil golf course. **Closed** Jan.

This friendly hostelry was founded in 1751. From the wing in the inner courtyard there is a stunning view of the Seine. Most of the bedrooms are large and light. The ones overlooking the river have just been entirely refurbished; very elegant and refined, they have gained in comfort what they have lost in traditional style. The rooms looking out over the church or the courtyard have period furniture, rugs, and engravings; foreign guests prefer them for their "Old France" atmosphere. In the great dining room with its cheerful bouquets of flowers and paintings, the warm color-scheme and the carefullylaid table add to the fine dining experience. Traditional, delicate, and light cooking is served in a courteous way. A beautiful place to stay, in a rare location, which has kept a bit of the charm of yesteryear.

***How to get there*** *(Map 8): 92km northwest of Paris via A13, Gaillon exit, then D316.*

## Auberge du Vieux Puits

27500 Pont-Audemer (Eure)
6, rue Notre-Dame-du-Pré
Tel. (0)2.32.41.01.48 - Fax (0)2.32.42.37.28 - M. and Mme Foltz
E-mail: vieux-puits@wanadoo.fr

**Category** ★★ **Rooms** 12 with telephone, bath or shower, 10 with WC and 6 with TV – 2 for disabled persons. **Price** Double 320-450F / 48,78-68,60€. **Meals** Breakfast 50F / 7,62€, served 8:00-9:30. **Restaurant** Service 12:00PM-2:00PM, 7:30PM-9:00PM; mealtime specials 220-330F / 33,54-50,31€, also à la carte. Specialties: Canard aux griottes; truite "Bovary". **Credit cards** Visa, Eurocard and MasterCard. **Pets** Dogs not allowed. **Facilities** Parking. **Nearby** Insect collection in the Canel museum in Pont-Audemer, Risle valley, Normandie Bridge, abbey of Le Bec-Hollouin – 18-hole Champ-de-Bataille golf course in Neubourg. **Closed** Mid Dec – end Jan; Monday and Tuesday in low season.

This inn in Pont-Audemer is easily accessible by the highway and is perfect for travelers who want to get aquainted with Normandy. The buildings, in typical 17th-century Norman timbered style, surround a flower garden, with an old well and two impressive willows, where you can have cocktails, coffee, and excellent afternoon snacks in summer. Inside, there are several cozy little lounges where you can have tea or read by the fireplace. The dining room is slightly larger and is decorated with antique china and gleaming copper. The savory cuisine is innovative yet based on traditional Norman recipes. You can choose between the simple, rustic, charming bedrooms in the old houses, or the modern comfort of those in another building, which is built in the same style.

***How to get there*** *(Maps 1 and 8): 52km west of Rouen via A13, Pont-Audemer exit, then D139 and N182 (300m from the town center).*

## Relais Moulin de Balisne

Balisne 27130 Verneuil-sur-Avre (Eure)
Tel. (0)2.32.32.03.48 - Fax (0)2.32.60.11.22
M. Gastaldi

**Category** ★★ **Rooms** 10 and 2 suites with telephone, bath, WC, TV and minibar. **Price** Single, double and suite 400-550F / 60,98-83,85€. **Meals** Breakfast 50F / 7,62€, served 8:00-11:00; half board 400-500F / 60,98-76,22€, (per pers., 2 days min.). **Restaurant** Closed Monday lunchtime in winter. Service 12:00PM-3:00PM, 7:30PM-10:00PM; mealtime specials 165-350F / 25,15-53,36€, also à la carte. Specialties: Duo de sole et langouste; cassolette d'escargots et gambas aux petits lardons; œuf d'autruche farci; lotte sauce caramel. **Credit cards** All major. **Pets** Dogs allowed. **Facilities** Lake and river fishing, parking. **Nearby** Senonches forest, Châteaux of Beauménil and Anet – 9-hole golf course in Coulonges. **Open** All year.

When you first see the hotel from the road, you may worry about its proximity to the road, but as soon as you enter, you will be assured that all is quiet inside. The only outside noise you hear is the babbling of the Avre and Iton rivers. The *Moulin* rests on a 13-acre estate, with two ponds and boats for lovers of fishing. The house is purely charming, with the board games in the lounges and the dining room bar. You will enjoy generous portions of food, which might benefit from a bit more finesse. The decor is incredibly inviting with mementos, rugs, Persian tablecloths, and a great fireplace. Some of the comfortable rooms are under the eaves, giving you the impression that you are "perched in the trees." The great hospitality and proximity to Paris make the Moulin a very attractive place indeed.

***How to get there*** *(Map 8): 75 km from Paris on the western highway heading toward Dreux. Take Bois-d'Arcy exit. Then N 12 toward Dreux, and then Alençon.*

## Hôtel du Château d'Agneaux

Agneaux 50180 Saint-Lô (Manche)
Avenue Sainte-Marie
Tel. (0)2.33.57.65.88 - Fax (0)2.33.56.59.21 - M. and Mme Groult
E-mail: rene-groult@wanadoo.fr

**Category** ★★★ **Rooms** 12 with shower, WC, TV and 10 with minibar. **Price** Double 445-615F / 67,84-93,76€, suite 765-915F / 116,62-139,49€. **Meals** Breakfast 59F / 9,15€. **Restaurant** Service 7:30PM-9:00PM; mealtime specials 140-340F / 21,34-51,83€, also à la carte. Specialties: Fish and the chef's desserts. **Credit Cards** Amex, Visa, Eurocard and MasterCard. **Pets** Dogs allowed (+50F / 7,62€). **Facilities** Tennis (30F / 4,57€), parking. **Nearby** Church and museum in Saint-Lô, Château of Torigni-sur-Vire – 9-hole golf course in Courtainville. **Open** All year.

Leaving the ugly suburbs of Saint-Lô, you'll find that the *Château d'Agneaux* has escaped the clumsiness of urban planners. A little stone and dirt road leads you away from the main road to the old chapel, the château and the watchtower which look out over the unspoiled and peaceful valley, with nothing in view but trees and the River Vire flowing gently through the green countryside. M. and Mme Groult owned a farmhouse inn for many years, and now *Agneaux* is their dream come true; they have refurbished it with love. Everything here reflects their passion for the place. All is well-renovated and pleasantly accommodated. The bedrooms are very comfortable and prettily though not overwhelmingly decorated, with some four-poster beds and lovely parquet floors. Room 4, with it's five windows, is well-lit all day. Also, take note of a few rooms, equally well-done, set up 30 meters away in the watchtower. A truly charming enclave of peace, nature, and tranquility.

***How to get there*** *( Map 7 ): 1.5km west of Saint-Lô via D900.*

## Hôtel Le Conquérant

50760 Barfleur (Manche)
16-18, rue Saint-Thomas-Becket
Tel. (0)2.33.54.00.82 - Fax (0)2.33.54.65.25 - Mme Delomenède

**Category** ★★ **Rooms** 13 with telephone, 10 with bath or shower, 3 with basin, 8 with WC and TV. **Price** Double 200-400F / 30,49-60,98€. **Meals** Breakfast 30-50F / 4,57-7,62€ (4 mealtime specials), served 8:00-10:00. **Restaurant** Crèperie only for residents, by reservation. Service 7:00PM-9:00PM; mealtime specials 80-130F / 12,20-19,82€, also à la carte. Specialties: Galette camembert sur beurre d'escargot; galette manchotte; crêpe Le Conquérant. **Credit cards** Visa, Eurocard and MasterCard. **Pets** Dogs not allowed. **Facilities** Parking (30F / 4,57€), bike rentals. **Nearby** Ile Tatihon, Valognes, Thomas-Henry Museum in Cherbourg – 9-hole golf course in Fontenay-en-Cotentin. **Open** Mar 16 – Nov 14.

Just off the port of Barfleur, you will find a charming, well-manicured garden hidden behind the granite walls of this 17th-century manor house, with an old Japanese pagoda tree and rare cordelines. The bedrooms, all differently furnished, are improved yearly, varying in size, modern amenities, and soundproofing (some rooms still share a shower and toilet on the same floor). The renovated rooms have been tastefully redone with Jouy-motif wallpaper and antiques. We like the green room, which overlooks both the street and the garden and has a large bathroom. On the *second étage*, the bedrooms are simpler and unfortunately are not soundproofed. Rooms 1, 2, 3, 9, 16, and 17 overlook the garden, while the others give onto the street in the back. For a long stay, you will enjoy the bedroom with a terrace in the small house in the garden. In the evening, on reservation, you can eat the hotel's special *crêpes*. For breakfast, you can order a classic French *petit déjeuner* or one of four more copious menus. A wonderful little place to stay.

***How to get there*** *( Map 7): 30km east of Cherbourg via D901.*

# Hôtel de la Marine

50270 Barneville-Carteret (Manche)
11, rue de Paris
Tel. (0)2.33.53.83.31 - Fax (0)2.33.53.39.60 - M. Cesne-Emmanuel

**Category** ★★ **Rooms** 31 with telephone, bath or shower, WC, TV and minibar. **Price** Double 425-620F / 64,79-94,52€. **Meals** Breakfast 52F / 8,29€, served 7:30-10:00; half board 425-520F / 64,79-79,27€ (per pers., 3 days min.). **Restaurant** Service 12:30PM-1:30PM, 7:30PM-9:30PM; mealtime specials 145-400F / 22,11-60,98€, also à la carte. Specialties: Fish and shellfish. **Credit cards** All major. **Pets** Dogs not allowed. **Facilities** Parking. **Nearby** Island of Jersey, Valognes, Museum of Thomas-Henry in Cherbourg, Cotentin Tour between Le cap de la hague, Barfleur and Le cap de Carteret – 9-hole golf course in Saint-Jean-de-rivière. **Open** Feb 16 – Nov 2.

The *Hôtel de la Marine* is right on the water in the delightful seaside resort of Carteret. Although the building itself is of no particular interest, its outstanding panoramic location makes it like an ocean liner. Towering high above the sea, the hotel showcases the tides and the boats. You will enjoy the view from the two dining rooms, the rotunda-shaped lounge, and from most of the bedrooms, notably those with a terrace or a balcony. The bright bedrooms are classical in decor, with antique-style furniture and pale fabrics, though the soundproofing isn't perfect. In a second building, the rooms are pleasant, although they have no balcony, and the toilet is equipped with a mechanical flush. The least attractive rooms are those overlooking the back street (Numbers 6, 9, 16, 20, 32, 34, 37). For five generations, the owners have proven that professionalism and hospitality can be inherited, and the Michelin Guide has awarded one star to their young son and chef for such delicate, inventive specialties as rack of Norman lamb in puff pastry. The breakfasts are delicious, too.

***How to get there*** *(Map 6): 38 km south of Cherbourg. On A 13, take the Barneville-Carteret exit. The hotel is in Carteret.*

## Hôtel des Ormes

50270 Barneville-Carteret (Manche)
Quai Barbey-d'Aurevilly
Tel. (0)2.33.52.23.50 - Fax (0)2.33.52.91.65
M. and Mme Le Guevel

**Category ★★★ Rooms** 10 with telephone, bath or shower, WC, satellite TV – 1 for disabled persons. **Price** Double 395-580F / 60,22-88,42€. **Meals** Breakfast 55F / 8,38€, served 7:30-10:30. No restaurant. **Credit card** Visa. **Pets** Dogs allowed (+50F / 7,62€). **Facilities** Parking. **Nearby** Island of Jersey; Valognes; Thomas-Henry Museum in Cherbourg; Cotentin trail along La Hague Cape, Barfleur and Carteret Cape – 9-hole golf course in Saint-Jean-de-Rivière. **Closed** Jan 5 – Feb 5.

Between sea and land, on the sailing port of Carteret with all its Breton charm, you will find this little, flower-bedecked hotel, full of great things. The ten rooms are small, but they have been furnished and decorated with a particular care. Some beautiful pieces of furniture, found here and there, and wallpaper that elegantly jibes with the colorful fabrics bear witness to the care taken to blend beauty with comfort. According to your taste, you might choose those that overlook the ever-changing sea; or those that have a view of the restful garden. The bathrooms are pleasant, and some even have large windows. The lounge bar in warm tones opens out to a little, sheltered terrace. In summer, breakfast is taken in the garden amongst the flowers. Simple and friendly hospitality. No restaurant in the hotel, but this shouldn't bother you too much, because the fine food of the *Hotel de la Marine* is nearby.

***How to get there*** *(Map 6): Via A 13, take the Caen exit, then N 13 toward Cherbourg, then take the Valognes exit. Head toward Barneville-Carteret; once there, head toward the sailing port.*

## La Beaumonderie

50290 Bréville-sur-Mer (Manche)
20, route de Coutances
Tel. (0)2.33.50.36.36 - Fax (0)2.33.50.36.45 - Mme Denèfle

**Category** ★★★ **Rooms** 12 with telephone, bath or shower, WC, TV, 8 with minibar – 1 for disabled persons. **Price** Double 570-870F / 86,90-132,63€. **Meals** Breakfast 55F / 8,38€, served 7:30-11:00; half board +195F / 29,73€ (per pers., 3 days min.). **Restaurant** Closed Sunday evening and Monday lunchtime in low season. Service 12:00PM-2:00PM, 7:30PM-10:00PM; mealtime specials 119-249F / 18,29-38,11€. Specialties: Fish and lobster. **Credit cards** All major. **Pets** Dogs allowed (+35F / 5,34€). **Facilities** Covered swimming pool, squash, tennis and parking. **Nearby** Thalasso center and casino in Granville; Mont Saint-Michel, Channel Islands, Avranches – 27-hole Granville golf course. **Open** All year.

Don't be discouraged by the road that runs along the east side of this elegant, turn-of-the-century house. Efficiently double-glazed windows keep out the noise, and the traffic all but stops at night. We were immediately impressed with the emphasis on decor, both youthful and classical; the beauty of the materials used and the attention to detail, all conferring the hotel with a charming, home-like ambiance. Ask for a room on the west side, which overlooks lush countryside near the sand dunes. You will see a small race track, a golf course and, above all, the sea and its promise of unforgettable sunsets. Wide, comfortable beds, harmonious color schemes, and pleasant baths combine to make the rooms truly lovely. On the ground floor, you will enjoy the same panoramic view, an English-style bar, which gives out to the dining room, and opens up to the outside world and where you will eat very well indeed. Warm hospitality.

***How to get there*** *(Map 6): 25km north of Avranches via D973 to Granville, then towards Coutances (3km from Granville).*

## Manoir de Roche Torin

50220 Courtils (Manche)
Tel. (0)2.33.70.96.55 - Fax (0)2.33.48.35.20
Mme Barraux
E-mail: manoir.rochetorin@wanadoo.fr

**Category** ★★★ **Rooms** 13 with telephone, bath or shower, WC and TV. **Price** Single and double 480-820F / 73,18-125,01€, suite 890F / 135,68€. **Meals** Breakfast (buffet) 62F / 9,46€, served 8:00-10:00. **Restaurant** Closed Monday, Tuesday lunchtime and Wednesday lunchtime. Service 12:00PM-1:00PM, 7:15PM-9:00PM, mealtime specials 120-350F / 18,29-53,36€, also à la carte. **Credit cards** All major. **Pets** Dogs allowed (+42F / 6,41€). **Facilities** Parking. **Nearby** "Jardin des Plantes" in Avranches, Mont Saint-Michel, museum and observatory in Avranches. **Open** Feb 16 – Nov 14 and Dec 16 – Jan 4.

A happy compromise between the old and the new best describes the decoration of this turn-of-the-century family mansion. Floral fabrics have been selected for the salon. The bedrooms, like the rest of the house, are appointed with a combination of modern, rattan, and period furniture. Three rooms enjoy a view over Mont Saint Michel, while those on the *second étage* beneath the eaves are beautifully bright and also have a lovely view. All the bedrooms are attractive, our favorites being those with cheerful striped or checked cotton fabrics. Only three bedrooms are still awaiting renovation. Smokers can dine in the small rustic room with a large fireplace where salt-marsh lamb and lobsters are grilled. Just next to it is the dining room for non-smokers, which is surrounded by panoramic picture windows overlooking the sunset. Although the cuisine is irregular, the staff is friendly and efficient. All around, the countryside and the polder where Normandy's famous sheep graze offer a quiet setting and an unrestricted view as far as Mont Saint Michel.

***How to get there*** *(Map 7): 12km southwest of Avranches via N175, then towards Mont-Saint-Michel via D43.*

353

## Château de la Roque

50180 Hébécrevon (Manche)
Tel. (0)2.33.57.33.20 - Fax (0)2.33.57.51.20
Famille Delisle
E-mail: mireille.delisle@wanadoo.fr - Web: chateau.de.la.roque.fr

**Rooms** 15 with telephone, bath or shower, WC and TV – 2 for disabled persons. **Price** Double 400-560F / 60,98-85,37€. **Meals** Breakfast incl. **Evening meals** Service 8:00PM; mealtime specials 100F / 15,24€ (wine incl.). Specialties: Regional cuisine. **Credit cards** All major. **Pets** Dogs allowed on leash by request. **Facilities** Bicycle, fishing, hunting, tennis, parking, golf course. **Nearby** Church and museum (Tenture des Amours de Gombault and Macé) in Saint-Lô, Château of Torigni-sur-Vire – 9-hole golf course in Couttainville. **Open** All year.

In the midst of the gentle Norman countryside, this very pretty château has been opened to guests by Raymond Delisle of cycle racing fame. It's a great success: All the rooms are comfortable and beautiful, with special attention paid to the choice of fabrics, which are complemented by antique furniture. The rooms in the château itself as well as in the outbuildings are all marvelously attractive and well-kept (Number 4, somewhat small, is best for one person.). Bread is made every day in an old oven here; it is served at the breakfasts which guests enjoy at a large communal table in the charming dining room. If you reserve ahead, you can enjoy the excellent *table d'hôtes* dinner presided over by Madame Delisle with charm and vivacity. The dinner is served in a huge, beautiful room located in the converted barn and adjacent to an attractive lounge. The *Château de la Roque* is one of our outstanding addresses in Normandy.

***How to get there*** *(Map 7): 6km northwest of Saint-Lô. Before Saint-Lô, take D972, towards Coutances, to Saint-Gilles, then towards Pont Hébert (D77) for 3km.*

## Le Gué du Holme

Saint-Quentin-sur-le-Homme 50220 Ducey (Manche)
14, rue des Estuaires
Tel. (0)2.33.60.63.76 - Fax (0)2.33.60.06.77
M. Leroux

**Category** ★★★ **Rooms** 10 with telephone, bath and WC – 1 for disabled persons. **Price** Double 400-500F / 60,98-76,22€. **Meals** Breakfast 55F / 8,38€; half board 500F / 76,22€ (per pers., 3 days min.). **Restaurant** By reservation. Closed Friday, Saturday lunchtime and Sunday from mid Sep – Easter. Service 12:00PM-2:00PM, 7:00PM-9:00PM; mealtime specials 150-390F / 22,87-59,46€, also à la carte. Specialties: Foie gras aux pommes; aumônière de homard. **Credit cards** All major. **Pets** Dogs allowed (+40F / 6,10€). **Facilities** Parking. **Nearby** Poilley-Ducey-Museum; garden and Museum of the Palais des Evêques (manuscripts of Mont Saint-Michel) in Avranches; Villedieu-les-Poêles-Museum; Mont Saint-Michel. **Closed** Jan 2 – 24; Sunday evening from Sep 15 – Easter.

Not too close to Mont Saint Michel nor too far away, this small village inn is ideally located for discovering the regional marvels without being too disturbed by the hordes of tourists who come to this part of Normandy. Charming and very tasteful, the interior decoration contrasts with a somewhat dull façade, making the surprise inside even greater. We were particularly impressed with the small details throughout, even in the corridors with their thick green carpet and pale antique furniture. Pleasant and very comfortable, the bedrooms are handsomely modern and perfectly kept. Most overlook a small garden where you can enjoy breakfast in good weather. Other meals are served in the very elegant dining room where the lithographs and brass sconces are highlighted by the orange walls. The chef's talented use of the excellent local produce the friendly, efficient staff scores many points for the beautiful *Gué du Holme*. Attentive and warm hospitality.

***How to get there*** *(Map 7): 40km southwest of Granville. Via A11, take exit 175.*

355

## Hôtel de France et des Fuchsias

50550 Saint-Vaast-la-Hougue (Manche)
20, rue du Maréchal-Foch
Tel. (0)2.33.54.42.26 - Fax (0)2.33.43.46.79
M. and Mme Brix

**Category** ★★ **Rooms** 34 with telephone, 29 with bath or shower, WC and TV. **Price** Single and double 290-480F / 44,21-73,18€. **Meals** Breakfast 45F / 6,86€, served 8:00-10:00; half board 325-400F / 49,55-60,98€ (per pers., 3 days min.). **Restaurant** Closed Monday lunchtime in May and Jun except national holidays. Service 12:00PM-2:00PM, 7:00PM-9:15PM; mealtime specials 86-300F / 12,96-45,73€, also à la carte. Specialties: Choucroute de la mer au beurre blanc; feuilleté de pommes tièdes à la crème de calvados. **Credit cards** All major. **Pets** Dogs allowed (+30F / 4,57€). **Facilities** Bicycle rental. **Nearby** Ile Tatihon, Valognes, Barfleur, Thomas Henry Museum in Cherbourg – 9-hole golf course in Fontenay-en-Cotentin. **Closed** Jan 3 – Feb 23 and Mondays from Sept 15 – Apr.

At Saint Vaast-la-Hougue on the eastern side of the Cotentin Peninsula the climate is so mild that mimosas flourish. The bedrooms in this old coachman's inn are simple but elegant, with muted colors and handsome furniture (Room 14 is a bit small, however). Those at the back of the garden, in the *Les Feuillantines* house, are decorated in the same spirit and most are more spacious. The last two weeks of August, chamber-music concerts are given in the pleasant small lounge (and the garden). They are very popular with guests, who attend them at no charge. Meals are served on a veranda opening onto the garden and feature seafood along with produce from the nearby farm at Quettehou. In addition, this beautiful hotel is in a part of Normandy where the climate is especially clement, near a small fishing port, a sandy beach, and hedgerows and woods.

***How to get there*** *(Map 7): 37km southeast of Cherbourg via N13 to Valognes, then D902 and D1 to Saint-Vaast-la-Hougue (it's in the town center).*

## Moulin de Villeray

61110 Condeau (Orne)
Tel. (0)2.33.73.30.22 - Fax (0)2.33.73.38.28
M. Eelsen

**Category** ★★★ **Rooms** 20 and 4 apartments with telephone, bath or shower, WC, TV and minibar – 1 for disabled persons. **Price** Single and double 390-1250F / 59,46-190,56€ , apart. 950-1500F / 144,83-228,67€. **Meals** Breakfast 80F / 12,20€; half board 495-925F / 75,46-141,02€ (per pers., obligatory in high season). **Restaurant** Service 12:00PM-2:00PM, 7:00PM-10:00PM; mealtime specials 145-360F / 22,11-54,88€, also à la carte. Specialties: Regional cuisine. **Credit cards** All major. **Pets** Dogs allowed (+50F / 7,62€). **Facilities** Swimming pool, mountain bike, canoeing, parking. **Nearby** Hills of the Perche (about 150km), museum of the philosopher Alain in Mortagne-au-Perche – 18-hole Perche golf course. **Open** All year.

The River Huisne flows peacefully by a lovely hamlet in the Perche region. A river branch, and turbulent downstream, borders the "Mill of Villeray". A carefully tended park full of flowers follows the watercourse. In the main building and two beautiful small houses, the bedrooms are very prettily redecorated with harmonious, charmingly colored fabrics, and antique or pine furniture. Located in the small houses, the most recent rooms are also the most attractive. Upstairs, some rooms have a balcony. Avoid the two or three bedrooms which are waiting to be redecorated. The bathrooms are being progressively renovated. Pleasant lounge that gives into a large dining room that opens out to the garden. Decorated in a rustic style, the dining room still has the great wheel from the era of the mills. While the prices are somewhat high, the light, beautifully seasoned cuisine is excellent, the staff pleasant and helpful, the setting restful and enchanting.

***How to get there*** *(Map 8): 9km north of Nogent-le-Rotrou; on A11, Chartes exit, Luigny or La Ferté-Bernard.*

## Manoir du Lys

La Croix Gauthier
61140 Bagnoles-de-l'Orne (Orne)
Tel. (0)2.33.37.80.69 - Fax (0)2.33.30.05.80 - M. and Mme Quinton

**Category** ★★★ **Rooms** 25 with telephone, bath or shower, WC, TV and minibar – Elevator; wheelchair access. **Price** Single and double 350-900F / 53,36-137,20€, suite 900-1100F / 137,20-167,69€. **Meals** Breakfast 65F / 9,91€; half board and full board 430-900F / 65,55-137,20€ (per pers., 3 days min.). **Restaurant** Service 12:30PM-2:30PM, 7:30PM-9:30PM; mealtime specials 150-350F / 22,87-53,36€, also à la carte. Spécialités: Dos de sandre fumé au hêtre et poêlé d'asperges au jus de persil; tarte friande d'andouille de Vire. **Credit cards** All major. **Pets** Dogs allowed (+35F / 5,34€). **Facilities** Covered swimming pool, tennis, parking. **Nearby** Andaine forest, Bonvouloir lighthouse, Château of Carrouges, Sées Cathedral – 9-hole golf course in Bagnoles-de-l'Orne. **Closed** Jan 5 – Feb 14, Sunday evening and Monday from Feb 14 – Easter and Nov 1 – Jan 5.

In the midst of the Andaine Forest very near the *Bagnoles-de-l'Orne* spa, the *Manoir du Lys* is beautifully quiet. The bedrooms, many large, are bright and very well equipped, with classic or discreetly modern decor and antiqued or lacquered furniture. Cheerful colors, beautiful baths in the recent part and effective soundproofing make them extremely pleasant. Some rooms have terraces and those with mansard ceilings overlook the orchard, where deer often search for fruit. The lounge and the piano bar are lovely. In the panoramic dining room, the alliance of yellow and pale green matches of the greenery in the garden (where you can have meals in summer.) Monsieur Quinton and his son Frank preside over the excellent cuisine, which combines traditional Norman recipes with the finesse of original creations. Warm hospitality from the whole family, who love their job as much as their region.

***How to get there*** *(Map 7): 53km west of Alençon via N12 to Pré-au-Pail, then N176 and D916.*

## Hôtel du Tribunal

61400 Mortagne-au-Perche (Orne)
4, place du Palais
Tel. (0)2.33.25.04.77 - Fax (0)2.33.83.60.83
M. le Boucher

**Category** ★★ **Rooms** 11 with telephone, bath or shower, WC and satellite TV. **Price** Single and double 220-320F / 33,54-48,78€. **Meals** Breakfast 40F / 6,10€, served 7:30-10:30; half board 290F / 44,21€ (per pers. in double room). **Restaurant** Service 12:00PM-2:00PM, 7:00PM-9:00PM; mealtime specials 90-190F / 13,72-28,97€, also à la carte. Specialties: Croustillant de boudin moutagnais, confit de canard au cidre. **Credit cards** Visa, Eurocard and MasterCard. **Pets** Dogs allowed (+20F / 3,05€). **Nearby** Museum Alain, Cloister of Bellême, Church of Notre-Dame in Moutagne-au-Perche; forest and hills of Perche (150 km) – 18-hole Bellême-Saint-Martin golf course. **Open** All year.

In the heart of a magnificent region and the pretty village of Mortagne with its historic architectural riches, the *Hôtel du Tribunal* is located in a landmarked building constructed in the 13th and 18th centuries. Set on a small square shaded with linden trees, the hotel appeals immediately with its warm, family atmosphere and its interior decoration, at once simple and elegant. The bedrooms are papered in different colors and decorated with a mixture of antique, period, or rattan furniture; the bathrooms offer comfortable amenities. Illuminated by three windows, the pink and blue family bedroom is especially lovely with its large farm table and its lounge area. Three bedrooms directly overlook the small interior courtyard, where several tables are set out in summer. In the charming dining room, its tables smartly laid with white linens, you can enjoy good regional cuisine. In place of lounge, there is a pleasant room at the entrance with several tables and a fireplace.

***How to get there*** *( Map 8): 38km west of Alençon via N12.*

## Hôtel du Mouton Gras

76390 Aumale (Seine-Maritime)
2, rue de l'Abbé-Dauchy
Tel. (0)2.35.93.41.32
M. and Mme Gauthier

**Rooms** 6 with bath or shower, and TV (3 with WC). **Price** Single and double 280-440F / 42,69-67,08€. **Meals** Breakfast 35F / 5,34€, served from 8:00; half board (except in weekends) 350F / 53,36€ (per pers.). **Restaurant** Closed Monday evening and Tuesday. Service 12:00PM-2:00PM, 7:30PM-9:00PM; mealtime specials 100-195F / 15,24-29,73€, also à la carte. Specialties: Shellfish; tête de veau; tarte aux pommes flambée au calvados. **Credit cards** All major. **Pets** Dogs allowed on request. **Facilities** Parking (30F / 4,57€). **Nearby** Le Pays de Bray: Fouges-les-eaux, Saint-Léger-aux-Bois, Rezancourt, Château of Mesnières-en-Bray, Saint-Saëns starting-point of the Varenne Valley and the forest of Eawy. **Closed** 15 days in Sep, for Christmas and New Year's Day.

It doesn't take much imagination to hear the jingling bells of the old postal express ponies, who once came to this relay station to catch their breath. Today, people come to the "Fat Sheep" mainly for its excellent restaurant. The dining room opens directly onto the enclosed courtyard, its brick walls hung with brightly shining antique copper pots, and its red checkered tablecloths creating a warm and inviting atmosphere, as does the large fireplace stocked with wines awaiting a taker. This is the perfect example of a little, country inn. To prolong the pleasure of a meal with good traditional regional dishes, there are several very simple bedrooms upstairs and in a small adjacent outbuilding. Don't ask to much from these rooms -- they are purely functional, and their prices are in keeping with that. In summer, the Norman weather willing, meals are served in the flowery courtyard.

***How to get there*** *(Map 1): 62km southeast of Dieppe towards Neuchâtel-en-Bray then Aumale.*

## Le Donjon

76790 Etretat (Seine-Maritime)
Tel. (0)2.35.27.08.23. - Fax (0)2.35.29.92.24
M. Omar Abodib
E-mail: ledonjon@wanadoo.fr

**Category** ★★★ **Rooms** 11 with telephone, bath, WC and satellite TV. **Price** Single and double 480-1180F / 73,18-179,89€. **Meals** Breakfast 50F / 7,62€, served 8:00-10:30; half board obligatory for the weekend 420-900F / 64,12-137,20€ (in double). **Restaurant** Service 12:00PM-2:00PM, 7:00PM-9:30PM; mealtime specials 130-260F / 19,82-39,64€, also à la carte. **Credit cards** All major. **Pets** Dogs allowed (+50F / 7,62€). **Facilities** Parking. **Nearby** Etretat cliffs, Lupin field, Benedictine museum in Fécamp – 18-hole golf course in Etretat. **Open** All year.

Below *Le Donjon*, the cove of Etretat is surrounded by little houses facing the stony beach, the chalk cliffs, and the famous "Needle's Eye" that all lovers of Arsène Lupin know so well. Nothing shocking in the fact that hotel has been outfitted with the gentleman burglar in mind. Inside, the lounge and the little dining rooms (two overlook the ocean) are decorated with glistening fabrics and many 1900 antique tables and furnishings. The rooms, of the same design, rival each other in beauty. The *"Suite Orientale"*, the *"Chambre Horizon"* and the "Marjorie Room" all enjoy a magnificient view. Necessary half board at the *Donjon*, which leads us to a few clarifications about dining. Good overall (read, excellent, like the veal salad), we prefer the meats to the fish dishes, which are sometimes overcooked, to the chagrin of the purists. Pleasant, cozy atmosphere and the greatest hospitality.

***How to get there*** *(Map 1): Via A 13, take Le Havre-Pont de Tancarville exit after the bridge, then head toward Saint-Romain-de-Colbose and then Etretat.*

## Les Hêtres

Le Bourg 76460 Ingouville-sur-Mer (Seine-Maritime)
Tel. (0)2.35.57.09.30 - Fax (0)2.35.57.09.31
M. Liberge

**Rooms** 4 with telephone, bath, WC and TV – Wheelchair access. **Price** Double 480-730F / 73,18-111,29€. **Meals** Breakfast 75F / 11,43€, served 7:30AM-12:00PM. **Restaurant** Service 12:00PM-2:00PM, 7:30PM-10:00PM; mealtime specials 165-380F / 25,15-57,93€, also à la carte. Specialties: Fish and local products. **Credit cards** Visa, Eurocard and MasterCard. **Pets** Dogs allowed (+50F / 7,62€). **Facilities** Parking. **Nearby** Beach (3 km), château and museum in Dieppe, Church and cemetery in Varengeville, villages in Caux Country (Luneray, Blosseville...), Fécamp, Château of Bailleul, Etretat. **Closedd** Jan 10 – Feb 11 and Monday evening and Tuesday in low season.

In a small hamlet not far from the chalk cliffs of the seashore, this small, welcoming hotel is lovely, even if you can see the nuclear power plant in the distance. You should reserve early, because *Les Hêtres* has only four bedrooms, but what rooms they are! Each is a model of good taste and ultra-modern amenities, with fabrics by Patrick Frey or Braquenier, a few pieces of handsome, smartly polished antique furniture, and an elegant series of engravings. Their price varies with the size of the room (the most expensive has a private terrace on the garden;) the baths are simply luxurious. Excellent breakfasts are served beneath the half-timbered eaves. On the ground floor, the long dining room is just as beautiful, with a lovely fireplace in one corner. Bertrand Warin's celebrated cuisine puts a delicious finishing touch on this special place.

***How to get there*** *(Map 1): 30km south of Dieppe via D925, to Saint-Valéry-en-Caux, then to Cany-Barville. After the traffic circle, head towards aero club and take 2nd right.*

## Le Saint-Pierre

76530 La Bouille (Seine-Maritime)
4, place du Bateau
Tel. (0)2.35.18.01.01 - Fax (0)2.35.18.12.76

**Rooms** 6 with telephone, bath or shower, WC and TV. **Price** Single and double 280-350F / 42,69-53,36€. **Meals** Breakfast 40F / 6,10€, served 8:00-11:00. **Restaurant** Closed Sunday evening and Monday. Service 12:00PM-2:00PM, 7:30PM-9:00PM; mealtime specials 160-260F / 24,39-39,64€, also à la carte. **Credit cards** All major. **Pets** Dogs allowed on request. **Facilities** Parking (30F / 4,57€). **Nearby** Rouen; Elbeuf (GR2 for the Roches Ouival, 4 km); church in Yvetot; the millenium oak in Allouville-Bellefosse, Nature Museum. **Closed** Sep – end Mar, Sunday evening and Monday.

An hour's drive from Paris takes you to this small 18th-century village on the banks of the Seine and the *Saint-Pierre* hotel, whose terrace offers a panoramic view of the river and the great barges that regularly pass by. Partly demolished during World War II, the building unfortunately no longer has its old charm, but the large bay windows in the dining room (and in the conference room upstairs) afford light and a beautiful view. Popular with the region's business people, the cuisine is delicate and refined. The interior decoration is classic throughout. The six bedrooms on the *second étage* are decorated in the contemporary Roche Bobois style, with bamboo furniture and dark Pierre Frey drapes. The bathrooms are well-equipped and comfortable. Ask for Rooms 1, 2, or 7 on the Seine side. Only Room 3 overlooks the village road in the back but it is spacious and can accommodate two children. The staff is courteous and professional, and the *Saint-Pierre* is a pleasant place to stay on the way to Normandy. But avoid the weekend traffic.

***How to get there*** *(Map 8): 20 km northwest of Rouen. Take A 13 toward Paris, then head toward Caen-Le Havre. Take the Maison-Brulée exit 24. After the second service station, take a right and head toward La Bouille.*

## Auberge du Val au Cesne

Le Val au Cesne 76190 Croix-Mare (Seine-Maritime)
Tel. (0)2.35.56.63.06 - Fax (0)2.35.56.92.78
M. Carel
Web: www.pageszoom.com/val.au.cesne. – E-mail: val-au-cesne@lerapporteur.fr

**Rooms** 5 with telephone, bath, WC and TV. **Price** Double 480F / 73,18€. **Meals** Breakfast 50F / 7,62€, served 8:00-11:00; half board and full board 690F / 105,19€ (in single) 440-550F / 68,60-83,85€ (per pers. in double). **Restaurant** Service 12:00PM-2:00PM, 7:00PM-9:00PM; mealtime specials 150F / 22,87€, also à la carte. Specialties: Terrine de raie; tête et fraise de veau; sole farcie à la mousse de langoustines; escalope de dinde "Vieille Henriette"; feuilleté aux pommes. **Credit cards** Visa, Eurocard and MasterCard. **Pets** Dogs allowed. **Facilities** Parking. **Nearby** Rouen Cathedral, church and museum in Yvetot, Abbey of Saint-Wandrille – 18-hole golf course in Etretat. **Open** All year.

The *Auberge* was initially a restaurant with an excellent reputation, consisting of two charmingly furnished rooms separated by a fireplace. At his customers' request, M. Carel opened five comfortable bedrooms in a house very near the *Auberge*. In a charming small valley, it has an elegant, welcoming atmosphere which is created by a very tasteful decoration, faithful to the regional style, as well as by the basic architecture which makes you feel very much at home. Part of the garden is home to various animals: you can admire a family of parrots, rare species of hens and doves… The five bedrooms are pleasant, but we like the Rose Room less. The small country road nearby will not disturb you as it luckily is quiet before nightfall in the heart of the *Pays de Caux*.

***How to get there*** (*Maps 1 and 8*): *30km northwest of Rouen via A15, towards Yvetot, then D5 for 3km heading towards Duclair.*

# Hôtel des Carmes

76000 Rouen (Seine-Maritime)
33, place des Carmes
Tel. (0)2.35.71.92.31 - Fax (0)2.35.71.76.96
M. Patrick Beaumont

**Rooms** 12 with telephone, bath or shower, WC and TV. **Price** Double 220-260F / 33,54-39,64€. **Meals** Breakfast 34F / 5,34€, served 8:00-10:00. No restaurant. **Credit cards** All major. **Pets** Dogs allowed. **Nearby** Rouen: Old Market square, Notre-Dame Cathedral, Court House, Saint-Maclou Church, Saint-Ouen Church, Fine-Art museum; Clères zoo. **Open** All year.

Located in the heart of Rouen, just a little ways from the cathedral and abbey church of Saint-Ouesn, the *Hôtel des Carmes* is a little, 4-story, 19th-century building. Completely renovated, it offers fresh and comfotable rooms. Those with baths open directly onto the trees of the delightful Carmes square, bursting with flowers in spring. The breakfast, made from regional produce, is served on the ground floor in an appealing area in warm colors. A tiny corner lounge faces the dining area. Very peaceful, despite its central location and too high prices, the hotel is perfect for a stopover in Rouen -- a town rich in artistic heritage and history. You will be greeted with a smile by Patrick Beaumont, the young owner, who will give you advice about where to go for dinner. The choices are overwhelming. We prefer *L'Ecaille* and *L'Episode* for gourmet dining, and *Le P'tit Zinc* for a pleasant dinner.

***How to get there*** *( Map 1 ): In the center of town.*

## Relais Hôtelier Douce France

76980 Veules-les-Roses (Seine-Maritime)
13, rue du Docteur-Girard
Tel. (0)2.35.57.85.30 - Fax (0)2.35.57.85.31
M. Bardot

**Category** ★★★ **Rooms** 13 suites with kitchenette, telephone, bath and satellite TV – 1 suite for desabled person. **Price** suites 430-600F / 65,55-91,47€. **Meals** Breakfast 55F / 8,38€, served 8:00-10:30, half board by reservation. **Restaurant** Service 12:30PM-2:30PM and 7:30PM-9:30PM, mealtime specials 150-250F / 22,87-38,11€, also à la carte. Specialties: Marmite de la mer. **Credit card** Visa. **Pets** Dogs allowed (+50F / 7,62€). **Facilities** Mountain bike rental. **Nearby** Albâtre coast, Caux Country, Châteaux of Angot, of Miromesnil and of Cany-Barville, Varengeville and Vasterival Gardens– 18-hole golf course in Dieppe, tennis, sea (100 m away). **Closed** 15 days in Nov and 3 weeks in Jan – Feb.

Located in the heart of the charming village of Veules-les-Roses, this former, 17th-century postal relay has been completely restored by the Friends of the Tour de France. Along the Veules that peacefully flows past the burg, the yellow walled and green half-timbered loggias have been outfitted as summer lounges with rattan chairs. Right next door, the thirteen suites, each with their own kitchen corner and little dining room, gaily display their contemporary look. Terra-cotta flooring, white beams, tannish pink patinated walls, billowing curtains, headposts in stylish, flowery fabrics go well with the furnishing and designer lamps. The bathrooms are modern and functional, with shower or bathtub, toilet and hair dryer. The garden, like a flowering cloister, offers a fresh, calm haven for the *apéritif*. The pretty restaurant offers a good selection of regional and traditional dishes.

***How to get there*** *( Map 1 ): At Rouen, take A 15 toward Le Havre, exit after Barentin, and head toward Pavilly, Yerville, and then Fontaine. Follow the signs.*

# Saint-Christophe

44502 La Baule (Loire-Atlantique)
Place Notre-Dame
Tel. (0)2.40.60.35.35 - Fax (0)2.40.60.11.74
M. Joüon

**Rooms** 28 and 5 suites, with telephone, bath or shower, satellite TV – 1 for disabled persons. **Price** Doubles 250-710F / 38,11-108,24€. **Meals** Breakfast 50F / 7,62€, served at all hours; half board (required in summer) 255-545F / 38,87-83,08€. **Restaurant** Service 12:30PM-2:00PM, 7:30PM-10:30PM; mealtime specials 125-195F / 19,06-29,73€. Specialties: Noix de Saint-Jacques de Saint-Quay en fine croûte persillée; moelleux au chocolat amer et brochettes de fruits. **Credit cards** All major. **Pets** Dogs allowed (+35F / 5,34€). **Facilities** Parking. **Nearby** La Baule; La Brière and La Guérande marshes – 18-hole La Baule golf course in Saint-Denac. **Open** All year.

In the heart of La Baule and bought by the Jouon family in the 70s, this family pension with its turn-of-the-century seaside architecture, bursting with greenery, is only 100 yards from the beach and is still very calm. Housed in three villas -- the *Sainte-Claire*, *Saint-Francois*, and *Saint-Christophe* -- the comfortable and antique furnished rooms come in double and small suite sizes, for families. The little English-style lounge is great for reading or for the *apéritif*. The large dining room next to the piano bar offers, under its modern paintings, fragrant fare that changes everyday. Fish is favored here, like the Dory filet roasted with pineapple and green pepper, along with the house's products, like the duck *foie gras*. The welcome and service could do with a little more attention.

***How to get there*** *(Map 14): 15 km from Saint-Nazaire. In the center of La Baule, near the big intersection, pass on your left the square with the merry-go-round and tourist office and head straight for Atlantia, Poulingen, then take the fourth road on your left (follow the signs), to the allee des Petrels.*

## Le Fort de l'Océan

44490 Le Croisic (Loire-Atlantique)
La Pointe du Croisic
Tel. (0)2.40.15.77.77 - Fax (0)2.40.15.77.80

**Rooms** 9 with air-conditioning, telephone, bath, WC, satellite TV and minibar – 1 for disabled persons. **Price** Single and double 800-1200F / 121,96-182,94€; suite 1500F / 228,67€. **Meals** Breakfast 80F / 12,20€, served 7:30-11:00; half board 730-1080F / 111,29-164,64€ (per pers., 3 days min.). **Restaurant** Closed Nov 17 – Dec 12 and Jan 5 – Feb 6 and Monday evening and Tuesday Sep 15 – Jun 10. Service 12:00PM-2:30PM, 7:30PM-9:30PM/10:30PM; mealtime specials 130F / 19,82€ (Chef's special), 265-420F / 40,40-64,12€, also à la carte. **Credit cards** Amex, Visa, Diners club. **Pets** Dogs allowed (+50F / 7,62€). **Facilities** Swimming pool, Bicycle, parking and garage. **Nearby** La Baule, La Brière and La Guérande marshes – 18-hole La Baule golf course in Saint-Denac. **Open** All year.

A fort often occupies a strategic position meaning that, once converted into a hotel, it enjoys an exceptional location. Such is the case of the *Fort de l'Océan*, which stands right on the rocks of Croisic Point, long abandoned but still a favorite hiking destination for summer vacationers. Built by Vauban, Louis XIV's Commissioner of Fortifications, the hotel has become one of character and charm thanks to the combined efforts of good local builders, the owners Monsieur and Madame Louis, and the talented Catherine Painvin, who has done a marvelous decorating job. The bedrooms are lovely and luxuriously comfortable, with beautiful fabrics coordinated with antique furniture, including some painted pieces, and elegant handicrafts created by Everwood. The "luxury-hotel white" style was chosen for the bathrooms and their soft, thick, numbered towels. We would have enjoyed tarrying in the elegant, refined public rooms, but we couldn't resist the comfortable chaises-longues in the garden and the sight of the sea: it was the next best thing to being on a boat.

***How to get there*** *( Map 14): 15km east of La Baule.*

## Hôtel Maris Stella

44490 Le Croisic (Loire-Atlantique)
1, avenue Becquerel - Plage Port-Lin
Tel. (0)2.40.23.21.45 - Fax (0)2.40.23.22.63
M. and Mme Garnier

**Category** ★★★ **Rooms** 10 with telephone, bath, WC, TV and minibar. **Price** Single and double 495-795F / 75,46-121,20€; suite 695-895F / 105,95-136,44€. **Meals** Breakfast 58F / 8,85€, served 8:00-11:30. **Restaurant** Closed Monday. Service 12:00PM, 7:30PM; mealtime specials 195-320F / 29,73-48,78€; also à la carte. Specialties: Lobster, fish. **Credit cards** Visa, Eurocard and MasterCard. **Pets** Dogs not allowed. **Facilities** Swimming pool and parking. **Nearby** La Baule, La Brière and La Guérande marshes – 18-hole La Baule golf course in Saint-Denac. **Closed** Nov 15 – Dec 20, Jan and Monday.

Facing the sea, the *Maris Stella* was one of the first resort hotels built in Le Croisic at the turn of the century. Behind its austere granite façade is hidden a marvelously comfortable interior, which has made the most of its magnificent view. The communal rooms are decorated identically, from their attractive, sand-colored modern furniture to the matching thick carpets and drapes. The bedrooms have a very restful atmosphere and you won't be disturbed by the small road (for local traffic only) which separates the building from the beach and the sea. Two small dining rooms are at your disposal, serving good breakfasts and refined cuisine. For families or groups of friends, we heartily recommend the duplexes located in the former outbuildings on the other side of the garden. Each is tastefully decorated, has a large lounge area, and note that the price is lower for a group of people. Reasonable prices throughout the hotel are offered in low season and during week days following a long weekend.

*How to get there* (*Map 14*): 15km east of La Baule.

## Abbaye de Villeneuve

44840 Les Sorinières (Loire-Atlantique)
Route de La-Roche-sur-Yon
Tel. (0)2.40.04.40.25 - Fax (0)2.40.31.28.45
M. Brevet

**Category** ★★★★ **Rooms** 20 with telephone, bath and WC (15 with TV). **Price** Single and double 390-890F / 59,46-135,68€, suite 1095-1245F / 166,93-189,80€. **Meals** Breakfast 70F / 10,67€, served 7:00-10:30; half board 430-970F / 65,55-147,88€. **Restaurant** Service 12:00PM-2:00PM, 7:00PM-9:30PM; mealtime specials 140-380F / 21,34-57,93€, also à la carte 195F / 29,73€. Specialties: Maraîchère de homard et sa vinaigrette parfumée; dos de sandre poché au beurre blanc primeurs nantais; charlotte moelleuse au chocolat amer. **Credit cards** All major. **Pets** Dogs allowed. **Facilities** Swimming pool, parking. **Nearby** Art Museum and Jules Verne Museum in Nantes, Valley of the Erdre, Clisson – 18-hole golf course in Nantes. **Open** All year.

This former Cistercian abbey, founded in 1201 by Constance of Brittany, was partially destroyed during the French Revolution, and then restored in 1977 is now a charming and luxurious hotel. The monastery's library is now the restaurant. The rooms, furnished with antiques, have kept their stately dimensions on the *premier étage*, and, on the next story, sport magnificent half-timbered beams. The line-up of lounges and dining rooms with their French-style ceilings and stone fireplaces creates a mood that is a bit majestic, but, when it comes to a stay, preferable to the austerity of an abbey. There is great comfort and real elegance here, only ten minutes from the Nantes city center. Service and reception worthy of a great hotel (despite some inexplicable absences, such as no hairdryers in the bathrooms). Classic, high-quality cuisine.

***How to get there***: *(Map 14): 10 km south of Nantes on A 83, heading toward Bordeaux, La Roche sur Yon, and then Viais.*

## Hôtel de la Bretesche

44780 Missillac (Loire-Atlantique)
Tel. (0)2.51.76.86.96 - Fax (0)2.40.66.99.47
M. Christophe Delahaye

**Category** ★★★★ **Rooms** 29 with telephone, bath, WC, satellite TV and minibar – Elevator; 2 for disabled persons. **Price** Single and double 450-1050F / 68,60-160,07€; suites 950-1500F / 144,83-228,67€. **Meals** Breakfast 80F / 12,20€, served 7:30-10:30. **Restaurant** Closed Sunday evening and Monday and Oct 15 – Mar 15; mealtime specials 165F / 25,15€ (lunchtime weekdays), 220-430F / 33,54-65,55€; also à la carte. Specialties: Foie gras landais cuit au naturel; brochette de pêches et abricots rôtis aux amandes sorbet passion. **Credit cards** All major. **Pets** Dogs allowed except in restaurant. **Facilities** Heated swimming pool (May-Sep), parking. **Facilities** La Baule; La Brière and La Guérande marshes – 18-hole golf course. **Closed** Jan 30 – Mar 10.

The area is enchanting: A little Renaissance château on a lake, with a rolling golfing green peaking through the centuries-old trees, and very elegant outbuildings strung out around a checkered courtyard. The hotel is in these 19th-century buildings, once used as a calash. The superbly renovated interior bathes in a quiet mood. The rooms are generally fitted out with fabrics, outfitted with *Directoire*-style furnishings. Prices are in accordance with their size, but the level of comfort is always high, and all enjoy a beautiful view. Why not have your excellent and well-presented breakfast in your room? The dining room also looks out on a beautiful panorama. The gourmet food lives up to its reputation, and you can extend your evening in the lounge bar, set up in the former stable with its wooden stalls. A very beatiful establishment, particularly hospitable.

***How to get there*** *(Map 14):Via A11, take Nantes exit, then N 165.*

# Hôtel Sud-Bretagne

44380 Pornichet (Loire-Atlantique)
42, boulevard de la République
Tel. (0)2.40.11.65.00 - Fax (0)2.40.61.73.70
M. Bardouil

**Category** ★★★★ **Rooms** 30 with telephone, bath, WC and TV. **Price** Double 600-1200F / 91,47-182,94€, suite 1500-1800F / 228,67-274,41€. **Meals** Breakfast 65F / 9,91€; half board 650-1050F / 99,09-160,07€. **Restaurant** Closed Sunday evening and Monday in low season. Service 12:00PM-15:00, 7:00PM-10:30PM; mealtime specials 165-225F / 25,15-34,30€, also à la carte. **Credit cards** All major. **Pets** Dogs allowed. **Facilities** Swimming pool, parking. **Nearby** La Baule, La Brière and La Guérande marshes – 18-hole La Baule golf course in Saint-Denac. **Open** All year.

Ideally located not far from the beaches at La Baule, the *Hôtel Sud-Bretagne* has been in the same family since 1912, and to this day every member of the family joins in running and improving the hotel. Their contributions range from interior decoration to the organization of excursions aboard *La Orana*, a 17-meter teak-and-mahogony ketch. You will feel at home here. And a magnificent home it is, where each room has its own style. There is a lounge with a cozy fireplace, a billiard room, and several dining rooms overlooking an indoor swimming pool. Outside, garden furniture invites you to relax in the sun. Each bedroom has a different theme (ducks, cherries, Joséphine, and so) on reflected in the choice of fabrics, furniture and objects. There are some small apartments, with a lounge, a terrace, and typical Breton box beds for children. The seafood, finely prepared by Madame Bardouile, is extremely fresh (the fishermen work "under contract" for the hotel). The *Sud-Bretagne* is one of a few luxury hotels which has retained all its charm and character.

***How to get there*** *(Map 14): 5km east of La Baule.*

## Hôtel Villa Flornoy

44380 Pornichet (Loire-Atlantique)
7, avenue Flornoy
Tel. (0)2.40.11.60.00 - Fax (0)2.40.61.86.47 - M. Rouault
E-mail: hotflornoy@aol.com - Web: www.villa-flornoy.com

**Category** ★★ **Rooms** 21 with telephone, bath or shower, WC and TV – Wheelchair access. **Price** Double 360-530F / 54,88-80,80€. **Meals** Breakfast 42F / 6,50€, served from 7:30; half board 340-415F / 51,83-63,27€. **Restaurant** Service 12:30PM-2:00PM, 7:30PM-9:00PM; mealtime specials 120-145F / 18,29-22,11€, also à la carte. Specialties: Filet de bar rôti, étuvée de poireaux à la crème; grenadin de porc au miel et son riz pilaf. **Credit cards** Visa, Eurocard and MasterCard. **Pets** Dogs allowed (+35F / 5,34€). **Nearby** La Baule, La Brière and La Guérande marshes – 18-hole La Baule golf course in Saint-Denac. **Open** Mar – Nov.

Guests at the *Villa Flornoy* are not disturbed by the summer hustle and bustle of the beaches at Pornichet and La Baule because the hotel is located in a quiet residential quarter 900 feet away. Its façade is very much in the "Norman Coast", turn-of-the-century style. Today completely refurbished in contemporary taste, the hotel offers lovely bedrooms with cheerful, classic, comfortable furnishings. Those with a third bed tend to lack this balanced feeling. All overlook the street and the neighboring villas, or the pleasant garden behind the hotel. On the ground floor, an elegant reception lounge with antique furniture, engravings, and carefully chosen objects could be in a private house; from the lounge, glass doors lead into the garden, and on the other side by a beautiful dining room in shades of orange. The food is good, but lacks a professional touch. The same goes for the reception and the service, which is courteous and well-meaning, but which can be a bit lacking in high season.

***How to get there*** *(Map 14): 5km east of la Baule. Opposite the Town hall of Pornichet.*

## Auberge du Parc - La Mare aux Oiseaux

44720 Saint-Joachim (Loire-Atlantique)
162, île de Fédrun
Tel. (0)2.40.88.53.01 - Fax (0)2.40.91.67.44
M. Guérin

**Rooms** 5 with telephone, bath or shower and WC. **Price** Single and double 380F / 57,93€. **Meals** Breakfast 35F / 5,34€. **Restaurant** Closed Sunday evening and Monday in low season. Service 12:00PM-2:00PM, 7:00PM-9:00PM; mealtime specials 150-195F/ 22,87-29,73€, also à la carte. Specialties: Croquant de grenouilles aux algues bretonnes, gingembre confit et beurre d'agrumes; anguilles rôties aux pommes acidulées. **Credit cards** All major. **Pets** Dogs allowed. **Facilities** Parking. **Nearby** Guérande, Salt Marshes, Regional Park of Brière – 18-hole Bretesche golf course, 18-hole La Baule golf course in Saint-Denac. **Closed** Mar and Sunday evening, Monday in low season.

Fédrun is an island village lost in the midst of the immense marshes of the Brière region. Eric Guérin, the young owner of the *Auberge du Parc* and a great admirer of the island's small, thatched-roof cottages and the wild countryside he knows so well, interrupted a promising career in Paris to exercise his talents here: he had been *maître d'art* the *Tour d'Argent* and head chef at the *Jules Verne*. It is in fact difficult to imagine a more charming combination of magnificent surroundings, fine and inventive gastronomy which completely captivated us, and ravishing bedrooms, deliciously decorated with natural shades, sober and beautiful furniture, amusing Eskimo lithographs.... The atmosphere throughout is artistic, elegant and amiable. This is a magic place. We recommend that you find a guide to explain the fauna and history of the marshland, if you don't wish to borrow a boat from the hotel and set out on your own mission of discovery.

***How to get there*** *(Map 14): 16km northwest of Saint-Nazaire via D47.*

## Hôtel du Mail

49100 Angers (Maine-et-Loire)
8-10, rue des Ursules
Tel. (0)2.41.25.05.25 - Fax (0)2.41.86.91.20
M. Dupuis

**Category** ★★ **Rooms** 26 with telephone, bath, shower, 1 with basin, TV and minibar. **Price** Single and double 150-325F / 22,87-49,55€. **Meals** Breakfast (buffet) 36F / 5,34€, served 7:00-10:00. No restaurant. **Credit cards** All major. **Pets** Dogs allowed (+20F / 3,05€). **Facilities** Parking (18F / 2,74€). **Nearby** Abbey of Solesmes, Abbey of Fontevrault, tapestry of the Château d'Angers, Loire Valley – 18-hole Anjou country club golf course. **Closed** Sunday and national holidays between 12:00PM-6:30PM.

This pleasant hotel is in the heart of Angers, set up in an 18th-century private manor. You will sleep well here because the street is quiet and the parking area closes at 11:30P.M., to ensure your peace and quiet. The diverse rooms are almost all renovated and carefully decorated in a panoply of colors, with stained or more modern furnishings. Only a few await their new decoration, planned very soon. The brightest rooms look out on the courtyard (three open onto the courtyard), where tables are set up in the shade of the linden in summer. With its antique furniture, the huge dining room houses the hearty breakfast buffet, and a little lounge in the back is a great place to relax in comfort. Monsieur and Madame Dupuis will welcome you vibrantly with a smile. For restaurants, try: *L'Auberge d'Eventard* and the *Provence Caffé*, our favorites, but there are also *Le Toussaint*, *Le Relais*, and *Lucullus*.

***How to get there*** *( Map 15 ): In front of the town hall ("mairie"), take first street on right (rue David-d'Angers) and another right on rue des Ursules.*

# Hôtel Le Castel

49320 Brissac-Quincé (Maine-et-Loire)
1, rue Louis-Moron
Tel. (0)2.41.91.24.74 - Fax (0)2.41.91.71.55
Cécile Bourron

**Category** ★★ **Rooms** 10 and 1 suite with telephone, bath, satellite TV. **Price** Double 305F / 46,50€, triple 340F / 51,83€, suite 450F / 68,60€ (4 pers.). **Meals** Breakfast 40F / 6,10€, served 7:00-10:00. No restaurant. **Credit cards** All major. **Pets** Dogs allowed (+25F / 3,81€). **Facilities** Parking. **Nearby** Château of Brissac, Angers, Doué-la-Fontaine, Layon vineyards, 18-hole golf course, riding. **Open** All year.

In the heart of the village, across from the entrance to the superb Brissac château, is an anonymous white structure with standard windows, built some thirty years ago. If it weren't for the flowery terrace and the large umbrellas, you might be tempted to just pass on by. And you would be wrong, for the hotel's interior deserves some attention. Totally renovated, the hotel offers a pleasant and uniform decoration, with thick, brick-red, spotted carpets, and pale yellow curtains with large blue interlacing in the common areas; and azure carpeting and coordinated, Persian-style fabrics for the rooms. For a small, 2-star hotel, things are well-done, not just in terms of decoration (the suite is great, as well as is the large family room), but also with the comfort of the bathrooms and the hotel's general upkeep. Equally well-tended, the breakfast buffet is very agreeable, especially when the first hints of sunlight make the tables come out, and the umbrellas open. And then, over the high branches of the cedars that crown the château's gate, one can make out the chiseled façade of the noble structure.

***How to get there*** *( Map 15): Via N 748, take Angers-Poitiers exit. At Brissac, in front of château gate.*

## Château des Briottières

49330 Champigné (Maine-et-Loire)
Tel. (0)2.41.42.00.02 - Fax (0)2.41.42.01.55 - M. and Mme de Valbray
Web: www.briottieres.com - E-mail: briottieres@wanadoo.fr

**Category** ★★★★ **Rooms** 10 with telephone, bath. **Price** Double 550-750F / 83,85-114,34€, "supérieures" 900-1500F / 137,20-228,67€. **Meals** Breakfast 60F / 9,15€; half board 1370-2220F / 208,86-338,43€ (per 2 pers.). **Evening meals** Only for residents on request. At 8:00PM (by reservation); mealtime specials 300F / 45,73€ (all incl.). **Credit cards** All major. **Pets** Dogs allowed (+50F / 7,62€). **Facilities** Heated swimming pool, bicycle, billiard, parking. **Nearby** Abbey of Solesmes, Abbey of Fontevrault, Château of Angers, Loire Valley – 18-hole Anjou country club golf course. **Open** All year (by reservation in winter).

The *Château des Briottières* is off the beaten path and surrounded by an immense English-style garden which is in itself worth a visit. The masters of the house are warm and friendly. A vast gallery leads to the reception areas. The lounges are furnished in 18th-century style, and the large dining room is brightened by pearl-grey woodwork and pink drapes. The owners join you for the excellent, friendly dinners, which are served on a magnificently set dining table. There is a library with a French billiard table. Upstairs, the comfortable bedrooms are all tastefully decorated with lovely fabrics and very beautiful antique furniture. Some rooms are intimate, while others are vast. The bathrooms are charming, read luxurious. The swimming pool is located in a beautiful garden. The food is healthy and unpretentious, served on porcelain plates and silver service. And if you stay on, the sixth night is free from October 15 to April 15!

***How to get there*** *(Map 15): From Paris A11 Durtal exit. 30km north of Angers towards Laval and immediately head towards Sablé in Montreuil-Juigné; follow signs from Champigné.*

## Le Prieuré

49350 Chênehutte-les-Tuffeaux (Maine-et-Loire)
Tel. (0)2.41.67.90.14 - Fax - 02.41.67.92.24
M. Doumerc

**Category** ★★★★ **Rooms** 35 with telephone, bath or shower, WC and TV – Wheelchair access. **Price** Double 600-1450F / 91,47-221,05€; suite 1250-1600F. **Meals** Breakfast 85F / 12,9€, served 7:30-10:30; half board 750-1200F / 114,34-182,94€ (per pers.). **Restaurant** Service 12:30PM-2:00PM, 7:30PM-9:00PM; mealtime specials 150F / 22,87€ (lunch in summer), 240-550F / 36,59-83,85€; also à la carte. Specialties: Raviolis d'anguille au vert; pomme de ris de veau aux noisettes; soupe de fraises au basilic et sorbet à l'orange. **Credit cards** Amex, Visa. **Pets** Dogs allowed (+60F / 9,14€). **Facilities** Swimming pool, tennis, evening concerts, wine tasting. **Nearby** in Saumur: Church of Notre-Dame de Nantilly, Château of Saumur (horse museum); Château of Montgeoffroy, Abbey of Fontevrault, Montreuil-Bellay (château), Mushroom Museum in Saint-Hilaire-Saint-Flouent, Château of Brissac. **Closed** Jan 9 – Mar 4.

Clinging to a cliffside far above the Loire, this Renaissance priory affords an absolutely splendid view. The bedrooms on the manor house side, the huge salon, the dining room, and the terraces all enjoy a sweeping view of this panorama, and that is only one of the hotel's strong points. We also loved the classic, cheerful decoration, the antique and period furniture, the way the hotel is kept, and the professional, efficient service. The tasteful bedrooms all offer modern amenities, their price varying with their size and their view. Somewhat farther away, ensconced in greenery (the park spreads over 62 acres), fifteen bedrooms are located in outbuildings constructed some twenty years ago. They are simpler but less expensive and each has a private terrace. It all adds up to a beautiful, luxurious place--with professional service to match.

*How to get there* (Map 15): 7km from Saumur, via A85, Saumur exit.

# Hôtel Anne d'Anjou

49400 Saumur (Maine-et-Loire)
32, quai Mayaud
Tel. (0)2.41.67.30.30 - Fax - 02.41.67.51.00
M. and Mme Camus

**Category ★★★ Rooms** 50 with telephone, bath or shower, WC and TV – 1 for disabled persons. **Price** Double 450F / 68,60€, suite 690F / 105,19€. **Meals** Breakfast 48F / 7,32€, served 7:00-10:00; half board 425-475F / 64,79-72,41€. **Restaurant** *Les Ménestrels*. Closed Sunday and Monday noon in low season. Service 12:15PM-1:30PM, 7:30PM-9:30PM, also à la carte. **Credit cards** All major. **Pets** Dogs not allowed. **Facilities** Parking. **Nearby** Notre-Dame Church of Nantilly, Horse Museum in Saumur, Château of Montsoreau, Abbey of Fontevraud, Montreuil-Bellay (château), Mushroom Museum in Saint-Hilaire-Saint-Florent. **Closed** Dec 23 – Jan 3.

The Anne d'Anjou is a beautiful 18th-century mansion which is ideally located between the Loire and the imposing medieval Château of Saumur. A magnificent Louis XVI stairway surmounted by a stunning trompe l'oeil ceiling leads to the bedrooms. Those on the *premier étage* still have much of their original charm, particularly the room with Empire bas-reliefs covered with gold leaf. The rooms are beautifully decorated with elegant fabrics and newly-renovated bathrooms. The price of the rooms varies according to their size and the floor they are on. (We are less enthusiastic about those on the *troisième étage*). Some rooms have a view on the garden and the château rising in the immediate background; others look out over the immense span of the Loire (guests here are somewhat disturbed by the noise of the road). With the first warm days of spring, tables are set out in the beautiful garden for breakfast. The restaurant is excellent and the overall atmosphere is pleasant for this urban hotel, which has just changed hands but has not changed in spirit.

***How to get there*** *(Map 15): 66km west of Tours. On A85 Saumur exit.*

## Haras de la Potardière

La Potardière
72200 Crosmières (Sarthe)
Tel. (0)2.43.45.83.47 - Fax (0)2.43.45.81.06 - M. and Mme Benoist
Web: haras-de-la-potardiere@wanadoo.fr

**Rooms** 17 (7 in château, 10 in the stables) with telephone, 16 with bath, 1 with shower, WC, TV, 16 with minibar – Wheelchair access. **Price** Simple and double 450-650F / 68,60-99,09€. **Meals** Breakfast 50F / 7,62€. No restaurant (room service in winter). **Credit cards** Visa, Eurocard and MasterCard. **Pets** Dogs allowed. **Facilities** Heated swimming pool (May – Sep), billiard, 3-hole golf course, tennis, riding by reservation. **Nearby** Château of Lude; Solesmes Abbey – 27-hole Sablé-Solesmes golf course. **Open** All year.

Located on a superb, rolling, green and forested landscape, this former equestrian ranch contains a 19th-century château, stables, and a chapel. In the château, the oak parquetry and panelling of the ground floor frames the large lounge, breakfast room, and a little library. The noble, spacious, and nicely-furnished upper floor rooms all have a southern exposure. The rooms above have high, sloped ceilings and have kept a lot of their charm. However, the stables, despite a great billiard room, are a bit impersonal, which doesn't diminish the rooms' comfort but makes them less attractive. Nearby is a pleasant pool, sheltered from the wind and particularly welcome in the summer. This is a beautiful, inviting, and extremely quiet place. There is no restaurant, but *La Petite Auberge* in Malicorne is not far; in La Fleche, our favorite restaurants are *Le Vert Galant*, *La Fesse d'Ange*, and *Le Moulin des 4 Saisons*.

***How to get there*** *(Map 15): 10 km northwest of La Flèche. Via A 11, take the La Flèche/Sablé, Crosmières, then head toward Bazouges until you reach La Potardière.*

## Relais Cicéro

72200 La Flèche (Sarthe)
18, boulevard d'Alger
Tel. (0)2.43.94.14.14 - Fax (0)2.43.45.98.96
Mme Chérel

**Category** ★★★ **Rooms** 21 with telephone, bath or shower, WC and TV. **Price** Double 525-675F / 80,04-102,90€. **Meals** Breakfast 50F / 7,62€, served from 7:00. No restaurant. **Credit cards** Amex, Visa, Eurocard and MasterCard. **Pets** Small dogs allowed. **Nearby** Chapel of Notre Dame-des-Vertus, Tertre Rouge zoological park, Château of Lude, Solesmes Abbey. **Open** Jan 7 – Dec 19.

Taken over by Madame Cherel three years ago now, this hotel in the center of La Flèche is set up in a pretty 16th- and 18th-century house, with its manicured little garden, which is so calm in summer. Tastefully furbished by the previous owner with refinement and comfort in mind, the main house's rooms are the most pleasant. You'll enjoy the ground floor's very-British-style bar, its lounge with piano and fireplace, and its charming dining room where breakfast is served if the weather is unfriendly. The upstairs rooms are decorated with the same care. Our favorites are Rooms 11, 16, 19, and 20 (really big, with a garden-view balcony). The books provided for you in your room bear witness to the homey atmosphere here. The annex rooms, of course, are just as comfortable and well-tended, even if a bit less personal. Two suites in another building are darker and more rustic, but are practical for families. No hotel in the restaurant, but *La Fesse d'Ange*, *Le Vert Galant*, and *Le Moulin des 4 Saisons* are nearby.

***How to get there*** *(Map 15): Via A 11, take Durtal exit, then N23 until La Flèche.*

## Auberge du Port-des-Roches

72800 Luché-Pringé (Sarthe)
Tel. (0)2.43.45.44.48 - Fax (0)2.43.45.39.61
M. and Mme Lesiourd

**Category** ★★ **Rooms** 12 with telephone, bath or shower, WC and 4 with TV. **Price** Double 240-310F / 36,59-47,26€. **Meals** Breakfast 35F / 5,34€, served 8:00-9:30; half board 260-290F / 39,64-44,21€ (per pers., 3 days min.). **Restaurant** Service 12:00PM-1:30PM, 7:30PM-8:30PM; mealtime specials 115-195F / 17,53-29,73€, also à la carte. Specialties: Blanquette de sandre aux noix et jasnières; ris de veau braisé aux oreilles de cochon; crème caramélisée au cidre en coque de pomme. **Credit cards** Visa, Eurocard and MasterCard. **Pets** Dogs allowed on request. **Facilities** Bicycle rental, boating, parking. **Nearby** Châteaux of Montmirail, Courtanvaux and Saint-Calais, Château of Lude, and of Bazouges – 18-hole Le Mans golf course in Mulsanne. **Closed** Feb and Sunday evening, Monday.

Recently taken over by a young couple, this small inn is reflected in the calm waters of the Loire, which is just across a small road. The inn is in the process of extensive interior renovation, which Thierry and Valérie Lesiourd spend their winters doing. The small bedrooms are attractive and tastefully decorated in cool, cheerful colors. Six rooms overlook the river, the others occupying a side wing. The lounge and dining room are decorated in a rustic, pleasing style, and have recently been updated for today's taste. You will find a very attractive terrace full of flowers, set up right on the river bank. Real progress is being made at this delightful inn, its prices are reasonable, and the region is full of attractions.

***How to get there*** *(Map 16): 40km southwest of Le Mans heading toward of La Flèche, then D13 to Luché-Pringé and D214 to "Le Port-des-Roches".*

## Le Relais des Etangs de Guibert

72600 Neufchâtel-en-Saosnois (Sarthe)
Tel. (0)2.43.97.15.38 - Fax (0)2.43.33.22.99
M. and Mme Gaultier
E-mail: gillesgaultier@wanadoo.fr

**Rooms** 15 with bath, WC, TV – Wheelchair access. **Price** Double 270-320F / 41,16-48,78€; triple 380F / 57,93€. **Meals** Breakfast 35F / 5,34€, served 7:30-11:00; half board 280F / 42,69€. **Restaurant** Service 12:00PM-2:00PM, 7:30PM-10:00PM; mealtime specials 85-190F / 12,96-28,97€, also à la carte. Specialties: Fish. **Credit card** Visa. **Pets** Dogs not allowed. **Facilities** Fishing. **Nearby** Perseigne Forest, Alps hills – golf courses at Arconnay and Bellème **Open** All year.

A little road winds through rolling hills and a few hamlets surrounded by vegetable gardens and green yards, and then down toward a forest which is reflected in the great pond that this inn looks over. The location itself deserves a stop, and out of the 15 rooms here, 9 are highly recommendable (but avoid 1, 8, 9, 10, 12, and 15). Often decorated in lacquered rattan furniture and cheerful colors, the rooms are rather simple, but all the same pleasant and always outfitted with comfortable bathrooms. On the ground floor, the roomy dining room with its exposed framework has a lordly fireplace, a dais graced with a piano, and bay windows that open out on the terrace which looks out on the pond, and where tables are set up in sunny weather. The decor is fetching and warm. Unfortunately, we haven't tasted the food, so we can say nothing about it. The overall effect is one of total peace and quiet, and *Le Relais* will make both nature lovers and fly-fishers happy. (The pond is to be restocked, and fishing gear supplied.)

***How to get there*** *(Map 8): Via D 311 between Mamers and Alençon. Take a right at Neufchâtel, coming from Mamers, when you get to the Renault station. Follow the signs.*

# Château de Saint-Paterne

72610 Saint-Paterne (Sarthe)
Tel. (0)2.33.27.54.71 - Fax (0)2.33.29.16.71
M. and Mme de Valbray
E-mail: paterne@club-internet.fr

**Rooms** 9 with telephone, bath and WC. **Price** Double 450-650F / 68,60-99,09€, suite 850F / 129,58€. **Meals** Breakfast 50F / 7,62€, served 7:30-12:00PM. **Evening meals** Service 8:00PM; mealtime specials 230F / 35,06€ (all incl.). **Credit cards** Amex, Visa, Eurocard and MasterCard. **Pets** Dogs allowed by reservation. **Facilities** Tennis, swimming pool, parking. **Nearby** Châteaux of Montmirail, Courtanvaux and Saint-Calais; Carrouges, Bazouges, Ludes; Pin horse farm; Alençon; Perche – 18-hole Mans golf course in Luisanne. **Closed** Jan 15 – Mar 15, by reservation in low season.

Alençon is on the doorstep of the village of Saint Paterne, but this château remains sheltered in its vast walled-in park. Its young owners will give you a hearty welcome, and the high quality of the place owes a lot to their good humor. On the ground floor, there is a superb salon with extremely elegant antique furniture, a beautiful dining room and a bedroom. There are other bedrooms upstairs, each with its own special style, including the Henri IV with its superb French polychrome ceilings. Enhanced by lovely pieces of family furniture, all the rooms are beautifully appointed and have faultless baths. For dinner, the hotel has opened a charming small *auberge* in one wing; decorated in Mediterranean colors, it serves cuisine that's spiced with sunshine and made with excellent fresh products, including the vegetables grown in the château's extraordinary garden. This is a superb place to stay with the charm of a private home and the amenities of a luxurious hotel.

***How to get there*** *(Map 8): 3km east of Alençon, towards Chartres-Mamers.*

## Hôtel du Martinet

85230 Bouin (Vendée)
1 bis, place de la Croix-Blanche
Tel. (0)2.51.49.08.94 - Fax (0)2.51.49.83.08
Mme Huchet

**Category** ★★ **Rooms** 21 with telephone, bath or shower, WC and TV. **Price** Double 280-360F / 42,69-54,88€. **Meals** Breakfast 37F / 5,84€; half board 280-320F / 42,69-48,78€ (per pers.). **Restaurant** Closed Oct – Mar. Service 12:30PM-1:30PM, 7:30PM-9:30PM, mealtime specials 110-160F / 16,77-24,39€ (60F / 9,15€ child), also à la carte. Specialties: Fish and shellfish. **Credit cards** All major. **Pets** Dogs allowed (+20F / 3,05€). **Facilities** Bicycles, swimming pool, parking. **Nearby** Church of St-Philbert-de-Grand-Lieu, Machecoul, oyster beds, Ile d'Yeu – 18-hole golf courses in Saint-Jean-de-Monts and in Pornic. **Open** All year.

Y ou will be enchanted by this late 18th-century residence where the smell of wax mingles with that of fresh-cut flowers. The furniture in the bedrooms on the ground floor and *premier étage* is plain but very comfortable. There are two other bedrooms under the eaves which are ideal for families of four. In a small wing of the hotel, five beautiful bedrooms have just been added. They are cheerful and very pretty, their bathrooms are immaculate and all are at ground level, opening onto a large flower garden and the swimming pool. Beyond the swimming pool in the distance, you will have a beautiful view over the countryside and the Vendée marshes. In the restaurant, the owner's oyster-farmer husband will be delighted to serve you oysters from his beds and other seafood. The *Hôtel du Martinet* is a delightful place to stay, perfect for visiting the Vendée marshes. Madame Huchet is an extremely kind manager, and the prices are truly reasonable.

***How to get there*** *(Map 14): 51km southwest of Nantes via D751 and D758 heading towards Noirmoutier.*

## Hôtel de l'Antiquité

85300 Challans (Vendée)
14, rue Galiéni
Tel. (0)2.51.68.02.84 - Fax (0)2.51.35.55.74
M. and Mme Belleville

**Category** ★★ **Rooms** 16 with telephone, bath, WC, TV – Wheelchair access. **Price** Doubles 260-400F / 39,64-60,98€. **Meals** Breakfast 35F / 5,34€, served 7:30-10:00. No restaurant. **Credit cards** All major. **Pets** Dogs not allowed. **Facilities** Swimming pool, parking. **Nearby** Château and market in Clisson; Church of Saint-Philbert-de-Grand-Lieu; Machecoul; Puy-du-Fou; beach (15km away). **Open** Jan 3 – Dec 22. Closed Sunday from Christmas – Easter.

Seen from the road, this hotel is no letdown, and it just gets better and better once you get inside. You'll discover the dining room with its venerable cupboard and amusing little tables in exotic wood, and then the winter-garden lounge with its rattan furniture from which you catch a glimpse of the flowery patio with the swimming pool behind. The hotel got its name from the former career of the present owners who set up the hotel twenty years ago and have left the mark of antique furniture everywhere. Despite this charming touch and the spirit behind it, most of the rooms are a bit outmoded. For the moment, we can only recommend those that have just been set up on the other side of the pool. Comfortable, well-furnished, and tastefully decorated, these rooms have luxurious bathrooms and are of a good quality for their price. A nice place, just a few minutes from the Ile de Noirmoutier. No restaurant here, but *Le Gîte de Tourne Pierre* in Challan is perfect for dinner, if you don't wish to drive to Saint-Gilles and dine at the excellent *Château de la Verie*.

***How to get there*** *( Map 14): 60 km south of Nantes, go to Saint-Philbert on D 65, then Machecoul via D 117, then D 32 until you reach Challans.*

## Château de la Vérie

85300 Challans (Vendée)
Route de Saint-Gilles-Croix-de-Vie
Tel. (0)2.51.35.33.44 - Fax (0)2.51.35.14.84
M. Martin

**Category** ★★★ **Rooms** 23 with telephone, bath, WC, TV, safe and minibar. **Price** Single and double 300-880F / 45,73-134,16€. **Meals** Breakfast 60F / 9,15€, served 8:00-10:30. **Restaurant** Service 12:00PM-2:00PM, 7:30PM-9:30PM; mealtime specials 100-320F / 15,24-48,78€, also à la carte. Specialties: Emietté de confit de lapin tiède, pommes macaires; canard de Challans au sang; brioche vendéenne aux framboises. **Credit cards** All major. **Pets** Dogs allowed (+50F / 7,62€). **Facilities** Swimming pool, tennis, parking. **Nearby** Le Puy du Fou, Château of Apremont, church of Sallertaine, château and market in Clisson, Church of Saint-Philbert-de-Grand-Lieu, Machecoul, Saint-Gilles-Croix-de-Vie, Fromentine (boats for Ile d'Yeu), Les Sables d'Olonne, beach (15km away). **Open** All year.

Converted into a hotel, the *Château de la Vérie* offers beautiful, comfortable bedrooms. Japanese wickerwork, vivid colors, charming little engravings and antique furniture – nothing is lacking: even the mirrors in the bathrooms have china frames. The dining room and lounge have been decorated in the same spirit; they are welcoming rooms, feel very much like a private house, and look out onto a large terrace where breakfast is served and you can look out over the verdant park. Not far away is the swimming pool, a welcome attraction in the second-sunniest *département* of France. Delicious, nourishing meals are pleasantly served, but with a touch of amateurism. This is a beautiful place to stay, just ten minutes from the beaches.

***How to get there*** *(Map 14): 60km south of Nantes via D65 to Saint-Philibert, then D117 to Machecoul, then D32 to Challans; it's 2.5km from the town hall (mairie) heading towards Saint-Gilles-Croix-de-Vie on D69.*

## Hôtel L'Escale

85350 Ile-d'Yeu (Vendée)
Port-Joinville
Tel. (0)2.51.58.50.28 - Fax (0)2.51.59.33.55
M. and Mme Taraud

**Category** ★★ **Rooms** 26 and 2 suites (15 with air-conditioning) with telephone, bath or shower and WC. **Price** Single and double 190-330F / 28,97-50,31€, suite 450F / 68,60€. **Meals** Breakfast 35F / 5,34€. No restaurant. **Credit cards** Visa, Eurocard and MasterCard. **Pets** Dogs allowed (+30F / 4,57€). **Facilities** Parking. **Nearby** Beach of Ker-Chalon, large lighthouse, Church of Saint-Sauveur, ruins of the old château. **Closed** Jan 3 – 14.

Five minutes from the port, this venerable hotel has just expanded into a new house with 15 rooms and is now the islands most beautiful place to stay, even if there is no seaside view. Comfortable and perfectly kept, the recent part is the only one we can recommend as the old part is of no particular interest. The new lobby has an elegant seaside atmosphere with its film-director armchairs, matching teak tables, and a corner fireplace. The beautifully decorated bedrooms combine sober, modern brown-red furniture with thick bedspreads in eggshell Mayenne cloth, and lovely curtains with broad stripes or colorful motifs matching the headboards; the small bathrooms are very pleasant. The *Escale* is as hospitable as they come and an ideal stopover, for walking or biking around the Island of Yeu. For lunch or dinner, we suggest the *Flux Hôtel*, very nearby, with its panoramic dining room overlooking the sea; and the restaurant on the port at La Meule.

***How to get there*** *(Map 14): Steamer connections with Port-Joinville (tel. 02.51.58.36.66) and Fromentine (tel. 02.51.68.52.32); on the harbour towards Saint-Sauveur.*

## Fleur de Sel

85330 Noirmoutier-en-L'Ile (Vendée)
Tel. (0)2.51.39.21.59 - Fax (0)2.51.39.75.66
M. and Mme Wattecamps
E-mail: F1eurdese1@france-mail.com

**Category ★★★ Rooms** 35 with telephone, bath, WC, TV, 22 with minibar – Wheelchair access. **Price** Double 400-720F / 60,98-109,76€. **Meals** Breakfast 55F / 8,38€, served 8:00-9:30 in lounge, 10:30 in room; half board 395-595F / 60,22-90,71€ (per pers., 2 days min.). **Restaurant** Service 12:00PM-1:30PM, 7:00PM-9:30PM; mealtime specials 138-225F / 21,34-34,30€, also à la carte. Specialties: Seafood, shellfish and fish, lobster. **Credit cards** Amex, Visa. **Pets** Dogs allowed (+40F / 6,10€). **Facilities** Swimming pool, tennis (30-50F / 4,57-7,62€ in high season), sauna (60F / 9,15€), tanning booth (50F / 7,62€) putting range, mountain bikes. **Nearby** Château and museum of Noirmoutier, passage du Gois and the woods of la Chaize, salt marshes, oyster beds – 18-hole Golf Course in Saint-Jean-de-Monts, 18-hole golf course in Pornic. **Open** Mid Feb – Nov 1.

A bit away from the village, the *Fleur de Sel* is a, rambling white house built around a superb swimming pool and carefully-tended garden. The rooms are bright and very pleasant. (The ground-floor rooms have their own private terraces.) Most have been renovated, either cozily in English pine and mahogany, or in a seaside, "ship deck" style with colored rattan armchairs and matching fabrics. The bathrooms, in white faience and blue and yellow sponge-painted walls, are impeccable. Inventive food, served in two huge dining rooms with French windows that allow food to be served outside. Next door, their are two inviting little lounges, where you could have a drink and linger around the fire, which is nice in the winter months. A beautiful and welcoming place, very well run by Monsieur and Madame Wattecamps.

***How to get there*** *(Map 14): 82 km southwest of Nantes. La Fromentine overpass. The hotel is 500 m behind the church.*

## Hôtel Les Prateaux

85330 Noirmoutier-en-l'Ile (Vendée)
Bois de la Chaize
Tel. (0)2.51.39.12.52 - Fax (0)2.51.39.46.28
M. Blouard

**Category** ★★★ **Rooms** 22 with telephone, bath or shower, WC and TV. **Price** Single and double 380-870F / 57,93-132,63€. **Meals** Breakfast 55-65F / 8,38-9,91€; half board and full board 402-775F / 61,08-118,15€ (per pers.). **Restaurant** Service 12:30PM-1:30PM, 7:30PM-8:30PM; also à la carte. Specialties: Fish and shellfish. **Credit cards** All major. **Pets** Dogs not allowed. **Facilities** Parking. **Nearby** Church of Saint-Philbert-de-Grand-Lieu, Machecoul, oyster beds, Ile d'Yeu – 18-hole golf courses in Saint-Jean-de-Monts and Pornic. **Open** Feb 13 – Nov 11.

*L*es Prateaux has been entirely renovated and nothing has been spared to make the new and old bedrooms beautifully comfortable. The newest rooms are larger, and one even has a private 144-square-foot terrace overloking the park. The other rooms have balconies. The principal building is composed of the dining rooms (which open onto a vast terrace) the lounge and some of the bedrooms. The other rooms are located nearby in the garden. The hotel is very attractively located; built in 1939 on the end of the Ile du Noirmoutier in the middle of the forest of La Chaize, it is very quiet. The sea is only about 300 meters away and a walk through the woods will bring you to a pretty beach. The atmosphere is very summery and the a scent of the pines and mimosas is reminiscent of the Côte d'Azur.

***How to get there*** *(Map 14): 82km southwest of Nantes by D751 and D758. Access by road bridge from Fromentine, 1.5km from Noirmoutier to Bois de la Chaize, then follow signs.*

## Logis de La Couperie

85000 La Roche-sur-Yon (Vendée)
Tel. (0)2.51.37.21.19 - Fax (0)2.51.47.71.08
Mme Oliveau

**Category** ★★★ **Rooms** 6 and 1 suite with telephone, bath or shower, WC and TV. **Price** Single and, double 275-520F / 41,92-79,27€. **Meals** Breakfast 45F / 6,86€, served 7:30-10:00. No restaurant. **Credit cards** Amex, Visa, Eurocard and MasterCard. **Pets** Dogs not allowed. **Facilities** Lake, bike, calash, small gym, parking. **Nearby** History museum and Château of Chabotterie, Saint-Sulpice-le-Verdon, Tiffauges, Vendée military school. **Open** All year.

The *Logis de la Couperie* is a former manor house which was rebuilt at the end of the 18th-century. It is located in open countryside, five minutes from the center of town, and surrounded by a 5-acre park with a small lake. Nature lovers will find peace here. In the large entrance hall there is a magnificent staircase which leads to the upper floors. The bedrooms are all comfortable and tastefully furnished with antiques and regional furniture. There is a well-stocked lounge/library, where a cheerful log fire burns in winter. The excellent breakfast, made only from organic foods, is served in the dining room or your room. You will enjoy, among other delights, the house's apple juice and brioche. *Le Pavillon Gourmand*, *Le Saint Charles*, and *Le Hunier* are among the very good restaurants in La Roche-sur-Yon.

*How to get there (Map 14): On D80 towards Château-Fromage, five minutes from the town center, via the Route Nationale from Cholet or Route Nationale from Niort.*

## Hôtel La Barbacane

85130 Tiffauges (Vendée)
2, place de l'Eglise
Tel. (0)2.51.65.75.59 - Fax (0)2.51.65.71.91
Mme Bidan

**Category** ★★ **Rooms** 16 with telephone, bath or shower, WC and TV. **Price** Double 310-479F / 47,26-73,18€. **Meals** Breakfast 33-46F / 5,03-7,02€. No restaurant. **Credit cards** All major. **Pets** Dogs allowed. **Facilities** Heated swimming pool, billiards, garage. **Nearby** Ruins of Château of Gilles de Retz ("Blue Beard"), spectacle of Puy-du-Fou, Vendée military school – 18-hole golf course in Cholet. **Open** All year.

This charming little hotel is in a village whose name made the entire surrounding region tremble in the 15th-century. The fortress of Gilles de Retz, alias Blue Beard, is located here. You will go past its imposing ruins to get to *La Barbacane*, where you'll find the friendly welcome of Mme Bidan. The hotel is also her home, which is why each room has travel souvenirs and family furniture. On the ground floor there is a billiards room and a dining room where you can have generous breakfasts. The bedrooms are on several floors and in a ground-floor wing which opens onto the main garden; they are charming, often with exotic wicker furniture and pretty bathrooms (terra-cotta and blond wood), and are reasonably priced. Behind the hotel, there is another garden, with a beautiful terrace around a swimming pool. For dinner, the village restaurant, *L'Auberge du Donjon*, is right next door. If you don't mind going a little further, visit the château at Clisson and the market before having dinner at *La Bonne Auberge*.

***How to get there*** *( Map 15 ): 20km west of Cholet via D753 towards Montaigu.*

## Auberge de la Rivière

85770 Velluire (Vendée)
Tel. (0)2.51.52.32.15 - Fax (0)2.51.52.37.42
M. and Mme Pajot

**Category** ★★ **Rooms** 11 with telephone, bath and WC (6 with TV). **Price** Single and double 400-490F / 60,98-74,70€. **Meals** Breakfast 60F / 9,15€, served 8:00-10:30; half board and full board 445-580F / 67,84-88,42€ (per pers., 3 days min.). **Restaurant** Closed Sunday evening and Monday in low season. Service 12:15PM-2:00PM, 8:00PM-9:30PM; mealtime specials 120-240F / 18,29-36,59€, also à la carte. Specialties: Feuilleté de langoustines; bar aux artichauts; pigeonneau sauce morilles. **Credit card** Visa. **Pets** Dogs allowed (+30F / 4,57€). **Nearby** Church of Notre-Dame and Museum of the Vendée in Fontenay-le-Comte, Poitou marshes – 9-hole golf course in Niort. **Closed** Jan 10 – Feb 20 and Monday in low season.

This hotel is in the little village of Velluire on the banks of the Vendée and is only a few kilometers from Fontenay-le-Comte. The calm of the locale is only sometimes broken broken by the splashing of a carp's tail, the whistle of a blackbird, or sometimes the far-off passing of a train. Spread out between the main building and the neighboring house, the rooms are pleasant, very comfortable, and completely renovated. All but one look out on the river, along which runs a foot path for your long, pastoral strolls. In the large, beautiful dining room, Mme Pajot serves excellent seafood and regional specialities. This is a pleasant and unpretentious place to stay, far from the tourist hordes. You will be warmly welcomed before heading off to discover the area marshlands and the Ile de Ré.

***How to get there*** *(Map 15): 45km northwest of Niort via N148 towards Fontenay-le-Comte, then D938 on 10km and D68 to Velluire.*

## Hostellerie du Maine Brun

16290 Hiersac (Charente)
Asnières-sur-Nouère
Tel. (0)5.45.90.83.00 - Fax (0)5.45.96.91.14
Mme Ménager

**Category** ★★★ **Rooms** 18 and 2 apartments with telephone, bath or shower, WC and TV. **Price** Double 590-750F / 89,94-114,34€; apart. 950-1300F / 144,83-198,18€. **Meals** Breakfast 65F / 9,90€; half board 485-560F / 73,94-85,37€ (per pers., 3 days min.). **Restaurant** Closed Monday. Service 12:00-2:00PM, 7:30PM-9:00PM, mealtime specials 98-198F / 14,96-30,22€, also à la carte **Credit card** All major. **Pets** Dogs allowed (+50F / 7,63€). **Facilities** Swimming pool, mountain bike, parking. **Nearby** Angoulême; Braconne; La Rochefoucauld; Romanesque churches of Angoumois (Cellefrouin, Lichères, Diran, Dignac, Villebois-Lavalette, Mouthiers-sur-Boëme, Saint-Michel, Saint-Amand-de-Boixe). **Open** Apr 15 – Oct 15.

The Nouère feeds the stream of this former mill located near Angoulême, in a green and quiet locale. With its white stone walls and almost flat roofs covered in tile, typical of the local architecture, the *Hostellerie* makes use of its outside terraces which are covered with tables and umbrellas in nice weather. Behind the cool, old walls, the two huge dining rooms and the lounge are furbished in a rustic, mongrelized Haute Epoque style which is a bit quaint but charming nonetheless. Upstairs, a few rooms are particularly well-decorated with a rich variety of antique or 18th- and 19th-century style furniture. The others are run-of-the-mill, but also very comfortable. Good meals served in an attentive and friendly way. Warm hospitality.

*How to get there (Map 22): 17 km east of Angoulême via D 699.*

## Les Pigeons Blancs

16100 Cognac (Charente)
110, rue Jules-Brisson
Tel. (0)5.45.82.16.36 - Fax (0)5.45.82.29.29
Famille Tachet

**Rooms** 7 with telephone, bath or shower, WC and TV. **Price** Double 360-550F / 54,88-83,85€. **Meals** Breakfast 50F / 7,62€, served 8:00-10:00. **Restaurant** Service 12:00PM-2:00PM, 7:30PM-9:00PM; mealtime specials 138-250F / 21,34-38,11€, also à la carte. Specialties: Filet de rouget poêlé au foie gras; pièce de bœuf des tonnellies charentais. **Credit cards** All major. **Pets** Dogs not allowed. **Nearby** In Cognac: museum of Cognac, Chais of Cognac, Detective Film Festival; Romanesque churches of Cherves and Saint-Hérie in Matha, Le Marestay, Châtres, Châteaux of Saint-Sauvan, Richemont and Garde-Epée; horsedrawn carriage tours from Martha, road along the banks of the Charente of Jarnac in Angoulême, cruises on the Charente from Jun to Sep. **Open** All year.

In the same family since the 18th century, *Les Pigeons Blancs* is a former postal relay station which is set in a quiet private park. The hotel is renowned for its restaurant, which is considered one of the finest in the region and is where merchants from the famous cognac houses often come for business lunches. But the *Pigeons Blancs* can also be proud of its lovely, comfortable bedrooms. They are decorated with elegant antique furniture, pretty coordinated fabrics and wallpaper. And they are kept immaculate, as are the bathrooms. There is a small, comfortable lounge with deep sofas, books and games which provide pleasant relaxation as you enjoy one of the region's famous brandies. Next to the lounge are two warmly decorated dining rooms with handsome family furniture.

***How to get there*** *(Map 22): 40km west of Angoulême via N141; road to Saint-Jean-d'Angély, Matha.*

# Hostellerie Château Sainte-Catherine

16220 Montbron (Charente)
Route de Marthon
Tel. (0)5.45.23.60.03 - Fax (0)5.45.70.72.00
Mme Crocquet

**Category** ★★★ **Rooms** 10 and 4 suites with telephone, bath or shower, WC and TV. **Price** Double 350-550F / 53,36-83,85€, suite (2 rooms, 2 bath) 600-800F / 91,47-121,96€. **Meals** Breakfast 49F / 7,62€, served 8:00-10:30; half board 350-450F / 53,36-68,60€ (per pers., 3 days min.). **Restaurant** Closed in Feb. Service 12:00PM-2:00PM, 7:30PM-9:00PM; mealtime specials-menu 120F / 18,29€ (lunchtime)-250F / 38,11€. Specialties: Foies gras; confits; magret; mousses; tarte tatin. **Credit cards** All major. **Pets** Dogs allowed. **Facilities** Swimming pool, mountain bikes and parking. **Nearby** Angoulême, forest of Braconne, La Rochefoucauld, source of the Tiouvre, caves and Château of Rancogne, Romanesque church of Angoumois (Cellefrouin, Lichères, Diran, Dignac, Villebois-Lavalette, Mouthiers-sur-Boëme, Saint-Michel, Saint-Amand-de-Boixe). **Closed** Feb.

Lying in the midst of a beautifully tended 20-acre park far from the beaten path, this handsome manor house was built for Joséphine de Beauharnais by Napoléon. Ten bedrooms and four suites (twelve give onto the park) have been discreetly arranged in light colors, offering recently renovated baths with all modern amenities. The two dining rooms, which have conserved their original character and charm, also overlook the park. The room in which breakfast is served is brightened with painted wood panels depicting country scenes, while the woodwork in the other dining room lends it the warm atmosphere of the past. The surrounding park is a haven of tranquillity in summer: a place you want to linger in. The cuisine, based on specialties of the neighboring Périgord, is excellent.

***How to get there*** *(Map 22): 17km east of Angoulême via D699.*

## Château de Nieuil

16270 Nieuil (Charente)
Tel. (0)5.45.71.36.38 - Fax (0)5.45.71.46.45
M. and Mme Bodinaud
E-mail: nieuil@relaischateaux.fr

**Category** ★ **Rooms** 11 with air-conditioning, telephone, bath, WC, TV and minibar. **Price** Double 750-1600F / 114,34-243,92€, suite 1600-2400F / 243,92-365,88€. **Meals** Breakfast 80F / 53,36€, served 8:00-11:00; half board and full board 790-1300F / 120,43-198,18€ (per pers., 3 days min.). **Restaurant** Closed Sunday evening and Monday except for reseidents and Jul – Aug. Service 12:00PM-2:00PM, 8:00PM-9:30PM; mealtime specials 200F / 30,49€ (lunch), 260-350F / 39,64-53,36€, also à la carte. Specialties: Fish and meat with fresh vegetables. **Credit cards** All major. **Pets** Dogs allowed. **Facilities** Swimming pool, tennis, art galery, parking. **Nearby** Forest of Braconn, Romanesque churches. **Open** Apr 20 – Nov 2.

In the 14th century, the *Château de Nieul* was a fortress; and in the 16th century, towers were added. In 1937, the present owner's grandparents transformed it into a hotel. The château today is a romantic ensemble lying behind the volutes of garden surrounded by moats and an immense park with a lake. Haute Epoque interior decoration is predominant in the reception rooms. Each bedroom has its special style, with superb decoration. Throughout, the antique furniture and paintings are of fine quality. More important still is M. Bodineau and his staff's hospitality, far from that stuffy "château" atmosphere. Luce Bodineau's excellent cuisine and the many sports and leisure activities available (you can even rent equipment) make the *Château de Nieul* a great place. Note that in winter the country restaurant of the château, the *Grange aux Oies*, offers a more rustic but equally savory version of the château's cuisine (190F).

***How to get there*** (*Map 23*): *40km northwest of Angoulême via N141 toward Chasseneuil, Fontafie and Nieul on D739.*

## Hôtel Le Chat Botté

Ile de Ré
17590 Saint-Clément-des-Baleines (Charente-Maritime)
Tel. (0)5.46.29.21.93 - Fax (0)5.46.29.29.97
Mmes Massé-Chantreau

**Category** ★★ **Rooms** 19 with telephone, bath or shower and WC – Wheelchair access. **Price** Single 330F / 50,31€, double 390-620F / 59,46-94,52€. **Meals** Breakfast 46 and 65F / 6,86 and 9,91€, served 8:15-10:30. No restaurant. **Credit cards** Visa, Eurocard and MasterCard. **Pets** Dogs allowed (+40F / 6,10€). **Facilities** Small health center, tennis, parking. **Nearby** Museum and citadel of Saint-Martin-de-Ré, Baleines Lighthouse – 9-hole Trousse golf course. **Closed** End Nov – mid Dec and Jan 5 – Fev 10.

The *Hôtel Le Chat Botté* ("puss in boots") is an adorable village house with a patio and a large flower garden on the delightful Ile de Ré. Bright wood panelling harmonizes with elegant terra-cotta floors, and the fabrics are perky, fashionable, and recall the sea. Everything is elegantly simple, impeccably kept and decorated, including the bedrooms. We noted that they were quiet, even in the summer vacation season: Saint-Clément is still spared the hordes of tourists who invade the Ile de Ré in July and August. Not only is the *Chat Botté* quiet, it is also relaxing, given the fitness and beauty-care facilities offered. Breakfast is served in a very pretty room overlooking the garden. There is no restaurant in the hotel but the excellent restaurant *Le Chat Botté* is just next door and run by the same family; *L'Auberge de la Rivière* in Les Portes-en-Ré, and in La Flotte, our favorite, *L'Ecailler*, where you will love the best fish of the coastal area accompanied by a stunning selection of wines.

***How to get there*** *(Map 22): 28km west of La Rochelle via the Pallice Bridge.*

## Hôtel de l'Océan

Ile de Ré - 17580 Le Bois-Plage-en-Ré (Charente-Maritime)
172, rue Saint-Martin
Tel. (0)5.46.09.23.07 - Fax (0)5.46.09.05.40 - M. and Mme Bourdet
Web: www.iledere.com

**Category** ★★ **Rooms** 24 with telephone, bath or shower, WC, TV – Wheelchair access. **Price** Single and double 350-500F / 53,36-76,22€. **Meals** Breakfast 50F / 7,62€, served 8:00-10:45; half board 350-580F / 53,36-88,42€ (per pers.). **Restaurant** Service 12:15PM-2:30PM, 7:15PM-10:30PM; mealtime specials 140-180F / 21,34-27,44€, also à la carte. Specialties: Homard au beurre de thym. **Credit cards** Amex, Visa. **Pets** Dogs allowed. **Facilities** Private parking (150m). **Nearby** Museum and citadel of Saint-Martin-de-Ré, Baleines Ligthouse – 9-hole Trousse Chemise golf course. **Open** Feb 6 – Jan 4.

Bois-Plage is a town that so far has not been affected by the fashions that are progressively overtaking the Ile de Ré. Along a small street, the pretty white and green façade of the *Hôtel de l'Océan* is a good indication of the charm you'll find inside. The dining room and fireplace, its colonial-style furniture painted pearl-grey, its white panelled walls hung with beautiful ocean-liner lithographs, is an invitation to tarry over the excellent meals served there. To the right of the entrance, two small lounges in eggshell colors reminded us that the owner used to be an antiques dealer. Across a terrace dining room outside, you'll find a long garden which several bedrooms overlook. Bullrush-covered floors, thick piqué bedspreads, beautiful drapes, natural plaster on the walls and antique furniture here and there are several sound decorative qualities that are sure to please. (If you reserve in time, ask for the bedrooms located above the restaurant: they are the largest and our favorites; avoid the scant rooms that have not yet been renovated.) Good breakfasts with delicious homemade preserves are served with a smile.

*How to get there (Map 22): 28km west of la Rochelle, via La Pallice bridge.*

## Hôtel France Angleterre et Champlain

17000 La Rochelle (Charente-Maritime)
20, rue Rambaud
Tel. (0)5.46.41.23.99 - Fax (0)5.46.41.15.19 - Mme Jouineau
Web: www.bw-fa-champlain.com - E-mail: hotel@bw-fa-champlain.com

**Category** ★★★ **Rooms** 36 with air-conditioning, telephone, bath or shower, WC, cable TV and minibar – Elevator. **Price** Single and double 320-580F / 48,78-88,42€; suite 700F / 106,71€. **Meals** Breakfast 50F / 7,62€, served 7:15-11:30. No restaurant. **Credit cards** All major. **Pets** Dogs allowed (+30F / 4,57€). **Facilities** Garage (35-48F / 5,34-7,62€). **Nearby** New World Museum, Lafaille Museum, Protestant and Fine Arts Museum in La Rochelle, Ile de Ré, Esnandes, church portal and dungeon in Vouvant, Poitou marshes – 18-hole La Prée golf course in La Rochelle. **Open** All year.

This 17th-century former convent hides a beautiful garden behind its walls, which is a good place for breakfast. To get to the garden you cross a large hall and some lovely reception rooms. Period woodwork, antique statues and lovely old furniture create a warm and elegant ambiance. The bedrooms, reached by elevator or by the splendid stone staircase, offer you the choice of a comfortable modern style or the charm and elegance of an earlier era. They are different in decor but all are comfortable, though you will probably prefer those with a view overlooking the garden; the rooms on the street have double glazing, and all will soon be air-conditioned. There is no restaurant, but a half board arrangement is possible. The staff is very pleasant, adding further to the hotel's many attractive features. For dinner, you have an embarrasingly wide choice of options, whether near the port or on the old streets of the town.

***How to get there*** *( Map 22 ): In the center of La Rochelle.*

## Le Moulin de Marcouze

17240 Mosnac-sur-Seugne (Charente-Maritime)
Tel. (0)5.46.70.46.16. - Fax (0)5.46.70.48.14
M and Mme Bouchet

**Category** ★★★ **Rooms** 10 with telephone, bath, WC, minibar, safe, satellite TV. **Price** Single and double 575-780F / 87,66-118,91€; suite 1300F / 198,18€ – 1 for disabled persons. **Meals** Breakfast 80F / 12,20€; half board 760-810F / 115,86-123,48€ (per pers.). **Restaurant** Service 12:30PM-1:00PM, 8:00PM-9:30PM; mealtime specials 160-275F / 16,77-41,92€, also à la carte. Specialties: Gigot d'agneau de sept heures. **Credit cards** Amex, Visa. **Pets** Dogs allowed (+50F / 7,62€). **Facilities** Swimming pool, parking. **Nearby** Romanesque churches of Saintonges – 18-hole Saintes golf course. **Open** Apr – Sep 30.

Dominique Bouchet was chef at Paris's *Tour d'Argent* for 8 years, and now mans the kitchen at the *Ambassadeurs*, the restaurant of the hotel *Crillon*. Yet, his heart has always been in Charente, and that is why you can now find him both in Paris and at the *Moulin de Marcouze*. Well, almost. Because it's his wife who looks after the place and one of his students who works in the kitchen. So there are a few good meals in your future, served in dining room that looks down on the clear waters of the Seugne. Sober though elegant, the eating area and rooms make the most of natural white, tan, and rust tones. Our favorites are those with picture windows that have a view of the river and the little island (each has a terrace). The others look out on shrubbery. With rustic, antique furnishings, terra-cotta floors graced with carpets, and contemporary paintings, these huge rooms are pleasant and have beautiful, grey marble bathrooms. The reception hall is a little chilly, but, from there, you can cast your eyes on the noble vintages (under glass) from the wine cellar.

***How to get there*** *(Map 22): Via A 10, take Pons exit. 11 km on the road to Bordeux (D 134). At Belluire, take your first right toward Mosnac.*

## Hôtel de Bordeaux

17800 Pons (Charente-Maritime)
1, rue Gambetta
Tel. (0)5.46.91.31.12 - Fax (0)5.46.91.22.25 - M. Jaubert - Mlle Muller
Web: www.hotel-de-bordeaux.com

**Category** ★★ **Rooms** 16 with telephone, bath, WC, TV. **Price** Single and double 220-260F / 33,54-39,64€. **Meals** Breakfast 40F / 6,10€, served 7:30-10:30; half board 240F / 36,59€, full board 315F / 48,02€ (per pers., 3 days min.). **Restaurant** Service 12:00PM-2:00PM, 7:30PM-9:30PM; mealtime specials 90-240F / 13,72-36,59€, also à la carte. Specialties: Salade fraîche de crustacés et haricots verts; rognonnade de veau au jus de thym. **Credit cards** Amex, Visa. **Pets** Dogs allowed. **Facilities** Parking. **Nearby** Dungeon of Pons, Château of Usson; Romanesque churches of Saintonges; Aulnay; Château of Damierre; Saintes – 18-hole Saintes golf course. **Closed** Sunday in low season.

From the street, this hotel is like many other establishments in the center of town, but inside, pleasant surprises abound. First, there is a small, quite British bar (reserved for hotel guests except on Saturday morning); an elegant lounge; and finally the patio, which is the very charming prolongation of the two dining rooms. Sheltered from the wind, bordered by shrubs and hollyhocks, it is perfect for dinner and relaxation in the gentle climate of the southern Charente-Maritime. In the kitchen, young M. Jaubert turns out masterful specialties and the prices are right. After having apprenticed with the greatest chefs, he has returned to his native town to open his own business, and his reputation is growing. As for the bedrooms, the conveniences and decoration are very ordinary but not unpleasant. Four look out onto the patio and the others onto a quiet street; all are perfectly maintained. Let us add that the atmosphere is very welcoming, youthful and informal, and you will understand why the *Hôtel de Bordeaux* is the delight of all who stay there.

***How to get there*** *( Map 22): 22km south of Saintes.*

## Résidence de Rohan

17640 Vaux-sur-Mer (Charente-Maritime)
Parc des Fées (près Royan), route de Saint-Palais
Tel. (0)5.46.39.00.75 - Fax (0)5.46.38.29.99
M. and Mme Seguin

**Category** ★★★ **Rooms** 41 with telephone, bath or shower, WC and TV. **Price** Single and double 300-700F / 45,73-106,71€. **Meals** Breakfast 57F / 8,70€, served 7:30AM-1:00PM. No restaurant. **Credit cards** Amex, Visa, Eurocard and MasterCard. **Pets** Dogs allowed. **Facilities** Heated swimming pool, tennis (+50F / 7,62€), parking, hotel golfing. **Nearby** Lighthouse of Cordouan, La Rochelle, Sablonceaux Abbey, Talmont-sur-Gironde, La Palmyre zoo – 18-hole Côte de la Beauté golf course in Royan. **Open** Mar 26 – Nov 10.

The elegant *Résidence de Rohan* stands in the Parc des Fées, a lovely small wood on the edge of the beach at Nauzan. The trees surrounding the house, the lawn ly sloping towards the sea and several chaise-longues scattered among the pines add charm to this pink-and-white 19th-century villa. Inside, the decor is quite different from what you might expect to find in a seaside house; the velvet-covered armchairs in the lounge, the mahogony Charles X-style furniture in the bar, the carpets and rugs create a rather opulent ambiance. All the bedrooms have their own style and beautiful fabrics; many are furnished with antique furniture. Some rooms, notably those in the annex, are very spacious, while others open onto the garden. You can enjoy an excellent breakfast on the terrace overlooking the sparkling ocean. The hosts are friendly and hospitable. A seaside swimming pool with snack bar offer further enjoyment of the water. Good restaurants nearby include *Le Chalet, Les Trois Marmites, Les Filets Bleus* and *La Jabotière*.

***How to get there*** *( Map 22 ): 3km northwest of Royan via D25, which follows the coast towards Saint-Palais-sur-Mer.*

403

## Au Marais

79510 Coulon (Deux-Sèvres)
46-48, quai Louis-Tardy
Tel. (0)5.49.35.90.43 - Fax (0)5.49.35.81.98
Martine Nerrière

**Category ★★★ Rooms** 18 with telephone, bath, WC and TV. **Price** Double 360-600F / 54,88-91,47€. **Meals** Breakfast (buffet) 40F / 6,10€, served 7:30-10:00. No restaurant. **Credit cards** Visa, Eurocard and MasterCard. **Pets** Dogs allowed (+30F / 4,57€). **Nearby** Poitou marshes – 18-hole golf course in Niort. **Closed** Jan.

All the magic of the Poitou marshland is here in front of the hotel: the Sèvre River is directly in front of the hotel and the cruise boats are nearby. The hotel is built in classic Poitou style and has been totally restored without being spoiled. The interior decoration is very carefully done. The rooms sport a beautiful variety of vibrant colors, many terra-cotta floors, and well-chosen fabrics and furnishings. Given their high quality, we highly recommend those which have been renovated in this spirit. They are all remarkably well-kept, and the bathrooms are immaculate. The hotel is quiet despite the numbers of tourists in July and August. This is an excellent small hotel which is ideal for visiting "Green Venice" and where you will find a young, very friendly staff. There is no restaurant in the hotel but the owners will give you good addresses. Our favorites are *Le Central*, on the Place de l'Eglise in Coulon, if you wish to remain in the village; and in Niort, we recommend the delightful *Belle Etoile*.

***How to get there*** *( Map 15): 10km west of Niort via D9 and and D1 (on the edge of the Sèvre).*

## Le Logis Saint-Martin

79400 Saint-Maixent-l'Ecole (Deux-Sèvres)
Chemin de Pissot
Tel. (0)5.49.05.58.68 - Fax (0)5.49.76.19.93
M. and Mme Heintz

**Category** ★★★ **Rooms** 10 and 1 suite with telephone, bath or shower, WC and satellite TV. **Price** Single and double 480-795F / 73,18-121,20€. **Meals** Breakfast 70F / 10,67€, served 8:00-10:00; half board 510-640F / 77,75-97,57€ (per pers., 3 days min.). **Restaurant** Service 12:15PM-2:00PM, 7:30PM-9:30PM; mealtime specials 175F / 26,68€ (lunch), 250-380F / 38,11-57,93€, also à la carte. Specialties: Pigeonneau rôti en cocotte julienne de citron confit sauce aux légumes et cardamome. **Credit cards** All major. **Pets** Dogs not allowed. **Facilities** Parking. **Nearby** Futuroscope in Poitiers; La Rochelle; île de Ré; Poitou marshes; Tumulus of Bougon Museum – 9-hole golf courses in Mazières-en-Gatine, Sainte-Maxire and Les Forges. **Closed** Jan.

This large, 17th-century stone house, so cool when it is hot outside, and so warm in the winter, is a great place to spend a weekend. From here you can walk along the Sèvre River which runs in front of the hotel, and through the countryside described by René Bazin in *L'Eglise verte*. The rooms are comfortable, bright, pleasantly decorated, quiet, and all have a nice view. A suite has even been recently set up in the tower. On the ground floor, the large dining room, where a fire is often crackling away, presents the inventive, flavorfully balanced, and well-cooked cuisine of Bertrand Heintz and his team. This food will last in your memories. A very charming place.

***How to get there*** *(Map 15): 24km northeast of Niort via N11.*

## Le Relais du Lyon d'Or

86260 Angles-sur-L'Anglin (Vienne)
4, rue d'Enfer
Tel. (0)5.49.48.32.53 - Fax (0)5.49.84.02.28
M. and Mme Thoreau

**Rooms** 10 with telephone, bath or shower, TV – 1 for disabled persons. **Price** Single and double 370-450F / 56,41-68,60€. **Meals** Breakfast (buffet) 40-75F / 6,10-11,43€, served 8:30-11:00; half board 260-360F / 39,64-54,88€ (per pers., 3 days min.). **Restaurant** Closed Wednesday and Thursday lunchtime in low season. Service 7:30PM-9:00PM; mealtime specials, also à la carte 110-190F / 16,77-28,97€, also à la carte. Specialties: Flan de foie gras et son coulis de langoustines. **Credit cards** Visa, Eurocard and MasterCard. **Pets** Dogs allowed. **Facilities** Painting classes, wellness center, parking. **Nearby** Romanesque churches of Saint-Savin; Antigny; Poitiers. **Closed** Dec – Feb.

Located in the heights of the beautiful village of Angles-sur-l'Anglin, the various buildings of this old postal relay surround a small courtyard. The very tastefully renovated interior is absolutely charming and very comfortable. Cheered by many floral and fruit stencil patterns, the sponge or brush painted walls always add a colorful touch. The rooms are set up in two buildings. Our favorites are in the older one. The others are pretty enough, but their linoleum flooring make them seem less genuine. The two attic rooms are very sweet. A nice antique yard piece of furniture here, beautiful fabrics and mosquito netting there, and pretty bathrooms all around. In the inviting dining room, where a fire burns, mouth watering food is served, but the recent change of chef prevents us from saying more. In nice weather, you can kick back, lunch, or dine on grilled meat under the pergola that overlooks one of the old village's little streets. A pretty, hospitable place at reasonable prices.

***How to get there*** *(Map 16): 16km north of Saint-Savin.*

# Les Orangeries

86320 Lussac-les-Châteaux (Vienne)
12, avenue du Docteur-Dupont
Tel. (0)5.49.84.07.07 - Fax (0)5.49.84.98.82 - M. and Mme Gautier
E-mail: orangeries@wanadoo.fr

**Rooms** 10 with telephone, bath, WC, TV, minibar and safe – 1 for disabled persons. **Price** Single and double 350-675F / 53,36-102,90€ (Same-day reservation stopover plan: 435F / 66,32€ ); suite 550-910F / 83,85-138,73€ (4 pers.). **Meals** Breakfast 50-80F / 7,62-12,20€, served from 8:00. No restaurant. **Credit card** Visa. **Pets** Dogs allowed (+30F / 4,57€). **Facilities** Parking. **Nearby** Romanesque churches of Saint-Savin; Antigny; Poitiers; Chauvigny. **Open** Feb – Dec 15.

In the Roman Poitou, *Les Orangeries* has been set up on the family estate of Jean-Philippe Gautier. An architect by trade, he has kept all the authentic charm of the huge areas. Soberly furbished, very comfortable, and decorated with refinement, the rooms all have spit-spot bathrooms. Upstairs, under an exceptional framework, an immense billiard room lined with many sofas also has many old games collected by Olivia. Below, an inviting lounge with a fireplace is for those who want their privacy. In nice weather, the great garden springs with wonders, with many flowers, shade trees, and a 35-meter swimming pool with a teak deck, which plays against the French-style garden and its manicured boxwoods and arbored terrace where breakfast and brunch is served every morning. Jean-Philippe and Olivia have much in mind for the other house and the estate's beautiful outbuilidngs. For now, while awaiting the soundproofing of the rooms facing the town, choose those near the garden. Attentive hospitatility at this very beautiful place to stay.

***How to get there*** *(Map 16): Via A 10, southwest of Poitiers, take N 147 (Poitiers-Limoges). The hotel is in the center of Lussac-les-Châteaux.*

## Auberge Charembeau

04300 Forcalquier (Alpes-de-Haute-Provence)
Route de Niozelles
Tel. (0)4.92.70.91.70 - Fax (0)4.92.70.91.83 - M. Berger
E-mail: charembeau@provenceweb.fr

**Category** ★★ **Rooms** 23 with telephone, bath or shower and WC. **Price** Single and double 300-500F / 45,73-76,22€. Rooms with kitchenette 1950-4000F / 297,28-610,68€ per week. **Meals** Breakfast 46F / 6,86€, served 8:00-10:00. No restaurant. **Credit cards** All major. **Pets** Dogs allowed (+20F / 3,05€). **Facilities** Swimming pool, tennis, bicycle rentals, parking. **Nearby** Lure mountain, Salagon priory, Ganagobie priory, Château of Sauvan, Saint-Michel observatory, delicacies at *Site remarquable du goût.* **Open** Mid Feb – mid Nov.

This little hotel in the middle of the lovely countryside of the Forcalquier region is run by a friendly couple who have given the old restored house a charming family atmosphere. You have a choice between the traditional bedrooms, smartly furnished, fresh, and all entirely renovated (like their bathrooms), and the suites with a small kitchen, which are just as charming. In front of the inn, you can relax around the swimming pool surrounded by the Provençal countryside. On request, the Charembeau rents bikes, including those with a baby-carrier, for exploring the region on marked bicycle trails. For restaurants, we recommend that you try the Provençale country cooking at the *Hostellerie des Deux Lions* in Forcalquier; the *Auberge Pierry* in Reillanne, the *Bello Visto* in Lurs, or the *Café de la Lavande* in Lardier.

***How to get there*** *(Map 34): 39km south of Sisteron via N96 (or A51, exit La Brillanne), then N100 towards Forcalquier. It's 4km from Forcalquier via N100 towards Niozelles.*

## Hostellerie de la Fuste

La Fuste 04210 Manosque (Alpes-de-Haute-Provence)
Tel. (0)4.92.72.05.95 - Fax (0)4.92.72.92.93
Famille Jourdan-Bucaille

**Category** ★★★★ **Rooms** 14 (4 with air-conditioning) with telephone, bath, shower, WC, cabel TV, safe and minibar – 1 for disabled persons. **Price** Single and double 650-900F / 99,09-137,20€; suite 1000-1400F / 152,45-213,43€. **Meals** Breakfast 90F / 13,72€, served 8:30-10:00; half board 980F / 149,40€ (per pers.). **Restaurant** Service 12:00PM-1:30PM, 7:30PM-9:30PM; mealtime specials 250-400F / 38,11-60,98€. Specialties: Agneau de pays; truffes and games in season. **Credit cards** All major. **Pets** Dogs allowed. **Facilities** Heated swimming pool (covered in winter), parking. **Nearby** Plateau of Valensole, Manosque: Carzou Foundation, Museum of Jean Giono, Moustiers, Gorges of Verdon. **Closed** Jan 10 – Feb 10; Sunday evening and Monday from Oct – mid Jun, except national holidays.

In Giono, that marvelous part of Haute-Provence where olive trees rub elbows with the lavender, this old basitde has become a gourmet stop. Served either in the garden in nice weather or around the fireplace, Daniel Jordan's cooking is prepared with passion and harmoniously intermingles creativity and tradition. The curious can watch the kitchen staff at work through a huge picture window that overlooks the kitchen. The rooms are classically decorated, well-cared-for, and always comfortable, no matter what their size. Some have huge balconies and overlook the orchard and herb garden, while others open onto the terraces' flora. Breakfast here is delicious. Everything is of a really high quality, even if the rates seem a bit high to us. While in Manosque, you can discover real Provençale specialties at *Dominique Bucaille* in the warm ambiance of a former spinning mill, also run by the family.

***How to get there*** *(Map 34): On A 51 (Aix-en-Provence/Manosque), take the Manosque exit. Hotel 6 km from Manosque on D 4.*

## Auberge du Clos Sorel

04400 Pra-Loup (Alpes-de-Haute-Provence)
Les Molanès
Tel. (0)4.92.84.10.74 - Fax (0)4.92.84.09.14
Mme Dominique Mercier

**Category** ★★★ **Rooms** 11 with telephone, bath, WC and TV. **Price** Double 520-850F / 79,27-129,58€. **Meals** Breakfast 50F / 7,62€, served 8:00-9:30; half board 400-600F / 60,98-91,47€ (per pers., 3 days min.), diet cooking in summer (+50F / 7,62€). **Restaurant** Service 12:30PM-2:30PM; mealtime specials 150F / 22,87€, also à la carte. Specialties: Ravioles; gigots; tourtes aux herbes; tartes. **Credit cards** Visa, Eurocard and MasterCard. **Pets** Dogs allowed (+35F / 5,34€). **Facilities** Swimming pool, aqua gym im summer. **Nearby** Skiing from hotel, Colmars, Bonette trail, Cayolles; Allos. **Closed** Beg Sep – Dec 10 and Apr 10 – end Jun.

Well-located on a hillside in a hamlet that seems not to have changed for centuries, the *Auberge du Clos Sorel* occupies the oldest farmhouse of the region, in immediate proximity to the ski slopes. The building has lovely stone walls and an entranceway built of logs, and blends in perfectly with the surrounding chalets. Inside, original features such as beams, an impressive fireplace, and sloping ceilings have been retained, and these combine with the polished furniture to create the kind of warm and cozy atmosphere one looks forward to after a long day spent skiing or walking. In the evening, dinner is served by candlelight in what used to be the main room of the farmhouse. The tables are pretty and the cuisine is refined. In summer, a swimming pool and tennis courts facing a magnificent panorama make the inn a lovely place to stay. The ambiance is a happy mixture of informality and sophistication.

***How to get there*** *(Map 34): 70km southwest of Gap via D900B and D900 to Barcelonnette, then D902 and D109 to Pra-Loup. (Les Molanès is just before the resort.)*

410

## La Bastide de Moustiers

04360 Moustiers-Sainte-Marie (Alpes-de-Haute-Provence)
Tel. (0)4.92.70.47.47 - Fax (0)4.92.70.47.48
M. Ducasse
E-mail: bastide@i2m.fr - Web: www.bastide-moustiers.i2m.fr

**Category** ★★★★ **Rooms** 12 with air-conditioning, telephone, fax, bath, WC, TV, safe and minibar –
1 for disabled persons. **Price** Single and double 850-1700F / 129,58-259,16€, according to the
season. **Meals** Breakfast 80F / 12,20€, served in dining room all day (coffee served in room)
**Restaurant** Closed Jan 5 – Feb 28. Service 12:00PM-2:00PM, 7:30PM-9:45PM; mealtime specials 215-
285F / 32,78-43,45€. Specialties: Regional cooking. **Credit cards** All major. **Pets** Dogs not allowed.
**Facilities** Heated swimming pool, mountain bikes, picnic baskets, parking. **Nearby** The Grand Canyon
of the Gorges of the Verdon via the road or GR4; Lake of Sainte-Croix. **Open** All year.

What a pleasure it is to visit this part of Haute-Provence, and this park,
recently registered and now protected against land development. Alain
Ducasse's estate now includes 5 new additions: a duplex attic room, a large
suite with lounge and fireplace that can includes a second room, making a little
villa for four people, and two equally charming rooms that open onto the lawn.
As in the bastide, you will find the same refined comfort, attention to detail,
antique furniture, and colors drawn from the world of flowers, fruits, and
vegetables, giving each room a fresh and cheerful Provençal comfort. The
kitchen offers you a menu which honors the local, Mediterranean flavors.
There is a superb swimming pool with a view, little nooks to enjoy the
countryside, and prices that make it possible to take a "bite" of what might be
called the Ducasse style.

***How to get there*** *(Map 34): On A 51, take the Cadarache-Vinon exit. Head
toward Greoux-les-Bains, Riez, and then Moustiers. On A 8, take the Le Muy
exit, head toward Draguigna, Aups, and then Moustiers.*

## La Ferme Rose

04360 Moustiers-Sainte-Marie (Alpes-de-Haute-Provence)
Tel. (0)4.92.74.69.47 - Fax (0)4.92.74.60.76
M. Kako Vagh

**Category** ★★ **Rooms** 12 with telephone, bath or shower and WC and TV. **Price** Double 390-640F /
59,46-97,57€. **Meals** Breakfast 48F / 7,62€ or brunch à la carte. No restaurant. **Credit cards** Visa,
Eurocard and MasterCard. **Pets** Dogs allowed. **Facilities** Mountain bikes and tandem. **Nearby** Church
and Pottery Museum in Moustiers, the Grand Canyon of the Gorges of the Verdon via the road or GR4;
Sainte-Croix Lake. **Open** Mar 16 – Nov 14.

From the terrace of "The Pink Farm," you will have a beautiful view over
the lovely village of Moustiers, which seems suspended between two cliffs.
The hotel is charming. The owner has decorated it in a very personal style,
combining his collection of 1950s objects, paintings done by his grandfather -
a well-known Provençal painter - and amusing pieces of furniture. Note the
tables, chairs and bar banquettes which came from the old *Brasserie Noailles* in
Marseilles. The bedrooms are very pleasant, bright and cheerful, with spit-spot
shower rooms decorated in pretty Salernes faience. A really terrific and simple
place, whose outlying areas sometimes draw criticism from our readers, but
which still deserves a place in this guide. Good places to eat include *Les
Santons*, in the village itself, and *La Bastide de Moustiers* nearby.

***How to get there*** *(Map 34): On A51, Cadarache/Vinon-sur-Verdon exit, towards
Gréoux-les-Bains, Riez, Moustier. On A8, Le Luc exit, towards Aups, Moustiers.
In Moustiers head towards the village of Sainte-Croix for 1km.*

## Auberge de Reillanne

04110 Reillanne (Alpes-de-Haute-Provence)
Tel. (0)4.92.76.45.95
Mme Marie-Anne Founès

**Rooms** 7 with telephone, bath, WC and free minibar. **Price** Single and double 280-380F / 42,69-57,93€. **Meals** Breakfast 45F / 6,86€; half board 410F / 62,50€ (per pers.). **Restaurant** Closed Wednesday except for residents. Service 7:30PM-9:00PM; mealtime 160F / 24,39€, also à la carte. Specialties: Piccata de fois gras aux navets confits; solimane d'agneau à la menthe et au miel; home-smoked fish, pintade à la crème d'ail et de sauge. **Credit cards** Visa, Eurocard and MasterCard. **Pets** Dogs allowed. **Facilities** Parking. **Nearby** Manosque, priories of Salagon and Ganagobie, Château of Sauvan. **Closed** Jan 11 – Mar 1.

Located in a part of the region which has remained unspoiled, this hotel is surrounded by greenery. The few bedrooms are large, a bit drearily furbished but comfortable all the same, with an emphasis on natural materials: light-colored wood or cane, unbleached wool, and flowery fabrics. All the bedrooms have pleasant views and large bathrooms with terra-cotta floor tiles. There is no charge to use the minibars in the rooms; guests decide how much they want to pay for the drinks - obviously trust is the keyword here. Marie-Anne Founes has created a tranquil mood here, while Ludovic Jans (formerly of *Guerard et Loiseau*) concocts good seasonal food with the freshest, regional produce, very simply highlighted by light herbs. You'll taste the results in a little dining room and continue the evening in the lounge area in front of a fireplace, lit if the weather demands. A unpretentious place to stay for those who like the simple things in life.

***How to get there*** *(Map 33): 15km northwest of Manosque towards Apt, then N100 and D214 towards Reillanne.*

## Le Pyjama

04400 Super-Sauze (Alpes-de-Haute-Provence)
Tel. (0)4.92.81.12.00 - Fax (0)4.92.81.03.16
Mme Merle

**Category** ★★★ **Rooms** 10 with telephone, bath, WC, TV and minibar. **Price** Double 350-450F / 53,36-68,60€; suite 490-640F / 74,70-97,57€. **Meals** Breakfast 20-45F / 3,05-6,87€. No restaurant. **Credit cards** All major. **Pets** Dogs allowed. **Nearby** Skiing from the hotel, Barcelonnette, The 7 Passes, Bonette road. **Closed** Sep 5 – Dec 15 and Apr 20 – Jun 25.

Having spent twenty years running another hotel in the resort, Geneviève Merle (ski champion Carole Merle's mother) had this hotel designed to integrate harmoniously with the surroundings. Eight of the ten bedrooms face south, their terraces overlooking a field of larch trees. They are tastefully decorated, with very pleasant bathrooms. M. Merle owns an antique shop nearby, and it has provided the hotel furniture. Four rooms have a mezzanine which can accommodate two extra people. In the annex there are four studios complete with kitchen areas which are very convenient for families. This is a comfortable, informal hotel at the foot of the ski slopes, with outstanding breakfasts, good value for the money, and a very friendly staff. *Le Pyjama* has no restaurant but there are many in the village, and *L'Optraken*, run by Madame Merle's children, is not far. This is an extremely comfortable establishment, at the foot of the slopes, offering a friendly and informal atmosphere.

***How to get there*** *(Map 34): 79km southeast of Gap via D900B and D900 towards Barcelonnette, then D9 and D209 to Super-Sauze.*

## Le Pi-Maï

05240 La Salle-les-Alpes (Hautes-Alpes)
Hameau de Fréjus
Station de Serre-Chevalier
Tel. (0)4.92.24.83.63 - M. and Mme Charamel

**Category** ★★ **Rooms** 6 with bath or shower, WC. **Price** Double 400-450F / 60,98-68,60€. **Meals** Breakfast incl.; half board 420-510F / 64,12-77,75€ (per pers.). **Restaurant** Service 12:00PM-3:00PM, 8:00PM-9:00PM; mealtime specials 140-160F / 21,34-24,39€. Specialties: Croûte au fromage de Bagnes; grillades de charolais aux braises de mélèze. **Credit card** Visa. **Pets** Dogs not allowed. **Nearby** Skiing from the hotel, golf courses, mountain bike, horse trekking. **Closed** Sep 15 – Dec 1 and May – Jul.

Entirely renovated after a fire, the *Pi-Maï* has refound that charming, cozy feel that made it so successful. First off, there is the restaurant known for its good, healthy food. A few bright rooms with larchwood beams, sometimes with a balcony, have just been set up with your pleasure in mind. ("Torrent" is the largest.) 2000 meters in altitude, on a slope a bit away from the beaten track, the hotel overlooks the valley. At the end of the day, the last skiiers go back to the slopes, and what a pleasure it is to stretch out and enjoy the last daylight and pure, mountain silence in almost perfect solitude. (In summer, the *Pi-Maï* is easier to get to, but the sense of calm and solitude is no longer there.) An almost one-of-a-kind address where you will find a sporty, refined, and attentive welcome.

***How to get there*** *(Map 27): 10 northwest of Briançon via N 91. At Villeneuve-la-Salle, Hauts de Frejus. 7 km to go, accessible by road, except during snowcover, or take the Frejus cable car from Villeneuve 1400 (last car at 4 pm), then 10 mins on foot, 3 mins skiing, or 20 mins by car in summer.*

# Hôtel Alliey

Serre-Chevalier 05220 Le Monêtier-les-Bains (Hautes-Alpes)
Tel. (0)4.92.24.40.02 - Fax (0)4.92.24.40.60
Hervé and Eliane Buisson
Web: www.alliey.com

**Category** ★★ **Rooms** 24 with telephone, bath, WC, 8 with TV. **Price** Single and double 290-420F / 44,21-64,12€; duplex 550F / 83,85€. **Meals** Breakfast 50F / 7,62€, served 8:00-10:30; half board 330-420F / 50,31-64,12€ (per pers.). **Restaurant** Closed Tuesday lunchtime. Service 12:30PM-1:30PM, 7:30PM-9:00PM; mealtime specials 130-160F / 19,82-24,39€. Specialties: fondue aux cèpes. **Credit cards** Visa, Eurocard and MasterCard. **Pets** Dogs allowed. **Nearby** Ski resort of "Grand Serre Che"; climbing, mountain bike; Montgenèvre – 9-hole course in Clavière 21 km away. **Closed** Apr 25 – Jun 24 and Sep 2 – Dec 16.

From several generations now, the Buisson family has held onto the traditions of this village, the best preserved town of the famous "Grand Serre Che" ski area. In the heart of the town, next to Saint-Pierre Chapel, this family home has kept its old stones and waxed ceiling beams. In winter and summer, there is a conviviality here that changes according to the season, and there is always someone on hand to satisfy your every whim. The rooms are sweet, charming, and flowery with comfortable bathrooms. The patio rooms are smaller but just as well-tended. In the restaurant, with its warm wood panelling, you'll sample "grandma's recipes" and many regional dishes with a fine bottle of wine from a cellar that has no less than 160 vintages. Hervé and Elian Buisson wanted to create a relaxed and friendly mood here, so that your stay might be remembered as a peaceful, pleasure-filled, and restoring one. Mission accomplished.

*How to get there ( Map 27): 13 km from Briançon.*

## Auberge du Soleil

06390 Coaraze (Alpes-Maritimes)
Quartier Porta-Savel
Tel. (0)4.93.79.08.11 - Fax (0)4.93.79.37.79
M. and Mme Jacquet

**Category** ★ **Rooms** 8 and 2 suites in annex, with telephone, bath or shower, WC and TV on request. **Price** Double 370-520F / 56,41-79,27€, suite 520-980F / 79,27-149,40€. **Meals** Breakfast 48F / 7,32€, served 8:00AM-12:00PM; half board 380-460F / 57,93-70,13€ (per pers., 3 days min.). **Restaurant** Service 12:00PM-2:00PM, 7:30PM-9:00PM; mealtime specials 142F / 21,67€, also à la carte. Specialties: Tourte maison; gibelotte de lapin; caille aux raisins. **Credit cards** Amex, Visa. **Pets** Dogs allowed (+35F / 5,34€). **Facilities** Swimming pool, lawn bowling, table tennis. **Nearby** Mercantour reserve, valley of Wonders, Turini forest, villages of Lucéram, Peille and Peillon – 18-hole Agel golf course in La Turbie. **Open** Mid Feb – Nov 1.

This hotel is only half an hour from Nice and not far from the magnificent nature reserve of Mercantour. It is splendidly located in a medieval village 640 meters up on a rocky outcrop. The maze of narrow village streets ensures total peace and quiet: you may need to call on the hotel to help you carry your luggage up the steep slopes. You will find an informal, almost bohemian atmosphere in the hotel but it is all in elegant taste. The rooms, though simple, are no less comfortable. There is also a billiard room. a summer lounge located in a cool, vaulted cellar, and an attractive dining room which extends out over a covered terrace with panoramic views of the valley. The cuisine is simple and good. The garden slopes down in steps to the swimming pool and orchard, where you can pick the fruit without feeling guilty.

*How to get there (Map 35): 2km north of Nice via A8 exit Nice-Est, then "voie rapide" (expressway) towards Drap-Sospel. At the Pointe des Contes, left towards Contes-Coaraze.*

## Hôtel L'Aiglon

06500 Menton (Alpes-Maritimes)
7, avenue de la Madone
Tel. (0)4.93.57.55.55 - Fax (0)4.93.35.92.39 - M. and Mme Caravelli
Web: http://perso.wanadoo.fr/aiglon - E-mail: aiglon.hotel@wanadoo.fr

**Category** ★★★ **Rooms** 28 (25 with air-conditioning), 1 apartment and 2 suites with telephone, bath or shower, WC, satellite TV, safe and minibar – Elevator. **Price** Single and double 295-720F / 44,97-109,76€, suite and apart. 690-1100F / 105,19-167,69€. **Meals** Breakfast 40F / 6,10€; half board 400-700F / 60,98-106,71€ (per pers.). **Restaurant** Closed Wednesday lunchtime. Service 12:30PM-2:00PM, 7:30PM-9:30PM; mealtime specials 110F / 16,77€ (lunchtime weekdays) and 190-300F / 28,97-45,73€, also à la carte. Specialties: Regional cooking. **Credit cards** All major. **Pets** Dogs allowed. **Facilities** Heated swimming pool and parking. **Nearby** in Menton: Museum of J.Cocteau, Palais de l'Europe, exotic garden; village of Gorbio; Lemon Festival in Feb; Royal Valley; the French Riviéra; garden of Villa Hambury – 18-hole Cannes-Mougins golf course. **Closed** Nov 5 – Dec 22.

This former mansion is a great village hotel. Its spacious reception rooms with their roccoco gilt, the many corner lounges with 1930s furniture, the daily papers attached to wooden poles: it all brings back the atmosphere of the great luxury hotels in the days when elderly English people came to winter on the Riviera. Decorated in old-fashioned sepia tones, the bedrooms with their comfortable beds and immaculate bathrooms (well-soundproofed, but best to choose the garden-side rooms in the summer) are nevertheless as appealing as anything modern. Their reasonable prices vary depending on their size and the season; some even have a view of the sea as the hotel is separated from the Mediterranean only by a row of small buildings. Served on the veranda or in the shady arbor, lunches and dinners offer simple, delicious specialties. Not far away, the luxuriant garden conceals a heated (86°F) outdoor swimming pool.

***How to get there*** *(Map 34): 29km from Nice, 7km from Monaco.*

## Le Manoir de l'Etang

06250 Mougins (Alpes-Maritimes)
66, allée du Manoir
Tel. (0)4.93.90.01.07 - Fax (0)4.92.92.20.70
Family Gridaine-Labro

**Category** ★★★ **Rooms** 16 with telephone, bath or shower, WC, TV and minibar. **Price** Double 600-1000F / 91,47-152,45€, suite and apart. 1350-1600F / 205,81-243,92€. **Meals** Breakfast 60F / 9,15€, served 8:00-10:30. **Restaurant** Service 12:00PM-1:30PM, 8:00PM-9:30PM; mealtime specials 150F / 22,87€ (lunchtime, wine incl.) and 190F / 28,97€, also à la carte. Specialties: Aïoli de lotte fumée et pommes de terres confites à l'huile d'olives; canette mijotée au miel et romarin; mendiant de figue rôtie et crème glacée à l'amande. **Credit cards** Amex, Visa ,Eurocard and MasterCard. **Pets** Small dogs allowed on request. **Facilities** Swimming pool, parking. **Nearby** The Riviera and its villages – 18-golf-courses in Cannes-Mougins. **Open** Mar – Nov.

Set up in a superb bastide dating from the early 19th century, this hotel looks down on a rolling, private park with a pond, cyprus trees, and rose laurels. Next to the manor and its tiled terrace, the garden flaunts a beautiful variety of flowers and trees that give off all the seasonal sensations of Provence. On the ground floor, an inviting earthy red lounge with terra-cotta flooring and Provençal furnishing looks on a bright dining room where flavorful, light, and inventive regional cuisine is served. The comfortable rooms are brightened up by beautiful fabrics and sport a few pieces of antique furniture. The swimming pool below, framed by two olive trees, has a sweeping view of the southern French countryside. Peace and quiet are guaranteed, as well as friendliness, because hospitality is a familly affair at *Le Manoir*. A beautiful, charming place to stay.

*How to get there ( Map 34): 5 km north of Cannes on the expressway.*

# Les Muscadins

06250 Mougins Village (Alpes-Maritimes)
18, boulevard Courteline
Tel. (0)4.92.28.28.28 - Fax (0)4.92.92.88.23 - M. Bianchini

**Category** ★★★★ **Rooms** 7 and 1 suite, with air-conditioning, telephone, bath or shower, WC, satellite TV. **Price** Doubles 750-950F / 114,34-144,83€; suite: 900-1100F / 137,20-167,69€. **Meals** 60F / 9,15€, served 8:00-11:00; half board (+200F / 30,49€). **Restaurant** Service 12:15PM-2:45PM, 7:30PM-10:00PM; mealtime specials 175-290F / 26,68-44,21€; also à la carte. Specialties: Risotto à l'italienne; raviolis de homard; fondant au chocolat. **Credit cards** All major. **Pets** Dogs allowed. **Facilities** Parking. **Nearby** Picasso Musuem in Vallauris; the Riviera and its villages; sea (10 km away) – 18-golf-courses in Cannes-Mougins. **Closed** Mid Nov – mid Dec.

At the entrance to Mougins, overlooking the bay of Cannes and the Lerins isles, this former boarding house has welcomed Eluard, Cocteau, Man Ray, and Picasso, who, some say, painted a few of the walls to pay his bill, only to have the miffed owner demand that he put them back in their former state. What a loss! *Les Muscadins* is now a small, discretely luxurious hotel. Upon entering, you will be struck by the refined atmosphere. The restrained comfort of the little bar, the dusky rose carpeting on the stairs, and the muffled light of the hallways say it all. The variegated rooms parade delightful art objects, rare antique furniture, and carefully chosen fabrics. Those that look out on the sea are delightful. The "junior-suite" is unforgettable, though the others have a look all their own. The marbled bathrooms are very nice. For several years now, the tyro Noel Mantel has been offering up a light, fragrant Mediterannean fare in the veranda-style dining room, or, in summer, on the shady neighboring terrace. A unique place with attentive and warm hospitality.

***How to get there*** *(Map 35): via A 8, take the Cannes Mougins exit, then head toward Grasse.*

## Hôtel La Pérouse

06300 Nice (Alpes-Maritimes)
11, quai Rauba-Capeu
Tel. (0)4.93.62.34.63 - Fax (0)4.93.62.59.41 - Mme Giometti
E-mail: lp@hroy.com

**Category** ★★★★ **Rooms** 64 with air-conditioning, telephone, bath or shower, WC, TV and minibar.
**Price** Single and double 600-1850F / 91,47-282,03€, apart. 2150-3000F / 327,77-457,35€. **Meals**
Breakfast 95F / 14,48€, served 7:00-11:00. **Restaurant** Closed Sep 15 – May 15. Service 12:00PM-
2:00PM, 7:30PM-10:00PM; à la carte. Specialties: BBQ in the hotel gardens. **Credit cards** All major.
**Pets** Dogs allowed. **Facilities** Swimming pool, sauna, whirlpool, solarium. **Nearby** Turini forest, valley
of La Tinée (Roure, Roubron), valley of La Vésubie, villages of Utelle, Belvédère, le Boréon, Venanson –
18-hole Opio golf course in Valbonne, 18-hole Bastide-du-Roy golf course in Biot. **Open** All year.

The *Hôtel La Pérouse* is in a large Mediterranean-style mansion at the foot of the château that dominates old Nice and the Baie des Anges. It is surrounded by aloe plants and lemon trees; to reach it you have to take one of the two elevators from the quayside. The bedrooms are spacious and quiet, and prices vary according to whether you have a view of the garden or the sea; some have a terrace with deck chairs. In summer you might take advantage of the barbecue, swimming pool, and solarium, panoramic solarium, or have a drink under the lemon trees that flourish on the smashing terrace. The terrific hospitality is a welcome surprise for a hotel of this caliber.

***How to get there*** *(Map 35): In the town center.*

## Hôtel Windsor

06300 Nice (Alpes-Maritimes)
11, rue Dalpozzo
Tel. (0)4.93.88.59.35 - Fax (0)4.93.88.94.57 - M. Redolfi-Strizzot
E-mail: windsor@webstore.fr

**Category** ★★★ **Rooms** 57 with telephone, bath or shower, WC, TV, minibar and air-conditioning – Elevator. **Price** Single and double 420-750F / 64,12-114,34€. **Meals** Breakfast 40F / 6,10€, served 7:00-10:30; half board +140F / 21,34€ (per pers.). **Restaurant** Closed Saturday lunchtime and Sunday. Service 12:00PM-2:00PM, 7:00PM-10:30PM; also à la carte. **Credit cards** All major. **Pets** Dogs allowed. **Facilities** Swimming pool, fitness room, sauna (70F / 10,67€), massage (240F / 36,59€), parking (60F / 9,15€). **Nearby** Turini forest, Valley of La Tinée, Valley of La Vésubie, villages of Utelle – 18-hole Opio golf course in Valbonne, 18-hole Bastide-du-Roy golf course in Biot. **Open** All year.

From the street, the *Hôtel Windsor* seems like a classic mid-town hotel. Once you step inside, however, you'll see that you can't read a book by its cover. In the modern reception area, there is an ornate Oriental bed encrusted with mother-of-pearl and a gilt shrine with a seated Buddha. Just outside, you will also discover a luxuriant exotic garden with an aviary in the hollow of an old tree; here, a few tables are hidden away not far from a small swimming pool. In the often large bedrooms, the furniture is deliberately 1950s-60s hotel style. Many are large and all are comfortable. Its owner offers sixteen contemporary "artists" bedrooms (Ben, Pete, Fend, Honegger, Panchounette...). It's best to let Monsieur Redolfi-Strizzot explain why: "An artist is related to an inherent reality. That's what attracts me. In the hotel business, we have gotten to a limit as regards material competition. We can always add an iron, a hair dryer, of course; but it's best to enrich the human fabric…".

***How to get there*** *( Map 35 ): In the center of town.*

## Hôtel Les Deux Frères

Roquebrune Village - 06190 Cap-Martin (Alpes-Maritimes)
Place des Deux-Frères
Tel. (0)4.93.28.99.00 - Fax (0)4.93.28.99.10
M. W. Bonestroo

**Category** ★★ **Rooms** 10 with telephone, bath or shower and TV. **Price** Single and double 495-545F / 75,46-83,08€. **Meals** Breakfast 45F / 6,86€. **Restaurant** Service 12:00PM-2:00PM, 7:30PM-10:00PM; à la carte. Specialties: Fish; duck; foie gras. **Credit cards** Amex, Visa, Eurocard and MasterCard, Diner's Club. **Pets** Dogs allowed. **Nearby** Rue Moncolet in Roquebrune, La Turbie Church, footpath to Cap Martin – 18-hole Monte-Carlo Golf Course in La Turbie. **Closed** Mid Nov – mid Dec.

The two brothers of the hotel's name are actually the two rocks that gave their name to the village of Roquebrune. The square named for them is one of the best sites in the medieval village, protected by its Carolingian castle. Here a school was built; 15 years after its closing a Dutch architect transformed it into a hotel. The classrooms were turned into pretty white-walled bedrooms, and the courtyard into a restaurant. Around the great fireplace, comfortable leather-covered sofas are grouped, creating a place that most guests find difficult to tear themselves away from in the evenings. You'll enjoy a very inviting atmosphere, always in flower, with many paintings and mementos. Warm hospitality.

***How to get there*** *(Map 35): 5km south of Menton via A8 or N98.*

## Auberge du Colombier

06330 Roquefort-les-Pins (Alpes-Maritimes)
Tel. (0)4.92.60.33.00 - Fax (0)4.93.77.07.03
MM. Wolff

**Category** ★★★ **Rooms** 18 and 2 suites with telephone, bath, shower, WC and TV. **Price** Double 270-650F / 41,16-99,09€, suite 450-800F / 68,60-121,96€. **Meals** Breakfast 50F / 7,62€; half board +170F / 25,92€ (per pers.). **Restaurant** Closed Monday evening, Tuesday from mid Oct – end Mar. Service 12:00PM-2:30PM, 7:30PM-10:00PM; mealtime specials 150-195F / 22,84-29,73€, also à la carte. Specialties: Ravioles de homard en nage de pistou; carré d'agneau en croûte d'herbes. **Credit cards** All major. **Pets** Dogs allowed (+40F / 6,10€). **Facilities** Swimming pool, tennis (+50F / 7,62€), parking. **Nearby** Nice, Grasse, gorges of Le Loup and Gourdon, Saint-Paul-de-Vence (Maeght Foundation) – 18-hole Opio golf course in Valbonne. **Closed** Jan 4 – Feb 13.

The trip between Nice and Grasse, long ago, lasted two days, and that's why this postal relay had to be built. It still makes a good overnight halt or a pleasant base from which to explore the many attractions of the French Riviera. The auberge was modernized in 1980 but preserves its old charm. Today it has a beautiful swimming pool, a tennis court and some more recently-built bedrooms in which, however, some of the atmosphere has been lost. You will find a pleasant welcome here and a restaurant which is renowned for its cuisine and its *spécialités de la maison*.

***How to get there*** *( Map 34): 25km west of Nice via A8, exit Villeneuve-Loubet, then D2085 towards Grasse. From Cannes, Cagnes-sur-Mer exit, towards Grasse.*

## Hôtel Brise Marine

06230 Saint-Jean-Cap-Ferrat (Alpes-Maritimes)
58, avenue Jean-Mermoz
Tel. (0)4.93.76.04.36 - Fax (0)4.93.76.11.49 - M. Maîtrehenry
E-mail: bmarine@nicematin.fr - Web: www.hotel-brisemarine.com

**Category** ★★★ **Rooms** 16 with air-conditioning, telephone, bath or shower, WC, TV and safe. **Price** Double 730-780F / 111,29-118,91€. **Meals** Breakfast 58F / 8,85€, served 8:00-10:00. No restaurant. **Credit card** Visa. **Pets** Dogs allowed. **Nearby** Saint-Pierre Chapel (Cocteau) in Villefranche, Villa Ephrussi-de-Rothschild in Saint-Jean-Cap-Ferrat, Villa Kerylos in Beaulieu – 18-hole La Bastide-du-Roy golf course in Biot. **Open** Feb 1 – Oct 31.

Located among the luxurious villas, grand hotels and noble residences in Saint-Jean-Cap-Ferrat, this is a little Italian house built in the 19th century. The *Hôtel Brise Marine* has a delightful garden with flowers, palm trees, espaliers, stone balustrades, fountains, and terraces. The owner has personally looked after the hotel and its sixteen elegant and comfortable little bedrooms for forty-five years. Many of them overlook the garden of an inaccessible château and the sea. Regularly redecorated, they invariably retain their touch of seaside charm (several rooms only, on ground level with a lovely small courtyard, are still somewhat old-fashioned). Great breakfasts taken in front of one of the most beautiful vistas imaginable, with the luxuriant vegetation of the garden, the sea just a bit below, and the bay of Monte Carlo far off. No restaurant in the hotel, but *La Voile d'Or* and *Le Provençal* are among the chic, expensive restaurants of Saint Jean. *Le Sloop* is a simpler, reasonably-priced fish restaurant.

***How to get there*** *( Map 35 ): 15km east of Nice via N98.*

## Hôtel Le Hameau

06570 Saint-Paul-de-Vence (Alpes-Maritimes)
528, route de La Colle
Tel. (0)4.93.32.80.24 - Fax (0)4.93.32.55.75
M. Huvelin

**Category** ★★★ **Rooms** 14 and 3 apartments with air-conditioning, telephone, bath or shower, WC, safe and minibar, 6 with satellite TV. **Price** Single and double 450-680F / 68,60-103,67€, apart. 780-800F / 118,91-121,96€. **Meals** Breakfast 60F / 9,15€, served 8:00-10:00. No restaurant. **Credit cards** Visa, Eurocard and MasterCard. **Pets** Dogs allowed. **Facilities** Swimming pool, garage (35F / 5,34€), parking, closed garage (35F / 5,34€). **Nearby** Chapel of Le Rosaire (Matisse), Perfume Museum in Grasse, Church of Saint-Charles-Borromée in Saint-Paul-de-Vence, les Cluses of Haute-Provence – 18-hole Opio golf course in Valbonne. **Closed** Jan 8 – mid Feb and mid Nov – end Dec.

This white 1920s house looks over the valley and the village of Saint-Paul-de-Vence, and is up a path bordered by lemon trees in a flowering garden. The hotel has terraces and arcades and is almost hidden by honeysuckle, fig trees, and climbing vines. The bedrooms are large and prettily decorated, and the furniture is traditionally Provençal. Numbers 1, 2 and 3 have a loggia and an impressive view of Saint-Paul. The rich iridescent green tiles of some of the bathrooms are superb. In the adjoining 18th-century farmhouse there are other smaller attic rooms but they all have a lovely view. This great place to stay is a bit spoiled by the noise of traffic in peak season, but is still one of the most charming places in the area. There is no restaurant but apart from a gastronomic pilgrimage for Picasso lovers to the famous *Colombe d'Or*, you can enjoy delicious Provençale cuisine at *La Brouette*.

***How to get there*** *(Map 34): 20km west of Nice via A8, exit Cagnes-sur-Mer, then D7 towards Vence via La Colle-sur-Loup; it's 1km before Saint-Paul-de-Vence.*

## La Tour de l'Esquillon

Miramar 06590 Théoule-sur-Mer (Alpes-Maritimes)
Tel. (0)4.93.75.41.51 - Fax (0)4.93.75.49.99
M. and Mme Dérobert
E-mail: esquillon@compuserve.com

**Category** ★★★ **Rooms** 25 with telephone, bath, WC, TV and minibar. **Price** Single and double 550-1100F / 83,85-167,69€, apartment (4-6 pers.) from 1600F / 243,92€. **Meals** Breakfast incl., served 8:00-10:00; half board 520-720F / 79,27-109,76€. **Restaurant** Service 12:00PM-2:00PM, 7:00PM-9:00PM; mealtime specials 160-220F / 24,39-33,54€, also à la carte. Specialties: Fish; bouride; aïoli. **Credit cards** All major. **Pets** Dogs allowed. **Facilities** Private beach, parking. **Nearby** Château of Napoule, Estérel slopes, Bay of Napoule – 18-hole Cannes-Mandelieu golf course. **Open** Feb – Oct 14.

At the edge of the winding road overlooking the deep-red Esterel Mountains, *La Tour de l'Esquillon* is perched like a bird's nest overlooking the Estérel Massif, its deep-red rocks forming a beautiful, jagged coastline between Cannes and Saint-Raphaël. Brilliant yellow broom, pink oleander, hydrangeas and fruit trees covering the terraced garden lie between the hotel and its private beach which you can reach by minibus, and where you can enjoy light meals. The *Esquillon* has a kind of old-fashioned charm, with its 1950s furniture and its discreet, friendly service. The roadside house with yellow shutters has something about it. The rooms, in both the hotel and the villa, are big, cool, and look out on the sea. Some more expensive rooms have a balcony, which is a pleasant place to have breakfast. In the restaurant, you will enjoy the savory, spicy specialties of Provence. From the dining room, you will have a panoramic view over Cannes. Note that there is noise from the road on days of peak traffic.

*How to get there (Map 34): Between Saint-Raphaël and Cannes, on A8 Mandelieu exit, then towards Théoule-Miramar.*

# Hôtel Villa La Roseraie

06140 Vence (Alpes-Maritimes)
Avenue Henri-Giraud
Tel. (0)4.93.58.02.20 - Fax (0)4.93.58.99.31
M. and Mme Ganier

**Category** ★★ **Rooms** 14 with telephone, bath or shower, WC, TV and minibar. **Price** Single and double 395-750F / 60,22-114,34€. **Meals** Breakfast 70F / 10,67€ (obligatory in summer), served 8:30AM-12:00PM. No restaurant. **Credit cards** Amex, Visa. **Pets** Dogs allowed. **Facilities** Swimming pool, bike (50F / 7,62€/day), parking. **Nearby** Maeght Foundation, Saint-Charles Church, Borromée Church in Saint-Paul-de-Vence, the valleys of Haute-Provence – 18 hole Opio golf course in Valbonne. **Open** All year.

This hotel, nestled in the village, is a former private home, built in the turn-of-the-century Mediterannean style. The garden's lush southern vegetation, mixed with contemporary sculptures, bronzes, and mobiles, holds a well-preserved intimacy. In the midst of this oasis, the house has but a few rooms in a sunny, youthful style, well-furbished with objects hunted down in antique yards, sprays of Olivades fabrics, Tiffany lamps, and Salernes faience. A charming feel, in which the fine work of local painters, ironworkers, tilemakers, and artisans mixes the Provence with the romantic. Monsieur and Madame Ganier, who are very hospitable and quite taken up with the hotel and the needs of its guests, never stop making improvements. The breakfasts are just as generous as they are delicious, with homemade pastries, jams, fresh orange juice, and eggs. You won't want to leave, but you'll have to for dinner, for there is no restaurant in the hotel. Luckily, *Le Vieux Couvent* isn't far, and its chef deserves to be counted among the greats.

***How to get there*** *( Map 34): 10km north of Cagnes-sur-Mer via D36.*

## Auberge des Seigneurs et du Lion d'Or

06140 Vence (Alpes-Maritimes)
Place du Frêne
Tel. (0)4.93.58.04.24 - Fax (0)4.93.24.08.01
M. and Mme Rodi

**Category** ★★ **Rooms** 10 with telephone, shower and WC. **Price** Double 364-394F / 55,64-60,22€. **Meals** Breakfast 55F / 8,38€, served 7:30-10:00. **Restaurant** Closed Sunday evening and Monday. Service from 12:30PM and 7:30PM; mealtime specials 170-250F / 25,92-38,11€; also à la carte. Specialties: Carré d'agneau à la broche; tian vençois. **Credit cards** All major. **Pets** Dogs allowed. **Nearby** Chapel of Le Rosaire (Matisse), Perfume Museum, Carzou Museum in Vence, Maeght Foundation, Church of St-Charles-Borromée in Saint-Paul-de-Vence, valleys of Haute Provence – 18-hole Opio golf course in Valbonne. **Open** Mar 16 – 14 Nov.

Located in a wing of the Villeneuve de Vence château, this *auberge* is on the square with the famous ash planted by Francis I. It has welcomed many famous guests such as King Francis I and, more recently, Renoir, Modigliani, Dufy, and Soutine. Mme Rodi knows the exact dates of their visits and will enjoy telling you about them. The reception rooms contain an eclectic collection of objects (a 16th-century washstand, an olive oil press, modern lithographs, etc.) all of which have a history. The bedrooms are large, furnished plainly but appropriately for the building, and there is always a basket of fruit and flowers awaiting every guest. The most attractive rooms look out on the square, the quietest over the rooftops. The whole *Auberge* is full of character and is very welcoming. The restaurant is famous for its lamb cooked on a spit in the century-old fireplace. Outside of that, the menu is a bit typical and a bit expensive.

*How to get there (Map 34): 10km north of Cagnes-sur-Mer via D36.*

## Hôtel Welcome

06230 Villefranche-sur-Mer (Alpes-Maritimes)
1, quai Courbet
Tel. (0)4.93.76.27.62 - Fax (0)4.93.76.27.66 - M. and Mme Galbois
E-mail: reservation@welcome.com - Web: www.welcomehotel.com

**Category** ★★★ **Rooms** 32 with air-conditioning, telephone, bath or shower, WC, TV and minibar.
**Price** Single and double 400-950F / 60,98-144,83€. **Meals** Breakfast incl, served 7:15-10:00; half
board 480-670F / 73,18-102,14€ (per pers.). **Restaurant** Service 12:30PM-2:00PM, 7:30PM-10:30PM;
mealtime specials 155F / 23,63€, also à la carte. **Credit cards** All major. **Pets** Dogs allowed (+35F /
5,34€). **Nearby** The Lower Corniche, Saint-Jean-Cap-Ferrat (Villa Ephrussi de Rothschild), Beaulieu
(Villa Kerylos) – 18-hole Opio golf course in Valbonne. **Closed** Mid Nov – end Dec.

On the quayside of the old port of Villefranche you will find colorful fishing
boats, a chapel decorated by Jean Cocteau, and a hotel in the pedestrian
area which is built on the site of a 17th-century monastery. The hotel is modern
with many balconies and large, comfortable, sunny rooms, decorated in
cheerful colors. All overlook the sea, and many have a balcony where you can
enjoy your breakfast. The top-floor rooms have been smartly decorated like
ship cabins, with a balcony that recalls the deck of an ocean cruiser. The
welcome is very courteous and attentive. Before leaving Villefranche, give
yourself a few minutes to walk about the tiny streets of the old village, just
behind the hotel. You'll find the fragrances of Italy here, and we're happy to
say that there are still places, just a few yards from the sea, that have escaped
the concrete jungle of the coast.

***How to get there*** *(Map 35): 6km from Nice via N559.*

## Le Mas d'Entremont

13090 Aix-en-Provence (Bouches-du-Rhône)
315, route nationale 7
Tel. (0)4.42.17.42.42 - Fax (0)4.42.21.15.83 - M. Marignane
E-mail: entremont@wanadoo.fr

**Category** ★★★★ **Rooms** 16 and 1 suite, with air-conditioning, telephone, bath, WC, minibar, safe and satellite TV. **Price** Single and double 670-1000F / 102,14-152,45€, suite 1400F / 213,43€ (2 pers.). **Meals** Breakfast 80F / 12,20€. **Restaurant** Service 12:30PM-2:00PM, 7:30PM-9:30PM; mealtime specials 210-250F / 32,01-38,11€, also à la carte. Specialties: Salade gourmande au foie gras; marmite de rascasse à la marseillaise. **Credit card** Visa. **Pets** Dogs allowed. **Facilities** Swimming pool, tennis, parking. **Nearby** Albertas Place, Hôtel de ville, Saint-Sauveur Cathedral (burning bush triptych by N. Froment) and Pavillon Vendôme in Aix-en-Provence; Roquefavour aqueduct – 18-hole Club des Milles golf course, 18-hole Fuveau golf course. **Open** Mar 14 – Oct 31.

For quite a long time now, *Le Mas d'Entremont* has been a restful, quiet, and verdant haven for vacationers. This is a great stone building, gently shaded by a manicured, flowery garden, and with open, inviting patios. A large fountain pool covered with water lillies offers that coolness so sought after in summer. In the house, the stone vaulting, great exposed beams and antique furniture play against a traditional atmosphere made from the most refined details. The rooms combine comfort and style with beautiful, polished antique furnishings and pleasant bathrooms. Most have a little terrace hidden away by abundant flowers and elegant, wrought-iron trellisses. Depending on the season, meals are taken in the inviting dining room, under the trees, or under tile-roofed arbor. You will enjoy subtle and fragrant Provençale cuisine. The fish really stands out. Thoughtful and courteous hospitality. A beautiful place to stay just 3 km from the heart of Aix.

***How to get there*** *(Map 33): After Aix, via N 7, heading toward Avignon.*

431

## Hôtel Le Pigonnet

13090 Aix-en-Provence (Bouches-du-Rhône)
5, avenue du Pigonnet
Tel. (0)4.42.59.02.90 - Fax (0)4.42.59.47.77 - MM. Swellen

**Category** ★★★★ **Rooms** 52 with telephone, bath or shower, WC, satellite TV and minibar – Elevator. **Price** Single and double 700-1650F / 106,71-251,54€; suite 2000F / 304,90€. **Meals** Breakfast 80-130F / 12,20-19,82€, served 7:00-11:00; half board +270F / 41,16€ (per pers., 3 days min.). **Restaurant** Closed Saturday lunchtime and Sunday lunchtime except Jul. Service 12:15PM-1:30PM, 7:15-9:30PM; mealtime specials 260-330F / 39,64-50,31€, also à la carte. Specialties: Baudroie du golf à la nîmoise, carré d'agneau rôti. **Credit cards** All major. **Pets** Dogs allowed. **Facilities** Swimming pool, parking. **Nearby** Albertas Place, Hôtel de ville, Saint-Sauveur Cathedral (burning bush triptych by N. Froment), Pavillon Vendôme in Aix-en-Provence; Roquefavour aqueduct – 18-hole Club des Milles golf course, 18-hole Fuveau golf course. **Open** All year.

Hôtel le Pigonnet has regained its intimate, familial atmosphere thanks to the two charming Swellen sons who have recently taken over and revitalized the hotel, profiting from their parents' long experience. Standing in the middle of a large park with a formal garden offering guests the historic view of the Mont Sainte-Victoire immortalized by Cézanne, the hotel is only some ten minutes from the center of Aix. In the lounges, a beautiful collection of paintings by Provençal artists and an elegant decor create an atmosphere of great comfort. The absolutely smashing rooms burst with charm and are found in the old house, the residence, and the villa (with two rooms, two bathrooms, and a lounge). For meals, guests may choose between the gastronomic cuisine served in the beautiful Riviera room overlooking the park, or lighter meals around the swimming pool or on the shady terrace.

***How to get there*** *( Map 33 ): A8 or A51, Aix/Pont-de-l'Arc exit, then to the town center and take the 3rd traffic light on the left (avenue Pigonnet).*

# Hôtel des Quatre-Dauphins

13100 Aix-en-Provence (Bouches-du-Rhône)
54, rue Roux-Alphéran
Tel. (0)4.42.38.16.39 - Fax (0)4.42.38.60.19
MM. Darricau and Juster

**Category** ★★ **Rooms** 12 with telephone, bath or shower, WC, TV and minibar. **Price** Single and double 295-420F / 44,97-64,12€, suite 520F / 79,27€ (3 pers.). **Meals** Breakfast 42F / 6,41€, served 7:00-10:00. No restaurant. **Credit cards** Visa, Eurocard and MasterCard. **Pets** Dogs allowed. **Nearby** In Aix-en-Provence: Albertas Place, Hôtel de ville, Saint-Sauveur Cathedral (burning bush triptych by N. Froment), Roquefavour aqueduct – 18-hole Club des Milles golf course, 18-hole Fuveau golf course. **Open** All year.

This three-story family house in a quiet side street near the famous Place des Quatre Dauphins in Aix has handily been converted into a hotel. On the ground floor there is a small reception area and a lounge which also serves as a breakfast room. The bedrooms are tiny and the closets basic but functional enough. Everything has been done with simplicity and much taste. The hotel, right in the center of town, is not air-conditioned, so if you need to close the window to block out the noise of the street in summer, you might be a bit hot. For restaurants try: *Maxime, Côté Cour* on the Cours Mirabeau; *L'Amphitryon* is good and very pleasing; *Le Petit Bistro Latin, Chez Gu,* and the gourmet *Clos de la Violette*; and don't forget to have a drink at the *Deux Garçons*. A charming restaurant, *Le Garde*, takes you to Vauvenargues for dinner in the heart of the country.

***How to get there*** *(Map 33): In the center of the town.*

## Villa Gallici

13100 Aix-en-Provence (Bouches-du-Rhône)
Avenue de la Violette
Tel. (0)4.42.23.29.23 - Fax (0)4.42.96.30.45
M. Gil Dez

**Category** ★★★★ **Rooms** 22 with air-conditioning, telephone, bath, WC, satellite TV, safe and minibar. **Price** Room and suite 1250-2950F / 190,56-449,72€. **Meals** Breakfast 80 and 100F / 12,20 and 15,24€. **Restaurant** Only for residents. Service 12:30PM-2:00PM, 7:30PM-9:30PM; also à la carte. Specialties: Regional cooking. **Credit cards** All major. **Pets** Dogs allowed (+100F / 15,24€). **Facilities** Swimming pool, parking. **Nearby** In Aix-en-Provence: Albertas Place, Hôtel de ville, Saint-Sauveur Cathedral (burning bush triptych by N. Froment); Roquefavour aqueduct – 18-hole Club des Milles golf course, 18-hole Fuveau Golf Course. **Open** All year.

In the *Villa Gallici*, Gil Dez found a bastide in which to exercise his talents as an interior decorator and create an elegant *hôtel de charme*. The villa has been decorated with exquisite style, and designed like a home rather than a hotel. The bedrooms are spacious, comfortable and individually decorated. *toile de Jouy* and gingham have been used in one, while another boasts a flowery cotton canopied bed along with boldly striped fabrics. In each room styles, colors and materials have been subtly and successfully combined. In the immaculate bathrooms, earthenware tiles, Carrara marble and glossy white wood panelling create an elegant decor. Breakfast beneath the plane trees is a delight. In an annex, new bedrooms have been added: veritable apartments which are even more luxurious. A place to remember that has blended charm and luxury. *Villa Gallici* is near *Le Clos de la Violette*, which should satisfy the most demanding of gastronomes.

***How to get there*** *(Map 33): Near the Archbishop's Palace (palais de l'archévèque).*

## Hôtel d'Arlatan

13200 Arles (Bouches-du-Rhône)
26, rue du Sauvage
Tel. (0)4.90.93.56.66 - Fax (0)4.90.49.68.45
M. Desjardin

**Category** ★★★ **Rooms** 48 with air-conditioning, telephone, bath, WC, satellite TV and minibar.
**Price** Double 498-850F / 76,22-129,58€, suite 980-1450F / 149,40-221,05€. **Meals** Breakfast 62F /
9,46€, served 7:00-11:00. No restaurant. **Credit cards** All major. **Pets** Dogs allowed. **Facilities**
Garage (+60-70F / 9,15-10,67€). **Nearby** Saint-Trophime Church and cloister, arenas, Alyscamps,
Réattu Museum in Arles, Abbey of Montmajour, the Camargue – 18-hole Servanes golf course in
Mouriès. **Open** All year.

Arles, the museum city has an archaeological counterpart in the *Hôtel
d'Arlatan*, where vestiges of the past span the centuries. Built on the
Basilica and the Baths of Constantine, the entire building is a veritable
architectural patchwork. The unique hotel, owned by the same family for three
generations, is regularly restored and renovated. It would indeed take a book
to describe the *Arlatan*'s bedrooms. Wall fragments from the fourth century
and beams from the eighteenth can be seen in Suite 43, and a monumental
17th-century fireplace in Suite 41. Ask for the rooms which have just been (very
well) redone and overlook the Rhône: Numbers 23 and 27 among others;
Room 34, with very beautiful stone walls and one of the least expensive; or one
of the suites, large or small. Nestling in a small street overlooking gardens, the
*Arlatan* is a hotel of singular character and charm. The most popular
restaurants in Arles are *L'Olivier* and *Le Vaccarès*. For a very fashionable spot,
try the restaurant or bar of the famous *Hôtel Nord-Pinus*.

*How to get there* ( *Map 33*): In the center of the town, signposted.

## Hôtel Calendal

13200 Arles (Bouches-du-Rhône)
22, place Pomme
Tel. (0)4.90.96.11.89 - Fax (0)4.90.96.05.84 - Mme Lespinasse-Jacquemin
Web: www.lecalendal.com - E-mail: contact@lecalendal.com

**Category** ★★ **Rooms** 27 with air-conditioning, telephone, bath, WC, satellite TV – Rooms for disabled persons. **Price** Double 290-420F / 44,21-64,12€, suite 450-500F / 68,60-76,22€. **Meals** Breakfast 40F / 6,10€, served 7:00-10:30 (buffet), 7:00-12:00PM (continental). **Tea Room** Slads, omelettes, English pastries. **Credit cards** All major. **Pets** Dogs allowed. **Facilities** Parking. **Nearby** Saint-Trophime Church, arenas, Alyscamps, Réattu Museum in Arles, Abbey of Montmajour, the Camargue – 18-hole Servanes golf course in Mouriès. **Open** All year.

Magnificiently located between the two main Roman ruins of Arles -- the ancient theater and the arenas (which some rooms overlook) -- this little hotel is a great base from which to easily explore the historic center. You get here by car, and because of parking problems, the hotel offers a card that lets you park on outer boulevards' parking lots. Recently renovated in traditional Provençal colors, the bedrooms are all spacious, fresh and spruce, and there are modern amenities in the bathrooms. The old-fashioned tea room, decorated with beautiful bullfight posters, serves light meals and delicious homemade pastries; in good weather, you will be served on the terrace or in a lovely garden shaded by palm trees and a two-century-old Provençal micoucoulier tree. The large garden is a real plus for this hotel in the center of town and is the perfect place to relax and have a drink away from the urban squall.

***How to get there*** *( Map 33 ): Near the arenas.*

## Grand Hôtel Nord-Pinus

13200 Arles (Bouches-du-Rhône)
Place du Forum
Tel. (0)4.90.93.44.44 - Fax (0)4.90.93.34.00 - Mme Igou
Web: www.nord-pinus.com - E-mail: info@nord-pinus.com

**Category** ★★★★ **Rooms** 25 with air-conditioning, telephone, bath, WC, TV and minibar. **Price** Double 840-990F / 128,06-150,92€, suite 1700F / 259,16€. **Meals** Breakfast 75F / 11,43€, served 7:00-11:00. **Restaurant** Service 12:00PM-2:00PM, 7:30PM-10:00PM; mealtime specials 120-180F / 18,29-27,44€, also à la carte. **Credit cards** All major. **Pets** Dogs allowed. **Nearby** Réattu Museum in Arles, Abbey of Montmajour, the Camargue – 18-hole Servanes golf course in Mouriès. **Open** All year.

Like Giono, you might wonder; "Why Pinus? Nord, I understand, but Pinus? It was simply the name of the founder. Nothing is more logical. I now realize that I have entered the land of the imagination and fantasy." Picasso, Cocteau, Dominguez are just some of the famous names in the visitors' book. The hotel was run for some time by Germaine, a *chanteuse*, and Nello, a famous clown, both of whom were well-known characters in Arles. When they died, the hotel lost its soul. It has returned under the care of Anne Igou, whose love for the place has brought back the magic and atmosphere, aided by a skillful restoration combining sensitivity and good taste. The bedrooms are large, with pretty furniture and Provençal fabrics, and the bathrooms have every facility. It is worth remembering to ask for Suite 10 or the bedrooms looking onto the courtyard; these are recommended for people who are concerned about the noise on the Place du Forum in summer. This is truly a charming hotel.

***How to get there*** *( Map 33 ): In the town center.*

# Hôtel Castel-Mouisson

13570 Barbentane (Bouches-du-Rhône)
Quartier Castel-Mouisson
Tel. (0)4.90.95.51.17 - Fax (0)4.90.95.67.63
Mme Mourgue

**Category** ★★ **Rooms** 17 with telephone, bath and WC. **Price** Double 280-400F / 42,69-60,98€. **Meals** Breakfast 40F / 6,10€, served 8:00-10:30. No restaurant. **Credit cards** All major. **Pets** Dogs not allowed. **Facilities** Swimming pool, tennis, parking. **Nearby** Barbentane Château, Avignon, Villeneuve-lès-Avignon, Abbey of Saint-Michel-de-Frigolet – 18-hole Châteaublanc golf course, 18-hole Vedène golf course in Grand Avignon, 4-hole Lou Compact golf course in Barbentane. **Open** Mar 1 – Oct 31.

This peaceful and reasonably priced hotel is at the foot of the Montagnette Mountain not far from Avignon. It was built twenty years ago in the style of a Provençal farmhouse and is surrounded by tranquil countryside. There are cypresses and fruit trees growing beneath the grey cliffs of the Montagnette, which overlooks the valley. Brightened with Provençal fabrics, the bedrooms are simple but reasonably comfortable. In hot weather you will enjoy cooling off in the pretty swimming pool. In Avignon, there are numerous good small restaurants such as *La Fourchette, L'Entrée des Artistes,* as well as charming places for lunch such as the *Les Félibres* tearoom and bookshop, *Le Bain Marie* and *Simple Simon.* For a lovely dinner, try the restaurant in the *Mirande Hotel* or *La Vieille Fontaine* in the *Hôtel d'Europe.*

***How to get there*** *(Map 33): 8km southwest of Avignon via N570, then D35 towards Tarascon along the Rhône.*

## Les Roches Blanches

13260 Cassis (Bouches-du-Rhône)
Route des Calanques
Tel. (0)4.42.01.09.30 - Fax (0)4.42.01.94.23 - M. Dellacase

**Category** ★★★★ **Rooms** 24 with telephone, bath or shower, WC, TV and minibar – Elevator. **Price** Single and double 480-970F / 73,18-147,88€, suite 1150-1350F / 175,32-205,81€. **Meals** Breakfast 75F / 11,45€, served 7:15-10:30. **Restaurant** Service 12:30PM-2:00PM, 7:30PM-9:30PM; mealtime specials 200-230F / 30,49-35,06€, also à la carte. Specialties: Provençale cooking. **Credit cards** All major. **Pets** Dogs allowed. **Facilities** Swimming pool, parking. **Nearby** The Calanques – 18-hole Frégate Golf Course, 18-hole Salette golf course in La Penne-sur-Huveaune. **Open** Mid Feb – mid Nov.

*L*es Roches Blanches is a former town house built in 1885 and then transformed into a hotel in 1930. Built next to the rocky inlets (*calanques*) of Cassis, this large house combines the charm of a beach hotel--the terraced garden slopes down to the water, where you can swim--with the charm of a family house whose large dining-room windows overlook the sea. The bedrooms are all comfortable, and some have terraces looking out over pine trees and either the sea or Cape Canaille. Very nicely renovated, the rooms marry up cheerful colors and Louis-Philippe style furnishings in painted wicker or cherrywood. Many have access to wonderful terraces overlooking the sea. In their concern for preserving the old charm of the house, the owners have kept several pieces of 1930s furniture, the door and the vast stairway in Art Déco wrought iron, and the pretty faïence mosaic tables of the garden. There is a very beautiful overflow swimming pool which plays against the deep-blue sea that beats against the rocks just a few meters below.

***How to get there*** *( Map 33 ): 23km east of Marseille via A50 towards Toulon, Cassis exit. In summer you cannot cross the village, so take the Calanques road and Le Bestouan beach.*

## Hôtel La Bastide

13810 Eygalières (Bouches-du-Rhône)
Chemin de Pestelade, route d'Orgon
Tel. (0)4.90.95.90.06 - Fax (0)4.90.95.99.77
Nathalie Calabrese

**Category** ★★★ **Rooms** 12 with telephone, bath or shower, WC, satellite TV and 10 with safe – 1 forr disabled persons **Price** Double 380-480F / 57,93-73,18€. **Meals** Breakfast 45F / 6,86€, served 8:00-10:30. No restaurant. **Credit card** Visa. **Pets** Small dogs allowed by reservation. **Facilities** Swimming pool, parking. **Nearby** Les Baux; Saint-Rémy-de-Provence; Fontvieille – 18-hole Servanes golf course in Mouriès. **Closed** Jan.

Here is a delicious little hotel, perfect for your stays in this wondrous region. In a 30-km radius, you have Les Baux, Saint-Remy, the Luberon, Arles, and Avignon. *La Bastide* is a sturdy, rambling house. Its beautiful, cool entryway opens up to a stairway that splits in two to serve the rooms in the two wings. Whether on the ground floor or upstairs, the rooms are discreetly comfortable, well-looked-after, and have a magnificient view of the countryside. The garden is made of olive trees and a thicket of lavender, thyme, and rosemary. The lounge, with its little couches next to Provençal settees, takes part in the soft peace and quiet that reigns everywhere here. For dinner, you have an abundance of options, with many great places nearby (*L'Auberge Provençale*, *Les Micocouliers*, *La Maison d'Adeline*, the *Crin Blanc*, and the *Bistrot d'Eygalières*). Finally, the kind welcome of Nathalie Calabrese adds a special touch to the place.

***How to get there*** *(Map 33): 13 km southwest of Cavaillon via A 7. Take Cavaillon exit, heading toward Saint-Remy. After Plan-d'Orgon, head toward Eygalieres. Once in the town, take the road to Orgon.*

## Mas doù Pastré

13810 Eygalières (Bouches-du-Rhône)
Quartier Saint-Sixte
Tel. (0)4.90.95.92.61 - Fax (0)4.90.90.61.75
M. and Mme Roumanille

**Rooms** 11 with telephone, bath or shower, WC, TV and 5 with minibar. **Price** Double 350-690F / 53,36-105,19€, suite (4 pers.) 1150F / 175,32€. **Meals** Breakfast 55F / 8,38€, served 8:00-10:30. No restaurant. In summer, salads served in garden. **Credit cards** All major. **Pets** Dogs not allowed. **Facilities** Heated swimming pool, whirlpool, winter garden, parking. **Nearby** Les Baux, Saint-Rémy-de-Provence, Fontvieille – 18-hole Servanes golf course in Mouriès. **Open** All year.

Mme Roumanille, who has just renovated this old farmhouse as she would have her own home, is a friendly and hospitable hostess. Throughout the house, the ceilings and walls are decked out in Provençal colors, and there is a wealth of antique furniture, paintings, engravings, prints, and local curios-enough to make you feel even better than you would at home. The evocatively named bedrooms are all different: their decor owes much to carefully chosen furnishings, and to the owners' boundless imagination in adding a touch of exuberance and humor. You can also sleep in an authentic, elaborately carved wooden trailer, which is very old but equipped with air-conditioning and every modern comfort. Breakfast is delicious (there are always fresh fruit juices), whether you have it outside or in the charming dining room. This is an excellent and very Provençal hotel. *L'Auberge Provençale* is the famous restaurant in Eygalières (whose hospitality, however, doesn't match), and the fashionable spot is *Sous les Micocouliers*.

***How to get there*** *( Map 33 ): 13km southeast of Cavaillon via A7, Cavaillon exit, then D99 and D74a.*

## Le Relais de la Magdeleine

13420 Gémenos (Bouches-du-Rhône)
Route d'Aix-en-Provence
Tel. (0)4.42.32.20.16 - Fax (0)4.42.32.02.26
M. and Mme Marignane

**Category** ★★★★ **Rooms** 24 with telephone, bath or shower, WC and TV. **Price** Double 600-890F / 91,47-135,68€, suite 1200F / 182,94€. **Meals** Breakfast 75F / 11,43€, served from 7:15; half board 680-780F / 103,67-118,91€ (per pers., 3 days min.). **Restaurant** Service 12:00PM-2:00PM, 8:00PM-9:30PM; mealtime specials 250F / 38,11€, also à la carte. Specialties: Galettes de grenouilles à la provençale; pavé de canard au miel de lavande; griottes au chocolat sauce pistache. **Credit cards** Visa, Eurocard and MasterCard. **Pets** Dogs allowed (+30F / 4,57€) but not in the swimming pool. **Facilities** Swimming pool, parking. **Nearby** Marseille, Aix-en-Provence, Cassis and the Calanques – 18-hole La Salette golf course in Marseille-La Valentine. **Open** Mar 15 – Nov 30.

To find this beautiful 18th-century country house covered in ivy and roses, you leave the highway, drive along an avenue of century-old plane trees and cross a formal garden designed by Le Nôtre. Monsieur and Madame Marignane, whose family has been in the hotel business for three generations, also love furniture and paintings. So the reception areas sport a superb collection of 17th- and 18th-century pieces, and each room's decor corresponds to a specific period. The ground-floor restaurant, run by the couple's son, offers a refined and cannily inventive fare. Just a few kilometers from Marseille and Aix-en-Provence, *Le Relais* is a one-of-a-kind and elegant place, which has avoided the trap of that trendy, "art deco" look. Really terrific hospitality.

*How to get there (Map 33): 23km from Marseille via A50 towards Toulon, Aubagne-Est or Aubagne-Sud exit, then D2 to Gémenos.*

## Le Mas de Peint

Le Sambuc 13200 Arles (Bouches-du-Rhône)
Tel. (0)4.90.97.20.62 - Fax (0)4.90.97.22.20
M. Bon
E-mail: peint@avignon.pacwan.net

**Rooms** 8 and 3 suites with air-conditioning, telephone, bath, WC, minibar, safe, and satellite TV. **Price** Double 1195-1550F / 182,18-236,30€; suite 1880-2180F / 286,60-332,34€. **Meals** Breakfast 100F / 15,24€, served 8:00-10:30. **Restaurant** By reservation. Service 12:00PM-1:30PM, 8:00PM-9:00PM; mealtime specials 190F / 28,97€ (lunch), 245F / 37,35€ (dinner). Specialties: Farm-fresh produce; home-raised beef; country rice. **Credit cards** All major. **Pets** Dogs allowed (+120F / 18,29€). **Facilities** Swimming pool, mountain bikes rentals, horseback tours, parking. **Nearby** Saintes-Maries-de-la-Mer (gypsy pilgrimage, May 24 and 25), Arles (féria for Easter) – 18-hole La Grande Motte golf course. **Closed** Jan 10 – Mar 10.

The *Mas de Peint* is a formidable compromise between the friendliness of a Camargue guest house and the modern accommodations of a luxurious hotel of character and charm. The owner of a famous herd of horses and bulls, Jacques Bon, is always proud to discuss (and show) his 1235 acres devoted to growing rice and breeding horses and bulls. Mme Bon has contributed her art as a talented architect and interior decorator to the Mas de Peint, which feels like a house for entertaining friends. There is a large table with a bouquet of fresh flowers in the entrance, and a comfortable sofa surrounded by bookshelves. You will find a small reading room and a larger room with a fireplace. In the kitchen, guests gather for an informal meal offering regional specialties. The bedrooms are extraordinarily large, some have bathrooms on a mezzanine, and every room has its personal charm.

***How to get there*** *(Map 33): 20km south of Arles via D36, towards Salin-de-Giraud; at the exit from Sambuc, 3km to the left.*

443

## Auberge de La Benvengudo

13520 Les Baux-de-Provence (Bouches-du-Rhône)
Tel. (0)4.90.54.32.54 - Fax (0)4.90.54.42.58
Famille Beaupied
E-mail: benvengudo@aol.com

**Category** ★★★ **Rooms** 22 with air-conditioning, telephone, bath or shower, WC and TV. **Price** Double 600-900F / 91,47-137,20€, suite 950F / 144,83€. **Meals** Breakfast 65F / 9,91€, served 7:30-10:00; half board 1170-1520F / 178,37-231,72€ (per 2 pers., 3 days min.). **Restaurant** Closed Sunday. Service 7:30PM-9:30PM; mealtime specials 240F / 36,59€. Specialties: Croustillant de ris d'agneau au coulis de tomate fraîches; pavé de mérou de méditerranée basilic rouge; soufflé glacé au marc de Châteauneuf-du-Pape. **Credit cards** Amex, Visa. **Pets** Small dogs allowed (+55F / 8,38€). **Facilities** Swimming pool, tennis, lawn bowling, parking. **Nearby** Contemporary Art Museum at the Hôtel des Porcelets in Les Baux, Queen Jeanne's pavilion, Alphonse Daudet's windmill in Fontvieille, the Val d'Enfer – 9-hole golf course in Les Baux, 18-hole Servanes golf course in Mouriès. **Open** Feb – Nov 1.

The Benvengudo nestles at the foot of the strange and beautiful Alpilles, whose jagged outline is reminiscent of some of the highest mountain peaks in the world, while their white rocks and vegetation lend an air of Greece to this part of Provence. Built twenty-one years ago, the mas seems to have been here forever. The bedrooms, all air-conditioned, are very comfortable, each with its style and its color scheme, and some with small private terraces. The lounge and dining room are decorated in lovely Provençal style. The son of the family is the chef, preparing dinners of savory regional recipes; for lunch in summer, there is a small menu of fresh salads. Prices might have changed, so best to ask when you reserve your room.

*How to get there (Map 33): 30km south of Avignon via A7, Cavaillon exit, then D99 to Saint-Rémy and D5 to Baux and D78 toward Arles.*

# L'Oustaloun

13520 Maussane-les-Alpilles (Bouches-du-Rhône)
Place de l'Eglise
Tel. (0)4.90.54.32.19 - Fax (0)4.90.54.45.57
M. and Mme Fabregoul

**Category** ★★ **Rooms** 10 with telephone, bath or shower, WC and 6 with TV. **Price** Double 295-420F / 44,97-64,12€. **Meals** Breakfast 40F / 6,10€, served 7:40-9:30. **Restaurant** Service 12:15PM-1:30PM, 7:15PM-9:30PM; mealtime specials 105F / 16,01€, 130-150F / 19,82-22,87€, also à la carte. Specialties: Provençale and Italian cooking. **Credit cards** Amex, Visa. **Pets** Dogs allowed. **Facilities** Parking. **Nearby** Avignon, Arles, Saint-Rémy-de-Provence, Les Baux and the Val d'enfer, Alphonse Daudet's windmill in Fontvieille – 9-hole golf course in les Baux, 18-hole Servanes golf course in Mouriès. **Closed** Jan 8 – mid Feb.

In 1792, this was the first town hall of the village, then the gendarmerie (and the prison). Today, *L'Oustaloun* is a typical small Provençal *auberge* looking out on - what else? - a square shaded with towering plane trees and a babbling fountain. The bedrooms are lovely and comfortable; all are decorated with Provençal fabrics and antique furniture. All the bathrooms have been renovated. One of the two rustic dining rooms is in the former "chapel", the other was the old olive-pressing room. With the first good weather, the *Oustaloun* spills out to the center of the square, where a bar-terrace is set up, shaded by large parasols. This is a charming spot just several minutes out of spectacular (and gastronomically acclaimed) town of Les Baux. The prices are reasonable and you will be welcomed with a very warm Provençal smile.

***How to get there*** *(Map 33): 40km south of Avignon via A7, exit Cavaillon, then D99 to Saint-Rémy and D5.*

## Le Pré des Baux

13520 Maussane-les-Alpilles (Bouches-du-Rhône)
8, rue du Vieux-Moulin
Tel. (0)4.90.54.40.40 - Fax (0)4.90.54.53.07
M. Pinchinat

**Category** ★★★ **Rooms** 10 with wheelchair access, air-conditioning, telephone, bath or shower, WC and TV. **Price** Double 450-500F / 68,60-76,22€, 3 pers. 650-700F / 99,09-106,71€. **Meals** Breakfast 60F / 9,15€, served 8:00-11:00. No restaurant. **Credit cards** Amex, Visa. **Pets** Dogs allowed (30F / 4,57€). **Facilities** Swimming pool, parking. **Nearby** Les Baux; Alpilles; Camargue – 2 golf courses (6km). **Open** Mid Mar – beg Nov.

Since its creation some ten years ago, *Le Pré* has managed to become both a village hotel and verdant little oasis of peace and calm. The ten rooms open onto the swimming pool area, which you get to by an anterior gangway, which reduces bothersome foot traffic. With their buoyant white walls and floors, the rooms are brightened up by colored rattan armchairs in the corner lounge. The bathrooms are pleasant and well-cared-for. Each room has a little shady terrace overlooking the garden that surrounds the pool. It is tranquil and restful here. The availability of Monsieur Pinchinat and his precious advice make this a particularly good place to stay while you discover the wonders of the area, such as the Camargue of Avignon, and from Saint-Remy to Aix-en-Provence, there is no wont of places to stroll. For dinner, *La Petite France* and *Le Margaux* are nearby, but there are many other great restaurants in the area.

***How to get there*** *( Map 33 ): 40 km south of Avignon via A 7. Take Cavaillon exit, then D 99 until Saint-Remy, then head toward Maussane. The hotel is 50 m to your right, on the little path across from the stop sign.*

## Le Berger des Abeilles

13670 Saint-Andiol (Bouches-du-Rhône)
Tel. (0)4.90.95.01.91 - Fax (0)4.90.95.48.26
Mme Grenier
E-mail: berger-des-abeilles@epicuria.fr

**Category** ★★ **Rooms** 6 with telephone, bath or shower, WC and TV. **Price** Single and double 320 and 370F / 48,78 and 56,41€. **Meals** Breakfast 60F / 9,15€, served 8:00-10:00; half board 480F / 73,18€ (1 pers.), 740F / 112,81€ (2 pers., 3 days min.). **Restaurant** Closed Monday lunchtime except for residents. Service 12:30PM-1:30PM, 8:00PM-9:30PM; mealtime specials 140-250F / 21,34-38,11€, also à la carte. Specialties: Provençale cooking; mousse au miel de lavande; vieux marc de Provence. **Credit cards** Amex, Visa, Eurocard and MasterCard. **Pets** Dogs allowed (50F / 7,62€). **Facilities** Parking. **Nearby** Les Baux, Saint-Rémy-de-Provence, Avignon. **Closed** Jan – Feb 10.

*L*e Berger des Abeilles is as welcoming as a hotel could possibly be. There are only six bedrooms and so the owners provide a personal style of service. All the rooms are perfectly comfortable, but you should choose our favorites if they're available, "Alexia" or "Caroline". (The rooms are named after the women in the family.) A few items of period furniture set the trend for the cheerful, intimate decor. Mme Grenier does the cooking herself and her cuisine has an excellent reputation. Dinner is served in a beautiful, rustic dining-room or outside in the shade of a gigantic plane tree. The noise of traffic on the main road, muffled by luxuriant vegetation, can hardly be heard in the hotel garden, and not at all indoors (thanks to the thick walls). This is a lovely place to stay.

***How to get there*** *(Map 33): 13km south of Avignon via N7 (2km from north of Saint-Andiol). On A7, Avignon-Sud exit, towards Cabannes, 5km south then towards Salon, Marseille.*

## Château de Roussan

13210 Saint-Rémy-de-Provence (Bouches-du-Rhône)
Tel. (0)4.90.92.11.63 - Fax (0)4.90.92.50.59
Mme McHugo
E-mail: chateau.de.roussan.@wanadoo.fr

**Rooms** 21 with telephone, bath or shower and WC – Wheelchair access. **Price** Double 440-750F / 67,08-114,34€. **Meals** Breakfast 60-80F / 9,15-12,20€, served 8:00-11:00; half board 415-575F / 63,27-87,66€ (per pers., 3 days min.). **Restaurant** Closed lunchtime in winter. Service 12:00PM-2:00PM, 7:30PM-9:30PM; mealtime specials and menu 145-170F / 22,11-25,92€. **Credit cards** Amex, Visa. **Pets** Dogs allowed. **Facilities** Parking. **Nearby** Museum Frédéric-Mistral in Maillane, Eygalières, les Baux, Avignon, Arles – 18-hole Servanes golf course in Mouriès. **Open** All year.

An avenue of superb, century-old plane trees leads up to this fanciful house which was built at the beginning of the 18th-century by the Marquis of Ganges. A hotel since 1951, the château has nevertheless retained all its original character. The salons, the dining room, the library, and many bedrooms are still furnished with beautiful antiques; and the floors still have beautiful old parquet and terra-cotta tiles. Also furnished with antiques, many of the bedrooms have charming storage niches and alcove beds. The interior decoration might not be to everyone's taste. There is an old-fashioned atmosphere here, a neglected and even dilapidated surrounding that will appeal only to those who love the charms of history and old places. They will certainly enjoy the magic of the château. However, avoid the *Laurier Rose* and *Lila* bedrooms, and don't expect much of the bathrooms. The château is surrounded by a 15-acre park, an orange grove, a basin, and a lake with a small island. It is said that the elegant Marquis used to give sumptuous suppers here.

***How to get there*** *( Map 33 ): 14km west of Cavaillon via A7, exit Cavaillon, then D99; 2km from Saint-Rémy on Tarascon road.*

## Château des Alpilles

13210 Saint-Rémy-de-Provence (Bouches-du-Rhône)
Ancienne route des Baux
Tel. (0)4.90.92.03.33 - Fax (0)4.90.92.45.17 - Mmes Bon
E-mail: chateau.alpilles@wanadoo.fr

**Category** ★★★★ **Rooms** 19 with air-conditioning, telephone, bath, WC, TV, and minibar.
**Price** Single and double 975-1200F / 148,64-182,94€, suite 1490-2000F / 227,15-304,90€. **Meals**
Breakfast 90F / 13,72€, served 7:30-11:30. Snacks available with reservation, also à la carte;
mealtime specials199-250F / 30,49-38,11€. **Credit cards** All major. **Pets** Dogs allowed (+50F /
7,62€). **Facilities** Swimming pool, tennis, sauna, parking. **Nearby** Frédéric Mistral Museum in
Maillane, Eygalières, Les Baux, Avignon, Arles – 9-hole golf course in Les Baux, 18-hole Servanes golf
course in Mouriès. **Closed** Nov 13 – Dec 28 and Jan 6 – Feb 17.

The château was built at the beginning of the 19th century by one of the
oldest families of Arles and became the meeting place of politicians and
writers staying in the region. The lounge, the bar, and the dining room, richly
decorated with plasterwork and mirrors, are all very pleasant rooms and open
out onto the garden. Their contemporary furniture (sofas and armchairs
upholstered in deep-red leather) harmonize well with this decor; the impressive
white ensemble in the dining room will delight those who like the Knoll style
but will perhaps shock others less sensitive to 1970s design. The bedrooms are
much more classic with their antique or period furniture, charming, tasteful
decoration, and large, functional bathrooms. If you wish to stay at the hotel for
dinner, you can enjoy simple but refined cuisine. The large park, with a
swimming pool and tennis courts, is planted with many trees, some a century
old and others of rare species.

***How to get there*** *(Map 33): 14km west of Cavaillon via A7, exit Cavaillon, then
D99; 1km from Saint-Rémy-de-Provence.*

# Domaine de Valmouriane

13210 Saint-Rémy-de-Provence (Bouches-du-Rhône)
Petite route des Baux
Tel. (0)4.90.92.44.62 - Fax (0)4.90.92.37.32 - M. and Mme McHugo
E-mail: domdeval@wanadoo.fr

**Category** ★★★★ **Rooms** 14 with air-conditioning, telephone, bath, and satellite TV – Elevator; 1 for disabled persons. **Price** Double 590-1350F / 89,94-205,81€; family rooms 1160-1550F / 176,84-236,30€. **Meals** Breakfast 70F / 10,67€, served 7:00-10:30; half board +300F / 45,73€ (per pers.). **Restaurant** Service 12:15PM-1:30PM, 7:45PM-9:30PM; mealtime specials 160F / 24,39€ (lunchtime weekdays), 230 and 290F / 35,06 and 44,21€; also à la carte. Specialties: Mini-ratatouille en croûte de raviolis. **Credit cards** All major. **Pets** Dogs allowed (+50F / 7,62€). **Facilities** Swimming pool, tennis, parking. **Nearb** Frédéric Mistral Museum in Maillane – 8-hole Servanes golf course in Mouriès. **Open** All year.

In the heart of a valley protected by the Alpilles, surrounded by great pines and a delightful rock garden accented by Mediterranean plants, this hotel is a huge bastide with thick walls. For a long time, it was the home of the car racer Olivier Gendebien. When you walk in, you will be stunned by the atmosphere of the house. The refined luxury of the 14 rooms (2 have a terrace, and 3 ground-floor rooms have their own entrance) remind us that everything here is of the highest quality. The inviting little bar with its dark panelling, the huge upstairs lounge, and the terrace are places dedicated to pleasure, rest, and relaxation. The active crowd might want to have a tennis match before cooling off in the swimming pool, sheltered from the wind. The restaurant is not the least charming thing about this hotel. You will enjoy inventive and light gourmet food in the Provençale style. Madame McHugo and her team are courteous and attentive.

***How to get there*** *(Map 33): Via A7, take Cavaillon exit, then D99. Before Saint-Rémy take the road towards Beaucaire, then D27 via Les Baux. The Hotel 2km away.*

# Le Mas des Carassins

13210 Saint-Rémy-de-Provence (Bouches-du-Rhône)
1, chemin Gaulois
Tel. (0)4.90.92.15.48 - Fax (0)4.90.92.63.47
M. and Mme Ripert

**Category** ★★★ **Rooms** 10 with telephone, bath and WC – Wheelchair access. **Price** Double 400-600F / 60,98-91,47€. **Meals** Breakfast 57F / 8,7€, served 8:00-9:30. No restaurant. **Credit cards** Visa, Eurocard and MasterCard. **Pets** Dogs not allowed. **Facilities** Parking. **Nearby** Frédéric Mistral Museum in Maillane, Eygalières, Les Baux, Avignon, Arles – 9-hole golf course in Les Baux, 18-hole Servanes golf course in Mouriès. **Open** Apr – end Oct.

This 19th-century farm is now a small family hotel. It is just outside the center of Saint-Rémy-de-Provence in what has become the residential quarter. In its pretty garden, however, you can imagine yourself in the middle of the country. The bedrooms are all different. In *Magnaneraie*, for example, there is a rustic ambiance with stone walls, while the *Jassé* room is the only one with a terrace. There is a pretty dining room and a small, pleasant lounge with cane furniture. There is no restaurant, but if you are staying in the hotel, the helpful Mme Ripert will prepare a snack for you. The restaurants we recommend are: *Bistrot des Alpilles, Café des Arts, Jardin de Frédéric* in the village, or *L'Oustalet Maïenen* in Maillane.

***How to get there*** *(Map 33): 14km west of Cavaillon. A7, take Cavaillon exit, then D99.*

## Hostellerie de Cacharel

13460 Saintes-Maries-de-la-Mer (Bouches-du-Rhône)
Route de Cacharel
Tel. (0)4.90.97.95.44 - Fax (0)4.90.97.87.97
M. Colomb de Daunant

**Category** ★★★ **Rooms** 15 with telephone, bath or shower and WC. **Price** Single and double 580F / 88,42€. **Meals** Breakfast 50F / 7,62€, served 8:00-10:00. Snacks available: 85F / 12,98€ "country plate". **Credit cards** Visa, Eurocard and MasterCard. **Pets** Dogs allowed. **Facilities** Swimming pool, horse trekking, parking. **Nearby** Church of Saintes-Maries-de-la-Mer, gypsy pilgrimage (May 24 and 25), seawall (30km), Arles – 18-hole Servanes golf course in Mouriès. **Open** All year.

Lovers of nature, wide open spaces, and the authenticity, this is the hotel for you. Located in the Camargue nature reserve, in the midst of pools, meadows, and marshes, this great stone house looks like it has been here since the beginning of time. You'll love the age-old feeling in the common room, with its adjoining corner lounge and huge fireplace framed by two stone benches, where breakfast and light meals are served. You'll ponder over the photos of the Camargue landscape and bullfight scenes taken by the owner's father. If you ask Monsieur Colomb about the rich local culture and fine regional restaurants, you'll receive precious advice about how to get to know the real Camargue. Opening out to a shady garden, the elegant, sober, and highly pleasant rooms are all in white, of a good size and overlook a wild and highly fascinating landscape. There is also a huge pool protected by white walls, as well as horses for the pleasure of the guests. A very beautiful and authentic place to stay.

***How to get there*** *(Map 33): 38km southwest of Arles. 4km north of Saintes-Maries-de-la-Mer by D85a, called the Route de Cacharel.*

## Mas du Clarousset

13460 Saintes-Maries-de-la-Mer (Bouches-du-Rhône)
Route de Cacharel
Tel. (0)4.90.97.81.66 - Fax (0)4.90.97.88.59
Mme Eysette

**Category** ★★★ **Rooms** 10 with telephone, bath, WC, TV and minibar. **Price** Single and double 780-970F / 118,91-147,88€. **Meals** Breakfast 60F / 9,15€, served 7:00-11:00; half board 960-1510F / 146,35-230,20€ (1-3 pers.). **Restaurant** Closed Monday lunchtime and Tuesday lunchtime. Service 12:00PM-2:00PM (by reservation), 8:00PM-10:00PM; mealtime specials 180-350F / 27,44-53,36€, also à la carte. Specialties: Sufrigi aux croûtons; terrine de canard sauvage; loup en croûte. **Credit cards** All major. **Pets** Dogs allowed (+50F / 7,62€). **Facilities** Swimming pool, gypsy evenings (on request), private garage. **Nearby** Church of Saintes-Maries-de-la-Mer, gypsy pilgrimage (May 24 and 25), sea wall (30km), Arles – 18-hole La Grande Motte golf course. **Closed** Nov 15 – Dec 16.

If you want to life the Provençale life and keep the memory of Frederic Mistral, who made this culture well-known, then the *Mas du Clarousset* is the place to do it. Henriette is the heart of this hotel; her family's heirlooms decorate the inviting fireplace nook in the lounge, and i she concocts some good local specialities in the kitchen. If you don't take the half-board plan, best to reserve a table if you decide to eat here. The ten ground-floor rooms run the length of the annex. They are comfortable, soberly outfitted, and personalized by antique cabinets. Each opens onto covered terrace with a sweeping view of the Camargue. Henriette, who knows everything about this area, will let you in on all the secret places here. A cozy, little hotel that will win you over with its hospitality.

***How to get there*** *(Map 33): 38km southwest of Arles, then D85a (7km from Saintes-Maries).*

## Logis du Guetteur

83460 Les Arcs-sur-Argens (Var)
Place du Château
Tel. (0)4.94.99.51.10 - Fax (0)4.94.99.51.29
M. Callegari

**Category** ★★★ **Rooms** 10 with air-conditioning, telephone, bath or shower, WC, TV and minibar. **Price** Double 600-800F / 91,47-121,96€. **Meals** Breakfast 48F / 7,62€, served 8:00-10:30; half board 500F / 76,22€, (per pers., 2 days min.). **Restaurant** Service 12:00PM and 7:15PM; mealtime specials 150-350F / 22,87-53,36€, also à la carte. Specialties: Saumon fourré à l'écrevisse; Saint-Jacques au beurre de muscat; pigeon de ferme aux truffes; ris de veau aux oranges, bourride. **Credit cards** All major. **Pets** Dogs allowed (+30F / 4,57€). **Facilities** Swimming pool, parking. **Nearby** Sainte-Rosaline Chapel (4km from Arcs), Château of Entrecasteaux, Thoronet Abbey, Seillans, Simon Segal Museum in Aups – Saint-Andiol golf course. **Closed** Jan 15 – Feb 15.

The old 11th-century Château du Villeneuve, houses the *Logis*. However, it was restored in 1970, and its rough stone medieval walls have been preserved. Upon your arrival, from the porch, you'll find a round courtyard, with an old stone well in its center, that embraces the entire region. In your comfortable, pleasantly furnished bedroom, you can be assured that no enemies will scale the castle walls. On the contrary, you can relax and take in the magnificent, panoramic views. The dining room, which is in the old cellars, has a covered terrace that looks out over the charming belltower and rooftops below. There is a lovely swimming pool, delicious cuisine, and a very kind welcome.

***How to get there*** *( Map 34): 12km south of Draguignan via N555 and D555; in the medieval village.*

## Hostellerie de la Reine Jeanne

RN 98 Forêt du Dom
83230 Bormes-les-Mimosas (Var)
Tel. (0)4.94.15.00.83 - Fax (0)4.94.64.77.89
M. Roux - Mme Héry

**Category** ★★★ **Rooms** 8 with telephone, bath or shower, WC, TV and minibar. **Price** Single and double 700-800F / 106,71-121,96€. **Meals** Breakfast 70F / 10,67€; half board 590F / 89,94€ (per pers., 3 days min.). **Restaurant** Closed Sunday evening and Monday lunchtime in low season. Service 12:00PM and 7:30PM; mealtime specials 170-300F / 25,92-45,73€; also à la carte. **Credit card** Visa. **Pets** Dogs allowed. **Facilities** Swimming pool, parking. **Nearby** Chartreuse de la Verne, Forest of Dom, Gulf of Saint-Tropez. **Closed** Jan.

Lying in the heart of the Dom Forest along the road to Saint Tropez, this inn offers bedrooms that have been intelligently arranged: you won't be disturbed by the traffic. Spacious and comfortably designed in an often retro style, all overlook a wood of pines and oaks with a little garden in the foreground, not far from a reflecting pool with fountains. Three ground-level rooms open directly onto the garden, and the others have a terrace. The group of buildings is arranged around a spacious, superbly furnished patio and a canopy that houses an enormous grill, as well as a shiny Harley Davidson. The grill is not just a key part of the decor; stoked and smoking at mealtime, it calls out to the hungry guests with its suckling pig slowly turning on a spit. (We also recommend the house speciality of grilled meats.) A great place midway between Toulon and Saint-Tropez, loving cared for by Madame Hery. Relaxed and hospitable mood.

***How to get there*** *(Map 34): 42 km fro Toulon. Head toward Hyeres-Saint-Tropez on N 98 through the Dom Forest.*

## Hostellerie Bérard

83740 La Cadière-d'Azur (Var)
Rue Gabriel-Péri
Tel. (0)4.94.90.11.43 - Fax (0)4.94.90.01.94 - Mme Bérard
E-mail: berard@hotel-berard.com - Web: www.hotel-berard.com

**Category** ★★★ **Rooms** 40 with air-conditioning, telephone, bath, WC, TV and minibar. **Price** Single and double 480-800F / 73,18-121,96€, suite 900-1200F / 137,20-182,94€. **Meals** Breakfast 90F / 13,72€, served 7:30-9:30. **Restaurant** Closed Monday lunchtime and Jan 4 – Feb 4. Service 12:30PM-2:00PM, 7:30PM-9:30PM; mealtime specials 85-120 / 12,96-18,29€ (lunch), 180-450F / 27,44-68,60€, also à la carte. Specialties: Lotte piquée aux anchois frais; filet de bœuf au mourvédre et fondue d'échalotes; glace au fenouil. **Credit cards** All major. **Pets** Dogs allowed (except in the room) (+40F / 6,10€). **Facilities** Swimming pool, sauna, fitness center, watercolor classes, cooking school, parking and garage. **Nearby** Cassis; Porquerolles Island; Bandol, village of Le Castellet, beach (3km) – 18-hole La Frégate golf course in Saint-Cyr-sur-Mer. **Closed** Jan 4 – Feb 4.

You will enjoy the festive atmosphere of the Thursday market and don't worry about being disturbed by it: the hotel has a quiet garden behind medieval walls. The bedrooms in the former convent are large, cool in summer, and decorated in shades of brown matching those of the baths, which are covered with Salernes tiles. In the bastide, the bedrooms are more classic but also more colorfully appointed with beautiful Provençal fabrics. All are comfortable and well-furnished. You can have a view of the rooftops, the garden, the ramparts, the village itself, or the countryside with the medieval village of Le Castellet in the distance. Monsieur Bérard's cuisine, which pays homage to regional products, makes this one of the outstanding restaurants of Provence. We were charmed by the friendly hospitality extended by Madame Bérard and her daughter.

*How to get there ( Map 34): 20km west of Toulon via A50, La Cadière d'Azur exit.*

## Hostellerie Les Gorges de Pennafort

83830 Callas (Var)
Tel. (0)4.94.76.66.51 - Fax (0)4.94.76.67.23
M. Da Silva

**Category** ★★★ **Rooms** 12 and 4 suites, with air-conditioning, telephone, bath, WC, satellite TV and minibar. **Price** Single and double 520-750F / 79,27-114,34€, suite 870-1000F / 132,63-152,45€. **Meals** Breakfast 70F / 10,67€, served 8:00-11:00; half board 600-780F / 91,47-118,91€ (per pers., 2 days min.). **Restaurant** Closed Monday in low season. Service 12:00PM-2:00PM, 7:30PM-10:00PM; mealtime specials 180F / 27,44€, (lunch weekdays) 250-350F / 38,11-53,36€, also à la carte. Specialties: Fricassée de petits gris et pied de porc aux asperges; filet de rougets au Sauterne et curry; lapereau rôti aux petits oignons et artichauts; ananas et pruneaux au gingembre glace à l'armagnac. **Credit cards** Amex, Visa. **Pets** Dogs allowed (+50F / 7,62€). **Facilities** Mountain bike, swimming pool, tennis, parking. **Nearby** Le Malmont, villages of Bargemon, Seillans, Salernes, Tourtour, Aups (Simon-Segal Museum), Les Arcs (Sainte-Roseline Chapel), Château of Entrecasteaux, Thoronet Abbey. **Closed** Jan 15 – Mar 15; Sunday evening and Monday in low season.

This pretty, ochre-colored Provençal hotel lies in the heart of dramatic mountain gorges. At night, the trees, the craggy cliffs, and the nearby lake are beautifully illuminated by invisible projectors. Fronted by a manicured and flowery garden, this hotel is right in the middle of the gorges. Decorated with colorful fabric wall coverings and white-leaded wood furnishings, the bedrooms are prim and modern, impeccably kept, and very comfortable; all have gleaming bathrooms. The lounges, the bar, and the dining room (where you will enjoy excellent Provençale specialties) are decorated in the same charming style. There is a ravishing shady terrace, and the service is always perfectly professional.

***How to get there*** *( Map 34): 20km northeast of Draguignan via D56 and D25. On A8, exit Le Muy and then D25.*

# Château de Valmer

83420 La Croix-Valmer (Var)
Route de Gigaro
Tel. (0)4.94.79.60.10 - Fax (0)4.94.54.22.68 - Mme Jouanny
E-mail: chateauval@aol.com

**Category** ★★★ **Rooms** 42 with air-conditioning, telephone, bath, WC and TV – Elevator; wheelchair access. **Price** Double 910-1700F / 138,73-259,16€. **Meals** Breakfast (buffet) 100F / 15,24€, served from 8:00. **Restaurant** Service 12:30PM-3:00PM, 7:30PM-9:00PM, Provençale lunch menu, mealtime specials 290-350F / 44,21-53,36€. **Credit cards** Amex, visa. **Pets** Dogs allowed (+50F / 7,62€). **Facilities** Swimming pool, private beach, tennis, parking. **Nearby** Saint-Tropez Gulf, Les Maures, islands of Porquerolles and Port-Cros. **Closed** Oct – Mar.

A luxurious hotel, elegant and comfortable, the *Château de Valmer* stands on a rise surrounded by a 12-acre park with a century-old palm grove leading down to a private beach. The interior decoration has been magnificently renovated. In the lounges, there are antiques and deep sofas which are elegantly covered with printed fabrics coordinated with those of the drapes. The decor matches the handsome paintings. The bedrooms are beautiful and impeccably kept, and they have very luxurious bathrooms. Prices vary according to the size of the room and the view. Lovely terraces with stone colonnades lend charm to the façade of the château, and there are also tables for breakfast. The château offers a Provençale lunch menu, but you can also head to the beach for lunchtime grilled meats and evening gourmet cuisine of *La Pinède*, also run by the hotel's owners. This is, indisputably, one of the most beautiful places on the Côte d'Azur.

***How to get there*** *(Map 34): Via A8, Le Luc exit, towards La Garde-Freinet, Gassin and La Croix-Valmer.*

## Moulin de la Camandoule

83440 Fayence (Var)
Chemin Notre-Dame-des-Cyprès
Tel. (0)4.94.76.00.84 - Fax (0)4.94.76.10.40 - M. and Mme Rilla
E-mail: moulin.camandoule@wanadoo.fr
Web: httpperso.wanadoo.fr/camandoule

**Category ★★★ Rooms** 11 with telephone, bath, shower, WC and TV. **Price** Double 330-750F / 50,31-114,34€, suite 760-970F / 115,86-147,88€. **Meals** Breakfast 75F / 11,43€, served 8:00-10:00; half board 515-735F / 78,51-112,05€ (obligatory Mar 15 – Oct 31). **Restaurant** Closed Wednesday lunch. Service 12:00PM-2:00PM, 7:30PM-10:00PM; mealtime specials 165-285F / 25,15-43,45€, also à la carte. Grill near the swimming pool Jun – Sep. **Credit cards** Visa, Eurocard and MasterCard. **Pets** Dogs allowed (+45F / 6,86€). **Facilities** Swimming pool, parking. **Nearby** Seillans, Bargenon, Sainte-Roseline Chapel (4km from Arcs), Château of Entrecasteaux, Abbey of Le Thoronet, Saint-Gassien Lake – 18-hole golf course in Roquebrune-sur-Argens. **Open** All year.

Surrounded by a huge park, this old olive oil mill has been well-preserved and today belongs to an English couple who run it like an old-fashioned English guest house. You will enjoy a warm, friendly welcome and all the services and comforts of a good hotel. The interior decoration is in excellent taste, even if it is starting to show its age. The bedrooms are furnished in an attractive Provençal style. In the unusual lounge the old machinery of the oil press has been cleverly incorporated into the decor, and the menus are framed on the walls of the swimming pool bar. The good things in life are appreciated here, and the Moulin likes to share these things with its guests. Mme Rilla, who has worked on many radio and TV food programs, has made *La Camandoule* a favorite destination for travelers and locals alike.

*How to get there (Map 34): 31km north of Fréjus via D4, then D19.*

## La Grillade au feu de bois

Flassans-sur-Issole
83340 Le Luc (Var)
Tel. (0)4.94.69.71.20 - Fax (0)4.94.59.66.11
Mme Babb

**Category** ★★ **Rooms** 16 with telephone, bath or shower, WC and TV. **Price** Single and double 400-600F / 60,98-91,47€, suite (with whirlpool) 900F / 137,20€. **Meals** Breakfast 50F / 7,62€, served 8:00-10:30. **Restaurant** Service 12:00PM-2:00PM, 7:30PM-9:00PM; mealtime 180F / 27,44€, also à la carte. Specialties: Traditional Provençale cooking. **Credit cards** Amex, Visa, Eurocard and MasterCard. **Pets** Dogs allowed. **Facilities** Heated swimming pool, parking. **Nearby** Abbey of Thoronet, Luc Tower, Abbey of La Celle, La Loube mountain – 18-hole Barbaroux golf course in Brignoles. **Open** All year.

This very well restored 18th-century Provençal mas is surrounded by lush vegetation and has a terrace shaded by beautiful trees, the oldest of which is a 100-year-old mulberry. Inside, the various living areas and the long vaulted dining room, with a fireplace at one end, are remarkably furnished. (Mme Babb, who is also an antiques dealer, has personalized the decor with numerous lovely objects, paintings, and pieces of furniture.) The comfortable rooms sport two styles: rustic in the main house; youthful and colorful in the other building (with pastel fabrics and white wicker furniture). All are well-looked-after and perfectly soundproofed. You'll never even notice that the N 7 is only 500 m away. Grilled meats and fine Provençale cuisine served in the superb dining room or on the terrace, in the midst of countless flowers and trees that brighten the garden.

***How to get there*** *(Map 34): 13km east of Brignoles via N7 between Flassans-sur-Issolle and Le Luc.*

## Auberge du Vieux Fox

83670 Fox-Amphoux (Var)
Place de l'Eglise
Tel. (0)4.94.80.71.69 - Fax (0)4.94.80.78.38
M. and Mme Staudinger

**Category** ★★★ **Rooms** 8 with telephone, bath or shower, WC and 4 with TV. **Price** Double 380-530F / 57,93-80,8€. **Meals** Breakfast 40F / 6,10€, served 8:00AM-12:00PM; half board 730-840F / 111,29-128,06€ (2 pers.). **Restaurant** Service 12:30PM and 7:30PM; mealtime specials 145-250F / 22,11-38,11€, also à la carte. Specialties: Agneau de Haute-Provence; galette du berger. **Credit cards** Amex, Visa, Eurocard and MasterCard. **Pets** Dogs allowed (+35F / 5,34€). **Facilities** Parking. **Nearby** Abbeys of Thoronet and La Celle, Verdon lake and gorges – 18-hole Barbaroux golf course in Brignoles. **Open** All year.

The old village of Fox-Amphoux, perched on its wooded crag, was first a Roman camp and then became a headquarters of Knights Templars. The hotel is in the old presbytery adjoining the church in the center of the village. Inside, the dining room, with its well-laid tables and beautiful antique furniture, is a little dark but full of character. In summer you can also have lunch on the enchanting little terrace in the shade of a large fig tree. Generous portions, though a bit lacking in refinement. Upstairs, all the rooms and bathrooms are comfortable and overlook the Saint-Victoire and Saint-Baume hills. Some have a truly magnificient view. A genuinely rural place, perfect for life at the pace of a little, out-of-the-way Provençal town. Reserved hospitality.

***How to get there*** *( Map 34): 32km north of Brignoles via A8, Saint-Maximin-la-Sainte-Baume exit, then D560 to Tavernes, D71 and D32.*

# L'Aréna

83600 Fréjus (Var) - 145, rue du Général-de-Gaulle
Tel. (0)4.94.17.09.40 - Fax (0)4.94.52.01.52
Mme Bouchot - M. Bluntzer
Web: www.arena-hotel.com - E-mail: info@arena-hotel.com

**Category** ★★★ **Rooms** 30 with air-conditioning, telephone, bath or shower, WC, satellite TV – 2 for disabled persons. **Price** Double 450-700F / 68,60-106,71€. **Meals** Breakfast 50F / 7,62€, served 7:30-10:30. **Restaurant** Closed Monday lunchtime and Saturday lunchtime. Service 12:00PM-2:00PM, 7:00PM-10:30PM; mealtime 140-250F / 21,34-38,11€, also à la carte. Regional cooking. **Credit cards** All major. **Pets** Dogs allowed (+40F / 6,10€). **Facilities** Swimming pool and parking (+50F / 7,62€). **Nearby** Fréjus: cathedral and cloister; Massif de l'Estérel between Saint-Raphaël and La Napoule, Saint-Tropez, Cannes – 5 golf courses nearby. **Closed** Nov.

Standing in the heart of the city, this small hotel has made admirable use of its garden so that apart from a little noise from the outside, we quickly forgot the *Arena*'s urban location (which is even an advantage if you want to visit the Roman ruins of the old city.) Inside, an elegant tiled floor, painted-wood furniture, and Provençal fabrics are a perfect expression of the Mediterranean *bonhomie* and carefree way of life. The simple bedrooms are pleasant and well-kept, and the soundproofing is totally effective. All the rooms are somewhat small except for those recently set up in a separate building and the one (our favorite) located on ground level near the swimming pool. Delicate and delicious meals are served on the terrace or in a lovely dining room. A pleasant place to stay where you are sure to be heartily welcomed.

***How to get there*** *( Map 34 ):40 km west of Cannes; via A7, Fréjus-Saint-Raphaël exit.*

## La Boulangerie

83310 Grimaud (Var)
Route de Collobrières
Tel. (0)4.94.43.23.16 - Fax (0)4.94.43.38.27
Mme Piget

**Category** ★★★ **Rooms** 11 (6 with air-conditioning, 4 with TV and 1 with minibar) with telephone, bath, WC. **Price** Double 660-690F / 100,62-105,19€, suite 780-1520F / 118,91-231,72€. **Meals** Breakfast 60F / 9,15€, served 7:45-11:00. **Restaurant** Only lunchtime. Service 12:00PM-1:30PM. Specialties: Aïoli de poissons; poulet fermier aux truffes; filet de loup aux fruits de provence; moelleux au chocolat. **Credit cards** Amex, Visa, Eurocard and MasterCard. **Pets** Dogs allowed (+60F / 9,15€). **Facilities** Swimming pool, tennis, table tennis, parking. **Nearby** La Garde-Freinet; ridgeway to the Notre-Dame-des-Anges Hermitage; Collobrières; Carthusian monastery of La Verne; Saint-Tropez – 18-hole Beauvallon golf course in Sainte-Maxime. **Open** Apr – Oct 10.

This place has nothing to do with bakeries as its name would suggest-it is named after a small village-and additionally, it has a very different atmosphere from a traditional hotel. Far from the crowds in a tranquil spot in the Massif des Maures, it is more like a holiday house in the interior of Provence. Everything conspires to produce this impression, with the terrace bordered by a swimming pool where you can have meals, the dining room, which is part of the lounge, and the terrifically one-of-a-kind hospitality of Madame Piget. This is an informal, cheerful, comfortable, and elegantly furnished place. Each bedroom has its own style. The rooms are simple and comfortable and seem more like guest rooms than hotel rooms, yet some should be brought up-to-date, to justify their price.

***How to get there*** *(Map 34): 10km west of Saint-Tropez via D14; 1km from the village.*

# Le Verger

83310 Grimaud (Var)
Route de Collobrières
Tel. (0)4.94.43.25.93 - Fax (0)4.94.43.33.92
Mme Zachary

**Rooms** 9 (3 with air-conditioning) with telephone, bath or shower, WC. **Price** Double 550-950F / 83,85-144,83€. **Meals** Breakfast 60F / 9,15€, served 8:30-11:30. **Restaurant** Service 12:00PM-2:30PM, 7:30PM-11:00PM; à la carte. Specialties: Filet de dorade à la crème d'olives vertes; salade de foie gras aux truffes, carré d'agneau au miel; bourride; sabayon chaud aux framboises; crème brûlée. **Credit cards** Visa, Eurocard and MasterCard. **Pets** Dogs allowed. **Facilities** Swimming pool, parking. **Nearby** La Garde-Freinet, ridgeway to the Notre-Dame-des-Anges Hermitage, Collobrières, Carthusian monastery of La Verne, Saint-Tropez – 18-hole Beauvallon golf course in Sainte-Maxime. **Open** Apr – Oct.

This pretty house looks like a private dwelling. The bedrooms have French windows which open onto a terrace or a lawn with fruit trees. The tasteful Provençal decor is enhanced with lovely fabrics and beautiful bathrooms. You will find your bed turned down every evening, and bouquets of flowers add a pleasant touch. Every day, the restaurant is filled with customers who come back regularly for Monsieur Zachary's fine cuisine, eaten on the ramade or, in case of wind, in the newly-opened, elegant veranda. Newcomers are delighted to have discovered his outstanding specialties made with aromatic herbs and vegetables from the kitchen garden. Shielded by a bamboo grove on the small river in back, the *Verger* is very quiet. And the hospitality is charming.

***How to get there*** *( Map 34): 9km west of Saint-Tropez. In Grimaud take D14 for 1km towards Collobrières and follow signs.*

# Les Glycines

83400 Porquerolles (Var)
22, place d'Armes
Tel. (0)4.94.58.30.36 - Fax (0)4.94.58.35.22
Mme Meyer

**Category** ★★ **Rooms** 11 with air-conditioning, telephone, bath or shower, WC and TV. **Price** Double with half board 390-850F / 59,46-129,58€. **Meals** Breakfast (buffet) 50F / 7,62€, served from 8:30. **Restaurant** Service 7:30PM-10:30PM: mealtime 99-169F / 15,24-25,76€, also à la carte. Specialties: Tartares de poisson; omelette aux oursins; loup grillé au fenouil; carpaccio de thon; aïoli. **Credit cards** Amex, Visa. **Pets** Dogs not allowed. **Nearby** Bike rides along island paths, beaches, boat rental. **Open** All year.

Located on the village square, *Les Glycines* ("wisteria") nestles behind a garden in the shade of a century-old fig tree, its whitewashed walls and blue shutters evoking the quiet charm of Provençal homes of yesteryear. In the bedrooms, all air-conditioned and comfortable, some overlooking the square and others the garden, the same soft atmosphere is created by Provençal fabrics, sandstone floor tiles, and walls in pastel colors. The baths also are comfortable and well-equipped. Breakfast and dinner are served in the cool shade of the garden on tables set with crimson linens. So before the first hordes of "day trippers" descend from the boats, it's best to enjoy your coffee on the terrace of *L'Escale*, and in the evening go to the *Plage d'Argent*, the "Silver Beach", for dinner (the return trip by bike at night is unforgettable): *Voilà*: the recipe for being an authentic *"Porquerollais"*.

***How to get there*** *( Map 34): Ferry connection from Hyères or La Tour Fondue - tel. (0)4.94.58.21.81). Also, boat taxis available (tel. (0)4.94.58.31.19. Phone at any time. Cars not allowed on the island. Airport Toulon-Hyères is 7 km away.*

## L'Oustaou

83400 Porquerolles (Var)
Place d'Armes
Tel. (0)4.94.58.30.13 - Fax (0)4.94.58.34.93
M. and Mme Garbit

**Category** ★★★ **Rooms** 5 with air-conditioning, telephone, shower, WC and TV. **Price** Double 500-850F / 76,22-129,58€. **Meals** Breakfast 45F / 6,86€, served from 8:00. **Restaurant** Service 11:30AM-3:30PM, 7:30PM-10:30PM; Chef's special 70F / 10,67€, mealtime specials 130F / 19,82€, also à la carte. Specialties: Fish; marmite du pêcheur; assiette provençale; tian d'aubergines. **Credit cards** Amex, Visa, Eurocard and MasterCard. **Pets** Dogs allowed. **Nearby** A lot of promenades by bicycle on the island, beach, boat rentals. **Open** Apr – Oct 31.

Standing on the port with its façade on the village square, the Oustaou on Porquerolles Island features charmingly simple bedrooms with modern amenities. Two overlook the Mediterranen, and three look out over the square. On the ground floor, the terrace restaurant offers a quiet view of the sea on one side, and on the other, you can follow the spectacle of village life without leaving the hotel. Good fish is served here, but you can also enjoy a dietetic plate. Note that it's indispensable to rent bikes to get to the beaches and creeks on the south shore of the island, or to discover the eighty kilometers of paths criss-crossing Porquerolles' 3125-acre national park.

***How to get there*** *( Map 34): Ferry connection from Hyères or La Tour Fondue - tel. 04.95.58.21.81) or boat-taxi (tel. 04.94.58.31.19 - at any time). Airport Toulon-Hyères, 7km. Cars forbidden on the island.*

## Le Manoir

83400 Port-Cros (Var)
Tel. (0)4.94.05.90.52 - Fax (0)4.94.05.90.89
M. Buffet

**Category** ★★★ **Rooms** 22 with telephone, bath or shower and WC. **Price** Double with half board 800-1100F / 121,96-167,69€ (per pers.). **Meals** Breakfast 65F / 9,91€, served 7:45-11:00. **Restaurant** Service from 1:00PM and 8:00PM; mealtime 260-300F / 39,64-45,73€, also à la carte. Specialties: Bourride provençale; carré d'agneau à la fleur d'oranger; tarte tatin de légumes. **Credit cards** Visa, Eurocard and MasterCard. **Pets** Dogs not allowed. **Facilities** Heated swimming pool. **Nearby** Nature trails in the Port-Cros national park, Porquerolles. **Open** Easter – beg. Oct.

The eucalyptus, palm trees, white walls, and graceful columns of the *Manoir* evoke an exotic dream, a lost island. And yet Toulon is so close. The island of Pont-Cros is a nature reserve and no vehicles are allowed. The hotel was opened just after the war in this private house, and it still preserves a family atmosphere, blending conviviality with elegance. There is a large lounge and several small ones, which card players frequent towards the end of the summer season. The bedrooms are cool and charming, and some have little terraces or mezzanines. A beautiful, quiet 30-acre park and a swimming pool built in the middle of the yard add to the considerable charm of this lovely hotel.

***How to get there*** *(Map 34): Ferry connection from Le Lavandou and Cavalaire - tel. (0)4.94.71.01.02, from Hyères - tel. (0)4.94.58.21.81. Cars not allowed on the island. Airport Toulon-Hyères.*

## Grand Hôtel des Lecques

Les Lecques 83270 Saint-Cyr-sur-Mer (Var)
24, avenue du Port
Tel. (0)4.94.26.23.01 - Fax (0)4.94.26.10.22 - Mme Vitré

**Category** ★★★ **Rooms** 58 with telephone, bath or shower, WC and satellite TV – Elevator. **Price** Single and double 435-740F / 66,32-112,81€. **Meals** Breakfast 75F / 11,43€, served 7:30-10:00, half board obligatory im summer 625-685F / 95,28-104,43€. **Restaurant** *Le Parc* Service 12:00PM-2:00PM, 7:00PM-9:15PM; mealtime specials 115-165F / 17,53-25,15€. Specialties: Regional cooking. Lunch near swimming pool 12:30PM-2:30PM, buffet: 130F / 19,82€. **Credit cards** Amex, Visa, JCB. **Pets** Dogs allowed. **Facilities** Swimming pool, tennis and parking. **Nearby** Exotic Garden in Sanary, Bandol, Le Castellet – 18-hole Frégate golf course in Saint-Cyr-sur-Mer. **Open** Apr 15 – Oct 31.

*L*e *Grand Hôtel des Lecques* was once summer home to wealthy Provençal families who came here to enjoy the beach and its dunes. Today, the long, duneless ribbon of sand attracts families and August vacationers from all over. Set back slightly from the main street along the sea, the recently renovated hotel has conserved the essential part of its original park and garden so as to offer a quiet oasis of trees and flowers. The big white building is charming and the skillful renovations have created a fresh, cheerful ambiance in the lounges and the dining room. The newly renovated bedrooms on the upper floors in the front, with a view over the sea, are the most beautiful. You simply cross the street, and you're on the beach, unless you prefer the hotel's swimming pool; snacks are served there, and the restaurant offers aromatic Provençale specialties. This is a good hotel for a vacation on the sea, in Provence, and in Saint-Cyr-sur-Mer itself, where a reproduction of the Statue of Liberty stands on the Place de l'Eglise. It's a traditional village where local farmers still come to animate the big open market on Sunday morning.

***How to get there*** *(Map 34): 20km west of Toulon via A 50, exit Saint-Cyr-sur-Mer, then to Les Lecques.*

# La Ferme d'Augustin

83350 Ramatuelle (Var)
Tel. (0)4.94.55.97.00 - Fax (0)4.94.97.40.30
Mme Vallet

**Category** ★★★ **Rooms** 46 with air-conditioning, telephone, bath (5 with shower), WC, TV, safe and minibar – Elevator. **Price** Double 580-1600F / 88,42-243,92€, suite 1600-1800F / 243,92-274,41€. **Meals** Breakfast 75 F / 11,43€, served 6:00-2:00PM. No restaurant but snacks available for residents only. **Credit cards** All major. **Pets** Dogs allowed (+70F / 10,67€). **Facilities** Heated swimming pool with hydromassages, parking. **Nearby** L'Annonciade Museum in Saint-Tropez, ridgeway to the Notre-Dame-des-Anges Hermitage, Collobrières, Carthusian monastery of La Verne – 9-hole Beauvallon golf course in Sainte-Maxime. **Open** Mar 20 – Oct 20.

This hotel is located on the former family farm, but, today, its rural character is just a far-off memory. As soon as you arrive, you will be captivated by the pine grove and the garden full of wisteria, bougainvillea, rambling roses, and the great, parasol-shaped mulberry trees. In the lounges, antique country-style furniture is tastefully combined with modern sofas. The bedrooms have pretty bathrooms with wall tiles from Salernes. They all overlook the garden and have a balcony or terrace commanding sea views. Some even have a smashing view of a private garden. The hotel occupies a truly enviable position, just off Tahiti Beach, 200 meters from hiking paths and mountainbiking trails. If you want to stay on the beach all day, ask for a box lunch; the bar serves light meals and provides 24-hour room service.

*How to get there ( Map 34): 5km from Saint-Tropez on the "plage de Tahiti" road.*

## La Ferme d'Hermès

83350 Ramatuelle (Var)
Route de l'Escalet - Val de Pons
Tel. (0)4.94.79.27.80 - Fax (0)4.94.79.26.86
Mme F. Verrier

**Category** ★★★ **Rooms** 8 and 1 suite with telephone, bath, WC, TV, minibar and kitchenette. **Price** Double 600-880F / 91,47-134,16€, suite 1100F / 167,69€. **Meals** Breakfast 80F / 12,20€, served 9:00AM-12:00PM. No restaurant. **Credit cards** Visa, Eurocard and MasterCard. **Pets** Dogs allowed (+50F / 7,62€). **Facilities** Swimming pool, parking. **Nearby** L'Annonciade Museum in Saint-Tropez, Ramatuelle festival in July and August, La Nioulargue in Oct, Grimaud. **Open** Apr – Oct 31 and Dec 27 – Jan 10.

A dirt path through the vineyards, a fragrant garden full of rosemary bushes and olive trees, a pink house: this is the address in the Midi you have always dreamed of, a place where you want to welcome your friends. The fireplace in the little reception lounge and in the suite, homemade jams and pastries for breakfast, and bouquets of flowers make this hotel worlds-apart from the anonymity you find elsewhere along the coast. The rooms, many with a kitchenette, are sassy and nicely decorated with pine furniture. Some have a little ground-level terrace divided by shrubbery and with a spray of ivy. Breakfast is served either in your room or on the terrace, for the hotel has no dining room. The overall effect is pleasing and inviting, without a touch of trendiness. As far as meals go, Madame Verrier is full of good advice. In Saint-Tropez, let's just mention: *Chez Fuchs*, *Le Café des Arts*, *Le Petit Charron*, or *Au Fil à la Pâte*.

***How to get there*** *( Map 34): 2km south of Ramatuelle on L'Escalet Road.*

## La Figuière

83350 Ramatuelle (Var)
Route de Tahiti
Tel. (0)4.94.97.18.21 - Fax (0)4.94.97.68.48
Mme Chaix

**Category** ★★★ **Rooms** 42 with air-conditioning, telephone, bath, WC, TV, safe and minibar – 2 for disabled persons. **Price** Double 500-1000F / 76,22-152,45€, duplex (4 pers.) 1500-1600F / 228,67-243,92€. **Meals** Breakfast 70F / 10,67€, served 8:00-11:00. **Restaurant** Service 12:00PM-3:00PM, 8:00PM-11:00PM; also à la carte. Specialties: Regional cooking. **Credit cards** All major. **Pets** Dogs allowed (+60F / 9,15€). **Facilities** Swimming pool, tennis, parking. **Nearby** L'Annonciade Museum in Saint-Tropez, Ramatuelle festival in July and August, La Nioulargue in Oct, La Garde-Freinet, ridgeway to the Notre-Dame-des-Anges Hermitage, Collobrières, Carthusian monastery of La Verne – 18-hole Beauvallon golf course in Sainte-Maxime. **Open** Apr 2 – Oct 4.

Yes, there are still some genuine houses with stately façades and cool rooms tiled in red terra-cotta like long ago; houses that resist fashion and trends. This is one of them. On the beach route, just a few minutes from Saint-Tropez, the *Figuière* hides its five little houses in a fig garden. The rooms are spacious, quiet, perfumed with flax, and many have their own private terrace. The regional decoration is sober and the bathrooms are comfortable–some have a double washbasin, shower, and bath. Our favorites have numbers ending in 30 and 40 and enjoy pretty, private terraces surrounded by lavender and lantanas; they have a panoramic view over the vineyards and hills covered with parasol pines. The large, comfortable bathrooms often have twin sinks, a shower, and a bathtub. Good breakfasts are served with the morning newspaper. Provençale dishes are served next to the swimming pool, surrounded by pink laurels and quince trees. Reasonable prices for the area. Warm and attentive hospitality.

***How to get there*** *( Map 34): 2.5km south of Saint-Tropez on L'Escalet Road.*

471

## Les Moulins

83350 Ramatuelle (Var)
Lieu-dit "Les Moulins" - Route des Plages
Tel. (0)4.94.97.17.22 - Fax (0)4.94.97.72.70
M. C. Leroy

**Category** ★★★ **Rooms** 5 with telephone, bath, satellite TV, safe and minibar. **Price** Single and double 1250F / 190,56€; suite 1450F / 221,05€. **Meals** Breakfast 90F / 13,72€, served 8:30-11:00. **Restaurant** Service 7:30PM-10:00PM; mealtime specials 290-480F / 44,21-73,18€; à la carte. Specialties: Tarte fine aux senteurs de Provence; soupe de pommes de terre aux truffes; tarte aux framboises et pignons. **Credit cards** Amex, Visa. **Pets** Dogs allowed. **Facilities** Parking. **Nearby** Saint-Tropez; La Garde-Freinet; Collobrières; Chartreuse de la Verne – 18-hole Beauvallon golf course in Sainte-Maxime. **Open** Mar 1 – Nov 1.

After *La Table du Marche*, Christophe Leroy reaffirmed his attachment to this area by founding this inn in a Ramatuelle farmhouse. Fragrant plants cover the old beautiful stones and climb up the arbors and trellises that shade the courtyard. Wanting to maintain its authentic feel, the house has but a few rooms, as well as a dinng room that is used on chilly days, so one can enjoy the extraordinary fireplace. In summer, meals are served in the courtyard, garden and veranda, which was added on but, over time, proved to fit right in. We praise the excellent food and the chef who is behind it. The rooms have a youthful freshness, with a white color scheme accented by tart colors, veils, and light, transparent organdies. The same refined comfort in the small bathrooms, in keeping with the original dimensions of the rooms. Great for a lovers' weekend or short holiday, rather than a family vacation.

*How to get there (Map 34): 3km east of Saint-Tropez, toward Salins.*

472

## Hôtel Le Pré de la Mer

83990 Saint-Tropez (Var)
Route des Salins
Tel. (0)4.94.97.12.23 - Fax (0)4.94.97.43.91
Mme Blum

**Category** ★★★ **Rooms** 3, 1 suite and 8 studios, with telephone, bath, shower, WC, TV, safe and minibar. **Price** Single and double 520-760F / 79,27-115,86€, studio 670-990F / 102,14-150,92€, suite 1060-1420F / 161,60-216,48€. **Meals** Breakfast 60F / 9,15€, served 8:30AM-12:00PM. No restaurant. **Credit cards** All major. **Pets** Dogs allowed (+50F / 7,62€). **Facilities** Parking. **Nearby** L'Annonciade Museum in Saint-Tropez; Ramatuelle festival in July and August; La Nioulargue in October, la Garde-Freinet, ridgeway to Notre-Dame-des-Anges Hermitage; Collobrières; Carthusian monastery of La Verne – 18-hole Beauvallon golf course in Sainte-Maxime. **Open** Easter – Sep 30.

This low, white house, built in the Mexican-Saint Tropez style, offers large and very pleasant rooms, some outfitted with a little kitchen. Comfortable and cooled by a great fan, they are all soberly decorated with white walls, superb terra-cotta flooring, printed cottons, and beautiful antique cabinets. All have their own private terrace with a table and white wood chairs that opens onto the walled garden, bursting with pink laurels, aletheas, pomengranate, and lemon trees. You will eat excellent breakfast, where jams made from the hotel's fruit have the place of honor. In love with her hotel, Joséphine Blum has thought of everything to make your stay pleasant. You'll even find a little candle, box of matches, and mosquito repellant in your wardrobe, in case you want to have an impromptu romantic dinner on the terrace. Restaurant fashions come and go here, but there are always *Le Café des Arts* on the Place des Lices, *Le Petit Charron*, *Chez Fuchs* (Tropezian favorite), or *Au Fil à la Pâte*.

*How to get there* (*Map 34*): *3km east of Saint-Tropez on the Salins road.*

## Hôtel des Deux Rocs

83440 Seillans (Var)
Place Font-d'Amont
Tel. (0)4.94.76.87.32 - Fax (0)4.94.76.88.68
Mme Hirsch

**Category** ★★★ **Rooms** 15 with telephone, bath or shower, WC and minibar. **Price** Double 300-580F / 45,73-88,42€. **Meals** Breakfast 50F / 7,62€, served 8:00-10:00; half board 350-490F / 53,36-74,70€ (per pers., 3 days min.). **Restaurant** Closed Tuesday and Thursday lunchtime. Service 12:00PM-2:00PM, 7:30PM-9:00PM; mealtime specials 90F / 13,72€ (lunchtime weekdays)-160-225F / 24,39-34,30€, also à la carte. Specialties: Saint-jacques à l'ail et aux amandes; foie gras poelé aux poires; filet de bœuf aux morilles. **Credit card** Visa. **Pets** Dogs allowed. **Nearby** Chapel of Saint-André in Comps-sur-Artuby, Fayence, les Arcs and the Sainte-Roseline Chapel (4km), Château of Entrecasteaux, Abbey of Le Thoronet – 18-hole golf course in Roquebrune-sur-Argens. **Open** Apr – end Oct.

Standing at the top of the splendid village of Seillans, close to the city walls and the old castle, is the *Hôtel des Deux Rocs*, a large Provençal house which is a modest, rustic replica of certain Italian residences. Variety is the keynote of the decor, which is exquisite. You will feel at home and relaxed in the small lounge with a fireplace. The bedrooms are all individually designed: period furniture, wall fabrics, curtains, and bathroom towels are unique to each one of them. (Just one downside: during our last visit, we noticed that the bathrooms were starting to show their age.) Breakfast can be served at tables set up in the pleasant little square not far from Max Ernst's *Génie de la Bastille*; homemade preserves are just one of the many delicious details which make a stay here memorable. You will love this hotel, and prices are very reasonable.

***How to get there*** *( Map 34): 34km north of Fréjus via A8, Les Adrets exit, then D562 towards Fayence and D19.*

## Les Bastidières

83100 Toulon (Var)
Cap Brun 2371, avenue de la Résistance
Tel. (0)4.94.36.14.73 - Fax (0)4.94.42.49.75
Mme Lagriffoul

**Rooms** 5 with air-conditioning, telephone, bath or shower, WC, TV and minibar. **Price** Double 450-800F / 68,60-121,96€. **Meals** Breakfast 60-70F / 9,15-10,67€, served 8:00-10:00. No restaurant. **Credit cards** Not accepted. **Pets** Dogs allowed. **Facilities** Swimming pool, parking. **Nearby** Mont Faron; gorges of Ollioules and Evenos; villages of the Castellet and the Cadière d'Azur; Siciè cove; Porquerolles; Port-Cros; Saint-Tropez. **Open** All year.

In a verdant, residential area of Toulon, this beautiful villa is surrounded by a garden where exoticism and the air of Provence mingle harmoniously. Palm trees, yuccas, and ancient pine trees cast shade over large earthenware jars overflowing with impatiens and geraniums. The owners live in the main house. Just next door, there is an annex with five spacious, elegantly and classically decorated bedrooms that are comfortably equipped with very functional bathrooms. Each room opens onto a small flowery terrace (15 square meters) where it is pleasant to have breakfast. The food is excellent and is presented on beautiful silver service. The quietest and most intimate rooms are near the swimming pool, which is beautifully large and surrounded by trees, exotic plants, and Mediterranean flowers. It is midway between the hotel and the guest house–"guest" in the sense that you live independently of the main house, and that all the services of a hotel are not provided (the lounge is in the owners' house). But *Les Bastidières* is a beautiful place to stay.

***How to get there*** *(Map 34): On A8, Toulon exit; towards Mourillon beaches, Cap Brun, Pradet.*

## Château de Trigance

83840 Trigance (Var)
Tel. (0)4.94.76.91.18 - Fax (0)4.94.85.68.99
Famille Thomas

**Category** ★★★ **Rooms** 10 with telephone, bath, WC and TV. **Price** Double 600-750F / 91,47-114,34€, suite 900F / 137,20€. **Meals** Breakfast 70F / 10,67€, served 7:30-10:00; half board 580-730F / 88,42-111,29€ (per pers.). **Restaurant** Closed Wednesday lunchtime in low season. Service 12:00PM-2:00PM, 7:30PM-9:00PM; mealtime specials 210-360F / 32,01-54,88€, also à la carte. Specialties: Duo de foie gras aux truffes noires et blinis au pain d'épices; aumônière d'agneau et caviar d'aubergine; pommes de terre "grenaille" au lard fumé; trigançois aux infusions de miel de thym et d'hypocras (medieval liqueur). **Credit cards** All major. **Pets** Dogs allowed. **Facilities** Parking. **Nearby** Verdon canyon, ridgeway from La-Palud-sur-Verdon, Moustiers-Sainte-Marie — 9-hole Château of Toulane golf course in La Martie. **Open** Mar 22 — end Oct.

Originally a fortress built in the 9th century by the monks of the Abbey of Saint-Victor, the *Château de Trigance* became a castle of the Counts of Provence two hundred years later. Bought in a state of near ruin, the château has been wonderfully restored, using local stones, with the desire to keep the medieval look always in mind. That's why the lounge and dining room might seem a little austere and rustic, with their exposed stone and little doorways. Located around a huge terrace overlooking the countryside, the rooms are very comfortable, decorated in Haute Epoque style, often with a plum or dusky rose color scheme. Excellent regional cuisine is only served indoors, which is a pity, but you can enjoy drinks at the bar on the terrace facing this fantastic panorama. In summer plays are performed on the esplanade by the ramparts. The owners extend a friendly welcome.

***How to get there*** *( Map 34 ): 44km north of Draguignan via D995 to Comps-sur-Artuby; then D905 to Trigance.*

## L'Anastasy

84000 Avignon (Vaucluse)
Ile de la Barthelasse
Tel. (0)4.90.85.55.94 - Fax (0)4.90.82.59.40
Mme Manguin

**Rooms** 5 with bath or shower. **Price** Single and double 350-450F / 53,36-68,60€. **Meals** Breakfast 50F / 7,62€. **Restaurant** For residents only. Service from 1:00PM and 8:30PM; mealtime 150F / 22,87€. Specialties: Provençal and Italian cooking. **Credit cards** Not accepted. **Pets** Dogs allowed. **Facilities** Swimming pool, parking. **Nearby** Palace of the Popes, Notre-Dame des Doms, Campana collection at the Petit-Palais, Calvet Museum, Villeneuve-lès-Avignon – 18-hole Châteaublanc golf course. **Open** All year.

L'*Anastasy* used to be a typical Avignon farm, where animals and harvests were the sole concern. The barns and stables is now a large family house for friends and guests. There is a spacious lounge and kitchen-dining room which is the heart of the house, for the friendly hostess, Olga Manguin, loves cooking for her guests. The Provençale and Italian specialties she excels at are delicious. The bedrooms are pretty. The attractions of the house are many, including the terrace and garden planted with lavender and rosemary, hollyhocks and acanthus. Although the atmosphere is convivial, you nevertheless can be left on your own, but do join in the activities here. Olga's friends, including journalists, directors, stage designers, and actors, wouldn't dream of staying anywhere else during the Avignon Festival.

***How to get there*** *(Map 33): At Avignon, go around the ramparts, and head toward Ile de la Barthleasse on the Daladier bridge (avoid the Pont de l'Europe). In the middle of the bridge, take a right to D 228 toward ile de la Barthelasse. Follow the Rhône River; at the traffic circle, take your first right, then toward the church. Second house on the left after the church.*

## Auberge de Cassagne

84130 Le Pontet - Avignon (Vaucluse) - 450, allée de Cassagne
Tel. (0)4.90.31.04.18 - Fax (0)4.90.32.25.09
MM. Gallon, Boucher and Trestour
E-mail: cassagne@wanadoo.fr - Web: www.valrugues-cassagne.com

**Category** ★★★★ **Rooms** 30 and 5 apartments with air-conditioning, telephone, bath, WC, satellite TV, safe and minibar. **Price** Single and double 620-1770F / 94,52-269,83€, suite 1770-2820F / 269,83-429,90€. **Meals** Breakfast 105F / 16,01€, served 7:30-10:30; half board 800-1375F / 121,96-209,62€ (per pers.). **Restaurant** Service 12:00PM-1:30PM, 7:30PM-9:30PM; mealtime specials 195-480F / 29,73-73,18€, also à la carte. Specialties: Terrine provençale au cœur de foie gras. **Credit cards** All major. **Pets** Dogs allowed (+60F / 9,15€). **Facilities** Tennis, swimming pool, sauna, fitness room, parking (+20F / 3,05€). **Nearby** Palace of the Popes, Campana collection at the Petit Palais and Calvet Museum in Avignon, Avignon festival in Jul, Villeneuve-les-Avignon – 18-hole Grand Avignon golf course. **Open** All year.

You will find the beautiful *Auberge de Cassagne* tucked away in an oasis of greenery where there isn't a trace of the outskirts of Avignon. The reception and service are perfectly complemented by the staff's professionalism and human touch. Most of the bedrooms are located in a group of Provençal-style buildings around or near the flowery swimming pool. They enjoy modern amenities, attractive interior decoration, and immaculate bathrooms. Philippe Boucher, who trained with Paul Bocuse and Georges Blanc, prepares renowned cuisine (one Michelin star), and the beautiful wine cellar is in the hands of André Trestour. Lunch and dinner are thus special moments, made even more enjoyable in summer by service under a gigantic plane tree. A beautiful, if expensive, place.

***How to get there*** *(Map 33): 5km east of Avignon via A7, Avignon-Nord exit, then 5 mins. and left on small road before the traffic lights.*

# Hôtel d'Europe

84000 Avignon (Vaucluse)
12, place Crillon
Tel. (0)4.90.14.76.76 - Fax (0)4.90.14.16.71
M. Daire

**Category** ★★★★ **Rooms** 47 with air-conditioning, telephone, bath, WC, TV and minibar.
**Price** Double 1700-2200F / 259,16-355,87€, suite 3000-3300F / 458,01-503,81€. **Meals** Breakfast
90F / 13,74€, served 6:30-11:00. **Restaurant** Closed Monday lunch and Sunday. Service 12:00PM-
2:00PM, 7:30PM-10:00PM; Sunday brunch 11:30AM-3:00PM, mealtime specials 180-400F / 27,44-
60,98€, also à la carte. **Credit cards** All major. **Pets** Dogs allowed (+50F / 7,63€). **Facilities** Private
garage (50F / 7,63€). **Nearby** Palace of the Popes, Notre-Dame des Doms, Campana collection at the
Petit-Palais, Calvet Museum, theater festival at Avignon in Jul, Villeneuve-Lès-Avignon, Roman
Provence, Alpilles, Luberon – 18-hole Châteaublanc golf course in Avignon. **Open** All year.

The seigneurial 17th-century *Hôtel d'Europe* was once the mansion of the
Marquis de Graveson. The refinement of the hotel has been carefully,
handily, and tastefully preserved: handsome antique furniture and paintings
along with brilliant Aubusson tapestries decorate the salons and the very
beautiful dining room. The bedrooms, which are of varying size, are all
furnished with antiques and have very comfortable accommodations. Three
suites have been opened and from their private terrace in the evening, you will
enjoy a unique view of the Palace of the Popes (lit in summer) and the medieval
ramparts surrounding the town. Weather permitting, you can dine in the pretty
patio, shaded by plane and palm trees, which are planted in huge traditional
pots made in the nearby village of Anduze. The cuisine is excellent, justly star
rated, and there is a very good wine cellar. You may also use the private garage,
which solves the thorny problem of parking in the old town.

***How to get there*** *(Map 33): Inside the ramparts.*

## Hôtel de la Mirande

84000 Avignon (Vaucluse)
4, place de la Mirande
Tel. (0)4.90.85.93.93 - Fax (0)4.90.86.26.85 - M. Stein

**Category** ★★★★ **Rooms** 20 with air-conditioning, telephone, bath, WC, TV and minibar. **Price** Single and double 1700-2400F / 259,16-365,88€, suite 3200F / 487,84€. **Meals** Breakfast 115F / 17,93€, served until 11:00. **Restaurant** Service 12:00PM-2:00PM, 7:30PM-10:00PM; mealtime specials 155F / 23,63€ (lunchtime weekdays), 240-480F / 36,59-73,18€, also à la carte. Specialties: Embeurrée de févettes au Jabugo; meringue croustillante au fromage blanc; sorbet thym-basilic. **Credit cards** All major. **Pets** Dogs allowed (+80F / 12,2€). **Facilities** Cooking lessons, parking (+80F / 12,20€). **Nearby** Palace of the Popes, Notre-Dame des Doms, Campana collection at the Petit-Palais, Calvet Museum, theater festival at Avignon in Jul, Villeneuve-Lès-Avignon, Luberon – 18-hole Châteaublanc golf course in Avignon. **Open** All year.

A palace of charm in Avignon. From the entryway, the inner courtyard has been turned into a delightful conservatory, with wicker armchairs in delicate caramel colors. Off the courtyard there is a stunning sequence of rooms with beautiful antiques, Provençal-style fabrics, and chintzes. The superb bedrooms are spacious, elegant and comfortable, and all have a lounge or anteroom. Those on the *premier étage* are more spacious, while those on the mezzanine and *deuxième étage* are more intimate. Some rooms on the last floor have a lovely terrace which is very pleasant at lunchtime. The ancient and baroque music evening concerts in the autumn or the cooking workshops directed by master chefs will give you the opportunity to discover this exquisite hotel. If you are simply passing through Avignon, the tea room and the piano bar are also very pleasant places to spend a lovely afternoon. Last, but not least, the people are very charming.

***How to get there*** *(Map 33): In the town center, at the foot of the Palais des Papes.*

# Les Géraniums

84330 Le Barroux (Vaucluse)
Place de la Croix
Tel. (0)4.90.62.41.08 - Fax (0)4.90.62.56.48
M. and Mme Roux

**Category** ★★ **Rooms** 22 with telephone, bath or shower and WC. **Price** Double 260-290F / 39,64-44,21€. **Meals** Breakfast 40F / 6,10€, served 8:00-10:00; half board 250-270F / 38,11-41,16€ (per pers., 3 days min.). **Restaurant** Service 12:00PM-2:00PM, 7:00PM-9:00PM; mealtime specials 90-180F / 13,72-27,44€, also à la carte. Specialties: Terrine de lapin à la sauge, foie gras au Muscat de Beame de Venise, lapin à la sarriette, parfait à la lavande. **Credit cards** All major. **Pets** Dogs allowed (+30F / 4,57€). **Facilities** Parking. **Nearby** Château of Barroux, Sainte-Madeleine Monastery, Pharmacy Museum at the Hôtel-Dieu in Carpentras, Mazan Gallo-Roman cemetery, Dentelles de Montmirail – 18-hole Le Grand Avignon golf course. **Closed** Nov 15 – Mar 15.

Lorded over by a superb château, Le Barroux is a village set high on a hill between the Ventoux and the jagged peaks of Montmirail, commanding stunning views of all the Comtat Venaissin, with its orchards, vineyards, and cypresses. The place has a charm all its own, and this small hotel provides pleasantly comfortable accommodation. It also serves as that typical French institution, the *café de la place*, thus offering first-hand insight into local village life. The bedrooms are simple but pleasant and have recently been improved. The nicest have a small terrace. The menu features good local dishes based on fresh products and is likely to include game in season. Meals can be served on the terrace or in the dining room.

***How to get there*** *( Map 33 ): 9km from Carpentras via D938; between Carpentras and Malaucène.*

# La Maison

84340 Beaumont-du-Ventoux (Vaucluse)
Tel. (0)4.90.65.15.50 - Fax (0)4.90.65.23.29
Mme Michèle Laurelut

**Rooms** 3 with bath and WC. **Price** Double 300-370F / 45,73-56,41€. **Meals** Breakfast 50F / 7,62€, served 8:30-10:00. **Restaurant** Closed Monday and Tuesday except in summer and Nov – Mar. Service 12:00PM and 7:30PM; mealtime specials 145F / 22,11€; also à la carte. Specialties: Aubergines confites à la provençale; tian d'agneau; petits farcis de saison; chausson aux pêches tièdes. **Credit cards** Visa, Eurocard and MasterCard **Pets** Dogs not allowed. **Nearby** Beaumont Chapel; Vaison-la-Romaine; Arc de Triomphe and old theater in Orange; Carpentras-Mornas; Henri Fabre Museum in Sérignan. **Open** Feb – Nov.

In this pretty, blue-shuttered house, surrounded by the vines and orchards of the village, Michèle Laurelut doesn't just invite you to come taste her stuffed treats, her eggplant delicacies, and hot peach compote, but also to stay a while in one of the three recently opened rooms. (Soon to be four, a suite for families joined by a communicating door and with a shared bathroom.) Provence was most definitely her inspiration for the rooms' simple decoration, brightened by colored, regional fabrics. The comfort here is well-looked-after and refined. Under the shade of linden trees, the terrace, where breakfast and meals are served in nice weather, bursts with fragrance in blossom time. In winter, *La Maison* seats its guests around a wood fire. Warm and friendly hospitality here. Those who know the restaurant will love the idea of making their pleasure last past dinner.

***How to get there*** *( Map 33 ): 9 km southeast of Vaison-la-Romaine.*

## Château de Rocher - La Belle Ecluse

84500 Bollène (Vaucluse)
156, rue Emile-Lachaux
Tel. (0)4.90.40.09.09 - Fax (0)4.90.40.09.30
M. Carloni

**Category** ★★★ **Rooms** 19 with telephone, bath or shower, WC and TV. **Price** Single and double 290-600F / 44,21-91,47€. **Meals** Breakfast 45-60F / 6,86-9,15€, served 7:00-10:00; half board 500-600F / 76,22-91,47€ (2 pers., 3 days min.). **Restaurant** Service from 12:00PM and 7:00PM; mealtime specials 100F / 15,24€ (lunchtime)-150-250F / 22,87-38,11€; also à la carte. Specialties: Foie gras mi-cuit et poêlé; filet de bœuf aux truffes; nougat glacé au miel de lavande; agneau de pays aux aubergines. **Credit cards** All major. **Pets** Dogs allowed (+30F / 4,57€). **Facilities** Parking. **Nearby** Arc de Triomphe and old theater in Orange, Henri Fabre Museum in Sérignan, Château of Grignan — 18-hole Grand Avignon golf course. **Open** All year.

Built in 1826 for Count Joseph Maurice de Rocher, this beautiful aristocratic mansion was decorated by Florentine artists. It stands on the edge of a large 10-acre park inhabited by domestic animals and some wild species, and culminates in a magnificent semi-circle of trees in front of the entrance. The bedrooms, many large, are bright and comfortable. Their decoration combines classic with retro styles, and some original touches such as Room 8, which is located in a chapel illuminated by stained-glass windows. The elegant cuisine can be served outside on the terrace, in summer, or in the Richelieu dining room, which has a painted wooden ceiling, a beautiful carved stone chimney and a portrait of the famous Cardinal above the mantel.

***How to get there*** *( Map 33 ): 20 km north of Orange on A 9, take the Bollene exit. Head toward "centre ville." After 600 m, turn left toward Gap on the Nyon road.*

## Auberge de l'Aiguebrun

RD 943 - 84480 Bonnieux (Vaucluse)
Tel. (0)4.90.04.47.00 - Fax (0)4.90.04.47.01
Mme Buzier

**Category** ★★★ **Rooms** 10 with telephone, bath, WC, satellite TV. **Price** Single and double 600-1200F / 91,47-182,94€. **Meals** Breakfast 85F / 12,96€, served 8:00-10:00; half board 600F / 91,47€ (per pers.). **Restaurant** Closed Tuesday and Wednesday lunch. Service 12:00PM-2:00, 8:00PM-10:00PM; mealtime specials 200F / 30,49€. Specialties: Tatin de laitue au saumon fumé; gâteau de châtaignes à la sauce au chocolat. **Credit cards** Visa, Eurocard, MasterCard **Pets** Dogs no allowed. **Facilities** Swimming pool, parking. **Nearby** Luberon Valley; rock-climbing at Buoux; La Roque-d'Antéron Festival; Market in Apt (Saturday) – 18-hole golf course in Saumane. **Open** End Feb – end Nov.

The Loumarin valley is the only pass through Mount Luberon. On this pretty road, you will make out poplars outside the wood, then bells of the village, telling you that you are almost there. You will have to go down to the edge of the Aiguebrun to find this inn, bought up by Madame Buzier, who ran the *La Treille* restaurant in Avignon. She used the original name and made it one of the great addresses in the area. The interior decoration accents the best Provençal trends, with furniture found at the antique yards of L'Isle-sur-la Sorgue, paintings patinated with Rousillon roan, mementos, and beautiful fabrics. The comfortable rooms are done in the same style, but a bit more soberly. The restaurant serves Provençale specialities made from fresh produce, fruity olive oil, and vegetables from the garden. In winter, there is meat roasted in the fireplace, *foie gras*, and, in all seasons, the desserts "just like Mom used to make." Warm hospitality.

***How to get there*** *( Map 33): Via A 7, take Cavaillon exit, then head toward Apt, take D 36 heading toward Bonnieux. 6 km from Bonnieux, head toward Lourmarin and then Buoux on D 943.*

## Bastide de Capelongue

84480 Bonnieux (Vaucluse)
Tel. (0)4.90.75.89.78 - Fax (0)4.90.75.93.03
Mme Loubet
E-mail: bastide@francemarket.com

**Rooms** 17 with telephone, bath, WC, satellite TV and minibar. **Price** Single and double 1000-1800F / 152,45-274,41€. **Meals** Breakfast 90F / 13,72€, served 8:00-11:00; half board and full board 950-1500F / 144,83-228,67€ (per pers., 2 days min.). **Restaurant** Service 12:15PM-2:00PM, 7:00PM-10:00PM; mealtime specials 270F / 41,16€, also à la carte. **Credit cards** All major. **Pets** Dogs allowed (+90F / 13,72€). **Facilities** Swimming pool, parking and garage. **Nearby** Avignon; Aix-en-Provence; Alpilles; villages of the Luberon -–18-hole Pont Royal golf course. **Open** Mid. Mar – mid. Nov.

From its hilltop scattered with shrubs and lavender, the *Bastide* enjoys a magnificent view over the old village of Bonnieux. Recently opened to the public, it is a mansion belonging to the Loubet family, who also own the *Moulin de Lourmarin*, one of the great restaurants of the region. The interior decoration highlights half-tones of pale grey, pastel blue, terra-cotta ochre, while beautifully patinated Provençal furniture--lovely remakes of 18th-century wardrobes, tables, and chairs--can be admired throughout the hotel. The overall effect is one of soft, serene refinement. Each bedroom is named after a character from the novels of Daudet or Giono; we loved their contemporary comfort and, here too, their delicate shades and materials. Served in a luminous dining room or on the terrace, the menus change daily depending on the vegetables from the hotel's 2 1/2-acre garden, and the meat, fish, and poultry on offer in the market. The *Bastide* is luxurious but worth it.

***How to get there*** *(Map 33): A7 Cavaillon exit; towards Apt, then D36 Bonnieux.*

## Hostellerie du Prieuré

84480 Bonnieux (Vaucluse)
Tel. (0)4.90.75.80.78 - Fax (0)4.90.75.96.00
Mme Coutaz - M. Chapotin

**Category** ★★★ **Rooms** 10 with telephone, bath, WC and TV. **Price** Double 540-670F / 82,32-102,14€. **Meals** Breakfast 50F / 7,62€, served 8:00-10:00. **Restaurant** Closed Tuesday – Friday lunchtime from Jul – Sep and Tuesday, Thursday lunch and Wednesday from Mar– Oct. Service 12:30PM-2:00PM, 7:30PM-9:00PM; mealtime specials 98-198F / 15,24-30,49€, also à la carte 150F / 22,87€. Specialties: Chartreuse d'agneau aux aubergines; crème brûlée à l'essence de truffes. **Credit card** Visa. **Pets** Dogs allowed (extra charge). **Facilities** Parking, garage (40F / 6,10€). **Nearby** Avignon, Aix-en-Provence, Luberon villages – 18-hole Saumane golf course. **Open** Mar – Nov 1.

Spared the gentrification that is slowly taking over the hotels of the Luberon, the *Hostellerie du Prieuré* has retained the charm of the old residences of the past. The grand stairway and its wrought-iron railing, the traditional red floor tiles, and the heavy oak doors evoke memories of the past which will delight those who love beautiful old architecture. We also like the comfortable bedrooms, many with antique furnishings, and their warm colors. The sizes of the rooms, their expositions (the darkest rooms are marvelously cool in summer, yet more somber in winter), and their furnishings are all different. In the spring and summer, the bar service and the dining tables are transported to the leafy garden but we are just as fond of the interior bar and dining room (the bar, in particular, has a highly interesting showcase with old layouts of the main Paris theatres). The reception is agreeable, though sometimes a bit nonchalant, but this spontaneity is also part of what makes this place charming. If you wish to dine out one night, *Le Fournil* serves fine cuisine on a terrace.

***How to get there*** *( Map 33): On A7, exit Cavaillon, go towards Apt, then D36 to Bonnieux.*

## La Bastide de Voulonne

84220 Cabrières-d'Avignon (Vaucluse)
RD 943
Tel. (0)4.90.76.77.55 - Fax (0)4.90.76.77.56
Sophie and Alain Rebourg-Poiri

**Category** ★★★ **Rooms** 5 and 1 suite, with telephone, bath, WC and TV. **Price** Room and suite 400-1000F / 60,98-152,45€. **Meals** Breakfast 55F / 8,38€, served 8:00-10:00. **Restaurant** Service 8:00PM-10:00PM; mealtime specials 150F / 22,87€. **Credit card** Visa. **Pets** Dogs allowed by reservation. **Facilities** Swimming pool, parking. **Nearby** Luberon villages; rock-climbing in Buoux; La Roque-d'Antéron Festival; Market in Apt (Saturday) — 18-hole Saumane golf course. **Open** All year, but by reservation in Jan and Feb.

Two great sycamores hide and cool the authentic façade of this manor house that used to belong to the local governor. This is the Luberon plain, with its fruit trees, only a few minutes from the famous villges that dot the two branches of the valley. Sophie and Alain fell in love with the house, and have just breathed new life and color into it. The famous earth tones of Rousillon, with orange, yellow, and brick red, are found on the walls as well as in the flooring and patterned, Provençal fabrics. With wrought iron, rattan, and an occasional old piece of furniture, all is cheerful and up-to-date -- still a bit "new" but pleasant all the same. Brightened by bow windows overlooking the interior courtyard, the huge dining room is in the former bakery, next to the bread oven. Alain serves Provençale food whipped up from market produce and family recipes. Flowers all around, with, a bit away, a large heated pool. Truly warm hospitality.

***How to get there*** *( Map 33): Via A 7, take the Cavaillon exit. Head toward Apt. At Coustellet, turn toward Gordes-Les Imberts. 2 km later, follow the signs on your right.*

## Château des Fines Roches

84230 Châteauneuf-du-Pape (Vaucluse)
Tel. (0)4.90.83.70.23 - Fax (0)4.90.83.78.42
Philippe and Jean-Pierre Estevenin

**Category** ★★★★ **Rooms** 6 with air-conditioning, telephone, bath, WC and minibar. **Price** Single and double 850-1100F / 129,58-167,69€. **Meals** Breakfast 80F / 12,19€, served 8:00-10:00. **Restaurant** Closed Monday. Service 12:00PM-2:00PM, 7:00PM-9:00PM; mealtime specials 175F / 26,68€ (lunch) and 270-340F / 41,16-51,83€, also à la carte. **Credit cards** Amex, Visa. **Pets** Dogs no allowed. **Facilities** Parking. **Nearby** In Châteauneuf-du-Pape: Père-Anselme Wine Museum; wine cellars and vintners (Château de la Gardine, Château of Nerte, clos du Mont-Olivet, clos des Papes, domaine Bousquet des Papes, domaine Durieu; in Bédarrides: domaine Font de Michelle); Avignon; Orange. **Closed** Nov 15 – 30.

Châteauneuf-du-Pape recalls more the Côtes- du-Rhône vineyards than the summer palace of the Pope at the time that the Comtat Venaissin belonged to Saint-Siège and when John XXII came to stay in Avignon. This is the château of the Marquis Folco de Baroncelli that has been changed into luxurious, charming hotel. The reception areas have the rich, romantic atmosphere of beautiful, country châteaux. The vibrantly colored rooms are more "decorated." With all the comforts, there are a few showers in the towers that have an exceptional view of the vineyards. The Estevin brothers run the kitchen and offer up tasty, gourmet specialities in the beautifully decorated, deep brown dining room, or on the terrace, where the great outdoors becomes part of your pleasure.

***How to get there*** (*Map 33*): *20 km from Avignon via A 7. Take Avignon-nord exit. Via A 9, then Roquemaure exit.*

## Le Mas de Magali

84110 Le Crestet (Vaucluse)
Tel. (0)4.90.36.39.91 - Fax (0)4.90.28.73.40
M. and Mme Bodewes

**Rooms** 10 with telephone, bath and satellite TV. **Price** Doubles 350-450F / 53,36-68,60€. **Meals** Breakfast 45F / 6,86€, served 8:00-10:00. **Restaurant** Service 7:30PM-9:00PM, mealtime specials 135F / 20,58€; also à la carte. Specialties: Rougets au pastis; poulet fermier aux morilles; moruette à la landaise. **Credit card** Visa. **Pets** Dogs allowed (extra charge). **Facilities** Swimming pool, parking. **Nearby** Vaison-la-Romaine, Séguret, Dentelles de Montmirail, wine trail. **Open** Apr – Oct 15.

A bit away from the little medieval town of Crestet, *Le Mas de Magali* seems to be lost in the countryside. The hotel overlooks a superb panorama of hills, vineyards, and cypresses, with the silhouette of Mont Ventoux far away. This view, the flowers, and the beautifully furbished pool area give this place the charm that its architecture lacks. Pleasant and cheerful, though a bit fussy, the interior decor uses a mostly yellow and blue color scheme, mixed and matched in the fabrics, that sing a song of Provence. To the right of the entrance, a bright dining room serves fresh, mouthwatering fare that changes from day to day. The rooms are on the ground floor and upstairs (where you will also find a comfortable library salon). The rooms are cute and rather well-tended. In off season, reserve those with a view and a terrace. In summer, you can also ask for the back rooms, which are cooler, but which sometimes suffer from the noise from the restaurant. A practical address at reasonable prices.

***How to get there*** *(Map 33): At Vaison-la-Romaine, take D 930 toward Malucene, then follow the signs.*

## Hostellerie de Crillon-le-Brave

84410 Crillon-le-Brave (Vaucluse)
Place de l'Eglise
Tel. (0)4.90.65.61.61 - Fax (0)4.90.65.62.86
MM. Chittick and Miller

**Category** ★★★★ **Rooms** 19 and 4 suites (2 suites and 1 room with air-conditioning) with telephone, bath or shower, WC and TV on request. **Price** Single and double 850-1900F / 129,58-289,65€, suite 1600-2600F / 243,92-396,37€. **Meals** Breakfast 90F / 13,72€, served 7:30-11:00; half board +310F / 47,26€ (per pers., 3 days min.). **Restaurant** Open just for the weekend lunchtime. Service 12:00PM-2:30PM — BBQ near the swimming pool in summer. Service 7:30PM-9:30PM; mealtime specials 160F / 24,39€ (lunch), 250-400F / 38,11-60,98€, also à la carte. **Credit cards** All major. **Pets** Dogs allowed (+80F / 12,2€). **Facilities** Swimming pool, bike, garage. **Nearby** Bédoin, Dentelles de Montmirail, Chapel of Le Grozeau, Château of Barroux, Pharmacy Museum at Hôtel-Dieu in Carpentras — 18-hole Grand Avignon golf course. **Closed** Jan — Mar.

Just next to the church stands this beautiful hotel: formerly a large family house, its bedrooms are still named after the former occupants. The building still has its worn flagstone floors and is tastefully decorated with terracotta objects and Provençal antiques found at nearby Isle-sur-la-Sorgue. The bedrooms are extremely comfortable and cozy, and their yellow-ochre walls evoke the Midi sun. The two lounges contain shelves loaded with old books, comfortable sofas and windows looking over the pink rooftops of the village. A terraced garden, with pretty wrought-iron furniture in its many shady corners, leads down from a waterlily pond to the swimming pool, where a grill has been set up.

*How to get there ( Map 33): 15km north of Carpentras via D974 and D138.*

## Hostellerie La Manescale

Les Essareaux 84340 Entrechaux (Vaucluse)
Route de Faucon
Tel. (0)4.90.46.03.80 - Fax (0)4.90.46.03.89
Mme Warland

**Rooms** 5 with telephone, bath or shower, WC, TV and minibar. **Price** Double 450-650F / 68,60-99,09€, suite 550-950F / 83,85-144,83€. **Meals** Breakfast 75F / 11,43€, served 8:30-10:00. **Restaurant** For residents only. Specialties: Cooking with fresh local produce. **Credit cards** All major. **Pets** Dogs allowed (+60F / 9,15€). **Facilities** Swimming pool, parking. **Nearby** Cathedral of Notre-Dame-de-Nazareth in Vaison-la-Romaine, Dentelles de Montmirail, Séguret – 18-hole Grand Avignon golf course. **Open** Easter – mid. Oct.

Formerly a shepherd's house and now carefully rebuilt and restored, this pleasant inn stands among vineyards and olive trees between the Drôme and the Vaucluse, facing Mont Ventoux. The bedrooms are luxuriously equipped and tastefully decorated, providing every thoughtful detail. Some of them are small suites (the Provence room, for instance). The pleasure of a hearty breakfast on the terrace is enhanced by the magical scenery: a peaceful valley, crowned by the Ventoux, displaying a subtle and ever-changing palette of colors and light. Hotel facilities also include a superb swimming pool. This is a place one would like to keep to oneself, but enthusiastic readers' letters have made sharing the secret a pleasure. In the evening, you can enjoy a good cold dinner, or you can go out to the *Saint-Hubert* or *Chez Anaïs* in Entrechaux. Note that only children over seven can stay in the hotel.

*How to get there (Map 33): 8km east of Vaison-la-Romaine via D205. Via A7, take Bollène exit.*

# Les Florets

84190 Gigondas (Vaucluse)
Route des Dentelles
Tel. (0)4.90.65.85.01 - Fax (0)4.90.65.83.80
Mme Bernard

**Category** ★★ **Rooms** 13 and 1 apart., with telephone, bath or shower, WC and TV. **Price** Double 450-700F / 68,60-106,71€. **Meals** Breakfast 60F / 9,15€, served 8:00-10:00; half board 900F / 137,20€ (2 pers., 3 days min.). **Restaurant** Service 12:00PM-2:00PM, 7:30PM-9:00PM; mealtime specials 100-190F / 15,24-28,97€, also à la carte. Specialties: Tian de morue aux artichauts; concassée de tomates au basilic. **Credit cards** All major. **Pets** Dogs allowed (+40F / 6,10€). **Facilities** Parking. **Nearby** Chapel of Notre-Dame-d'Aubune, Séguret, Dentelles de Montmirail, cathedral and Roman bridge in Vaison-la-Romaine – 18-hole Grand Avignon golf course. **Closed** Jan, Feb and Wednesday.

*L*es Florets occupies an enviable position in the middle of the countryside at an altitude of 1200 feet facing the peaks of Montmirail and overlooking the Gigondas vineyards. This is a simple country hotel, traditional in style, with a pleasant family atmosphere. The jagged peaks above can be viewed from the terrace, where an arbor provides welcome shade. The bedrooms are simple and unpretentious, but comfortable enough and have a view of the trees. We recommend the new and very charming bedrooms in the annex. Each opens directly onto the garden. The furniture is tasteful and the rooms and baths have modern conveniences. The restaurant serves regional specialties accompanied by local Gigondas wines. The staff are very friendly and the owner will be happy to show you his cellars and have you taste his wines.

***How to get there*** *(Map 33): 25km east of Orange via D975 towards Vaison-la-Romaine, then D8 and D80; on the Dentelles de Montmirail road.*

## Hôtel La Gacholle

84220 Gordes (Vaucluse)
Route de Murs
Tel. (0)4.90.72.01.36 - Fax (0)4.90.72.01.81- Eric Bongert and Hervé Sabat
E-mail: la.gacholle.gordes@wanadoo.fr

**Category** ★★★ **Rooms** 11 with telephone, bath, WC, minibar and TV, 3 with safe. **Price** Double 450-750F / 68,60-114,34€. **Meals** Breakfast 60F / 9,15€. **Restaurant** Service 12:00PM-2:00PM, 7:00PM-10:30PM; mealtime specials 85F / 12,96€ (lunch weekdays) and 195F / 29,73€, also à la carte. **Credit cards** Amex, Visa. **Pets** Dogs allowed. **Facilities** Swimming pool, tennis, parking. **Nearby** Gordes and Luberon villages; Sénanque Abbey; Marcket in Apt (Saturday) – 18-hole golf course in Saumane. **Closed** Jan 10 – Mar 15.

Gordes is probably the best known and the most visited village in Luberon, which can be a problem in high season. We are only all the more pleased to find this quiet, little hotel just a bit away from the village with an awesome view of the plain. To take advantage of this panorama, the whole building looks out on the vista. The little, comfortable rooms have just been renovated in a tastefully, current style, with thick, greyish-brown bedcovers with white, arabesque piqué, tan walls, gorse flooring, diverse modern furniture, and tobacco or yellow curtains. Private terraces for the ground-floor rooms. A beautiful lounge with a fireplace, done up in Provençal colors with some baroque, wrought-iron pieces, opens onto the panoramic dining room bordered by an awning. The fare is truly excellent, heartily flavoured, perfectly cooked, and well-accompanied with vegetables. There is an pleasant outside bar next to the pool

***How to get there*** *(Map 33): At Avignon, take N 100 toward Apt. At Coustellet, take a left toward Gordes. At the château, turn left toward Murs. The hotel is 1.5 km away.*

## Domaine de la Fontaine

84800 Isle-sur-la-Sorgue (Vaucluse)
920, chemin du Bosquet
Tel. (0)4.90.38.01.44 - Fax (0)4.90.38.53.42
M. and Mme Sundheimer

**Rooms** 3 and 2 suites with telephone, shower, WC and TV. **Price** Double 490-580F / 74,70-88,42€; suite (3 pers) 820F / 125,01€, extra bed 100F / 15,24€. **Meals** Breakfast incl. **Restaurant** For residents only by reservation. Service at 8:00PM, mealtime specials 140F / 21,34€. Specialties: Lotte à la provençale, lapin aux pruneaux, magret de canette. **Credit cards** Not accepted. **Pets** Dogs not allowed. **Facilities** Swimming pool and parking. **Nearby** l'Isle-sur-Sorgue, flea market and Provençal market on Sunday, Fontaine de Vaucluse, Gordes, the Bories, Abbey of Sénanque; Avignon; the Luberon – 18-hole Saumane golf course.

Once directors of two restaurants in Munich, Irmy and Dominique Sundheimer fell in love with this old Provençal mas and the surrounding countryside. Just minutes from Isle-sur-la-Sorgue, the *Domaine de la Fontaine* is surrounded by an immense cultivated plain with hedgerows for protection from the *mistral* wind. The Domaine has few rooms and is so intimate, like a cross between a small hotel and a bed and breakfast. The bedrooms have been entirely renovated, each with its predominant color, simple, pleasant furnishings, lovely beds and bedding, and huge bathrooms. The dinner menu, which varies with the market and Irmy's inspiration. The dining tables are set up in the spacious dining room (its decoration still lacks warmth and patina) or on the terrace under a three-century-old plane trees. Breakfast is also served there, and we enjoyed lingering over our coffee while listening to the murmur of the *Domaine*'s "fountain".

***How to get there*** *( Map 33): A7, Avignon-sud or Cavaillon exit. In the town, take N100 to Apt, after "Citroën/Total" garage on the right, take first left.*

## Mas de Cure Bourse

84800 Isle-sur-la-Sorgue (Vaucluse)
Carrefour de Velorgues
Tel. (0)4.90.38.16.58 - Fax (0)4.90.38.52.31
M. and Mme Pomarède

**Category** ★★★ **Rooms** 13 with telephone, bath, WC and TV. **Price** Double 400-600F / 60,98-91,47€. **Meals** Breakfast 50F / 7,62€; half board 455-530F / 69,36-80,80€. **Restaurant** Closed 3 weeks in Nov and 2 weeks in Jan, Monday and Tuesday lunch. Service 12:00PM-1:30PM, 8:00PM-9:30PM; mealtime specials 165-260F / 25,15-39,64€, also à la carte. Specialties: Chèvre pistou et tapenade; moelleux chocolat-griottes. **Credit card** Visa. **Pets** Dogs allowed (+50F / 7,62€). **Facilities** Swimming pool, parking. **Nearby** Isle-sur-Sorgue, flea market and Provençal market on Sunday, Vaucluse fountain, Gordes, the Bories, Abbey of Sénanque – 18-hole Saumane golf course. **Open** All year.

The *Mas de Cure Bourse* is a former postal relay station which was built in 1754 on the plain of Isle-sur-la-Sorgue and you'll probably have the impression of getting lost in a labyrinth of tiny roads before reaching the *mas*. Recently taken over by the Pomarède family, the tradition of fine food seems to continue here. Seasonal specialities are served in the pretty dining room in front of a a crackling fireplace or under the shady terrace. (You can watch the food being prepared thanks to a large window between the reception area and the kitchens.) The decoration and the modern amenities in the bedrooms are impeccable. We prefer *La Chambre du Bout*, the Room at the End, with its small balcony and view over the swimming pool.

***How to get there*** *(Map 33): On A7, exit Avignon-sud or Cavaillon. 3km from Isle-sur-la-Sorgue, on D938, road from Carpentras to Cavaillon, Velorgues cross road.*

## Auberge du Cheval Blanc

84240 La Bastide-des-Jourdans (Vaucluse)
Tel. (0)4.90.77.81.08 - Fax (0)4.90.77.86.51
Mme Agnès Maillet

**Rooms** 4 (3 with air-conditioning), with telephone, bath, WC, TV and minibar. **Price** Double 380-500F / 57,93-76,22€. **Meals** Breakfast 55F / 8,38€, served 8:00. **Restaurant** Closed Thursday. Service 12:00PM-1:30PM, 7:30PM-9:30PM; mealtime specials 150-215F / 22,87-32,78€, also à la carte. Specialties: Rougets poêlés à l'huile d'olive; tartare de tomates aux avocats; carpaccio d'artichauts au parmesan; ragoût d'artichauts à la caillette provençale. **Credit cards** Visa, Eurocard and MasterCard. **Pets** Dogs allowed. **Facilities** Parking. **Nearby** Tour-d'Aigues; châteaux of Ansouis and de Lourmarin; Manosque – 18-hole Pierrevert golf course. **Closed** End Jan – end Feb.

Between Cavaillon and Manosque, the old mounts of Luberon have become, over the years, a refuge for Parisians and wealthy foreigners. On the border between the Vaucluse and Alpes-de-Haute-Provence regions, this village has kept the genuine look of the Giono country. This *auberge* is a former horse station that Agnes and Serge Maillet bought up, some years ago, to make a gourmet stop inspired by the food of Provence. Today, the pretty house has added some charming, upstairs rooms. Tradition and elegance inspired the decor, while not forgetting comfort and refinement. Roomy, cool, and bright, all of them have a little lounge, and the streetside rooms are air-conditioned. Only 15 km away from Manosque, this nice inn and good eatery invites you to come spend some time in lavender country. And once the proposed pool is finished, you'll find it hard to leave the place.

***How to get there*** *( Map 33): 37 m from Aix-en-Provence; 15 km from Manosque. On the D 956 between Pertuis and Manosque.*

496

## Le Mas des Grès

84800 Lagnes (Vaucluse)
Route d'Apt
Tel. (0)4.90.20.32.85 - Fax (0)4.90.20.21.45 - M. and Mme Crovara
E-mail: mas.des.gres@wanadoo.fr

**Category ★★ Rooms** 14 and 2 suites with telephone, bath, WC (6 with TV). **Price** Double 390-750F / 59,46-114,34€, suite (4 pers.) 1100F / 167,69€. **Meals** Breakfast 55F / 8,38€, served 8:00-11:00; half board +425-650F / 64,79-99,09€ (per pers. in double room). **Restaurant** For residents only by reservation. Cold lunches in July and August. Diner: 8:00PM-9:30PM, mealtime specials 100F / 15,24€ (lunch), 165F / 25,15€. Specialties: Provençale cooking. **Credit card** Visa. **Pets** Dogs not allowed. **Facilities** Swimming pool, parking. **Nearby** Isle-sur-la-Sorgue, Vaucluse Provençale, Gordes, the Bories, Sénanque Abbey – 18-hole Saumane golf course. **Closed** Nov 15 – Mar 15 (except by reservation).

A little bit guest house, a little bit inn, *Le Mas des Grès*, right next to the heavily visited Isle-sur-la-Sorgue, is still a wonderful place to stay. The hotel is beautiful, everything cheerful and in good taste. It's a lovely place, a hotel that is the contrary of a hotel, more like a vacation home filled with laughter and *joie de vivre*. The lounge and the bedrooms are elegantly simple, as charming as the guest room you'd find in a friend's house; and some also have some great advantages: Room 8 and two adjoining rooms can accommodate an entire family, and Room 6 is perfect for children. In the evening, the restaurant, reserved for residents, offers seasonal Provençale cuisine, which you can enjoy outside beneath an arbor; in July and August, a small cold buffet is served at lunch. A swimming pool (yes, next to the road) is a great place to cool off. Surrounded by orchards, the Mas des Grès is your home away from home in the Luberon.

***How to get there*** *(Map 33): On A7, take Avignon exit toward l'Isle-sur-la-Sorgue, then toward Apt via N100 for 5km.*

## Ferme de la Huppe

Les Pourquiers 84220 Gordes (Vaucluse)
Route D 156
Tel. (0)4.90.72.12.25 - Fax (0)4.90.72.01.83 - M. Konings

**Rooms** 9 (4 with air-conditioning) with telephone, bath, shower, WC, TV and minibar. **Price** Single and double 400-700F / 60,98-106,71€. **Meals** Breakfast incl., served 8:30-10:30. **Restaurant** Open evenings and Saturday noon, closed Thursday. Service 12:00PM-1:30PM, 7:30PM-9:00PM; mealtime specials 150-210F / 22,87-32,01€, also à la carte. Specialties: Seasonal cooking. **Credit cards** Visa, Eurocard and MasterCard. **Pets** Dogs not allowed. **Facilities** Swimming pool, parking. **Nearby** The Bories, Sénanque Abbey, Roussillon, l'Isle-la-Sorgue, Vaucluse Fountaine – 18-hole Saumane golf course. **Open** End Mar – Dec 19.

The small road winding across the Luberon plain gradually turns into a track, leading to this beautifully restored, secluded old farmhouse. Everything revolves around the fig tree, the olive trees, and the well in the middle of a small inner courtyard. It gives access to the six delightful bedrooms named after the old parts of the building: *La cuisine*, *L'écurie*, *La cuve*... the "kitchen", the "stables", and the "wine vat". Their terracotta floors, thick walls and small windows ensure both privacy and coolness, but make the rooms a bit dark, which might not please everybody. They are decorated with old objects and elegant fabrics, and all are very comfortable. A covered patio adjoining the dining room looks onto a beautiful swimming pool screened by flowers and lavender. Young chef Gérald Konings' inspired cuisine is fast gaining him a reputation. The *Ferme* offers an excellent reputation in this region of high gastronomic standards. Last but not least, the hospitality is charmings and the prices are still very reasonable.

*How to get there ( Map 33 ): 25km northeast of Cavaillon to Gordes via D2; then toward Joucas for 2.5km, then right toward Goult for 500 meters.*

## Auberge La Fenière

84160 Lourmarin (Vaucluse)
Route de Cadenet
Tel. (0)4.90.68.11.79 - Fax (0)4.90.68.18.60 - Reine and Guy Sammut

**Rooms** 7 with air-conditioning, telephone, bath, WC and TV — 1 for disabled persons. **Price** Double 600-800F / 91,47-121,96€; suite 1000F / 152,45€. **Meals** Breakfast 85F / 12,96€, served at any time. **Restaurant** Closed Monday lunchtime in high season, Monday in low season. Service 12:00PM-1:30PM, 7:00PM-9:30PM; mealtime specials 200-550F / 30,49-83,85€. Specialties: Saint-pierre à la vanille et huile d'olive de Cucuron; pigeonneau fermier rôti en cocotte à l'ail confit. **Credit cards** All major. **Pets** Dogs allowed (+40F / 6,10€). **Facilities** Swimming pool, parking. **Nearby** The Luberon, Aix-en-Provence, La Roque d'Anthéron (Piano Festival in Aug), Market in Apt (Saturday) — 18-hole Pont Royal golf course in Mallemout. **Closed** Jan.

Reine Sammut is famed as one of the France's leading women chefs, and the name "La Fenière" will surely bring back mouthwatering memories for many a gourmet. Today, the restaurant has moved from the center of Lourmarin and opened nearby in the heart of the countryside. Madame Sammut has opened seven bedrooms with all the amenities, each dedicated to an art or a craft. Designed to reflect their name, the rooms are fashionable, warm, and original in decor. Five rooms also have a pleasant terrace with a view of the Durance Valley: they're our favorites. On the ground floor, the reception lounge has a colonial feel with tables and small armchairs in exotic wood, while the large, more modern dining room adjacent to it is the soul of Provençal *joie de vivre* with its high, bright-red chairs and its stunning, rainbow-colored plates. The newly planted gardens are as carefully tended as Reine Sammut's *grande cuisine*.

***How to get there*** *( Map 33): 30km northeast of Aix-en-Provence; via A7, take Sénas exit, via A51 Pertuis exit.*

## Le Mas du Loriot

Murs 84220 Gordes (Vaucluse)
Route de Joucas
Tel. (0)4.90.72.62.62 - Fax (0)4.90.72.62.54
Mme Thillard

**Rooms** 8 with telephone, bath or shower, WC, TV and minibar – Wheelchair access. **Price** Double 550-700F / 83,85-106,71€ (1 room 270F / 41,16€). **Meals** Breakfast 70F / 10,67€, served 8:30-10:30; half board 575F / 87,66€ (per pers., in double, obligatory in summer). **Restaurant** Closed Nov 15 – Mar 6. Service from 8:00PM; mealtime specials 185F / 28,20€. Specialties: Filet de bœuf à l'anchoïade; lotte aux petits légumes; pavé de cabillaud à l'huile d'olive et tapenade. **Credit cards** Visa, Eurocard and MasterCard. **Pets** Dogs allowed (+50F / 7,62€). **Facilities** Swimming pool and parking. **Nearby** The Bories, Abbey of Sénanque, Roussillon, Isle-sur-la-Sorgue, Fontaine de Vaucluse - 18-hole Saumane golf course. **Closed** Dec 15 – Mar 6.

The small road winds around Joucas, begins to climb the slope and a few hundred feet farther up, a lane leads into the garrigue and to this minuscule hotel surrounded by lavender, pine trees, and green oaks. Eight recently installed bedrooms offer modern amenities, a private terrace for each, charming decoration in cool colors, and a magnificent view: perfect for those who love an intimate, quiet place to stay. The restaurant has a single menu, different every evening. Lovingly prepared by Madame Thillard, its good family cooking is made with fresh farm products; you will be served in a dining room with elegant wrought-iron furniture, or on the terrace overlooking the Luberon. The welcome extended by the owners and their young children, Julien and Sophie-Charlotte, made us want to return. Soon.

***How to get there*** *( Map 33): 25km northeast of Cavaillon via D2, then towards Joucas, then Murs.*

## Mas des Capelans

84580 Oppède (Vaucluse)
Tel. (0)4.90.76.99.04 - Fax (0)4.90.76.90.29
Monsieur and Madame Poiri

**Rooms** 8 with telephone, bath, WC and TV. **Price** Double 400-900F / 60,98-137,20€; suite 600-1000F / 91,47-152,45€. **Meals** Breakfast 60F / 9,15€, served 8:30-10:30; half board 400-650F / 60,98-99,09€ (per pers., 3 days min.). **Evening meals** Closed Sunday and 2 nights in low season. Service at 8:00PM; mealtime specials 160F / 24,39€. Specialties: Lapereau au romarin, navarin aux petits légumes, pintade aux cerises. **Credit cards** All major. **Pets** Dogs allowed on request (+70F / 10,67€). **Facilities** Heated swimming pool, billiards, parking. **Nearby** Northern Luberon (Ménerbes, Lacoste, Bonnieux, Saint-Symphorien priory, Buoux, Apt) – 18-hole Saumane golf course. **Open** Mar – Nov 15.

A former silk worm nursery of the Senanque Abbey, the *Mas des Capelans* offers 8 spacious, comfortable, and well-tended guest rooms. Each one is named after the view it has, like *Rousillon*, *Gordes*, or quiet simply *Les vignes* ("Vineyards"). The reception area, with its high exposed frame, is outfitted with comfortable furniture of various styles set up around the fireplace. Some evenings, Monsieur and Madame Poiri set a mouthwatering communal table with Provençale food, either in the main area or outside under the gazebo, which quickly becomes a cosmopolitan occasion that finishes late at night. The good breakfast is served on separate tables in either the veranda decorated with Southern French objects or the interior courtyard under the shade of the blackberry trees. The surroundings are particularly flowery, the swimming pool included, which is such a hard place to leave.

***How to get there*** *( Map 33 ): 10 km east of Cavaillon. On A 7, take the Avignon-sud exit, then N 100 toward Apt. Between Coustellet and Beaumette. Follow the signs.*

# Hôtel Arène

84100 Orange (Vaucluse)
Place de Langes
Tel. (0)4.90.11.40.40 - Fax (0)4.90.11.40.45
M. and Mme Coutel

**Category** ★★★ **Rooms** 30 with air-conditioning, telephone, bath or shower, WC, minibar, safe and TV. **Price** Single and double 350-550F / 53,36-83,85€. **Meals** Breakfast 46F / 6,86€, served 7:00AM-12:00PM. No restaurant. **Credit cards** All major. **Pets** Dogs allowed. **Facilities** Garage. **Nearby** Old theater and Arc de Triomphe in Orange, Mornas, Henri Fabre Museum in Sérignan, gorges of Ardèche, Vaison-la-Romaine – 18-hole Grand Avignon golf course. **Closed** Nov – Dec.

Driving around in Orange requires nerves of steel, but once you get to the hotel (the street there is also for pedestrians), you'll quickly forget this inconvenience because their are many garages for the guests. You will be next to the ancient theater on a little pedestrian square under the shade of centuries-old sycamores. The city now takes on all its charm. The rooms, all different, are more or less large, comfortable, remarkably well-looked-after, and cheerful on the average (some are a bit dark). Well-prepared breakfasts are served in dining room bursting with Provençale color. The hotel has no restaurant, but *Le Garden* is right next door and offers good food served under a shady terrace in summer. *Le Parvis* is another good Orange restaurant (reservations necessary, particularly during the summer vacation season).

***How to get there*** *( Map 33 ): Enter Orange by the Avenue de l'Arc de Triomphe, go straight ahead until rue Victor-Hugo. The hotel is almost at the end of the street on the left.*

## Mas La Bonoty

84210 Pernes-les-Fontaines (Vaucluse)
Chemin de la Bonyoty
Tel. (0)4.90.61.61.09 - Fax (0)4.90.61.35.14 - R. Ryan - P. Cuff
E-mail: bonoty@aol.com - Web: bonoty.com

**Rooms** 8 with telephone, bath or shower, some with TV. **Price** Single and double 300-350F / 45,73-53,36€. **Meals** Breakfast 45F / 6,86€, served 8:00-10:00; half board 360F / 54,88€ (per pers.). **Restaurant** Closed Sunday evening and Monday in low season. Service 12:00PM-2:00PM, 7:30PM-9:00PM; mealtime specials 110F / 16,77€ (lunchtime weekdays), 165-220F / 25,15-33,54€; also à la carte. Specialties: Foie gras de canard poêlé au rasteau sur risotto d'épautre; gratinée de queues de langoustines et Saint-Jacques; fondant de chocolat au lait d'amandes. **Credit cards** Amex, Visa. **Pets** Dogs allowed by reservation. **Facilities** Swimming pool, parking. **Nearby** Mazan; Comtat Venaissin, Crillon-le-Brave, Bédouin, Chalet-Reynard, Malaucène, Barroux, Caromb, Carpentras. **Closed** 2 weeks in Nov and 3 weeks in Feb.

A former 17th-century farm, the *Mas La Bonoty* has been carefully restored and is far from the beaten path. Refined Provençale food is served here, in a very nice dining room with stone walls, warmed by a grand fireplace. In summer, breakfast is under the shade of the pines, and dinner is taken on the terrace next to the pool. Red hexagonal floor tiles, polished wood furniture, and cotton fabrics give the rooms that Provençal look of yesteryear. They are not all that large, but are perfectly comfortable. The surrounding park, planted with apricot trees, cherry trees, olive trees, and lavander, adds to the tranquility of the locale. The polite hospitality of Richard Ryan and Peter Cuff, who founded the beautiful *Auberge d'Enrose* in Gers a few years ago, make this a high-quality place to stay.

***How to get there*** *( Map 33): Via A 7, take Avignon nord exit, then head toward Carpentras. In the center of Pernse, head toward Manzan on D 1, then follow the signs.*

## L'Orangerie

84420 Piolenc (Vaucluse)
4, rue de l'Ormeau
Tel. (0)4.90.29.59.88 - Fax (0)4.90.29.67.74 - Mme de La Rocque
E-mail: orangerie@wanadoo.fr

**Rooms** 5 with bath or shower, WC and telephone. **Price** Single and double 300-480F / 45,73-73,18€, apart. 600F / 91,47€ (4 pers.). **Meals** Breakfast 50F / 7,62€, served 8:30-10:30; half board from 340F / 51,83€ (obligatory in summer). **Restaurant** Service 12:00PM-2:00PM, 7:30PM-9:30PM; mealtime specials 90-200F / 13,72-30,49€. Specialties: Foie gras; crabe farci; zarzuela; magret aux airelles. **Credit card** Visa. **Pets** Dogs allowed by request with extra charge. **Facilities** Parking. **Nearby** Henri Fabre Museum in Sérignan, old theater and Arc de Triomphe of Orange, Chorégies of Orange in July and August, Mornas – 18-hole Moulin golf course. **Open** All year.

Vegetation has overrun the inner courtyard of this hotel. Set back on a small road, *L'Orangerie* is a quiet hotel. Meals are served in a beautiful barrel-vaulted dining room with huge French windows, the outside tables make for cool summer dinners beneath flowers and climbing plants. The food is copious, and the wine and whisky selection is superb. (We recommend the simple dishes.) An amateur artist, Monsieur de la Rocque exhibits his strikingly faithful reproductions of chiaroscuro paintings by Georges de la Tour. His wife has turned the bathrooms into miniature museums. The charming bedrooms, have antique objects and 19th-century furniture. The most beautiful room, Delatour, even has a terrace-solarium. However, some rooms deserve a makeover. If you prefer Provençal decor and more modern accommodations, reserve rooms at *La Mandarine*, just 1.5 km away and part of the hotel. Friendly hospitality.

***How to get there*** *(Map 33): 6 km north of Orange. Via A 7, take Orange centre exit. (Or the Bollene exit if you are coming from Lyon on N 7 to Marseille.)*

# Mas de Garrigon

84220 Roussillon (Vaucluse)
Route de Saint-Saturnin
Tel. (0)4.90.05.63.22 - Fax (0)4.90.05.70.01 - Mme Druart
E:mail: mas.de.garrigon.@wanadoo.fr

**Category** ★★★ **Rooms** 9 with telephone, bath, shower, WC, TV and minibar. **Price** Single and double 650-820F / 99,09-125,01€, suite 1080F / 164,64€. **Meals** Breakfast 90F / 13,72€, served 7:30-10:30; half board 600-850F / 91,47-129,58€. **Restaurant** Closed Monday and Tuesday noon. Service 12:00PM-2:00PM, 8:00PM-9:00PM; mealtime specials 145F / 22,1€ (lunchtime), 195-360F / 29,73-54,88€, also à la carte. Specialties: Agneau des Alpes et jus au romarin; poissons de Méditerranée; desserts gourmands. **Credit cards** All major. **Pets** Dogs not allowed. **Facilities** Swimming pool, parking. **Nearby** Gordes, the Bories, Sénanque Abbey, Isle-sur-la-Sorgue, Luberon – 18-hole Saumane golf course. **Open** All year.

An attractive place to stay in all seasons, the *Mas de Garrigon* is a Provençal-style house built in 1978 and surrounded by luxuriant vegetation with the marvelous smell of Provence. Around the swimming pool, reserved exclusively for residents of the hotel, the chaises-longues are a veritable invitation to sit back and relax; you can also have lunch there. The comfortable lounge-library has the appeal of a private room with its objects, paintings, and its beautiful fireplace. All the bedrooms have been decorated with similar care, and we felt very much at home in them (each room has a private terrace facing due south, with a superb view over the ochre soil of Roussillon). Light cuisine is made with fresh produce from the local markets and prepared so as to enhance the innate taste of the ingredients. Roussillon is truly a jewel in the crown of the Luberon.

***How to get there*** *( Map 33): 48km east of Avignon via N100 towards Apt, then D2 towards Gordes and D102.*

## Auberge du Presbytère

Saignon 84400 Apt (Vaucluse)
Place de la Fontaine
Tel. (0)4.90.74.11.50 - Fax (0)4.90.04.68.51 - M. and Mme Bernardi
E-mail: auberge.presbytere@provence-luberon.com.

**Rooms** 10 with bath and WC. **Price** Double 280-580F / 42,69-88,42€. **Meals** Breakfast 50F / 7,62€, served 8:30-10:00. **Restaurant** Service 12:30PM-1:30PM, 8:00PM-9:00PM; mealtime specials 170F / 25,92€. Specialties: Provençale cooking; ruchamandier. **Credit cards** Amex, Visa. **Pets** Small dogs allowed on request. **Nearby** Saignon Church, Luberon, Buoux, Saint-Symphorien priory, Bonnieux, Lacoste, Ménerbes, Oppède, Maubec, Robion – 18-hole Saumane golf course. **Open** By reservation.

When Monsieur and Madame Bernardi left Saint-Tropez, their idea was to open a bed-and-breakfast here in the heart of the Luberon. Things turned out differently, but the idea is the same: welcoming guests at their *Auberge du Presbytère* as if they were friends. The *auberge* is made up of three village houses which have been combined, creating a complex of rooms on charmingly different levels. The interior is furnished with antiques, as in a country house. The bedrooms are delightful. Charming and of a great variety of sizes, the rooms have kept their unique authenticity. Some have a view, others don't. When you make your reservation, best to ask for a description of the available rooms. The restaurant offers two daily menus with appetizing traditional, regional recipes served in the dining room or on the terrace at noon and in the interior garden in the evening. A fun, vacation house located on an irresistible little square in the heights of a charming Luberon village. Reasonable prices for the area.

***How to get there*** *(Map 33): 35km southeast of Apt; in the high part of the village.*

## Hostellerie du Val de Sault

84390 Sault (Vaucluse)
Route de Saint-Trinit
Tel. (0)4.90.64.01.41 - Fax (0)4.90.64.12.74

**Rooms** 11 and 5 suites with telephone, bath, WC, TV and minibar – 1 for disabled persons. **Price** Double 510-790F / 77,75-120,43€. **Meals** Breakfast 72F / 11,43€, served 8:00-10:00; half board 420-560F / 64,12-85,37€ (per pers.). **Restaurant** Service 12:30PM-2:00PM, 7:30PM-9:00PM; mealtime specials 129F / 19,82€ (lunchtime)- 230-495F / 35,06-75,46€ (mealtime with truffles). Specialties: L'œuf frais du jour cuit minute à l'infusion de truffes du Ventoux et ses mouillettes à l'épeautres. **Credit cards** Amex, Visa, Eurocard and MasterCard. **Pets** Dogs allowed. **Facilities** Swimming pool, tennis, fitness center, parking. **Nearby** Mazan, Venasque, Pernes-les-Fontaines, Comtat Venaissin; Luberon. **Closed** Beg Nov – beg Apr.

As you head up the mountain, you might find it hard to imagine that there is a hotel up there, lost in the midst of oak trees at an altitude of 2400 feet, and just above a superb valley speckled with lavender. Recently constructed, the buildings blend in perfectly with the spectacular site. One houses the spacious restaurant with a high, beamed ceiling, which opens out onto a beautiful terrace. Its reputed cuisine seems fine and creative: unfortunately, we were not able to taste it during our visit, but we are told that the half board is excellent. The bedrooms are located in the upper. Very comfortable with their veranda lounge that opens out to a large, panoramic private terrace; the rooms are simply and cheerfully decorated, somewhat reminiscent of a chalet (natural or streaked pine, carpets, colorful fabrics). The new suites with room and lounge are level with the garden in front of the Ventoux. You will enjoy total quiet at the *Val de Sault*, and a most friendly welcome.

***How to get there*** *(Map 33): 50km east of Carpentras via D1, to Mazan and Sault, towards Saint-Trinit.*

## La Table du Comtat

84110 Séguret (Vaucluse)
Tel. (0)4.90.46.91.49 - Fax (0)4.90.46.94.27
M. Franck Gomez

**Category** ★★★ **Rooms** 8 with telephone, bath, WC and TV. **Price** Double 470-600F / 70,13-91,47€.
**Meals** Breakfast 80F / 12,19€, served 8:00-10:00; half board 580-640F / 88,42-97,57€ (per pers.).
**Restaurant** Service 12:30PM-2:00PM, 7:30PM-9:00PM; mealtime specials 170-460F / 25,92-70,13€,
also à la carte. Specialties: Regional cooking. **Credit cards** Amex, Visa, Diners. **Pets** Dogs allowed.
**Facilities** Swimming pool, parking. **Nearby** Dentelles de Montmirail; Mont Ventoux; Séguret; Vaison-
la-Romaine. **Closed** Feb.

Hanging on the little rocky foothills that turn into the delicate, Montmirail
range a bit further away, Seguret is definitely one of the most beautiful
villages of Vaucluse. The hotel is on the heights, next to the church, and its
exceptional location made us choose it. How could you be unmoved by the
enormous plain that spreads out below you, sumptuously ablaze when the last
light of day spreads the shadows of cypresses over the green vineyards and
gilds the distant, hillside village of Sablet below? You will enjoy this vista from
the little rooms (white, simple, and rustically decorated), and especially from
the beautiful dining room, which looks out over this wide, open space. It's also
the case with the charming terrace, shaded by a blackberry tree, and the little
pool set up amongst the rocks. The gourmet food is highly reputed, a bit
expensive, but indisputably well-prepared. The salon is pleasantly furnished in
antiques. The fireplace sports a stunning nativity scene representing the
inhabitants of the village.

***How to get there*** *(Map 33): Via A7, take Bollène exit coming from north.*
*Orange exit from south, then D 8 and D 23.*

## Hostellerie du Vieux Château

84830 Sérignan (Vaucluse)
Route de Sainte-Cécile
Tel. (0)4.90.70.05.58 - Fax (0)4.90.70.05.62 - M. and Mme Truchot

**Rooms** 7 with telephone, bath, WC, TV and minibar – Wheelchair access. **Price** Double 400-800F / 60,98-121,96€. **Meals** Breakfast 50F / 7,62€, served 8:00-10:00. **Restaurant** Closed Sunday evening and Monday in low season. Service 12:30PM-1:30PM, 7:30PM-9:00PM; mealtime specials 155-260F / 23,63-39,64€, also à la carte. Specialties: Foie gras au Beaume-de-Venise; canard au cassis. **Credit cards** Amex, Visa. **Pets** Dogs allowed (+50F / 7,62€). **Facilities** Swimming pool, parking. **Nearby** Arc de Triomphe and old theater in Orange; Mornas, Henri Fabre Museum in Sérignan. **Closed** 1 week in Nov, Dec 6 – 31 and Sunday evening and Monday in low season.

This was originally a farmhouse with a mill in the back whose only remaining trace is a tiny canal that runs the length of the building. Today, the hotel is a large village house flanked by a small vegetable garden and a pleasant flower garden filled with fragrant lavender around the swimming pool. The owners run a very traditional hotel, with M. Truchot in the kitchen and his wife at the reception. The atmosphere is that of a quiet, simple, family-style provincial *auberge*. The bedrooms are comfortable and each decorated in a personalized way. Room 1 has a lot of charm with its alcove bed. 2 flaunts a little lounge (furnished in a rather chilly way, to our minds). Rooms 3 and 6 are charming with their antique or retro furniture. The others are also recommendable, except for 5, which is small and has too-high windows. In summer, meals are served in the shade of the beautiful plane trees in the garden, making for a very Provençal setting.

***How to get there*** *( Map 33): 7 km northeast of Orange. Via A 7, take Orange centre exit ( or Bollène exit if you're coming from Lyon). Then N 7 and D 976 toward Serignan.*

## Domaine de la Ponche

84190 Vacqueras (Vaucluse)
Tel. (0)4.90.65.85.21 - Fax (0)4.90.65.85.23
M. Jean-Pierre Onimus

**Rooms** 4 and 2 suites, with telephone, bath and satellite TV. **Price** Double 500-900F / 76,22-137,20€, 3 pers. 600-750F / 91,47-114,34€; suite 1180F / 179,89€ (2 pers.). **Meals** Breakfast 40F / 6,10€, served 8:00-10:30; half board 160F / 24,39€. **Restaurant** Closed Tuesday lunchtime and Saturday lunchtime. Service 12:00PM-2:00PM, 8:00PM-9:30PM; mealtime specials 135-190F / 20,58-28,97€, also à la carte. Specialties: Pigeon au Rasteau. **Credit card** Visa. **Pets** Dogs allowed (+50F / 7,62€). **Facilities** Swimming pool, parking. **Nearby** Dentelles de Montmirail, Séguret, Vaison-la-Romaine, wine trails – 18-hole golf price in Vedène. **Open** All year.

On this wine-producing plane, not far from the famous Dentelles de Montmirail, this inviting, former 17th-century bastide is one of this year's great discoveries. We particularly like the subdued elegance of the spacious rooms, some with a functioning fireplace, with plain pastel walls, polished red tile floors, and one or two pieces of regional furniture. A calming, scaled-down aesthetic reigns here, with excellent, big beds and superb bathrooms. The difference in price depends on whether or not the room has a lounge nook. (Those without are still roomy and very comfortable.) No need to go far for dinner, because the hotel's restaurant is another strong point about this address. The fare, bursting with Southern French flavors, is always concocted from the freshest produce. You will sample it in a beautiful dining room, or outside, under the gazebo or next to the fountain. Great pool area, full of flowers, where you can have a light meal.

*How to get there* (*Map 33*): *Via A 7, take Bollène exit, then D 8 toward Carpentras. The way to the hotel is marked 2 km before Vacqueras.*

## Hostellerie Le Beffroi

84110 Vaison-la-Romaine (Vaucluse)
Rue de l'Evêché
Tel. (0)4.90.36.04.71 - Fax (0)4.90.36.24.78 - M. Christiansen
E-mail: lebeffroy@wanadoo.fr

**Category** ★★★ **Rooms** 22 with telephone, bath or shower, WC, TV and minibar. **Price** Double 465-700F / 70,89-106,71€. **Meals** Breakfast 50F / 7,62€, served 7:30-9:45; half board 405-605F / 61,74-92,23€ (per pers., 3 days min.). **Restaurant** Closed Nov – end Mar. Service 12:00PM-1:45PM (except on weekdays), 7:15-9:30PM; mealtime specials 98F / 15,24€ (lunchtime), 195F / 29,73€ also à la carte. Specialties: Feuilleté de petits-gris à la provençal; gigot d'aubergines; râble de lapereau au romarin; crème brûlée au miel de lavande. **Credit cards** All major. **Pets** Dogs allowed (+35F / 5,34€). **Facilities** Swimming pool, minigolf, games, garage (40F / 6,10€). **Nearby** Arc de Triomphe and old theater in Orange, Mornas, Henri Fabre Museum in Sérignan. **Closed** End Jan – end Mar.

This hotel high up in the medieval part of Vaison consists of several mansions joined together. The buildings' character has been preserved with tiled floors, polished panelling, spiral staircases and beautiful antiques, paintings and curios. The bedrooms are all different; antique lovers will be especially taken by the quality of the period furniture. The lounges are also pleasantly furnished and have open fireplaces. A superb terrace garden offers a lovely view over the rooftops of Vaison. If you crave a heartier meal at lunch, Robert Bardot's *Le Moulin à Huile* is a delicious address.

***How to get there*** *(Map 33): 30km northeast of Orange via D975; at the top of the town.*

## Hostellerie La Grangette

84740 Velleron (Vaucluse)
Chemin Cambuisson
Tel. (0)4.90.20.00.77 - Fax (0)4.90.20.07.06
M. and Mme Blanc-Brude

**Category** ★★★ **Rooms** 16 telephone, bath or shower, WC, TV on request. **Price** Double 550-1200F / 83,85-182,94€. **Meals** Breakfast 70F / 10,67€, served 8:00-10:00; half board +250F / 38,11€ (per pers.). **Restaurant** Service 12:00PM-2:00PM, from 8:00PM; mealtime specials 180-250F / 27,44-38,11€, also à la carte. Specialties: Calamars à l'encre; ris de veau au melon; gratin des charmettes. **Credit cards** All major. **Pets** Dogs allowed (+140F / 21,34€). **Facilities** Swimming pool, parking. **Nearby** Isle sur Sorgue; Fontaine de Vaucluse; Gordes; the Bories; Abbey of Sénanque; Avignon; the Luberon – 18-hole Saumane golf course. **Open** All year.

The *Hostellerie La Grangette* occupies a beautiful old farmhouse surrounded by nature, in a flurry of ivy and creepers. The interior parades a very elegant Provençal look. The line-up of little, ground-floor lounges have beautifully upholstered and polished antique furniture. Sixteen beautiful bedrooms, all different, are decorated in antiques, fine fabrics, and bric-a-brac and offer you comfort and calm. There are the *Mistral, Mule de Pape,* and *Mireío,* and the stupendous *Arlesiènne* with its terrace and windows filled with the light of the setting sun. There is an immense swimming pool surrounded by hedges, a shady terrace for meals and a large garden with trees which can be the starting point for pleasant walks. Add the friendly hospitality and you have a very pleasant hostelry. A touching place, where luxury and the right price meet.

***How to get there*** *(Map 33): Via A 7, take the Avignon exit toward L'Isle sur la Soruge. Once at L'Isle, head toward Pernes-les-Fontaines on D 938 for 4 km, then follow the signs.*

## Auberge de la Fontaine

84210 Venasque (Vaucluse)
Place de la Fontaine
Tel. (0)4.90.66.02.96 - Fax (0)4.90.66.13.14 - M. and Mme Sœhlke
E-mail: Fontvenasq@aol.com

**Rooms** 5 suites with air-conditioning, telephone, bath, WC, TV, minibar. **Price** Suite 800F / 121,96€. **Meals** Breakfast 50F / 7,62€. **Restaurant** Closed Wednesday and mid Nov – mid Dec. Service every evening 8:00PM-10:00PM; mealtime specials 220F / 33,54€, also à la carte. Specialties: Assiette du pêcheur; choucroute au foie gras; gibier frais en saison; pigeonneau aux airelles. *Bistro* mealtime specials 90F / 13,72€, mealtime-truffes 190F / 28,97€, also à la carte (closed Sunday evening and Monday). **Credit cards** Visa, Eurocard and MasterCard. **Pets** Dogs allowed. **Facilities** Mountain bikes, parking in the village. **Nearby** Venasque Church, Gallo-Roman cemetery in Mazan, Pernes-les-Fontaines, Carpentras – 18-hole Saumane golf course. **Open** All year.

The *Auberge de la Fontaine* is a beautiful old village house which Ingrid and Christian Soehlke have completely restructured inside, creating an amusing maze of mezzanines, terraces, and stairways. While conserving the structure's noble appearance, they particularly sought to create the informal atmosphere of a house for friends. And it would be difficult not to feel at ease: each suite includes a bedroom and a lounge with a fireplace, tastefully decorated and furnished in very Provençal style and equipped with a direct-dial phone, television, and cassette, CD players, fax and minitel. Each has a secluded terrace and a kitchenette, but the charming dining room and the Soehlkes' succulent cuisine should not be missed. There is a dinner concert each month, and in the low season, the hotel proposes a 5-day package with cooking lessons.

*How to get there* ( *Map 33): 11km south of Carpentras via D9.*

## Auberge Les Bichonnières

01330 Ambérieux-en-Dombes (Ain)
Route de Savigneux
Tel. (0)4.74.00.82.07 - Fax (0)4.74.00.89.61 - M. Sauvage
E-mail: bichonnier@aol.com

**Category** ★★ **Rooms** 9 with telephone, bath or shower, TV and WC. **Price** Double 250-380F / 38,11-57,93€. **Meals** Breakfast 40F / 6,10€, served 8:00-10:00; half board 300F / 45,73€ (per pers. in double room, 3 days min.). **Restaurant** Closed Monday, Thursday in Jul and Aug. Service 12:15PM-1:45PM, 7:30PM-8:45PM; mealtime specials 135-250F / 20,58-38,11€, also à la carte. Specialties: Grenouilles fraîches, volaille de Bresse. **Credit cards** Amex, Visa, Eurocard and MasterCard. **Pets** Dogs allowed. **Facilities** Parking. **Nearby** Trévoux, bird reserve in Villard-les-Dombes, Montluel, Pérouges — 18-hole Le Clou golf course in Villard-les-Dombes. **Closed** Christmas holiday, Sunday evening and Monday from Sep — Jun.

The Dombes is a lush, green region of lakes and birds, yet it has few good hotels. Some thirty kilometers from Lyon on the edge of a roadside, yet in a quiet setting, the *Bichonnières*, an old farmhouse with country charm, is one of those few. In the comfortable small bedrooms, the light-brown shades of the plaster and beams are brightened with bucolic fabrics, and the bathrooms are quite presentable. On each floor, you will find a small corner lounge. For meals, depending on the season, the dining tables are set in an attractive dining room, on a covered terrace, or beneath the large parasols on a flowery interior courtyard. Chef Marc Sauvage prepares excellent regional specialties, including the region's famous Bresse chicken. As the hotel-restaurant business is a demanding one, the owners close for several days during the year. It's best to reserve in advance.

***How to get there*** *(Map 26): 30km north of Lyon via A6, Villefranche exit, then D904 towards Bourg-en-Bresse, then Villars-les-Dombes.*

## Hôtel de France

01210Ferney-Voltaire (Ain)
1, rue de Genève
Tel. (0)4.50.40.63.87 - Fax (0)4.50.40.47.27
M. and Mme Boillat

**Rooms** 14 with telephone, bath, WC, safe and satellite TV. **Price** Single and double 320-430F / 48,78-65,55€; half board 410F / 62,50€ (per pers.). **Meals** Breakfast 45F / 6,86€, served 7:00-10:00. **Restaurant** Service 12:00PM-2:30PM and 7:30PM-10:00PM; mealtime specials 110-260F / 16,77-39,64€, also à la carte. Specialties: Ballotine de pintade aux morilles et vin jaune. **Credit cards** All major. **Pets** Dogs allowed. **Facilities** Parking. **Nearby** Château of Fernet-Voltaire, Geneva, Lake Léman – 4 18-hole golf course. **Open** Jan – end Dec.

On the Swiss border, Ferney-"Voltaire", named after its most famous resident, parades its delicately painted homes with their chiselled stone. This hotel fits in well, and its charming façade really makes you want to go inside. There's no vaste reception area here, just a bar where you check in and get your room key. You will then catch a glimpse of the newly renovated, slightly rustic, slightly refined dining room, with its yellow walls, engravings, beautiful, natural wood beams, and antique furniture. This is a smashing, beautifully tended area that opens out to a veranda and a shady terrace where meals are served in nice weather. You'd be right to get a table here, because the hotel is heavily frequented by the Genevese who appreciate fine, savory food. The rooms are on the three upper stories (No elevator). They are pleasant and simple with their colored fabrics, carpeting, and retro furniture. Comfortable and impeccably clean, these high-quality rooms are a great value for the money.

***How to get there*** *( Map 27): From Geneva, head toward the airport, then take the road to Ferney-Voltaire. The hotel is at the entrance to the village.*

## Auberge des Chasseurs

Naz-Dessus - 01170 Echenevex (Ain)
Tel. (0)4.50.41.54.07 - Fax (0)4.50.41.90.61
M. and Mme Lamy

**Category** ★★★ **Rooms** 15 with telephone, bath or shower, WC, safe, radio and TV. **Price** Single and double 450-800F / 68,60-121,96€. **Meals** Breakfast 58F / 9,15€, served 8:00-10:00; half board 530-650F / 80,80-99,09€ (per pers.). **Restaurant** Closed Sunday evening and Monday. Service 12:00PM-1:30PM, 7:00PM-9:30PM; mealtime specials 85-110F / 12,96-16,77€ (lunchtime except Saturday and Sunday), 175-290F / 26,68-44,21€, also à la carte. Specialties: Aiguillette de féra du lac rôtie au vin d'Arbois; feuilleté aux fruits rouges. **Credit cards** All major. **Pets** Dogs allowed (+40F / 6,10€). **Facilities** Swimming pool, tennis, parking. **Nearby** Le Pailly and La Faucille Pass, Château of Fernet-Voltaire – 27-hole Maison Blanche golf course in Echenevex. **Open** Mar – Nov 15.

Standing on the slopes of the Jura, amidst fields and woods, and yet just 15 minutes from Geneva, the *Auberge des Chasseurs* is an old farmhouse which has been very well restored. The homey atmosphere inside is very charming. The beamed ceilings, chairs, and bedroom doors are decorated with floral frescos recently done by a Swedish artist. In the restaurant, there is a magnificent series of photographs by Cartier-Bresson. Upstairs, you will find a very inviting lounge and bar. The bedrooms are beautifully decorated with Laura Ashley fabrics and wallpapers, English-pine furniture and their charming bathrooms are just as lovely. Outside, the oak garden furniture was designed by an artist, as was the mosaic of the terrace floor. The garden is full of flowers and shady spots, and the view is splendid. The cuisine is excellent, the service attentive, and Dominique Lamy is a very hospitable owner.

***How to get there*** *(Map 20): 17km northwest of Geneva via D984 towards St-Genis-Pouilly, then D978c towards Gex. Echenevex 2km before Gex on the left.*

## Ostellerie du Vieux Pérouges

01800 Pérouges (Ain)
Place du Tilleul
Tel. (0)4.74.61.00.88 - Fax (0)4.74.34.77.90
M. Thibaut

**Category** ★★★★ **Rooms** 28 with telephone, bath, shower, WC and TV. **Price** Single and double 550-1100F / 83,85-167,69€. **Meals** Breakfast 70F / 10,67€, served 8:00AM-12:00PM. **Restaurant** Service 12:00PM-2:30PM, 7:00PM-9:00PM; mealtime specials 200-450F / 30,49-68,60€, also à la carte. Specialties: Filet de carpe farci à l'ancienne; volaille de Bresse; panaché pérougien; galette de l'hostellerie. **Credit cards** Visa, Eurocard and MasterCard. **Pets** Dogs allowed. **Facilities** Parking. **Nearby** Trévoux, bird reserve in Villard-les-Dombes, Montluel – 18-hole Le Clou golf course in Villard-les-Dombes. **Open** All year.

Pérouges is an exceptional small medieval town that you must visit to plunge yourself into the atmosphere, and what more appropriate place than this inn which is made up of several very old houses. Stone stairways, stained glass windows, French ceilings, fireplaces… nothing is amiss. The most luxurious bedrooms are resplendent with Haute Epoque furniture and marble baths. The other, simpler rooms are also well-furnished and offer excellent modern amenities. Each house borders a small paved lane with, here and there, a small garden or open ruins overgrown with vegetation. The house opens onto the main square where the restaurant is located. Here too, the medieval atmosphere is prevalent; a wide-board floor, a baker's kneading trough, china cupboards, a large fireplace in which several large logs are often burning, all combine to whet the appetite for the *Ostellerie*'s regional cuisine which is served by waiters in traditional dress.

***How to get there*** *( Map 26 ): 35km northeast of Lyon via A42, Pérouges exit.*

# La Huchette

01750 Replonges (Ain)
Tel. 03.85.31.03.55 - Fax 03.85.31.10.24
Mme Gualdieri

**Rooms** 12 with telephone, bath, WC, TV and minibar – Wheelchair access. **Price** Single and double 400-650F / 60,98-99,09€, suite 1000-1200F / 152,45-182,94€. **Meals** Breakfast 60F / 9,15€, served from 7:00. **Restaurant** Closed Monday and Tuesday lunchtime. Service 12:00PM, 7:30PM; mealtime specials 160-230F / 24,39-35,06€, also à la carte. Specialties: Gâteau de foie bressan; suprême de poulet de Bresse aux morilles; nougatine au coulis de fraises. **Credit cards** All major. **Pets** Dogs allowed. **Facilities** Swimming pool and parking. **Nearby** Mâcon, Church of Saint-André-de-Bagé, Lamartine tour (65 km): Solutré rock, Pouilly, Fuissé, Chasselas, Grand Vert pass and lake of Saint-Point, Berzé-le-Châtel and chapel of Berzé-la-Ville, Milly-Lamartine and Château of Pierre-Clos, Château of Monceau. **Closed** Mid Nov – mid Dec and Monday.

Replonges is on the border of Burgundy and Bresse, though still part of the Rhône-Alpes region. At first glance, the inn's location might frighten you away (the highway borders the garden), but it would be a shame to pass this old home up, because its comfort, beauty, and hospitality really deserve a stop. Well-soundproofed, spacious, and comfortable, the rooms have a view of the owner's private wood. The English-style lounges, done up in bottle greens, yellows, and burgundy, are intimate and very comfortable. Next door, the dining room, with its slender beams, fireplace, and subtle, *trompe-l'oeil* wallpaper depicting a panoramic hunting scene, is one of the most charming of places to enjoy delicate, flavorful food made from excellent local produce. That should work up your appetite by the time the village's bell tolls noon.

*How to get there (Map 26): 4km from Mâcon.*

## Hôtel de la Santoline

07460 Beaulieu (Ardèche)
Tel. (0)4.75.39.01.91 - Fax (0)4.75.39.38.79
M. and Mme Espenel
E-mail: santolin@club-internet.fr - Web: http://perso.club-internet.fr/santolin

**Category** ★★★ **Rooms** 7 with telephone, bath, WC and minibar (some with air-conditioning).
**Price** Double 350-580F / 53,36-88,42€. **Meals** Breakfast 48F / 7,62€, served 8:30-10:00; half board
355-465F / 54,12-70,89€ (per pers., 3 days min.). **Restaurant** Closed lunchtime. Service 7:30PM-
8:30PM; mealtime specials 165F / 25,15€, also à la carte. Specialties: Market fresh fare. **Credit cards**
Visa, Eurocard and MasterCard. **Pets** Dogs allowed (+30F / 4,57€). **Facilities** Swimming pool,
parking. **Nearby** La Cocalière cave, Païolive woods, Vivarais slopes, Les Vans to la Bastide-
Puylaurent. **Open** Apr – end Sep.

In the middle of Ardèche, surrounded by scrubland, *La Santoline* is in an old
stone hunting lodge. You can see the Cevennes from here; all is peace and
quiet. Below, a swimming pool cools you off in summer, when you can also
enjoy the flowering terrace. Dinners and breakfast can be served there. The
food is delicate, and the "menu-carte" plan, though it limits your choice,
insures the freshest fare. You'll find it hard to resist the charm of the rooms,
with their Provençal colors, smashing cotton prints, old furniture, and
patchworks. The bathrooms are unparalleled. The vista is splendid. The perfect
pool area surrounded by lavender and santolina, the owners' kindness and the
reasonable prices make this charming inn a great place for a long stay

***How to get there*** *( Map 32): 84km north of Nîmes via N106 to Alès, then D904
and D104 to La Croisée-de-Jalès, then D225.*

## Château d'Urbilhac

07270 Lamastre (Ardèche)
Tel. (0)4.75.06.42.11 - Fax (0)4.75.06.52.75
Mme Xompero

**Category ★★★ Rooms** 12 with telephone, bath or shower and WC. **Price** Double 550-700F / 83,85-106,71€. **Meals** Breakfast 65F/ 9,90€, served 8:00-10:30; half board 650-700F / 99,09-106,71€ (per pers.). **Restaurant** Closed lunchtime except weekends. Service at 12:00PM and 7:30PM; mealtime specials 250F / 38,11€. Spécialités: Carpaccio de magret de canard à l'huile d'olive et vinaigre balsamique; grenadins de veau sautés au vin de Cornas; cocotte de petits légumes paysans. **Credit cards** All major. **Pets** Dogs allowed. **Facilities** Heated swimming pool, tennis, parking. **Nearby** Tournon, Vivarais steam train between Tournon and Lamastre – 18-hole golf course in Chambon-sur-Lignon. **Open** May – end Sep.

The *Château d'Urbilhac*, built in the last century in Renaissance style over the cellars of a 16th-century fortified house, is set in 148-acres of parkland. In the reception rooms, 19th-century style is predominant. The bedrooms, each with its own style, are equally beautiful. Restful and comfortable, they are further enhanced with superb bathrooms and often look out on a sublime panorama. In the spring, the dining room is moved out onto a vast veranda. You will enjoy outstanding cuisine from the chef, Fabrice Redon. The fare is intelligently original and shows great respect for the local produce. (The prices are expensive at first but the reasonable demi-pension price is applicable beginning with the first night.) Mme Xompero is especially attentive, going from table to table, ensuring that everyone is pleased and generally contributing to the excellent atmosphere here. Finally, you should not leave Urbilhac without first stepping onto the immense terrace and looking out over the valley where distant Ardèche farms are scattered between pastures and chestnut groves.

***How to get there*** *( Map 26 ): 36km west of Valence via D533.*

# Domaine de Rilhac

07320 Saint-Agrève (Ardèche)
Tel. (0)4.75.30.20.20 - Fax (0)4.75.30.20.00
M. and Mme Sinz

**Category** ★★ **Rooms** 8 with telephone, bath or shower, WC and TV. **Price** Single and double 400-500F / 60,98-76,22€, apart. 800F / 121,96€. **Meals** Breakfast 65F / 9,91€, served 8:00-10:30; half board 460-520F / 70,13-79,27€ (per pers., 2 days min.). **Restaurant** Service 12:00PM-1:30PM, 8:00PM-9:30PM, mealtime specials 135-430F / 20,58-65,55€ (80F / 12,20€ child), also à la carte. **Credit card** Visa. **Pets** Dogs allowed (+40F / 6,10€). **Facilities** Parking. **Nearby** Mont-Gerbier-des-Joncs; Eyrieux gorges – 18-hole Chambon-sur-Lignon golf course. **Closed** Jan, Feb, Tuesday evening and Wednesday.

This huge plateau, in front of Mount Gerbier-de-Jounce and Mezenc, is 1000 meters in altitude. The air is pure, brown cows graze on grassy meadows criss-crossed by trout streams that wind through the hollows. Ludovic Sinz is not only a talented young chef, but with his wife Florence, he knows how to turn a stodgy Ardechois farm into a charming place. A stairway with a beautiful wrought-iron railing crafted by a local artisan leads to the comfortable bedrooms. They are named after flowers and each has a framed alphabet. The colors of the embroideries are repeated in the coordinated bedcover fabrics, drapes and table skirts, all contributing to a fresh and tasteful decor. The view is magnificent throughout, with large bay windows affording fine panoramas. The yellow plaster in the entrance, the small lounge and the dining room creates a joyful, almost Provençal atmosphere in all seasons. You will find the same refinements in the shady walled garden outside. The gourmet food is a flavorful wonder, proving that Ludovic got a lot from his time with Bernard Loiseau. The *Domaine* is a charming place to get back to nature without giving up all the modern comforts.

*How to get there* ( *Map 26* ): *56km west of Valence via D533.*

## La Châtaigneraie

07130 Soyons (Ardèche)
Tel. (0)4.75.60.83.55 - Fax (0)4.75.60.85.21
M. Philippe Michelot
E-mail: musard@club-internet.fr

**Rooms** 18 with air-conditioning, telephone, bath, WC, TV and minibar – 1 for disabled persons. **Price** Double 420-650F / 64,12-99,09€, 3 pers. 750-1000F / 114,34-152,45€. **Meals** Breakfast 55-90F / 8,38-13,72€, served 8:00-10:00; half board from 450F / 68,60€ (per pers.). **Restaurant** Service 12:00PM-2:00PM, 7:00PM-10:00PM; mealtime specials 120F / 18,29€ (lunchtime)-280F / 42,69€. Regional and Provençale cooking. **Credit cards** All major. **Pets** Dogs allowed (+50F / 7,62€ ). **Facilities** Swimming pool, tennis (1 covered), sauna, whirlpool and parking. **Nearby** Museum of Soyons, Château of Crussol; wine tasting in Château de Saint-Peray and Cornas, Valence (Museum of H. Robert) – 18-hole golf course in Saint-Didier-de-Charpey. **Open** All year.

As the Rhône Valley is one of the most frequented thoroughfares in the world, this hotel would seem a practical place to stay, despite its roadside location. Every effort has been made to make us forget the proximity of the autoroute: perfect soundproofing, air-conditioning, many leisure activities, not to mention the lovely decoration and hospitality of the staff. The *Châtaigneraie* is made up of two houses: *La Musardière*, a four-star hotel with all amenities, smart decoration and prices to match. We most highly recommend the three-star *La Châtaigneraie*, with comfortable amenities and a more youthful decor hinting of Provence. Several bedrooms designed for families or groups have a kitchenette, and some an extra bed on a loggia. For couples, we highly recommend Rooms 701, 702, 703 and 704, which are lovely. Delicious cuisine is served in an intimate dining room, on the veranda, or on the terrace. A convenient place to stay that we recommend for your short stop-overs.

***How to get there*** *( Map 26 ): 10km south of Valence, toward La Voulte-sur-Rhône.*

## La Bastide du Soleil

07110 Vinezac (Ardèche)
Tel. (0)4.75.36.91.66 - Fax (0)4.75.36.91.59
MM. Labaune and Chatel
E-mail: la.bastide@en.arcdèche.com

**Rooms** 6 with air-conditioning, with telephone, bath, WC, TV, minibar – Elevator. **Price** Single and double 390-490F / 59,46-74,70€; 3 pers. 680F / 103,67€. **Meals** Breakfast 40-60F / 6,10-9,15€, served 8:00-10:30; half board 390-420F / 59,46-64,12€ (3 nights min.). **Credit cards** All major. **Pets** Dogs allowed (+30F / 4,57€). **Facilities** Balazuc, Ardèche gorges, Chauvet cave. **Restaurant** Service 12:00PM-2:00PM, 7:30PM-10:00PM; mealtime specials 98F / 15,24€ (lunchtime) 140-265F / 21,34-40,40€; also à la carte. Specialties: Raviolis de picodon à la sauge; consommé à l'aïl. **Closed** End Jan – beg Mar.

A bit in the highlands, Vinezac is a medieval hamlet with roan sandstone that blazes in the light of the setting sun. The hotel, in a former 17th-century château, is on the little main square, bursting with laurels, geraniums, and rosemary. Breakfast and dinner are served under an awning in front of the entrance, where you will really enjoy this place. Because *La Bastide* is above all else an excellent restaurant where you will taste delicately flavoured and well-prepared Southern French cuisine. The comfortable, quiet rooms -- redone good as new with light wooden parquetry -- are also worthy of attention. Many have a beautiful view (even if you might have to bend over backwards to see it from a few rooms). They are youthfully decorated, colorful, and furnished with *Directoire* style furniture in cherrywood, made by an Aubenas carpenter. This place is, too say the least, very comfortable. With the lounge-bar and its huge fireplace, ravishing and spacious dining room with French-style ceiling, and balustraded, stone stairway, you will see why this hotel is one of this year's great discoveries.

*How to get there (Map 32): 13 km south of Aubenas, on the road to Alès.*

## La Treille Muscate

26270 Cliousclat (Drôme)
Tel. (0)4.75.63.13.10 - Fax (0)4.75.63.10.79
Mme Delaitre

**Category** ★★★ **Rooms** 12 with telephone, bath, WC and TV. **Price** Double 350-650F / 53,36-99,09€. **Meals** Breakfast 48F / 7,62€, served 8:00-10:00. **Restaurant** Closed Wednesday. Service 12:00PM-1:30PM, 8:00PM-9:30PM; mealtime specials 90-145F / 13,72-22,11€, also à la carte. Specialties: Beignets d'aubergines; croustillant de pigeon laqué au miel d'épices; bouillabaisse sur rouille citronnée. **Credit cards** Visa, Eurocard and MasterCard. **Pets** Dogs allowed. **Facilities** Parking. **Nearby** Mirmande, Poët-Laval; Forts area in Nyons – 18-hole Valdaine golf course. **Closed** Jan and Feb.

*L*a Treille Muscate is exactly the kind of small hotel you hope to find in a Provençal village. Beautiful sunny yellow walls brighten the on the ground floor rooms; here you will find the dining room with its bright Provençal table linens, the corner bar, and the small TV room. There are several pieces of handsome regional furniture, large watercolors, varnished jugs, and splendid dinnerware crafted by a skilled potter, a neighbor and friend; all create a decor that makes you feel truly at home. Upstairs, pretty bedrooms have recently been installed and beautifully decorated. They have a lovely view out over the quiet village or the countryside.The excellent cuisine is enhanced with aromatic herbs and local products. In good weather, a few tables are set out on the village side or in a small garden, bordered with terraced walls and overlooking the countryside. The hospitality and service at "The Muscat Arbor" are informal.

***How to get there*** *( Map 26 ): 16km north of Montélimar via A7, Loriol exit. Then 5km. N7 toward Loriol-Montélimard.*

## Au Clair de la Plume

26230 Grignan (Drôme)
Place du Mail
Tel. (0)4.75.91.81.30 - Fax (0)4.75.91.81.31
Mme Filliette-Neuville

**Category** ★★★ **Rooms** 8 with telephone, bath, WC and satellite TV. **Price** Single and double 400-880F / 60,98-134,16€. **Meals** Breakfast 8:00AM-12:00PM. No restaurant. **Credit cards** All major. **Pets** Dogs allowed (+40F / 6,09€). **Facilities** Parking free (300 m). **Nearby** Château and Museum of Mme de Sévigné in Grignan; Letter Writting Festival (1st weekend in Jul); Fort area in Nyons; Poët-Laval; Dieulefit; villages of the Drôme – 9-hole Valaurie golf course. **Closed** End Jan – beg Feb.

Almost at the foot of an impressive château made famous by Madame de Sévigné, the elegant 18th-century mansion houses delightful guest rooms, which all look out over the front garden. Wisteria, rosebushes, and ivy clamber up the trellises and gazebos to make many shady corners. The main area is set up with Zélige faience tables, where breakfast is served in the morning and tea in the afternoon. Inside, the lounge with its fireplace, little dining room, and huge kitchen have kept their original size. All is decorated soberly and tastefully, with 19th-century furnishings, a delicate variety of fabrics, and engravings. You find this same restraint in the rooms. High-ceilings on the *premier étage* and more cozy on the second, these rooms are well-tended, comfortable, always with beautiful Provençal bedcovers and very nice bathrooms. Many nice touches at this hotel that has just opened and which should soon become a great success. Youthful, friendly, and attentive hospitality. For dinner, we recommend *Le Poème*, *L'Eau à la Bouche*, and the more gourmet *La Roseraie*.

***How to get there*** *(Map 33): Via A 7, take the south Montelimar exit, the N 7, and then D 133.*

## Manoir de la Roseraie

26230 Grignan (Drôme)
Tel. (0)4.75.46.58.15 - Fax (0)4.75.46.91.55
M. and Mme Alberts
E-mail: roseraie.hotel@wanadoo.fr

**Category** ★★★★ **Rooms** 15 and 2 suites with telephone, bath, WC and satellite TV – Wheelchair access. **Price** Single and double 860-1150F / 131,11-175,32€, suite 1650-1900F / 251,54-289,65€. **Meals** Breakfast 90F / 13,72€, served 8:00-10:00; half board 755-820F / 115,10-125,01€ (per pers., 3 days min.). **Restaurant** Service 12:00PM-1:30PM, 8:00PM-9:15PM; mealtime specials 195-260F / 29,73-39,64€. Specialties: Pigeonneau fermier rôti, sauce au verjus et betterave. **Credit cards** All major. **Pets** Dogs allowed (+60F / 9,15€). **Facilities** Heated swimming pool, tennis, parking. **Nearby** Château and Museum of Mme de Sévigné in Grignan, Fort area in Nyons; Poët-Laval; Dieulefit – 9-hole Valaurie golf course. **Closed** Jan 5 – mid Feb; Monday in low season.

In this beautiful private mansion built in 1850 by the mayor of Grignan, Michèle Alberts and her husband have tastefully refurbished and decorated the bedrooms and the suite. With comfortable amenities, their decor is elegant and cheerful. Particularly roomy on the *premier étage*, they are more cozy on the *second*. Two rooms in the outbuilding are on ground-level with the garden; others are very roomy with their sloped ceiling. Each bathroom vies with the next in luxury and originality. Some of the suites can even serve as lounges with a pull-out bed. Tables in the dining room, its skylight in a rotunda shape, are elegantly set facing a panoramic view over the ravishing park, which is planted with some 400 rose bushes, bougainvillea, lindens, cedars, and perennials. The heated swimming pool, beautifully integrated into the park, is perhaps the ideal spot for enjoying the lovely setting.

***How to get there*** *(Map 33): 90km north of Avignon via A7, Montélimar-Sud exit, then N7 and D133.*

## Auberge de la Rochette

26400 Vaunaveys-la-Rochette (Drôme)
Tel. (0)4.75.25.79.30 - Fax (0)4.75.25.79.25
MM. Cordonier and Danis

**Rooms** 5 with telephone, bath or shower, WC, TV, safe and minibar. **Price** Double 420-520F / 64,12-79,27€, duplex (4 pers.).680F / 103,67€. **Meals** Breakfast-brunch 65F / 9,91€, served 8:30-10:00; half board 390-420F / 59,46-64,12€ (per pers., 3 days min.). **Restaurant** Service 12:00PM-1:15PM, 7:30PM-9:00PM; mealtime specials 175-210F / 26,68-32,01€. Specialties: Foie gras de canard maison; crème brûlée à la lavande. **Credit cards** Visa, Eurocard. **Pets** Dogs not allowed. **Facilities** Swimming pool, parking. **Nearby** Facteur Cheval's Palace in Hauterives, Vercors Monts, villages of the Drôme. **Closed** 3 weeks in Oct, 3 weeks in Feb and Wednesday in low season.

After having run a restaurant in Lyon, this charming inn's owners chose a more tranquil job in the beautiful Provençal Drôme. The *Auberge* is an old barn which has been restored in the regional style. The small size allows the owners to receive guests, like friends. The beautiful rooms have been carefully designed. (A room with a mezzanine and high ceilings was designed with families or groups of friends in mind). The decor includes warm sand-colored walls, Provençal quilted bedspreads and matching drapes, terra-cotta floors, and painted furniture. An elegant small dining room opens onto a flower-filled terrace where regional specialties are served. You will love this delicate and flavorful food, always made from the freshest produce. Very well-looked-after, with very kind hospitality and reasonable prices, this is a truly great place to stay.

*How to get there ( Map 26): On D 538 between Crest and Chabeuil, 20 km south of Valence. Coming from the south on A7, take Loriol exit (then head toward, Crest, Romans, and Chabeuil). Coming from the north, take Valence south (heading toward Romans, Grenoble, Chabeuil, and Crest).*

## Domaine des Buis

Les Buis 26140 Albon (Drôme)
Tel. (0)4.75.03.14.14 - Fax (0)4.75.03.14.14
M. and Mme Kirch

**Rooms** 6 avec bath and TV – Telecard phone. **Price** Double 460-630F / 70,13-96,04€; suite 690F / 105,19€. **Meals** Breakfast 55F / 8,38€, all the morning. No restaurant. **Credit cards** Visa, Eurocard and MasterCard. **Pets** Dogs not allowed. **Facilities** Swimming pool, garage. **Nearby** Facteur Cheval's Palace in Hauterives; Condrieu and Tain-L'Hermitage caves; Distillery Museum; Vivarais railway – Golf d'Albon in 500m. **Open** All year.

There is a reason why the *Domaine des Buis* is known as the "Guest Meeting Place." This huge 18th-century house in country stone has all the good qualities of a hotel and a guest home. The rooms have just been tastefully renovated and have impeccable, spacious, bright, and often luxurious bathrooms. The light walls, parquetried or tiled floors, and elegantly colorful fabrics grant the place the highest level of quality and comfort. Hélène and Didier Kirch, who also live here, look out for the well-being of their guests for whom they have meticulously outfitted lounges and a garden. The environs are particularly green and peaceful. Beautiful trees shade the park. At times, if the wind is just right, you can make out the noise of traffic from the highway, but never to the point of it being a distraction. This is a beautiful place for a restful stay, or just to discover an area that is sometimes passed up for southern Drôme. This is also an ideal place for golfers, because there is a green just next door. For restaurants, we recommend *L'Albatros* and *A. Lecomte's*.

***How to get there*** *(Map 26): 40km north of Valence via A7. Take Chanas, exit and head toward Valence via N7. 500m after Albon golf course.*

# Le Domaine du Colombier

26780 Malataverne (Drôme)
Route de Donzère
Tel. (0)4.75.90.86.86 - Fax (0)4.75.90.79.40
M. and Mme Chochois

**Category** ★★★ **Rooms** 22 and 3 suites with telephone, bath, WC, minibar and TV. **Price** Single and double 480-880F / 73,18-134,16€, suite 1200-1300F / 182,94-198,18€, 3-4 pers. 580-1080F / 88,42-164,64€. **Meals** Breakfast 70F / 10,67€, served 7:30-11:00; half board +260F / 39,64€ (per pers.). **Restaurant** Service 12:15PM-2:30PM, 7:15PM-9:30PM; mealtime specials 150F / 22,87€ all incl. (lunchtime except Sunday) 195-360F / 29,73-54,88€. Specialties: Omelette aux truffes du Tricastin; carré d'agneau de pays au romarin. **Credit cards** All major. **Pets** Dogs allowed (+50F / 7,62€). **Facilities** Swimming pool, bowling alley, bicycles, helicopter pad, parking. **Nearby** Nyons, Château and Museum of Mme de Sévigné in Grignan, villages of the Drôme between Montélimar and Orange. **Open** All year.

Formerly a 14th-century abbey, the *Domaine du Colombier* maintains its tradition of hospitality to travelers to this day, as it is now a pleasant hotel conveniently located on the road south. Although only minutes from the highway, it seems to be in the middle of the countryside. When you walk through the door, be prepared to find furniture and fabrics piled up in the entrance hall, for it is also a shop. The bedrooms are bright, colorful, and comfortably decorated; three of them have a small mezzanine. In the garden, the swimming pool, surrounded by chaises longues, is a lovely place to relax. The lavender-blue furniture in the dining room is Provençal in style, and dinner or an evening drink can also be served on the patio.

***How to get there*** *( Map 33): 9km south of Montélimar via N7 and D144a (2km after Malataverne dir. Donzere). Via A7, take Montélimar exit and head toward Malataverne.*

## Auberge de la Gloriette

26170 Mérindol-les-Oliviers (Drôme)
Tel. (0)4.75.28.71.08
M. and Mme Mina

**Rooms** 4 with bath or shower and WC. **Price** Single and double 250-300F / 38,11-45,73€. **Meals** Breakfast 30-50F/ 4,57-7,62€, served 8:30-11:00. **Restaurant** Only by reservation. Closed Thursday (except in summer) and Sunday evening. Service 12:00PM-2:00PM, 7:30PM-9:00PM; mealtime specials 100F / 15,24€, also à la carte. Specialties: Provençal. **Credit cards** Visa, Eurocard and MasterCard. **Pets** Dogs allowed. **Facilities** Swimming pool and parking. **Nearby** Orange, Mornas, Museum of Henri Fabre in Sérignan. **Closed** Jan, Feb and Sunday evening; open on weekend in Nov – Dec.

The son of a baker, Jacques Mina grew up watching his father rolling out dough and removing hot, aromatic batches of golden pastries from the oven. In 1988, the bakery in Mérindol was up for sale and, with his companion Michèle, Jacques left Paris, bought the bakery, and opened a small restaurant with several bedrooms next door: the *Auberge de la Gloriette*. The Minas' savory experience and their natural friendliness quickly made the inn a success. And it's not surprising. The Provençale specialties fresh from the baker's oven and served in generous portions are irresistible; the lovely dining room and the shady terrace overlooking vineyards and olive trees, and the charming little bedrooms all play their part in making the *Gloriette* a special play to stay (not to mention the swimming pool, a godsend when the summer heat wave sets in.) It's a hotel right out of Marcel Pagnol, tailor-made for guests who enjoy friendly people and the simple pleasures of life.

***How to get there*** *(Map 33): 9km east of Vaison-la-Romaine, dir. Buis-les-Barronies, Puymerols, Mérindol.*

## La Capitelle

26270 Mirmande (Drôme)
Rue du Rempart
Tel. (0)4.75.63.02.72 - Fax (0)4.75.63.02.50 - M. and Mme Melki
E-mail: capitelle@wanadoo.fr

**Category** ★★ **Rooms** 19 and 2 apartments (3-4 pers.) with telephone, bath or shower, WC and satellite TV. **Price** Double and apart. with half board 410-440F / 62,50-67,08€ per pers. **Meals** Breakfast incl. served 8:00-10:00. **Restaurant** Service 12:00PM-1:45PM, 7:30PM-9:00PM; menu 170-275F / 25,92-41,92€, also à la carte. Specialties: Terrine de foie gras aux pommes confites; aumônière d'agneau au thym; filet de daurade en marinière de coquillages; pyramide de chocolat et mousse à l'orange. **Credit cards** All major. **Pets** Dogs allowed (+35F / 5,34€). **Facilities** Garage (+60F / 9,15€). **Nearby** Mirmande church, Pöet-Laval, Nyons – 18-hole Valdaine golf course. **Open** Dec, Jan and Feb; Tuesday and Wednesday lunchtime except Jun – Sep).

*L*a Capitelle is a tall Renaissance building with mullioned windows. The lounge and dining room have vaulted ceilings and handsome stone fireplaces. Items of period furniture combine well with more simple contemporary furnishings to create an elegant and yet warm atmosphere. A sober and sure taste is also in evidence in the bedrooms, most of which have a beautiful antique wardrobe with a bouquet of dried flowers. All the rooms are different, and most enjoy a magnificent view over the plain below. Breakfast and drinks can be served on the ramparts, while meals are served in the dining room or on the shady terrace in summer: the regional cuisine is excellent. To enjoy optimum service as well as the beauty of the site, guests are kindly requested to arrive by 8:30PM at the latest. The staff is hospitable and very friendly.

***How to get there*** *( Map 26): 35km south of Valence; Via A7 take Montélimar-north exit, then N7 until Saulce then D204.*

# La Maison

26130 Saint-Restitut (Drôme)
Tel. (0)4.75.04.46.30 - Fax (0)4.75.04.46.39
Mme Nurys Seligmann

**Rooms** 2 and 4 apartments, with telephone, bath, WC and satellite TV, 4 with minibar. **Price** Double (2 nights min.) 790-990F / 120,43-150,92€; apart. 1390-1690F / 211,90-257,64€. **Meals** Breakfast incl., served 8:00-10:30. **Evenings meals** Service 12:00PM-1:30PM, mealtime specials 190F / 28,97€. Light dinner 8:30PM. **Credit cards** Amex, Visa. **Pets** Dogs not allowed. **Facilities** Swimming pool, parking. **Nearby** Grignan; Orange; Avignon; villages of the Drôme – 9-hole Valaurie golf course. **Open** End Mar – Nov.

What makes the charming Miss Seligmann tick? Born in the Dominican Republic, raised in Rome, and married in Switzerland, she became a designer and interior decorator, then took to restoring and furbishing this large estate, while all the while bringing up four adorable daughters. The family could have just contented itself with welcoming friends and family, but Nurys's desire to show her work and welcome others inspired her to open up a few guest rooms. The house is certainly suited for it, because even if the lounge and dining room are shared, the rooms in the outlying buildings leave you a lot of independence. They are superb, roomy, and some even have a little lounge. Decorated in a white and tan color scheme, accented by homey furniture and perfectly chosen bric-a-brac, the rooms are very refined. The bathrooms have also been carefully and comfortably furbished, with beautiful linens. Good Provençale food, with a great wine cellar and Olympic-size swimming pool in the immaculate garden to enjoy the countryside. A great place to get to know.

*How to get there ( Map 33): 7km from Bollène. Via A7, take Bollène exit; head toward Saint-Restitut on D 160. 1.5km from town, right of "La Plaine", then follow signs.*

## La Ferme Saint-Michel

26130 Solérieux (Drôme) - D 341
Tel. (0)4.75.98.10.66 - Fax (0)4.75.98.19.09
M. Laurent

**Category** ★★ **Rooms** 14 (5 with air-conditioning) with telephone, bath, WC and TV. **Price** Single and double 360-560F / 54,88-85,37€. **Meals** Breakfast 38F / 6,10€, served 7:00-10:00. **Restaurant** Closed Dec 23 – Jan 24, Sunday evening and Monday by reservation. Service 12:00PM-2:00PM, 7:30PM-9:15PM; mealtime specials 130-180F / 19,82-27,44€, also à la carte. Specialties: Menu-truffe. **Credit cards** Visa, Eurocard and MasterCard. **Pets** Dogs not allowed. **Facilities** Swimming pool, parking. **Nearby** Château of Mme de Sévigné and Grignan musuem; villages of the Drôme – 18-hole Valaurie Golf Course. **Open** All year.

Partially renovated and under new ownership, the Ferme Saint-Michel is a traditional old Provençal *mas*, isolated from the road by thick vegetation, whose origins go back to the 16th century. The Ferme opens onto an inviting terrace where, in summer, a few tables are set for dinner. You will savor excellent local products such as the truffles harvested on the property, and game seasonal. Large trees afford lovely shade over the terrace, while a few steps away, there is the swimming pool. Quiet, well-kept, and attractive, all the bedrooms have been renovated. Their decor remains simple but comfortable, and the local Souleïado fabrics go well with the Provençal painted furniture. On the ground floor, there is a cool dining room, a small bar, and inviting lounges with fireplaces.

***How to get there*** *(Map 33): North of Bollène. On A7, Bollène or Montélimar-Sud exit, toward Saint-Paul-Trois-Châteaux. On D341, head toward Beame-de-Transit.*

# Maison Pic

26001 Valence (Drôme)
285, avenue Victor-Hugo
Tel. (0)4.75.44.15.32 - Fax (0)4.75.40.96.03 - David Sinapian
E-mail: pic@relaischateaux.fr - Web: www.pic-valence.com

**Category** ★★★★ **Rooms** 15 with air-conditioning, telephone, bath, satellite TV, minibar – Elevator; 1 for disabled persons. **Price** Single and double 750-1250F / 114,34-190,56€, suite 1100-1600F / 167,69-243,92€; extra bed 200F / 30,49€. **Meals** Breakfast 90 and 120F / 13,72 and 18,29€, served 7:00-11:00; half board 1300F / 198,18€ (per pers.). **Restaurants** *Pic*: Closed Sunday evening, Monday and Thursday lunchtime Jan 2 – 18. Service 12:00PM-2:00PM, 8:00PM-10:00PM; mealtime specials 290F / 44,21€ (lunchtime except Saturday and Sunday), 660-840F / 100,62-128,06€. *L'Auberge du Pin* (tel. 04.75.44.53.86); menu 155F / 23,63€. **Credit cards** All major. **Pets** Dogs allowed. **Facilities** Swimming pool, parking and garage. **Nearby** Grignan; Orange; villages of the Drôme – 9-hole Valaurie golf course. **Open** All year.

The legendary N 7 that joins Paris and Sète is spotted with famous gourmet establishments that have held onto, that is to say, enlarged their services. This hotel's story started in a country cafe in Saint-Peray where Sophie Pic concocted dishes that attracted more and more food lovers. In 1936, she "moved down" to Valence to be closer to her southern clientele. Today, her great-granddaughter, Anne Pic-Sinapian, who runs the kitchen, has created this all new hotel as a place to stop over. Sure, the stucco is new and there is not that attractive, aged look, but charm is here, nevertheless. The rooms are fanciful, gracefully arranged, the vaulted lounge is intimate, and the comfort here is refined and totally inviting. What a success! As for dining, if your budget isn't cut out for good living AND fine dining, then know that *L'Auberge du Pin* offers delicious, rustic food, with all the tastes of nature.

***How to get there*** *( Map 26 ): Via A 7, take Valence south exit, towards "centre ville".*

## Le Hameau de la Valouse

Grange-Basse 26110 Valouse (Drôme)
Tel. (0)4.75.27.72.05 - Fax (0)4.75.27.75.61
M. Eric Gaulard
E-mail: egauhdv@aol.com

**Category** ★★★ **Rooms** 12 and 8 apartments, with telephone, bath or shower, WC, TV – Wheelchair access. **Price** Double 340-430F / 51,83-65,55€; apart for 1 week 2600-5900F / 396,37-900,76€ (2-6 pers.). **Meals** Breakfast 30F / 4,57€, served 8:00-10:00; half board and full board +120-190F / +18,29-28,97€ (per pers., 3 days min.). **Restaurant** Closed Monday evening and Tuesday in low season. Service 12:00PM-1:30PM, 7:00PM-8:30PM; mealtime specials 98-180F / 15,24-27,44€. Specialties: Ravioles; truites; carré d'agneau. **Credit cards** Amex, Visa. **Pets** Dogs allowed (+30F / 4,57€). **Facilities** Swimming pool, parking. **Nearby** Grignan; Nyons; Valréas; Vaison-la-Romaine; Saint-Jalle; Poët-Laval; Dieulefit – 9-hole Valaurie golf course. **Closed** Nov, Jan and Feb, Monday evening and Tuesday in low season.

The hamlet of Valouse is a charming village in Provençal Drôme, where you can still find olive trees, broom, and fields of lavender. The hamlet's various buildings are clustered on a verdant hill in the great outdoors. A great restoration project has conserved the impressively large dimensions of the buildings' architecture. The interiors have also been completely rehabilitated to make not just rooms, but also apartments that are rented by the week. The spacious rooms are furnished with regional furniture, decorated in a singular way, and some have a fireplace. In winter and summer (when meals are served on the terrace), the restaurant looks over the 60 acres that make up the estate. A large swimming pool accommodates the guests without the fear of overcrowding. An ideal place for your family vacation plans.

***How to get there*** *(Map 33): 15km north of Nyons. In Nyons take the D 94 via Ga. Then on the left, via the La Valouse pass.*

## Les Séquoias

38300 Bourgoin-Jallieu (Isère)
54, Vie de Boussieu - Ruy
Tel. (0)4.74.93.78.00 - Fax (0)4.74.28.60.90
M. Laurent Thomas

**Rooms** 5 with telephone, bath, WC, TV and minibar. **Price** Double 600-800F / 91,47-121,96€. **Meals** Breakfast 60F / 9,15€, served 8:30-10:00. **Restaurant** Closed Sunday evening and Monday. Service 12:00PM-1:30PM, 7:00PM- 9:30PM; mealtime specials 160 F / 24,39€ (Lunchtime except Saturday and Sunday), 210-400F / 32,01-60,98€. Specialties: Noix de Saint-Jacques poêlées; nage de coquillages de Bretagne au naturel. **Credit cards** All major. **Pets** Dogs allowed (+40F / 6,10€). **Facilities** Swimming pool, parking. **Open** Sep – Aug.

Built in the mid-19th century by a silk manufacturer, this opulent manor rises up from the middle of a 5-acre park full of aromatic cedars, ginkos, and sequoias. The large rooms are stunning, a witness to the modernist style of the architect. The superb marble stairwell that leads to the rooms is truly eye-catching. The rooms themselves are spacious with high ceilings and very luxurious with beautifully classical decor in a white and blue color scheme. Both the rooms and the huge suites are very comfortable and have pleasant bathrooms. Their limited number and the protection of the park insures a peaceful and quiet stay. The two smashing ground-floor restaurant rooms show, through their elegance and comfort, the high priority that good food takes here. And the justly praised cuisine does nothing to diminish that impression.

***How to get there*** *(Map 26): Via A 43, around Bourgoin-Jallieu, take the "Le Rivet, Ruy-Montceau" exit. Take a right on N 6 toward La Tour-du-Pin. At the Nissan garage, take a right on the Boussieu road, and follow the signs.*

# Château de Passières

38930 Chichilianne (Isère)
Tel. (0)4.76.34.45.48 - Fax (0)4.76.34.46.25
M. Perli

**Category** ★★ **Rooms** 23 with telephone, bath, shower and 20 with WC. **Price** Double 280-450F / 42,69-68,60€. **Meals** Breakfast 40F / 6,09€, served 7:30-9:30; half board from 310F / 47,26€ (per pers., 3 days min.). **Restaurant** Closed Monday in low season and Nov – Jan. Service 12:15PM-1:30PM, 7:15PM-9:00PM; mealtime specials 120-200F / 18,29-30,49€, also à la carte. Specialties: Escalope de saumon au miel de pissenlit; crêpes d'agneau; truffes. **Credit card** Visa. **Pets** Dogs allowed (+20F / 3,05€). **Facilities** Swimming pool, tennis, parking. **Nearby** Mont Aiguille, Vercors plateau, Grenoble. **Closed** End Nov – Jan, Sunday evening and Monday in low season).

Restored by a very friendly family, this 15th-century château occupies a truly exceptional position at the foot of Mont Aiguille, a magnificent rock wall which creates a somewhat unreal atmosphere throughout the region. We particularly recommend Rooms 1, 4, and 5 with their dark-brown antique wood panelling, exposed beams, walnut finishings, and old furniture. (The showers are a little spartan.) Room 16 isn't bad either, where as the others are modern and a bit impersonal, with white stucco and blue or brick carpeted walls, pine wardrobes, and 70s lacquered white headboards. On the ground floor there is a very retro lounge, with almond-green, figured panelling, antique furniture and, above all, a superb collection of paintings. In good weather, dining tables are set out on the terrace and in winter, the good regional cuisine is served in the large dining room. On the walls, several paintings by Edith Berger remind art lovers that a small museum dedicated to her works is located on the top floor. A smashing little hotel-museum for lovers of art, hominess, and quiet strolls.

*How to get there (Map 26): 50km south of Grenoble via N75 towards Sisteron until Clelles, then D7.*

## Domaine de Clairefontaine

38121 Chonas-L'Amballan (Isère)
Tel. (0)4.74.58.81.52 - Fax (0)4.74.58.80.93
M. Girardon

**Category** ★★ **Rooms** 28 and 2 apartment, with telephone (18 with air-conditioning, bath, WC, TV, minibar). **Price** Single and double 200-600F / 30,49-91,47€, 3 pers. 370F / 56,41€. **Meals** Breakfast 45F / 6,86€, served 7:30-9:00. **Restaurant** Closed Sunday evening, Monday and Thursday lunchtime in low season. Service 12:00PM-1:45PM, 7:00PM-9:00PM; mealtime specials 175-450F / 26,68-68,60€, also à la carte. Specialties: Homard breton cuit minute à la courte nage; mi-cuit au chocolat, glace verveine. **Credit cards** All major. **Pets** Dogs allowed. **Facilities** Tennis, garage and parking. **Nearby** Vienne; Côtes-du-Rhône vineyards. **Closed** Jan and Dec.

This family business is getting more and more well-known because of its food, rightly "starred" due to the talents of Philippe Girardon and served in a ravishing dining room highlighted in yellow. So you will love it here at *Clairefontaine*, and the magic continues right up to the after-dinner drink, because the hotel has an outstanding wine cellar containing some very rare Chartreuse liqueurs. The upstairs rooms, with their squeaky floors, classic furniture, and old wallpaper, have a very country charm. This year, there are a few more rooms available in a new "old-fashioned" building, modeled on old walnut drying sheds. These very comfortable, "simply" decorated rooms have huge bathrooms and outside loggias, with aromatic plants grown in herb boxes at the foot of the hotel. A very inviting and beautiful place that we recommend as heartily as *Le Marais Saint-Jean*, another hotel run by the same family just a few hundred meters away.

***How to get there*** *(Map 26): On the A 7, Vienne exit, then N 7 or N 86 and D 7 towards Le Péage-en-Roussillon; or Chonas exit, then N 7, towards Vienne.*

## Hôtel du Golf

Les Ritons 38250 Corrençon-en-Vercors (Isère)
Tel. (0)4.76.95.84.84 - Fax (0)4.76.95.82.85
M. Sauvajon
E-mail: hotel-du-golf@planete-vercors

**Category** ★★★ **Rooms** 8 and 4 duplexes with telephone, bath, WC, satellite TV and minibar. **Price** Double 450-790F / 68,60-120,43€; duplex (4 pers.) 650-960F / 99,09-146,35€. **Meals** Breakfast 60F / 9,15€, served 7:30-11:00; half board 440-615F / 67,08-93,76€ (per pers.). **Restaurant** Service 12:30PM-1:30PM/3:00PM, 7:30PM-8:30PM/9:00PM; mealtime specials 100-180F / 15,24-27,44€; also à la carte. **Credit cards** All major. **Pets** Dogs allowed. **Facilities** Swimming pool, sauna and parking. **Nearby** Skiing in Courençon and in Villard de Lans (5 km), caves of Chouanche – 18-hole Courençon golf course. **Closed** End Mar – beg May, mid Oct – mid Dec.

Especially well-located at the entrance to the immense Vercors Natural Park, the *Hôtel du Golf* is in immediate proximity to all the sports activities of this resort: golf, hang gliding, mountain biking, and others. The Sauvajon family is outstandingly hospitable and does its utmost to make your visit enjoyable. The bedrooms, some with lofts, are comfortably appointed and well-kept (Number 2 is somewhat small). They are very quiet and pleasant although their decoration could do with a bit more personality. On the ground floor, an inviting lounge-bar with comfortable, beigeleather armchairs is a lovely spot to relax over a drink before dinner. The food, particularly the fish dishes, is mouthwatering. The former chef of *La Marée* in Paris obviously isn't there for nothing. Generous brunches and the half board deal is a great value for the money.

***How to get there*** *(Map 26): 40km southwest of Grenoble, Villard-de-Lans exit.*

## Hôtel Chalet Mounier

38860 Les Deux-Alpes (Isère)
Tel. (0)4.76.80.56.90 - Fax (0)4.76.79.56.51
M. and Mme Mounier

**Category** ★★★ **Rooms** 47 with telephone, bath or shower, TV (46 with WC). **Price** Double 450-980F / 68,60-149,40€. **Meals** Breakfast incl., served 7:30-9:30; half board 415-695F / 63,27-105,95€ (per pers., 3 days min.). **Restaurant** Service 12:30PM-2:00PM, 7:30PM-9:00PM; mealtime specials 140-300F / 21,34-45,73€, also à la carte. **Credit card** Visa. **Pets** Dogs not allowed (extra charge). **Facilities** Heated swimming pool, covered swimming pool, sauna, hammam, health center, massage (80F / 12,20€), tennis half court (summer). **Nearby** Ski lifts (100m), village of Venosc, Bézardé valley, Ecrins park, La Meije Mounts. **Closed** May – Jun 29 and Sep – Dec 15.

This chalet was originally a mountain refuge and farm but since 1933 has grown into a large and modern hotel while retaining its charm. The welcoming entrance hall immediately establishes the atmosphere of the hotel. You will be charmed by the decor of the lounge and the restaurant, whose large windows open onto the garden and the swimming pool and onto the snow-clad slopes in winter. The bedrooms are all comfortable and have balconies with unrestricted views of the mountains. Chef Robert Mounier prides himself on his hearty, succulent cuisine, which is very professionally served (on the terrace or next to the swimming pool in summer). The hotel is very quiet and the people are very friendly.

***How to get there*** *( Map 27): 74km southeast of Grenoble (detour from Grenoble via Pont-de-Claix) via N85 to Vizille; then N91 to the barrage (dam) on the Chambon via Bourg-d'Oisans, then D213 to Les Deux-Alpes.*

# Château de la Commanderie

Eybens 38320 Grenoble (Isère)
17, avenue d'Echirolles
Tel. (0)4.76.25.34.58 - Fax (0)4.76.24.07.31 - M. de Beaumont
E-mail: chateau.commanderie@wanadoo.fr

**Category** ★★★ **Rooms** 25 with telephone, bath or shower, WC, satellite TV and minibar. **Price** Double 475-715F / 72,41-109,00€. **Meals** Breakfast 61F / 9,15€, served 7:00-10:00. **Restaurant** Closed Saturday lunchtime, Sunday evening and Monday. Service 12:00PM-1:15PM, 8:00PM-9:45PM; mealtime specials 170-275F / 25,92-41,92€, also à la carte. **Credit cards** All major. **Pets** Dogs allowed (+52F / 7,62€). **Facilities** Swimming pool, parking. **Nearby** Grenoble museum, massifs of Vercors, Chartreuse and Oisans – 18-hole Bresson-Eybens golf course. **Open** All year.

Formerly a hospice of the Knights of Malta, the *Château de la Commanderie* is ideally located just 5km from the center of Grenoble and half an hour from the Olympic ski slopes. A large, lovely walled garden planted with centuries-old trees insures a high level of peace and quiet at this half-city, half-country address. The bedrooms combine modern comforts and facilities with period furniture, old engravings, and carefully chosen fabrics. (We only recommend Room 16 for families.) Breakfast is a substantial affair served on the terrace in summer, or in vast 18th-century rooms decorated with family portraits. Next to it is a large dining room decorated with pastoral Aubusson tapestries. The superb cuisine is intelligently innovative and respect ful of its ingredients. A great value for the money. A friendly, family atmosphere prevails.

***How to get there*** *(Map 26): 4km east of Grenoble via the bypass (south), exit Eybens (Route Napoléon); in the town center.*

# Chavant

Bresson 38320 Grenoble (Isère)
Rue de la Mairie
Tel. (0)4.76.25.25.38 - Fax (0)4.76.62.06.55
M. and Mlle Chavant

**Category** ★★★★ **Rooms** 7 with telephone, bath, TV and minibar. **Price** Double 680-720F / 103,67-109,76€. **Meals** Breakfast 70F / 10,67€, served 7:30-11:00. **Restaurant** Closed Saturday lunchtime and Monday. Service 12:00PM-2:00PM, 7:30PM-9:30PM; mealtime specials 194-270F / 29,73-41,16€, also à la carte. Specialties: Lobster; cailles à la Chavant; gratin de fruits rouges au Grand Marnier. **Credit cards** All major. **Pets** Dogs allowed (+40F / 6,10€). **Facilities** Swimming pool, parking and garage (70F / 10,67€). **Nearby** Museum in Grenoble, massifs of Vercors, Chartreuse and Oisans – 18-hole golf course in Bresson-Eybens. **Closed** Dec 25 – 31.

Just a few minutes from central Grenoble, the *Chavant* is an "old-fashioned" inn that is friendly and comfortable. Come here, above all else, for the food and great wine cellar, stocked with regional vintages. In winter, you'll dine in a huge dining room with blond panelling, reheated by a large fireplace; in summer, in a delightful, shady garden bursting with flowers. You will dine on the lobster that Jean-Pierre Chavant, truly his father's son, knows how to prepare in a thousand ways. He and his sister Danielle strive to keep the traditional qualities of the place, while adding the modern comfort of the seven rooms, all different but all inviting. A large, softly-lit lounge and a beautiful, shady swimming pool add to the tranquility and restfulness that this place emanates. Attentive hospitality.

***How to get there*** *(Map 26): 4 km east of Grenoble via the south. Take exit 6 toward Bresson (Route Napoléon).*

## Hôtel des Skieurs

38700 Le Sappey-en-Chartreuse (Isère)
Tel. (0)4.76.88.82.76 - Fax (0)4.76.88.85.76
M. Jail
Web: www.lesskieurs.com - E-mail: hotelskieurs@wanadoo.fr

**Category** ★★★ **Rooms** 18 with telephone, bath or shower, TV. **Price** Single and double 310F / 47,26€. **Meals** Breakfast 35F / 5,34€, served 7:30-9:30; half board and full board 345-395F / 52,59-60,22€ (per pers., 3 days min.). **Restaurant** Closed Sunday evening and Monday. Service 12:00PM-1:30PM, 7:30PM-9:30PM; mealtime specials 130-250F / 19,82-38,11€, also à la carte. Specialties: Ragout de noix de saint-jacques aux ravioles du Dauphiné. **Credit card** Visa. **Pets** Dogs allowed (+30F / 4,57€). **Facilities** Swimming pool, parking and garage. **Nearby** Skiing, Chartreuse Mounts: gorges of the Guiers-Vif; Museum of Fine Art in Grenoble. **Closed** Apr, Nov and Dec; Sunday evening and Monday.

From Grenoble, the road bravely climbs the flank of the Chartreuse Mountains before arriving in this small mid-mountain (3000 feet) village and the *Hôtel des Skieurs.* Run by a hard-working young couple, the big chalet has just undergone extensive renovation during which the small lounge-bar, the stairway, and the bedrooms were entirely paneled in larch. Today, they exude a warm, cheerful, mountain atmosphere, with a delicate aroma of pine in the air. On the ground floor, a spacious dining room opens wide onto an equally spacious terrace where meals are served with the first rays of sun: the excellent cuisine, nutritious and traditional, is prepared by the owner and served by his wife. The hotel is simple, comfortable, and professionally run: great for those who love walking and the fresh mountain air.

***How to get there*** *(Map 26): 12km north of Grenoble, toward Saint-Pierre-de-Chartreuse.*

## Hôtel Le Christiania

38250 Villard-de-Lans (Isère)
Tel. (0)4.76.95.12.51 - Fax (0)4.76.95.00.75
Mme Buisson

**Category** ★★★ **Rooms** 18 and 5 junior-suites with telephone, bath or shower, WC and TV – Elevator. **Price** Double 460-660F / 70,13-100,62€, suite 640-790F / 97,57-120,43€. **Meals** Breakfast 60F / 9,15€, served 7:30-10:00; half board 395-615F / 60,22-93,76€, full board +80F / 12,20€ (per pers., 4 days min.). **Restaurant** Service 12:00PM-2:00PM, 7:30PM-9:00PM; mealtime specials 130-190F / 19,82-28,97€, also à la carte. Specialties: Terrine de foie gras au vin de noix; carré d'agneau; truite d'eau vive; tarte au chocolat; croustillant aux poires caramélisées. **Credit cards** All major. **Pets** Dogs allowed (+40F / 6,10€). **Nearby** Mountain of Vercors, caves of Choranche; skiing – 18-hole Corrençon golf course. **Closed** Apr 20 – May 22, Sep 26 – Dec 19.

From the outside, the *Hôtel Le Christiania* is architecturally classic, and its location on the edge of the road is not a plus. But you will be pleasantly surprised once you have gone inside and seen how charming it is. The very friendly owners have in fact decorated the hotel like their own home. Paintings, family furniture and objects lend special touches to the small lounge on the left. And a corner of the elegant dining room is bright with a collection of shining antique carafes. Mme Buisson herself is the artist behind the small floral motifs on each door. In the same spirit, the green and red tartan fabrics, the drapes and the checked eiderdowns have been tastefully selected, all creating a lovely effect. The last suites are very beautiful. The owner's son is the chef, while his wife presides over the dining room. They maintain a reputation for excellent meals, which are served outdoors with the first good weather.

***How to get there*** *( Map 26): 35km southwest of Grenoble.*

# Les Iris

42160 Andrézieux-Bouthéon (Loire)
32, avenue Jean-Martouret
Tel 04.77.36.09.09 - Fax (0)4.77.36.09.00
Mme Sylvie Fontvieille

**Category** ★★★ **Rooms** 10 with telephone, bath, TV and minibar. **Price** Single and double 450F / 68,60€. **Meals** Breakfast 50F / 7,62€, served 7:00-10:30; half board 515F / 78,51€ (per pers.). **Restaurant** Closed Sunday evening and Monday. Service 12:00PM-1:30PM, 7:00PM-9:30PM, mealtime specials 85-215F / 12,96-32,78€. **Credit cards** Visa, Amex. **Pets** Dogs allowed. **Facilities** Swimming pool, parking. **Nearby** Modern Art musuem in Saint-Etienne – 18-hole golf course in Saint-Etienne. **Closed** Nov 1 holidays and winter holidays, 2 weeks in Aug.

This Saint-Etienne town might scare you off, with its overpasses, airport, and industrial zone. And yet, it is in this unromantic area that *Les Iris* sprung up under the cedars. Loved by a business clientele attracted to the fine food and the hotel's "homey" feel, this is a useful place in a region where charming hotels are sparse. The restaurant is indisputably elegant, with its tables surrounded by *Directoire* chairs, orange-tinted walls, and huge windows overlooking the garden and terrace (where meals are served in summer). The more standard, small bedrooms are panelled with plain, green, or orangish pink Japanese cane, furnished in lacquered rattan, with fabrics in green floral patterns brightened by pinks. All rooms are in a separate building open to the greenery and the swimming pool. Their limited number and the kind of reception from Sylvie and Yves make it possible for you to choose your own breakfast place, whether in the dining room, on the terrace, next to the pool, or in front of the French window of your room (especially for those that open onto the garden).

***How to get there*** *( Map 25): Via A 72-E 70, take Exit 8B toward Andrezieux center. Once in town, head toward the train station, then toward Saint-Just-bord de Loire.*

# Hôtel Troisgros

42300 Roanne (Loire)
Tel: 04.77.71.66.97 - Fax: 04.77.70.39.77
Marie-Pierre and Michel Troisgros

**Categ** ★★★★ **Rooms** 18 with air-conditioning, telephone, bath, TV and minibar – Elevator. **Price** Single and double 900F / 137,20€, suite 1350-2000F / 205,81-304,90€. **Meals** Breakfast 125F / 19,06€. **Restaurant** *Michel Troigros*, Service 12:00PM-1:30PM, 7:00PM-9:30PM; mealtime specials 690-830F / 105,19-126,53€, also à la carte. **Credit cards** All major. **Pets** Dogs allowed. **Facilities** Parking. **Nearby** Déchelette Museum; Roannais Church. **Closed** Thursday and Wednesday, winter holidays and Aug 1 – 15.

It wasn't the famous food at *Troisgros* that occasioned our trip to Roanne. We had intended to combine a stop-over at the hotel and at *Le Central*, the charming new "spin off" from *Troisgros*, totally made over by Christian Liaigre. If the reception area and bar of the original establishment have kept the coziness that often comes with great houses, the duplex bespeaks the classical refinement of the designer, with wengee furniture, beautiful fabrics, and a subtle color scheme. Note that the peerless, original bathroom-boudoirs are still here. Some ravishing though less spectacular rooms, smaller and less expensive rooms also pleased us. The *Central* illustrates everything that is artistic decoration. There is a little spice shop before the bright dining room, where the justly praised, flavorful, "home-style" food is served. Roanne itself deserves a stop as well, all the more so because of the gourmet food of Michel Troisgros and the exceptional hospitality of his wife Marie-Pierre. You now have a choice between a charming place and an exceptional one in this house that has "lived in the (Michelin) stars for thirty years."

***How to get there*** *(Map 25): Avoid Lyon. On A7, coming from the north, Villefranche-sur-Saône south exit. Coming from the south, go past Saint-Etienne.*

## Hôtellerie Beau-Rivage

69420 Condrieu (Isère)
2, rue du Beau-Rivage
Tel. (0)4.74.56.82.82 - Fax (0)4.74.59.59.36
M. Humann

**Category** ★★★★ **Rooms** 21 and 4 suite (20 with air-conditioning) telephone, bath, shower, WC, satellite TV, minibar. **Price** Single and double 525-850F / 80,04-129,58€. **Meals** Breakfast 70F / 10,67€, served 7:30-10:00. **Restaurant** Closed Monday in low season and Nov – Jan. Service 12:00PM-1:30PM, 7:30PM-9:00PM; mealtime specials 295-430F / 44,97-65,55€, also à la carte. Specialties: Quenelles de brochet au salpicon de homard. **Credit cards** All major. **Pets** Dogs allowed (+50F / 7,62€). **Facilities** Parking, garage (70F / 10,67€). **Nearby** Vineyards of Condrieu, Côtes Rôties and Saint-Joseph; Archeological Museum in Saint-Romain-en-Gal, Vienne Roman ruins. **Open** All year.

Stuck between the fine vineyards of Côtes Rôties and the Rhône meadows, Condrieu is a little, spread-out town. The hotel is just on the river bank and enjoys a tranquil setting, rarely troubled by passing swans or a boat coming from the neighboring little nautical club. The *Beau-Rivage* is a very classic place, frequently up-dated to today's tastes, but never far from its original subdued and cozy style. The dining room, a semi-circle that overlooks the terrace and the river, is itself a star. For many years now, delicious cuisine has been served here, washed down, as is the custom, by some venerable bottles of Côtes-du-Rhône. Shared between the main house and a neighboring building, the rooms are always comfortable, with very elegant fabrics and stylish furniture. Some have a terrace or veranda, at times of an impressive size. Friendly hospitality and very professional service.

***How to get there*** *(Map 26): Via A 7, take the Condrieu exit (coming from the north) or the Chanas exit (coming from the south), then head toward Serrieres, Annonay, and then N 86 until Condrieu.*

# Hôtel des Artistes

69002 Lyon (Rhône)
8, rue Gaspard-André
Tel. (0)4.78.42.04.88 - Fax (0)4.78.42.93.76 - Mme Durand
Web: www.hartiste@club-internet.fr

**Category** ★★★ **Rooms** 45 with telephone, bath or shower, WC, TV (36 with minibar). **Price** Single and double 370-510F / 56,41-77,75€. **Meals** Breakfast 50F / 7,62€, served 7:00-11:30. No restaurant. **Credit cards** All major. **Pets** Dogs not allowed. **Facilities** Parking. **Nearby** Hôtel de Ville, art museum in Lyon, Yzeron, Mont d'Or Lyonnais, Trévoux, Pérouges – 18-hole Lyon Verger golf course, 9-hole Lyon Chassieux golf course. **Open** All year.

The *Hôtel des Artistes* (a favorite haunt of artists, as its name and many autographs indicate) is in that old quarter of Lyon, which lies between the embankments of the Rhône and Saône, close to the Place Bellecour and the Célestins Theatre. The bedrooms are decorated with very simple, modern furniture, differing only in the cheerful colors of the fabrics. Effectively soundproofed, comfortable, and equipped with lovely small baths, they overlook either the back of the hotel, the side façade of the *Théâtre des Célestins*, or the elegant *Place des Célestins*. Avoid those that overlook the tiny courtyard. Breakfast is very good, and there is a friendly atmosphere. Special weekend rates are available. Lyons has a number of world-famous restaurants that deserve a pilgrimage. There are also many "up and comings", such as the excellent *Soupière* (rue Moliere). Don't forget the unbeatable bistrots that also made Lyon famous, such as *Le Bistrot de Lyon*, *Le Bouchon aux Vins*, *Le Garet*, the *Brasserie Brotteaux*, the *Café Comptoir Abel*, the *Café des Fédérations*, and many more.

**How to get there** *(Map 26): In the town center near "Place des Célestins".*

## Château de Candie

73000 Chambéry-le-Vieux (Savoie)
Rue du Bois-de-Candie
Tel. (0)4.79.96.63.00 - Fax (0)4.79.96.63.10
M. Lhostis

**Category** ★★★★ **Rooms** 19 with telephone, bath, WC and satellite TV – 1 for disabled persons;
Elevator. **Price** Double and suite 700-1200F / 106,71-182,94€. **Meals** Breakfast 65F / 9,91€; half
board 505-1145F / 76,99-174,55€ (per pers., 3 days min.). **Restaurant** Closed Sunday evening.
Service 11:30AM-2:00PM, 7:00PM-10:00PM; mealtime specials 160-400F / 24,39-60,98€, also à la
carte. Specialties: Ravioles de champignons aux truffes; filets de lavaret à la grenobloise. **Credit
cards** Amex, Visa. **Pets** Dogs allowed. **Facilities** Parking. **Nearby** Château of Miolans, Les Charmettes
(Rousseau's house), Guiers-Vif gorges, Bourget Lake; Aiguebelette Lake. **Open** All year.

Built as a fortress more than four centuries ago to keep watch over the valley,
the typically Savoyard *Château de Candie* proudly towers over Chambéry.
Eight years ago, it had the good luck to catch the eye of a château lover, who
devoted himself to beautifying the fortress and sharing his passion with those
with the great idea to stop by. Everywhere, in the bedrooms, the salons, and
even the corridors, the result is magnificent: without ever betraying the search
for a "decorative effect", it is the height of modern comfort with the nobility
of beautiful antique furniture, paintings, objects, chandeliers, fabrics....Not
surprisingly, the bedrooms are as lovely as they can be, with great exposure.
(Five are less than 700F.) Meals are served in a recently built part, decorated
on the outside in the regional *trompe-l'oeil*, and on the inside with white or
waxed antique woodwork. The talented chef Gilles Hérard skillfully exploits
Savoy's wealth of delicious regional products. Particularly warm hospitality, in
keeping with the highly exceptional place.

*How to get there* (*Map 27*): *5km from Chambéry.*

## Château de la Tour du Puits

73000 Coise-Saint-Jean (Savoie)
Tel. (0)4.79.28.88.00 - Fax (0)4.79.28.88.01
Mme Carlo
E-mail: ctp@prevot.fr

**Category** ★★★★ **Rooms** 8 with telephone, bath, WC, satellite TV, 3 with air-conditioning. **Price** Double 850-1250F / 129,58-190,56. **Meals** Breakfast 95F / 14,48€, served 7:30AM-12:00PM; half board from 750F / 114,34€ (per pers.). **Restaurant** Closed Sunday evening. Service 12:00PM-2:00PM, 7:30PM-9:30PM; mealtime specials 195-550F / 29,73-83,85€, also à la carte. Specialties: Cappucino de grenouilles et cresson; poissons de nos lacs. **Credit cards** All major. **Pets** Dogs allowed (+25F / 3,81€). **Facilities** Parking, helicopter pad **Nearby** Château of Miolans; Chambéry; Les Charmettes (Rousseau's house); Bourget Lake; skiing. **Closed** Nov and 2nd week in Apr.

On a peaceful mesa, midway between the Bauges mounts and the Belledonne range, this little château, in an English-style park, has some beautiful views of the countryside. No fustian ambiance here, no parade of lounges, no gilt and crystal. No, *La Tour* stands out because of even rarer qualities -- the singularity of the place, the discretion, the attention to the guests, and the care given to each and every detail. There are no more than 8 rooms of incredible comfort. All are different, more or less large, more or less classic, but always very elegant, with irresistible bathrooms in delicate faience, pastel tones, and studied decor. Many touches deserve at least a stop over. Not having had the chance to try the food, we can say nothing about it, but we ask you, even so, to trust the young Hervé Thizy, who, after working in some of the best kitchens in Lyon, was chef at the famous restaurant of the Pourcel brothers.

***How to get there*** *( Map 27): Via A 43, take Exit 23 to Châteauneuf. Then follow the signs.*

## Lodge Nogentil Hôtel

73120 Courchevel 1850 (Savoie)
Tel. (0)4.79.08.32.32 - Fax (0)4.79.08.03.15
Mme Deleuze

**Category** ★★★ **Rooms** 10 with telephone, bath, WC, TV, safe and minibar – Wheelchair access. **Price** Single 650-880F / 99,09-134,16€, double 800-1180F / 121,96-179,89€. **Meals** Breakfast incl., served 8:00-10:00. No restaurant. **Credit card** Visa. **Pets** Dogs not allowed. **Facilities** Parking. **Nearby** Skiing from hotel – 9-hole Courchevel golf course, 18-hole Méribel golf course. **Closed** May (open by reservation in summer).

Located along the Bellecôte slopes, the *Lodge* is one of the chalets that was built in keeping with the new architectural tradition of Courchevel. The mood here is just as pleasant as the number of charming rooms is limited. Bright with blond wood panelling, these rooms are decorated in a sober way, but with a little piece of rustic furniture here, and a wardrobe brought back from Afghanistan there, you'll find they have a very personal touch. Same thing goes for the lounge where tradition is spiced with the exotic. Next door, the bar is a great place to end the day before or after you have gone to one of the many restaurants in Courchevel. A hotel that seems like a big family chalet. Reasonable prices for a ski area that is all the rage.

***How to get there*** *( Map 27 ): To Albertville, Moûtiers, then take D 915 and D 91 until Courchevel 1850. The hotel is on Rue de Bellecôte.*

# Hôtel Adray-Télébar

73550 Méribel-les-Allues (Savoie)
Tel. (0)4.79.08.60.26 - Fax (0)4.79.08.53.85
M. Bonnet

**Category** ★★ **Rooms** 24 with telephone, bath or shower and WC. **Price** Single and double 550-750F / 83,85-114,34€. **Meals** Breakfast 60F / 9,15€, served 8:00-11:00; half board and full board 620-800F / 94,52-121,96€ (per pers., 3 days min.). **Restaurant** Service 12:00PM-4:00PM, 8:00PM-10:00PM; menu 190F / 28,97€, also à la carte. Specialties: Escalope à la crème; steak au poivre; tarte aux myrtilles; fondue savoyarde; raclette. **Credit cards** Visa, Eurocard and MasterCard. **Pets** Dogs allowed. **Nearby** Skiing from hotel, Les Trois Vallées, mountain excursions – 9-hole Courchevel golf course, 18-hole Méribel golf course. **Closed** Apr 25 – Dec 19.

This pretty chalet is only a few steps from the chairlift and the ski runs but it is well-located above the valley, with spectacular views of pinewoods and mountains. You reach it via Méribel 1600, where you must leave your car; the hotel staff meets you and to take you to the chalet. The Adray is unrivalled at Méribel, and at lunchtime the large sunny terrace is invaded by skiers. The atmosphere is cheerful and the home cooking excellent. The bedrooms are simple but welcoming, with comfortable rustic furniture. The service is friendly and attentive. This is the place for making the most of the mountains without paying the higher prices of hotels in the village center.

***How to get there*** *( Map 27 ): 39km south of Albertville via N90 and D95, then D90.*

# Le Yéti

73553 Méribel-les-Allues (Savoie)
Tel. (0)4.79.00.51.15 - Fax (0)4.79.00.51.73
M. and Mme Saint-Guilhem
E-mail: le.yeti@laposte.fr

**Category** ★★★ **Rooms** 37 with telephone, bath, WC and satellite TV. **Price** Room with half board in winter 830-990F / 126,53-150,92€, in summer 540-750F / 82,32-114,34€ (per pers.). **Restaurant** Service 12:00PM-2:30PM, 7:30PM-10:00PM; mealtime specials 98-235F / 15,24-35,83€, also à la carte; gourmet fare: 315F / 48,02€. **Credit cards** All major. **Pets** Dogs not allowed. **Facilities** Swimming pool, sauna. **Nearby** Skiing from hotel, Les Trois Vallées, mountain excursions – 9-hole Courchevelle Golf Course, 18-hole Méribel Golf Course. **Closed** Apr 21 – Jun 30 and Sep 1 – Dec 16.

This chalet-hotel is located on the western slopes of Méribel, just next to the ski runs. Sophie and Frédéric Saint Ghilhem, who are both mountain guides, have decorated the hotel lovingly, and it shows. The walls are panelled in rough, hand-polished wood; the handsome furnishings include pretty objects, kilims, and comfortable armchairs in the bar and in front of the fireplace. The view is magnificent from all vantage points. The bedrooms are extremely comfortable and furnished in the loveliest mountain-chalet style. The panoramic restaurant has a terrace facing due south over a small swimming pool. Finally, when you set out for the lofty summits, Frédéric is there to advise you and to share the adventure.

***How to get there*** *(Map 27): 39m south of Albertville via N90 and D95, then D90.*

## La Tour de Pacoret

Montailleur - 73460 Grésy-sur-Isère (Savoie)
Tel. (0)4.79.37.91.59 - Fax (0)4.79.37.93.84
M. Chardonnet

**Category** ★★ **Rooms** 9 with telephone, bath or shower, WC and TV. **Price** Single and double 280-450F / 42,69-68,60€. **Meals** Breakfast 50F / 7,62€, served 8:00-10:00; half board and full board 300-490F / 45,73-74,70€ (per pers., 3 days min.). **Restaurant** Service 12:00PM-1:30PM, 7:30PM-9:00PM; mealtime specials 90-280F / 13,72-42,69€ , also à la carte. Specialties: Mitonnée fondante de joues du cochon; filet de fera en croûte de sésame; moelleux chaud au chocolat. **Credit cards** Visa, Eurocard and MasterCard. **Pets** Small dogs allowed (+30F / 4,57€). **Facilities** Swimming pool, parking. **Nearby** Conflans, Mont Fortress, Château of Miolans – 27-hole Giez-Faverges golf course. **Open** Apr – Nov.

This beautiful 14th-century watchtower, standing in the middle of the countryside on a hilltop at the foot of the Alps, has been converted into a charming small country hotel. A magnificent spiral staircase of black stone leads to the bedrooms. All different, they are regularly redecorated, prettily furnished, and comfortable. The ground-floor rooms form several attractive dining rooms, and just next to them, the garden-terraces offer a splendid view. Here, in the shade of the wisteria or the parasols, dining tables are laid, inviting the first arrivals to have lunch or dinner facing the snowy Alps and overlooking the Isère River as it snakes through the valley. When we stayed here, we took special note of the excellent cuisine and the staff's kind hospitality.

***How to get there*** *(Map 27): 19km southwest of Albertville via N90 towards Montmélian until Pont-de-Grésy, then D222 and D201 towards Montailleur.*

# Hôtel Le Calgary

73620 Les Saisies (Savoie)
Tel. (0)4.79.38.98.38 - Fax (0)4.79.38.98.00
M. Berthod

**Category** ★★★ **Rooms** 40 with telephone, bath, TV and minibar – 2 for disabled persons. **Price** Double and 3 pers. with half board and full board 360-620F / 54,88-94,52€, 460-720F / 70,13-109,76€ (per pers.) **Restaurant** Service 12:15PM-1:30PM, 7:15PM-9:00PM; mealtime specials 145-230F / 22,11-35,06€, also à la carte. Specialties: Cuisses de grenouilles à la crème de miel et tilleul; filet de féra du Léman croustillant à la peau; coulis de betteraves au suc de racine; carré d'agneau avec beurre de menthe fraîche et coriandre au cumin; marquise au chocolat et beurre de cacao tradition; glace aux pruneaux. **Credit cards** All major. **Pets** Dogs allowed (+50F / 7,62€ per days). **Facilities** Swimming pool, hammam, sauna, garage (50F / 7,62€ per day). **Nearby** Skiing from hotel, Olympic cross-country stadium 200m away – 18-hole Mont d'Arbois golf course in Megève (15 km). **Closed** except May, Oct and Nov.

*L*e *Calgary* was built in Tyrolean style by the French ski champion Frank Piccard, who returned from Austria in love with the hotels there. Thus the reason for the flower-covered balconies which run along the façades and the two traditional oriel windows. Inside, the lounge recalls an Austrian pub and the dining room, with its colorful tablecloths, is very cheerful. Although the bedroom decor is somewhat standard, the rooms are spacious, and some can accommodate three people. All have a balcony with a lovely view over Beaufort and the ski trails of Les Saisies. In summer, the hotel offers a large choice of study sessions, including some for children. *Le Calgary*, by the way, is named after the town where Frank Piccard won an Olympic medal.

***How to get there*** *(Map 27): 31km northeast of Albertville via D925, towards Beaufort, and D218, towards Col des Saisies. Or 30 km southwest of Sallanches, Praz-sur-Arly, and then head toward Notre-Dame-de-Bellcombe.*

# Les Campanules

73320 Tignes (Savoie)
Le Rosset, BP 32
Tel. (0)4.79.06.34.36 - Fax (0)4.79.06.35.78 - MM. Reymond
E-mail: campanules@wanadoo.fr

**Category** ★★★ **Rooms** 33 and 10 suites with telephone, bath, WC and satellite TV – 1 for disabled persons – Elevator. **Price** Double 600-1100F / 91,47-167,69€; suite 800-1400F / 121,96-213,43€. **Meals** Breakfast incl., served 7:30-9:30; half board 430-860F / 65,55-131,11€ (per pers., 2 days min.). **Restaurant** *Le Chalet*. Service 12:00PM-1:45PM, 7:30PM-9:45PM; mealtime specials 135-280F / 20,58-42,69€, also à la carte. Regional cooking. **Credit cards** All major. **Pets** Dogs not allowed. **Facilities** Sauna, hammam, jacuzzi. **Nearby** Skiing, Vanoise Park. **Closed** May – Jun, Sep – Oct.

At the time of its complete rehabilitation, this hotel decided to make up for its huge size with many little details that give it a "family lodge" feel, with its blond wood panelling, Savoyard-style pine furniture, and inviting atmosphere. The rooms are wonderfully soundproofed, impeccably clean, and comfortable throughout. Arranged in a simple though pleasant way, they all have the same decor, with varnished panelling, thick carpeting, and cream fabrics with colorful floral patterns specifically designed for the hotel. You'll also love the little extras that make the ends of the day so pleasant, like personal closets for your skis, a hot air system that dries your socks, and a little sauna to relax in before enjoying the refined, regional food (half board included). Add to all this a privileged location, in summer as in winter, with the lake and Killy area nearby.

***How to get there*** *( Map 27): 85km southeast of Albertville, highway to Moûtiers, N90 to Bourg-Saint-Maurice and Tignes.*

## Le Blizzard

73150 Val-d'Isère (Savoie)
Tel. (0)4.79.06.02.07 - Fax (0)4.79.06.04.94
M. Cerboneschi

**Category** ★★★★ **Rooms** 60 and 14 suites (some with fireplace, jacuzzi and minibar), with telephone, bath, WC and TV – Elevator. **Price** Single and double 820-1630F / 125,01-248,49€ (650-800F / 99,09-121,96€ in summer). **Meals** Breakfast incl.; half board 590-995F / 89,94-151,69€ per pers. (500-600F / 76,22-91,47€ in summer per pers.). **Restaurant** Service 12:00PM-3:00PM, 7:30PM-10:00PM; mealtime specials from 180F / 27,44€, also à la carte. **Credit cards** All major. **Pets** Dogs allowed (+70F / 10,67€). **Facilities** Swimming pool, sauna, hammam, jacuzzi, parking (65F / 9,91€). **Nearby** Ski lift (100m), Vanoise Park, riding, mountain bikes, tennis. **Open** Jul – end Aug and Dec – end Apr.

**B**ringing together charm and good hotel management is well-nigh impossible. Nevertheless, that is exactly what *Le Blizzard* has managed to do, and we praise them for their decorative and organizational talents. The many lounges, the billiard room, bar, restaurant and all the guest areas display the venerable look of a mountain chalet -- intimate, elegant, and inviting. Redone in the same manner, the rooms are equally impressive and help us forget the lackluster façade of the hotel. The southern rooms are quieter and also have a balcony and a nice view of Bellevarde's Olympic slope. The restaurant, under the direction of Stéphane Benchérif, offers very good traditional food, served outside when the weather permits. The large, heated swimming pool, next to the terrace, becomes the center of activity during the summer vacation months, as soon as the blizzards turn into refreshing breezes.

***How to get there*** *( Map 27): 85km southeast of Albertville, take highway towards Moûtiers, then Bourg-Saint-Maurice, and D 902 to Val-d'Isère.*

# Hôtel Fitz Roy

73440 Val-Thorens (Savoie)
Tel. (0)4.79.00.04.78 - Fax (0)4.79.00.06.11
Mme Loubet

**Category** ★★★★ **Rooms** 30, 3 apartments, 3 with mezzanine telephone, bath, hairdryer, TV and minibar – Elevator. **Price** Double in half board and full board 800-1900F / 121,96-289,65€ (per pers.). **Meals** Breakfast incl., served 7:00-11:00. **Restaurant** Service 12:00PM-3:00PM, 7:00PM-10:00PM; mealtime specials 220-500F / 33,54-76,22€, also à la carte. Specialties: Regional cooking. **Credit cards** Amex, Visa. **Pets** Dogs allowed only in room (+90F / 13,72€) and small dogs allowed in restaurant. **Facilities** Swimming pool, sauna, health center, beauty salon, parking. **Nearby** Skiing from hotel. **Open** Dec 1 – May 6.

In the heart of Val Thorens, the *Fitz Roy* is a luxurious modern chalet. The interior is decorated very elegantly, with blond woodwork, predominantly white and pastel fabrics, and tasteful furniture. The large lounge, where vast sofas surround the fireplace, looks out due south over the ski runs. The bedrooms, which are all different, are spacious, with very refined decor and accommodations. Each has a balcony and a bathtub with whirlpool. In the evening, enjoy traditional Savoyard country cooking and professional service by candlelight. From the large terrace-solarium, you will also enjoy the superb sunsets over the resort. For *l'après-ski*, there is a swimming pool and excellent exercise equipment. In a resort which can be criticized for being artificial, the *Fitz Roy* has successfully combined luxury, modernity, and the finest hotel tradition.

***How to get there*** *( Map 27): 62km southeast of Albertville via N90 to Moûtiers, then D915 and D117.*

## Chalet-Hôtel Peter Pan

Les Houches 74310 Chamonix (Haute-Savoie)
Tel. (0)4.50.54.40.63
M. and Mme Bochatay

**Rooms** 13 (2 with bath, 4 shower and 2 with WC). **Price** Double 200-280F / 30,49-42,69€. **Meals** Breakfast 38,50F / 6,10€, served 8:00-10:00; half board and full board 260-310F / 39,64-47,26€ (per pers.). **Restaurant** Service at 12:30PM and 7:30PM; mealtime specials 145F / 22,11€ lunchtime, 98F / 15,24€, also à la carte. Specialties: Crépinette de pied de porc aux cèpes; salade gourmande, filet de féra à la crème de genépi; foie de veau à l'aigre-doux, braserades; bourguignon de canard à la crème de cassis; cake au chocolat. **Credit cards** Not accepted. **Pets** Dogs allowed. **Facilities** Parking. **Nearby** Ski lifts (1km) – 18-hole Praz golf course in Chamonix (7km). **Closed** except in May and Oct 15 – Dec 15.

This beautiful converted 18th-century farm is on a hilltop near Les Houches and has a superb view of the valley of Chamonix. In this delightful place, the owners have created an original and welcoming ambiance, with excellent food at reasonable prices. The two chalets are constructed entirely of wood and are veritable small museums. Meals are served by candlelight on prettily set little wooden tables bright with bouquets of flowers. The rooms, and let's be clear here, are more than just quaint and of a rather spartan comfort, especially as concerns the sanitary facilities. Rooms 1 and 2 are, however, very roomy and have bathrooms. It is above all else because of the hospitality, good prices, and charming atmosphere that the *Peter Pan* is in the 2000 edition of this guide.

*How to get there* ( Map 27): 59km northeast of Albertville via N212, then N205. By A40, LeFayet exit. 7km west of Chamonix.

## Hameau Albert Ier

74402 Chamonix (Haute-Savoie)
119, impasse du Montenvers
Tel. (0)4.50.53.05.09 - Fax (0)4.50.55.95.48 - Pierre and Martine Carrier
E-mail: info@hameaualbert.fr - Web: www.hameaualbert.fr

**Category** ★★★★ **Rooms** 27 (hotel), 12 (farmhouse), 2 chalets with telephone, bath, satellite TV and minibar – Rooms for disabled persons; elevator. **Price** Double 690-1700F / 105,19-259,16€. **Meals** Breakfast 80F / 12,20€, served 7:30-10:30; half board and full board 585-1475F / 89,18-224,86€ (per pers.). **Restaurant** *Albert I<sup>er</sup>* Closed Wednesday lunchtime except national holidays. Service 12:00PM-2:00PM, 7:30PM-9:30PM; mealtime specials 190-385F / 28,97-58,69€. *Maison Carrier* Closed Monday lunchtime except national holidays. Service 12:00PM-2:00PM, 7:30PM-9:30PM; mealtime specials 145-240F / 22,11-36,59€, also à la carte. **Credit cards** All major. **Pets** Dogs allowed. **Facilities** Sauna, swimming pool, parking. **Nearby** La Flégère (250 m), Chamonix (3 km) – 18-hole Praz golf course. **Closed** Nov 2 – Dec 3.

For three generations now, the cozy and comfortable *Albert Ier* has been the great hotel and gourmet restaurant of Chamonix. Pierre and Martine Carrier have just finished their ambitious expansion project, setting up three farmhouse and two chalets made from original materials on their park. A dozen rooms have been created where Alpine charms meets Italian design. Traditional comforts are coupled with a pleasing fireplace and comfortable bathtubs, and a tip-top view of the Red Needles and Mont Blanc. Another farmhouse shelters the *Maison Carrier*, a "country restaurant" with a naturalist decor where you will sample the refined recipes of the Savoy. This hamlet also has a leisure area with a beautiful, half-covered swimming pool. With this new development, this generation of Carriers shows once more their desire to match the tradition of service with a high level of sophistication.

*How to get there (Map 27): On the road to Montenvers.*

## Hôtel du Jeu de Paume

Le Lavancher 74400 Chamonix (Haute-Savoie)
705, route du Chapeau
Tel. (0)4.50.54.03.76 - Fax (0)4.50.54.10.75
Mme Prache

**Category** ★★★★ **Rooms** 18, 4 suites and 1 chalet (with 3 rooms), with telephone, bath, shower, WC, TV, hairdryer and minibar. **Price** Single and double 960-1160F / 146,35-176,84€, suite 1500F / 228,67€. **Meals** Breakfast 70F / 10,67€, served 7:15-10:00 (in dining room); half board 741-1011F / 112,81-153,97€ (per pers.). **Restaurant** Service 12:00PM-2:00PM, 7:30PM-9:30PM; mealtime specials 185-350F / 28,20-53,36€, also à la carte. **Credit cards** All major. **Pets** Dogs allowed in rooms (+50F / 7,62€). **Facilities** Swimming pool, tennis, car rental, parking. **Nearby** Skiing in Argentières (Les Grands Montets, 3km), and in Chamonix — 18-hole Praz golf course. **Closed** Beg May — beg Jun and Sep 10 — beg Dec.

A residential, preserved locale, Le Lavancher is 5 km from Chamonix, on the edge of a pine wood overlooking the Argentière Valley. This chalet-hotel is luxurious, refined and very comfortable with wood playing a major role in the decor. The bedrooms are all very functional and furnished with warmth and good taste; nearly all have balconies. There is the same comfortable coziness in the bar and lounges. The traditional, hearty gourmet food, changed to keep with the change in season, is served in a sometimes too hurried way for a dinner in the mountains. Very warm hospitality. In winter, a hotel car drives guests to the slopes.

***How to get there*** *(Map 27): 67km northeast of Albertville via N212. By A40, Le Fayet exit.*

561

# Hôtel Le Labrador

Les Praz 74400 Chamonix (Haute-Savoie)
101, route du Golf
Tel. (0)4.50.55.90.09 - Fax (0)4.50.53.15.85 - M. Bartoli
E-mail: labrador@cyberaccess.fr - Web: www.hotel.labrador.com

**Category** ★★★ **Rooms** 32 and 1 apartment with telephone, bath, WC, TV, safe and minibar. **Price** Double 660-860F / 100,62-131,11€, apart. 1100-1600F / 167,69-243,92€ (2 pers., 250 F / 38,11€ per extra pers.). **Meals** Breakfast incl., served until 10:30; half board and full board 450-670F / 68,60-102,14€ (per pers., 3 days min.). **Restaurant** Service 12:00PM-2:00PM, 7:15PM-9:30PM; menue specials from 160F / 24,39€, also à la carte. **Credit cards** All major. **Pets** Dogs allowed. **Facilities** Sauna, fitness center, whirlpool, parking. **Nearby** Skiing from hotel, Alpine skiing: La Flégère (250 m), Chamonix (3 km) – 18-hole Praz golf course. **Closed** Beg Nov – beg Dec.

Built on the Chamonix Golf Course facing Mont Blanc, the *Labrador* enjoys an outstanding location, even if the highway is not far away. A combination of Scandinavian and Savoyard architecture, the various buildings of the hotel fit harmoniously into the natural setting. The bedrooms are not very large but they are comfortable, those on the front have balconies, and the suite sports a fireplace. *La Cabane* offers good *cuisine* with specialties which vary with the seasons. The only drawback is its large size, which interferes a bit with the cozy atmosphere. Pleasant and attentive hospitality, nevertheless. Advice about the tourist attractions of Chamonix is gladly given. The hotel also offers ski, golf or mountain package trips.

***How to get there*** *(Map 27): 67km northeast of Albertville, via N212. Via A40, exit Le Fayet. (3km north of Chamonix via N506, toward Argentière; on the golf course).*

# Le Montagny

490, Le Pont 74310 Les Houches
Chamonix (Haute-Savoie)
Tel. (0)4.50.54.57.37 - Fax (0)4.50.54.52.97 - M. Ravanel
E-mail: montagny@wanadoo.fr - Web: http://perso.wanadoo.fr/hotel.montagny

**Category** ★★ **Rooms** 8 with telephone, bath, WC and TV. **Price** Double 380F / 57,93€. **Meals** Breakfast 42F / 6,86€, served 7:30-10:30. No restaurant. **Credit cards** Visa, Eurocard and MasterCard. **Pets** Dogs not allowed. **Facilities** Parking. **Nearby** Ski lift (3 km) – 18-hole Praz golf course in Chamonix (7km). **Closed** Nov – Dec 15.

One of the oldest families in the valley here has just opened this small chalet-hotel where the slope leads up to the Dôme du Goûter peak. Its location and the small number of rooms make the Montagny marvelously quiet, an impression heightened by the crystal-clear mountain air. -We loved the interior with its light pine panelling, the green tartan fabric upholstery on the benches in the room where breakfast (delicious) is served, as well as on those in the lounge (often with an open fire, a must for a mountain evening.) We found the bedrooms just as inviting, with modern amenities and pretty blue and white fabrics with honey-colored panelling and bathroom tiling. Room 104 is ideal for families; Numbers 206 and 207, located beneath the eaves of the roof, are equipped with charming alcove bathrooms. We can heartily recommend all the rooms. It's no wonder the delightful little Montagny already has its regular customers. Several restaurants for *fondues*, *raclettes* and Savoyard products: *L'Impossible* and *Le Peter Pan* in Les Houches.

***How to get there*** *(Map 27): Via A 40, head toward Chamonix. 5 km before Chamonix, get off the expressway at the the last exit to "Les Houches". Go 50m on D 243, then take the first road on your left, the "route du Pont" for 500m.*

# Hôtel La Savoyarde

74400 Chamonix (Haute-Savoie)
28, route des Moussoux
Tel. (0)4.50.53.00.77 - Fax (0)4.50.55.86.82 - M. and Mme Carrier
E-mail: savoyarde@silicone.fr.

**Category** ★★★ **Rooms** 14 with telephone, bath, WC and TV. **Price** Double 490-740F / 74,70-112,81€. **Meals** Breakfast 46F / 6,86€, served from 7:00. **Restaurant** Service 12:00PM-2:00PM, 7:30PM-9:30PM, mealtime specials 88F / 13,72€ (38F / 6,10€ child), also à la carte. Specialties: Raclette, tartiflette, fondue. **Credit card** Visa. **Pets** Dogs allowed. **Facilities** Garage (+50F / 7,62€), sauna and spa in Auberge du Bois-Prin (60F / 9,15€), parking. **Nearby** Skiing, mountain excursions – 18-hole Praz golf course. **Open** End Dec – May 14 and Jun – end Nov.

This hotel at the foot of Mount Brévent is surely one of the best located hotels in Chamonix. It overlooks the village and has a superb view of the Aiguille du Midi. Refurbished in the last two years, its style evokes both an English country cottage and an Alpine chalet. There are two adjoining buildings, both well-cared for and, in summer, surrounded by flowers. The attractive entrance hall sets the tone of the house: painted ceilings, white walls and a cozy atmosphere. The owners have resisted the temptation to go in for a pseudo-rustic decor. The bedrooms are light and airy and have specially designed furniture. All have balconies or terraces and only two are at the back of the hotel. Among our favorites are Room 5, which has a large balcony, and Room 14, with its exposed beams. One drawback: in the bedrooms near the stairs, early-morning skiers can sometimes wake guests who are less enthusiastic early risers. Good mountain specialties are served by the fireside or on a terrace facing Mont Blanc.

***How to get there*** *( Map 27): 67 km from Albertville. On A 40, take the Chamonix south exit. Hotel next to the cable car station at Brévent.*

## Les Chalets de la Serraz

74220 La Clusaz (Haute Savoie)
Rue du col des Aravis
Tel. (0)4.50.02.48.29 - Fax (0)4.50.02.64.12
Mme M.-C. Gallay

**Category** ★★★ **Rooms** 12 with telephone, bath, WC and satellite TV – 1 for disabled persons. **Price** Single and double 450-750F / 68,60-114,34€; suite 520-850F / 79,27-129,58€. **Meals** Breakfast 65F / 9,91€, served 8:00-10:30; half board 395-650F / 60,22-99,09€ (per pers.). **Restaurant** Service 12:00PM-2:30PM, 7:15PM-9:30PM; mealtime specials 125-165F / 19,06-25,15€. Specialties: Péla traditionnelle au reblochon des Aravis; cocotte de canard au cidre et navets confits; rognons d'agneau façon grand-mère. **Credit cards** Amex, Visa. **Pets** Dogs allowed (+65F / 9,91€). **Facilities** Swimming and garage (65F / 9,91€). **Nearby** Skiing; lake of Annecy **Closed** May and Oct.

Leaving La Clusaz in the direction of the Aravis Pass, you will come to this group of traditional chalets on the picturesque route through the summer mountain pastures. The valley itself, dotted with spruce and traversed by a small river, ensures each bedroom a lovely view. Choose the small, mazot farmhouses with kitchenettes and lofts (ideal for families), or the bedrooms in the main building: a renovated old Savoyard, wood-shingled farmhouse. Their furnishings, including mountain furniture and red-and-white checked fabrics, are in keeping with the chalet style. (Only the bathroom fixtures are somewhat sad.) All the bedrooms, some with ground-floor terraces, are well-kept and comfortable. We admired the elegance of the dining room and its pale panelling. The kitchen offers delicately gourmet meals, and, once a week, Savoyard specialties, which are served at a communal table. Warm ambiance and hospitality.

*How to get there* ( Map 27): 32 km from Annecy.

## Au Cœur des Prés

74920 Combloux (Haute-Savoie)
Tel. (0)4.50.93.36.55 - Fax (0)4.50.58.69.14
M. Paget

**Category** ★★★ **Rooms** 35 with telephone, bath, WC and TV. **Price** Single and double 410-570F / 62,50-86,90€. **Meals** Breakfast 50F / 7,62€, served from 7:30; half board 410-490F / 62,50-74,70€ (per pers.). **Restaurant** Service 12:00PM-2:00PM, 7:30PM-8:30PM; mealtime specials 155-190F / 23,63-28,97€, also à la carte. **Credit cards** Visa, Eurocard and MasterCard. **Pets** Dogs allowed. **Facilities** Tennis, sauna, jacuzzi, heated swimming pool, billiard, garage (35F / 5,34€), parking. **Nearby** Ski lifts (1km), Megève, Chamonix – 18-hole Mont d'Arbois golf course in Megève. **Closed** Sep 25 – Dec 19, and Apr 6 – Jun.

This hotel has the advantage not only of a superb view of Mont Blanc and the Aravis Mountains, but it is also surrounded by a large, quiet meadow. Most of the bedrooms overlooking Mont Blanc have a balcony; they are comfortable and all have now been renovated. Those on the *troisième étage*, which have mansard ceilings, are the most charming. The lounge has comfortable armchairs and a big fireplace, and the dining room is charming with its tiled floor, exposed beams, pink tablecloths and panoramic view. Guests very much enjoy Chef Nicola's cuisine. The hotel has been awarded prizes by the community for its summer flower display and is ideal for those who like peace and tranquility amid impressive scenery. During the winter-sports season, the hotel has a shuttle to take clients to the various ski areas.

***How to get there*** *(Map 27): 36km northeast of Albertville via N212 to Combloux through Megève. Via A40, LeFayet exit.*

## Les Roches Fleuries

74700 Cordon (Haute-Savoie)
Tel. (0)4.50.58.06.71 - Fax (0)4.50.47.82.30
J. and G. Picot
E-mail: lesrochesfleuries@hct.net

**Category ★★★ Rooms** 25 with telephone, bath, WC and satellite TV. **Price** Single and double 555-780F / 84,61-118,91€; suite 900-1200F / 137,20-182,94€. **Meals** Breakfast 70F / 10,67€, served 7:30-10:00; half board 470-740F / 71,65-112,81€ (per pers.). **Restaurant** Service 12:00PM-2:00PM, 7:30PM-9:30PM; mealtime specials 150-340F / 22,87-51,83€, also à la carte. Specialties: Fricassée de queues d'ecrevisses aux cèpes de Cordon. La boite à fromages. Menu 160F / 26,39€. **Credit cards** All major. **Pets** Dogs allowed (+50F / 7,62€). **Facilities** Heated swimming pool, health center, tanning salon, whirlpool, hammam, mountain bikes rental, parking, garage (30F / 4,57€). **Nearby** Ski lifts (700m), Megève, Chamonix – 18-hole Mont d'Arbois golf course in Megève. **Closed** Sep 22 – Dec 17 and Apr 8 – May 6.

Cordon lies between Combloux and Sallanches on the threshold of Mont Blanc and is a delightful village, more charming and genuine than its fashionable neighbors. The mountains are beautiful in all seasons, even in summer, when the chalets nestle among cherry and walnut trees, and there are sensational views of the Aiguilles de Chamonix and the Aravis Mountains. This hotel takes advantage of this wonderful vista, with the individual terraces that many of the bedrooms have. The lounge and dining room are furnished in a comfortable rustic style. In winter the blaze in the fireplace creates a warm and cozy ambiance. The cuisine is light and elegant, and you can also enjoy regional specialties in the hotel's second restaurant, *La Boîte à Fromage*.

***How to get there*** *(Map 27): 40km northeast of Albertville via N212 to Combloux, then D113. Via A40, Sallanches exit, then 5 km.*

# L'Ancolie

Lac des Dronières 74350 (Haute-Savoie)
Cruseilles
Tel. (0)4.50.44.28.98 - Fax (0)4.50.44.09.73
M. Lefebvre

**Category** ★★★ **Rooms** 10 with telephone, bath, WC and satellite TV. **Price** Single and double 380-510F / 57,93-77,75. **Meals** Breakfast 50F / 7,62€, served 7:30-10:30; half board 420-475F / 64,12-72,41€ (per pers., 3 days min.). **Restaurant** Service 12:00PM-2:00PM, 7:00PM-9:15PM; mealtime specials 130-375F / 19,82-57,17€, also à la carte. Specialties: Foie gras frais de canard landais; Rissoles de reblochon fermier; croustillant de pigeon de la ferme de monsieur Trottet. **Credit cards** All major. **Pets** Dogs allowed (+30F / 4,57€). **Facilities** Parking and garage (30F / 4,57€). **Nearby** Annecy Lake, Le Semnoz by the ridgeway, gorges of Le Fier, Geneva – 18-hole Bossey golf course, 18-hole Annecy golf course in Talloires. **Closed** Nov 1 holidays and winter holidays, Sunday evening in low season.

Recently built in the style of a mountain chalet, the *Ancolie* stands facing Mount Salève and is reflected in the waters of a small artificial lake with newly landscaped banks. The location could be splendid if only Electricité de France had not put up three giant highlines !... This reservation aside, the hotel is still greatly enjoyed by hikers and mushroom gatherers. We also love the interior decoration of the Ancolie, where waxed pine furniture, thick carpets and ravishing coordinated fabrics form an ensemble which is comfortable and smartly kept, as are the bedrooms; some have a terrace and all are well-soundproofed. Our favorites are those on the lake. Yves Le Febvre directs the hotel's hospitable staff and the kitchen, whose menu is highly tempting. While waiting for the opportunity to taste his cuisine, we will rely on his fine reputation to recommend it to you.

***How to get there*** *( Map 27 ): 20km from Annecy*

# Marceau Hôtel

Marceau-Dessus 74210 Doussard (Haute-Savoie)
115, chemin de la Chapelière
Tel. (0)4.50.44.30.11 - Fax (0)4.50.44.39.44
M. and Mme Sallaz

**Category ★★★ Rooms** 16 with telephone, bath or shower, WC, hairdryer, minibar and TV. **Price** Single and double 480-700F / 73,18-106,71€; apart. 900F / 137,20€. **Meals** Breakfast 55F / 8,38€, served 8:00-11:00. No restaurant, but light meals available. **Credit cards** All major. **Pets** Dogs allowed (+50F / 7,62€).**Facilities** Tennis, parking. **Nearby** Lake of Annecy, Semnoz by the ridgeway, gorges of Le Fier – 18-hole Annecy golf course in Talloires. **Open** All year.

It's great to find a quiet place just a few minutes from one of the most visited areas in France! In the countryside, with a beautiful view of the lake and valley, this inviting and comfortable hotel has a lot going for it. There is a reading and television lounge, beautifully outfitted with a fireplace. A huge terrace opens in good weather, amongst the flowers and near the vegetable garden. Breakfasts are served here (or in your room), as well as meals. Inside, flowers from the garden bear witness to the attention given to the guests needs. The well-tended rooms have kept their slightly outdated, though overall charming look. The well-selected furniture even gives them a certain panache. Only the hallways are a little drab. You can also order a light dinner, carefully prepared by Monsieur Sallaz and served in the half-rustic, half-refined ambiance of the large dining room, with its pink table linens and light wood. If not, you can also go to the excellent *Chappet* nearby. Daily supplied with fish from the lake, this restaurant offers remarkable food at a good price, with a waterfront terrace.

***How to get there*** *(Map 27): 20km south of Annecy via N508 towards Albertville, Bout-du-Lac, Doussard and Marceau-Dessus.*

## Hôtel des Cimes

Le Chinaillon 74450 Le Grand-Bornand (Haute-Savoie)
Tel. (0)4.50.27.00.38 - Fax (0)4.50.27.08.46
M. and Mme Losserand
E-mail: info@hotel-les-cimes.com - Web: www.hotel-les-cimes.com

**Category** ★★★ **Rooms** 10 with telephone, bath, WC, TV and minibar. **Price** Double 450-750F / 68,60-114,34€, in Jan week 3400F / 518,33€ per pers., rental fees included. **Meals** Breakfast incl., served 8:00-11:00. Meal trays 80-120F / 12,20-18,29€. **Credit cards** Visa, Eurocard and MasterCard. **Pets** Small dogs allowed. **Facilities** Sauna, parking and garage. **Nearby** La Clusaz, Aravis Pass, gorges of the Fier, Annecy Lake. **Closed** Apr 23 – Jun 19, Sep 11 – Nov 27.

Le Grand Bornand: 2000 inhabitants, 2000 cows, and a landmarked site where you can admire several magnificent old chalets including, nearby, this marvelous small hotel run by Kiki and Jeannot, a young couple from the mountains who have the gift of hospitality and good taste. From the entrance, we were charmed by the few pieces of old furniture from the area, decorative objects, bouquets of dried flowers. Fragrant with roses and lily-of-the-valley, the hotel has walls covered with broad, golden pine boards; furniture and doors decorated with friezes or painted motifs by Kiki or an artist friend. We loved the bedrooms with their checked eiderdowns and their small bathrooms. There is a table here and there for the delicious breakfasts or the dinner trays (the family's kitchen is occasionally open to guests in the hotel.) The *Hôtel des Cimes* is one of our most beautiful recent discoveries. Reserve now!

***How to get there*** *( Map 27): 35km east of Annecy. On A3 Annecy-nord exit, then towards Thones and Saint Jean de Six; On A10, Bonneville exit to Le Grand-Bornand.*

# Hôtel de La Croix Fry

74230 Manigod-Thônes (Haute-Savoie)
Tel. (0)4.50.44.90.16 - Fax (0)4.50.44.94.87
Mme Guelpa-Veyrat

**Category** ★★★ **Rooms** 12 with telephone, bath (5 with whirlpool), WC and satellite TV. **Price** Double 500-2000F / 76,22-304,90€ (suite). **Meals** Breakfast 100F / 15,24€, served 8:00-10:00; half board 550-950F / 83,85-144,83€ (per pers., 3 days min.). **Restaurant** Service 12:30PM-1:30PM, 7:30PM-8:30PM; mealtime specials 150-400F / 22,87-60,98€, also à la carte. Specialties: Tartifflette maison; viande et omelette avec bolets et chanterelles; foie gras maison; desserts aux fruits sauvages. **Credit cards** Amex, Visa. **Pets** Dogs allowed (+25F / 3,81€). **Facilities** Heated swimming pool, tennis, fitness room, parking. **Nearby** Skiing in La Croix Fry/l'Etoile (1km), La Clusaz, Manigod Valley, village of Chinaillon, gorges de Le Fier, Annecy lake – 18-hole Annecy golf course in Talloires. **Closed** Mid Sep – Mid Dec, mid Apr – mid Jun.

This is the kind of hotel we would like to find more often in the French Alps without having to go to the five-star establishments. It is comfortable and cozy and its bedrooms – all named after mountain flowers – have had great care lavished on them over the years: beamed ceilings and old furniture create a snug chalet atmosphere. The ones facing the valley have breathtaking views and are very sunny. All have either a balcony, a terrace or a mezzanine to make up for the tiny bathrooms. (Some have balneotherapy bathtubs.) The former stables, converted into a bar with seats covered in sheepskin, lead into the dining-room, which faces the Tournette Mountains. This is a great spot in summer or winter, and you are strongly advised to reserve well in advance, for the hotel has a large and faithful following.

*How to get there (Map 27): 27km east of Annecy via D909 to Thônes, then D12 and D16 to Manigod, then La Croix Fry.*

## Le Coin du Feu

74120 Megève (Haute-Savoie)
Route de Rochebrune
Tel. (0)4.50.21.04.94 - Fax (0)4.50.21.20.15
M. and Mme Sibuet

**Category** ★★★ **Rooms** 23 with telephone, bath, WC and TV. **Price** Single and double 820-1280F / 125,01-195,13€. **Meals** Breakfast 35F / 5,34€; half board 740-890F / 112,81-135,68€ (per pers.). **Restaurant** Open only in winter. Service 7:30PM-10:30PM; specials 250F / 38,11€. **Credit cards** Amex, Visa, Eurocard and MasterCard. **Pets** Dogs allowed (extra charge). **Nearby** Ski lifts (200m), Chamonix valley – 18-hole Mont d'Arbois golf course. **Closed** Apr 6 – Jul 24, Sep – Dec 19.

This hotel has long been known to those who like tradition as the most appealing place to stay in Megève. Among al the hotels created or taken over by the Sibuet family, this one is our favorite because of its coziness, seasoned look, and its relatively affordable rates, given its situation near a trendy ski area, where prices are sometimes higher than the mountains themselves. Its success lies in its handsome pine furniture, oak panelling, the flowered fabrics, and above all, its welcoming fireplace. All the rooms are wonders of comfort and good taste, perfectly in keeping with what one expects from a mountain chalet. The hotel's restaurant, the *Saint-Nicholas*, attracts Megève regulars who come here for its simple but delicious cuisine. Lastly, the friendly and attentive welcome of the staff adds a bit of warmth to the *Coin du Feu* that any hotel, no matter how beautiful or comfortable, must have to be truly charming.

***How to get there*** *(Map 27): 34km northeast of Albertville via N212. By A40, LeFayet exit. (The hotel is on the road to Rochebrune).*

## Le Fer à Cheval

74120 Megève (Haute-Savoie)
36, route du Crêt-d'Arbois
Tel. (0)4.50.21.30.39 - Fax (0)4.50.93.07.60
M. Sibuet

**Category** ★★★ **Rooms** 37 and 9 suites with telephone, bath, WC, satellite TV and minibar. **Price** Double with half board 650-980F / 99,09-149,40€ (per pers.). **Meals** Breakfast 65F / 9,91€, served 7:45-10:30. **Restaurant** Service 7:30PM-9:30PM; Savoyard specials, also à la carte. **Credit cards** Amex, Visa. **Pets** Dogs allowed (+55F / 8,38€). **Facilities** Swimming pool, sauna, whirlpool, hammam, health center, parking, garage. **Nearby** Ski lifts (450m), Chamonix valley – 18-hole Mont d'Arbois golf course. **Closed** After Easter – Jun 30, Sep 11 – Dec 14.

This is one of the most charming hotels in Megève, from every point of view. The chalet has been very well refurbished; exposed beams and lovely wood panelling create a warm and comfortable decor, as do the patinated and polished antique furniture and the variety of fabrics and *objets d'art*. We can't recommend any particular bedroom - they are all delightful and any variation in price is only due to size. In winter, meals are served by the fireplace in the dining room, and in summer by the swimming pool. (A bit of a downside. Not all of our readers thought the quality of the food was reflected in its price.) The hotel shuttle can take you to the slopes and in the summer, you can spend a day in the Les Moliettes mountain pasture, lying at an altitude of 4680 feet, which you can get to in a four-wheel drive or on foot (one hour), followed by lunch and a discovery of the local flora and fauna. Guests receive a warm welcome.

*How to get there (Map 27): 34km northeast of Albertville via N212. By A40, Sallanches exit.*

## Les Fermes de Marie

74120 Megève (Haute-Savoie)
Chemin de Riante-Colline
Tel. (0)4.50.93.03.10 - Fax (0)4.50.93.09.84 - M. and Mme Sibuet
E-mail: contact@fermesdemarie.com - Web: www.fermesdemarie.com

**Category** ★★★ **Rooms** 68 with telephone, bath, WC and TV. **Price** Single and double with half board 890-2200F / 135,68-335,39€ (per pers.). **Restaurant** Service 12:00PM-2:00PM, 7:30PM-10:00PM; mealtime specials 300F / 45,73€; also à la carte. Specialties: Regional cooking, fish. Cheese restaurant: menu 230F / 35,06€. Rôtisserie: menu 260F / 39,64€. **Credit cards** All major. **Pets** Dogs allowed (extra charge). **Facilities** Steam bath, fitness center, sauna, jacuzzi, health center, swimming pool, piano-bar. **Nearby** Ski lifts (500m), Chamonix Valley – 18-hole Mont d'Arbois golf course. **Open** Dec 17 – Apr 12 and Jun 20 – Sep 16.

"Marie's Farms" actually make up a Savoyard hamlet consisting of chalets reconstructed from old mazots-traditional tiny mountain chalets. The reception, the three restaurants, the library, and the bar occupy the large main chalet. All the bedrooms face due south and are superbly furbished in the best mountain style, with comfortable amenites, a balcony/terrace, and a small lounge. Jocelyne scoured the region for all the antique furniture in the hotel. You can enjoy three restaurants: a rôtisserie, another specializing in cheese, and finally, the restaurant serving regional gastronomy. Similar care has been given to the breakfast, which includes delicious homemade preserves, good country bread, and crusty baguettes. *La Ferme de Beauté* offers one-week beauty and fitness treatments with special rates in January, March, June, and July. An excellent, luxurious, and charming hotel.

***How to get there*** *(Map 27): 34km northeast of Albertville via N212. Take A40, exit Sallanches. (The hotel is at the Megève exit, heading toward Albertville).*

# Hôtel Le Mégevan

74120 Megève (Haute-Savoie)
Route de Rochebrune
Tel. (0)4.50.21.08.98 - Fax (0)4.50.58.79.20 - M. Demarta
E-mail: netarchitects.com/megevan

**Category** ★★ **Rooms** 11 with telephone, bath, WC, minibar and TV. **Price** Double 350-650F / 54,88-99,09€. **Meals** Breakfast incl., served from 7:00. No restaurant. **Credit cards** Amex, Visa, Eurocard and MasterCard. **Pets** Dogs allowed. **Nearby** Skiing from hotel (100 m), Valley of Chamonix – 18-hole Arbois golf course. **Open** All year.

The *Mégevan* is an unpretentious little hotel, full of extra touches and much loved by its regulars. No uptight mood here, like some places where breakfast service stops at 10:03; the schedule changes to hospitably suit your needs. Below the Rochebrune road, just 100 m from the cable car, this establishment houses 11 rooms that are pleasant despite their somewhat outdated decor. Each has a little balcony overlooking the larches. The little lounge-bar with its deep couches let's you kick back around a fireplace after skiing. Here you might best get a feel for the kind of "homey" atmoshere that made this hotel such a success. Each morning, the low table, the bar counter, and the little tables are cleared for the breakfast plates and coffee cups. The guests settle in, and good conversation soon begins in this friendly meeting place. Megeve has many dining options, including *Le Delicium* and *Le Grenier de Megève*. There is the fondue at *Chamois*, and the trendier *Le Saint-Nicolas* (even if the chef has unfortunately left). For breakfast, try *L'Alpette* at Rochebrune with its beautiful terrace.

***How to get there*** *(Map 27): 34km northeast of Albertville via N212. Via A40, exit Sallanches. The hotel is on the road to Rochebrune.*

## Le Mont-Blanc

74120 Megève (Haute-Savoie)
Place de l'Eglise, rue Ambroise-Martin
Tel. (0)4.50.21.20.02 - Fax (0)4.50.21.45.28
M. and Mme Sibuet

**Category** ★★★★ **Rooms** 40 with telephone, bath, WC, TV, minibar and safe. **Price** Single and double 990-3320F / 150,92-506,13€. **Meals** Breakfast 80F / 12,20€. No restaurant. **Credit cards** Amex, Visa, Eurocard, MasterCard. **Pets** Dogs allowed (extra charge). **Facilities** Sauna, jacuzzi, health center. **Nearby** Ski lifts (50m), Chamonix Valley – 18-hole Mont d'Arbois golf course. **Closed** May – Jun 15.

Successful, talented Jocelyne and Jean-Louis Sibuet are in charge of the *Mont Blanc's* "new life". The *Mont Blanc*! This was one of the symbolic places of the prosperity and carefree spirit of the 1960s when anybody who was a celebrity emigrated from Saint Tropez to Megève for the winter. Guests came down to enjoy the hotel's cozy comfort late in the day because most had spent the wee hours in *Les Enfants Terribles*, the hotel's famous, sophisticated bar which was decorated by Jean Cocteau (since outfitted with an inviting tea room where delicious, homemade hot chocolate is served). Reviving this spirit was a difficult challenge: Times have changed, and most guests no longer have the whimsical insouciance of that Golden Age. Today, the *Mont Blanc* has taken on a very beautiful look, happily marrying English, Austrian and Savoyard styles. Everything is luxuriously perfect. A high level of comfort and very good service that attracts an international clientele that demands discretion with their luxury.

***How to get there*** *( Map 27): 34km northeast of Albertville via N212. Take A40, exit Sallanches. Toward Rochebrune road, on the left of the corner of the Maison de la Montagne. ( Call the hotel when you get there so they can open the barriers to the pedestrian street.)*

## La Bergerie

74110 Morzine (Haute-Savoie)
Rue du Téléphérique
Tel. (0)4.50.79.13.69 - Fax (0)4.50.75.95.71 - Mme Marullaz
E-mail: hotelbergerie@portesdusoleil.com

**Category** ★★★ **Rooms** 27 rooms, studios and apartments with telephone, bath, WC, TV (21 with kitchenette). **Price** Room and studio (1-2 pers) 400-800F / 60,98-121,96€, apart. (4-6 pers.) 600-1000F / 91,47-152,45€. **Meals** Breakfast 60F / 9,15€, served 7:00-11:00. **Evening meals** 1 day a week. **Credit cards** Visa, Eurocard and MasterCard. **Pets** Dogs allowed. **Facilities** Heated swimming pool, sauna, solarium, health center, game room, garage. **Nearby** Ski lifts (50m), Avoriaz, Evian – 9-hole Morzine golf course, 18-hole Royal Hôtel golf course in Evian. **Open** Dec 20 – mid Apr and end Jun – mid Sep.

This is the favorite hotel of Morzine residents. There are now studios and apartments as well as individual bedrooms, all sharing the hotel's services. All is pleasant in this hotel run by the truly wonderful Marullaz family, who have created a cheerful and witty look here. The best bedrooms are those facing south which look out over the garden and the swimming pool. The restaurant offers a small menu and once a week, a *table d'hôtes* dinner is served, featuring Savoyard specialties. In winter, the heated outdoor swimming pool is accessible via a covered passageway. The most popular restaurants with the resort's regulars are *Le Cherche Midi* on the road to *Les Gets*, or *La Crémaillère* in Les Lindarets-Montrionds, which you can also get to in winter via the ski trails.

***How to get there*** *( Map 27): 93km northeast of Annecy via A41 and A40, Cluses exit, then D902. The hotel is near the E.S.F (ski school).*

## Chalet Hôtel L'Igloo

74170 Saint-Gervais (Haute-Savoie)
3120, route des Crêtes
Tel. (0)4.50.93.05.84 - Fax (0)4.50.21.02.74
M. Chapelland

**Category** ★★★ **Rooms** 12 with telephone, bath, WC, satellite TV, 9 with minibar. **Price** Double with half board 630-980F / 96,04-149,40€ (per pers., discount in summer). **Meals** Breakfast 70F / 10,67€, served 8:00-10:00. **Restaurant** Service 12:00PM-4:00PM, 7:00PM-9:00PM; mealtime specials from 130F / 19,82€, also à la carte. **Credit cards** Amex, Visa, Eurocard and MasterCard. **Pets** Dogs allowed (+50F / 7,62€). **Facilities** Swimming pool. **Nearby** Skiing, Chamonix, Megève – Mont d'Arbois golf course in Megève (15km). **Open** Dec 16 – Apr 19 and Jun 16 – Sep 19.

When the evening sun gilds the mountain peaks and the last skiers have disappeared behind the snowdrifts and into the valley, it's lovely to sit in silence and contemplate the gorgeous mountain scenery. The *Chalet Hôtel Igloo*, located just at the arrival of the chairlift, makes this dream a reality for the few lucky people who can do just that and then stay overnight in one of its eight comfortable bedrooms. The contrast is striking between the busy daytime, with customers constantly coming in and out of the restaurant, the cafeteria or the bar, and the pastoral quiet which descends on the chalet at six in the evening. Then, you can quietly enjoy a drink on the terrace facing Europe's highest peak, before going into the restaurant to enjoy its excellent gastronomic cuisine.

***How to get there*** *(Map 27): In winter, access only by the Mont d'Arbois and Princesse chairlifts leaving from Megève; in summer, via Saint-Gervais, Le Ballex (in a 4X4) and Mégève Mont d'Arbois.*

## Chalet Rémy

Le Bettex
74170 Saint-Gervais (Haute-Savoie)
Tel. (0)4.50.93.11.85 - Fax: 04.50.93.14.45
Mme Didier

**Rooms** 19 with basin; hallway baths and showers. **Price** Double 250F / 38,11€. **Meals** Breakfast 35F / 5,34€, served 8:00-10:00; half board (obligatory in winter) 300F / 45,73€ (per pers., 3 days min.). **Restaurant** Service 12:00PM-2:00PM, 7:00PM-9:00PM; mealtime specials 100F / 15,24€, also à la carte. Specialties: Family cooking. **Credit cards** Visa, Eurocard and MasterCard. **Pets** Dogs allowed. **Nearby** Ski lift (300m), Chamonix, Megève – Mont-d'Arbois golf course in Megève (15km). **Open** All year.

This exceptional hotel is housed in an 18th-century farmhouse which through the centuries has preserved all its old woodwork. Panels, ceilings, moldings, and the staircase leading to the superb gallery serving the bedrooms, all create a lovely harmony of dark red tones. The dining room is set with small tables lit by candles, and the family cuisine is excellent. Mme Didier loves classical music, which accompanies meals. It is the simplicity of the bedrooms that makes them charming; and though the bathroom facilities are merely basic, the bedrooms are absolute jewels with their lovely wood walls, floors, and ceilings. The location of the *Chalet Rémy* is another major asset. It is on the outskirts of Saint-Gervais and is reached by a winding road surrounded by pine woods and meadows facing the impressive snowy peaks of Mont Blanc.

***How to get there*** *(Map 27): 50km northeast of Albertville via N212 and D909 to Robinson and Le Bettex. By A40, Le Fayet-Passy exit.*

## Hôtel Beau Site

74290 Talloires (Haute-Savoie)
Tel. (0)4.50.60.71.04 - Fax (0)4.50.60.79.22
M. Conan

**Category** ★★★ **Rooms** 29 with telephone, bath or shower, WC and TV (10 with minibar). **Price** Double 450-825F / 68,60-125,77€, suite 900-1000F / 137,20-152,45€. **Meals** Breakfast 60F / 9,15€, served 7:30-10:30; half board and full board 470-760F / 71,65-115,86€ (per pers., 2 days min.). **Restaurant** Service 12:00PM-2:00PM, 7:30PM-9:15PM; mealtime specials 175-280F / 26,68-42,69€, also à la carte. Specialties: Fish from the lake. **Credit cards** All major. **Pets** Dogs allowed. **Facilities** Tennis (+65F / 9,91€), private beach, parking. **Nearby** Saint-Germain Hermitage, Château of Menthon-Saint-Bernard, Thorens and Montrottier Château, lake, museum and old city in Annecy – 18-hole Annecy golf course in Talloires. **Open** May 8 – Oct 14.

With grounds reaching right down to the banks of Lake Annecy, the *Hôtel Beau Site* is reminiscent of a hotel on the Italian lakes. This family estate was converted into a hotel at the end of the 19th century. With its look of yesteryear, this hotel will move those nostalgiac for those days gone by. Overlooking the lake, the ground-floor dining room-veranda is a perfect example of this, mostly thanks to its tiled floor, its huge windows, and its old platters that play against the monastic whitness of the walls. Nearby, the salon, with its antique furniture, is a place to linger in the evening over an herbal tea or liqueur. The charming bedrooms have been neatly refurbished; they have a terrace and many look out on the lake. Some are decorated with antiques, others are more modern, and some have a mezzanine. The food is excellent. The hotel is specially noted for its warm and friendly welcome.

***How to get there*** *(Map 27): At Annecy, take east bank of lake towards Thônes until Veyrier, then Talloires.*

# Les Prés du Lac

74290 Talloires (Haute-Savoie)
Tel. (0)4.50.60.76.11 - Fax (0)4.50.60.73.42
Melle Marie-Paule Conan
E-mail: les.pres.du.lac@wanadoo.fr

**Catégorie** ★★★★ **Rooms** 16 with telephone, bath or shower, WC, TV and minibar. **Price** Double 860-1120F / 131,11-170,74€; 3 pers. 1100-1250F / 167,69-190,56€. **Meals** Breakfast 80F / 12,20€, served from 7:30. **Restaurant** Only room service. **Credit cards** All major. **Pets** Dogs allowed (+60F / 9,15€). **Facilities** Tennis, parking. **Nearby** Saint-Germain Hermitage, Château of Menthon-Saint-Bernard, Thorens and Montrottier Château, lake, museum and old city in Annecy – 18-hole Annecy golf course in Talloires. **Open** Mar 15 – Oct 15.

With its limited rooms, homey atmosphere, proximity to the lake (and a private beach), warm hospitality, and complete tranquility, the exceptional *Prés du Lac* makes us want to sing its praises. Founded by Madame Conan and her daughter on a bit of the family estate, thwis little hotel has its rooms in "*La maison principale*," "*Les Trémieres*," and the "*Villa Caron*." Almost all have a superb lakeside view, some even with a ground-level terrace or a balcony. Light decor, English fabrics, engravings, paintings, wide and comfortable beds, lacquered rattan furniture (progressively replaced by antiques) make it hard to not fall in love with this place. Especially when the hotel encourages our lacksadaisical side by serving breakfast until a very late hour. You'll linger in your room, in the corner lounge, or on the terrace in front of the everchanging waters of the lake and the Duingt château on the opposite bank. For dinner, the *Beau Site* is just a stone's throw away.

*How to get there (Map 27): At Annecy, take the lake's east bank toward Thônes until Veyrier, then head toward Talloires.*

# LOW PRICE LISTING

## ALSACE-LORRAINE

### BAS-RHIN

### HAUT-RHIN

### MEURTHE-ET-MOSELLE

### MEUSE

### VOSGES

582

# A Q U I T A N I E N

# A U V E R G N E - L I M O U S I N

## CANTAL

## CORRÈZE

## CREUSE

## HAUTE-LOIRE

## PUY-DE-DOME

# B  U  R  G  U  N  D  Y

## CÔTE-D'OR

# CENTRE - LOIRE VALLEY

## CHER

## INDRE

## INDRE-ET-LOIRE

## LOIR-ET-CHER

## LOIRET

# C H A M P A G N E - P I C A R D I E

## AISNE

## MEUSE

## SOMME

# C O R S I C A

## CORSE-DU-SUD

## HAUTE-CORSE

# F R A N C H E - C O M T É

## DOUBS

## JURA

# I L E - D E - F R A N C E

## SEINE-ET-MARNE

## YVELINES

## ESSONNE

# L A N G U E D O C - R O U S S I L L O N

## AUDE

## GARD

# P A Y S - D E - L A - L O I R E

591

## BOUCHES-DU-RHÔNE

## VAR

## VAUCLUSE

# R  H  Ô  N  E  -  A  L  P  E  S

## AIN

## ARDÈCHE

*The prices given in parentheses are those for a double room, sometimes with half board. For more details, please refer to the specific page.

# INDEX OF HOTELS

## IN ALPHABETICAL ORDER

# A

# B

# C

# D

# K

# L

# M

# Q

# R

# S

# T

# U

# V

# W

# Y

# Z

# HUNTER RIVAGES

#### 4TH EDITION

# BED AND BREAKFASTS
## of Character and Charm
# IN FRANCE

• WITH COLOR MAPS AND PHOTOS •

# HUNTER RIVAGES
### 3RD EDITION

# H O T E L S
## of Character and Charm
# I N   P A R I S

• WITH COLOR MAPS AND PHOTOS •

**HUNTER** RIVAGES

4TH EDITION

# HOTELS AND COUNTRY INNS

of Character and Charm

# IN ITALY

• WITH COLOR MAPS AND PHOTOS •

**HUNTER** RIVAGES

3RD EDITION

# HOTELS AND COUNTRY INNS
of Character and Charm
# IN SPAIN

• WITH COLOR MAPS AND PHOTOS •

# HOTELS AND COUNTRY INNS
## of Character and Charm
# IN PORTUGAL

# HUNTER RIVAGES GUIDES

## *The Guides Europeans Use.*

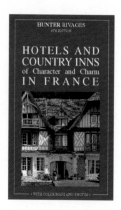

US $ 22.95
ISBN 1-55650-899-9

US $ 19.95
ISBN 1-55650-902-2

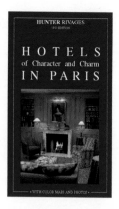

US $ 16.95
ISBN 1-55650-901-4

US $ 22.95
ISBN 1-55650-900-6

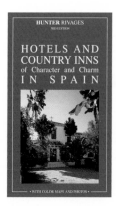

US $ 18.95
ISBN 1-55650-903-0

US $ 16.95
ISBN 1-55650-904-9

# Notes

# Notes

Printed in Italy
Litho Service (Verona)